Peter Norton's
Inside the PC,
Eighth Edition

Peter Norton
John Goodman

SAMS

A Division of Macmillan Computer Publishing
201 West 103rd Street, Indianapolis, Indiana 46290 USA

Peter Norton's Inside the PC, Eighth Edition

Copyright © 1999 by Peter Norton,

EIGHTH EDITION

International Standard Book Number: 0-672-315327

Library of Congress Catalog Card Number: 98-88367

Printed in the United States of America

01   00   99   4   3   2

Interpretation of the printing code: The rightmost double-digit number is the year of the book's printing; the rightmost single-digit, the number of the book's printing. For example, a printing code of 99-1 shows that the first printing of the book occurred in 1999.

Trademarks

Executive Editor
Angela Wethington

Acquisitions Editor
Jamie Milazzo

Development Editor
Robert Bogue

Technical Editors
Nancy Ives
Shareef Batata
Loyd Case
Vince Averello

Managing Editor
Thomas Hayes

Copy Editor
Nancy Albright

Proofreaders
Carl Pierce
Sean Medlock

Indexer
Erika Millen

Production
Louis Porter, Jr.

Cover Designer
Aren Howell

Book Designer
Gary Adair

Overview

Contents

Acknowledgments

Creating a wholly new version of an old standard can be a daunting task. I was fortunate to have the assistance of many people in this effort.

First among them is Dr. John M. Goodman. For the seventh edition, I and my editor for that edition, Sunthar Visuvalingam, invited him to completely rethink this book from a new perspective and then execute his plan for it. For this edition he was again available to bring that work up to date with all the news in this very rapidly expanding field.

We also relied heavily on the expertise of many other professionals. Priceless among them was our Development Editor, Robert Bogue. The positive impact that Rob had on this project simply cannot be overstated. Rob contributed well beyond what is expected of any Development Editor. Key contributions were also made by Emmett Dulaney and Scott Clark, who wrote or rewrote several complete chapters and sections. Others who made major contributions to the project are Andrew Schulman, James Kelsey, John Levine, John Lunsford and [insert name of multimedia writer here]. And we are grateful to have had the very valuable assistance of our technical editors, Nancy Ives, Shareef Batata, Loyd Case, and Vince Averello. We are most grateful to all of these people for helping keep us from error. Still, the responsibility for any errors that remain is ours alone.

After the manuscript arrived at the publisher, many additional talented and dedicated people contributed their special skills to making this the best possible book. The Executive Editor, Angela Wethington, and Acquisitions Editor, Jamie Milazzo, were chief among them. Without all this help, many places in the book would have been harder to understand. We also want to acknowledge with great thanks for their patient efforts to shepherd this revision through what was a rather protracted and, at times, trying process our agents Bill Gladstone, Matt Wagner, and the rest of the good folks at Waterside Productions.

We both want to thank wholeheartedly the many companies who assisted us, often surprisingly generously. Dell Computer provided the sample desktop and laptop systems that are shown and described at various points throughout the book. You can learn more about Dell's fine products by going to its Web site: http://www.dell.com /buydell.

Rise Technologies provided the motherboard and CPU that you will see pictured and discussed in Chapters 7 and 16. Nokia made one of its flat-panel displays available, and Matrox provided the video cards we discuss and show in Chapter 13, including its cutting-edge quad PCI video board. Microsoft provided its sound system and several mice plus a USB-enabled keyboard shown in Chapters 12 and 23. Hitachi provided a DVD-RAM drive and its very fine high-resolution monitors both of which are described and shown in Chapters 4 and 10. Olympus provided the digital still-image camera used to create the figures in this edition. Zoom Telephonics provided its voice-data-fax-video modem and video camera. These last two items are also described and shown in Chapter 13. Kinesis, Pace, and Datahand provided their unique keyboards for us to try out, and you'll learn more about them in Chapter 13, as well.

Without the help of all of these companies, plus many helpful discussions with key technical personnel within each of them, we would not have had the necessary hands-on experience and insiders' knowledge to help us discern hype from fact in these areas.

What's New in this Edition

This edition has been completely updated from the seventh edition. Although the core computer technologies remain much the same, we've highlighted coverage of the following new content:

- **Microprocessors**: Evolution of *x*86 architecture, including Intel's Pentium II Xeon, Celeron, Pentium III and Pentium III Xeon, and all the clone x86 processors now on the market or about to arrive there (from AMD, Cyrix, IDT, and Rise), local bus and cache technology, RISC/CISC/VLIW (aka ILP or EPIC) differences and confluence, multiprocessor systems and the future. See Chapter 7, "Understanding PC Processors," and Chapter 25, "PCs That Think They're Mainframes: Multiprocessor PCs and Other Servers."

- **Disks**: Removable hard disks, super-floppies, magneto-opticals, CD-RW, and DVD-ROM to DVD-RAM. See Chapter 9, "You Can Never Have Too Much Closet (or Data Storage) Space," and Chapter 10, "Digging Deeper Into Disks."

- **Memory**: ROM (mask programmed, EPROM, EEPROM, and so on), RAM (flash, EDO, FPM, SDRAM, VRAM, DDR SDRAM, and the newest flavor, Direct Rambus). Cache, video, expanded, disk controller, NIC, and printer memory. See Chapter 11, "Giving Your PC's CPU Enough Elbow Room—PC Memory."

- **Display**: CRTs, LCD (double scan, active matrix, and the newest flat panel desktop or wall-mounted displays); all the latest standards; video image RAM. See Chapter 13, "Seeing the Results: PC Displays."

- **Input/Output**: All the ways people put information into PCs, from keyboards and mice to digital cameras, including information on repetitive stress injuries and ways to avoid them. See Chapter 12, "Getting Your PC's Attention: Input Devices." Also the Universal Serial Bus (USB), FireWire (IEEE 1394), Advanced Graphics Port (AGP) in all its versions (1X, 2X, 4X, and Pro), CardBus (zoomed video, CIS, card and socket services), enhanced SCSI coverage, detailed PCI architecture, and system chips. See Chapter 16, "Faster Ways to Get Information Into and Out of Your PC."

- **Operating Systems and Programming**: All versions of Windows including Windows 95, 98, NT and Windows CE, the Windows memory models compared, Linux, UNIX, and Java virtual machine. See Chapter 17, "Understanding PC Operating Systems." Also learn how computer programs are created and how they work, including assembly language, code reuse (linking, modularity, libraries, object-oriented programming) in Chapter 8, "How Your PC 'Thinks,'" and Chapter 18, "Understanding How Humans Instruct PCs."

- **Multimedia**: Audio and video compression/decompression techniques, audio-video hard disks, audio synthesis, speech recognition and synthesis, wave guide technology, 3D modeling, virtual reality (force transducers, data mining, and so on). See Chapter 19, "Some PCs Can Understand Speech and Talk to Us," Chapter 20, "How to 'Wow' a Human," and Chapter 21, "Immersive PC Experiences."

- **Portables**: Space constraints on components, proprietary parts, upgrading issues, battery technologies, including "smart" batteries. See Chapter 22, "Why Mobile PCs Must Be Different."

- **Networking and Communications**: Network topologies (bus, star, modified star, ring, linking LANs), video conferencing, whiteboard, group calendaring and scheduling; modem standards and specifications, data compression and error correction, ISDN, T1, xSDL, cable and fiber-optic connection to the Super Highway, satellite communications. See Chapters 23, "The PC Reaches Out, Part One: Modems and More" and 24, "The PC Reaches Out, Part Two: Through the NIC Node."

- **Internet**: Protocols, gateways, firewalls, World Wide Web, HTML, CGI, Java, JavaScript, JavaBeans, ActiveX, NetPC. See Chapter 26, "You Can Touch the World, and It May Touch You, Too!

Tell Us What You Think!

As a reader, you are the most important critic of and commentator on our books. Our editors, and we as authors, value your opinions and we all want to know what we're doing right as well as what we could do better. Our publisher furthermore wants to know what books in other areas you'd like to see it publish, and any other words of wisdom you're willing to pass their way. You can help them make the other strong books that meet your needs and give you the computer guidance you require.

If you have access to the World Wide Web, we hope you will check out our publisher's site at http://www.mcp.com.

> **Note:** If you have a technical question about this book, you may call the Macmillan technical support line at 317–581–3833 or send email to support@mcp.com. Or, you may send email directly to Dr. John Goodman at john@agoodman.com.

The team leader of the group at Macmillan Computer Publishing that created this book is Angela Wethington. She particularly welcomes your comments. You can fax, email, or write her directly to let her know what you did or didn't like about this book—as well as what could have been done to make this and Macmillan's other books stronger. Here's the information you'll need to do that:

Fax: 317–581–4669

E-mail: awethington@mcp.com

Mail: Angela Wethington
            Sams Publishing
            201 W. 103rd Street
            Indianapolis, IN 46290

Introduction

You're about to embark on an amazing voyage of discovery, understanding, and productivity. Welcome!

From the day it first appeared, the IBM PC stirred excitement and fascination: The PC marked the coming of age of "personal" computing, a drastic change from the days when all computers were managed by other people who doled out computer power to users on an as-needed, as-available basis. Today, the PC is the tool without equal for helping business and professional people improve their personal performance and the quality of their work. Students of almost all ages and other home-based users have successfully expanded personal computing into near ubiquity. The exploding home-PC market has accelerated the development of an ever-growing range of applications from word processors for homework, to technologies that allow people to actually work at home. Users also have utilized the technology to find recipes, play with games, work on their education, and research topics.

The original IBM PC also spawned a great many other computers—some from IBM, but most from the makers of IBM-compatible computers—that make up the PC family. In fact, when I first wrote this book, it was actually called *Inside the IBM PC*, but the strong influence that companies other than IBM now exert on the PC industry inspired me to change the title a few years ago. The term *PC* is now universally used in the computer industry to refer to any IBM-compatible computer, and that's exactly how I use the term in this book.

I am excited and enthusiastic about the PC family, and I want you to be, too. I want to lead you into understanding the workings of this marvelous machine and to share with you the excitement of knowing what it is, how it works, and what it can do. Armed with that knowledge, you'll be positioned to make intelligent decisions about computers for yourself, your family, or your company.

My Approach

If you know anything about me or the first edition of this book, you know that I made my reputation by explaining the technical details of the PC. In the early days of the PC, that was what PC users needed most—an inside technical explanation of how the PC worked.

The world of the PC has matured and changed since then—a lot—and so have the needs of mainstream PC users. My approach seems to have withstood the test of time, however, and it occurs to me that you might want to know how I look at what I do.

From my perspective, the most useful approach to a subject such as this one has always been to assume that you, my reader, are an intelligent, curious, and productive person. That means that you'll never find me endlessly repeating elementary stuff, as though my books were for "dummies," and you're spared from all the dysfunctional oversimplification and condescension that such writing makes inevitable.

I like to write in the same way that I talk, and you may already know that my conversational approach was something of a novelty back when this book was first published. I don't mind saying that I'm proud to see my basic belief—that people can talk about technology like people, not like machines—has been adopted by hundreds of other writers. I think you'll intuitively agree that you'll learn more about your computer from "talking" with me about it than you would if I just handed you pages of technical lists and hieroglyphic diagrams and told you that the test will be on Thursday. But, when this book premiered, that's exactly what most computer documentation was like.

I would never, of course, suggest that computer professionals have maintained their personal job security by keeping computers as mystical and unfathomable as possible. But I will observe that many companies have experienced notable jumps in productivity at all levels when certain types of technology management people are made obsolete. These companies have taken steps to empower everyday computer users to make many of their own decisions, to solve their own problems. You may not be employed by a large multilevel company—you may work in a small company, or you may be a student, retired, self-employed, or not employed at all. Still, this book will lead you to the same power and enable you to make the same sorts of productivity jumps by giving you a personal, direct, and complete understanding of the essential technologies used in your PC.

About This Book

This isn't a book for people who are having trouble finding the on/off switch on their computers. Instead, it's for people who have enough experience and curiosity to begin examining in greater depth these wonderful machines. My goal is to make understanding the PC easy and fun.

This is, more than anything else, a book written to help you learn what you really need to know about the PC. You can successfully use a PC without really understanding it. However, the better you understand your PC, the better equipped you are to realize the potential in the machine and—don't forget this—to deal with circumstances that almost certainly will arise someday. After all, when something goes wrong, the better you understand, the more likely you are to make the right moves to fix the problem and reduce its adverse impact on you and your business.

There are many other reasons you might want to understand the inner workings of your PC. One reason, a really good one, is simply for the intellectual satisfaction and sense of mastery that comes with understanding the tools with which you work. Another is to open up new realms for yourself. After all, there is plenty of demand these days for people who have PC savvy. But perhaps the most practical reason is the one that I suggested before. By analogy, think back to the early days of the automobile when you had to be an amateur mechanic to safely set out on a journey by car. It doesn't take the skills of a mechanic to drive a car today because cars have been tamed for everyday use. I'd like it to be that way with computers, but, frankly, computing hasn't yet progressed quite that far. Today, to efficiently and successfully use a personal computer, you need at least some degree of expertise; the more expertise you have, the better you can deal with the crises that sometimes arise as well as everyday issues.

Vitally important, too, in today's economy, is the realization that by understanding what goes on inside your PC, you'll be much better equipped to make intelligent decisions when it comes time to pull out your or your company's wallet. You won't end up paying for what you won't use. You'll really minimize your risk of "driving home with an Edsel," when you can look at technological trends and understand where things are and where they're likely headed. With high technology, more than anything else, advances tend to antiquate much of what came before. Last year's innovation will probably be this year's low-end model, and in the grand scheme of things, we wouldn't want it any other way. For you and me personally, however, this type of evolution-by-replacement can make buying equipment extremely stressful. After we're finished here, you'll be in a strong position when it comes time to analyze all of your purchase options and make a purchase choice that will give you the most for your buck—the greatest longevity.

Finally, PCs are now an integral part of our lives. Children learn to use them in schools, at home, or at a public library. You may not see yourself becoming all that heavily invested in computing as a part of your life, but it certainly is an ever-increasing part of most of our lives, and it appears that computers will be even more at the core of our children's lives. Thus, to understand your PC is in a way to understand more fully the social and technical environment in which we live. That puts the contents of this book right up there in importance: on a par with that to be found in books on politics, economics, and history.

For Readers of the Previous Edition

If you already own a copy of a previous edition of *Peter Norton's Inside the PC*, some natural questions you'll be asking yourself are these: Do I need yet another version of this book? What's new here that I want? And if I do buy this version, is there any reason to save the previous version I have? Here are my answers.

This is an update from the seventh edition, so if you have carefully read that version you may recognize familiar content in this edition. However, almost every chapter required substantial revision to bring it up to date—indeed, I was amazed to find out just how much this was true, inasmuch as it had been only a little more than a year since I completed the seventh edition. Several chapters have been rewritten in their entirety. And all the figures in this edition are either wholly new, or have been redrawn for greater clarity and, in some cases, to reflect updated facts about the technology.

If you own the sixth or any earlier edition of this book, you will find that absolutely everything in this version is new. The seventh edition was a new look at the topic. We started at ground zero and rebuilt this exposition from the bottom-up, using a new notion of what was appropriate to include and what was not.

We did this for several reasons, chief among which is that the world of PCs has changed dramatically. It was time to update this book in more than just minor ways. New perceptions and perspectives enabled the book to evolve along with the PC itself.

New Topics and New Organization

PCs are no longer just hackers' toys, nor even mere programmers' tools. They have become nearly "ubiquitous information appliances." (That phrase, literally, is one commonly cited vision of where PCs are going, even if they aren't yet quite there.)

Today, as never before, you can use a PC quite successfully without much or any appreciation of what is inside it. That this has happened is no accident. Many companies have expended enormous effort trying to make PCs so easy to use that you won't have to think about how they do their jobs.

Still, you can be even more effective if you do understand them—more effective as a PC user, and especially more effective when it comes to choosing additions or upgrades to your PC's hardware or software. The more savvy you are, the less likely you are to be taken in by unwarranted hype over the "latest and greatest" innovations.

Also, having a sound understanding of the technologies equips you to have more influence on the companies that create all the new products, both hardware and software, that we all want to see made as useful as possible. These companies actually do listen quite carefully to the "end users" of their products—but they listen much more attentively when they think these customers actually understand what they are talking about, and aren't merely making the mistakes of the misinformed.

Acquiring that understanding now can be harder than ever. In part, this is because there is so much more to know; and in part, it is because some of the new ideas are so complex and arcane. However, I firmly believe that any intelligent person who wants to understand these topics can, if only they are willing to give them some focused attention, and if only someone—such as I—is there to guide their learning.

Look at the table of contents. This book gives you first a fast overview, then a much more in-depth treatment. It is broken down into parts to help you know how the different topics relate to one another.

New Angles on Old Topics

When PCs were simply standalone machines, a look inside could be just that. It could be confined to an exploration of what each part of your PC is and does, and how it can do those things. But now, with PCs connected to the world, mainly through the Internet, and with local area networking becoming common not only in offices, but also in homes, any in-depth look inside a PC must be extended. In a sense, we will dive into the PC and then find ourselves coming out "the other side" where I will show you, in addition to what we found inside the PC itself, the world of technical marvels to which your PC gives you access.

Therefore, this edition clearly separates the inside-inside story on PCs from the inside-and-out-the-other-side story, and then gives you considerable detail about both. Also, as our industry matures and as the focus of my exploration with you in this book changes, some topics that were central in previous editions become merely background material or warm-up events before the main show in this edition. For example, you will find that I explain what DOS is and how it still underlies the Windows operating system most of you are using, but you won't find nearly the focus on DOS that has been the case in previous editions.

What's Not Still Here

Something had to go. Not only could we not put in everything we said before, plus all the new material without making this book so large and heavy that you wouldn't even want to pick it up, it was time for some things to go. I don't mean to suggest that those things are no longer true, nor even that they no longer matter. It simply is the case that they no longer deserve the prominence they had in earlier editions.

So, if you own previous editions of this book, I hope you will keep them and keep them handy. You may well find that something I said in one of them was said in just the right way for you to understand it most easily. Or, there may be a table or figure there that made some details apparent that you can't find so easily in the current edition.

Sometimes, when you approach a new topic, you will find it easier to understand if you read what I say about it here, in this version, and then go back and compare that to what I said in a previous version. Two different statements of the same thing sometimes make a point clear that you might otherwise miss.

Navigation Aids for Our Journey

Some people think they'll get lost in a book as big as this one. Well now, I wouldn't want that to happen. So I've made sure you'll have plenty of ways to keep the big picture in view, and to find each nook or cranny that especially interests you.

The table of contents is a good place to start. Or, if you want to find some specific bit of information, check the index. That is an especially good way to find something when you remember reading it, but can't recall where in the book you found it. Also look at the jump table on the inside front and back covers. That points you directly to certain hot topics, and points out some that may be treated partially in each of several chapters.

New in this eighth edition is the glossary. The glosssary includes a lot of the "buzz-words," phrases, and acronyms you will run across when reading about PCs. For each one, I have tried to give you a very concise definition of what the term means, plus in many cases, I have given an reference to a chapter in this book where you will find that topic treated at greater length.

Technical Note: Some of you want really detailed, technical information—the "real goodies," as you might put it. And there is quite a lot of that in here. Just look for paragraphs that look like this one.

Maybe really "hard" stuff frightens you. Should you avoid these paragraphs? I suggest you try reading a few and see. You might find that you can understand more than you thought you could. And you might even enjoy them. On the other hand, I've been careful to ensure that your overall grasp of the book's story line will not suffer if you skip these paragraphs entirely.

Historical Aside

Some of you are interested in the broad picture, and would enjoy some histori- cal perspective. You'll want to keep a lookout for paragraphs that look like this one. Not only will you find some interesting background on today's technology, you may also discover the reasons that we still must do certain things the way we do, because of past decisions—the influence of which still lingers.

Tip: Looking for some hot tips? I have them in here, too. This is how they will appear in the body of the book.

Note: Sometimes, I have a note flagged in the manner of this paragraph. These are not necessarily technical points, nor are they asides. They are just something I found, well, noteworthy.

Standards: The PC field is full of jargon and other things that may confuse you. Fortunately, there are some standards that help us keep things straight. Whenever you see this sort of paragraph, please read it carefully. It will help you keep out of many of the potholes you might otherwise fall into on your journey.

Warning: Speaking of tripping up, there are some important cautionary notes. These are warnings I give you so you won't hurt yourself, your PC, or your data. Please read them, too, and follow them every time they apply. You'll be glad you did, and so will I.

Peter's Principle: Peter's Principles Point the Way

Finally, there are a number of what I like to think are wonderfully useful ideas scattered throughout the text. These are discoveries I have made that I want to share with you—the fruits of my experimentation that may, when shared in this manner, save you some painful learning experiences.

To help you find them, I have given each one a title, like the one above this paragraph.

A Point of View

Where you stand often defines what you can see. That's true when you are out hiking in the mountains, and it is no less true when you come with me on a "hike" through PC land.

If you're looking for interesting and useful technical information about the PC from the inside out, you won't be disappointed. I am dedicated to making this book a guide to what makes the PC tick. But, just as the hardware has changed dramatically over the past couple of years—and seems poised for more, even more dramatic changes in the next few years—so has the focus of the user. The Internet is all the rage and for some pretty good reasons. PCs today can be understood only in the context of these larger changes. To that end, I shall address both the technology as it is and as it seems likely to be in the near future, and also how all this is changing what PC users are doing, thinking, and wanting.

A lot of this book focuses on hardware. That is the stuff you can see, feel, heft, and for which you feel pretty sure you got something for your money. But software is also important. In fact, without good software, your PC's hardware is good only as a doorstop or decoration.

So some chapters will take you into hardware depths and practically ignore the software, while others will assume the hardware and explain the technologies behind today's operating systems and application programs. You can discover which chapters serve which purposes pretty well just from the table of contents, and I will point out the relationships among different parts and chapters in this book from time to time in the text, as well.

At the end of several chapters, you'll find some suggestions for things you may wish to think about or try. These exercises are examples of what I think is the most powerful way to get to know your PC. Get in and get your hands dirty—figuratively, at least. This is so important, in fact, that I have devoted an entire chapter to teaching you how to do this safely and effectively: Chapter 6, "Enhancing Your Understanding by Exploring and Tinkering" If you haven't ever played around much inside your PC, you might want to wait until after you read that chapter before you start tinkering.

PART I

The Big Picture

The View from Afar

Welcome to a journey of adventure! This book is going to take you on a tour inside the modern personal computer (PC). You'll learn how it is built (and why), how it works (at least in a general sense), and gain insight into where this amazing technology is headed. The knowledge you'll gain will empower you in several ways. You'll become a more educated consumer, better able to make wise choices when selecting or upgrading your PC. When the inevitable problems arise, you'll be better equipped to understand what's happening and thus to take appropriate corrective actions. And your new insights will help you position yourself on this incredible, ever-breaking wave of new technology so that you won't, as surfers say, "wipe out."

Previous editions of this book have begun with what was once a deceptively simple question: What is a PC? Today, unless you've been hidden away somewhere, it's very unlikely that you don't already have a fairly accurate answer. Those transitional days of "you think you know what a PC is, but you don't," are largely behind us. In fact, today the opposite is more likely true: You might not think you know what a PC is, but you probably do. Most of us use a computer every day that we would recognize as a "PC," or, if we don't use one ourselves, our partners or children do.

Historically, a computer that was a "personal computer" existed in contrast to the many corporate-owned mainframe computers, which were accessed through terminals. For the most part, these terminals didn't have any computing power of their own. All tasks, from scientific calculations taking weeks to complete to rudimentary game programs, were run in the mainframe's central processing unit. This processing power had to be shared by everyone using the mainframe. If you had a particularly complex task to perform, you might have had to make an appointment to use the processor power you needed, so that everyone else's work wouldn't be interrupted.

Today, while the PC on your desk at work may be connected to a corporate mainframe via a network, it probably contains several times the computing power of yesterday's mainframes. (If any of these terms, such as mainframe and network, are new to you, don't be concerned. As we continue, I'll take the time to make certain you understand the jargon and abbreviated terms which are rife in the computing world.)

Today, of course, the term PC serves almost no function other than succinctly naming a class of devices we all recognize, much like "television." PC still distinguishes your desktop or notebook unit from a mainframe computer or minicomputer, yes. That's hardly an important distinction. Similarly, the term PC sets apart what we increasingly think of simply as "the computer," from all of the microchips and embedded computers that are quietly running your washing machine, your microwave oven, and your VCR. No one would expect you to say, "I'm going to go write a letter on the computer," and then stick your head inside the microwave.

As you'll see, there is convergence coming between these computer-based appliances and the computer—the PC—on your desk or your lap. But most of those appliances will always be just that: appliances. Perhaps, then, more than anything else today, it is the multi-purpose functionality of a computer—its ability to perform hundreds of very different tasks—which cues us, almost subconsciously, to recognize that *this* is a PC, but *that* is not. Still, we've largely reached the point of saturation. We don't internally analyze what a friend means when she announces that she's going to purchase a PC. We simply understand.

Don't Blink

One of the greatest frustrations for PC manufacturers in recent years has been this same universal understanding. If we all already know what a PC is, we become resistant to industry attempts to tell us that it's something else. For example, if you're already perfectly happy with your old computer, which has no support for sound or motion video and no Internet access, simply being told that you're using an antiquated machine won't be very convincing.

For a very different group of users, most such attempts to tell us what a *viable* PC is—through the creation of industry standards, like the Multimedia PC (MPC)—have failed because industry standards have a way of following behind what these users already possess. By the time a standard is adopted, it's often outdated. This is because PC technology changes at an unbelievable rate, and this second group of early adopters wants new tools as soon as they're available. This ongoing evolution is altering how many people go about living their lives.

What's the State of the Art?

Let's talk about the evolution of PCs: how they got here and where we think we see them going. Let's look at the ever-changing state of the art.

Up until fairly recently, if you asked someone who was supposed to know these things what a state-of-the-art PC was, you'd probably get an answer something like this: "It's an arrangement of particular kinds of computing hardware pieces plus a collection of software programs designed to run on that hardware. It's a tool that you use to do word processing, create and manipulate spreadsheets, store and retrieve data using a database application, or several similar tasks." More recently, of course, the answer would include a reference to the PC's growing capacity for helping artists create interesting visual effects or for musicians to compose and perform electronic music, or for you and me to work with data from distant locations via an online connection.

Tomorrow's State of the Art

As you probably know, it's this last factor—remote accessibility—that is in the forefront of today's news. Industry visionaries (some would say alchemists) are prophesying a world of ubiquitous computing. In this world, every computer would have access to every other computer (to the degree that this is desirable, and within strict security guidelines, of course). Anything that is known that you want to know could be made available to you, anywhere. You could retrieve email from your car and have it read aloud while you drive. The population of India could appear on a public-use computing panel in your doctor's office. You could visually look in on your children and their babysitter from a small handheld device that fits in your purse. You could work interactively with your boss on an emergency presentation while you're sitting with a fishing rod in Yosemite National Park, and so on.

For this grand vision of a world of fully interconnected computers and of software that can be anywhere and yet be used by anyone to be possible, all those computers have to be *fully interoperable*. That means that no longer may PCs run only PC software, Macintosh computers run Mac software, and UNIX computers run UNIX software. Every computing device must run any program. If that sounds like a pipe dream, guess again. We're fast approaching that point now. In some limited ways, it's already upon us. You will learn more about this hot topic in Chapter 26, "You Can Touch the World, and It May Touch You, Too!," and Chapter 27, "Looking Back and Looking Ahead."

The Plague: Jargon

Wherever the world of computing is going, you're holding this book because you already know that you want to understand more about issues which may impact your life. One of the things that often annoys newcomers to this exploration is the heavy load of jargon that they encounter. Jargon and acronyms (which are just one form that jargon can take) are common in almost every area of human endeavor. It serves at least two purposes. The first (and laudable) one is that it's a form of shorthand. After you know what the acronym (or other jargon item) means, mentioning it recalls the entire definition and its context. This makes for more efficient communication. The second purpose of most jargon (a much more negative one) is that the insiders in a field use it as a weapon to intimidate, and a barrier to exclude, the outsiders. This latter use of jargon, regrettably, appears to be human nature. It is, if you will, the book burning of the late twentieth century. So you should expect to have to learn the insider language that applies to PCs, just as you would with any other field of comparable complexity.

Tip: Still, the level of jargon and the number of acronyms used in the personal computer field are unusually high. Any time you encounter an acronym, or even just a word or phrase that you suspect means something other than what it appears to mean at first glance, look in the Index for a reference to the place in this book where I discuss the concept in more detail. You may find additional explanations available in the Glossary at the end of this book.

But enough of this for now. You will learn about much of the other jargon used in the PC world soon, and by putting it in its proper context later in the book, the meanings will be much clearer than they'd be if I tried to define them all right here. There's no question that an awareness of this nomenclature is an important part of understanding—and being able to interact with—the world of PCs. But where did all of this come from?

Do the Time Warp, Again

Personal computers of any sort are a recent phenomenon. Many say that the first one was the MITS Altair computer, created in 1974. It was a big box with a tiny capability. The user interface was just a lot of little switches and lights on the front panel. You could demonstrate the principles behind the operation of any computer, but you really couldn't do much computing.

An amazingly short time later, the Apple Computer company was born and its Apple II became the definition of what a computer was for an entire generation of people. At about the same time several other companies made small computers that were quite distinct from one another in their designs, but which all ran an operating system called CP/M. (You learn a little bit about what an operating system is in Chapter 5, "How to Get Your PC to Understand You," and revisit that subject in more depth in Chapter 17, "Understanding PC Operating Systems.")

These CP/M computers could do quite a few useful tasks, but learning how to use them required a level of dedication that relatively few people wanted to bring to bear. Still, they were successful products and people did a lot of work using them.

1981 saw a quantum jump in the capability of small computers. IBM's original PC (that was its name for it, which we presume stood for personal computer, not play computer, as was once suggested) cost about the same as many of the other small computers on the market, but it was a big technological step forward in some important ways. That fact was not at all obvious to many people at the time, but it became quite clear within about one or two years after the PC's introduction.

What Have We Done?!

When it introduced its PC, IBM did three things that were totally out of character. First, it told everyone almost all the details about how its PC was built. It did this to invite others to make hardware pieces that would work with its PC. A lot of companies took IBM up on its offer. Second, it bought the PC's operating system from a third party, Microsoft. Third, its license agreement with Microsoft let Microsoft license that operating system to other companies that made small computers as well as to IBM.

At first, IBM offered only a very limited number of optional hardware pieces and software programs that one could buy for its PC. This meant that although the basic design was impressive for its time, the kinds of things one could actually *do* with a PC were quite limited.

However, very soon the marketplace was overflowing with PC add-ons that could enable a PC to do almost anything. In short order, the IBM PC became hugely popular. It soon far outsold all the competition put together. And just as the Volkswagen "Bug" is history's most customized car, the IBM PC soon became history's most customized computer.

That, no doubt, made the folks at IBM very happy. What happened next did not. Some people said to themselves, "Because IBM has told us all about how they build their PC, we can build ones just like theirs. And we can do it cheaper. And we can buy our microprocessor chips from Intel and our operating system from Microsoft (and the other parts from yet other manufacturers), so IBM can't stop us." All of which was absolutely true. Of course, one major reason why those "clone makers" could create and sell their products more inexpensively was that they didn't have to pay for all the engineering effort IBM had expended.

In a very few years we had a whole industry making computers that were so nearly alike that they all could run the same programs and one could freely exchange data between them (carrying the data on diskettes, usually). And equally significantly, soon no one manufacturer, including IBM, could claim control of that "industry standard PC" design. The dominant small computer became some sort of a PC-compatible or PC-clone. And the number of them grew way beyond anything that anyone at IBM had ever thought possible—or, very likely, would have found desirable. There are, however, some terrible consequences.

Tied to the Past

This market development defined the PC originally as any small computer that conformed to IBM's general design and that would run the same programs that could run on any other PC. The downside of these events is that this industry standard became pretty much the definition of what was acceptable as a small computer, especially for use in business. And as the years went on and even more people got those PC-compatible computers, this standard became more solidly entrenched. Now, almost no company would dare to introduce a new computer design or a new operating system design for the PC that isn't fully "backward compatible."

By this we mean that those new computers or PCs running those new operating systems will be able to run virtually any program that could run on any earlier PC or

PC-compatible computer. This has been very important in terms of letting PC owners feel free to upgrade to the newer machine or newer operating system, but it also has served as a heavy anchor limiting companies' freedom to innovate. (This is beginning to change today, but only in the most minute of ways.)

Intel—the company that made the microprocessor IBM chose to put at the heart of its original PC, and the company that still makes most of the CPU (*central processing unit*) chips for PCs today—has ridden this huge wave of computer industry growth precisely because it promised vociferously that every x86 family member is totally backward compatible with the original 8088. (You can find out all about what the x86 family is in Chapter 7, "Understanding PC Processors.")

Similarly, Microsoft, by being the vendor with the operating system that IBM used, rode the same wave to dominate the computer operating system market. And its family of first DOS, then Windows operating systems are, *de facto*, the industry standards for PC operating systems.

By contrast, IBM, who started this whole show, is now only a peripheral player. It no longer can single-handedly set any meaningful standards for the industry. And not only is it not the only maker of PCs, it isn't even the one that makes the largest number of units each year.

The Bottom Line: What You Must Know and Why

Who needs to know all these things? Perhaps you do. Understanding how we got where we are, as an industry, and having some insight into where we're probably going in the near future will explain a lot about what's happening now. And it will help you see which of the hot, new products (hardware or software) are likely to be important, and which are likely to serve only niche markets, blooming briefly and then passing from the scene.

Clearly, if you can see in advance which hot new technologies are likely to have a lasting impact and which are not, then you can choose to invest more heavily in the former and steer clear of the latter. That will get you the best return on your investment in both PC hardware and software, especially over the long haul. Furthermore, if you see the computing industry as having a significant place in your personal future, perhaps forming the basis of your livelihood itself, your knowledge must be fairly deep about certain aspects of the PC's design, as well as about how its software is built and operates. And, it should come as no surprise that giving you this information is exactly what the rest of this book is all about.

Can You Learn It All?

When I first began working with PCs shortly after IBM first introduced them in 1981, they weren't very complicated. It was perfectly practical for one individual to aspire to understand in full detail every aspect of the design of the PC hardware, as well as learn how nearly all PC software was programmed.

Back then, PCs were rare, and there were very few companies that made anything to do with them. That's why it was all so simple. Now, however, PCs are a *very* big business. Increasing interconnectivity simply makes understanding the big picture and all the details in it a much harder task.

Arguably, modern PCs—including their natural extensions via the Internet and other similar computer-to-computer connections—have become, as a whole, the most complex creation of mankind. Collectively, they form the most sophisticated consumer and business tool ever devised.

This complex creation was not made by a single company, or even by a few companies. A huge number of companies and their brilliant, hard-working employees were needed to build it all. This means that there are far too many diverse products that enhance or work with PCs for any one individual to understand them all fully.

Indeed, to write this book, I needed the help of several people with expertise that went beyond mine in various ways. You'll find them mentioned in my acknowledgments in the front of this book.

But don't despair. You *can* learn enough. You can learn the basics of how a PC is built and how it works, and you can learn the principles behind the programs it can use. You can learn how networks of PCs are created and, at least generally, how they operate. And those kinds of knowledge are exactly what you must learn to be newly empowered in ways that could change your life.

The OBE (Out of Box Experience) and You

With the push to make PCs into a sort of information appliance, hardware vendors began to give serious attention to various ways of helping new owners of their products have an easy time setting them up and getting them to work. The jargon term for this is the *OBE*, or the *Out of Box Experience*. It refers to the overall experience you're likely to have when you take home a new box containing some PC accessory—or even an entire new PC—open it up, and try to get it to work.

The goal, of course, is to make the OBE an easy and satisfying one. Achieving that goal has turned out to be quite a challenge for manufacturers. And, as often happens with laudable but difficult developments, even before a vendor's engineering department has worked out how to give the customer a good OBE, its marketing department will already be trumpeting to one and all that its products now offer a great OBE. So, my advice to you is this: *Caveat emptor.* Or, in common speech: Don't believe everything you read or hear—especially from a manufacturer or salesman.

No matter how nice he or she says your OBE will be, you should plan on spending some time getting to know your new PC (or PC peripheral) and its capabilities rather intimately. And then you will find that it takes even more time if you want to be able to upgrade those capabilities.

One error too many people make is to choose a PC based on how easy it is supposed to be to upgrade later. In the process, they can let themselves be talked into buying a PC with lesser capabilities than they really know they need (in order to avoid having to spend so much money up front). This rarely works out as smoothly as consumers are told.

In practical terms, this might mean that, unless you're very confident of your abilities to work inside the PC system unit (box), you should never buy a PC with less RAM than you'll need to run the programs you want to use in the next six months. (After that, the whole PC might be obsolete, or you might save so much on the new RAM you need by waiting until you need it—because prices on almost all PC parts have historically fallen quite rapidly—that you can afford to pay someone to install it.) At the end of Chapter 11, "Giving Your PC's CPU Enough Elbow Room—PC Memory," I give you some specific suggestions on how much RAM is enough. Also, be sure you buy as much storage space (as big a hard disk) as you can afford. That's another item that sounds easier to upgrade than it can turn out to be in practice.

A Method and Plan for Our Journey

Okay. You know what a PC is and you know something of how this industry came to be and where the illuminati think it's headed, at least in general terms. I'll close this chapter by telling you a bit more about how this book is organized, and how you might choose to organize your safari into the deepest, darkest parts of your PC, and the new world that opens up beyond it.

Like many other books about computers, this one is both a general learning tool and a reference tool. That is, it can be read from cover to cover, in a totally linear manner, or you can browse in it, or dip in first here, then there, until you get the specific facts you want or need to find. Choosing a particular path is up to you.

As you can see from the Table of Contents, the book is divided into eight parts. Furthermore, throughout each part you will find that the material has been layered and peppered with signposts for your convenience.

PCs and the World in Eight Parts

Part I, "The Big Picture," looks at PCs from the outside. That is, it tells you about them without actually referring to the nitty-gritty details.

Part II, "A First Look Inside Your PC," is a fast trip into the interior. Think of it as a chance to get your feet wet, or in another metaphor, as a high-altitude pass over the territory, to let you get a general sense of how the land is situated.

The story continues in Part III, "The Standalone PC." If yours is a fairly basic PC, and if it's never connected to another computer, then these chapters will have most of what you need to understand your PC's construction and function.

Part IV, "PC Programs: From Machine Language Bytes to Human Speech," is a bit different. It returns to something closer to the flavor of Part I, but this time goes a lot deeper into how computers in general, and PCs in particular, are programmed.

Next come three parts that describe the main ways in which some PCs are different from their simpler brethren. Part V, "Splendiferous Multimedia PCs," describes fancy PCs. Part VI, "PCs Are Frequent Flyers, Too," focuses on mobile PCs. Part VII, "The Connected PC," explains the special features of PCs that connect to other computers.

Finally, Part VIII, "PCs, the Internet, the Future, and You," takes you beyond merely going *inside* your PC. It takes you, in effect, out the other side of your PC and into the world beyond.

Use the Layers to Fine-Tune Your Travels

There are three main levels on which the text is written. There is the basic story, which is suitable for any reader. There are historical asides that might interest only readers who aren't in a tearing hurry to find some instantly useful facts, and are seeking enjoyable anecdotes and background information. And there are the particularly technical portions, clearly marked so you can either avoid them (if you fear they might spook you), or hone in on them (if you want to find the absolute last word on a topic).

And, of course, don't forget the Index and Glossary. They are often the best way to find the information you want in the fastest possible way.

Bon Voyage!

How (Almost) Any Computer Works

Computers are tools used to process information. (In the next chapter, I explain exactly what I mean by *information*. For now, I shall assume that you have at least a pretty good notion of what it is.) Having said that fairly obvious yet basic fact about computers, I have actually implied quite a bit about how they must be built. Let me explain.

The Logical Parts of Any Computer

Any computer, to qualify as a computer, must have internal parts that serve the following five functions:

- Input
- Output
- Processing
- Information holding
- Control

I want to be very clear here—I am referring to the functional roles played by these parts. The parts themselves need not be distinct from one another; it is perfectly possible for one physical component or module to do at least a portion of more than one of these essential tasks. There also may well be (and usually are) multiple physical pieces that together serve the totality of any one of these five functional parts.

In this section and its subsections, I will go over each of these five parts, explaining why it is essential, and then describe some examples of how particular pieces of your PC serve in each of those roles—at least some of the time.

First, if you are going to process some information, you must be able to get into the computer the information to be processed. So, all computers must have a functional part (or more than one) that serves as an *input path* for information.

Second, processing information is pretty pointless if you never get to find out the results of the processing. So, all computers must have another functional part (or more than one) that serves as an *output path* for the processed information.

Third, and this might be said to be the (logically) most central part, there must be some part that can do the information processing. We call this part the *information processing* part.

Fourth, it wouldn't be possible to do any information processing if every bit of it that came in went back out immediately. The information must linger for at least a while so the computer can work on it. This implies that all computers must have some sort of *information-holding* part (or parts).

There is another reason why some information-holding mechanism is necessary: The computer must know what it is to do. That means that somewhere inside it must be a place where the instructions about the processing it is to do can be kept. That takes more information holding.

Finally, there must be some part that *controls* what all the other parts do. Leave this out, and you have something that is almost a computer, but not quite. It has all the parts it needs to do everything, but no "head" to tell those pieces when to do the required tasks.

To repeat myself a little more concisely: Every computer has a means for information input, a means for information output, a place for information to linger while it is waiting to be processed, a portion that does the processing, and finally, a portion that directs the work of all the other parts.

When you get into the details of how a particular computer is built, you will find some significant differences. This book concerns itself with the details of how only PCs are built, which is why the chapter title doesn't promise that you will learn the details of every computer ever built. Funny thing, though: If you just count how many mainframe computers have been built, how many minicomputers, and how many of each kind of smaller computer, then add together all the varieties of PC, you will find that their total numbers far exceed all the other computers ever built. So to understand PCs is to understand almost all general-purpose computers.

Actually, I have left out one very important logical part, because it isn't also a functional part as such. I mentioned that there must be some place in which to hold the instructions describing what the computer is to do. These instructions, taken as a whole, are referred to as the *program* or *programs* the computer contains and is being called upon to *execute* (that is, to perform the instructions they contain). Those programs themselves can be thought of as yet another logical part of your PC. They differ from the other parts, though, because for all the other parts, you must have actual hardware of some sort. Programs, in their purest form, are merely abstract collections of numbers. True, they will end up residing in some physical medium somewhere, but you never need to possess physically that program-containing medium; all you really need is the capability of retrieving those numbers from it and transporting them into your PC. (This is, for example, what you often end up doing when your PC is connected to the Internet.)

Functional Hardware Parts of a PC

That was a pretty quick and abstract overview of how a computer is built. Now I am going to go back over each of these five functional physical parts of any computer in a bit more detail, this time showing you which pieces of a PC typify each one.

Information Input Devices

The input device you probably use most often on your PC is the keyboard. You also input information any time you load a program from a disk. Most PCs have a floppy disk drive. Some also have tape drives or removable cartridge drives. When you bring information on a floppy disk, tape, removable cartridge, or optical disc from some other computer to your PC, the drive that enables your PC to read that information is another form of input device.

You might be confused. You might be thinking that a floppy disk, optical disc, or removable disk is a place where information is held. That is true, but it is not the point I am trying to make here.

I am talking about the *functional input parts* of a computer, not about the physical pieces of which it is composed. Sometimes a physical piece can serve in two or more different functional roles. That is the case, for example, for a disk drive. When you bring information to your PC from some other computer on a floppy disk, that disk drive serves, at that time, as an input device. I'll explain a bit later in this chapter how that same physical piece can also serve as an information-holding device or an output device, depending on what you are doing with it.

> **Note:** Your hard drive could conceivably also serve as an input device, but only if you remove it from one PC and then install it in your PC. Because most hard drives don't normally migrate between PCs, we normally consider them to be only information-holding devices, not input or output devices.

Another very common way to put information into your computer, although you might not have thought of it in those terms before, is by moving and clicking your mouse. (Or, of course, doing the equivalent things using a trackpad, trackball, graphics tablet, joystick, or the like.)

Other types of input some people use these days include scanners, digital cameras, microphones, and videocassette recorders. These are the essential inputs for creating multimedia presentations on a PC.

Connect your PC to another computer, and you are likely to use that connection as a means of getting even more information into your PC. Such connections include connecting to other desktop PCs over a local area network, a mainframe host session connection, or using a modem to connect your PC to an electronic bulletin board or an Internet service provider. In effect, when your PC is connected to any of the other computers "out there," you are able to access the information they contain, and that makes them "input devices" that are "attached" (albeit temporarily) to your PC.

Of course, these same remote computers can also be used as recipients of information from your PC. But that is the subject of the next section, "Information Output Devices."

These are merely examples of some of the more common PC input devices. After you understand the concept, I am sure you can think of at least a few more you've heard about, and possibly even some you personally have used.

Information Output Devices

The most common output device for a PC is the monitor, on which words and pictures can be displayed for the PC user to see. It is a very efficient output device because it can display a lot of information at once, and it can alter that displayed information quite rapidly.

Another common form of output is a printer. In the early days of computers, almost all output that was in human-readable form was printed on paper. If that were still the case, and if all the information that is now shown on screens had to be printed, I think this planet would have no trees left. But when you do need to keep some output for later reading, printing to paper is a convenient way to accomplish that.

Remember that most printers print more than just words. In fact, a very large portion of PC output to printers today is in the form of highly formatted pages of text (information about how the individual letters are to look and where they are to be placed is sent to the printer in addition to the actual letters themselves), and those pages can also include photographic or other images.

But not all computer output must be put into a form that humans can read. Indeed, it is essential that we be able to put much of it out in a computer-readable form. Every time you save your work to disk—at least if the disk in question can be removed from your PC and attached to some other computer—you have created some output that some computer (yours or another) could later use for input. So your PC's floppy disk drives can serve as output devices. (And, as you learned in the preceding section, they also can serve as input devices. It just depends on what you are doing with them.)

We don't normally count saving files on the PC's hard disk as output, because you can't easily take your hard disk out and put it in another PC. (This is not to say that can't be done—just that it is not normally done.) But when you save a file to a floppy disk, to tape, or to a disk cartridge, and if you plan to take the information you put on those media to some other computer so that the content can be loaded into that other computer, those acts on your PC are clearly information output.

Multimedia creations often show up as output to audio loudspeakers (in addition to showing their images on the monitor), or they can be saved to a recordable CD (called a CD-R or CD-RW disc) or on a video cassette recorder. Perhaps you have given a presentation in which your PC was attached to a liquid crystal display panel on an overhead projector or to a video projector, as well as to a sound system, so an entire room full of people could see and hear what you had created. That is just another form of computer output. And, of course, any time you connect your PC to another computer (over a local area network or a modem connection), you can use that link for output (or for input).

Finally, let me describe a really unusual kind of PC output that certain people are using daily right now. One name for this activity is *rapid prototyping*. There are several ways in which this can be done. One common method, called *stereolithography,* uses a computer-controlled laser to solidify (*polymerize*) selected regions in a thin layer of a liquid plastic—thus turning those regions into a solid form—and then to do the same thing for the next layer, and so on until a full, three-dimensional object is created.

At the end of the process, one can paint the output, plate the finished product with metal, or do whatever may be appropriate for its intended use. No longer must a highly skilled craftsperson labor for many hours to craft these prototype objects; a suitable machine, driven by a small computer (which often is a PC), can do it all for you instead.

One person who is using this technique in some very intriguing ways is Michael Rees. He is a sculptor working and teaching at the Kansas City Art Institute in Kansas City, Missouri. You can learn more about his work at these Web sites:

http://www.wired.com/news/news/culture/story/16244.html

http://www.sound.net/~zedand00

The immediate output of the PC in this sort of rapid prototyping is the flow of numbers to the laser that causes it to do its job. But in another sense, the ultimate output is the object created. So in that sense, the entire rapid prototyping subsystem (with its supply of raw material) is an information output device for the PC. This is analogous to the way you often use a PC with a printer and its supply of paper to make what amounts to a small book.

Eventually, most manufactured items might be made under the control of a PC in just such a fashion. This just-in-time approach has the great advantage that only the parts that are going to be used are made, and each one can be custom-crafted to meet the most exacting details of the customer's every whim.

Information Processing Devices

Most of the work of information processing in your PC is done by a device called the *arithmetic-logic unit* (ALU), which is only a part of what is on the particular integrated circuit chip we call the *central processing unit* (CPU). The ALU adds, subtracts, multiplies, and divides numbers, and it also performs "logical operations," such as comparing two numbers to see which one is greater.

In the original IBM PC, that CPU chip was a part made by the Intel Corporation and they called it an 8088. Chapter 7, "Understanding PC Processors," tells you about all the other CPUs that have been used in later models of IBM PCs or in various PC-compatible and clone PC computers. You'll also learn there about some of the processors that have been used in some computers that aren't what we are calling a PC.

The name *central processing unit* suggests that there might be other processors in your PC, elsewhere than at the center of the action. Indeed, there are. A typical PC contains about half a dozen (and often many more) separate microprocessors, each doing its own, separate job.

The central processor is so important that often people refer to their entire PC by just the name of its CPU. For example, if you say you have a Pentium machine or a 486, you are doing that. This shorthand way of speaking is understandable and quite acceptable because the nature of the CPU prescribes most of the details for how all the other parts must be built.

Chapter 5, "How to Get Your PC to Understand You," explains what types of processing the CPU chip is capable of doing. For now, just know that it is the part or module that contains the subparts with their actual circuits that do most of the information processing that is done in your PC.

Information-Holding Devices

Earlier in this chapter, I mentioned several reasons why any computer must be able to hold information, at least briefly. One is to have it hang around long enough to be acted upon (processed). The other is that the instructions specifying what processing is to be done must be held inside the computer for them to be acted on.

> **Note:** There are two kinds of information-holding places in your PC. Some hold it while it is being worked on; others hold information for the longer term. They are so different that the industry has come to use two separate terms for these two forms of information-holding places (detailed for you in a moment). Please see the Warning at the end of this section.

Once again, I am focusing here on the essential *function* in any computer of the parts that hold information. The same devices that can serve this function might also be able to serve the function of carrying information to (or from) another computer, as was described in the preceding two sections. In doing so they will, of course, have to retain that information during its transit to (or from) the remote computer. They are not by that fact serving as what I am here calling the essential information-holding function of the computer, but rather as a suitably persistent medium of data transfer.

Because both types of information (data to be processed and instructions on what processing is to be done) are just numbers, they can both be held in the same information-holding devices. In PCs, that is precisely what is done.

Peter's Principle: Choose Data File Locations and Your Backup Strategy Independently

I *don't* recommend that you try to separate data and programs onto separate hard disks or disk partitions, despite the advantages that might seem to be offered when doing backups. Some PC programs won't allow you to do this, and there are other disadvantages as well. I describe my recommended method of doing backups in Chapter 6, "Enhancing Your Understanding by Exploring and Tinkering," in the section "How to Protect Your Data."

Chapter 18, "Understanding How Humans Instruct PCs," explains how sometimes the identity of these two types of information becomes even more confused—when data can act as instructions, or instructions can be treated as just so much more data.

Right now, I want to point out a different way to divide the places in a PC where information is held: a three-way division.

The first is a set of places that keep information that never changes (called *non-volatile electronic memory*). The second is a set of places that forgets any information it contains whenever you turn your PC off or reboot it (called *volatile electronic memory*). The third is a set of places that can keep information for a long time, and yet can enable that information to be changed (called *data storage places*).

Non-Volatile Electronic Memory

In the first set of places for information holding are some very high-speed ones whose content is changed either only rarely or not at all. In a PC, this is any number of non-volatile electronic memory chips. There must be at least one of these, because there must be at least a little bit of permanently and instantly available information to let the PC know how to start working when you first turn it on. Other programs that are held in non-volatile electronic memory include ones that are needed to activate the various hardware parts (such as the input and output devices) and that are used too often to make it worthwhile to get fresh copies of them from a disk whenever they are needed.

Some non-volatile electronic memory chips have their information content manufactured into them when they first are built. It can never be changed. We call these chips read-only memory (ROM) chips.

Other non-volatile electronic memory chips hold their information content for long periods of time without needing an outside power source, yet are able to have that information changed when necessary. As a generic group, these can be referred to as *NVRAM* (non-volatile, random-access memory) chips. Other names are also often used for these chips, each one describing how a particular kind of NVRAM chip is built. These names include *EEPROM, Flash RAM* (or *Flash ROM*), and *FERAM* (or *FEROM*). You'll learn more about each of these technologies in Chapter 11, "Giving Your PC's CPU Enough Elbow Room—PC Memory." Still others are actually volatile memory chips that have been outfitted with a battery to keep them from losing their data contents when external power is removed. The CMOS chip on your PC's motherboard is an example of this last type of NVRAM.

Volatile Electronic Memory

In the second set of places, your PC keeps information only temporarily. These places forget whatever information they contain any time you reset or turn off your computer. In a PC, these are found in some larger number of electronic read-write memory chips. Because it is possible to go directly to any of the stored bits of information in these chips, they are called *random-access memory* (RAM) chips.

Often in modern PCs, small groups of these chips are mounted on little plug-in circuit cards, and those assemblies are called *memory modules*. (Several different types of these memory modules exist, some called SIMMs and some called DIMMs. They are not all interchangeable; when adding more of them, you must get just the right kind for your PC.)

Both volatile and non-volatile electronic information-holding devices (RAM and ROM) are covered in much more detail in Chapter 11. For now, the most important other thing you must know about these devices is that they work very quickly—almost as fast as the CPU chip. And a whole lot faster than the third type of information storage device.

I've pointed out that this second group of memory chips (the volatile electronic ones) forgets easily. That can be disastrous if your PC becomes "hung" and must be reset when you are in the middle of some long task and have forgotten to save your work. But it also can be a blessing if your PC is so confused that it cannot do anything (which is what being "hung" really means). In that case, you can clear out all that confusing mess simply by turning off the power or pressing the reset button and letting it start afresh.

Because in modern PCs the CPU often runs too fast even for the RAM and ROM chips, some smaller amount of extra-fast RAM is needed to keep the CPU from having to twiddle its thumbs, chew its fingernails, or otherwise waste time waiting for the information it needs to reach it.

This faster RAM is organized into something called *cache memory* (composed of what are termed *SRAM* chips). In 486 and later processors, some of that cache memory is actually located on the CPU chip. Often, more of it is placed on the motherboard. You learn more about those details in Chapters 4 and 7.

Data Storage Places

The third set of places to store information is in the various types of disk, disc, and cassette drives on your PC or remotely on some other computer. The good news about these places is that they can accept new information and that they can preserve it even when your PC is shut off.

The bad news is that they cannot take or deliver back that information nearly fast enough to satisfy the CPU. In fact, these data storage places typically require hundreds to thousands of times as long to accept or retrieve information as is the case for RAM memory (which in a modern PC is itself several times slower than the CPU). So before any of the information is used as a program of instructions or as data to be processed, it must be loaded from that remote location into some place in the PC's RAM.

A useful shorthand to keep clearly in mind the differing nature of the fast information-holding places and the slow ones is to call the former ones "memory" and the latter ones "storage." From now on in this book I will do just that, and in fact, that is a standard distinction used almost all the time throughout the PC industry. Chapters 9, "You Can Never Have Too Much Closet (or Data Storage) Space," and 10, "Digging Deeper into Disks," are about PC storage. Chapter 11 talks exclusively about PC memory.

> **Warning:** Let me repeat myself: Memory and storage are two entirely different things. Many folks who are new to the PC business get them confused. Until you get clear about this, you will have no end of trouble trying to understand how your PC is built and how it works. Here is how I suggest you remember this distinction: Memory is the collection of fast information-holding places (RAM and ROM). Storage is the collection of long-term information-holding places (usually magnetic and/or optical disks or tapes).
>
> Typically, in a PC you will have tens or hundreds of times as much capacity in storage as you have in memory. For example, a pretty good system these days might have anywhere from about 64 megabytes (MB) to 1 gigabyte (GB) of RAM (and a small fraction of that much ROM), and it might have a few or perhaps a few dozen gigabytes (GB) of disk storage. One GB is the same as 1024MB.

Control Devices

Computers process information. They don't just do it automatically; something must direct their various parts to do their jobs. The input devices must be told to bring in the information to be processed. They also must be told to bring in the instructions describing the processing to be done. Both of these kinds of information are placed in information-holding places (typically, in a portion of your PC's main memory).

The parts of your PC that cause all this to happen are referred to as the *control portion*. Most of them are located on the CPU chip, along with its processor part (and, perhaps, an extra fast memory part, the cache memory). Some other parts of the control portion of your PC are on some other integrated circuit chips elsewhere in the PC—including several that are commonly referred to by the names *chip set* and *embedded controller* chips. I'll tell you quite a bit more about these other control chips in Chapter 16, "Faster Ways to Get Information Into and Out of Your PC."

Without a control portion, your PC would be no more than a fancy calculator. After all, any calculator has a means of information input (pressing the number keys (0–9) and the operations keys (+, −, ×, and ÷). It has a means of information output (the numerical display). It has an information-holding device at least large enough to hold the numbers it is using in the current calculation. And it obviously has processing power enough to do those calculations. What it lacks is any part that can "push the various buttons" automatically—which is precisely what the control portion of a PC does for you. (A calculator, despite having four of my five essential functional parts, is not a computer, because it lacks that fifth part.)

I'll close this section with a table that recaps what I have told you about how the many diverse pieces of which your PC is constructed—and the many peripheral devices you may connect to it—can in many cases serve more than one of the five vital roles that must be met in order for the whole assemblage to be a computer.

In Table 2.1, a bullet in one of the columns indicates that this device serves as a portion of this vital part of your PC as its primary purpose (or as one of them if it usually serves in more than one role). In the "Information Holding" column, I have replaced the bullets with the letters *S* for storage or *M* for memory.

A checkmark indicates that this role is not primary, but still a common usage for this device. A question mark indicates that this device can, in some cases, be made to serve this role—but that is definitely not a commonplace usage.

Table 2.1 The Vital Roles Served by Some PC Parts and Peripherals

PC Part or Information Peripheral	Information				
	Input	Output	Processing	Holding	Control
Keyboard	•				
Mouse	•				
Joystick	•				
Force feedback joystick	•	•			
Trackball or trackpoint	•				
TouchPad	•				
Microphone	•				
Digital camera	•				
Analog camcorder or VCR	•	•			

PC Part or Information Peripheral	Input	Output	Information Processing	Holding	Control
Digital camcorder or VCR	•	•	4		
Remote Weather Station	•				
Floppy disk (includes LS-120 Super Floppy)	•	•		S	
Optical disc (Audio CD)	•				
Optical disc (CD-ROM)	•				
Optical disc (CD-R)	•	•			
Optical disc (CD-RW)	•	•		S	
Optical disc (DVD-ROM)	•				
Optical disc (DVD-RAM)	•	•		S	
Magnetic fixed disk (ordinary hard drive)	•	•		S	
Removable disk drive (for example, PC card or ZIP disk)	•	•		S	
Digital tape drive	•	•		S	
Speakers		•			
Remote computer	•	•	4	S	•
Video monitor		?			
Video monitor (with touch screen)	•	•			
Printer		•			
Video projector		•			
Rapid Prototyping System		•			
Other PC-controlled devices (includes printed circuit board layout machines, automated car painting machines, automated sign makers, numerically controlled machine tools, and so forth)		•			

continues

Table 2.1 *Continued*

PC Part or Information Peripheral	Information				
	Input	Output	Processing	Holding	Control
ALU in CPU			•		
Cache memory in CPU				M	
Control circuits in CPU					•
Motherboard chip set					•
Motherboard ROM and NVRAM				M	
Motherboard RAM (both main memory and cache)				M	
NVRAM on plug-in card (such as video display adapters,network interface cards, modems, and so forth)			•	M	•

What Makes a Computer More than a Calculator?

Here is where programs fit into the story. Even with all the different hardware parts I described earlier, if it has no programs to run, a computer will do nothing. (Well, if you want, it can serve as a pretty good doorstop or boat anchor. To be precise, I should have said that it will do no computing.)

A *program* is nothing more than a precise prescription for what is to be done. In mathematical language, we say that it implements an *algorithm* (which is just a fancy word for a set of rules for doing something). Ah, if only making really good, error-free computer programs were as simple as that sounds.

Two Problems Programmers Face

There are two things that make writing computer programs harder than writing instructions to another human being. The first is that, unlike human beings, computer chips are able to "understand" and act on only a very few, rather simple instructions. So any task must be broken down into minute detail before it is ready to hand to a computer for execution. The second problem arises from the difficulty people have in anticipating absolutely every possible thing that might happen.

A perfect computer program must have specific built-in instructions saying precisely what is to be done in each and every possible situation that could arise, no matter how unlikely some of them might be. Figuring out all those possibilities is, to say the least, a challenge to the best minds. Deciding what actions are to be taken and incorporating the correct instructions to make those actions happen for every single contingency, without even once making a mistake, is asking for a perfection mere humans cannot seem to master.

In fact, many computer programs are now so complex that despite literally hundreds of millions of tests run on each one, some "bugs" are never found, simply because the conditions that would expose them never occur in those tests. Because computers run so rapidly and there are so many PCs in existence with such a wide diversity of add-on parts and running such an eclectic mix of software, even those rare bugs can surface, sometimes years after the product's introduction, in many thousands of computers.

An Example of the Problems

To get some sense of just how hard this might be, let's play a little game. Pretend that you are asked to tell a willing, but very literal-minded and not too smart, boy to do some task: taking out the trash.

First, you might write the task like this:

1. Go to kitchen.

2. Get kitchen wastebasket.

3. Take wastebasket to trash container outside house.

4. Return kitchen wastebasket to kitchen.

5. Come back here.

That would suffice for you and me; in fact, it might be insultingly overly specific. But for the prospective executor of this task, it might be appallingly vague.

Look at the first instruction. We can assume that the child knows how to walk. But where is the kitchen? How will the boy recognize it when he gets there? Then how is he to know what the kitchen wastebasket looks like?

We might assume that once he has the wastebasket he will know how to pick it up and carry it. But does he know the way to the outside trash container? You probably must spell it all out for him.

And then consider this: Suppose that when he gets to the back door it is closed. Did you remember to tell him to check for that, and if it is, to open the door before trying to go out? (And to close it after himself?) If you don't put in that sort of contingency checking and contingent instructions, the child might end up trying to open a door that is already open (and getting stuck at that point, unable to comply with what you have said he should do) or trying to walk through a closed door. Neither will work. Either will stop the execution of the program right there.

And so on. I don't think I need to carry this much further for you to get the general idea that writing computer programs takes a much more precise and attentive approach than directing human beings.

Two Ways Computer Designers Make Computer Programmers' Jobs Easier

To help programmers get their jobs done with fewer errors—either of omission (leaving out needed code to deal with unlikely conditions) or commission (including erroneous code)—computer designers have come up with two general strategies. The first is to make the computer chips understand more complex instructions. That saves the programmer from having to break down each task quite so far into its elemental sub-steps. The second method is to create programs that write programs. The human programmer writes only a general overview of what the program is to do and the order in which those tasks are to be done. The compiler then crafts the actual machine-language program from those more general instructions.

The first of these strategies goes by several names, each describing a different way of approaching the same problem. The data handling and processing portions of a microprocessor chip are built with functional parts (such as the ALU) that can respond to only some very primitive commands. The instruction decoder (which is a key part of the control section of the processor chip) can be built to read instructions that assume more complex actions and, by reference to some microcode stored on the chip, translate those instructions into the more primitive ones on which the functional processing parts can act.

This general strategy can be applied in several ways. One way, in which the complexity of the apparent processor instruction set is only minimally more complex than what the actual functional parts use, is called *reduced instruction set computer* (RISC) design. Another way, and the one used in the CPUs that are at the heart of almost all PCs built today, is to use that microcode instruction decomposition and elaboration strategy more heavily. The result is that the set of things the programmer can ask of the CPU is greatly expanded. This approach is called *complex instruction set computer* (CISC) design. Finally, we are beginning to see some processor chips that are designed to pack many elemental instructions into one, very long instruction. This *very long instruction word* (VLIW) strategy hasn't yet made it into mainstream PCs, but it very likely will within another generation or two.

Chapter 7 briefly describes the different CPU chips that have been or are now being used in PCs. That chapter also identifies which are more nearly pure CISC and which have more RISC in their designs.

The second strategy, crafting computer programs to write computer programs, also carries several names, such as *assemblers, interpreters,* and *compilers.* You learn more about each of these in Chapter 18. In that chapter, you will also learn about another, related strategy, which, in effect, bridges the two I have described here. In this strategy, the crafting of computer programs is broken down into layers of code. Each layer "clothes" the processor and all the layers beneath it with a new appearance, and that new appearance includes the apparent capability of understanding and performing even more complex tasks.

Summary

In this chapter, you have gotten a pretty good sense of what the five functional parts of any computer are (input, output, information-holding places, processing, and control) and how they can be exemplified in the pieces that make up your PC. Some additional, and quite necessary, parts, such as the power supply and box and other hardware that holds all the pieces together support these five functional parts. You now also should have at least a glimmering of both how complex the job of instructing a computer is and of some of the general strategies computer hardware and software engineers have devised to deal with that complexity.

These are topics you will return to in more depth later in this book. Chapter 4 goes over all the hardware parts in a little more detail and in the actual context in which they appear in a PC. There you learn why a power supply is vital, even though it doesn't do any of the essential tasks of the functional parts; why PCs have a motherboard and, usually, several daughter boards; the purpose of having a system unit with some parts inside and some outside it; and a lot more. In Chapters 7–16, 21, and 23–25, you will find each of the individual parts discussed in much greater detail. Chapters 5, 18, and 26 explain the ins and outs of the PC programs that activate all this hardware and cause it to do all the things you or I want it to do.

For now, though, you have gotten enough of an understanding of both the problems and their solutions that you can move on to examine in more depth just what information is and just what it means to process data.

Understanding Bits, Nybbles, and Bytes

You cannot really understand how a PC, or any other computer, is built and how it works unless you first learn what information is. That, after all, is the raw material a computer works with. In this chapter, I'll explain what information is. We'll also explore the many ways in which it is represented inside a PC. At the very end of this chapter, I'll explain how data and data processing (which is after all what PCs are used for) are related to information.

You might think this is all very arcane stuff that only a geek would want to know. Actually, this topic is very important for anyone who wants to know *how* computers work. If that's your goal—and presumably it is, because you're here—there are three aspects of digital information you really need to understand:

- The main advantage of digital information processing is the inherent "noise immunity" that digital data enjoys.

- The fundamental "language" of all digital computers is written in binary numbers, but those are often reexpressed for easier human perception in the hexadecimal numbering system—and make no mistake: You will encounter hexadecimal numbers many times in your use of PCs.

- Most data documents contain redundant information; knowing this enables us to compress those data files.

My purpose in this chapter is to explain each of these fundamental and very significant concepts in ways that you will, I trust, find relatively easy to understand.

What Is Information? How Much Room Does It Take Up?

You probably think you know what information is, at least in a general sense. And, no doubt, you do. But can you define it precisely? Probably not. In the day-to-day workings of the world, most people never need to know this, and so they've never thought about it.

Mathematicians do study such things, and they have come up with a really clear way for understanding information. They say that information can best be understood as *what it takes to answer a question.*

The advantage of putting it this way is that it then becomes possible to compute exactly how much information you must have in order to answer particular questions. This then enables the computer designer to know how to build information-holding places that are large enough to hold the needed information.

Measuring Information

The simplest type of question is one that can be answered either yes or no, and the amount of information needed to specify the correct answer is the minimum possible amount of information. We call it a *bit*. (If you like to think in terms of the ideas of quantum physics, the bit could be said to be the quantum of information.)

In mathematical terms, the value of the bit can be either a 1 or a 0. That could stand for true or false, or for yes or no. And in electrical engineering terms, that bit's value could be represented by a voltage somewhere that is either high or low. Similarly, in a magnetic information storage medium (such as a disk or tape, for example), the same bit's value could be stored by magnetizing a region of the medium in some specified direction or in the opposite direction. Many other means for storing information are also possible, and we'll meet at least a few later in this story.

The next marvelous fact (which isn't initially obvious) about information is that we can measure precisely, in bits, the amount of information needed to answer any question. The way to decide how many bits you need is to break down the complex question into a series of yes-no questions. If you do this in the optimal way (that is, in the way that requires the fewest possible yes-no questions), the number of bits of information you require is indicated by the number of elemental (yes-no) questions you used to represent the complex question.

How Big Is a Fact?

How many bits do you need to store a fact? That depends on how many possible facts you want to discriminate.

Consider one famous example: Paul Revere needed to receive a short but important message. He chose to have his associate hang some lighted lamps in a church tower. Longfellow immortalized the message as, "One if by land and two if by sea." This was a simple, special-purpose code. Computers work in much the same way, except that they use a somewhat more complex and general-purpose code.

Actually, Paul's code was a little more complex than the phrase suggests. There were three possibilities, and the lamp code had to be able to communicate at each moment one of these three statements:

- "The British are not yet coming." (Zero lamps)
- "The British are coming by land." (One lamp)
- "The British are coming by sea." (Two lamps)

Paul chose to use one more lamp for each possibility after the first. This is like counting on your fingers. This works well if the number of possibilities is small. It would have been impossible for Paul to use that strategy if he had needed to distinguish among 100 facts, let alone the thousands or millions that computers handle.

The way to get around that problem is to use what mathematicians call *place-value numbering*. The common decimal numbering system is one example. The binary numbering system is another (binary numbering is used in the construction of computers). The next example will help make this concept clear.

The Size of a Numeric Fact

Suppose someone calls you on the telephone and asks you how old you are (to the nearest year). You could tell them, or you could make them guess. If you do the latter, and if you say you will answer only *yes* or *no* in response to various questions, the following is the questioner's best strategy. (This assumes that over the phone the questioner is unable to get any idea of how old you are, but because you are a human, it is reasonable to guess that you are less than 128 years old.)

The first question is, "Are you at least 64 years old?" If the answer is *yes,* then the second question is, "Are you at least 96 years old?" However, if the answer to the first question is *no,* the second question would be, "Are you at least 32 years old?" The successive questions will further narrow the range until by the seventh question you will have revealed your age, accurate to the year. (See Figure 3.1 for the numbers to choose for each question.)

As the questioner gets the answers to each of the seven questions, he or she simply records them, writing a 1 for every *yes* and a 0 for every *no.* The resulting 7-bit binary number is the person's age. This procedure works because the first question is the most significant one. That is, it determines the most about the person's age. And if, like most of us, the questioner writes down the answer bits from left to right, the result will be a binary number stated in the usual way, with the most significant bit (MSB) on the left end of the number.

Here is what that process might look like. Assume you are 35 years old. Here are the answers you would give: "Are you at least 64 years old?" (no), 32 (yes), 48 (no), 40 (no), 36 (no), 34 (yes), 35 (yes). Your age (in binary) would be written 0100011.

This is an example of a place-value number. The first place is worth 64. The next is worth 32, then 16, and so on all the way to the last place, which is worth 1. By the *worth* of a place, I mean simply that you must multiply the value in that place (in binary this is always a 0 or a 1) by the worth of that place and add all the products to get the value of the number. In the example, add no 64s, one 32, no 16s, no 8s, no 4s, one 2, and one 1. The result of this addition (32 + 2 + 1) is, of course, 35.

FIGURE 3.1
Optimal strategy for the age-guessing game.

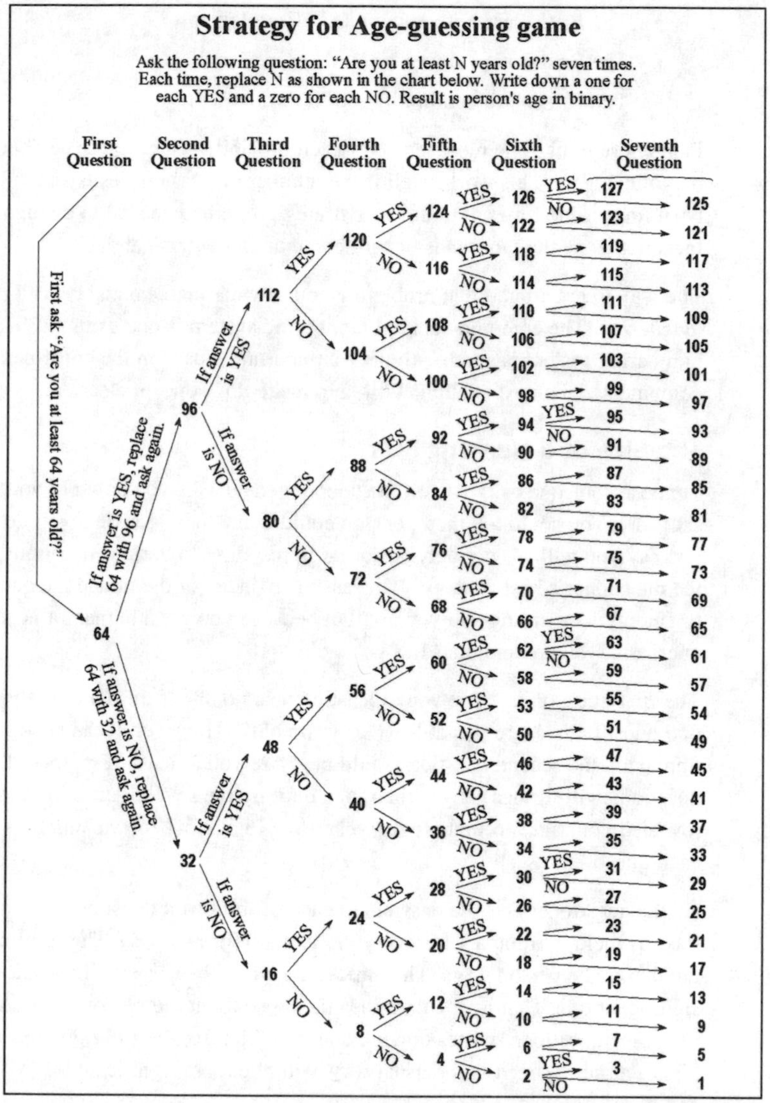

Strategy for Age-guessing game

Ask the following question: "Are you at least N years old?" seven times. Each time, replace N as shown in the chart below. Write down a one for each YES and a zero for each NO. Result is person's age in binary.

When you answer seven yes-no questions, you are giving the questioner 7 bits of information. Therefore, it takes 7 bits to specify the age of a human being in years (assuming that age is less than 128). And that means that 7 bits is the size of this numeric fact.

The general rule is this: The number of bits of information in a number is given by the number of places you need to represent that number in binary notation (which is to say, by using a place-value numbering system that uses only 1s and 0s).

But wait a minute, you might say, this is all well and good for numbers, but how much information is there in a non-numeric fact? That is an important question, because most things for which we use computers these days involve at least some information that is not naturally stated in a numeric form.

The Size of a Non-Numeric Fact

To decide how much information a non-numeric fact contains, you first must decide how you will represent non-numeric information. To see one way in which it might be done, consider this very common use for a computer—text editing.

In text editing, you create and manipulate what are termed *pure text documents*. A pure-text document normally isn't filled just with numbers. It is filled with words, and they are made up of letters separated by spaces and punctuation symbols. One way to represent such a document is as a string of symbols (letters, numbers, punctuation symbols, special symbols to represent the end of a line, tabs, and other similar ideas). How much information is there in such a document?

If you write down all the possible symbols that could occur in the document, you'll see how many different ones there are (disregarding how often each one occurs). Then you could give each of those unique symbols a numeric label. I claim it is easy to see how many simple questions, like those used earlier in this section to establish a person's age, it would take to pick each symbol out of that character set. Here's how.

Suppose you had a document with 43 different symbols occurring in it. This means you have a *character set* with 43 members. You could label those symbols with the numbers 0 to 42. After you have specified this collection of symbols and their order, you can designate any particular one of them by a number that gives its location in the collection. We call such a number an *index value*. The size of the non-numeric fact that you are indicating—for example, the size of the letter j—is now considered to be simply the size of the binary number needed as an index value to pick out the specified character from this collection of symbols. The size of the entire document is the number of symbols it contains times the size of each index value.

It is important to realize that these index values make sense only in the context of a given collection of symbols. Therefore, you must have that collection in hand before you can use this strategy. You will return to this point in more depth in the section "Symbols and Codes" later in this chapter.

Table 3.1 shows how many bits you need for an index value that can pick out one member of a collection of symbols. In our sample case, the answer is 6 bits, because 43 is less than 64. (With 6 bits, you could pick out each member of a collection of up to 64 symbols. You can pick out the members of a collection with only 43 members by thinking of them as the first 43 members of those 64. You could not get away with using a 5-bit number as an index value, because that would let you discriminate only among members of a set of 32 items.)

Table 3.1 How Big Is a Fact?

Number of Possibilities This Fact Can Distinguish	Number of Bits Needed to Hold This Fact
2	1
4	2
8	3
16	4
32	5
64	6
128	7
256	8
.	
.	
.	
65,536	16
.	
.	
1,048,576	20

This strategy provides a way to represent symbols as numbers (indices into collections of symbols). In the process, it also provides a measure of just how big a fact you need to specify those symbols. That is, it measures their information content. Each symbol holds as many bits of information as the size of the index value needed to pick it out of the collection of symbols to which it belongs.

This also provides a way to transform the original document (a string of symbols) into a string of indices (numbers). In the example, each index value would be 6 bits long. In that case, the entire document would be 6 bits times the number of index values (which is the same as the number of symbols, and this time I mean the total number of symbols in the document, not just the number of unique symbols). This is a form you could hold in a computer. This is a form much like the one actually used by typical text editors.

How Much Space Does Information Need?

Now you know the size of information in a mathematical sense—that is, how many bits you need to specify a certain fact. But how much room does it take to hold this information inside a computer? That depends, of course, on exactly how those information-holding spaces are built.

All PCs are built on the assumption that every information-holding place will contain a binary number. That is, each location can hold either a 1 or a 0. In this case, you need at least as many locations to hold a number as there are bits in that number.

> **Technical Note:** Because the information-holding spaces in PCs are organized into groups of 8 bits (called *bytes*), sometimes a number will fit into some number of bytes with space left over. In that case, any remaining highest-order bit locations are simply filled in with 0s. (That is true for positive numbers. For negative numbers, which typically are represented in a "two's-complement" style, the filled-in bit locations would all receive ones. I'll explain more about this way of representing negative numbers a little later in this chapter.)

The alternative to binary information-holding places is to put information in locations that could each represent more than two values. That enables you to hold more information in fewer locations.

If each location could have four discernible states (speaking electrically, let's say a nearly zero voltage, a low voltage, a medium voltage, and a maximum voltage), the numbers would be held in those locations using a quaternary (base-4) numbering system. This system is distinctly more space-efficient than binary because only half as many locations are needed to hold the same amount of information. However, building reliable and inexpensive information-holding cells that operate on any number base higher than 2 has proven to be very difficult. Therefore, until very recently, all modern computers have used only binary number holding places.

In what may herald a new movement away from purely binary systems, Intel has recently proclaimed that it has achieved "a major breakthrough" that enables it to manufacture flash memory products that store 2 bits per location (essentially using a base-4 number system). Whether this will remain an isolated application of a nonbinary number system in PCs or whether most of the computing parts will one day become quaternary (or based on some other, higher number base) remains to be seen.

Noise Versus Information

You may have realized that the number of bits that one cell can hold determines the number base in which the hardware can natively represent numbers. This implies that you could hold an enormous amount of information in a very few cells just by using some very high number base. But doing that means that you would have to be able to distinguish as many different possibilities for the value held in each cell as the base of that numbering system.

What if you chose a number base such as 1 million? Could you hold a value that could take on any of a million possibilities in one cell? If the value were held electrically, as a voltage, that would mean the cell might hold voltages between

continues

0 and 1 volt, and you would have to be able to set and read that voltage accurate to 1 microvolt. And indeed, you could do this—in principle. But in practice, you'd find that the inevitable noise in the circuit would probably swamp the tiny variations you intended to hold in that cell. Therefore, you couldn't *reliably* place —and then later on retrieve—numbers with that fine-grained a resolution after all. Even if you could, the circuit would work far too slowly to be useful in a computer.

This chain of reasoning hints at what is perhaps the biggest advantage of any digital circuits: They eliminate the effect of noise altogether. This is very important. At every stage of a digital circuit, the values are represented by voltages that inevitably will vary somewhat from their ideal values. That variation is called *noise*.

But when those values are sensed by the next digital portion of the circuit, that portion makes decisions that are simple, black-and-white, go/no-go decisions about what the values are. Then it re-creates those voltage values more nearly at their ideal levels.

This means that you can copy digital data any number of times and be reasonably sure that it still has *exactly* the same information content that it had when you started out. (This is in sharp contrast to what happens in analog circuitry. If you were to try to copy an analog tape recording of a chamber music concert, for example, and then copy the copy and keep on repeating this process hundreds of times, you would most likely end up with a tape recording that contained nothing but noise. All the original information—the pleasing sounds and very quiet background—would have been lost beneath the huge overlay of noise.)

To accomplish this noise-defying act, the digital elements of the circuit must each have a generous difference between significant input values. This is how it is possible for each stage to throw away the minor variations from the nominal values and be sure it isn't throwing away anything significant. And the faster you want that circuitry to make these noise-discarding decisions, the larger the differences must be between significantly different input levels. In the end, this is why computer circuit designers have almost always settled on binary circuits as the basic elements. They have the simplest decisions to make ("Is this level high or is it low?") and, therefore, they can make them most rapidly.

Document Size, Redundancy, and Information Content

Putting more information into fewer memory cells by using a number base other than binary is only one way to reduce the number of memory cells you need. It is not, in fact, normally used. One way that often *is* used is to remove redundancy.

I told you earlier that the amount of information you have can be assessed by seeing how many well-chosen questions you are able to answer using that information. Another way of viewing information is as news. That is, if you get some information and then you get the same message again, the second time it carries no (new) information. The relationship between the two points of view is clear when you consider that the repetition of a message doesn't help you answer any more questions than you could by using only the first copy. This shows that an exact repeat of some message does not really deliver twice the original information content. Furthermore, many individual messages deliver less information than they might appear to hold at first glance. The word that describes this fact is *redundancy*.

Real documents usually contain quite a lot of redundancy. That is, knowing some of the document enables you to predict the missing parts with an accuracy that is much better than chance. (Try reading a paragraph in which all the vowels have been left out. You can do surprisingly well.) The presence of this redundancy means that you must encode only some fraction of the symbols in the document to know all of what it contains. And that means the true information content of the document might be significantly less than the raw size (number of symbols times bits per symbol).

Exploring: Here is a paragraph of simple English with all the vowels removed. Can you read it? After you try, check your understanding by going to the end of the chapter where you will find the same paragraph with its vowels restored.

Ths s tst. f y cn rd ths prgrph, nd gt th mnng t lst mstly rght, y hv shwn tht nglsh s rdndnt t sch dgr tht lvng t ll th vwls dsn't stp y frm rdng t prtty wll.

For convenience, most text editors put every symbol you enter directly into your documents. They make no attempt to reduce the document size to the bare minimum. This saves time, but it bloats the documents, which, among other things, wastes disk storage space.

Most of the time that is just fine, but sometimes you want to minimize the size of your files. You might plan to send some of them over a phone line and want to minimize the time and cost that this will require. Or you might find yourself running out of space on your hard disk.

Technical Note: Various strategies have been used to minimize file sizes by getting rid of redundant information. One popular strategy is to use a *data compression* program. This is a program that can analyze an input file and then produce from it a smaller, nonredundant file—and then later be able to use that smaller file to reproduce the original file flawlessly. (Often these programs also are designed to take in several files, make nonredundant versions of each of them, and then put all these smaller, nonredundant "copies" into one overall "archive" file. This is very convenient, because it means that if you have a set of related files and you put them into such an archive, you will not only be able to store the collection of files in less space, you also will be assured of keeping all the members of that collection together.)

continues

I am speaking here only about data compression programs that do not, in fact, throw away any of the actual information in the input files. That is, they can reproduce those original files from their compressed versions without losing so much as a single bit anywhere within those files. We call this type of compression program *lossless*.

The essential strategy used in all lossless data compression programs is to build a table of the essential elements in the file to be compressed, followed by a list of which of those elements occur in the file and in what order. The degree to which a program of this sort can compress a file depends on two things: the inherent amount of redundancy in the input file, and the cleverness with which the program is able to determine what, in fact, are the truly essential and nonredundant elements that make up that file.

Another approach is a software or hardware data-compression disk interface product (also called an *on-the-fly file data compressor*). These products squeeze out the redundancy in files in exactly the same way as the standalone lossless data compression programs, but they do so as the files are stored on your disk or tape drives. Then they expand them back to their original, redundant form as those files are read from the tape or disk.

When you use an on-the-fly data compressor, you will have the illusion that your disks are larger than they really are. That is, you can put "ten gallons (of files) into a five gallon hat (or disk)." Because some computation must be done to compress and decompress the files, this apparent increase in disk size carries with it a slight slowdown in your PC's apparent performance.

Typical PC files will compress (on average) to about half their original size. Some files will turn out to be very nearly totally incompressible. They simply have very little redundancy to be eliminated. And some other files are so redundant that their compressed versions may be less than a tenth of the original size.

Things can become even more subtle. The information content of a file might depend on who is looking at it. If you have never seen a document before, it will contain much that is news to you. This means it will contain a lot of information. You could not guess all of its content without using a lot of yes-no questions. Essentially, you must see every symbol in the document, or nearly every one. That means that the information content of the document is fairly close to being the number of symbols it contains times the information content of each symbol. Because most of those symbols are completely unpredictable (by you), the information content of each one is simply the size of the index value you need to pick out that particular symbol from the character set being used.

Someone who knew ahead of time that this document was one of a certain small group of documents might find that it contained very little information (news). All that person needs in order to know all of what it contains is to figure out which one of the given sets of documents this one is. This will take a rather small number of questions (at least the number indicated in Table 3.1 for the size of the group of known documents). For that person, the document could be adequately replaced with just one index value. The size of that number is all the information that document contains *for that person*.

> **Note:** To see how powerful this approach can be, imagine that you work in an office that creates custom documents out of a limited number of standard parts (pieces of boilerplate text) along with a customer-specific header. You could replace each custom document with just that header followed by a short list of small numbers, one number per standard part you were including. The numbers could be small because each one needs to contain only enough information to indicate which of the limited number of standard parts it represents.
>
> This shortened representation of the document is adequate for you to re-create the full document. This means you need store only this small file on your hard disk to enable you to print out the full document any time you want.
>
> To put numbers to this, suppose your office used only 256 standard document parts. Each one could be any length. Suppose they averaged 10,000 bytes. Because an 8-bit index value (1 byte) would suffice to indicate any one of the 256 (2^8=256) documents, your custom documents could each simply consist of the customer-specific header followed by a string of bytes, one per standard part to be included. This would enable you to compress your documents for storage on average by a ratio of 10,000:1.
>
> Of course, because your customers don't have your collection of standard parts, you must assemble the full document for them before you can ship it.
>
> Is such an approach actually practical? Yes. Something much like this is often used in law offices, by architectural specifiers, and in the writing of computer programs, for example.

Bits, Bytes, Nybbles, and Words

Early teletypewriters used 5 or 6 bits per symbol. They were severely restricted, therefore, in the number of distinct symbols a message could contain (to 32 or 64 possibilities). To see just how restrictive this is, consider the following facts: There are 26 letters in the alphabet used by English-language writers, and every one of them comes in an uppercase (capital letter) form and a lowercase (uncapitalized) form. In addition, we use 10 numerals and quite a few punctuation symbols (for example, the period, comma, semicolon, colon, plus and minus sign, apostrophe, quotation mark, and so on). Count them. Just the ones I have mentioned here come to 70 distinct characters, and this is too many for a 6-bit code. Even leaving out the lowercase letters, you'll have 44 characters, which is too many for a 5-bit code.

To accommodate all these symbols in messages, for most of the past century the standard has been to use 7 bits. That allows 128 symbols, which is enough for all the lowercase and uppercase letters in the English alphabet, all 10 digits, and a generous assortment of punctuation symbols. This standard (which now has the formal name of the American Standard Code for Information Interchange, or ASCII) uses only 96 of the 128 possibilities for these printable symbols.

The remaining 32 characters are reserved for various *control characters*. These values encode the carriage return (start typing at the left margin once again), the line feed (move the paper up a line), tab, backspace, vertical tab, and so on. The ASCII standard also includes symbols to indicate the end of a message and the famous code number 7, to ring the bell on the teletypewriter. Presumably, this last one was needed to get the attention of the person to whom the message was being sent. (I go into more detail about the control characters and printable characters included in ASCII in the section "Symbols and Codes," later in this chapter.)

Starting with the IBM 360 series of mainframe computers in the early 1960s, the most commonly handled chunk of information was a group of 8 bits, which has been named the *byte*. Many other mainframe and minicomputer makers used other size chunks, but all modern PCs have used the byte exclusively as the smallest chunk of information commonly passed around inside the machine, or between one PC and another.

Although they never explained it this way, I am sure the engineers at IBM were concerned with two things when they decided to switch from 7-bit symbols to 8-bit ones. First, this change enabled them to use symbol sets with twice as many symbols, and that was a welcome enriching of the possibilities. Second, this was a more efficient use of the possibilities for addressing bits within a minimal chunk of information.

Standards: I can now explain exactly what is meant by a term I used earlier in this chapter and that may have confused you then. The term is "a pure text file," sometimes called "a pure ASCII text file."

This is any file that contains only symbols that can be represented by ASCII characters. More particularly, it must contain only bytes whose values are in the range 33 to 126 (which are the ASCII codes for various letters, numerals, and symbols that you could see typed on a page) plus some bytes with the special ASCII codes values 13 and 10 (which represent a carriage return and line feed, respectively), and perhaps also ones with the value 9 or 12 (which are, respectively, the ASCII codes for a tab and for the form feed command that causes a printer to start a new page).

The opposite of a pure text file could be a word processing document (which contains, in addition to the text that is to appear in the document, instructions as to how those text characters are to be formatted), or a program file (which typically will contain an almost random assortment of byte values, including all those between 127 and 255 that are a part of the -extended-ASCII code set— more on this topic later in this chapter).

Occasionally, dealing with half a byte as a unit of information is useful. This is enough, for example, to encode a single decimal digit. Some droll person, noting the resemblance of byte and bite, decided that this 4-bit chunk should be called the *nybble*. This name became popular and is now considered official.

More powerful PCs can also handle groups of 2, 4, or even 8 bytes at a time. There is a name for these larger groupings of bits. That name is *word*. Unfortunately, unlike a byte, a word is an ill-defined amount of information.

> **Technical Note:** This is not unlike the situation in the English language. Each letter, number, or punctuation symbol takes up roughly the same amount of room, but a word can be as small as a single letter or it may contain an almost unlimited number of letters. (Consider the words *I* and *a* and then remember the famous 34-letter word *Supercalifragilisticexpialidocious*; there are also a good many less artificial words that are nearly that long.) Things are not quite that bad in the world of computers; but still, a computer word is far from being a clearly defined constant.

One notion of a computer word is that it contains as many bits as the computer can process internally all at once. This rule makes the size of a word dependent on which computer you are talking about.

Another popular idea has been that one computer word has as many bits as can be carried at once across that computer's data bus. (The next chapter introduces you to the notion of a computer bus in detail.) This definition also gives us a size that depends on the particular model of PC.

If you use the first of these definitions, you can say the earliest PCs had 16-bit words, more modern ones have 32-bit words, and the Pentium and Pentium Pro have a 64-bit word. By the second definition, the earliest PCs had 8-bit words, and again the most modern ones have 32-bit or 64-bit words.

Either of these definitions can lead to confusion. The good news is that all the different models of PCs are more alike than different, so choosing one definition for word size and sticking to it can help you keep your sanity.

Fortunately, most people have now settled on 16 bits as the size of a PC's word, independent of which model of PC they are discussing. Thus, in programming one often speaks of handling words, double words (32 bits, referred to as *DWORDs*) and quadruple words (64 bits, referred to as *QWORDs*). However, these definitions are not universally used. So be careful when reading technical descriptions of PC hardware. A "word" might be something different from what you expect.

Representing Numbers and Strings of Characters

Information-holding places in a PC hold only binary numbers, but those numbers stand for something. Whether that something being represented is a number or something non-numeric, some group of bytes must be used. The strategy most commonly used to hold non-numeric information is simpler than that for numbers, because having several definitions of how to hold a number has proven more efficient, with each of the different ways being used in particular contexts. I'll explain the details of how numbers are held first and then explain how non-numeric entities are held.

How Numbers Are Held in a PC

Mathematicians distinguish among several type of numbers. The ones you probably use every day can be classified as *counting numbers*, *integers*, or *real numbers*. Counting numbers are, of course, the ones you use to count things. That is, they are the whole numbers beginning with 0 (1, 2, 3…). Integers are simply the counting numbers and the negatives of the counting numbers. Real numbers include integers and every other number you commonly use (for example, 45, –17.3, 3.14159265). Any of these three types of number (counting, integer, or real) can be arbitrarily large.

Computer engineers categorize numbers a little differently. They speak of short and long integers and short and long real numbers, for example. They also often distinguish integers that are always positive from those that are allowed to take on either positive or negative values. There also are some limitations on the acceptable sizes of those numbers in order to allow them to be represented inside your PC.

Counting Numbers and Integers

The exact definitions of a short integer and a long integer vary a little between different computer designs and sometimes between different computer languages for the same computer. The key point of difference with the mathematical definition is that although mathematical integers can be of any size, computer integers are limited to some maximum size, based on the number of information-holding places to be allocated to each one. Counting numbers are typically stored in either a single byte, a 2-byte (16-bit) word, or a 4-byte (32-bit) double word.

Short integers typically are held in a pair of bytes (16 bits). If counting numbers were stored in that space, it could have any value between 0 and 65,535. But, because integers can be either positive or negative, 1 bit must be used for the sign. That cuts down the largest size positive or negative integer to about half the foregoing value. Now the range is from –32,768 to +32,767.

Long integers typically are held in 4-byte locations (32 bits). This gives a range of from –2,147,483,648 to +2,147,483,647.

In the latest generation of PCs, information is often moved around 64 bits at a time. So far, most programs don't store integers with that many bits. Surely, someday soon some of them will. When that day comes, the range of poss,ible counting numbers could be expanded to a whopping 0 to 18,446,744,073,709,551,615 (or, in engineering notation, approximately 1.8×10^{19}). Similarly, signed-integers would be able to range from –9,223,372,036,854,775,808 to +9,223,372,036,854,775,807.

When giving the values of these long and short integers, the common notation for PCs uses hexadecimal numbers. (I explain exactly what these are in the next section. For now, you just need to know that hexadecimal, or base-16, numbers use two symbols chosen from the numerals 0–9 and the letters A–F to represent the value of 1 byte.) Thus, a short integer might be written as 4F12h or AE3Dh, and a long integer as 12784A3Fh or 83D21F09h. (The trailing lowercase letter *h* is merely one of the conventional ways to distinguish a hexadecimal number from a decimal number.)

Negative integers can be represented in two ways. In one plan, the first, or high-order bit is called the *sign bit*. Its value is 0 for positive numbers and 1 for negative numbers. The remaining bits are used to hold the absolute value of the number. Thus, +45 would be represented as the binary number 0000000000101101 and the number –45 as 1000000000101101. I'll call this the "obvious" way to represent a signed binary number. (Its formal name is *sign-magnitude representation*.)

The more commonly used way to represent negative numbers is called the *two's-complement* of the representation I have just described. To generate this representation for any negative number, you first figure out what the "obvious" representation would be, then flip all the bits ("complement" them) from 0 to 1 or from 1 to 0, and finally add 1 to the result.

Why would one want to do something so weird as using a two's-complement notation? For simplicity, actually. Let me explain why this is so.

Table 3.2 shows you 10 numbers starting with +4 at the top and decreasing by one on each succeeding line to –5 at the bottom. Each of these numbers is shown as a decimal value in the first column, as an ordinary binary number in the second column, and in two's-complement notation in the third column. (You can test your understanding of what I am doing here by extending this table several lines above the top and below the bottom.)

Table 3.2 Three Ways to Represent Integer Numbers

Decimal Value	"Obvious" Binary Notation	Two's-Complement Binary Notation
4	0000000000000100	0000000000000100
3	0000000000000011	0000000000000011
2	0000000000000010	0000000000000010
1	0000000000000001	0000000000000001
0	0000000000000000	0000000000000000
−1	1000000000000001	1111111111111111
−2	1000000000000010	1111111111111110
−3	1000000000000011	1111111111111101
−4	1000000000000100	1111111111111100
−5	1000000000000101	1111111111111011

In both the second and third columns, the first bit is the sign bit, with a 1 indicating a negative value. In the two's-complement notation is that the sign bit is, in a sense, automatic. Notice that if you start anywhere in the table and add 1 to the value in the third column (treating all the bits, including the sign bit, as if this were simply a 16-bit positive integer), you get the number on the line just above. Similarly, if you subtract 1 you get the number just below. This works whether the starting point is a positive or a negative value.

However, if you try this in the middle column, you'll find that you must use different rules for negative and positive numbers. That makes those ordinary binary numbers much more complicated to use in doing arithmetic. So computers typically are built to expend the effort to figure out the two's-complement form of negative values, knowing they will more than save it back in the ease with which arithmetic operations can be done on them later.

Here is another way to look at two's-complement notation for negative numbers. In Figure 3.2, I show you all the possibilities for a 4-bit number in two ways. First (on the left side of the figure) you see them in ordinary numerical order (going from bottom to top) and aligned against a "number line" in the usual position. The numbers on the number lines at left and right are, of course, in everyday decimal.

On the right side of the figure you see the same 16 binary numbers, but now the top 8 have been shoved under the rest, and as a consequence, they are aligned with the first 8 negative numbers. Because I have shown all the possible combinations of four 1s or 0s, adding 1 to the top one of the 16 binary numbers (1111b) causes it to "roll over" to 0 (like an odometer when it reaches the maximum mileage it can indicate).

FIGURE 3.2
Values of all the 4-bit binary numbers are interpreted both as counting numbers (on the left) and as two's-complement signed integers (on the right).

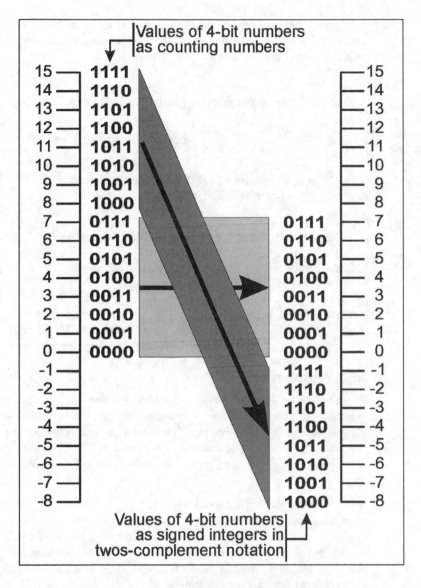

Values of 4-bit numbers as counting numbers

Values of 4-bit numbers as signed integers in twos-complement notation

In Figure 3.3, you see a summary of how all the kinds of whole numbers are held in your PC. Counting numbers can be stored either in a single byte or they may use an entire (16-bit) word. The value of a single-byte counting number can range from 0 to 255, because a byte has 8 bits, and $2^8 = 256$. Similarly, a double-byte counting number can range from 0 to 65,535, because $2^{16} = 65,536$.

Similarly, signed integers can be stored in a 2-byte word (16-bits) or in a 4-byte (32-bit) double word (DWORD). Because 1 bit is taken for the arithmetic sign (with a 0 indicating a positive number and a 1 indicating a negative number), the maximum positive value (and the minimum negative value) are about half as large as the largest counting number that could be stored in 16 or 32 bits.

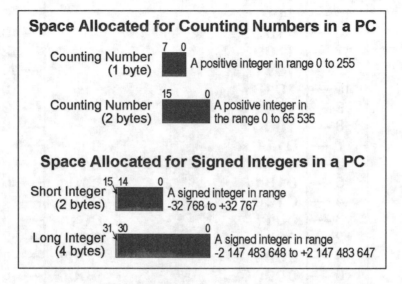

Space Allocated for Counting Numbers in a PC

Counting Number (1 byte)   7   0   A positive integer in range 0 to 255

Counting Number (2 bytes)   15   0   A positive integer in the range 0 to 65 535

Space Allocated for Signed Integers in a PC

Short Integer (2 bytes)   15 14   0   A signed integer in range -32 768 to +32 767

Long Integer (4 bytes)   31 30   0   A signed integer in range -2 147 483 648 to +2 147 483 647

Real Numbers

Real numbers are, I remind you, all the numbers you normally use. They can have the same value as a counting number or an integer, but they also can have fractional values. That is, the number 14 could be a counting number, a positive integer, or a real number that just happens to be a whole number. The number 14.75, on the other hand, can be only a real number. How these numbers get represented inside your PC can be very complex.

In the preceding paragraph, I spoke about the numbers 14 and 14.75, and I wrote both of them in their normal decimal form. You can easily show that these numbers, converted to binary, are 1110b and 1110.11b respectively. (The trailing *b* is, in all cases, simply there to show that these are binary numbers.) The period (we'll continue to call it a decimal point even though we're talking about binary numbers) serves the same function in 1110.11b that it does in the more-familiar 14.75.

This is how to represent a binary real number in what is termed *fixed point* notation. To store such numbers in a computer, you would have to allocate enough room to hold all the bits to the left and to the right of an imaginary decimal point.

Storing real numbers this way is infeasible, however. Because in everyday use we let these numbers be as large as we like or as small as we like, they potentially have an infinitely large number of possibilities. Setting aside potentially infinite blocks of information-holding places for each one is not possible. Therefore, some decisions have to be made as to how to represent these numbers adequately.

The only reasonable way to proceed is by breaking down such numbers in three distinct facts:

- The first fact about the number indicates whether it is positive or negative.
- The second fact indicates roughly how large the number is.
- The third fact describes what the actual number is, to some defined relative accuracy.

Finally, we write the number as a product of a numerical representation of each of those three facts.

Technical Note: In mathematical terms, this looks like a product of these three terms:

- Sign (plus or minus), called (not surprisingly) the sign part of the number and often symbolized by the letter S.
- An integer power of two, called the exponent part of the number and often symbolized by the letter E.
- A number between and 1 and 2, called the mantissa part of the number and often symbolized by the letter M.

Each of these portions is given a definite number of holding places in the computer. Because the first part, called the *sign*, indicates only 1 bit of information (plus or minus), it needs only a single bit as its holding place. The next part, called the *exponent*, and the final part, called the *mantissa*, each could potentially use an arbitrarily large number of holding places.

The amount of space our PCs use for the E and M parts of a real number represented in this fashion was set by a standard referred to as the "IEEE 724-1985 standard for floating point numbers." (I'll explain in a moment what "floating point" means in this context.) As the term implies, an industry *standard* ensures that numbers are maintained in the same manner.

The name *floating point* for this way of representing a number simply means that the mantissa M is assumed to have a decimal point, but because the mantissa must be multiplied by two raised to the power of the exponent, the effective location for the decimal point in the actual number must be imagined to have "floated" to the left or right by a number of places equal to the value of that exponent E.

Let's go back to our friend, the decimal number 14.75. You will recall that this could be written in binary as 1110.11b. Now imagine floating the decimal point to the left three places to get a mantissa that is between one and two. Now that number would be written as a floating point number this way:

$$14.75 = +2^3 \times 1.1101100000000b$$

For this number, the three parts are S = 0, E = 3, and M = 1.11011000000b. (The sign bit is 0 for positive real numbers and a 1 for negative real numbers, just as was the case for signed integers. Notice also that there are several 0s at the end of the mantissa. This, of course, doesn't change the value of the number. In practice, as many 0s are appended as necessary to fill up the standardized, allotted space in the computer.)

Strings of Non-Numeric Information

Back to the easy stuff. The representation of non-numeric information is *much* simpler than that of numeric information. Non-numeric information refers mostly to characters and strings of characters. Each character is chosen from some set of symbols. In a PC, we normally deal with a set of 256 characters (the extended-ASCII set I mentioned earlier) or with a Unicode character that comes from a much larger set. (I'll explain just what Unicode is later in this chapter.) In either case, we can represent each character by a number, and that number can be stored in one or—in the case of Unicode—in 2 or 4 bytes.

When you put a bunch of these characters together, you get what computer professionals call a *string*. So, from the perspective of the PC, a string is simply a collection of bytes, strung out one after another, which go together logically. Making sense of such a string of byte values is up to the program that produces or reads that string.

There are two methods that are often used to indicate the length of a string of characters representing a string. One is to put the length of the string, expressed as an integer, into the first 2 (or sometimes 4) bytes. The other is to end the string with a special symbol that is reserved for only that use. (The most common such symbol is given the name NUL or NULL and has the binary value 0.) Figure 3.4 shows these ideas graphically. Here, I have shown each character as taking up 1 byte—which has been the most common way to represent characters up until recently. Near the end of this chapter, I will detail an alternative way characters are now sometimes represented in 2- or 4-byte blocks. That method is most commonly used with the second of the two length-indicating strategies shown in Figure 3.4.

The advantage of the first strategy is that you can see the length of the string immediately. The advantage of the latter strategy is that, in principle, you can have strings of any length you want. However, in order to discern what length a particular string has, you must examine every one of the symbols in it until you come across that special string-terminating symbol.

FIGURE 3.4
The two most common ways non-numeric information is represented inside a PC.

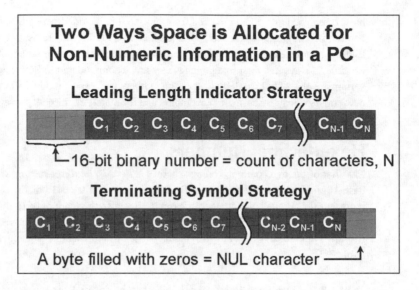

Symbols and Codes

Codes are a way to convey information. If you know the code, you can read the information. I've already discussed Paul Revere's code. His was created for just one occasion. The codes I am going to discuss in this section were created for more general purposes.

Any code, in the sense I am using the term here, can be represented by a table or list of symbols or characters that are to be encoded. The particular symbols used, their order, the encoding defined for each symbol, and the total number of symbols define that particular coding scheme.

> **Tip:** In order not to be confused by all this talk of bits, bytes, symbols, characters sets, and codes, you must keep clearly in mind that the symbols you want to represent are *not* what gets held in your PC. Only a coded version of them can be put there. If you actually look at the contents of your PC's memory, you'll find only a lot of numbers. (Depending on the tool you use to do this looking, the numbers might be translated into other symbols, but that is only because the tool assumes that the numbers represent characters in some coded character set.)

You'll encounter two common codes in the technical documentation on PCs:

- Hexadecimal
- ASCII

The hexadecimal code is used to make writing binary numbers easier. (Some people see hexadecimal as simply a counting system, and would object to seeing it here, but it is most often used as a coding method for 4 bits, so it is included here.) ASCII is the most common coding used when documents are held in a PC. If you are using a PC with non-English language software, you might be using yet another coding scheme. In fact, there are several ways in which foreign languages are accommodated in PCs. Some simply use variants of the ASCII single-byte encoding. Others use a special double-byte encoding. A new standard way is starting to encompass and ultimately replace all those possibilities. Its name is Unicode. I'll describe it in more detail in just a moment.

Hexadecimal Numbers

The first of the two common coding schemes is *hexadecimal numbering*, which is a base-16 method of counting. As you have now learned, it takes 16 distinct symbols to represent the "digits" of a number in base-16. Because there are only 10 distinct Arabic numerals, those have been augmented with the first six letters of the English alphabet (usually capitalized) to get the 16 symbols needed to represent hexadecimal numbers (see Table 3.3).

Table 3.3   The First 16 Numbers in Three Number Bases

Decimal	Binary	Hexadecimal	Decimal	Binary	Hexadecimal
0	0 0 0 0	0	8	1 0 0 0	8
1	0 0 0 1	1	9	1 0 0 1	9
2	0 0 1 0	2	10	1 0 1 0	A
3	0 0 1 1	3	11	1 0 1 1	B
4	0 1 0 0	4	12	1 1 0 0	C
5	0 1 0 1	5	13	1 1 0 1	D
6	0 1 1 0	6	14	1 1 1 0	E
7	0 1 1 1	7	15	1 1 1 1	F

The advantages of using hexadecimal are twofold: First, it is an economical way to write large binary numbers. Second, the translation between hexadecimal and binary is so trivial, anyone can learn to do it flawlessly.

Any binary number can be written as a string of bits. A 4-byte number is a string of 32 bits. This takes a lot of space and time to write, and it is very hard to read accurately. Group those bits into fours. Now replace each of the groups of 4 bits with the equivalent hexadecimal numeral according to Table 3.3. What you get is an 8-numeral hexadecimal number. This is much easier to write and read accurately!

Converting numbers from hexadecimal to binary is equally simple. Just replace each hexadecimal numeral with its equivalent string of 4 bits.

For example, the binary number

011010110011010110001100101000001

can be written in groups of 4 bits as

0110 1011 0011 0101 1000 1100 1010 0001

This can, in turn, be written as a hexadecimal number. Look up each group of 4 bits in Table 3.3 and replace it with its hex equivalent. Putting a lowercase *h* at the end (to indicate a hexadecimal number), you'll get this:

6B358CA1h

You can recognize a hexadecimal number in two ways. If it contains some normal decimal digits (0, 1, ... 9) and some letters (A through F), it is almost certainly a hexadecimal number. Sometimes authors will add the letter *h* or *H* after the number. The usual convention is to use a lowercase *h*, as in this book.

Another convention (and one that is very often used by C programmers) is to make the hexadecimal number begin with one of the familiar decimal digits by tacking a 0 onto the beginning of the number if necessary (or to put *0x* in front of every hexadecimal number). Thus, the hexadecimal number A would be written 0Ah (or 0xA).

Unfortunately, not everyone plays by these rules. In some cases, you simply have to go by the context and guess.

The ASCII and Extended-ASCII Codes

The other very common code you'll encounter in PCs is ASCII. As you've already read, ASCII now is the almost-universally accepted code for storing information in a PC. If you look at the actual contents of one of your documents in memory (or on a PC disk), you usually must translate the numbers you find there according to this code to see what the document says (refer to Figure 3.2).

Of course, because ASCII is so commonly used, many utility programs exist to help you translate ASCII-encoded information back into a more readable form for humans. One of the earliest of these utility programs for DOS is one of the external commands that has shipped with DOS from the very beginning. Its name is DEBUG. You'll meet this program and learn how to use it safely for this purpose in Chapter 6, "Enhancing Your Understanding by Exploring and Tinkering."

ASCII uses only 7 bits per symbol. When you create a pure-ASCII document on a PC, typically the most significant bit of each byte is simply set to 0 and ignored. This means there can be only 128 different characters (symbols) in the ASCII character set. About one-quarter of these (those with values 0 through 31, and 127) are reserved, according to the ASCII definition, for control characters. The rest are printable. (Some of the control code characters have onscreen representations. Whether you see those symbols or have an action performed depends on the context in which your PC encounters those control code byte values.) Those symbols and the ASCII control code mnemonics are shown in Figure 3.5. Add the decimal or hexadecimal number at the left of any row to the corresponding number at the top of any column in order to get the ASCII code value for the symbol shown where that row and column intersect. Table 3.4, later in this chapter, shows the standard definitions for the ASCII control codes.

Control Codes ASCII Printable Characters

Hex	Dec	00 / 0	10 / 16	20 / 32	30 / 48	40 / 64	50 / 80	60 / 96	70 / 112
0	0	NUL	DLE ►		0	@	P	`	p
1	1	SOH ☺	DC1 ◄	!	1	A	Q	a	q
2	2	STX ☻	DC2 ↕	"	2	B	R	b	r
3	3	ETX ♥	DC3 ‼	#	3	C	S	c	s
4	4	EOT ♦	DC4 ¶	$	4	D	T	d	t
5	5	ENQ ♣	NAK §	%	5	E	U	e	u
6	6	ACK ♠	SYN ▬	&	6	F	V	f	v
7	7	BEL •	ETB ↨	'	7	G	W	g	w
8	8	BS ◘	CAN ↑	(	8	H	X	h	x
9	9	HT ○	EM ↓	)	9	I	Y	i	y
A	10	LF ◙	SUB →	*	:	J	Z	j	z
B	11	VT ♂	ESC ←	+	;	K	[	k	{
C	12	FF ♀	FS ∟	,	<	L	\	l	¦
D	13	CR ♪	GS ↔	-	=	M	]	m	}
E	14	SO ♫	RS ▲	.	>	N	^	n	~
F	15	SI ☼	US ▼	/	?	O	_	o	⌂

FIGURE 3.5
The ASCII character set, including the standard mnemonics and the IBM graphics symbols for the 33 ASCII control characters.

Extensions to ASCII

Even before IBM's PC (and the many clones of it), there were small computers. Apple II was one popular brand. Many different brands of small computers running the CP/M operating software were also popular. These computers, like the IBM PC, all held information internally in (8-bit) bytes.

Because they held bytes of information, they were able to use a code (or character set) with twice as many elements as ASCII. Each manufacturer of these small computers was free to decide independently how to use those extra possibilities.

And that many different companies did make many different choices for what uses to make of what we now sometimes call the *upper-ASCII* characters (those with values from 128 through 255). Because the binary representation for those values all have a 1 in the most significant place, these characters are also sometimes called *high-bit-set* characters.

When you are at a DOS prompt, the symbols you will see on your PC's display in any place where an upper-ASCII character is displayed will be whatever IBM chose to make it. If you print that screen display on a printer, the symbol at that location will be transformed into whatever the printer manufacturer chose. In the pre-Windows days, this was a source of much confusion.

Fortunately, now most people print documents only from within Windows, and thus end up using the same set of symbols onscreen and on paper. In both cases the only symbols are those chosen by Microsoft and implemented in everyone's Windows video and printer drivers.

Not everything in your PC uses ASCII coding. In particular, programs are stored in files filled with what might be regarded as the CPU's native language, which is all numbers. Various tools you might use to look inside these files will show what at first glance looks like "garbage." In fact, the symbols you see are meaningless to people. Only the actual numerical values (and the CPU instructions they represent) matter.

These numbers are, in fact, what is sometimes referred to as "machine language," as they constitute the only "language" the CPU can actually "understand." (I will return to this point in more detail in Chapter 18, "Understanding How Humans Instruct PCs.")

Control Codes

Any useful computer coding scheme must use some of its definitions for symbols or characters that stand for actions rather than for printable entities. These include actions such as ending a line, returning the printing position to the left margin, moving to the next tab (in any of four directions—horizontally or vertically, forward or backward).

Only the special codes stand for various ways to indicate the beginning or the end of a message (SOH, STX, ETX, EOT, GS, RS, US, EM, and ETB). Another special code (ENQ) lets the message-sending computer ask the message-receiving computer to give a standardized response.

Four quite important control codes for PCs are the acknowledge and negative-acknowledge (ACK or NAK) codes, the escape code (ESC), and the null code (NUL). These are used when data is being sent from one PC to another, for example, by modem. The first pair are used by the receiving computer to let the sending computer know whether a message has been received correctly, among other uses. The escape code often signals that the following symbols are to be interpreted according to some other special scheme. The null code is often used to signal the end of a string of characters.

Table 3.4 shows all the officially defined control codes and their two- or three-letter mnemonics. These definitions are codified in an American National Standards Institute document, *ANSI X3.4-1986*.

Table 3.4 The Standard Meanings for the ASCII Control Codes

ASCII Value Decimal (Hex)	Keyboard Equivalent	Mnemonic Name	Description
0 (0h)	Ctrl+@	NULL	Null
1 (1h)	Ctrl+A	SOH	Start of heading
2 (2h)	Ctrl+B	STX	Start of text
3 (3h)	Ctrl+C	ETX	End of text
4 (4h)	Ctrl+D	EOT	End of transmission
5 (5h)	Ctrl+E	ENQ	Enquire
6 (6h)	Ctrl+F	ACK	Acknowledge
7 (7h)	Ctrl+G	BEL	Bell
8 (8h)	Ctrl+H	BS	Backspace
9 (9h)	Ctrl+I	HT	Horizontal tab
10 (Ah)	Ctrl+J	LF	Line feed
11 (Bh)	Ctrl+K	VT	Vertical tab
12 (Ch)	Ctrl+L	FF	Form feed (new page)
13 (Dh)	Ctrl+M	CR	Carriage return
14 (Eh)	Ctrl+N	SO	Shift out
15 (Fh)	Ctrl+O	SI	Shift in
16 (10h)	Ctrl+P	DLE	Data link escape
17 (11h)	Ctrl+Q	DC1	Device control 1
18 (12h)	Ctrl+R	DC2	Device control 2
19 (13h)	Ctrl+S	DC3	Device control 3
20 (14h)	Ctrl+T	DC4	Device control 4
21 (15h)	Ctrl+U	NAK	Negative acknowledge
22 (16h)	Ctrl+V	SYN	Synchronous idle
23 (17h)	Ctrl+W	ETB	End of transmission block
24 (18h)	Ctrl+X	CAN	Cancel
25 (19h)	Ctrl+Y	EM	End of medium
26 (1Ah)	Ctrl+Z	SUB	Substitute
27 (1Bh)	Ctrl+[	ESC	Escape
28 (1Ch)	Ctrl+\	FS	Form separator

ASCII Value Decimal (Hex)	Keyboard Equivalent	Mnemonic Name	Description
29 (1Dh)	Ctrl+]	GS	Group separator
30 (1Eh)	Ctrl+^	RS	Record separator
31 (1Fh)	Ctrl+_	US	Unit separator
127 (3Fh)	Alt+127	DEL	Delete

In Table 3.4, note that Ctrl+x means to press and hold the Ctrl key while pressing the x key, and Alt+127 means to press and hold the Alt key while pressing the 1, 2, and 7 keys successively on the numeric keypad portion of your keyboard.

Unicode

By now you understand why the early 5- and 6-bit teletype codes weren't adequate to do the job of encoding all the messages and data that needed to be sent or that are now being handled on our PCs. What might be less obvious to you is why even an 8-bit code such as extended ASCII isn't really what we need. If everyone on the planet spoke and wrote only in English, 8 bits might be plenty. But that clearly is not reality. By one count, there are almost 6,800 different human languages. Eventually, we will want to be able to communicate in nearly every one of them using a PC. And to do that, some serious improvements must be made in the information-encoding strategy we use.

The importance of this is becoming clearer and clearer. At first, people tried some simple tricks to extend extended ASCII. That was enough for a while, but soon the difficulties of using those tricks outweighed their advantages. And in any case, it was becoming apparent that these types of tricks just wouldn't do at all for the broader task ahead.

In the beginning, the heavy users of computers of all kinds were people who used a language based on an alphabet, usually one that was quite similar to the one used for English. Simple variations on the ASCII code table were worked out, one for each language, so that the set of symbols would include all the special letters and accents used in that country. These "code pages" could then be loaded into a PC, and it would be ready to work with text in that language.

However, this strategy can work only if two conditions are met. First, the computer in question must be used for only one of these languages at a time. Second, the languages must be based on alphabets not too dissimilar to English.

However, there are some very important languages that use too many different characters to fit into even a 256-element character set. This is clearly true for the Asian languages that are based on ideographs. What you might not realize is that this also holds true for many other languages, such as Farsi (used in Iran), where the forms of characters are altered in important ways depending on their grammatical context.

At first, people thought they could solve this problem by devising more complex character sets, one per language to be encoded. And the really difficult languages were handled by making up short character strings that would encode each of the more exotic characters.

One difficulty with this approach is that not all symbols are contained in a single-size information chunk. Another difficulty is that there are still many different encoding schemes, each one tuned to the needs of some particular language, and none will work for arbitrary mixed-language documents.

Obviously (in retrospect, at least) the solution ultimately must be to devise an entirely new encoding scheme—one that will have enough capacity to hold all the symbols used in any of the 6,800 languages of the people on this planet. This is exactly what has been done. The result of this effort is *Unicode*.

Unicode has been developed in a lengthy process, including input from linguists and computer scientists around the world. It is being codified in several documents issued by several international standards groups, each document describing some aspect of Unicode. The designers of Unicode have taken great pains to be sure that this strategy has enough room to grow in order to make it last a very long time.

The basic approach is to represent each symbol in Unicode with a 16-bit number. This means that it is possible to represent every symbol in a pair of bytes (which is one computer "word" in the most common definition of that term for PCs). Normally, this would allow representing at most 65,536 distinct characters or symbols. This set of symbol possibilities is called, in Unicode jargon, the *Basic Multilingual Plane* (BMP). This space is very large but, the designers thought, it might someday prove to be inadequate. Therefore, they built in a way to extend this representation even further.

When you use only 2-byte (16-bit) numbers to represent Unicode characters, *UCS-2 encoding* is being used. However, the standard enables inserting within the body of some UCS-2-encoded text some UCS-4 characters. To do this, two 1,024-location blocks were reserved in the BMP. Each of those locations cannot be used to represent any symbol. Instead, pairs of those numbers, one chosen from each group, will be used to encode up to about a million UCS-4 characters. Figure 3.6 compares the extended-ASCII way of representing a character with the Unicode UCS-2 and UCS-4 methods.

Why not simply use 4 bytes per character from the outset? The answer is that this is too wasteful of space. Almost all the time you can get away with double-byte characters, and only when you need to use something more exotic will you have to dedicate 4 bytes per symbol. This still means that a document that is stored all in Unicode will be at least twice the size of that same document stored in ASCII (assuming it could be represented accurately in ASCII), and possibly just a little bit more if it includes some of those special characters that require 4 bytes each.

FIGURE 3.6

Three ways characters are represented in PCs.

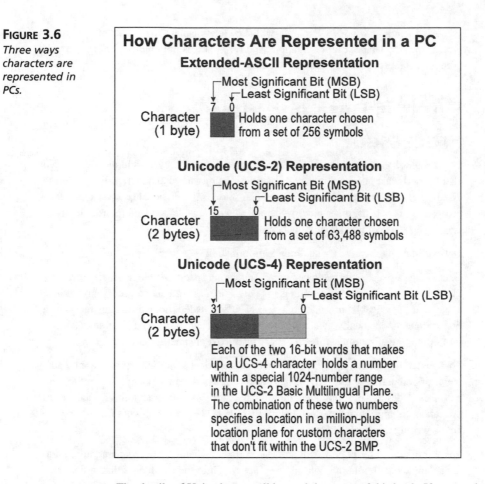

How Characters Are Represented in a PC

Extended-ASCII Representation

Most Significant Bit (MSB)
Least Significant Bit (LSB)
7   0

Character (1 byte)   Holds one character chosen from a set of 256 symbols

Unicode (UCS-2) Representation

Most Significant Bit (MSB)
Least Significant Bit (LSB)
15   0

Character (2 bytes)   Holds one character chosen from a set of 63,488 symbols

Unicode (UCS-4) Representation

Most Significant Bit (MSB)
Least Significant Bit (LSB)
31   0

Character (2 bytes)

Each of the two 16-bit words that makes up a UCS-4 character holds a number within a special 1024-number range in the UCS-2 Basic Multilingual Plane. The combination of these two numbers specifies a location in a million-plus location plane for custom characters that don't fit within the UCS-2 BMP.

The details of Unicode are well beyond the scope of this book. If you are interested, you can find most of them on the World Wide Web. Point your browser to the Unicode home page at

`http://www.unicode.org/`

and follow the links you find there.

Is Unicode being used today? Most certainly. If you are running Windows 95, Windows 98, Windows NT, or Windows 2000, you are using it (probably without knowing that you are). Every directory entry pointing to a file on your disk drives is stored using Unicode. Directories on UDF-formatted optical discs also use Unicode. And Office 95 and Office 97 use Unicode extensively in the document files they create. This makes it much easier for these programs to support users with different language needs. You set your language preference once (and it is recorded in the Windows Registry). Thereafter, every program you use, including Windows Explorer, will show you displays in your language, interpreted from the Unicode representation. And surely this is only the beginning. No program can claim to be truly international unless it supports Unicode.

What Is Data and How Is It Processed?

This chapter has covered much. You have learned what bits, bytes, and nybbles are; you also learned what information is and how it can be measured and stored. What's left to discuss about information in the most general sense is its relationship to data and data processing. This is the other piece of the puzzle you must understand in order to appreciate how a PC is built and how it operates.

Data is, in many ways, the same thing as information.

Data is the raw resource that, when combined with a specific context, creates meaning. The point of much data processing is to take some mass of data and reorganize it in such a way that the valuable information in it is clearly revealed. Sometimes this reorganization is done automatically by a computer, under the control of some program. Other times the reorganization is done in a more interactive manner.

This description clearly applies to the types of statistical analysis that were the bread and butter of computing in the early days. However, today we do so many different things with PCs. Does this description apply to graphic artists creating stunning visuals, or to musicians composing and performing music on a PC? How about what I am doing now—writing this book?

Yes, I think the description is still apt. For example, when I write this paragraph, I am taking some data I hold in my head and delivering it to the PC in a particular context. Therefore, I do some of the data processing in my brain. But I then expect the PC to capture that output and hold it for my editor's, and eventually my readers', use. After I have put the thoughts down, I often find I must use the PC as a tool to help me rearrange or modify those thoughts in an effort to make their meanings even more clear.

> **Exploring:** Remember the test earlier in the chapter? Here is the same paragraph with the vowels put back in. See how closely you got the meaning of this paragraph from the earlier version with no vowels.
>
> This is a test. If you can read this paragraph, and get the meaning at least mostly right, you have shown that English is redundant to such a degree that leaving out all the vowels doesn't stop you from reading it pretty well.

PART II

A First Look Inside Your PC

Understanding Your PC's Parts

At this point, you have seen an overview of the PC industry and its role in our society. You also have at least a general notion of how any computer is designed and works, and know something of what information is and how data is processed. It's finally time to get down and dirty, to go inside the PC and see how the parts look and what they are. The previous chapters focused on functionality and logical organization. This one focuses on the physical parts and how they're interconnected.

A PC as a Chamber Orchestra

Some people, and perhaps you, find computers intimidating. They feel reluctant to open the box and muck around inside. Others relish doing this. Whichever group you belong to (or even if you don't identify with either), you must know one very important fact up front and keep it clearly in mind as you continue on your safari into PC land.

> **Peter's Principle:** Look at the Parts Separately and Then at Their Interconnections
>
> The simple but overwhelmingly important fact is that PCs are made up of many parts, and each part is much simpler than the whole. To understand a PC, therefore, you are well advised to look first at the simpler parts that make it up. But to make sense of those explorations, you must also keep in the back of your mind some image of the interconnection and interaction of all these parts.

In this chapter you will meet the parts that make up a typical PC, and you will see the scheme by which they are interconnected. These introductions are fairly cursory, but they give you a necessary background image of the whole as the sum of its parts. The following chapters (especially those in Parts III, V, and VII) take you through a much more intimate look at each of the different parts of the PC, one at a time.

If you see a PC as some wonderfully capable multifunctional machine, you might believe that understanding how it works is almost impossible. Breaking down that image into many parts will be very helpful. Each of those parts might also be quite wonderful, but none is nearly as complex as the overall combination. Now look at each part in turn.

Understand the parts, one by one, in as much detail as you want, then see how they fit together and work as a whole. This is the most direct way to an overall understanding of the total PC.

I also want to give you some important cautionary tips. You really don't want to hurt either yourself or your PC, so before you open up any of your PC's constituent pieces, please carefully read the section later in this chapter titled "Safe System Unit 'Surgery'."

The Three Main Pieces

Most PCs have a lot in common. The essential core of the typical desktop PC comes in three pieces: a keyboard, a monitor, and one other box called the system unit. Of course, you might also have a printer and a mouse and other things, but nearly every PC has these three parts, and it must have them in order to do anything useful.

This is not to say that other PC designs are not possible. For example, a laptop computer has all three of these parts bundled into a single unit, mainly for convenience in carrying it around. In Part VI, "PCs Are Frequent Flyers, Too," I will go into detail on the many design differences between portable, laptop, and palmtop computers. This chapter focuses on the more typical desktop systems, such as that shown in Figure 4.1. This rather complex-looking system is built around a mainstream desktop PC system (in terms of its features and price) made by Dell Computer Corporation. I have enhanced it with an additional monitor, but when you analyze the fundamentals you'll see that it represents what most PC users have on their desktops today (This is definitely *not* the fastest PC around. But then, I have had it for awhile. The speed of technological progress in our industry is astounding—and that pretty much guarantees that any system you have had for any noticeable length of time won't be as fast as the latest and greatest systems on the market.)

FIGURE 4.1

A typical desktop PC has at least four parts: a keyboard, mouse (or other pointing device), a monitor, and a system unit. This system has one additional monitor.

Monitor   Microsoft Natural Keyboard   Microsoft IntelliMouse Pro   Dell Dimension XPS R350 system unit

I created the system shown in this figure both to show you what is common in some of today's desktop systems, and to show you some ways in which you might wish to extend that common desktop system for a variety of special purposes.

The multiple monitors, for example, show off one of the coolest new features in Microsoft Windows 98. You can spread your desktop across multiple monitors and thus show the output of multiple programs simultaneously.

Being able to see multiple programs on two screens is appropriate for a growing number of PC users today. Financial market traders are one group who have adopted this strategy enthusiastically, as have graphic design and CAD professionals. And I expect others will follow their lead, once the benefits of such a system are well-known.

This system unit has an Intel Pentium II 450MHz CPU and 320MB of RAM. It is built around an Intel motherboard with Intel's 440BX motherboard chip set, which includes a 100MHz front-side bus. I have plugged several option cards into this system which you'll encounter as examples as you read through this book. (These are also sometimes called I/O plug-in cards, because they contain mostly circuits used for getting information into or out of the PC. They are also commonly called adapters or adapter cards.)

This system unit stands taller than it is wide. We call such a PC system unit enclosure a *tower* case. The original PCs—both from IBM and from most of the clone PC makers— came with system units that were wider than tall (which we now call *desktop* cases). You'll also commonly encounter the term *mini-tower*, which is simply a shorter version of the tower case.

In the early years of PCs, many a PC owner tried putting the monitor on top of the PC's system unit. But that raised it up too high for comfortable viewing. People next tried pushing the system unit to one side, but that took up too much desktop space. So, they often turned the system unit on one end and stood it on the floor. Manufacturers simply adopted that idea in creating the first tower systems. And, indeed, when you look inside one of the older-style wide and low system units and compare it to a typical modern desktop PC, you'll find pretty much all the same things inside.

Most desktop PCs now conform to one of three industry-standard designs. They go by the names *ATX*, *micro-ATX*, and *NLX*. I'll tell you a bit more about these designs later in this chapter. The arrangement of components in these systems is a bit different than in the earliest PC-compatible designs. Many of those early systems, built more or less in accord with the arrangement IBM introduced with its IBM PC AT model, are still in use today.

In the near future, we can expect to see two more designs being built. One will be a new *closed-box PC* that will have some set of standard features included, but won't offer any place to add anything inside the box. Instead, these PCs will have just a few, very powerful ports into which one may plug all manner of external peripheral devices. The other new design I expect to see enter the market this year will be boxes called *workstation PCs,* built around a descendent of the ATX design called the *WTX*. This design will be of special interest to those of us who would like to have a really powerful PC with lots of extra gadgets built in or added in later on.

Of course, there are some other PCs that don't conform to one of these industry standard designs. The most prominent category are the mobile PCs, which I will discuss in detail in Chapter 22, "Why Mobile PCs Must Be Different." And there are a number of manufacturers who make custom-designed PCs for specialized uses.

Which form of PC you choose limits in some ways which options you can put into (or attach onto) that PC, but in general how those sub-systems are built and how they work are pretty much the same. So, learning about one system's pieces in detail will tell you about almost all the PC parts you might run across.

What Goes Inside the Box

There might be only three main pieces to a typical PC, but one of those pieces, the *system unit*, is a pretty complex object. It contains many other, smaller objects. It also contains the essential interconnection infrastructure that lets those pieces work together effectively and amicably.

> **Note:** A theme that I will return to over and over again in this book is this: PCs are made by many manufacturers out of pieces made by other, even more numerous, manufacturers. This diversity is the source of much of the flexibility and power of PCs. It has allowed each customer to buy a PC that includes almost any conceivable collection of features that the customer wants (and is willing to purchase).

This diversity is also the principal source of most peoples' problems with their PCs. I will go into more detail on this point in the section "Controlling Chaos," later in this chapter.

This diversity came about, and it could only have come about, after there were some industrywide agreements about how the pieces should interconnect. I discuss that point in the section "Information Rides the Bus," later in this chapter. But first, I must explain just what all those pieces are that live inside the typical PC's system unit.

Safe System Unit "Surgery"

This section introduces you to some basic considerations that are relevant to a physical exploration of your PC. Some of what follows will seem obvious to you; some of it won't. But there are a few simple precautions it's wise to take whenever you're going to be opening up your computer. These precautions will protect your PC's components and you as well.

The first thing to consider is the potential for hardware to be damaged by stray static electricity. Fortunately, the best defense is simply common sense and awareness of the dangers. The second and equally vital line of defense is a heightened awareness of exactly the impact you have, both electrically and physically, even if you just reach inside to touch something with no intent of moving it.

Of the three principal pieces that make up your PC—keyboard, monitor, and system unit—only the system unit is something you will want to open up. The keyboard contains little of interest (and often a whole lot of tiny springs that may fly all over the place if you aren't careful). I'd suggest opening it only if you need to clean it after a very bad spill of liquid into it. (Even then, it often will be better simply to replace the keyboard with a new one.) The monitor presents a different issue. At least it does if it's a typical *CRT* (*cathode ray tube*) monitor—that is to say, one that somewhat resembles a television set.

> **Warning:** You *really* don't want to open up your monitor. There is actual, physical danger there—high electrical voltages may remain on the cathode long after the monitor is turned off and unplugged. If these discharge into your body, *you could die*. At best, you'll have the worst day you can remember. Furthermore, there is nothing going on inside a monitor that is relevant to your understanding of how a PC works.

The system box, in contrast to the keyboard and monitor, was designed to be opened by anyone. And opening it is going to be necessary to fully understand its construction and workings.

What about other pieces your PC may have, such as a mouse, scanner, printer, modem, or whatever? These other pieces might or might not be safe to open. And usually you won't learn much of importance if you do open them, so at least for now I recommend you leave them alone.

Guidelines for Avoiding Static Electricity Damage

Now what about the static electricity hazard? It turns out that you are a lot more dangerous to your PC than it is to you—at least in terms of what could go wrong when you open up the system unit. The voltages used by the integrated circuit chips in your PC's system unit are anywhere from a little less than 3 volts up to 12 volts. These are so low that you won't hurt yourself touching any of them. On the other hand, people normally walk around with static electric charges of several hundred volts, or up to several thousand on a dry, cold day. That's more than enough to totally fry the delicate innards of your computer.

An electric current won't flow unless there's a voltage difference to drive it. Therefore, the actual voltage of your body isn't very important by itself. What matters is how much difference there is between the voltage at your fingertip and the voltage at the places you're about to touch. If you first touch the power supply or an unpainted portion of the metal chassis of your PC system unit, and then touch whatever you want inside, you will, by this first step, have brought your entire body (including your fingers) to essentially the same voltage as the chips you'll be touching. In this case, no damage will be done.

> **Warning:** It may seem counterintuitive, but it's vitally important that you keep your PC plugged into its grounded power outlet whenever you're looking or working inside it. The ground is central to carrying dangerously high voltages away from both you and your PC. You should, however, unplug your motherboard from the power supply if you have an ATX-based system.
>
> You may read the opposite instruction elsewhere, but don't be swayed. Your PC should remain plugged-in and turned off.

If you get a nasty, or even a painful, shock when you touch the case, be glad. That shock might have pained you, but it could have killed your PC's inner workings if they had received it instead of you.

If the pain of those shocks is just too great to bear, then there are several steps you can take. First, think about reducing the static electric charge you carry around. You can get static-reducing carpet or a chair pad and put it where you sit or stand when you work on your PC. An even easier solution is to get some fabric softener, dilute it with three to four times as much water as softener, and then spray the diluted mixture on your carpet. Repeat this as necessary, probably no more often than once a month, and then only in especially dry weather. (Make certain that you test the solution on a small, out-of-view section of carpeting to guarantee that it doesn't cause a color change.)

You can reduce your personal pain from these shocks another way. Get a one million ohm radio resistor. (Radio Shack is one convenient source.) The exact value of the resistor isn't important; anything from a few hundred thousand ohms to a few million will do, and the wattage rating of the resistor is also unimportant. Hold one end of the resistor and touch the other end to the PC case before you reach over and touch it directly. This will let your excess electric charge bleed off slowly, and you won't even feel the resulting current. It might take a second or two, but not longer. Finally, touch the case directly, just to be sure you're fully discharged and, thus, are safe to explore inside. For only a little more money, you can purchase a static-guard wrist strap. The simplest of these are disposable: They're made of paper with a conductive strip attached. You attach one end to your PC's case (it's self-adhesive) and place your wrist through a loop in the other end. Any static that builds up across your skin while you work is drained down the wrist strap. If you do a lot of work inside PCs, a non-disposable variety is also available.

When you move around a room, you're potentially picking up more static charge. This is why you must re-discharge yourself *each and every time* you are about to reach inside the PC. Likewise, if you're carrying an option card and are about to install it, by touching the case while you hold the card you are ensuring that the card and the case are at the same voltage. It is then safe to insert the card. (Of course, you should be discharged before you pick up an option card, too). Additionally, while you're working on your PC, try to keep a hand on the case at all times (or use one of the static straps I mentioned, above). This will provide a route for continuous discharging of any static electricity that might build up around your body while you're working.

Beware Line Current—It Can Kill…You!

To be totally safe working inside your PC you must guard against static electric discharges. You must also be sure that the electricity from the wall socket doesn't come out and bite you. There are two easy ways to guard against this. First, if your PC has a power switch in back, on its power supply, in addition to the power-switch or startup-switch on the front, make sure that this switch is Off. Many modern PCs don't turn off completely until and unless you turn this switch off, too. The second way merits some special attention:

> **Warning:** Never, under any circumstances, for any reason, *ever* open up the sealed power supply inside your PC. Like your monitor, the power supply contains voltages that could easily kill you. It's sealed for a reason. Leave it sealed.

If you ever hear strange sounds coming from your power supply—weird fan noises or what sounds like electricity shorting out—replace your power supply if you know how to do so, or pay someone who does know how. Never open your power supply for *any* reason.

Keeping Track of Changes—And Reversing Them Correctly

Once your system is well and truly powered-off, and any static has been discharged from your body, you can start looking or working inside, making changes if necessary. If you do choose to unplug something, or to unscrew something, you'll want to carefully record just what the connection looked like before you made the change. (Some people find taking digital camera or Polaroid photos a handy way to capture some of this information.) Then, if something you change doesn't work out, you can at least put it back the way it was.

Often, a particularly troublesome kind of connection in this regard are the places where flat, multi-conductor ribbon cables attach to printed circuit boards. Typically, there will be a field of gold-plated pins sticking up from the board. On the end of the cable is a rectangular block of plastic with some holes in one side. You plug in the cable by pressing the block down over the pins.

Two types of problem can arise. One is when the plug is turned around 180 degrees. The other is when it gets offset from the correct position by exactly the spacing of one pair of pins (typically, just one-tenth of an inch). Doing either of these things will mean that the wires in the cable will connect with the wrong pins, or they will fail to connect with any pins.

Two things can help: First, the usual practice is to identify one of the pins as the *number one* pin. This is often shown by a small numeral 1 printed next to that pin on the printed circuit card. (It is usually indicated by having a square bit of copper on the bottom side of the circuit board around the hole into which the pin is soldered, instead of the round ones used for all the other pins.) Ordinarily, the number one wire in the ribbon cable has a different color insulation than the rest of the cable. (Sometimes, this stripe of color on one edge of the cable is blue, sometimes black, and sometimes red. Or, you might find that all the wires are different colors, in a rainbow pattern. In that case, the brown wire will be number one.)

If you're lucky, the manufacturers of both the cable and the board with the field of pins will have taken one or two more precautions to keep you from plugging in the cable incorrectly. If they did the first good thing, there will be one or more missing pins and one or more of the holes in the block will be plugged up (at locations that match up with the missing pins). This arrangement of missing pins and matching plugged-up holes ensures that the block can only be plugged onto the pins in the correct position and orientation. If they did the second good thing, there will be a housing around the pins so the block cannot get offset by a pin-spacing distance. (And sometimes the block will have a small bump on one side that fits into a slot in that housing, preventing you from plugging in the cable backwards.)

Figure 4.2 shows just such a ribbon cable and its connectors. In this case, one pin is missing and one hole is plugged up. We say that this cable is *keyed* to ensure that it is installed correctly. There is also a housing, with a slot, but there isn't any bump on the connector so the plugged hole *key* is the only way used here to make sure the connector isn't turned around.

Notice in this figure the indicated small triangle on the motherboard that shows you where pin number one is on the post and header connector. Also visible (only barely visible in this figure, but easily seen when you can see the actual colors) is that the number one wire in the ribbon cable is red instead of gray. (This cable and connector must be turned over 180 degrees to the right in order to fit into the connector on the motherboard.) I've shown that "sandwich" opened like a book to let you clearly see the mating keys.

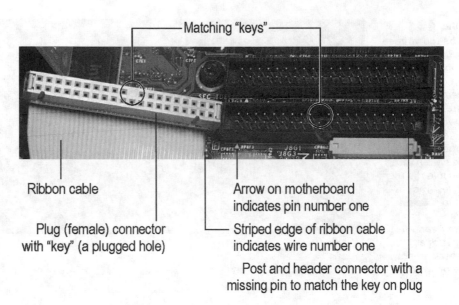

FIGURE 4.2
Ribbon cables and the header connector can be tricky to align. But keys (missing pins and plugged or missing holes) can make it easy. Shown here are the two EIDE connectors on the motherboard of our sample desktop system and one of the EIDE cables that attach to them.

Matching "keys"

Ribbon cable

Plug (female) connector with "key" (a plugged hole)

Arrow on motherboard indicates pin number one

Striped edge of ribbon cable indicates wire number one

Post and header connector with a missing pin to match the key on plug

Another trouble some people have, closely related to the difficulty I just described with ribbon cables, has to do with placing or moving shorting jumpers. These are little blocks that contain a metal insert. You slide them down over a pair of pins and the metal insert shorts those two pins together. (They are like a two-wire ribbon cable connector without the ribbon cable.) But, of course, if you miss the correct pair of pins, you won't short what needs to be shorted, and you may short something else that shouldn't be shorted. The only solution to this problem is to get a bright light and, if you need it, a strong pair of glasses or a magnifying glass. Then look very closely at what you're doing. You may also find that a pair of needle-nose pliers, commonly available at hardware or electronics stores, may enhance your physical dexterity when you're working with these little nuisances.

> **Warning:** Something to remember whenever you're working inside your PC is that, with very few exceptions, the force needed to seat connectors and cables inside your PC is slight. In fact, the amount of pressure you exert on a key when you type will usually be sufficient to put things in their place. If you encounter resistance, first pull back and double-check that everything is aligned properly before you try pushing harder.

Figure 4.3 shows one such jumper, both in a photograph and in a drawing to make clearer what you are seeing in the photograph. Here there are three "posts" (just like the pins in a post-and-header ribbon cable connector) and a metal-lined sleeve that can cover (and in the process short together) two of them. The jumper is normally installed either over the left and center posts or over the right and center posts.

Note: This particular jumper is an important one to know about. Moving it to the other position causes the BIOS configuration CMOS memory chip to forget everything you have told it. Later on, after you have booted up at least once, you can move it back and the BIOS configuration CMOS will hold only the default data it had when this PC was shipped from the factory.

That process is useful if you ever mess up the BIOS configuration settings so badly you don't know any other way to restore them to their original values. And it is the only easy way to recover if you enter a password for your system and then forget it.

However, this is an all-or-nothing sort of erasure of data. So, you are warned right now to record somewhere what all the BIOS configuration setup program screens show you about what the BIOS settings are now. That way, if any of them have been customized in useful ways, you will be able to restore those customizations relatively easily.

A Platform to Build Upon: The Motherboard

Every PC has one printed circuit card in it that serves as its foundation (logically, and often mechanically as well). This circuit card is commonly called the *motherboard*. This name comes from the fact that in most PCs this card has some connectors on it into which other circuit cards are plugged. The other, and perhaps more technically correct term is *mainboard*. That term can be used to refer to the main printed circuit board in any PC, but because almost all of them have places in which to plug other boards, the term motherboard has become the more common term for this item, even in those relatively few cases in which it really is only a mainboard.

There are, as I mentioned earlier in this chapter, three common standards used in the design of desktop PCs today. They go by the names ATX, micro-ATX, and NLX. These standards begin with the design of the motherboard and then specify a chassis and various other features designed around the needs of that motherboard for housing, cooling, and power—plus the space needed for option cards and disk drives.

The first of these standard designs, referred to by the name ATX, arose as a simplification and standardization of the several slightly different ways in which clone makers made PC desktop motherboards a few years ago. Their designs all stemmed from the design of IBM's PC model AT—hence the name ATX for the new, more standardized and easier-to-manufacture PC desktop motherboard.

The second design, NLX, is very different. And, as you might suspect, it sprang from a different source. When I described how tower case PCs came into being, I mentioned that putting a monitor on top of an old, AT-style PC made it too high to see comfortably. The tower unit was one response to this, but there was also another response. Some manufacturers started making "low profile" desktop PCs. These were boxes that were low enough that they actually could be placed underneath a typical monitor without raising it up too much.

The only way to do this, at that time, was to have the motherboard lying on the bottom of the case, with a small "riser" card plugged into the only slot connector that was on that style of motherboard. On its surface, this riser card had several more slot connectors into which a few option cards could be plugged. This arrangement made the option cards lie down parallel to the motherboard, which kept the overall height acceptably small.

The NLX design is much the same, but with one significant change. Now the riser card is the mechanical foundation. It is mounted to one side of the case, and it has one big slot connector for the motherboard as well as several ordinary slot connectors for option cards. The motherboard now has an edge connector much like that on an option card, but with provision for more connections. These connections not only let the motherboard communicate with the option cards, they provide the motherboard with all the different voltages of electrical power that it needs.

The third common design, the micro-ATX, is simply a further simplification and reduction in size of the ATX design. You can learn more about all of these design specifications, and also about the new WTX workstation design, by checking these URLs:

```
http://www.teleport.com/~atx/
http://www.teleport.com/~nlx/
http://www.teleport.com/~microatx/
http://www.wtx.org/
```

Diverse as they are, these designs all have a lot in common. In all cases, the motherboard has a socket or slot connector for the CPU and most or all of the RAM plus a number of logic circuits whose job is to convey information to and from all the other circuits on the motherboard and to the connectors leading to the option card circuits and the disk drives.

The most common generic name for these logic circuits is the motherboard *chip set*, or the motherboard *glue logic*.

Figure 4.4 shows the ATX motherboard from our example desktop system. The callouts indicate where you can find various key features. In this figure, you see the motherboard removed from its case and viewed from a position above and in front of it.

FIGURE 4.4

The motherboard from our sample desktop PC, here seen from above the front edge of the board, with several key features marked.

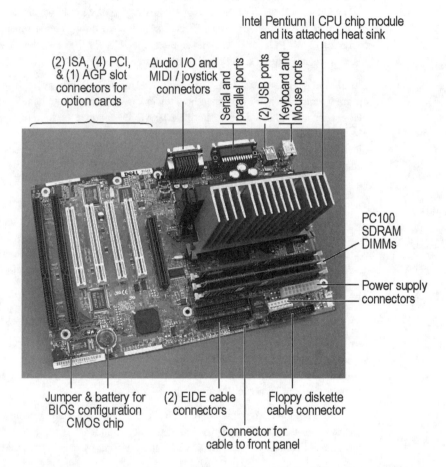

The largest object, sticking way up above the board's surface, is the heat sink attached to the CPU module. That is a vital part. It's designed to draw away the tremendous heat generated by the normal operation of the CPU itself. Without it, the CPU would simply cook itself to death. I'll tell you more about this topic later in this chapter in the section titled "Getting the Heat Out."

This CPU module (nearly entirely hidden in this view) is what Intel called a Single Edge Contact Cartridge (SECC). It plugs into what Intel originally called a *Slot 1 connector*, but now simply refers to as its *242-contact slot connector*. (Intel also has what was originally termed a *Slot 2 connector* for some of its other CPU modules, but that has been renamed to the Intel *330-contact slot connector*.) I'll tell you more about all of the CPUs available for PCs today, including both of those that go into conventional sockets, and those like this Pentium II that come in SECC modules, in Chapter 7, "Understanding PC Processors." You can get a better view of this module in Figures 4.5 and 4.6, which show this module. Figure 4.6 shows you how to unlock it from its socket and retaining mechanism.

The long rectangular objects at the left are the *I/O (input/output) slot connectors*. On this motherboard are two black ISA slot connectors (these are the older, so-called Industry Standard Architecture design), four (smaller, white) PCI slot connectors, and one additional black connector (on the right in this figure, and set farther back from the rear edge of the motherboard) which is an AGP (Advanced Graphics Processor) slot connector. A plug-in card with any of a wide variety of functional parts can be plugged into any of these slots other than the AGP slot; that one is used only for one of the newest and best kind of video display adapters. You'll get to meet the variety of I/O slot designs that have been used in PCs in Chapter 16, "Faster Ways to Get Information Into and Out of Your PC." I'll explain all about AGP in that chapter and in Chapter 13, "Seeing the Results: PC Displays."

Behind the CPU module in this figure are some special-purpose input-output connectors that are stacked up along the rear edge of the motherboard. I will describe them in more detail in a moment, in connection with Figure 4.5, which shows this motherboard from the other side.

Just in front of the CPU module are three memory modules plugged into special *DIMM* (dual in-line memory module) sockets. And in front of them on the left are the connectors you saw earlier in Figure 4.2 for the EIDE cables that connect to hard drives, CD-ROMs, DVD drives, and the like. To the right of those connectors are two white connectors for power cables and at the very front of the motherboard are two more black connectors. The smallest one is for a cable that goes to the front panel indicator lights and the switches for power and reset. The other connector is for the cable to the built-in floppy diskette drive. Finally, in the lower-left corner of the motherboard, is a round battery and the jumper you saw close up in Figure 4.3. This area contains the circuits that must run even when the PC is disconnected from the power supply. That includes the CMOS memory chip that holds configuration information about this PC, as well as the clock circuit that keeps track of the date and time of day.

This motherboard is a bit unusual in that it doesn't have a whole lot of jumpers on it. Many motherboards have lots of them so the person setting up the PC can make it work correctly with any of a variety of CPU modules and memory modules. This motherboard was built by Intel just for use with its CPU modules, and only for a particular few of them.

Still, this motherboard is like most in that it has a lot of setup options you can choose to alter. They simply are accessed through the BIOS configuration setup program instead of by moving jumpers around.

Warning: The BIOS setup program typically has several screens of settings. The basic screen contains very simple information. Some of the others get pretty arcane. If you are going to experiment with any of these settings, please record what they are before you begin so you can easily restore them if you find that what you have done doesn't work as you expected.

If your motherboard has a lot of jumpers, please don't move them at random. The only way to be sure which jumpers or switch positions do what is to check the manual that came with your motherboard or system unit.

Figure 4.5 shows this motherboard from the rear. Now you can see the front face of the CPU module as well as the details of the rear-mounted special-purpose input-output connectors.

FIGURE 4.5

The motherboard from our example desktop PC, here seen from above the rear edge of the board, with several key features marked.

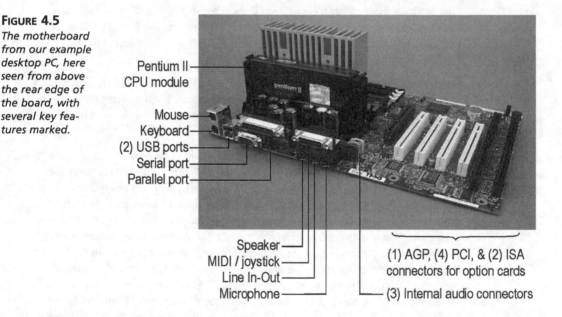

Pentium II CPU module

Mouse
Keyboard
(2) USB ports
Serial port
Parallel port

Speaker
MIDI / joystick
Line In-Out
Microphone

(1) AGP, (4) PCI, & (2) ISA connectors for option cards

(3) Internal audio connectors

I've labeled each of the individual, special-purpose input-output connectors in this figure. The three internal audio connectors serve the same purposes as the external ones (line, microphone, and speakers), but they are used with cables from internal devices that generate or use audio, most commonly a DVD or CD drive or a television tuner option card. From the number of these connectors you can see that this motherboard incorporates within its own circuitry most of what used to be supplied only on plug-in option cards. That is a trend we can expect to see continue, with one exception: Intel is supporting an initiative that would move all the audio functionality, plus modem functionality, to a specialized *Audio Modem Riser* (AMR) card that would plug into its own, specialized connector. That design will appear first in the WTX systems, and it may also be incorporated into other arrangements.

The Pentium II's SECC is held in place by a couple of different mechanisms. If you want to remove the CPU module from your motherboard (and that's an okay thing to do, provided you're careful to follow all the precautions I gave you earlier), you need to know how to disengage them. And before that, you need to know not to attempt this unless your PC has been turned off for a good while, to let the CPU module and its heat sink cool down. These CPUs get hot enough to burn you quite badly!

Figure 4.6 shows a close-up view of the Pentium II and its attached heat sink. Also shown are two views of one of the retaining locks located at each end of the top of this device. Notice how when these locks are in their locked position a small wedge-shaped piece sticks out of the side. That locks the module in a retaining channel that sticks up from the motherboard on either side of the Slot 1 connector.

FIGURE 4.6

The Pentium II comes in a Single Edge Contact Cartridge. There are locking devices on both sides that must be released before you can remove this module from its socket, and there may be a retaining device for the heat sink as well.

There may also be a retaining device of some sort at the top of the heat sink (that is, the side away from the CPU), down near the motherboard. If there is, be sure to remove it before you try to lift out the CPU. And when you do remove it, lift the CPU module straight up. Don't rock it back and forth or side to side. If it doesn't come out quite easily, don't simply tug harder. Look very carefully at the module and its connector and see where you are encountering resistance. Follow those tips and you are unlikely to cause any damage to either the motherboard or the CPU.

By the way, these tips also apply when you are removing an AGP video card or, to a lesser extent, any option card. You can damage them if you rock them side to side, laterally. They do often require a strong push or pull to get them into or out of their slot connector. This can be facilitated by pushing in one end at a time. However, you *must* be certain to push the card in (or pull it out) perfectly vertically. Lateral rocking or bending can easily damage the card and your motherboard. The risk is higher for AGP cards and SECC devices because they have much smaller contacts.

Looking at the bottom of the SECC package, you can just barely see the edge of the circuit board it contains and the CPU chip on that board (plus some of the other components located there). It isn't easy to see the dual-level edge contacts, because the circuit board doesn't stick out beyond the edge of the SECC module housing. Figure 4.7 shows a very similar set of edge contacts (from an AGP video card), plus the view of the SECC module from below and a view looking down into a Slot 1 (SC-242) CPU slot connector. Also visible in the bottom portion of this figure is the Heat Sink Retaining Bracket that secures the heat sink to the motherboard independently, and the end rails that help keep the SECC module from wobbling in its socket.

You Must Feed Your PC: The Power Supply

In some ways, the most fundamental piece attached to the motherboard is the power supply. After all, without electricity, the computer can do nothing. The power supply has two jobs:

1. Convert wall outlet AC electrical power into suitable DC voltages.
2. Remove the heat that results from the consumption of that electrical power.

This is easy enough to say, but for you to understand what these things mean, I must tell you a bit more.

From AC to DC, and Holding Some Energy in Reserve

The power supply's first job is to accept energy from the electric utility company via the power cord. It converts this AC power to direct current (DC) at several different voltages, and it stores some of that energy so it can bridge over small intervals in which the electric power input stops.

Figure 4.8 shows the power supply for our example desktop PC. Notice that it has a lot of wires coming out and ending in a number of power output connectors. The largest two go to a pair of connectors on the motherboard that you can see in Figure 4.4.

The rest of the connectors are for powering drives of various sorts and, in some PCs, additional fans. (In the sample PC, the supplemental fans are powered from connectors on the motherboard.)

FIGURE 4.7

The special, dual-level edge contacts used for the Pentium II in an SECC module; a bottom view of the module, and a top view of the SC-242 (Slot 1) connector into which it plugs.

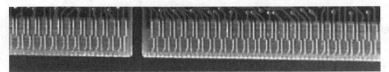

Close-up view of dual-level edge connector
(Shown here is an AGP card, but its edge
connector is the same as that on a Pentium II.)

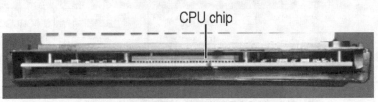

Bottom view of Pentium II SECC showing
the circuit board, CPU, and some other parts

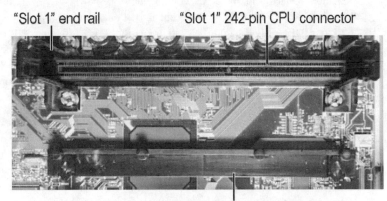

Heat Sink Retaining Bracket

The disk drive cables carry two voltages (+12 volts, +5 volts,) plug ground (two wires for ground, typically). The cables to the motherboard carry both of those and −5 volts, and −12 volts (with more than one wire for each voltage that is used a lot). In addition, they may carry some lower voltages (3.3 and 2.8 volts the most common) to power the CPU and other extra-fast chips on the motherboard that require those lower voltages to operate properly without cooking themselves as they work.

FIGURE 4.8
*The power supply
for our example
desktop PC.*

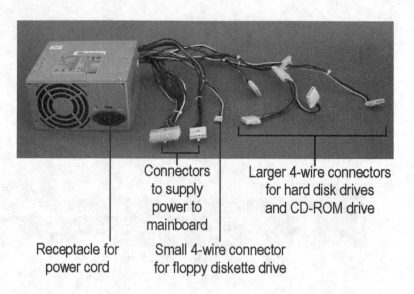

Connectors
to supply
power to
mainboard

Larger 4-wire connectors
for hard disk drives
and CD-ROM drive

Receptacle for
power cord

Small 4-wire connector
for floppy diskette drive

The other connectors on the cables coming out of the power supply are used to power
disk drives. Most modern PCs can accept at least one or two floppy diskette drives and
up to four IDE or EIDE hard disks, and/or CD-ROM, LS-120, tape, ZIP, or other kinds
of drive. Each of these devices needs electrical power to do its job, and none gets that
power from the motherboard. Instead, they use power connectors that hook directly to the
power supply. (The drives also connect to the motherboard through one or more cables
that carry data to and from the drives.)

Notice that the drive power connectors are of two kinds, large and small. Most 3-1/2"
drives require the smaller connectors. In this PC, only the floppy diskette drive uses that
size. All other PC drives use the larger connectors. This power supply didn't have quite
enough of those connectors, so I had to add a Y-adapter to give me one more usable connection. If you do this in your PC, be careful that you don't overload the power supply,
or it might not function correctly, and then your whole PC becomes useless until you
replace that power supply with a more capable one.

The electrical power coming from the wall socket is alternating current (AC). This means
that the voltage across the wires in the power cord varies smoothly from zero, up to some
maximum positive value, down to zero, further down to about the same maximum
negative value, and then back up to zero. And it continues this pattern, in the United
States repeating 60 times per second. Some other countries use AC with a different frequency; 50 cycles per second is another common value. Because the voltage is repeatedly going to zero, for times that are short in human terms but which are nearly eternal for
the very rapid circuits in a PC, the power supply must store up enough energy to at least
bridge the gaps that come 120 times each second.

A typical PC power supply can keep the PC going for considerably longer than that, though often not for as much as one second. You can buy special power supplies that incorporate a battery and battery charger, and these uninterruptible power supplies (UPS) can keep the PC working much longer during a power outage—sometimes for more than an hour. You can find out more about UPSs in Chapter 25, "PCs That Think They're Mainframes: Multiprocessor PCs and Other Servers" in the section "Steady Electrical Power Prevents Many Problems."

Monitoring the PC's Power and Rebooting

Part of the first job of the PC's power supply is to monitor the quality of the DC voltages it's supplying to the other parts of the PC. Whenever any of these voltages deviates from its nominal value by more than a preset amount (typically 5 percent), the power supply will indicate this to the motherboard.

The power supply tells the motherboard that its output voltages are within range by raising a voltage on one of the wires going into the motherboard power supply connector. This wire is called the *power-good line*. When you first turn on your PC, the power supply starts to work. When it has all its output DC voltages stabilized at their nominal values and after some short time delay, it raises the power-good line's voltage. That signals the CPU to start computing.

Whenever the power supply sees that line's voltage fall below some critical value, it lowers the voltage on the power-good line. In response to that, the computer simply resets itself, and when that line's voltage returns to the high state, the CPU again starts computing as if the PC had just been turned on. This action is called *rebooting*.

> **Tip:** If your PC reboots itself from time to time for no obvious reason, one possible cause is an inadequate power supply. You might have installed more power-hungry components than your PC's power supply was meant to support, or you might have a particularly poor supply of AC electricity to the PC from the wall socket. Or, of course, your PC's power supply could be dying.

One way to implement a reset button on a PC is simply to hook up a momentary contact switch so that when you press it, it shorts the power-good line to ground. That simulates the power supply saying that the DC voltages are not right and reboots the PC.

> **Tip:** One way discount PC vendors sometimes shave their costs is by including very low-wattage power supplies. When you are comparison shopping, be sure to ask about the number of watts supported by the power supply in each PC you are considering buying. Most power supplies today support 200–400 watts, which is adequate for most users.

Getting the Heat Out

Finally, the PC's power supply has one or more fans in it to remove waste heat from the PC. Not only must it remove the heat it generates in converting the AC input power to DC, it usually must remove almost all the energy used by all the other parts of the PC. Except for a tiny amount of electric energy that makes its way outside the PC through the attached cables to the monitor, keyboard, printer, and other peripheral devices, all the electric energy that the power supply dumps into the motherboard and the disk drives is used by those parts, which, in using it, convert that energy ultimately to heat.

The power supply makers ideally incorporate a fan they think is large enough to remove all the waste heat that will result from the power supply being run at its maximal output, in terms of watts. However, often that fan isn't really enough to ensure the optimum health of your PC. This is especially true if you have a PC loaded with many plug-in cards, any plug-in cards that have a lot of power-hungry components on them, or a CPU that runs at a high clock frequency.

If your CPU becomes too hot, it might self-destruct. Fortunately, most modern CPUs are built to protect themselves. If they are overheated, they turn down the internal clock speed to a very low frequency and make the PC crawl through its tasks—or else they actually shut down altogether and refuse to do anything until they cool off. This last behavior is what you'll get with the latest CPU chips from Intel.

If the CPU chip, or any other electronic component, becomes almost hot enough to die or stop working, it will have a much shorter life before it ultimately dies. Although this is true of all electronic components, the CPU chip is the one chip that dissipates the most power in most PCs, and thus is the one that will get the hottest unless it's kept cool by a heat sink with or without a fan.

A good heat sink may be able to keep the CPU chip quite cool. Instead of nearly burning yourself—as you would if you were to touch any PC CPU that had been running for awhile without a heat sink—if you touch a CPU with a good heat sink after it has been on for awhile, you might barely be able to detect any warmth from it at all. On the other hand, the latest, fastest CPUs give off so much heat that they are routinely expected to run hot—even with the best heat sinks system manufacturers can install.

A heat sink with an attached fan might do an even better job of cooling the CPU, although sometimes the amount of heat sink metal that is removed to make room for the fan makes the combination less effective than the heat sink would have been by itself.

This problem, combined with the greater capability of a really large, properly oriented heat sink to do as much cooling by itself as a smaller fan-cooled one, has led some manufacturers to avoid installing CPU fans in their machines. In this way, not only do they get adequate cooling, but by avoiding fan failures they increase the mean time between overall system failures (MTBF) for their PCs.

After you have made sure your CPU chip won't overheat, you also might want to look into adding one or more fans to keep the rest of the parts of your PC cool. This isn't really necessary for a run-of-the-mill PC without much in the way of special, power-hungry goodies inside it. It is a very good idea if you have a top-of-the-line screamer of a PC with all the bells and whistles you could stuff into it. Our sample desktop PC has an extra fan besides the one in the power supply, just to be sure it keeps cool enough inside.

One other issue concerning PC fans is noise—most of them put out more than you want them to. It's possible to buy special power supplies with extra-large and super-quiet fans. And you can, if you look around enough, find similar quiet and very capable fans to install in your PC where they will cool the plug-in cards. The only fan that usually makes too little noise to hear is the one on your CPU chip. (That is a pity, because it's the fan that's most likely to fail.)

> **Tip:** This raises a meaningful issue. It's a good idea to periodically—twice a year, perhaps—check and verify that all fans installed in your PC are functioning properly. Even if you have to replace an entire power supply because of a broken fan, it will cost you *much* less than replacing the whole computer because you've allowed your PC to fry. This is one—the only one—exception to the rule about making sure your PC is completely off before you open the case. You will be able to see the power-supply fans from outside, but you will need to open the case and turn the power on in order to check a CPU fan's operation. *Do Not* reach inside the case while the power is on. Just look to see that the fan works, and turn the PC back off.

Finally, I want to comment on the question of whether taking off the cover (or in the case of a PC like our example system, removing the side panel) helps your PC keep cool. You may think it obvious that removing the side or top panel from a PC would let it have more and better air flow and thus keep its internal parts cooler than being shut up in a nearly closed box. That seems reasonable; too bad it isn't true.

A well-designed fan and ventilation hole pattern in an otherwise closed case can direct more cooling air flow across the critical components than will occur simply by opening the case and allowing the heat to rise at its own pace. Indeed, many of today's high-end systems use a ventilation plan which is almost a forced-air cooling, in which very large quantities of cool air are brought into the PC. But this works only in a properly closed, sealed case.

This is not to say that your PC will necessarily overheat if the case is open while it's running. Goodness knows, I would have destroyed a lot of PCs by now if that were true. But it does mean that if your PC was well designed, it's likely to keep its internal parts coolest if you leave it closed up. And unless you are constantly adding or removing parts, or otherwise need frequent access to the interior, why not keep the cover on? In addition to the probable enhanced cooling of critical parts inside the PC, that will certainly reduce the amount of radio frequency energy—and audible noise—that will escape to pollute your environment, an effect which is certainly desirable.

Room to Grow: Slots and Bays

Any functional part of your PC that lives inside the PC system unit and that isn't on the motherboard must be attached to the motherboard to let information flow between those pieces and the circuits on the motherboard. Normally, that means the parts in question will either be mounted in a drive bay and connected to the motherboard or an adapter via ribbon cables, or be mounted on printed circuit cards that are plugged into one of the motherboard's I/O slot connectors.

The pieces of the PC that go outside the box also must connect to the motherboard. They do so either via some ports on the motherboard that stick through the back panel or else by plugging into connectors on the backs of printed circuit cards that are themselves plugged into one of the motherboard I/O slot connectors.

I have already shown you a fairly comprehensive collection of special-purpose input-output connectors on the back of our sample desktop PC. The only ones that aren't there and that you are likely to find on other PCs are an *IrDA* (infrared data communications) port and a FireWire (IEEE 1394) connector.

It wouldn't be possible to include here a comprehensive list of all the types of plug-in cards that you can add to a PC. Suffice it to say that if you can imagine something a PC might do, somebody has probably made a plug-in card to facilitate that function.

A few of the more common plug-in cards include a video display adapter, a network interface card, an SCSI adapter, process control cards for chemical engineers… and the list goes on and on. (Sometimes, you can get more than one kind of functionality on a single plug-in card. Those are, naturally, referred to as "multifunction" I/O cards.) You will learn about many of these cards in later chapters in this book, and the rest you will be able to understand from their manufacturer's literature after you have learned about the ones I describe.

Many people are concerned about whether or not they can upgrade their PCs at a later time. As I suggested in Chapter 1, "The View from Afar," this is not always an economically wise thing to do, but it does sometimes make sense. The ultimate limit on what upgrading you can do in a given PC system unit and with a given motherboard is set by three things:

- The power supply wattage
- The number and type of I/O slot connectors on the motherboard
- The number and size of the drive bays (and which of them are accessible from the front panel)

A few years ago, one PC manufacturer captured this concern by saying, "All my customers seem to care about is the number of watts, slots, and bays we give them."

If your present case, power supply, and motherboard are not ones that will gracefully accept the upgrades you want, you might be able to change one, two, or all three of these things. Mostly standard AT style replacement PC cases (and that includes the ATX and micro-ATX designs) come with a power supply that's sufficient for almost anything you'd care to put into them. Extra high power (or extra low-noise, or extra efficient) power supplies are also available. And if you need more slots, you might want to upgrade your motherboard and probably get a better CPU and many other important improvements at the same time.

What Goes Outside the Box

Not every part of a PC can go inside the system unit, nor would you necessarily want all of those parts to be integrated. The keyboard, monitor, and printer of most PCs are located outside the system. And some people connect an external modem, a scanner, external disk drives, and many other types of peripheral devices outside the system unit.

If the projected "closed box" design for PCs reaches the marketplace, you can expect to see many more peripheral devices outside the box (including hard drives, removable magnetic media disk drives, and optical disk drives). This will likely happen, and it will be acceptable, because these PCs will sport USB and FireWire (IEEE 1394) ports that will make hooking up those external devices easy and reliable. And sealing the box may make them more reliable as well—mainly because they will contain only what the manufacturer put into them initially, and those innards won't have been messed with by any end user.

One very good reason why many people prefer not having everything integrated into the system unit is that they like having a choice about each of those extra parts. Today's direct-order PC vendors (who essentially build each computer to a customer's specific order) allow a customer quite a range of choice in terms of what features are included inside the system unit, but they offer even more choice when it comes to the pieces that go outside.

Figure 4.1, for example, shows a standard system unit (with some added RAM and hard drives in it), but it also shows two larger-than-standard monitors. I also chose a different keyboard and mouse than were standard for this system at the time I put this together (and, as I'll describe more fully in Chapter 12, "Getting Your PC's Attention: Input Devices," you, too, may wish to change your pointing device, especially, but also your keyboard from time to time simply to help avoid suffering from what some people call a repetitive stress injury, or *RSI*). I'll describe a number of alternatives for external input and output devices in Chapters 12–14, "Getting Your PC's Attention: Input Devices," "Seeing the Results: PC Displays," and "Getting It All Down on Paper: Printers."

Information Rides the Bus

At the beginning of this chapter, I told you in part why it's important you realize a PC is composed of many quasi-independent subpieces. Now I'm going to discuss another reason.

The many pieces that make up your PC often come from many different manufacturers. This is true even when you buy the PC completely assembled from a vendor that ships all the pieces of your PC system in a single box. They might have made some of the parts, but they also might simply have assembled that PC out of the separate parts for you.

You could buy separate parts and assemble your own PC. You would sacrifice the convenience of having a ready-to-run PC immediately, and more importantly, you would lose the substantial benefits of getting a pre-tested system and of having a warranty on the operation of that system by the company that sold it to you. If you become your own system designer, then you are the responsible party when the pieces don't work together properly. Building your own PC can be an amazing education. In fact, it's probably the single-best way to really understand how everything works together inside the system unit. However, it can be as frustrating as any other complex educational experience— indeed, probably more so, because you'll also be waiting to be able to *use* your new system until its assembly is complete.

However, although I don't necessarily recommend that you build your own PC, understand that it certainly is possible. And what makes it possible is the notion of having standard interfaces between the various parts. That is what it takes to let pieces made, at least potentially, by many different manufacturers interconnect and work. The common name for any such standard information transfer interface is a *bus*.

A Bus Implies a Standard

Any time you connect one piece of computer hardware to another, if you expect them to work together, the interface between the two (where they plug together—which is the essence of an information bus) must meet four conditions: The two halves of the interface must be physically, logically, and electrically compatible, and the signals must be timed suitably.

Let me explain each of these points in turn. The first one is pretty obvious. If you try to push a plug with fifteen pins into a socket with only nine holes, it just won't go. Likewise, two plugs with 15 pins won't connect; one of them must be a 15-hole socket.

The second one is less obvious, until you think about it. Even when the connectors mate properly, there must be agreement between the manufacturers that, for example, data is going to go out of device A on pin number three and come into device B on socket hole number three.

The third condition is yet more subtle. If I intend to send data from device A to device B, the makers of both must agree on what levels of voltage and current will be available on each power-supplying pin (and, of course, on which side is supplying power and which is using it). Furthermore, with respect to all the pins that carry data, the manufacturers must agree on the voltage levels that mean a zero bit or a one bit.

The final condition is merely a refinement of the third one. It says that the two device makers also must agree that when they put a signal on any of the pins it will stay there for some prescribed amount of time, and perhaps that it will not rise or fall in voltage either faster or slower than some prescribed speeds.

Any time we have such an agreement among computer hardware makers we call it a *bus definition*. This applies especially if the agreement is not just between a few companies but is shared by the entire industry.

Historical Aside

Some bus standards are created after a lengthy negotiation between companies, possibly under the aegis of some national or international standards organization. Others just happen when one company makes a lot of one kind of device, call it A, (and, at first, all the other devices [B] that can connect to it) and then many other companies jump into the marketplace, offering their alternative devices to connect to the first maker's device A.

The first way, via a standards committee, is necessary when many companies want to enter a new marketplace more or less at once. This is how the VESA I/O bus and the SCSI interface were defined and refined through several versions (see Chapter 16 for more details).

The second way standards arise, by a *de facto* standard-creating process, is exemplified by how IBM came to define most aspects of what we today call a PC. IBM published its design for the original PC in 1981 (and again in 1983 for the PC/XT, and in 1985 for the PC/AT) with the hope of inducing others to make plug-in cards that would work in a PC. Not only did that happen, but the PC clone makers also used that information to help them make products that would directly compete with IBM's PCs. And thus was born what we now call the *industry standard architecture* (ISA) I/O slot definition, and more generally, the standard notion of what constitutes a PC.

Recently, a third way to create a standard—a full-system standard, however, not merely a bus standard—has emerged as the most common method. In this variation, one company solicits input from several or many other companies. Then the first company publishes its notion of a new standard. If the company doing

continues

continued

so is very prominent (for example, Microsoft or Intel), then very likely this new standard will be adopted by a lot of companies (including at least those who were consulted during its creation) and a new industry standard will have been born. The PC98 and PC99 sponsored and promoted jointly by Intel and Microsoft are very good examples of this last form of the standards-creation process.

I am using the term bus standard a bit more broadly than some authors have. I include any standardized interface between two kinds of PC hardware that must be able to connect and work together. Other authors have limited the term to only a few of the more famous buses, such as the I/O bus, which in its several forms is called by the jargon acronyms ISA, EISA, VESA, MCA, AGP, and PCI.

Given my broader usage, there are a lot of buses in your PC. Although some of them have received a lot of attention, and their names are, if not household words, at least relatively familiar jargon, others you might never have heard of before. The ISA bus and PCI bus variant forms of the I/O slot connector are two examples of famous PC buses. The IDE interface standard (and its descendent, the EIDE interface) for connecting a PC's motherboard to disk drives is another. Likewise, you probably have heard of the standards called the serial and parallel ports. Other, less familiar PC buses include the video interface (between the monitor and the display adapter or, more accurately, between each of them and the intervening cable), the SCSI device interface (between host adapter and cable and from cable to SCSI slave device), the IrDA infrared device standard, and so on. (That last one is interestingly different in that its physical definition relates to how two devices "attach" via light waves instead of by direct contact.) The newest of the important buses to join this list are the Universal Serial Bus (USB) and the FireWire (IEEE 1394) bus. In time, they may be the only widely used bus connections from a PC to the outside world, and thus may become the only ones most people will care about.

You will learn a lot more about these and many other PC buses in the chapters to come. In particular, you will find this topic treated in Chapters 15, "Understanding Standard PC Input and Output," and 16, "Faster Ways to Get Information Into and Out of Your PC."

Controlling Chaos by Leaving the Legacy Behind

The most wonderful fact about PCs is that their open design has led to a truly vast marketplace where a huge number of vendors have made a rapidly expanding variety of both hardware and software. The resulting mix-and-match environment has given PCs enormous flexibility and power. But it also has, inevitably, edged us close to chaos. This chaos must be managed or PCs will be so complex and difficult to set up and keep running that only a tiny fraction of the potential users will be willing to endure the needed effort.

To prevent this near chaos from curtailing a booming market, industry leaders have tried several things. Some of those companies proposed new standards for how a PC should be built. Other times, these companies—normally fierce competitors—have cooperated in the development of new industry standards for PC design (in other words, the PC99 standard I mentioned previously).

The Critical, Limited Resources in a PC

In Chapter 8, "How Your PC 'Thinks,'" you will learn about the details of the PC's design. You will learn about the several kinds of resources that a PC offers its constituent parts and the programs that run within it. (I'll explain just what a *resource* means in this context in just a moment.) Each piece of hardware and software must use some of one or more of these resources. Managing their demands and resolving conflicting requests for resources are major tasks in today's PCs.

With some exceptions, only one bit of hardware can use any given resource at a time. When that resource is allocated to that device, only that device can use it until its allocation is canceled. And often those allocations can't be canceled until the next time you reboot your PC. The exceptions include the possibility that some devices that normally would use an IRQ line, for example, can be operated in a polling manner, so as to free up that IRQ for some other device to use. This strategy, which is often used for printers to free up an otherwise occupied IRQ, is explained fully in Chapter 8. Another exception is that in systems with an advanced bus, such as PCI, it is possible for the system to see which cards are in which slots, and as a consequence for cards plugged into different slots on that bus to use the same interrupts.

Indeed, the fact that the ISA bus cannot share interrupts is one of the most powerful reasons cited for the fact that the PC99 standard has virtually eliminated the inclusion of any ISA bus slots, and certainly of all ISA-bus-using factory-installed components. By the end of 1999, all PCs being sold for general use will, therefore, have no ISA devices and, in almost all cases, no place to plug one in. Or at least, that's what some of the major players in the industry have agreed to do. Whether it actually happens is yet to be seen.

The following are the PC's critical, and limited, resources:

- The memory addresses that the CPU can see
- The input-output (I/O) port addresses it can use
- The interrupt request lines (IRQs) through which external hardware can get the CPU's attention
- The direct memory access (DMA) channels by which data can flow without the CPU's direct intervention

PC disk drives are divided further into logical drives, each of which gets its own letter designation. That lettering constitutes another critical and potentially limiting PC resource.

When only technical types used PCs, manufacturers could get away with requiring every user to understand all this, and those companies could reasonably expect the PC users to open the box and move jumpers or flip switches to set up the motherboard and each option card so they wouldn't conflict with one another. Now that PCs are mass-market items, that just won't do.

The industry's response has been to develop several *Plug and Play* (PnP) standards. These form a framework for making PCs more or less auto-configuring. This attempt has been only partially successful, mainly because of the need to keep including older hardware and software that was designed before there were any PnP standards.

I'll describe how Plug and Play systems work later in this chapter. For now, I want to cover how well it is working in commercially available operating system software and available PCs.

The first fully PnP-compatible operating system for the PC, Windows 95, does a reasonable job of recognizing the hardware you put in your PC, supplying the resources required for each piece, and resolving conflicting resource requests. But it is far from perfect. When it works, it's wonderful. When it doesn't, the user must get involved in solving the resulting problems, and often Windows 95 makes that process less easy than otherwise might be the case. (You may have heard the following variation on Plug and Play: "plug and pray.")

Windows 98 improved greatly on Windows 95 in this respect. Things are still far from perfect, but having to manipulate resources manually is much less common. Windows NT (versions 3.x and 4) minimally supports Plug and Play, but not by default. All in all, the Plug and Play support in NT leaves much to be desired. The forthcoming version, currently called Windows 2000, was supposed to support Plug and Play at least as well as Windows 98, but it now appears that this plan has been scaled back until the release that will follow Windows 2000.

All of the alternative PC operating systems, including OS/2, UNIX, Linux, and BeOS, offer some attempt at automatic configuration of whatever hardware they find in the PC when they are installed. They vary widely in how well they accomplish this intention, and in how well they are able to sense and support newly added hardware.

The trend toward removing ISA devices is going to make the job of doing Plug and Play much easier. When almost all peripherals are attached via the PCI bus, SCSI bus, USB, and FireWire, I expect to see nearly perfect Plug and Play implementations of most of these operating systems.

> **Peter's Principle:** A Snaphot of Your Resources
>
> From the Windows 95 or 98 *Start* button on the taskbar, select Settings, Control Panel, System. The System Properties dialog box will appear. Select the Device Manager tab, and click the Print button. Select All Devices and System Summary, and click OK. This lets you print out a listing of pretty much all that Windows knows about the resource usage in your machine.
>
> To keep this information in electronic form for ready comparison with other snapshots, print it to a file. If you haven't already done so, set up a printer definition for the purpose.
>
> To do that, from the Start button select Settings, Printers. In the resulting Explorer frame you will see Add Printer; select it. The wizard that pops up will walk you through the necessary steps. Choose Local Printer of type Generic/Text Only. Choose to Keep Existing Driver and for the printer's connection choose FILE: (which means print to a file).
>
> Now return to the Device Manager, and this time, before you print the summary, use the Print Setup button to select your Generic/Text Only printer. You will be prompted for a filename and location. Choose some folder that you reserve for configuration information and a file name that shows you on what date you took this snapshot of your PC. Finally, copy this file to a diskette to provide you with extra protection against catastrophic troubles.
>
> If you do this each time before and after you install new hardware, you can see from a file comparison of these snapshots just what Windows changed to accommodate the new hardware. If it isn't what you think should have changed, this will probably give you the information you'll need to help resolve any problems that might have resulted from installing the new hardware.

Why ISA Means Chaos

The biggest headache for the designer of any new PC is the success of all the earlier designs. That success means that many millions of prospective customers for the new PC design will already have a PC and that most of those PC owners will want to move some or all of the peripheral devices and plug-in cards from their older machine to the newer one. The headaches come from trying to make the new design accommodate those older parts.

This is a particular problem for plug-in cards designed for the original ISA bus. That bus design, unlike many newer I/O bus standards, didn't allow for the sharing of IRQ lines or DMA channels. And the cards designed for the ISA bus in the past typically didn't have any provision built in to let the motherboard turn them off or reassign their resource usage if that usage conflicted with another card in the system. A recent trend, even with so-called legacy ISA cards, is for them to include some Plug and Play controllability.

The ISA bus design didn't anticipate having the system configure the cards, nor having it disable them. But if the cards themselves include the proper provisions, a more modern

PC can use those cards as compatible Plug and Play cards, even when they're plugged into an ISA slot.

Modern PCs are expected to spot any new hardware and adapt themselves to it, and sometimes they can. But ISA cards, in particular the older, non-PnP compatible ones, are resource consumers that the newer PCs can't control. Even worse, the PC motherboard can't know, without some help, what resources this type of card is using. That means the use of these cards can totally defeat the automatically self-configuring PC.

The Limitations Imposed By the ISA Bus Standard

The continuing use of the ISA bus in modern PCs presents several difficulties. The lack of Plug and Play support is only one. A plug-in option card designed merely to the original ISA specification will have these, unnecessarily limiting, features:

- Only 16 data lines, thus limiting data transfers to two bytes at a time
- 8.33MHz maximum clock speed
- No sharing of interrupts or DMA channels between cards in different slots
- No provision for configuring the card's use of regions of main memory, I/O port addresses, IRQ lines, or DMA channels by the system
- No provision for being disabled by the system in case of resource conflicts

This specification needed to be improved before a truly modern PC could emerge. These improvements have evolved through several intermediate standards (with variable market success) before reaching their present state. And, of course, even that is just a way station on the way to some future, even-better PC design, with the next step being the total elimination of ISA-bus connected devices (as is required by the PC99 standard).

PC Cards (PCMCIA) and CardBus

Another development that later converged with the modern Plug and Play PC is a technology that started out as a means for adding functionality to microprocessor-based game machines. Only later did it become one of the popular features on a portable PC, and it is just now becoming an option that's available for a significant number of desktop PCs.

You probably know these devices by the name *PC Card*. Originally, they had the cumbersome name *PCMCIA cards*. The PC Memory Card International Association began as a trade association of several manufacturers of RAM and ROM chips. They designed a credit-card size carrier for memory chips with a connector on one end, and they published a specification for these cards, as well as the slot into which they would fit. When it became clear that this was a convenient form factor for adding something to a portable PC, other manufacturers joined the PCMCIA, and they began the push to broaden the applicability of this standard.

For example, Hewlett-Packard and Western Digital, among others, produced miniaturized hard disks that fit on these cards and figured out how to support them through appropriate device driver software. Manufacturers of other PC peripherals, including modems and network interface cards, also saw an opportunity here.

The PC Card design has undergone many developments, leading to two fully standardized and one proprietary form factor, called Type I, Type II, and Type III cards. They are all the same size, but differ in thickness. (That is, in three-dimensional space, all of these cards are the same size on the x- and y-axes, but differ in their size on the z-axis.) A PC Card slot can be made to accept a single Type I card, a single Type II card, or a pair of Type I or Type II cards. Many PC makers, especially those making mobile PCs, have also built oversize slots that can accept a Type III card.

Any PC Card slot must support the original 16-bit bus (based on the ISA bus). Newer ones usually support what is termed *CardBus*, which is simply a 32-bit version of that interface, derived from the PCI bus standard. The 32-bit CardBus standard was developed to facilitate the implementation of high-speed functionality in the small PC Card form factor. I will explain all these concepts in Chapter 16. I'll tell you more about PC Cards themselves in Chapter 22, "Why Mobile PCs Must Be Different," because so far they are far more common in this context than in desktop, workstation, or server PCs.

Plug and Play

There is a constant theme to all of these enhancements to the original PC architecture. It is to make the machine do more of what it is good at (detail work) and let the human operator concentrate on what humans are good for (seeing the big picture and the general application of the PC to some task humans value).

This means that PCs have become more and more capable of doing just work rather than first requiring extensive configuration tweaking by the user. That makes for a better OBE (Out of Box Experience), and hence for happier purchasers—and it also allows for easier upgrades.

All of these developments have been guided by a vision of a PC that's fully automatic in its configuration. The name given to this vision by the industry is Plug and Play. The difficulty in implementing this vision has been two-fold. One is to incorporate backward compatibility—which means the capability to use older, legacy devices with even the newest PC—and the other is preserving the open marketplace with all its wild and woolly freedom for innovation.

The Essentials of Plug and Play

Plug and Play is first and foremost a philosophy describing how a PC should operate without needing much in the way of user setup effort. More formally described, Plug and Play is a whole series of formal standards describing a number of ways to achieve this goal. And only PCs that conform to these standards are entitled to be described by the trademarked term, Plug and Play. Plug and Play builds upon the pioneering work of mainframe computer designers and of the developers of the various bus standards, and it also goes well beyond all of them.

Essential to this effort is the notion that every part of a PC (whether it's built onto the motherboard or is added to the PC on a plug-in option card or by plugging it into some other connector) shall have a device identifier. This *device ID* implies all the technical details that the PnP-controlling software must know about the device. For some devices, the ID identifies them as being able to be turned on or off and perhaps to have some or all of their resource usage controlled by the PnP management software. For other devices, it indicates that they are old (legacy) ISA cards or are otherwise inherently unable to be disabled or controlled.

The PC must learn about all of the PnP devices it contains. So, one of the jobs that must be done during the bootup process is *enumeration* of all those devices. Responsibility for this task is divided among several different players. The PCI controller chip has this job for devices plugged into PCI slots. Likewise, the EISA bus controller chip will report on EISA cards installed into those slots (if your PC has any of them). And PC Cards identify themselves to the PC Card controlling software as soon as they are plugged in. The PnP BIOS coordinates all this information and adds to it information for devices that are built into the motherboard, attached across the IDE bus plus the keyboard and a few other devices.

If you are running Windows 95 or 98, go into the Control Panel, System dialog box. Click the Device Manager tab, and select the View Devices By Connection radio button. Now click the plus sign in front of Plug and Play BIOS to see all the sources of this information and how the BIOS brings them all together.

After the devices in the system have been enumerated, two more tasks remain. One is to decide which ones get what resources. This is the job of the *arbitrators*. Once again, the overall task has been divided up so those subsystems, such as the PCI or EISA buses or the PC Card bus, can take care of the work for the devices they handle. The system arbitrator will does the rest. Finally, a *configurator* program must go out and set up each configurable PnP device so it uses the resources that have been assigned to it. The configurator also configures the device drivers for any nonconfigurable legacy ISA devices (at least for those for which the necessary information has been supplied) so they will access those devices via the resources they are known to use.

If, when you look at the Device Manager tab in the System Properties dialog box, you see any device listed with an exclamation point in a yellow circle on top of it, that device is in conflict with some other device. (So, you will likely see either none of these symbols or more than one.) That is a sign that you must help the system resolve things because it has tried and failed to do so on its own. Figure 4.9 shows an example of this. Here you see the exclamation point on top of the Logitech Serial Mouse and the Crystal PnP Audio System MPU-401 Compatible device names.

Alternatively, you might see some devices listed with a red X or a black X in a red circle over them. These are disabled devices. If you didn't choose to disable them yourself, then Windows did so to resolve some resource conflict. In Figure 4.9, there is one of these also. The Zoom Video Camera has a red X over it, showing that I have disabled it.

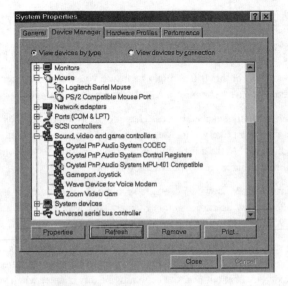

By highlighting one of the devices with the exclamation point or red X over it and then clicking the Properties button, you'll call up a dialog box that might tell you just what the problem is. Go to the Resources tab and see if it lists the conflict.

Sometimes, you will be able to alter the resource usage manually right in that dialog box to remove the conflict. Other times, after you have discovered what the conflict is, a general knowledge of what resources different devices use and of how those uses can be altered (by jumpers, switches, or running some software program) will let you quickly resolve the problem.

The more worrisome cases occur when Windows hasn't even noticed there's a conflict. This can happen when you have legacy devices, if those devices haven't been described properly to Windows. Only by knowing what resources those devices use and then making sure that Windows is reserving the required resources for those devices, can you eliminate that source of problems.

Of course, if you're running the older Windows 3.x and DOS or just DOS as your operating system, instead of Windows 95, then you most likely won't have the advantages of Plug and Play. (A software add-on package for Windows 3.x is available that gives partial Plug and Play capability, but it isn't a standard part of that operating environment.) Without Plug and Play support, you're totally on your own identifying and resolving resource allocation conflicts. And after you do that a few times, you really will appreciate a machine that can do that chore for you, even if it works correctly only most of the time.

What Parts Are Where in *Your* PC;
Some Things to Think About and Try

I've told you about a lot of things that might be inside your PC or attached to it. What pieces do you actually have? The only way to know for sure is to look.

First, look at the externally attached pieces. They are pretty much obvious. You surely have a keyboard and, most likely, a mouse. You might have one or two monitors. Do you have any external drives? Make a list of all of these pieces, and leave room beside each one to record all the resources it must have to do its job.

Now, if you are running Windows 95 or 98, look at the Device Manager listing you printed out if you followed my tip earlier in this chapter. That will show you all the resource allocations that Windows has managed or is otherwise aware of.

Finally, nothing replaces actually opening up the system unit and peering inside. You might have to remove some of the pieces in order to see just what they are. Just be sure you follow the cautions I set out near the beginning of this chapter when you do so.

Making this sort of exploratory trip inside your PC will help you visualize the parts as I describe them in more detail later in this book. If you also list the pieces and their resource uses, you will have taken the first step necessary to troubleshoot any difficulties you might have later when you install new hardware or when some portion of your PC starts misbehaving. And, when you have finished that exploration, you will be ready to learn how PCs and people communicate. In particular, in the next chapter, you will learn how programmers tell PCs what they are to do.

Summary: IBM's Grand
Innovation/IBM's Great Folly

This chapter has pointed out that PCs are collections of parts, each one doing its job independently of the others but all coordinated by the lead player—the CPU. What is both most wonderful and most terrible about PCs is that IBM (in its wisdom or folly) did something totally uncharacteristic when it introduced the PC. Namely, it told the world how it built them, and thus told the world how they could either build parts to work with the PC, or actually clone PCs.

Telling the world how to build parts led to the vast array of optional hardware for PCs, which in turn opened up the market as nothing else could have. This was very good for IBM. But with everyone able to build PCs, IBM not only lost its leadership position as a maker of PCs, it almost left that marketplace altogether. It's still there, but now competing with the many manufacturers of IBM-compatible PCs.

How to Get Your PC to Understand You

You must be able to communicate with your PC. But whenever you try to communicate with any other entity, be it another person or a machine, you must have some language you share with that other entity. It could be your native language, the native language of the other entity, or some common third language. Or, of course, you could employ the services of a translator.

The next question is, What language is your PC's native tongue? (I'll get to the other obvious questions—such as If I don't understand its language, and it doesn't understand mine, what common ground language might we use? and Where do I find a translator?—in Chapter 18, "Understanding How Humans Instruct PCs.")

What Language Does Your PC Understand?

There is only one language your PC can directly utilize: its "machine language," which is just a bunch of numbers. Every PC program is made up of a lot of these numbers. In other words, if you use a diagnostic program to look at a fragment of a program (which is what you might consider "text" in this special language), all you will see, usually, is just a lot of numbers. The PC reads these numbers as binary values, but for human convenience, most programs that display these numbers show them as pairs of hexadecimal symbols, each pair representing the binary value held in a 1-byte location.

You will usually look at such a program fragment either in the PC's main memory or on one of its disk drives. Figure 5.1 shows one such display of a program fragment in its hexadecimal form. This figure was generated by capturing the output from the DOS "external command" DEBUG. This is a program that has been included with every version of DOS, and is also available in Windows 95 and Windows 98. In Chapter 6, "Enhancing Your Understanding by Messing Around," I will show you how to use DEBUG (safely). For now, I want to discuss some of the things it can be made to show you.

The first column, consisting of two groups of four hexadecimal symbols separated by a colon, indicates a particular location in the PC's main memory. The 16 pairs of hexadecimal symbols just to the right of the location numbers are the values at that and the 15 following byte locations. The characters that appear at the right are the ASCII characters corresponding to some of those values (with a period standing in for any ASCII character that isn't a number, a letter, or a common punctuation mark). Sometimes the ASCII translation will help you understand what information is being held at those locations. More often, though, these characters have no real meaning. That is especially true when you're looking at a program such as the one in Figure 5.1.

FIGURE 5.1

DEBUG's display of the contents of some locations in a PC's main memory.

```
>debug
-d 0715:0180
0715:0180  2E FF 2E 18 01 E8 25 00-1E 0E 2E FF 2E 1C 01 E8  ......%.........
0715:0190  1B 00 1E 0E 2E FF 2E 20-01 E8 11 00 1E 0E 2E FF  ....... ........
0715:01A0  2E 24 01 E8 07 00 1E 0E-2E FF 2E 28 01 9C 2E 80  .$.........(....
0715:01B0  3E 34 01 00 74 1A 50 53-B4 07 2E FF 1E 30 01 0B  >4..t.PS.....0..
0715:01C0  C9 75 9B B4 95 2E FF 1E-30 01 0B C0 74 04 5B 58  .u......0...t.[X
0715:01D0  9D C3 EB FE EA 35 01 16-07 50 A0 86 05 0A C0 75  .....5...P.....u
0715:01E0  03 58 F9 C3 E8 A8 00 E8-23 00 26 C6 06 86 05 00  .X......#.&.....
0715:01F0  E8 03 00 58 F8 C3 32 FF-8A 1E 8B 05 B8 03 58 CD  ...X..2.......X.
-q
```

Location   Content in hexadecimal   ASCII translation

DEBUG, like most similar low-level PC diagnostic programs, can also be made to display another version of the meaning of these numbers. In Figure 5.2, you see the contents of the beginning of that same region of this PC's main memory, but this time displayed in a form known as *assembly language*. This is a more-or-less readable language for humans, but one that has been especially designed to be easy to translate into real machine language. This ease of translation grows from the fact that an assembly language provides a mnemonic code for each command in the PC's instruction set. (You'll learn more about assembly languages and other computer languages in Chapter 18.)

Each line in Figure 5.2 represents one machine language instruction. The first column in this figure, as in Figure 5.1, shows a location in memory. The second column shows the actual numbers stored in that location and enough of the subsequent locations to make up one entire instruction and its associated parameter values, if any. (Those numbers are shown here in hexadecimal format). The rest of that line is that instruction as it is written in assembly language. (Because this display takes up more space, one screenful in this format covers fewer memory locations than the display shown in Figure 5.1.)

FIGURE 5.2
A DEBUG's "disassembly" display of the same memory region.

```
>debug
-u 0715:0180
0715:0180  2E          CS:
0715:0181  FF2E1801    JMP       FAR [0118]
0715:0185  E82500      CALL      01AD
0715:0188  1E          PUSH      DS
0715:0189  0E          PUSH      CS
0715:018A  2E          CS:
0715:018B  FF2E1C01    JMP       FAR [011C]
0715:018F  E81B00      CALL      01AD
0715:0192  1E          PUSH      DS
0715:0193  0E          PUSH      CS
0715:0194  2E          CS:
0715:0195  FF2E2001    JMP       FAR [0120]
0715:0199  E81100      CALL      01AD
0715:019C  1E          PUSH      DS
0715:019D  0E          PUSH      CS
0715:019E  2E          CS:
0715:019F  FF2E2401    JMP       FAR [0124]
```

Location   Machine   Assembly language
               code

From the number of hexadecimal symbols in the second column, you can see that the instructions shown here vary in length from 1 byte (2 symbols) up to 4 bytes.

How Big Are the Words in PC Machine Language?

The numbers that represent a computer's machine language come in natural groupings, called instructions. Some are only 1 byte long. Others can stretch for up to about a dozen bytes. The maximum length of an instruction for your PC depends on which kind of central processor chip it has.

When the PC's central processing unit (CPU) reads one of these strings of numbers, it analyzes the first byte to decide how many bytes are in this particular instruction and then reads the rest of those bytes. Next, it looks at a table of super-detailed instructions, called the *microcode*, that is built into the CPU to find out what that particular instruction is asking it to do. Finally, it does that task.

In most modern PC CPUs, many of the more common instructions are "understood" and executed directly by the CPU, without having to look up any microcode. Only the most complex or least frequently used instructions force the CPU to refer to its microcode library. In Chapter 7, "Understanding PC Processors," I will explain more fully the difference between CISC and RISC processors. That discussion will cover the notion of microcode in more detail.

Technical Note: A very important point to realize is that because every instruction is just a group of numbers, you can't tell by looking at them whether they are part of some instructions or merely just data, and—more importantly—neither can your PC's CPU.

This becomes much more than just an interesting bit of trivia when you realize that it means your PC can do computations and logical operations on data that, in another context, can be considered a program. Therefore, your PC can create or modify programs as well as simply execute them. This capability is vital to the process of translating programs from a human-friendly language into real machine language.

What Can Your PC Do, at the Lowest Level?

What can one instruction command a PC to do? Not much. Basically, in a single instruction, all the CPU can do usually is some little bit of arithmetic or some logical operation on at most a few data items. For example, it can add a few numbers. It can move a number, or even move a whole string of bytes, from one place to another. It also can compare two numbers and decide which one is larger. That's just about it.

Well, some of the more recent and powerful CPU chips can do some fairly fancy bits of logic or arithmetic in a single, rather complex instruction, but I hope you are getting the idea that it can't do something really complex, such as check your spelling or compute your tax liability. To do such things requires an entire program with many, many instructions.

Still, even though a CPU can do only a relatively few and fairly simple operations, inherent in them is the power to accomplish all the manifold and wonderful things PCs can be made to accomplish. Provided, of course, that enough of the correct instructions are strung together properly (and presuming that the correct combination of peripheral hardware is in place and working).

A key aspect of this is that the CPU executes these strings of instructions so quickly that this execution speed is commonly measured in Millions of Instructions per Second (MIPS). When you look at the structures at Giza, you see pyramids rather than individual stones. When you execute a program, the great speed at which instructions are executed means that you see program functionality rather than the serial execution of each instruction.

Where Are Instructions and Data Kept?

In order for the CPU to execute instructions, they must be kept somewhere the CPU can get at them—quickly. The CPU is always in a hurry, and if you value your PC's speed, as most folks do, you never want its CPU to have to "twiddle its fingers" waiting for its next instruction to arrive. Likewise, for the CPU to process some data, it must be kept where the CPU can get at it—again, quickly.

In practice, this means that every bit of data and all the instructions that the CPU executes to process the data must be in some part of the machine's RAM (random access memory) or ROM (read-only memory) at the time the processing takes place. RAM and ROM are very fast electronic holding places for numbers, and they are composed of small integrated circuit chips.

Historical Aside

When PCs were first introduced, the RAM chips that were available and (relatively) inexpensive were about as fast as the CPU chips. Over the years since then, the CPU chips have gotten faster much more rapidly than affordable RAM chips. So now it is common to have some small amount of super-fast RAM between the CPU and the main RAM or ROM chips. This small area is called the *cache*, and it helps keep the CPU supplied with data and instructions (and to take from the CPU-processed data) at the full speed of the CPU. I'll explain cache memory in more detail in Chapter 11, "Giving Your PC's CPU Enough Elbow Room—PC Memory."

There are two reasons why you don't want to keep all your data and programs in RAM all the time. The first has to do with the inherent nature of RAM and ROM. The second has to do with their cost.

Programs or data that are kept in ROM cannot be changed. Therefore, ROM is a suitable place to keep only things that don't need to change. This is okay for any program you expect to run often and for data that is fixed (for example, the value of pi, or the conversion factor from centimeters to inches), but not for most of the data with which you work.

One of the most vital programs for a PC is the one that starts as soon as it is turned on. This is the BIOS (basic input/output system), and it was commonly stored in ROM so that it would be essentially indestructible and available as soon as the PC's power supply stabilized. The BIOS is discussed in greater detail later in this chapter. As with most ROM applications, this one has been replaced with newer, semipermanent solid-state storage devices such as the FlashEPROM. This ability to change their contents facilitates upgrades to the programs stored in these new devices.

Programs or data that are kept in RAM can be altered at will. But, unfortunately, they also can be altered in other ways that result in lost or unintentionally modified data. In particular, when you shut off your computer, or even merely reboot it, all the contents of RAM are lost.

For this reason, there are magnetic and optical disk drives, in both fixed and removable cartridge designs, (and tape drives and other media) for the semipermanent storage of both programs and data. These types of media, except for read-only optical discs (standard CD-ROMs or DVDs are examples), enable you to alter their contents. Between such alterations they faithfully hold the contents more or less indefinitely—at least for several years—even when you turn off power to them. There are even recordable (CD-R) and rewritable (CD-RW) versions of the optical media available for mass storage.

The matters of relative cost and relative speed also enter in. When PCs were new, RAM and ROM chips and magnetic disks cost a whole lot more than they do today. In fact, the ratio of cost for the two kinds of information-holding places, per unit of information held, has stayed more or less constant, with magnetic media having an advantage of close to 100:1 over electronic media.

Optical media have, in the past, been more expensive than magnetic media, but they are coming down in cost to where they are competitive with magnetic media today. However, with all the improvements in each of these areas, only the electronic information-holding devices have any hope of keeping up with today's speedy CPU chips.

Today, because RAM costs around a dollar per megabyte (except for special-purpose RAM such as that used in some laptop PCs) and the typical CPU chips cost about a hundred times as much, it is reasonable to have several dozen, or perhaps a hundred megabytes, of RAM. However, for about the same expenditure you can buy several gigabytes (thousands of megabytes) or tens of gigabytes of magnetic or optical disk capacity. Therefore, it has become quite common to have many dozen or hundreds of megabytes of RAM and several tens or more of gigabytes of disk storage space on a good PC.

What Is a BIOS ROM and Why Do I Need One?

Some programs must be kept where the CPU can find them without having to load them off a disk drive (in particular, those programs that are used to start the PC). Until it has gone through quite an extensive Power On Self-Test (POST) process, your PC doesn't know that it has any disk drives to work with at all.

For this reason, that startup (POST) program is kept in a ROM chip called the motherboard BIOS ROM. The contents of this ROM are located in a special region of the CPU's memory address space—one where the CPU automatically goes (it actually jumps to address FFFF0h to start the program) when it first wakes up in order to find out what it is to do.

Tip: After your PC has "booted up" (run the POST program and then started the operating system) successfully a number of times, you can save yourself a little bit of time on subsequent bootings by altering a setting in the motherboard BIOS.

Watch the screen when your PC starts up to learn how to enter the BIOS. The method varies from machine to machine, but most explain how to do it onscreen early in the POST process. (If that doesn't work, try holding down a key until the PC complains that there is a key stuck down. After that message, there is usually a prompt telling you how to enter the BIOS.)

In the BIOS, look for an option you can change to enable "fast boot" or to "skip testing memory on startup." In many cases, you will thereby not only cut out the time normally taken to count all the memory locations (and test them). You also will skip testing some other parts that rarely fail, and so don't really need to be retested every time you restart your PC.

Certain other programs are also kept in the motherboard BIOS ROM. In fact, it gets its name from these other programs. Their job is to activate the standard PC hardware, such as reading keystrokes from keyboard, putting information on the video display, sending information to the printer, and so on. Such programs are called *device drivers*.

As you'll learn in more detail in Chapter 18, computer designers have learned that it makes everyone's task easier if the actual details of operating the hardware are handled by one programmer or one group of programmers, and the details of what you want that hardware to do are handled by a different individual or group. The first programmer writes the device driver. The second writes what is most often called an *application program*.

The device driver programs that actually command the hardware to work are so often called upon by application programs (and by the operating system, which is another kind of program that sits between the other two) that it is more efficient to always keep them in memory than to fetch a copy of them each time you want to operate the hardware. The collection of programs that performs the most basic information input (such as reading keystrokes) and output (such as writing to the screen) is the BIOS, and it is the main resident in the motherboard BIOS ROM.

Some PCs also have their hardware setup programs located in a portion of the motherboard BIOS ROM. They can also have other programs in other ROMs. I'll mention a few of these in the section "Other Tasks, Other BIOSs," later in this chapter, and you'll see several other examples in later chapters.

Technical Note: Occasionally, you might need to change one or more of the programs that are kept in one of these ROMs. But if the motherboard BIOS were really a true read-only memory chip, that just wouldn't be possible. On some older PCs, that is the situation. Therefore, for those machines you would have to replace one such chip with another one that has been manufactured with the updated program in it.

All modern PCs use a variety of NVRAM (non-volatile random access memory) for their motherboard BIOS chips. Yet another term for this kind of memory is Flash ROM (or Flash RAM or Flash EPROM). This term comes from the notion that you can update an entire collection of locations in one fell swoop—an operation that is sometimes called "flashing" the chip. So, to update the motherboard BIOS in any such modern PC, you download a special program, start the PC in what Microsoft has termed MS-DOS mode (the "real mode" of CPU operation is the mode it starts in and remains in until the operating system starts protected-mode operation), and then run that program. (You can learn about the real and protected modes of CPU operation in Chapter 8, "How Your PC 'Thinks.'")

There are two ways to make these changeable, yet semipermanent, memory devices. Most often they are integrated circuit chips that have been specially built to enable them to hold information indefinitely, even if no electrical power is supplied to them. Yet, by special means (involving higher voltages applied briefly to special programming pins), they are able to have that information changed.

Alternatively, this facility may be provided simply as a small amount of normal RAM that has a tiny battery built into the chip package itself in order to enable it to remember its contents even when external power is removed. The choice of which kind of non-volatile memory technology to use is dictated by the relative costs of each kind, as well as the anticipated frequency of updates plus the anticipated time periods during which external power will be unavailable. Each manufacturer must go through a design evaluation to conclude which kind to use in its PCs.

No matter how the long-term information-holding arrangement is constructed, and no matter which programs are kept there, these programs are called *firmware*. This name suggests their basic nature (in that they are a kind of software), yet they are intrinsically linked to some particular piece of hardware as well.

Programs That Get Loaded Off a Disk and Firmware That Can "Disappear"

If you always want your PC to do exactly the same task over and over, then it would be best if you simply put the program needed for that task into firmware. However, most of us use our PCs sometimes to do one task, and other times to do different things. For us, the most sensible course is to store the programs for each of these purposes on a disk drive and load each of them into memory (RAM) only when we need it.

Conversely, sometimes you might want a program that really must be in ROM to be able to disappear. One example is the computer's configuration or BIOS Setup program. If you can call that program up at any time with some hot-key sequence, you could summon it accidentally. If at that moment you were in the middle of some important work and you hadn't saved that work, you could end up losing it all. This is because most setup programs don't let you exit from them without rebooting.

> **Note:** There are two strategies in this regard. As of this writing, Dell's Optiplex computers, for example, save the system state, including even the video display, before entering the Setup program. Then, after you finish making whatever changes you want to make you are permitted to return to exactly the point in your work where you were when you left it to go into the Setup program.
>
> Dell used the other strategy in its Dimension line of computers. This is the more usual (and less expensive) industry practice in which the user is forced to reboot the PC upon each exit from the Setup program. However, in these computers, Dell protects the user from the sort of accidental data loss described earlier by allowing you to enter the Setup program only during the boot process.

Another case in point is when you perform memory management. In Chapter 11, I explain just why this is so and how you can make ROMs, or even just portions of a ROM, disappear from the CPU's view.

Data Available on Demand Versus Data That's Always Available

Just as some programs must be kept in memory all the time, either because the CPU can't access a disk to get them without already having them to use or because the CPU will be using them often, some data values must be kept always at hand. And, just as most programs are kept on disks most of the time, so is most data.

The only data your PC must have instant access to, or access to before it can access the disk drives, are details about how the PC is configured, including the parameters that describe the disk drives attached to it. This type of data typically is stored in the Complementary Metal-Oxide Semiconductor (CMOS), which is a particular kind of integrated-circuit manufacturing technology. Although not exactly correct, common usage now refers to the data stored in this device as the "CMOS data."

You might wonder why this data isn't simply stored in the BIOS ROM along with the POST program that uses it. The reason is simple. The POST program never changes (except if you update it to a new version—something most users never do). This means that the POST program can be (and usually is) stored in an NVRAM or EEPROM chip whose contents are rarely (if ever) changed. The configuration data I'm referring to here is subject to relatively frequent change, so it must be stored in some easily alterable, yet non-volatile memory. And that is exactly what the CMOS is. This chip is also used to store the date and time of day, and that information gets updated every other second all day, whether the PC is turned on or not.

Historical Aside

The key advantage to the CMOS chip-manufacturing technology is the very low power needed to operate chips that are made using it. When PCs were young, this technology was relatively expensive, so it was used only when it really was needed. IBM decided when it introduced its PC/AT to use this technology to provide a small amount of ordinary "static" RAM that was made non-volatile by having a small battery associated with it. This combination of a battery plus a CMOS chip was soon nicknamed "the PC's CMOS." That name has stuck, even though now most of the integrated circuits in every part of your PC are manu-factured by a variation of the same CMOS technology.

All the other data your PC uses is stored on some disk, somewhere. This might be the hard disk inside your PC's system unit or a floppy disk you put into the A: drive, or it might be on a disk on some remote computer you access across the Internet. From the point of view of your CPU, there is no difference. These are all examples of data that can be made available upon demand but that aren't where the CPU can use them instantly.

Other Tasks, Other BIOSs

I have told you how these special hardware device drivers that control the standard PC hardware are normally placed into the BIOS ROM on the PC's motherboard. There are some other tasks that are done by similar device driver programs that can be located in other ROMs or can be programs that are loaded off a disk drive, just like any application program.

One example of a program that lives in a special ROM is the video display adapter's BIOS. The original IBM PC came with device drivers to operate either the original monochrome character display or the earliest color graphics adapter (CGA) as a part of the motherboard BIOS ROM.

Now, though, almost no one uses either of these video display adapters. A few PC manu-facturers have built in better video display circuits to their motherboards, and in those cases they have incorporated alternative device drivers to operate that alternative video circuitry right into the motherboard BIOS ROM.

More commonly, PCs are built with plug-in video display adapters. These option cards almost always carry a video BIOS ROM as well as the video display circuitry. By a special technique that I will explain in Chapter 8, each time you reboot your PC, the POST program looks for these "option ROMs" and, in effect, logically bonds them seamlessly with the programs in the motherboard BIOS ROM.

Still other augmentations to the BIOS programs don't need to be in a ROM. An example of this is the mouse driver. Normally, when your PC boots, it loads from the disk (at some fairly advanced point in the boot process) a small program that knows how to take information from the mouse and convey it to application programs as well as how to put a mouse cursor on the video display. That bit of addition to the BIOS code ends up somewhere in your PC's RAM where it stays until the next time you reboot.

How Mere Humans Can Manage All This

If you are getting the idea that a PC is stunningly complex, you are quite right. Arguably, individual computers (mainframes, minicomputers, and PCs), and even the whole interconnected set of computers that make up the Internet (many of which are PCs), are mankind's most complex creation yet.

And it all has been done by ordinary mortals. Complexity can be understood by nearly everyone who tries, if only he considers it one piece at a time.

In the chapters before this one I gave you an overview of computers, and specifically of the various pieces of hardware that makes up a typical PC. In this chapter, I gave you an overview of the native language of any computer. These overviews provide a context for understanding the details you will learn in the later chapters, where I go back over each of these areas in much greater detail.

Part III, "The Standalone PC," covers all the hardware issues plus the operating system software that activates it. Part IV, "PC Programs: From Machine Language Bytes to Human Speech," covers the rest of the software story. Part V, "Splendiferous Multimedia PCs," extends the discussion to the PCs that have been optimized for multimedia uses—which, it turns out, is fast becoming almost every PC sold today. Part VI, "PCs Are Frequent Flyers, Too," explains what is different about portable and laptop computers. Part VII, "The Connected PC," explains the details of how PCs get connected to one another and to other computers. And finally, Part VIII, "PCs, the Internet, the Future, and You," tells what is different now that our PCs are connected to so many other computers, and then attempts to tie everything I've told you together.

However, before I go into any of those detailed areas, I want to show you just how you can safely explore the information spaces within your PC—which, of course, leads us to the next chapter.

Enhancing Your Understanding by Exploring and Tinkering

Most people learn better when they actually experience something instead of simply reading about it. The text and figures in a book like this can take you only so far. To get a deeper understanding of how your (and for that matter, any one else's) PC works, you must get your hands dirty.

In Chapter 4, "Understanding Your PC's Parts," I told you about all the different pieces that make up a typical PC—and I encouraged you to examine your own PC and make a list of what it contains. That is the sort of hands-on exploration that I think will help give you a better understanding of the hardware. (And if you didn't do that exploration then, I encourage you to do it now. But first, review the precautions discussed in Chapter 4.)

In Chapter 3, "Understanding Bits, Nybbles, and Bytes," and Chapter 5, "How to Get Your PC to Understand You," I explained the fundamentals of binary and hexadecimal numbers, and I told you how your PC functions logically, as well as how it is instructed to do its tasks through software (programs).

Armed with this background, you are now ready to explore the logical insides of your PC. By this I mean a mostly software-oriented look at what's going on in your PC. To do this, you will have to use some programmers' tools, as mere human eyes cannot, by themselves, see the contents of your PC's memory or any other logical innards no matter how closely you stare at the hardware parts.

Think of this as a journey into your PC's private information spaces. What you'll see there turns out to be crucial to your gaining a full understanding of your PC.

Why Is This Valuable? And, Is It Dangerous?

You might be reluctant to try some of the experiments I suggest. You might think you don't need to do them, or you might fear hurting something if you do them wrong. I'll admit it up front: Some of the techniques I am about to explain can damage data. None of them will, however, harm your PC's hardware in any permanent way. So, although it might appear that I am encouraging the equivalent of giving of chain saws to babies, I actually am going to show you how to protect your computer quite fully before you start doing anything that is even possibly dangerous.

How to Protect Your Data

Because you are about to go inside your PC logically (through the use of some diagnostic program), and because in that process you possibly could damage some of your data, your common sense should tell you to protect your data against that possible harm. There is really *only* one good way to do that. You must make—*and test*—backups of your data.

Just as a dentist might say, "You have to floss only the teeth you wish to keep," I'll point out that you must back up only the data you don't want to lose. That might sound trivial, but it's not.

By now, most PC users know they should do backups. And, in fact, many people—perhaps most people who use PCs—do create backups. But most of them use a poorly thought-out process for that purpose. They typically just run some backup program on Friday afternoon, and expect it to do all the work. On Monday morning, they return to their desks, confident that all their work is now safe.

I have several concerns about this strategy. First, these people are vulnerable all week long. What if disaster strikes in midweek? This type of PC user stands to lose all the work he or she has done so far that week. (And, of course, if a fire burns down the building over the weekend, both the PC and any locally stored backups will be lost.)

Second, this strategy does too much. It commonly backs up *all* the files on your PC. The problem with doing too much is that you will soon fill up the backup media. This completely defeats the delightful capability of backup software to do its job while you're away from the computer. If your backup media fills each time you do a backup, the backup will pause until you return to the PC and insert another tape or diskette. The inconvenience and annoyance of this problem are two of the most oft-reported reasons why people stop doing backups altogether.

Additionally, a backup scheme that requires multiple tapes or diskettes does, by definition, require more pieces of media than otherwise. This can get very expensive. Because of the cost, one is strongly tempted to use the same media over and over for each backup. But if you find out later that this week's backup overwrote the only valid backup copy of some file, you might well be out of luck. Once the media that held that valid and potentially useful backup has been reused…Oops!

One improvement is to use a backup program that can be configured to back up only files that have been created or changed since the last backup. If you choose this approach, you are making incremental backups. Doing daily incremental backups that are supplemented by twice-weekly full backups—each made on a piece of media with sufficient capacity for the job—is a reliable, noninvasive backup scheme.

> **Tip:** As I mentioned before, you have the option of backing up everything on your computer every time you do a backup *or* having the backup software automatically back up only files that have changed since the previous backup. You can almost always configure a combination of these two as well, performing a complete backup two evenings a week, for example, and incremental backups every other night. My strong recommendation is that you use, at least, this combination scheme.
>
> I also would urge you to purchase ten pieces of backup media (tapes, for example), one for each work day of the week, for two weeks. Each morning, make it part of your daily habit to change to the next tape. The reason for this is simple: As they age, backup media can become unreliable. Tapes slowly stretch or distort, becoming unreliable. By spreading your daily backups out across several tapes, you minimize the likelihood of discovering that the backup you really need is resting on damaged media. The next week, use the second set of media. In this way, you doubly safeguard against the possibility that today's backup might overwrite your only good copy of a needed file. Completely replace your backup media at least three times a year.
>
> I would also encourage you to periodically verify the tape contents to be certain that your data is being stored reliably. All backup software provides this option, which is usually one of the preferences you select when you define a backup set. Doing this, say, for your full backup on Friday nights—after all, you won't have to watch it happening or wait for it to finish if you set your backups to run while you're away or asleep—will give you the added assurance that the tape is actually storing your data reliably.

This is, in fact, the strategy I most commonly recommend. It balances cost, time, and reliability. Of course, if you have a backup drive with sufficient speed and backup media with sufficient capacity, you can perform a full backup every night. Even in a total system failure, this scheme will cost you only one day's work. But even this plan has its drawbacks. First, all of your media must be large enough to hold a full backup. In the combination full/incremental scheme, you can use much smaller, less expensive, media for all of your daily incrementals. Second, if your backup hardware or your PC itself is too slow to perform a full backup during the time you're away from your PC, you'll find the backup still in progress when you return.

In the preceding tip, I mentioned using your backup software's built-in ability to verify that a backup has been made reliably. While this method is extremely trustworthy, it's not 100 percent trustworthy. The only way to achieve the latter is to restore the files to some place different from their origin, and then compare each restored file with its original.

(Most backup software can do this automatically, too, although it will take *hours* on a large full backup. This is a good job for your business PC to perform over the weekend, perhaps once a month. If your backup software doesn't support this, you can restore the backup and then use a standalone file comparison program such as Norton File Compare, from the Norton Utilities). Only if every single one of the restored files matches its original *exactly* is your backup strategy truly guaranteed.

An important part of any serious backup scheme is keeping one full set of backups offsite. That means in some other building, far enough away from your PC that if the building burns down or is robbed, flooded, or whatever, your spare set of backups will be safe. Insurance can replace all the hardware; it can even replace the programs you own, but nothing other than a valid set of backups will replace your data. There's just no other way to go. If you are the systems administrator of a company that has not yet implemented an offsite backup scheme, it's something you should recommend—or implement, if that is within your power—at your next opportunity.

You have many options for backup media. Many people now are using either CD-R or CD-RW (write-once or re-writeable CD data disks). Others find tape drives in one format or another to be their choice. Certainly, digital magnetic tape can be the least expensive medium for backup storage as well as the one with the greatest data storage capacity per physical volume, and tape is often chosen at the largest installations, mainly for those reasons.

After you learn about the different options for backup storage, choose one that works well for you. Then use it, test it, and go on using it regularly (and testing it periodically as well). And remember to keep refreshing your offsite copies of those backups—especially of your most critical files.

If you wait until you really need a backup copy of some files—to replace all the files on a disk that died, for example—before following this advice, I'm fairly sure that you'll decide that you definitely realized too late that doing backups (and testing them) is worth the effort. Please, just take my word on this one.

Archives Are Not Backups, But They're Useful

Besides your regular backup scheme, let me encourage you to give serious consideration to the benefit of archiving files you no longer need to keep online. Archiving allows you to immediately retrieve important files without keeping them on your hard drive. While this may sound like what a backup does, archives are different. Your complete backup scheme covers every file on the drives you back up. Archives, by their nature, are only selective. Further, while you *might* make your backups on disk media, you will *always* do archiving on disk. You may use CD-R or CD-RW or JAZ or ZIP disks, or even diskettes, but because you want to immediately retrieve files from your archives, you won't be using tape. (I strongly urge you to use some type of removable disk media for archiving; don't just copy files to a second hard disk installed in your PC.)

All that's involved in archiving files is copying them to your media of choice. For example, when you complete an important project, gather all of the project files together and either write them to a CD or drag them to a JAZ drive. If something happens to your PC, or if you need access to those project files at a location other than your own office, just pull out the archive and have instant gratification. You don't have to run any backup software; you don't have to illegally *install* the backup software on someone else's PC just so you can share the project files with them. Just drag and drop. Archives certainly can help guard you against catastrophic failure—just like backups—but they do far more to guard you against catastrophic inconvenience.

Incidentally, don't confuse archives in this context with compressed files, such as .ZIP files. You certainly may choose to compress the files you archive to other media, but you need not. Indeed, I recommend that you don't. Compressing your archived files just means that the decompressing software must be available whenever you want to access your archive. Decompressing also adds time to how quickly you can access your files. Finally, if you've used compressed files much, you know that they sometimes fail. Don't introduce an additional level of uncertainty into the mix.

Windows 98's Best Hidden Secret

Now I'm going to introduce you to one of the hidden gems in Windows 98. It isn't directly going to help you see inside your PC's information spaces, but I think you will find it useful. Mainly, it will help you get out of some difficult situations more easily— such as system lockups that can happen if you alter some bit of software or system settings—and it also can routinely make running Windows 98 a little bit smoother.

I am referring to the Windows 98 System Configuration Utility (see Figure 6.1). If you have Windows 98, then you have this program and it is already installed on your hard drive. But it isn't something you are very likely to find on your own.

The utility is in a file named MSCONFIG.EXE, and you'll find it in C:\WINDOWS\SYSTEM (if you installed Windows 98 to the default location). I value it enough that I have created a shortcut to it and located that shortcut on my Quick Launch toolbar.

Figure 6.1 shows the first screen you see when you run this program. As you can see in this figure, I have chosen to use this program to specify that each time Windows starts, it will not do *all* the things it usually does, just the ones I have selected. My normal setting for this program has it doing all of the usual CONFIG.SYS, AUTOEXEC.BAT, SYSTEM.INI, and WIN.INI file processing, but only a subset of the usual startup group items.

What this program refers to as the startup group items includes everything that gets run automatically when Windows starts, including not just those that are specified by short-cuts in the Startup folder, but also those that are mentioned in any of several Run and RunOnce entries in the Registry. I find it valuable to have such a convenient list of all those items in one place—and better yet to have the ability to temporarily suppress any of them. (To see what I mean, go to the Startup tab from within this program.)

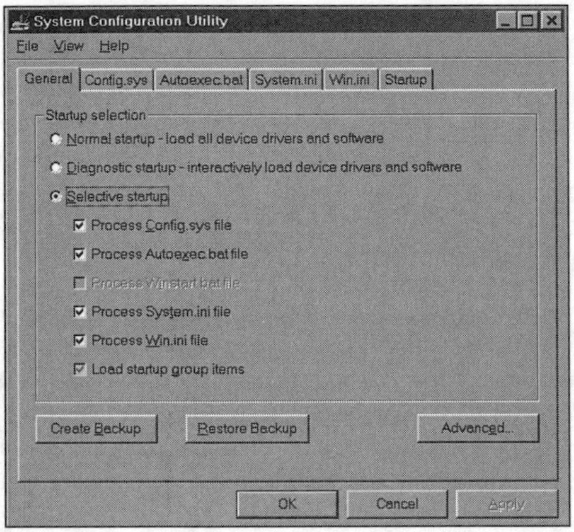

FIGURE 6.1

*The Windows 98
System
Configuration
Utility is one of
the best hidden
programs in that
operating system.*

I use this capability to keep from having some programs run that get loaded, but that I don't want always running. (One example is the AOL Instant Messenger program that Netscape Communicator loads with all its other pieces). The only other way to suppress some of those files is to edit the Registry—which even experts very properly wish to avoid doing except when it's truly necessary.

Similarly, the tabs in the System Configuration Utility for the four usual startup files (CONFIG.SYS, AUTOEXEC.BAT, SYSTEM.INI, and WIN.INI) enable you to temporarily suppress the execution of individual lines in those files. But my real favorite feature of this program is hidden behind the button you see in Figure 6.1 labeled Advanced. The options it contains are shown in Figure 6.2.

If you ever had to troubleshoot a balky Byzantine Windows 3.x installation, you probably learned about the many command line switches you could add to the WIN command to suppress features that might be causing your problems. The equivalents of those switches are all here on this screen. Here, too, are a few new options including my favorite, which you see checked in this figure. Choosing this option forces a Startup menu to appear once real-mode MS-DOS 7.1 has loaded, and before Windows 98's protected-mode operation begins. At that point, you can run any program that needs to run in MS-DOS mode, or execute any real-mode DOS commands.

To summarize: The Windows 98 System Configuration Utility is not a program you must use. It is, however, an easy way to perform a variety of diagnostic modifications on how your system starts Windows. That can be of invaluable troubleshooting assistance if Windows becomes corrupted. And this program's option for always running the Startup menu makes it easier to get to a pure, real-mode DOS command prompt which you will need to do if, for example, you wish to run a Flash RAM update program.

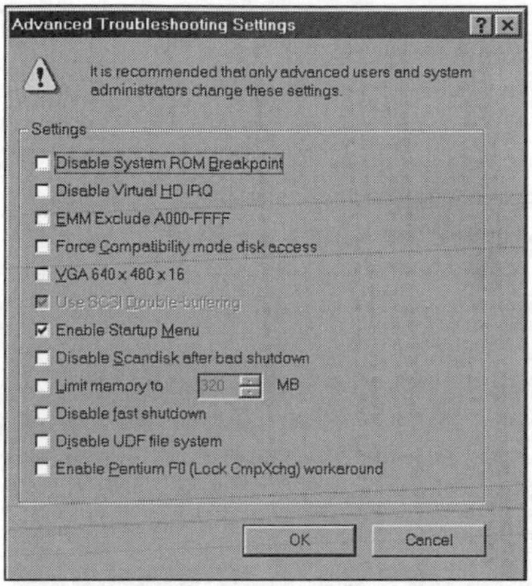

FIGURE 6.2
The Advanced settings screen in the System Configuration Utility offers several options.

An Introduction to DEBUG

Back when the PC was young and most of the people using one were programmers, engineers, or other tech types, a tool program was bundled with DOS to help programmers find and eliminate flaws, or *bugs*, from their programs. That tool's name was DEBUG.

How to Run (and How to Quit) DEBUG

DEBUG still is a part of DOS, and it even comes with Windows 95 and Windows 98. It is not a user-friendly program. If you simply type DEBUG at the DOS prompt and press Enter (or double-click DEBUG.EXE in the Windows 95 Explorer), you will be confronted with just a hyphen as a prompt. That is DEBUG's way of letting you know it is ready to do something for you. What you must do next is something you should already know.

There are two ways you can get a little bit of help from DEBUG itself. First, if you type DEBUG /? and press Enter at the DOS prompt, you'll get a very brief statement about the legal syntax for invoking the program. Second, if you are at the hyphen prompt and type ? and press Enter, you get a list of legal commands you can type there.

DEBUG is a very useful snooping tool.

You can use it to look at the contents of any place you want in the first megabyte of your PC's memory, or at any file or sector on any disk attached to the PC. A *sector* is a physical location on the disk; a *file* is a logical construct stored there. You'll find more details about these notions in Chapter 9, "You Can Never Have Too Much Closet (or Data Storage) Space."

> **Peter's Principle:** Nothing Beats Knowing How to Stop
>
> The most important thing to know about any program is how to get it to quit. (Mickey Mouse, in Disney's *Fantasia*, demonstrated just how essential this can be. As a sorcerer's apprentice, he got a water-carrying spell to start working, but he didn't know how to stop it. Before the sorcerer returned and stopped the spell, Mickey was almost washed away.) To get DEBUG to quit, type q and press Enter when you are at the hyphen prompt.

The reason DEBUG is limited to looking at the first megabyte has to do with its history. It is what we now call a *real-mode*, or *16-bit* program. As such, it cannot see any more than the first megabyte of RAM—a restriction shared by all real-mode programs unless they have been enhanced with a DOS extender.

Using DEBUG to Look at Memory Locations

You saw in Chapter 5, "How to Get Your PC to Understand You," (Figures 5.1 and 5.2) two examples of using DEBUG to look at a location in memory. (If that discussion is a bit hazy in your mind, you might want to go back and skim it before continuing here). One of these two examples shows what is called the dump display; the other shows a program disassembly (or, to help you associate the word with the letter u that is the DEBUG command to generate it, you can call this an *un*assembly). In the first display, you see the actual numeric values held at each physical memory location. In the second display, those values are interpreted as instructions, much as the CPU might interpret them.

How do you know at which memory addresses you should snoop to see something interesting? Well, the first step is to go to a DOS prompt (either by booting your computer to DOS without Windows or by opening a DOS prompt window inside Windows). Then enter the command MEM /D /P. This displays all the programs currently running in the first megabyte of your machine's main memory. The first column in the MEM display shows the segment portion of the address. Suppose that one of the lines begins with the number 1234. Then, if you snoop at 1234:0000, you'll see the beginning of that program. Actually, the first 16 bytes at this address are the memory control block for the program. I'll explain just what this means in Chapter 11, "Giving Your PC's CPU Enough Elbow Room—PC Memory."

In Chapter 11, you'll find out more about some of the interesting memory locations you can examine in this way. Right now, I want to point out some of the other things you can do with this program to further your exploration.

Other Things You Can Do with DEBUG

Looking at memory isn't all you can do with DEBUG—not by a long shot. It has 23 different commands it can execute. The d command merely displays the information it finds in memory. The u (unassemble) command, as you saw in Figure 5.2, interprets that information and displays the result. Other commands, in particular e (edit) and f (fill), let you alter the information that is held in memory.

> **Warning:** You might put some information into a place in memory that the PC must have to hold some other information. In this way, you could make your PC very confused, and perhaps hang. If that happens, you can recover simply by rebooting the PC. Of course, this means that you shouldn't do this sort of experimenting while you have any unsaved data in another program.
>
> Perhaps the worst thing that could happen would be if you were to alter the image in main memory of the FAT table for one of your disk drives. If you did this without realizing it, and if afterward you wrote anything to that disk, you could lose some of the files stored on that disk. So, in general, I'd recommend that you feel free to *look* at the contents of any memory location, but only alter ones whose purpose you understand. For even greater security, perform your disk exploration using the Norton Disk Editor, which can be run in a read-only mode. You'll read more about this in the section "Using the Norton Disk Editor," later in this chapter. (NDE can also be used for viewing the contents of memory.)

Still other DEBUG commands let you see information from a disk drive (or alter that drive's contents). The l (standing for load) command brings in one or more sectors of information from an absolute sector address on a disk and places that information in memory. After it's there, you can use the d command to display that information.

You can also read input from a port or send output to a port, and you can read or set the CPU's registers using DEBUG. (You'll learn in Chapter 8, "How Your PC 'Thinks,'" just what registers and ports are.)

Furthermore, you can make the PC run a program by using the proper DEBUG commands. Doing these things will give you a better sense of how your PC does them itself. But please be careful. I strongly suggest that you begin exploring with disks by using a *scratch* floppy disk—that is, any disk whose contents you don't care about. (If you have a disk whose contents you want to look at but want to be sure you don't alter, then first make a copy of it and then do your snooping on the copy.)

Because this isn't a book focused on DOS and DOS utilities, I won't take the time to explain in detail all the things you can do with DEBUG. Instead, I am going to move on to some other tools you might want to use for snooping around your PC.

> **Note:** If you want to find out more about DOS, I suggest you look at *Peter Norton's Complete Guide to DOS 6.22, 6th Edition*, Sams Publishing, 1994, ISBN 0-672-30614-X.

Using the Norton Disk Editor

I'll end this chapter by telling you about another PC exploration tool—Norton Disk Editor (NDE)—which comes as a part of the Norton Utilities.

Historical Aside

Peter Norton started his career in the personal computer field with an observation about human nature: People make mistakes.

He noticed that the designers of the first PCs and the early versions of DOS didn't really allow for that. The designers assumed that every PC user would know all the ins and outs of the machine and its software, and that the user never would do something unless he or she knew what effect it would have, and that the user really intended for that effect to occur.

But Peter recognized this wasn't always the case. In fact, a lot of early PC users came to great grief by erasing files they wished they hadn't erased. And from an understanding of just how the PC stored files, and how it erased them, Peter realized that it was quite possible to unerase files—at least much of the time.

So, Peter built a tool to do just that. This was the beginning of the Norton Utilities.

Before Peter could create the Norton Utilities and its Norton UnErase tool, he had to understand how PC disks are organized at a very deep and intimate level. The tool he created to help himself do that is what finally became known as the Norton Disk Editor (NDE).

As I explained earlier, you can look at almost anything you want on a disk simply by using DEBUG—at least you can if you know what you are doing with it. But it isn't easy. The Norton Utilities in general, and the NDE in particular, show you arcane information about your PC in a very straightforward manner. After you have used it even for a short time, I think you will agree with me on the importance of this feature.

The first important thing to know about NDE is how to find and run it. You can run this program from within Windows, but you will be limited to working in read-only mode if you do so. The easiest way to launch DISKEDIT from Windows is to open the Norton Utilities directory in the Windows Explorer. Find the file DISKEDIT.EXE and double-click it. A dialog box will pop up pointing out that you are using a multitasking environment. When you click OK, you'll be informed that NDE has been put into read-only mode to avoid causing disk-write conflicts with other running programs. Simply click the Continue button and you can explore away!

When you actually want to make changes to memory or disk, you must run NDE from within real-mode DOS. (To do this, use the Start menu's Shutdown command to restart your PC in MS-DOS mode). Then navigate the directory tree to the proper directory and run DISKEDIT from that command prompt. The only hard part here is that the directory names you will see, using the DIR command, are the short names. (At most, they will have eight characters in the filename plus an option three-character maximum extension.) Run in this fashion, NDE will still launch in read-only mode, but you can change it to write-enabled mode from NDE's Tools menu.

When you start NDE, it will most likely tell you that it is configured in read-only mode. That's wonderful. It means you can explore all you like, and you will never alter any of the data on your disks. Still, I suggest that your first explorations be done on a spare floppy diskette. Then, if you switch to write-enabled mode and improperly alter its contents, no harm will be done.

To see how important these precautions are, you need only realize that if you were to change just one crucial byte on a disk, you could render it totally inaccessible. The only way to recover from that sort of error is to use either NDE or the Norton Disk Doctor (NDD) to set that critical byte back to the right value. There are several different places you could alter the disk's data in ways that would render it unusable. One advantage to using NDD to recover from such an error is that it knows all those places and can set them back to their proper contents with little or no input on your part.

If someone has modified your copy of NDE so that it isn't set to always launch in read-only mode, then setting it to that mode is your first order of business. From the main menu (see Figure 6.3) select Tools, then select Configuration.

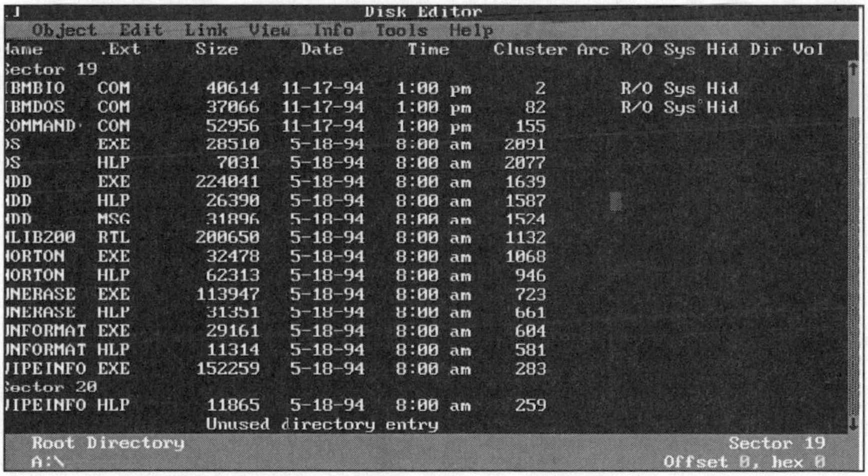

FIGURE 6.3

The Norton Disk Editor (NDE) program's display and main menu.

Figure 6.4 shows the screen that pops up when you choose Tools, Configuration and indicates the checkbox you will want to select to protect yourself. If there is a × in it, you're safe. Now click OK and you are ready to start exploring.

Rather than walk you through a lengthy exploration of a diskette at this point, I would rather encourage you to, as the title of this chapter puts it, mess around a bit. Try out the various menu items in NDE. You're in read-only mode, so just play with it. Try anything that comes to mind.

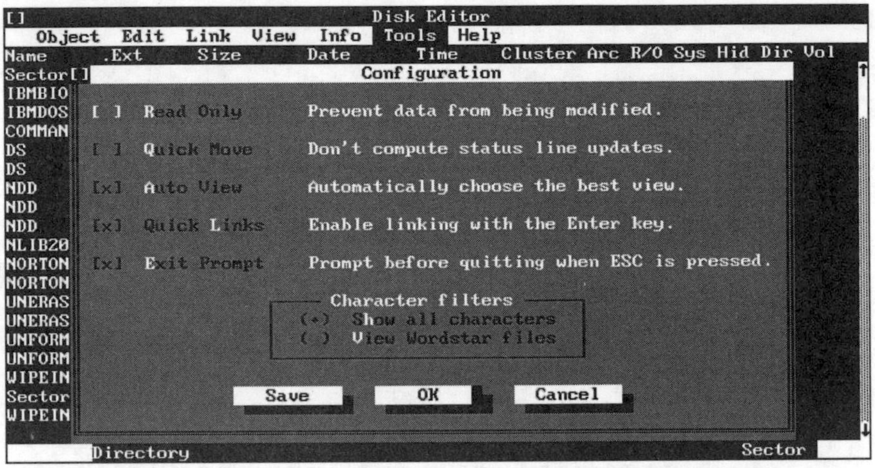

FIGURE 6.4
Explore safely; read-only mode will guarantee that you don't change disk contents inadvertently.

Note: When you're ready to put NDE to real use and you'd like a more detailed understanding of it—and, indeed, all of the Norton Utilities and more—check out *Peter Norton's Complete Guide to Norton SystemWorks 2.0*, by Scott Clark, Macmillan Computer Publishing, 1999, ISBN 0-67231-528-9.

Some More Things to Think About and Try

In this section, I'll give you suggestions for some explorations to try. And after you have read Chapter 9, you'll no doubt be able to think of many more.

Looking at the DOS Clock Values in the BIOS Data Area

Using DEBUG, retrieve the values held at memory locations 0040:006C through 0040:006F. Now do it again. You'll notice that the numbers you retrieve change each time you do it. These four locations hold a long integer number that tells how many times the PC's motherboard "timer" circuit has "ticked" since the PC was last rebooted. The timer ticks are events that happen once every 55 milliseconds. Knowing that, and if you know how to write simple programs in assembler (or most any other computer language), can you write a program to retrieve the value at this location repeatedly and to use them to display the time of day? (You'll have to give that program the current time when you start it. After that, it should be able to update the display on its own, using the information from these memory locations. This is what most onscreen PC clock programs do.)

Warning: There are two warnings that could save you some unnecessary grief, or at least some extra work.

The first is that the addresses I'll give in the next sections are stated in hexadecimal notation. Address 70h is the same as 112 in decimal, for example. Be careful when you enter them to use the number base expected by the program you're using. DEBUG normally expects all numbers to be entered in hex.

The second point is that you are going to send data only to port 70h (which is port 112 in decimal). You'll be reading data only from port 71h (113 decimal). If you accidentally write data to port 71h, you will *alter* the contents of the CMOS instead of inspecting them.

If you do alter the contents of your CMOS, this won't keep your PC from booting. There is a checksum in the CMOS that allows the POST to discover whether these data have been corrupted. If so, the POST will restore the factory default values and go on to boot up the PC. But this means, of course, that all of the configuration information you provided through the Setup program will have been lost.

You'll have to re-enter manually such things as the types of drives you have and any non-default choices you have made in other areas of the CMOS. For this reason, it is only prudent for you first to go into the CMOS setup program, inspect all the values displayed there (on each of the many pages, if your PC's setup program has many pages), and write down on paper all the values you see displayed. That way, you have a record from which you can help your PC rebuild its CMOS to the state it was in before corruption occurred.

Looking at the CMOS Real-Time Clock Values

Again using DEBUG, send a number to I/O port address 70h. The value you send will be an address in the CMOS nonvolatile RAM. Now read a byte in from I/O port address 71h—that is, the byte held at that address in the CMOS. The first 10 bytes (at addresses 00h through 09h) in the CMOS hold the current time according to the real-time clock on the motherboard. This is where the PC keeps track of time when it's turned off. One of the tasks your PC performs during the boot process is reading these locations to set the main operating system clock. Thereafter, that clock keeps time by reference to the timer tick BIOS data area locations you examined in the preceding paragraph.

If you retrieve this data (and it will take you 10 separate accesses to the CMOS to do so), then you'll find you can interpret it to get the time your PC thinks it is, without having to enter the current time manually. The format for this information is as follows: The first byte (at address 0) holds the current second. The third byte (address 2) holds the current minute. The fifth byte (address 4) holds the current hour. (Addresses 1, 3, and 5 hold the same information for the alarm time, if you have set one.) The seventh byte (address 6) holds the day of the week in numeric form (Sunday = 1). The next two bytes hold the date and current month. The last byte (address 9) holds the current year.

Two decimal digits are held in each of these bytes in what is called a *packed BCD format*. That is, each nybble (four bits) holds one decimal digit. Therefore, when the value is written in hexadecimal, you can simply pretend it is in decimal and read it directly.

> **Technical Note:** Alternatively, you can say that the tens place of the two-digit decimal value is the binary value divided by 16, with the fractional part discarded. The units place of the two-digit decimal value is the binary value modulo 16. This formulation suggests what calculations you'd have to do in a program to unpack the packed BCD values into a normal decimal value.

Here is one place, incidentally, where the now-infamous year 2000 problem pops up. Location 9 in the CMOS is only big enough to hold the last two digits of the year. Therefore, if you look only there, you (and your PC) won't be able to tell the difference between the year 2000 and the year 1900 (or 2100). There are other storage locations in the nonvolatile RAM that weren't at first designated for any particular use. One of these is now used to hold the century in modern PCs.

Just which CMOS location holds the century value can depend on what brand of computer you have. If yours is an IBM PS/2, for example, the century (two-decimal digit) value is held (as a packed BCD number) in CMOS location 37h. Most other PCs hold that value at CMOS location 32h. See if you can find out where this information is held in your PC.

If you want to learn a lot more about the Y2K problem, how it may affect you, and what you might do to get ready for it, I suggest you check out the following URLs:

```
http://www.zdnet.com/zdy2k/
```

```
http://www.readyfory2k.com/
```

Snooping Around on Your Disk Drives

If you have a copy of the Norton Utilities, use the NDE program (DISKEDIT.EXE) to look at a floppy diskette. From the Tools menu, select Configuration. Be sure the checkbox for Read Only is checked. This will keep you from accidentally altering something important on one of your disk drives.

Next, from the Object menu, choose Drive, and then your logical A: drive. (That is, the Logical Disks radio button should be selected—have a dot in it—and then from the list of logical disks, choose A:.)

Notice that there's no partition table on a floppy diskette. (That option on the Objects menu is grayed out.) The first sector of a floppy diskette is the Boot Sector. (The partition table option on the Objects menu will also be grayed-out on a hard disk if NDE is running in logical view mode. You must switch to physical view mode by selecting Physical Disk in the Change Drive dialog box, accessed through the Object menu.)

Look at the contents of that Boot Sector (by selecting it from the Object menu). The Norton Disk Editor, by default, displays a table of information about that disk that it has read from the boot sector. You can see the actual hexadecimal values stored in that sector by pressing the F2 function key, or by selecting View as Hex from the View menu. Notice that near the beginning of the boot sector you will see ASCII characters spelling out the name of the operating system, and its version used to format this disk.

Now try looking at your first physical hard drive, which is usually where your logical C: drive is located. Here you'll find a partition table. If you have a physical disk divided into two or more logical disks, then the partition table shows you the beginnings of that logical division. (If three or more drive letters are allocated to this physical disk, most likely you'll find additional partition tables, called *extended partition tables*, farther out on the disk.)

Now try looking at a directory. Again, you can have it displayed in a very readable format (the default directory display) or in hexadecimal if you want to see what really is stored in each location within each entry. This is particularly interesting to do if you are running Windows 95 and have some files with long names.

You can jump from one interesting place to another on the disk. Keep watching the location indications at the bottom of the screen as you do so. Often, the easiest way to jump is to highlight some piece of information and then press Enter. You will be transported to another location on the disk involving that particular piece of information. Using the Link menu is another way to jump around.

Yet Other Things to Try

When you tire of these experiments—and they may be more interesting after you read Chapter 9—you can return to this narrative and continue your journey. Any time along the way that some idea for an experiment pops into your mind—an experiment of any kind, not just one relating to memory, disks, DEBUG, or NDE—I encourage you to put the book down, go to your PC, and try it. This is, without a doubt, the very best way to learn about these intricate and fascinating machines.

Summary

Hands-on learning is the very best kind. What you hear you remember for awhile. What you hear and see, you remember longer. What you hear, see, and experience in every other possible way, you remember the longest and it leads most directly to a real sense of understanding.

Fortunately, getting this very valuable hands-on experience with various aspects of your PC isn't hard. In this chapter, I have shown you, first, how to protect yourself, your PC, and your data from danger while you are experimenting. Next, I pointed out how to use DEBUG and the Norton Disk Editor to explore the ways information is held both in your PC's main memory and on its disk drives. And finally, I gave you a few exercises with which you can expand your understanding.

PART III

The Standalone PC

Understanding PC Processors

The original IBM PC was built around an Intel 8088 chip as its central processing unit (CPU). This was not the first microprocessor that Intel made, and it was not the only kind Intel sold, even back then. It certainly wasn't the only one on the market. However, after the IBM PC (and its clones) swept the marketplace, the Intel 8088's close cousin, Intel's 8086, became pretty much the only processor chip most people needed to know about.

Historical Aside

This is, of course, not completely true. Apple, Atari, Commodore, and some other companies made non–IBM-compatible personal computers that were still selling fairly well. In a short time, though, all of these small computer makers (except Apple) fell by the wayside, and Apple's market share never rose very far past 10 percent of the personal computers sold each year. So the fact that Apple's computers were built using non–Intel-designed CPU chips was and continues to be only a minor side note in the history of this industry.

That was then. This is now. And, oh boy, now sure is different.

In the past twenty years, Intel has produced seven generations (including several dozen different models) of CPU chips that are closely enough related to the original 8086 that they deserve to be called members of a "family" of chips. Because the first member of that family was the 8086 microprocessor, and every model until recently had an 86 at the end of its name, they are called the *x86* family of CPU chips.

There are other, non-x86 (yet clearly important) central processor chips being manufactured by other vendors for use in small computers. Most notable, perhaps, are the PowerPC chips made by IBM and Motorola and used in the recent members of the Apple Macintosh computer line, and the Alpha chip family developed by Digital Equipment Corporation (DEC), which is now a part of Compaq. The chips in both of these families are powerful and important in their niche markets, but none of them are used in any model of what I am calling "a PC" for the purposes of this book.

Technical Note: Alpha-based computers are very similar to Intel-based PCs. Alpha-based computers use PCI cards and have 1.44MB floppy drives, SCSI hard drives, and all of the other standard components that we talk about for an Intel-based PC. Their primary difference, which is a big one, is that they utilize a different CPU. In fact, they are so similar that Windows NT can be run on either system, although it must be compiled in the Alpha's native language.

Thus, if you are after an understanding of PCs and how they work, you don't need to learn all about all those other microprocessors. Understanding just Intel's x86 family of CPU chips (and their *clones*—the functionally compatible CPU chips made by other vendors) will take you a very long way toward your goal.

This chapter gives you an overview of this crowd of PC processor possibilities and perhaps some insight into how you can navigate your way through the resulting confusion to find the perfect processor for your PC.

A Sea of Change in PC CPUs

For 90 percent of the time since the introduction of the first x86 microprocessor and the first PC, Intel totally dominated the market for PC CPUs. All the innovations came from it, and it sold something close to 90 percent of all the CPU chips used in PCs. In the past two years, there have been some very interesting and significant changes happening in this marketplace.

Intel has always had competitors who made clones of its x86 CPUs. In fact, in the beginning, Intel licensed its designs to several other manufacturers and helped them get into production. The products made by those vendors really were, quite literally, clones of the Intel chips. Intel did this because it would help them sell chips to OEMs (Original Equipment Manufacturers) who might otherwise have been reluctant, fearing that someday Intel might not be able to make and deliver enough chips. Knowing that there were some "second source" manufacturers was reassuring to those OEMs.

By the time Intel brought out its 386 CPU in 1985, it was feeling more confident and thus attempted to bring to an end the making of clone x86 CPUs. AMD (Advanced Micro Devices) resisted this move and ended up suing Intel. This lawsuit triggered some consequences none of us could have foreseen at the time.

AMD won the right to make clone 386 chips, but was denied permission to clone any future generations of Intel x86 chips. This forced AMD to assemble a team that could design functionally compatible, yet clearly different, CPU chips—a first step on the path to making x86-family members with innovations of its own devising. No longer would Intel completely own the x86 architecture—just as IBM no longer owned the overall PC architecture, but had to follow the needs and wishes of a larger industry of IBM-compatible PC makers and their customers.

Intel also responded to this legal battle in two ways. The first was that starting with generation five, it chose names that would clearly enjoy trademark protection (which by then the courts had ruled mere numbers did not). Instead of 586, the new chip was christened the Pentium. And with the sixth generation, Intel moved into a new and patent-protected packaging and interconnection scheme. I'll tell you more about the famous series of Intel Sockets (most notably Sockets 7, 8, and 370) and their Slots (1 and 2) later in this chapter. This latter move turned out to resemble the dead-end approach to protecting a monopoly position that IBM had attempted several years earlier with its Micro Channel architecture.

Today there are at least five major makers of independent, competing, and yet compatible designs of CPU chips for PCs: Intel, Advanced Micro Devices (AMD), Cyrix (now a division of National Semiconductor), Integrated Device Technology (IDT), and Rise. Each of these companies offers multiple versions of their CPU chips. (In addition to these vendors, there are several others that make x86-compatible clone CPU chips for use in the "embedded PC" marketplace, such as STMicroelectronics. I will not again mention those manufacturers, because their exclusive focus on embedded systems makes them not really a part of the main story.)

AMD and Cyrix started out with devices that simply copied the functionality of Intel's x86 chips, albeit in slightly different ways in terms of their internal design details. When Intel developed MMX technology, for example, 3Dnow was innovated by these clone chip makers in an attempt to compete. But it works both ways. In their most recent versions, these vendors have added significant new functionality that Intel had not innovated but is now being forced to copy. Several companies have aimed from the very beginning at making x86-equivalent CPU chips that were radically different from Intel's designs, with—supposedly—some attendant benefits for their customers.

Figure 7.1 shows the Intel Pentium II, which is unquestionably the most popular CPU chip for today's desktop PCs, along with a new entry in the chip market, the Rise mP6. I'll explain just what is special about these and the other x86 chips currently on the market later in this chapter.

With that as background, I now want to go back to the beginning and describe for you how we got to where we are today. Only with that as a foundation is it possible to understand some of the oddities of the present PC CPU landscape.

I will first concentrate on Intel to the exclusion of its competitors. This is only proper, because it did control the development of the x86 architecture for almost two decades, and it is still by a very large margin the predominant supplier of those chips. After that, I will tell you a bit about each of the four principal competitors in this marketplace. I'll close with what I hope you will find are sage words on what all this diversity means, and how you'll most likely want to let it affect your PC buying decisions now and in the next several years.

FIGURE 7.1
*The industry-
standard CPU for
desktop PCs,
Intel's Pentium II,
and one of many
competing prod-
ucts, the Rise mP6.*

Intel, IBM, and You

At the beginning of the PC revolution, IBM was the leader, and Intel and Microsoft were simply the most important of several major suppliers to IBM. That picture has now been turned upside down, with IBM only a minor player and Microsoft and Intel on top of the heap. Furthermore, this picture may be about to undergo yet another upheaval as a consequence of both the legal battles that Microsoft and Intel are facing, and of some fierce competition coming from other vendors. (In Microsoft's case, the most obvious alternative vendors that may threaten its position are Netscape, Sun, and the "Open Source" operating system, Linux. Intel's competitive threats are coming primarily from the makers of clone x86 CPU chips.)

So far, Intel still holds a very commanding lead in the race to supply all the CPUs needed for the hundreds of millions of PCs produced each year. However, its market share for CPUs for all desktop and mobile PCs has fallen recently, from around 90 percent to about 80 percent, and in some portions of that market—most notably the sub-$1,000 PCs—Intel no longer has even the majority of the market, according to some statistical sources.

Who has taken this much market share from Intel? AMD has been the leader, with approximately half of the sub-$1,000 PC market and around 15 percent of the total market for PC CPU chips. Cyrix has captured a modest fraction of AMD's market share, but its numbers are also rising. The other two players, IDT and Rise, are just beginning to make inroads, and it isn't possible to say yet how likely it is that they will surpass either AMD or Cyrix. Of course, with a market as large as that for PCs, having only a modest share of a small corner of the market can still mean a very healthy business.

As always happens when markets are open and competitive, the consumer comes out the ultimate winner. Intel has been forced by the competitive threat from AMD, Cyrix, and others to lower its prices, add features, and accelerate the development of new designs, and the competitors still are nipping at Intel's heels. So the race goes on, while we sit back and reap the benefits.

The *x*86 Family Tree

You cannot understand present PC processors without knowing something of their family history. The reason for this necessity is precisely the qualities of similarity and compatibility that have made these many, quite different, processors a "family." Intel named its line of CPU chips for PCs the *x*86 family. This includes (so far) at least a dozen major models introduced over the past 20 years.

The point of calling this a "family" of CPU chips is that they share many things in common. Their basic architecture has evolved over time, but it still reflects a particular approach to making a CPU. The way memory is addressed is fundamentally the same, although later models have more ways of doing so. Similarly, the instructions that the CPU understands (its native language, in other words) is the same, although again the later models have added substantially to the original vocabulary.

There is an important reason for this constancy. Intel didn't want to upset a very valuable apple cart. When the original IBM PC became a smash hit, Intel had a wonderful and rapidly expanding market for its products. But if it had introduced new, better, but incompatible designs for its subsequent microprocessors, there would have been a substantial risk that those new designs would not be acceptable to the marketplace. Indeed, all the clone PC experience to date has strongly suggested that the nearly total backward compatibility of every new PC is one of the most essential qualities it must have in order to succeed.

All this means that we are still saddled with some (unfortunate) architectural decisions the Intel designers made nearly a quarter-century ago. The most prominent of these was the way Intel's designers decided to expand the address space from what had been commonplace in even earlier models of microprocessor.

PC Prehistory

Before there were PCs, there were some other small computers. The Apple II was the king in schools. Various brands of CP/M machines ran many small businesses. All of these microprocessor-based small computers had two things in common. They all handled information internally in 8-bit (1-byte) chunks, and they all used no more than 64KB of RAM. (Well, with some clever page-switching mechanisms, some of them managed to use up to 128KB, but this was quite rare.)

When it came time to create a new generation of microprocessors, one thing that obviously was needed was to enable them to address more memory. The reason for the previous 64KB limit was simply that the memory addresses always had to fit into a 1-byte *register* (information holding space) inside the processor. To get a larger amount of addressable memory meant using larger memory address pointers.

It might, in retrospect, seem obvious that the next step should have been to double the length of the memory address pointers. That would jump the upper limit of RAM from 64KB to 4GB. The CPU chip designers at Motorola opted for exactly that choice at about the same time Intel's designers were making their choice in a very different way.

You must understand that there was a very powerful conflicting pressure on the Intel designers. They wanted to make it as easy as possible to transfer business programs from the earlier CP/M machines (some of which used Intel CPU chips, although the Zilog Z80 was the chip of choice for this OS) to their new machines. One way they felt they could facilitate that process was to make the new CPU chips address memory in a rather odd way. (This strategy was understandable, but it seemed odd even then, and it seems odder still today—and even more regrettable.)

In Chapter 8, "How Your PC 'Thinks'," and in Chapter 11, "Giving Your PC's CPU Enough Elbow Room—PC Memory," I'll tell you all about the Intel `segment:offset` method of combining two 16-bit numbers to get a single 20-bit number for addressing memory. For now, I'll just note that this strategy served Intel's goal. It did make it easy to "port" programs from CP/M to the PC, but it also imposed an upper limit of 1MB to the amount of RAM any computer using these new Intel chips could have. (At the time, this didn't seem so harsh a limit. After all, it was a factor of 16 larger than anything anyone had been able to use previously.)

Where the PC Began: Intel's 8086 and 8088

PC history starts with Intel's introduction of the 8086 CPU chip in 1979 and the 8088 the following year. These chips handled information internally in 16-bit (2-byte) chunks—twice as much as had been the case for the previous generation of microprocessor chips. The 8086 had 16-bit registers (information holding places) internally, and it had 16 data pins to carry information onto and off of the chip. The 8088 differed from this only in that it had just 8 data pins and an internal mechanism to enable it to move data in and out in single bytes, while still computing with that information internally in 2-byte chunks.

IBM chose the 8088 as the CPU for its new PC (which it introduced in August of 1981) over the slightly more powerful 8086, in part because having only 8 data lines meant that all the ancillary circuits could be only half as complex as would be needed to support 16 data lines. In today's terms, the difference is trivial. At the time, that difference really *was* a big deal in both engineering and financial terms.

Many Stops Along the Way

As you know, the PC was a great success, and with it, Intel's fortune was greatly boosted. So of course, Intel wanted very much to continue to be the preferred supplier of CPU chips for all of IBM's later PC models. To do that, Intel needed to keep coming out with improved versions of its 8086 CPU chip. Intel gave the subsequent members of the *x*86 family names such as 80186, 80286, and 80386. Each new member had substantial improvements in some of its features. (The 80186 was never used as the CPU in any model of IBM PC, for some arcane reason. All the rest were.) To make selling the idea of these chips to the mass market easier, Intel's marketing folks dropped the 80 off the front end. At that point, they talked only of the Intel 386.

The 386 was eventually made in two flavors, the 386SX and the 386DX. The next chip in the family also came in two flavors, the 486SX and 486DX. (The suffixes in the two cases meant very different things, but to Intel's marketers they were just memorable labels and didn't have to carry any additional meaning per se.)

Historical Aside

Each new generation of integrated circuits is noticeably more powerful than its predecessors because it is more complex. This has been possible only because the industry is constantly learning new and better ways to make the features on those chips smaller and, at the same time, make the size of the overall wafers on which the chips are created ever larger.

Gordon Moore, who was one of Intel's founders and its chief executive at the time, made an interesting observation about this back In the late 1960s. He said he had noticed that if one plotted the industry's progress on semilogarithmic paper (that is, with a scale that allots equal horizontal space to equal *intervals* of time and equal vertical space to equal *ratios* of performance or size), the points representing the complexity or fineness of scale of ICs and their dates of development would lie very nearly on a straight line. Another way to say this is that the economically feasible chips get about a hundred times more complex every decade. (And a related statement is that the price of a given level of complexity falls to about half every eighteen months or so.)

Most remarkable to me is that this so-called "Moore's Law" has *no* basis in any known physical facts. Instead, it seems to be, as much as anything, an observation about the rate of human invention. This exponentially increasing rate of progress has continued for many decades now, and still it shows no signs of stopping. Every time we seem to be about to run into an absolute brick wall in terms of some physical limit on what a particular integrated circuit manufacturing process can achieve, someone invents a new process that skirts that limitation. Truly this "law" is a remarkable observation—and so far it is completely inexplicable!

The feature-set improvements in this progression of chips came in several areas. First, each new type of chip worked faster than all its predecessors. Second, most new generations introduced at least a few new instructions (new words or phrases in the CPU's native language). Third, the size of the chunks of data being handled internally or being shipped in and out of the chip increased in several steps. Fourth, some new ways to address memory were added.

Protections and Paging—The 386 Brought Significant Change

Of all of these changes, perhaps the most historically significant is the innovation in memory access that was introduced with the 386. The 80286 already had introduced a version of what Intel called *protected mode*. This was a way to access more than just 1MB of RAM. The 286 version of protected mode allowed access of up to 16MB. The

386 supported this mode of access, plus another one that pushed the upper limit all the way up to 4GB (4,096MB). Of much greater importance is that the 386 also introduced a new mechanism called *paging*, by which the relationship between actual, physical memory addresses and the logical addresses seen by the CPU could be manipulated almost arbitrarily. I'll tell you all about both protected mode (in both its 286 and 386 flavors) and memory paging in Chapter 11.

The effect of these two improvements was to foster a whole new generation of software, all of which requires at least a 386-level CPU to run. This is why the introduction of the 386 in 1985 marked a watershed in the development of the Intel x86 CPU family. At no time since then has there been an improvement in the *x*86 CPUs so great as to render obsolete all previous generations of software as thoroughly. You can run nearly any PC program on the market today on an archaic, 386-based PC—if you have sufficient patience. (Today's PCs are a whole lot faster than the old, 386-based models, but they aren't capable of doing much that the earlier PCs couldn't do if given enough time.)

The next most significant feature upgrade was the increase in the size of information chunks that could be handled at once. From the initial 16-bit chunk for internal handling and 8-bit chunks for input and output, the *x*86 processors were extended by the time of the 386 to handle information internally and for input-output in 32-bit chunks. They still could put out or bring in just 1 byte, but they also could transfer up to 4 bytes in parallel. And almost all the processing internally proceeded 4 bytes at a time.

The 486—With Math on Board, Coprocessors Not Needed Anymore

By the time the 486 was introduced in 1989, the increased complexity that was made possible by new developments in integrated circuit manufacturing techniques allowed the chip designers to bring on board all the math processing power that up to that time had been relegated to a secondary, optional *floating-point coprocessor* chip. (You can learn all you could possibly want to know about floating-point issues in Chapter 3, "Understanding Bits, Nybbles, and Bytes.")

Furthermore, Intel added a small amount of what is usually referred to as Level 1 (L1) cache memory to the CPU chip. This is some very fast RAM that acts as a sort of loading dock where information can be parked briefly while it is on its way into or out of the CPU chip. I explain all about the various levels of cache memory (L1, L2, and now L3) in Chapter 8.

Pentium

Intel's Pentium CPU chip was introduced in 1993. This was the first of the named (rather than merely numbered) Intel *x*86 CPU chips. It also has become the foundation for Intel's entire line from then until now.

The Pentium upped the ante for motherboard makers because it sported 64 input/output pins. This meant it could move information on and off the chip 8 bytes at a time. Also, it doubled the amount of cache memory on the CPU chip. But now, instead of one 16KB cache, it has two 8KB caches—one for data and the other for instructions. This change helps the cache serve its main purpose of keeping significant information readily at hand, thus reducing the number of main memory accesses that are needed. That helps performance, because each main memory access makes the CPU wait, instead of it being able to sail along processing at its full speed. Internally, however, the Pentium (and all the more recent x86 CPUs from Intel) moves data around and processes it in 32-bit chunks. The principal exception to this is that the floating-point unit handles 64-bit chunks.

As with every other member of this family, the Pentium supports all the instructions of every previous *x86* processor, and it sports a few new ones all its own. But the most significant fact about the Pentium is simply that it can run significantly faster than any 486.

A major reason for the increased speed is that in addition to using a somewhat faster clock frequency so that it executes more instructions per second in each internal part, it also can process two instructions at a time. Actually, it can process two integer instructions simultaneously, but only one floating-point instruction at a time. This is accomplished by having two integer processing units (each very much like the corresponding parts of a 486) and one floating-point execution unit (which is an improved version of the one in the 486).

Technical Note: Overlapping the execution of separate instructions is an extension of an earlier idea called *pipelining*. In pipelining, the various stages of performing an instruction are broken up, with dedicated circuitry on the chip doing each instruction. The chip is designed so that while one section is executing an instruction, another section is gathering the data to be processed by the next instruction, and a third is figuring out (decoding) what is to be done to perform the instruction after that.

In a way, pipelining is similar to an assembly line or an automated car wash. When some local group assembles a group of volunteers to raise money by washing cars, the cars usually are washed one at a time. However, automated car wash machines can do several cars at once. While one is being rinsed, another is being washed, yet another is dried or waxed, and so forth. It is a production line. The time it takes to wash any one car remains about the same, but more cars can pass through the automated car wash each hour than can be washed by a single team of people working on one car at a time.

Intel's CPU designs have incorporated pipelining, in varying degrees, almost from the very beginning. The extent and sophistication of the pipelining has, however, been greatly increased with each succeeding generation. And now, with what amounts to multiple assembly lines in parallel, each is fed from a set of preprocessors that decode instructions and gather data. Then, through feeding a set of postprocessors that put the processed data back into memory, the Pentium raised the performance that is possible much more than you would expect if you only looked at the clock speed.

The Pentium shows what is called a *super-scalar* increase in performance over the 486. With the early members of the *x*86 family, Intel increased speed mostly by making each new CPU chip perform better than its predecessors. But with the Pentium, the major speed improvements could be attributed to something else—in this case, the doubling up of the integer execution units. (In general, any time you encounter the term *super-scalar,* you can assume that it refers to having multiple, parallel execution engines of one or another sort, and probably more of them than in previous models.)

Improving a Good Thing—The Pentium Pro and Pentium MMX

Intel's next two steps in the development of the *x*86 family were the Pentium Pro and the Pentium MMX. The former was a module that incorporated both a slightly improved Pentium and a separate chip that held the Level 2 (L2) cache memory. The latter was simply a Pentium with a few added instructions (and, because time had passed and more transistors could now be incorporated on the chip, some additional RAM to enlarge the on-board L1 cache).

Each of these improvements (L2 cache located physically inside the CPU module and augmentation of the *x*86 instruction set) has had some very significant echoes, both in later Intel *x*86 designs and in the offerings from the clone x86 CPU makers. I cover each of these innovations in more detail in later sections of this chapter, after I introduce the remaining members of Intel's *x*86 family.

The Pentium Pro also introduced a variation on pipelining, called *speculative execution* or, as Intel prefers to call it, *Dynamic Execution*. This feature enables the logic pieces inside the CPU to keep busy more of the time. If there is nothing to be done with the instructions that would normally come next (for example, because they involve some data that must be fetched from main memory), the logic unit will pick out a future instruction whose data is already on hand and figure out what the result of that instruction would be. That result is held in reserve, and if that instruction actually gets to be executed with the anticipated data, the result is instantly made available. Otherwise, that result is discarded and the logic unit's efforts are wasted. Then again, that unit couldn't have been doing anything more useful, so nothing really is lost.

Although instructions are often executed out of order, their results are always made available to subsequent instructions only in the originally specified order. That makes this process work transparently; the programmer and the user don't need to be concerned with how the CPU acts as though it is working more quickly—they simply will notice that it does.

Technical Note: The utility of speculative execution depends on several things. First, most of the time, most computer programs execute the instructions that are held in successive memory addresses one after the other, in the same order in which they are held in memory. But every once in awhile, the program will *jump* (also called *branch*) to another location in memory to get the next instruction to be executed.

Speculative execution works well for sequential instructions. It also can work well for a branch instruction, but only if the execution unit is clever enough to guess correctly which way the branch will go (or can work on both branches simultaneously—which would, of course, mean that more execution units would have to have been idle). The decision of which branch will be followed ultimately depends on the results of some calculation or comparison. Because the execution unit cannot know in advance how the branch calculation is going to come out, it must guess. CPU designers spend a lot of time trying to figure out clever ways of doing this guessing in order to maximize the percentage of the time that their chosen process will guess correctly.

This works well enough that speculative execution almost always gives some performance benefit. This benefit can be much enhanced if the programs being processed are of a special sort. The most recent versions of PC operating systems support a concept known as *threads*. This is the idea that you can sometimes divide up the work in a program into several related, yet at least partially independent tasks. Each of those tasks is called a thread or a *process*.

Now the programmer writes code to cause the processor to perform the work of each thread. The compiler does what it can to interleave these threads so that they will proceed in parallel. Now, if the CPU picks up a number of instructions out of main memory, it may be able to schedule the instructions for one thread to go through one execution unit and those for the other thread to go through the second execution unit. Because of the relative independence of the two processes, there is likely to be almost no time when the instructions that have been executed in this fashion will turn out to have been "wasted."

Achieving this clever routing of instructions through the two parallel execution units in the Pentium requires careful coordination between the programmer and the compiler (which must be specially designed to do this sort of optimization), and it also takes a good deal of luck. It won't work all the time. But if it works even a good fraction of the time, that will translate to a significant increase in performance.

Finally, the subunit in the CPU that handles information going in and out on the bus that connects the CPU to the system board has been modified to give priority to information being fetched from the external memory over information being sent out. Intel explains that its simulations show that this prioritizing of memory accesses speeds up the overall working of the system more than any other method it has tried.

Pentium II

In the middle of 1996, Intel brought out its next *x*86 family member, the Pentium II. Effectively, the Pentium II is a Pentium Pro with some slight tweaks to its design to enable it to handle 16-bit programs more speedily, plus the MMX technology. Thus, it combines the best of both the Pentium MMX and the Pentium Pro. (However, it goes backward in one minor, yet significant way. The L2 cache in the Pentium II operates at half the clock speed of the CPU, rather than at the same speed, as was the case for the Pentium Pro.)

What was really new about the Pentium II was how it was packaged and how it connected to the motherboard. Beginning with the 386, Intel had been packaging its *x*86 CPU chips in square, thin, black ceramic wafers with an array of gold-plated pins sticking out of the bottom. Those pins were then inserted into a socket on the motherboard.

Every new generation of *x*86 processor came in a larger package and needed more pins than any of its predecessors. Intel kept designing new sockets to accept them, and it labeled those socket designs with sequential numbers. By the time we got to the final Pentium releases, the socket was called Intel's Socket 7. But Intel has departed from that, putting the Pentium II into a much larger module with an edge connector that fits into what Intel termed its Slot 1 CPU connector.

These new Pentium II CPU modules were given the name Single Edge Contact Cartridge (SECC). Essentially, they are a box surrounding a printed circuit card with an edge connector. That printed circuit card carries, in the case of the Pentium II, the CPU chip, the L2 cache memory chip, and a few other components (such as bypass capacitors) that are necessary to make it all work well.

Figure 7.2 shows the SECC from the side and from below. You cannot see the innards very clearly here, but you can at least get a sense of the construction. Also shown here is the Slot 1 connector viewed from straight above. You can see how the Pentium II fits into the Slot 1 end rails (the "retention mechanism," in Intel speak) in Figures 4.4 and 4.5 in the section "A Platform to Build Upon: The Motherboard" in Chapter 4, "Understanding Your PC's Parts."

FIGURE 7.2

Intel introduced its new Single Edge Contact Cartridge (SECC) packaging for the Pentium II and the Slot 1 connector into which it fits.

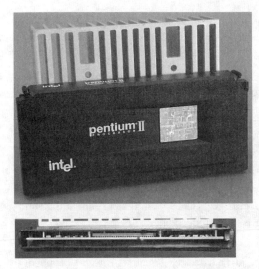

The Pentium II Xeon Series

In addition to introducing new Pentium II models with ever higher clock speed, Intel also brought out a minor variation on the theme that it termed the Xeon series. This was one step in its plan to divide up the PC marketplace into server, workstation, desktop, budget, and mobile segments, and to offer products for each with features chosen to appeal especially to that segment.

The Pentium II Xeons are essentially Pentium II processors with even more L2 cache memory included in the CPU module (and, more importantly, with that L2 cache running at the full CPU clock speed), and with some other minor features added to facilitate multiprocessing (using more than one CPU in a single PC) and enterprise system management.

The Pentium II Xeons are packaged in a slightly different SECC module, and they fit into a different socket that Intel named its Slot 2. Since then it has renamed the Slot 1 to simply SC-242 (242-pin slot connector) and the Slot 2 to SC-330 (330-pin slot connector).

One of the key differences in the Slot 2 (or SC-330) connector design is that the edge connectors are stacked in a three-high pattern, rather than the two-high pattern used on the Slot 1 (SC-242) connectors and the AGP connector. (You can see the difference between a one-high and two-high pattern of edge connector contacts in Figure 13.5 in the section "What Does the Image Painting On the Screen and How?" in Chapter 13, "Seeing the Results: PC Displays.")

The Pentium III series

The latest member of Intel's x86 family is the Pentium III (which was known widely in the industry prior to its release by its internal name, Katmai.) This is in many ways not a very new design at all. It merely updates the Pentium II design. There are both "regular" Pentium III and Pentium III Xeon models being offered at various clock speeds and with various amounts of L2 cache, up to a rather stunning 2MB at the high end.

The only real news about the Pentium III design is its inclusion of some new registers and a new set of instructions that expand on what MMX added. These new instructions are called the Streaming SIMD Enhancements (SSE), formerly referred to as the Katmai New Instructions (KNI). I explain them in some detail in the section "Growing the x86 Instruction Set—MMX, 3DNow!, and SSE," later in this chapter.

Attacking the Low-End Market—Intel's Celeron Models

As the number of PCs sold each year grew, and Intel's sales grew along with it, Intel decided to segment that market. The Pentium II and Pentium II Xeon product lines are one example. Another is the introduction of a lower-cost version of the Pentium called the Celeron.

This product is, in fact, just a repackaged Pentium II with a couple of feature differences. First, these CPUs are designed to work only with a 66MHz front-side bus, rather than the 100MHz front-side bus supported by the "full" Pentium IIs and Pentium II Xeon processors. Second, the initial Celeron models (which worked at clock frequencies of 266 and 300MHz) came with no L2 cache built into the CPU module. Finally, these processors are shipped on circuit boards without a surrounding housing that fit into a Slot 1 socket, just as the housed Pentium II modules do. This new packaging is termed the Single Edge Processor Package (SEPP), in contrast to the Pentium II's Single Edge Contact Cartridge (SECC).

That last step, making the packaging cheaper to manufacture (and ending up with something that also looks considerably less expensive) was important, because Intel was now facing very serious competition from AMD, in particular, for the low-end of the PC CPU market. Even with the omission of the L2 cache and reducing the packaging costs, Intel could not lower prices quite far enough to effectively counter AMD's pricing. As a result, Intel's market share has plummeted to an unprecedented less-than-a-majority of all sales in this segment.

Also contributing to Intel's poor sales showing was the very poor computing performance of the initial Celeron models, compared to their competition. This mainly was caused by the omission of the L2 memory cache in the CPU module and the failure to provide that cache on the motherboard.

Intel rectified this error in later Celeron models (starting with one that also ran at 300MHz, but which was termed the A version, and others running at clock speeds ranging from 333MHz up to—so far—a top speed of 433MHz). These models included a 128KB L2 cache, which is smaller than the Pentium II cache, but which works even better because it is located on the same chip with the CPU and thus works at the full CPU clock speed. In effect, Intel upgraded these Celerons to be nearly as good as the Pentium

II Xeon chips—the only significant shortcoming is in their limitation to a 66MHz front-side bus.

Intel also went back to a socketed design for the Celeron. The newest Celerons come in a package that looks exactly like the original Pentium, but with more pins. The socket these new Celerons fit into, now termed Intel's Socket 370, is very much like the earlier Socket 7, with (of course) more holes into which those pins can go. A Socket 7 accepts 321 pins; a Socket 370 accepts 370, which is just what the Celeron package has. Figure 7.3 shows a Pentium MMX and a new Celeron chip side-by-side from the top and the bottom. (You'll see a Socket 7 in Figure 7.4, later in this chapter.)

FIGURE 7.3

Intel's older Pentium MMX chip and its latest Celeron chip share a common package design, except that the Celeron has 370 pins and thus requires a Socket 370 (which is a modified Socket 7 with 370 holes for pins).

The real significance of Intel's decisions with these new Celerons is likely to be felt when even newer CPU chips are produced. Most likely they also will have the L2 cache on the CPU chip and therefore will not need the large, expensive SECC packaging. They may come in an SEPP version for backward compatibility with motherboards that have a Slot 1 or Slot 2 connector, but they also will very likely come in a Socket 370–compatible design as well. Eventually, all the Intel CPUs seem destined to return to a socketed design. (Third-party vendors already offer SEPP boards with Socket 370 sockets on them to enable use of the PPGA chips with Slot 1 motherboards.) The only likely exception to this future is trend that Intel might retain the SECC design to package multiple CPUs per modules for use in high-end servers.

More RAM Can Be Accessed Now—But When Will Anyone Use It?

Intel very quietly made one other architectural change to the x86 design, which was introduced with the Pentium Pro and has appeared in every Pentium II and III model since then. This is a change that may eventually have a great deal of impact, but which for now is almost going unnoticed. I am referring to the expansion of the memory address space from 4GB (which is the most for which a 32-bit memory address can serve) to 64GB (requiring 36-bit memory addresses). We can be glad Intel was planning ahead, but until people need that much RAM and operating system designers incorporate support for the larger memory address numbers, this will remain just another arcane fact about these CPU chips.

Growing the *x*86 Instruction Set—MMX, 3DNow!, and SSE

Until very recently, Intel did all the innovating in the x86 architecture. A couple of years ago, it decided to add a new group of instructions to the machine language understood by its processors. Because these 57 new instructions were designed to enhance performance in multimedia applications, they were termed the Multimedia Extensions to the x86 instruction set, or the MMX instructions for short.

Intel based this innovation on the observation that in many cases a program needs to do the same calculation to a number of data values, essentially in parallel. For example, it may need to multiply all of them by a constant. Instead of loading each one into a register, doing the multiplication, and then storing the answers in memory, with the new instructions it is possible to load several of those data items side-by-side into a larger (wider) register and then do a common action on all of them at once.

All of Intel's *x*86 processors from the 486 on have included a set of very wide (80-bit) floating-point processors. The MMX instructions are merely additions to the microcode inside the control unit that enables a new use for those existing registers. This new use is for what are termed SIMD (Single Instruction, Multiple Data) operations. The only kinds of data that can be used with the MMX instructions are integer values, which may be 8, 16, or 32 bits wide. The MMX instructions use just 64 bits of the 80 bits in the floating-point registers to store anywhere from 2 to 8 data values, depending on their size.

Naturally, because the same registers are being used for MMX and floating-point calculations, they cannot be used for both of those purposes at the same time. Anytime the program comes to an MMX instruction, it must save the floating-point register contents and block any floating-point calculations until it finishes with the MMX operations.

Intel's MMX instructions were originally proprietary, but this did not last long. The only way that customers would value the new MMX instructions would be if software developers decided to enhance their programs to use them. The best way to make that happen was to let every *x*86 clone CPU maker use them as well.

AMD originally did this with its first K6 processors. Then, it decided that instead of merely copying Intel's MMX instruction set enhancement, it would do something different and better. So it added some more registers to its *x*86 clone CPUs and added even more new instructions with the overall label 3DNow!—referring to the fact that its set of enhancements were particularly valuable for games and other programs that did a lot of 3D graphics calculations. Most particularly, AMD's 3DNow! instructions support floating-point as well as integer operations on multiple data elements in parallel.

Furthermore, AMD got Microsoft to support the 3DNow! instructions at the operating system level in Windows 9*x* and Windows NT. This means that the 3DNow! instructions help improve performance even for programs that are unaware of their existence.

Cyrix toyed with doing its own set of enhancements, but soon decided the best approach was to adopt AMD's. IDT also decided to support 3DNow! in its WinChip series of CPUs.

Finally, though, all the clone x86 vendors (AMD, Cyrix, IDT, and Rise) decided that they had to support both MMX and 3DNow! if they were going to be able to compete. So now, the only *x*86 CPUs being made that don't support both MMX and 3DNow! are Intel's.

But Intel was not resting. It was hard at work developing an answer to the 3DNow! initiative. As mentioned previously, its response came in the form of what were first termed the Katmai New Instructions (KNI)—now called the Streaming SIMD Extensions(SSE)—a set of enhanced SIMD operations supported in the new Pentium III and Pentium III Xeon CPUs.

The SSE enhancement to the MMX technology comes in two ways. First, Intel has added some new registers specifically for the use of these instructions. This is similar to, yet different from, what AMD did with its 3DNow! instructions and new registers. Second, the SSE instructions now work on both integer and floating-point numbers—just as the 3DNow! instructions have all along.

Presumably, soon there will be support for the SSE enhancements included in many of the major software programs, including both game packages and business applications. Microsoft will probably add support for them in its operating systems, too. When (or if) that happens, at least for its Pentium III family of CPU chips, Intel will have regained parity with its competitors on the SIMD front.

Perhaps the most important observation in all of this is that Intel no longer "owns" the *x*86 design totally. It still makes most of the x86 CPU chips, but now any vendor may propose innovations and, if they are good enough, other x86 vendors will accept them and software makers will support them. In that fashion, they will become an integral part of the ever-evolving x86 architecture.

Intel's Dual Independent Bus (DIB)

I have mentioned several times that Intel put the L2 cache for the Pentium Pro, Pentium II, Pentium II Xeon, Pentium III, and Pentium III Xeon processors on a separate chip housed inside the CPU module. I want to talk a little bit more about why this is so significant, and about how the future seems likely to play out in this connection.

First, the inclusion of the L2 cache in the CPU module enables those memory chips to run much faster. Instead of being clocked at a front-side bus speed of 66, 100, or soon 133MHz, they can run at the full clock speed of the CPU (or in some models, half that fast). Because the clock speeds in these processors can be up to 550MHz, these L2 caches are running much faster than the front-side bus.

> **Technical Note:** All the Intel processors that fit into its Slot 1 (SC-242) connector run the L2 cache at half the processor speed and use industry-standard SRAM chips for that L2 cache. All Intel processors that fit into the Slot 2 (SC-330) connector run the L2 cache at the full processor speed and use Intel-designed and Intel-built SRAM chips for the L2 cache. The newest processors (the ones that fit into the Socket 370) have the L2 cache on the CPU chip, running at the full CPU clock speed. Of course, that RAM clearly is manufactured by Intel in the process of making those CPU chips.

Furthermore, these CPU-module–included L2 memory chips are accessed independently from the front-side bus. That is, the CPU can be "talking" over the front-side bus to the Northbridge chip and at the same time over this new back-side bus to the L2 cache. This overlap of two independent conversations further increases the overall speed of the CPU.

After very quietly introducing this feature in the Pentium Pro, Intel has been trumpeting it as a highly significant innovation termed the Dual Independent Bus (DIB).

In the latest Celeron products, Intel has moved the L2 cache onto the CPU chip itself. This has become possible because the relentless advances in microminiaturization now permit putting many more transistors on the same size chip than would fit there even one year ago.

Intel's competitors, in particular AMD and Cyrix, have also benefited from the same advances in integrated circuit fabrication technology. They now can put their L2 memory caches on their CPU chips as well.

The biggest difference is that, while Intel has eliminated the external memory cache on its newest motherboards, AMD, Cyrix, and the rest of Intel's competitors are using Super7 motherboards with external cache memory on them. That used to serve as the L2 cache; now it can serve as L3 cache memory instead.

Until they can put even more cache memory on the CPU chips, external cache will be valuable. I expect to see Intel either go back to using external cache memory on the motherboard (running at the front-side bus speed) or include L3 cache chips inside its CPU modules—perhaps on SEPP boards, or more likely in a package similar to that used for the Pentium Pro.

Note: Finally, a word on jargon: The levels of memory cache are about to be renumbered. What is on the CPU chip and closest to the CPU (and which used to be termed L1 cache) will soon become L0 cache memory—at least if AMD has its way. The also on-chip, now L2 cache will become L1, and thus the external cache will be able to be referred to once more as L2 cache memory. Are you confused by this? It's just a kind of marketing shell game, designed not to confuse people with a new "L3" designation for that external cache or at least not the people who never bother to learn about the changes to the cache memory inside the CPU modules.

A Further Complication (CPU Steppings and Other Submodel Variations)

In all the preceding sections, I have glossed over one very important point. Since the beginning of the time covered so far in this chapter, whenever Intel introduced a new and improved processor—at least if the improvements were major—it would give that new processor a new model number. Usually, many months or even several years would go by between each of these introductions. This is no longer the case.

All along, Intel has, from time to time, improved its CPU designs in minor ways. These improvements might be likened to reprintings of a book, with the major revisions corresponding to new editions. Just as publishers often use the opportunity of a new printing to correct typographic and other minor errors in a book, so does Intel use these revisions of the masks used to "print" the integrated circuits to make corrections (and other integrated circuit manufacturers do this as well). These corrections to its manufacturing process improve performance or remove some of the bugs in its chip designs. These iterations are called *chip steppings*. To really know what the capabilities and limitations of your CPU are, you must know not only its model number, but also from which step it was made.

Now the situation gets even muddier. Intel lately has been marketing new processor submodels. For the most part, these involve different clock speeds at which they operate. However, some also involve different packages (such as the tape-bond chips and mobile modules that are sold to notebook computer makers) or other variations in the way the chip is packaged or how it operates.

I have described each of the major generations of the *x*86 family, with a focus on the most recent ones, which are the only generations that still are being built into new PCs. A complete list of even all the members of just Intel's *x*86 family would have many times this many entries, however. Fortunately, a typical user normally can ignore the subtle details of the submodels' differences. You'll learn some of the unique qualities of the chips used in portable computers in Part VI, "PCs Are Frequent Flyers, Too."

Others Yet to Come

We can be sure of one thing in this industry: The pace of change is relentless. More and better is always on the way. We'll surely see several more generations of CPUs from Intel before the end of the century.

What might we expect these later CPUs to offer that today's don't? For one thing, more speed. That is almost a given. They also will include a lot more processing power, and come in more varieties.

Finally, look for future chips to include even more self-test circuitry. This is essential, because already they are too complex to be tested fully by any external test machine.

What If It Isn't Intel Inside?

A few times so far in this chapter—and then only briefly—I've mentioned all the other makers of CPU chips for PCs besides Intel. That is mostly because Intel has a lion's share of the market.

But this isn't the full picture. There are alternatives to having an Intel processor inside your PC, and some of them make very good sense.

Another reason I have emphasized the Intel designs is because they exemplify most of the industry's trends. When you understand all that Intel has to offer, you'll find yourself well prepared to evaluate where the competition's offerings fit. (Recently the clone x86 makers have innovated in significant ways, but these innovations are easily understood in terms of what Intel did previously or what Intel has done since then in response.)

When you are number two (or three or four or five) in a market dominated by the number-one supplier, one of your main tools for convincing people to buy your product is to offer a lower price for the same quality and quantity of goods. This is nicely exemplified by the clone processor market.

Until very recently, the most successful clone CPU chip makers limited themselves to making cheaper or faster versions of what were essentially Intel design-equivalent chips. The details of the designs for these chips differed enough from Intel's to avoid patent or copyright infringement, but the basic philosophy behind their design was the same. However, in their latest designs we have the option of choosing from some truly new, alternative CPU designs that are still fully compatible with Intel's x86 CPUs.

Advanced Micro Devices (AMD)

Advanced Micro Devices (AMD), Intel's primary second-source supplier for its earlier x86 chips, has offered faster, yet cheaper and fully compatible CPU chips for many years. Its 386 designs were essentially identical to Intel's. The AMD 486SX was different but arguably a better design than Intel's, and it certainly ran faster and cost a lot less. AMD's next offering, the AM5x86, used a 486-like 32-bit I/O bus, but had an instruction set that more nearly resembled that of the Pentium. This began the real departure from the Intel x86 standard to one of AMD's own devising.

AMD's next design, called the K5, was a fully functional equivalent to the Pentium. It followed this with the K6, which used a radically new architecture that resulted in an improvement over Intel's Pentium Pro and Pentium II designs. However, manufacturing difficulties kept AMD from taking full advantage of those design superiorities.

AMD has since released two upgrades to the K6: the K6-2 and, most recently, the, K6-III. (The latter's name is reminiscent of Intel's Pentium III, which is surely no accident.) AMD claims that the K6-III will match the Pentium III in all important ways.

> **Technical Note:** One subtle change that AMD has made to the x86 architecture is that the registers in its K6 family of CPUs can be reassigned on-the-fly. This means that instead of transferring a number from one register to another, which could take an entire clock cycle, an instruction can simply rename that register and then reference it as if it were the newly named register. This enables some important speed gains, especially when you're doing speculative execution, where the results of alternative paths through the program could be simultaneously calculated and deposited in different registers, and then the appropriate one is used when the branch instruction comparison is complete. There are many other ways in which AMD's design differs from Intel's. You can learn more by accessing AMD's Web site, which I list at the end of the section "It's an Increasingly RISC-y Business," later in this chapter.

One very obvious difference between the K6 (and K6-2 and K6-III) and the Pentium II and III is that AMD's chips all fit into a standard Socket 7. Well, to get full performance from them, you need what is now termed a Super7 motherboard, which I discuss in the next section. This was necessary because Intel wouldn't permit AMD to license its Slot 1 connector design, and it also is a very popular choice because the motherboard makers knew how to make good, inexpensive Socket 7 motherboards. With only slight changes, they could adapt that design to the needs of the AMD K6.

A significant development in terms of market penetration is that Compaq (who makes more PCs than any other single manufacturer), Gateway, and some other PC OEMs (Original Equipment Manufacturers) have agreed to offer AMD CPUs as standard equipment in certain of their PC models. This means that many more AMD CPU chips are likely to be sold than was the case when the only markets were the independent PC consultants and small PC stores that built PCs from parts, plus the upgrade market.

AMD's next chip, the K7, is supposed to appear shortly after this book reaches bookstores in the middle of 1999. It is initially going to appear in a cartridge design similar to, Intel's SECC design. AMD's K7 will go into a proprietary slot connector it is calling Slot A. By early 2000, AMD plans to release K7 models in socketed form once more, most likely ones that will fit into Socket 370 motherboards.

The technical details of the K7 design are quite interesting and seem well beyond anything Intel has yet released. Still, because it is not yet an actual product, and we have no way of being sure that AMD will be able to manufacture it successfully, we can't anticipate how well it will do. What is most interesting about it is that, while most of AMD's market success to date has been at the very low end of the market (where the much lower prices of its CPUs have given it a distinct advantage over Intel), the K7 is clearly targeted at the high end of the market—the segment that Intel now holds most securely, and the one with the highest percentage of profit for the CPU vendor. If AMD succeeds in breaking into that market, it truly will have altered the PC CPU landscape in a very significant manner.

Super7 Motherboards

Intel felt that it needed to go to the proprietary Slot 1 for the Pentium II because of the need to support faster chip set features such as AGP and a faster front-side bus. AMD responded by tweaking the design of the then–industry-standard Socket 7 motherboard to include both of those features.

The resulting design was given the trademarked name Super7. AMD licensed this design to all the motherboard makers other than Intel, as well as making it available to the other clone x86 CPU makers. This is now the new industry-standard design for motherboards for all but the Intel x86 CPUs.

Intel has announced plans in the near future to increase the speed of the front-side bus on both its Slot 1 or Slot 2 motherboards and on its newest Socket 370 motherboards from 100MHz to 133MHz. The Super7 motherboard makers have already incorporated support for front-side bus speeds at least that high. And the SDRAM vendors are preparing DIMMs rated for that speed (to be called, naturally, PC 133 DIMMs).

The clone *x*86 portion of our industry (both the CPU and motherboard vendors) would like you to believe that its products are fully as good as Intel's. In many ways they clearly are. Still, some observers have declared Intel's motherboards to have better quality control. However, an Intel motherboard, not surprisingly, will work only with Intel CPUs. Not everyone agrees on the question of quality, but it is an issue you may wish to consider when evaluating your alternatives.

Cyrix, IBM, and Texas Instruments

The next most important Intel competitor, in terms of market share, is Cyrix. This company has developed a strong design team, and it has contracted with Texas Instruments and IBM Microelectronics for fabrication services. The IBM contract also lets IBM use Cyrix designs in the other CPU chips IBM makes under its own label. Recently National Semiconductor purchased Cyrix, but the Cyrix name still appears on the x86 CPU chips that National (Cyrix division) now sells.

Cyrix has two sixth-generation x86 products, and it now offers a seventh-generation one. One sixth-generation chip, the Cyrix 6x86, is comparable to the Pentium Pro. The other, the Cyrix 6x86MX, is comparable to the Pentium II. Both fit in a Socket 7 motherboard. The pinout of the 6x86 is identical to Intel's original Pentium (sometimes referred to as the P54C). Cyrix's 6x86MX has the same pinout as Intel's Pentium MMX (which is also known as the P55C). The seventh-generation offering from Cyrix is the M-II (pronounced *em-two*). The M-II is competitive with AMD's K6-2 or Intel's Pentium II.

> **Note:** Pinout, in case you were wondering, is jargon for which pins serve what function on an integrated circuit chip. Saying that two chips have the same pinout implies that either of them can be placed into a particular motherboard and, with perhaps some tweaks to the motherboard jumpers, each will function properly.

Reportedly, Cyrix is about to introduce yet another generation of *x*86 CPU chips (which it is calling the Jalepeno during its development). The rumors about this chip suggest that it also may compete well against the high-end Intel offerings. Of course, we'll have to await its appearance before that comparison can be properly evaluated.

The designs of these Cyrix chips differ significantly from both Intel's and AMD's designs. However, their performance is comparable. In practice, this means that each of the three companies' designs will be better for some tasks than its competitors and worse for others—but in all cases, they are quite comparable. For a typical end user, there shouldn't be much reason to prefer one over another, except of course for the price (and the less easily quantified matter of vendor support, because some vendors use only one manufacturer's CPUs in their systems). If you want to learn more about the details of how the Cyrix designs differ from Intel's and AMD's, you can get them at the Cyrix Web site, which I list later in this chapter.

Integrated Device Technology and Centaur Technology

Integrated Device Technology (IDT) has established itself as a major vendor of memory parts and other integrated circuits. A couple of years ago, it set up a wholly owned subsidiary called Centaur Technology to produce a line of WinChip microprocessors. The first product, the WinChip C6, is functionally a clone of Intel's Pentium MMX. However, it is a pure RISC design. (I explain that jargon term in some detail later in the section "It's an Increasingly RISC-y Business.") By innovating, IDT has made this chip much smaller than the Pentium, yet—for at least some uses—as fast and as powerful. Since then, it has brought out a WinChip 2 and is about to release a WinChip 4.

According to IDT's numbers, the WinChip 2 competes well with the Intel Pentium II, Celeron, AMD K6-2, and Cyrix M-II at similar clock rates. However, IDT has yet to make its chips work at clock rates as fast as its competitors. IDT says the WinChip 4 will use a new core design and will compete head-to-head with Pentium II or AMD K6-3, and will finally equal them in clock speed as well.

Most different about the IDT approach is its commitment to making very small die size chips. This enables IDT to make the chips less expensively, and they use far less power than their competition. By using very large on-chip L1 cache memory, plus very deep pipelines (11 stages versus 6 at most in the competition), they manage to get almost the same performance.

In testing, the WinChips are clearly the slowest of the competing *x86* designs—at least today—but they have equally clear advantages in size, cost, and power dissipation. If IDT's plans work out as it has announced them, the WinChip 4 may equal its competition in performance without giving up any of its other advantages. Clearly, this is one alternative vendor to watch.

Rise Technology

The newest of the *x86* clone CPU makers is Rise Technology. Its initial chip is called the mP6. It is not quite as fast as the best Pentium II chips, nor as cheap or small as the WinChip 2. But it gives a balanced value in terms of the ratio of performance to cost and power, as compared to the other x86 offerings on the market today.

The Rise mP6, at an initial clock speed of 200MHz and with a front-side bus speed of 100MHz, is targeted initially at entry-level desktop PCs and mobile PCs, where its power and cost advantages will be most appreciated and its slight performance drawbacks will be tolerable.

Figure 7.4 shows a Rise mP6 CPU chip in a Socket 7 on a Super7 motherboard from First International Computer (FIC). Also visible in this photograph are the two external L2 memory cache chips.

FIGURE 7.4
A Rise mP6 in a Socket 7 on a Super7 motherboard with 1MB of external cache memory.

The mP6 has no L2 cache on the chip, but when it is used in a Super 7 motherboard with 1MB of external (L2) cache, I have found that it performs comparably to the Intel Pentium II for many tasks.

Rise's next model will include L2 cache on the chip, which may enable Rise to become a contender at the higher end of the clone x86 CPU market. This, too, seems a company to watch.

Other Intel Competitors

This doesn't exhaust the list of Intel's competitors in the CPU market. Perhaps the most important three are these:

- The Apple-IBM-Motorola consortium that produces the PowerPC chips. These are not *x*86-compatible CPUs, although they can be made to emulate *x*86 chips through software. These chips are also the foundation for the PowerPC line of Macintosh computers.
- The DEC-Compaq Alpha family of processor chips, which, although not x86-compatible, are supported natively by a version of Windows NT. The Alpha chips are the speed demons of the PC world so far, running at higher clock speeds, performing floating-point math blazingly fast, and, when running Windows programs on native-alpha Windows NT, doing so at higher speeds than on any other Windows platform.
- TeraGen Corporation, which has not yet produced an actual product, but which has announced plans to create a flexible architecture processor chip that can act as if it has any of several CPU architectures, altering which one it seems to be on-the-fly, as a program dictates. This approach is not yet proven, but it is based on the RISC approach—which I'll discuss in detail next—and that approach certainly has borne some valuable fruit in the hands of the designers at AMD, Cyrix, IDT, and Rise.

Furthermore, there are several makers, Cyrix and IBM among them, that have announced plans to create PC-on-a-chip products. The Cyrix MediaGX is already on the market and has achieved some success as an embedded *x*86 solution for some information appliance designs.

Eventually, as these integrated solutions become more capable, they may threaten the traditional way of making a PC. After all, if you can get the CPU, the Northbridge and Southbridge chips, video controller, memory controller, storage controller, audio and modem functionality, and more in a single chip—just add some RAM, disk drives, and connectors for USB and IEEE 1394 devices, and you'll have a full PC— then what is to keep people buying Intel's CPU chips, or AMD's, or anyone else's?

It's an Increasingly RISC-y Business

The x86 processors "understand" (can execute) any of a very large set of instructions. Over 100 different instruction types exist, and most of them can accept modifiers, which essentially turn one instruction type into a family of instruction types. In all, a program can tell the processor to do literally several hundred different things. Some of these things are extremely simple; others are pretty complicated. (However, none of them is nearly as complicated as what is implicit in nearly any even moderately complicated human language sentence.)

You learned in Chapter 5, "How to Get Your PC to Understand You," that the individual instructions for the x86 processors vary in length from one to over a dozen bytes. The simplest actions are encoded in single-byte instructions. The most complex one, with all its modifiers, can stretch way out—to 20 bytes in an extreme case.

These characteristics are typical of what is referred to as a Complex Instruction Set Computing (CISC) machine. With each new generation of x86 processors, CISC computers are becoming more and more complex. Curiously, at the same time they also are becoming more and more like Reduced Instruction Set Computing (RISC) machines. RISC machines are characterized by a relatively meager set of individual instructions, all of which are exactly the same length.

For many years, there has been a debate in the computer science world about the relative merits of these two ways to design a processor. The resolution of that debate is turning out to be more of a merger than the declaration of a winner.

The RISC advocates point out that although this type of machine cannot do as many different things in one instruction, instructions can be decoded into logical unit operations more quickly because they are of a uniform size. On average, a RISC instruction takes fewer clock cycles to be executed than an average CISC instruction. In fact, RISC machines commonly can perform several of their instructions each clock cycle, whereas a CISC machine might take more than 100 clock cycles to perform a single particularly complex instruction.

CISC advocates have maintained that their favored processor design has two big advantages. First, they claim that programming a CISC processor is easier because it "understands" more of the things a programmer regards as elemental operations. Second, if it is built correctly, a CISC processor can do the overall tasks just as fast, or maybe even faster, than a comparable RISC machine, because its more complex instructions can encode the task with far fewer instructions.

There is some truth on both sides, of course. Ten or so years ago, all the very high-performance workstations used by engineers, programmers, and graphic artists were built around a RISC processor (or more than one). Now it is possible to buy a CISC-based PC that performs at the workstation level.

To get to this point, the makers of CISC processors have been incorporating in their designs many of the aspects of RISC design. In fact, the Intel Pentium was the first in the x86-compatible family to do so. In some cases (the AMD-K6 is just one example of this), the processor can break down the complex *x*86 instructions that the programmer thinks it uses into many smaller RISC instructions that are what its logical units actually execute. In effect, the RISC-based machine is built to emulate a CISC machine.

So even Intel, formerly the foremost producer of chips based on the CISC approach, has chosen to use the RISC approach at the microcode level to create what appears to programs to be a very fast CISC machine, but which works internally as a RISC one. (I discuss just what microcode is, and how it relates to the instructions a programmer actually uses, near the end of Chapter 2, "How (Almost) Any Computer Works," in the section "Two Ways Computer Designers Make Computer Programmers' Jobs Easier.")

Even in less extreme cases, the modern CISC processor uses concepts such as pipelining and speculative execution, which were first developed for RISC machines.

The picture gets more muddled when you learn that the newest development goes in a third direction, referred to as Very Long Instruction Word Computing (VLIWC). This concept has also been referred to by two other names. ILP stands for Instruction Level Parallelism and refers to specifying multiple actions within a single, typically very long "instruction word." This name has fallen into some disfavor of late, and Intel has therefore rechristened it EPIC (Explicitly Parallel Instruction Computing). By any name, the idea is to put many relatively simple instructions together into one long instruction and then build the processor so that it can process all of them at once. If it is done right, this can provide the best of both the RISC and the CISC approaches. Hewlett-Packard and Intel have been collaborating on their new Merced 64-bit processor design using this approach. The latest prediction is that we will be able to purchase this processor (also known as the first of Intel's IA-64 architecture CPUs) in mid-2000.

However, the bottom-line question for many of us is "Do I care?" My simple answer is "No." If the computer does what you want it to do, unless you are a heavy-duty programmer or a chip designer, you really don't care how it can accomplish its feats at this level—other than, perhaps, to satisfy your intellectual curiosity. It certainly isn't a reasonable basis for making a purchasing decision for most of us.

If you want to learn more about how your PC's CPU chip actually works at this level, you can find a good deal of information at the Web site of its manufacturer. Here are some URLs you might want to check:

```
http://www.intel.com/intel/product/index.htm
http://www.amd.com/
http://www.cyrix.com/
http://www.winchip.com/
http://www.rise.com/
```

Are More Brains Better than One?

Much of the thrust of processor development has focused on getting them to run faster. This has worked stupendously well. However, if you want a computer that goes faster than the fastest available processor can run, there is really only one way to accomplish this: Use more processors at once.

Multiprocessing, as this approach is termed, is nothing new. Mainframe computers did this decades ago. As PCs are becoming more capable and are being assigned to ever more complex tasks, it is becoming common to give some of them additional power in the same way.

This works, sometimes. But it isn't appropriate for all PC applications. Furthermore, in order for this approach to work, several things must be true. First, the individual processors must be designed in a way that permits them to cooperate with one another. The system design must support multiprocessing. Finally, both the operating system and the application programs must be rewritten to utilize this power.

This is a complex subject. I'll return to it in Chapter 25, "PCs That Think They're Mainframes: Multiprocessor PCs and Other Servers." For now, I just want to point out that this is one way in which speeding up a PC without having to speed up the processor itself is sometimes possible. Before leaving this discussion, I want to anticipate and clear up one possible confusion: This multiprocessing idea involves using several comparable CPU chips, each doing comparable work. It is completely independent of another idea that is used every day in all our PCs, namely having subprocessors dedicated to doing subtasks. That strategy is the subject of the next section.

Other Processors in Your PC

This entire chapter up to this point has focused on the CPU, which is, after all, the processor at the center of what your PC does. However, it is certainly not the only processor inside a typical PC.

In the distant past (about 20 or 30 years ago), if a designer wanted to design a subassembly for a complicated apparatus, and if that subassembly had to do some logical operations to perform its task, the designer would create a custom array of logic chips that did just the one thing needed for that subassembly's operation. This no longer is the best way to proceed. Now, it is much more common, and much cheaper, for a manufacturer to use an embedded processor. This is a processor that, in some other contexts, could do any of a wide variety of tasks, but in this particular context does just one because it has a single program built right into it.

Technical Note: There are still sometimes very good reasons to design and make custom Application-Specific Integrated Circuits (ASICs) to do these jobs. For example, if you can anticipate selling millions of them, you may save enough on the production of the ASICs to save more than their development cost. Another example is that an ASIC may be absolutely required If you cannot get sufficient performance from a more general-purpose processor plus an application-specific program. If you can get away with using a more general-purpose CPU, and if you aren't going to sell millions of them, clearly the preferable way to go now is not the ASIC approach.

Of course, if you aren't designing the systems that use these embedded processors, you won't have to make that choice. I'm only describing what is involved in that decision so you will understand why you will sometimes see ASICs and at other times see more familiar, older-generation CPU chips used as embedded processors.

One of these little embedded processors controls the keyboard for your PC. Another controls the floppy disk drives, and there is one on every hard disk. Yet another creates the video signals needed to put images on the monitor. Others control the PCI bus and the SCSI bus, as well as generating sounds or doing other specialized tasks.

For the most part, the processors used in these applications are not the same ones used as CPUs. But as some of those subtasks become more complicated, and as the earlier generations of CPU chips become less expensive, some of what were originally the CPU designs for PCs are finding a second life after they have become hopelessly too slow for CPU usage—as embedded controllers of peripheral PC subsystems.

I'm not going to go into a lot of detail about how any of these many dedicated embedded processors does its job. You will, however, see many of them mentioned in later chapters as I describe the subsystems they control.

Major and Minor Improvements

PC processors have improved in two ways: They have become faster, and they have become more complex.

The x86 chips made today run a lot faster than their predecessors. The first PC used a 5MHz clock frequency. Today's best machines run at better than 500MHz, with still faster ones promised very soon. The Pentium II, for example, is hugely more complex than the 8086. The Pentium II has nearly 7,500,000 transistors on the chip; the 8086 had only 29,000. But not every improvement is a major one. Some are valuable, yet only minor in nature.

The two biggest landmark events in the x86 family's history are certainly the introduction of virtual 86 mode and memory paging in the 386, and the development of the

Pentium chip with its dramatic changes in internal design and, accordingly, performance. Everything else pales by comparison.

For the PC user, this means that when software that exploited all the 386 could do became popular, any older CPU-based PC really was obsolete. Even today, you can run any of today's software you want on even the oldest 386-based PC, if only you have enough RAM installed (and not all 386 motherboards will let you do this), and provided you have enough patience. (Not many of us have enough patience, so the issue of being able to install enough RAM is mostly moot.)

When to Upgrade Your PC

That last discussion brings us to an important issue that every PC user must face sooner or later: "Should I upgrade my PC now?"

You can always find an article in a trade magazine that praises some newly improved PC as having the best performance or the greatest new features. That doesn't mean you must rush out and buy each new machine as soon as it comes on the market.

Most folks are well served by their PCs, even though they might be several years old. Remember, the trade press exists to sell magazines, and it does that by making each improvement sound like a revolution.

Two Rules of Thumb

For my money, the only important upgrades are ones that either give you some new functionality you really want or at least double the speed of your PC. For example, if you don't have a CD-ROM drive now, you probably must upgrade to a machine that does have one—or else add one to your present PC. If you are about to make this addition, you might prefer to get a DVD-ROM drive that can also read CDs. Every modern PC has a PCI bus, plus perhaps one or two ISA slots. If your present PC doesn't have a PCI bus, moving up to a new motherboard that does have PCI and new video and hard disk controller cards to take advantage of that new bus will certainly be beneficial.

Although reviewers love to measure performance and declare one PC "a clear winner" over the others because of its 10 percent greater speed, the truth is that most users won't notice anything less than about a doubling of speed, which is why I set this as my rough measure of when upgrading just to increase speed is worth it. (Exceptions exist, of course, particularly if the applications that are important to you are high-performance games. In that world, every little bit helps.)

Upgrading Versus Buying a New System

When you notice that you can get a truly significant increase either in functionality or speed, you must then decide whether to upgrade your existing PC or simply replace it with a newer, bigger, better model. That decision is often not an easy one.

One thing to look at is which pieces you must replace to get the functionality or performance you want. If you only must add an option card or plug in a new drive, you should upgrade. But if you must replace the processor, you usually also will want to replace the motherboard. And at that point you are getting pretty close to justifying the purchase of a whole new PC.

You often can move some of the pieces from your old PC into the new one and use them there. This is especially true for disk drives including removable media magnetic storage devices like ZIP drives, optical drives (CD-ROM or DVD), and so on, and it might be true for a PCI-bus video card or network interface card. It is often not true for an obsolete ISA-bus–based video card or a sound card. Today's systems often bundle in the video or sound circuitry, if not on the motherboard, then on an included option card, or they include a newer, more capable PCI-based version of that functionality. The old card you have might not function correctly with the new, faster PC.

For some practical advice on what to do with your old PC, refer to the Appendix of *Peter Norton's Complete Guide to PC Upgrades,* by Sams Publishing (ISBN: 0-672-31483-5).

How Your PC "Thinks"

Traditionally, the folks at IBM (and most computer scientists) have been extremely careful to make the point that computers don't think; only people do. Recently, even as IBM's Deep Blue computer beat Gary Kasparov at chess, the IBM representatives still insisted that Deep Blue didn't think; instead, it just computed the right moves to make. The members of Gary's team, on the other hand, often felt otherwise.

You might also believe at times that your PC "thinks." Well, it doesn't, at least according to the experts on the subject; but what it does often *looks like* thinking to most of us. This chapter introduces just what it *really* is that the PC does that so much resembles thinking.

What Is a Computer Architecture?

People who design computers often speak of the *architecture* of a given computer. What are they talking about? Isn't architecture something that applies to buildings but not to computers?

My dictionary says, as its third definition, that an *architect* is "the designer of anything." Its sixth definition of *architecture* is "the structure of anything." So, the architecture of a computer is just a fancy way of referring to how its parts are arranged and how they have been designed to work together.

In Chapter 2, "How (Almost) Any Computer Works," I showed you the basic components of a PC and explained how they work together to create a computing machine. Here, I want to go a bit deeper and tell you a little about how those parts are built and also how they are connected.

I am also going to take the opportunity to teach you some of the more important jargon that so litters this field. Knowing what the terms mean can make lots of things you read turn from apparent gibberish into something that is merely curiously obtuse, or—if you are very lucky (or work at it a bit)—into something that you actually understand.

It All Begins with the CPU

The core of any computer's design is its CPU. The designer of this chip ends up defining in many important ways what is possible for this computer. For example, the CPU has only so many pins on it. Their number, and their specific uses, define how much memory it can be connected to, what particular sorts of information manipulation it can perform, whether or not it responds to events outside itself when they occur, and so on.

The *x*86 CPU chips have many common features. It is that common set of features that defines the *x*86 architecture, and the PC architecture is a subset of the *x*86 architecture.

Details of the *x*86 CPU's Architecture

I could easily fill the rest of this book with arcane details about how the various *x*86 processors work. But if I did, your eyes would glaze over, and in any case you don't need to know all those things to get an accurate, even if general, notion of how the processors do their jobs. So, I am going to limit myself here to just an overview of the most important architectural features of these chips. I will, in this process, blur some of the lines between different parts of the CPU or lump several related parts together. This will let you see a unified picture that applies to all the members of the family more clearly than would be the case if I pointed out all the detailed ways in which the family members differ from one another.

> **Standards:** For the rest of this chapter, I will be referring many times to the *x*86 chip family members. By this designation I mean the Intel family of microprocessor, including the variety of Pentium models, but I also include any of the clone CPU chips that have been built by Intel's competitors, such as the AMD, National (Cyrix), IDT (Centaur), and Rise CPU chips I described in the previous chapter. For simplicity, I shall omit saying this each time it might apply. If your PC uses one of the clone chips, realize that what I am saying about the *x*86 chips probably also applies to the CPU chip in your PC. Where there are significant differences between the different brands, I will point them out.

The Bus Interface Unit

Pretend you are "visiting" the CPU. Your first impression will be a view from the outside, followed by what you see as you enter the "lobby." The actual CPU is connected to the outside world, in logical terms, by a portion of its internal circuitry we call the *bus interface unit*. This section "listens to" (monitors the voltage on) some of the pins, looking for input signals; "speaks to the outside world" (asserts a voltage) on some other pins; and for some pins can do either "listening" or "speaking," depending on the value of the voltage on yet another pin.

This section of the CPU is also responsible for *buffering* the input and output signals. This means that it contains amplifiers to make the output signals strong enough to be "heard" by any number of receiving circuits, up to some specified maximum. It also contains receivers capable of detecting the input signals while extracting very little power from their sources.

In some members of the *x*86 family, the bus interface unit also must translate voltage levels. In those chips, the external circuitry might operate from a 5-volt power supply, while the internal circuitry might be running on a 3.3-volt, or 2.5-volt power supply. This means that the valid voltage level to represent a binary 1 on any of the external pins is anything greater than about 2 volts, but on the corresponding internal connections the valid voltage level for a binary 1 is anything over about 1 volt. (In both cases, the level for a binary 0 is any voltage less than some threshold value that is very close to 0 volts.) The bus interface unit's receivers and output amplifiers are designed to accept and generate the valid voltage signals for each of its input and output connections, depending on whether they connect to the internal CPU circuits or to the outside world.

Note: The fact that the data signal receivers interpret any signal over one threshold as a binary 1 and any signal below another (lower) threshold as a binary 0 is the basis of the greatest virtue of all digital circuits: their capability of rejecting noise and thus carrying data through an unlimited number of processing circuits or making an unlimited number of copies—all with absolutely *no* loss of the information represented by these data.

In this context, the word *noise* means simply any inadvertent alteration of the signal voltage that may occur between the output of one circuit and the input to the next circuit. This could include some stray voltage that got transferred into the wire that carries the signal between the two circuits from some other, nearby wire (*crosstalk*), or a difference in the "ground" voltages to which the signal is compared by the sending and receiving circuits, or from any number of other sources.

In analog signal-handling circuits, any such noise that gets added to a signal simply gets carried along through each succeeding stage of signal processing. In digital signal-handling circuits, the noise gets canceled out and the signal regenerated to its nominal value within each stage.

As long as the noise alteration of the signal isn't large enough to confuse the receiving circuit as to whether that signal value was meant to be a 1 or a 0, this process will work perfectly. Conceivably, this process of perfect repair of digital signals might fail if the noise signals were simply too large. The job of the designers of these circuits and the larger circuits in which they are used is simply to ensure that this won't happen in any likely scenario for the use of their designs.

Finally, some members of the *x*86 family have internal clocks (occasionally known as the CPU's *frequency*) that run at some multiple of the external clock (also known as the *bus frequency*). The bus interface unit is also responsible for generating the internal clock from the external one, and for keeping information flowing into and out of the CPU in synchrony with both those clock frequencies.

Separating Instructions from Data

When the signals get inside the CPU, they must be routed to the correct internal parts. If you think of a CPU as analogous to an office, this job is that of the receptionist.

The incoming signals consist of a mixture of two kinds of information: instructions and data. (Think of orders for finished goods and raw material, if you prefer the factory analogy. Think of employees who do the office work and clients for whom they perform their services if you prefer the office analogy.)

Instructions are placed in a queue for the instruction decoder. ("Go over to Window 3 and wait in line, please.") Data, on the other hand, is parked in some waiting rooms, called *registers*. ("Follow me. Now, please wait in here. Someone will be with you shortly.")

Figuring Out What to Do and Making It Happen

The instructions are taken out of the queue, interpreted, and put to work by a group of parts called the *code prefetch unit*, the *instruction decoder*, and the *control unit*. I will refer to this collection of parts from here on simply as the *instruction handler*. This section of the CPU has several jobs to perform.

First, because the *x*86 processors are complex instruction-set computer (CISC) machines, their instructions come in a variety of lengths. The shortest is a single byte; the longest can consist of well over a dozen bytes.

The instruction handler examines the first byte and from what value it contains deduces how many bytes there are to this particular instruction. It must then make sure that the rest of the bytes of this instruction are ready for its further use, and if they are not, invoke the help of other sections of the CPU to go out to main memory and fetch them.

Next, the instruction handler must decide what data this instruction needs. Some instructions carry some or all of their data inside themselves. These are called *immediate* data items. Other instructions operate on data that is already present in one or more of the CPU registers. Yet others operate on, or return results to, locations outside the CPU in main memory. The instruction handler must ensure that the data items needed by this instruction are in place and ready to be operated on. If they are not, the instruction handler must arrange for them to be fetched into the CPU.

Finally, the instruction handler has the job of figuring out just what the instruction is telling the CPU to do and then activating the relevant parts of the CPU to get that job done. The simplest instructions correspond directly to some elementary task that some element of the CPU's circuitry can do. The more recent members of the *x*86 family have specialized circuitry dedicated to performing even some of the more complex instructions—if they are used often enough. This is done to make the CPU execute those instructions as fast as possible. In fact, most of the instructions an *x*86 processor understands require multiple actions by different parts of the computing machinery in the

CPU. The instruction decoder looks up these steps in an internal library called the *microcode store*. It then delivers those microinstructions to the relevant parts of the CPU for execution.

Registers Are Temporary Information-Holding Places

Registers are important in any processor. As I explained to you in Chapter 2, every computer—and a microprocessor such as an *x*86 processor, which is actually a full computer in its own right—must have some place to hold information while it is being processed.

The many different *x*86 family members have different numbers of registers and, in many cases, registers of different sizes. The original 8086 and 8088 designs include 14 registers, each capable of holding a single 16-bit number. The latest Pentium II has many more registers. Most of the Pentium II's registers hold 64-bit numbers; a few hold many more bits. (In the case of these largest registers [called *translation look-aside buffers*], only a portion of the bits it holds is visible to a program running on the CPU. The rest are hidden from the program's view, but are accessible to the CPU to help it do its job more quickly.)

One reason for the much larger number of registers in the most recent *x*86 family members is that they have gotten so complex that some special, extra registers were needed to facilitate automatic testing of the processor at the end of its production cycle—as the manufacturers attempt to make certain that their chips work before they leave their hands. Another reason is that these models include, in addition to the hardware needed to do the basic computing job they were designed to do, other hardware referred to as the *system management* hardware, which supports various special operations such as powering down to save power during times of inactivity.

To keep my story as simple as possible, I am going to focus at first just on the set of registers that were defined for the 8086. All the registers that were added in later members of the *x*86 family are similar to these, at least in concept. I will introduce some of those other registers when I discuss the functions that they serve. In the 8086 (and 8088), the 14 registers can be grouped into five categories. Here is a brief description of each category and the names of the corresponding registers.

General-Purpose Registers

Of the 8086's 14 registers, four are designated as general-purpose registers. These are used mainly for data values being processed. (That is, they can be added to, subtracted from, or multiplied by one another. They can be compared with one another, or a number in a general-purpose register can be combined with a number somewhere out in main memory. There are still other ways in which these data values can be processed.)

If the instruction being executed needs only 1 byte of data, that byte can reside in either half of a general-purpose register, and it can be accessed by that instruction without altering whatever byte value is in the other half of that register.

These registers have simple names. These names are used within statements in what is called assembly language programming as a way to refer to particular registers. (See Chapter 18, "Understanding How Humans Instruct PCs," for an explanation of this and the other special "languages" used in computer programming.) The names we use were defined by Intel, and they are based—in turn—on the names of the smaller, single-byte–wide registers in Intel's 8080 generation of CPU chips—a generation that immediately preceded the first of the x86 family.

When a program refers to registers that are being used to hold 16-bit numbers, the names of the most commonly used registers are AX, BX, CX, and DX. (The older generation CPU chips had A, B, C, and D registers—each able to hold only a single byte. You may think of X in this context as standing for *extended*.) When you want to refer to just one-half of one of these 16-bit registers, the lower half is called AL, BL, CL, or DL. The upper half is referred to as AH, BH, CH, or DH.

In more recent members of the x86 family of CPUs, there are a number of wider registers, and these often carry very similar names, such as EAX or EBX, meaning simply something twice as wide as the AX or BX register. Here, a letter (A, B, C, and so forth) is used alone to refer to a byte-wide (8-bit) register; that letter followed by an X means a double-byte-wide (16-bit) register. If that letter is followed by either an L or H, it refers to the lower or upper half of that register, and if the letter is followed by an X and preceded by an E, it refers to a 4-byte–wide (32-bit) register with much the same purpose as the similarly named, narrower one.

Technical Note: You might think that these names were chosen just because they are the first four letters of our alphabet. That might be so, but they also have mnemonic value. (That is, they have longer names that are suggested by these short ones.) These four registers, despite being called general-purpose, have some restrictions on their use and also some customary uses. Here are the details.

The AX (or AH plus AL) register is most often used as the *accumulator*—the place where the result of some calculation ends up. For example, you can add the value in some other register or in a memory location to the value in the A register, and the result will wind up replacing the value originally in the A register.

The BX register is often used to hold the segment portion of an address. When it is used for this, you may think of it as the *base* register, because the segment address value indicates the beginning (or base) of a region of memory. The BX register (or BL or BH) may also be used to hold data of other sorts.

The CX register is normally used to hold a number that indicates how many times some operation has been done. When that number reaches a specified target value, the program must jump to a different place in the program. Only if the *count* of operations that have been performed so far is held in this particular register is it possible to do the necessary comparison and jump in a single instruction.

The DX register (or DH and DL) commonly is called the *data* register. It sometimes is used to hold a port address. Other times, it is used in combination with AX to hold a 32-bit number (for example, the result of multiplying two 16-bit numbers).

The Flags Register

One very special register is called the *flags register*. (Its mnemonic name is, quite simply, FLAGS.) This is a place that holds a collection of 16 individual bits, each of which indicates some fact. One of the simplest examples of a flag bit's meaning is the one that indicates whether the last comparison of 2 bytes found that they were or were not equal. Other flags indicate whether the result of the last arithmetic operation was positive or negative, whether it was zero, or whether it overflowed the capacity of the register. Still other flags indicate something about the state of the processor. Examples of this include the following: Is the processor supposed to respond to or ignore external interrupts? Is it supposed to run in single-step mode? When processing a string of bytes, is it working its way "up" the string or "down" the string?

Because the more recent members of the *x*86 family have wider registers for both data and flags, they are able to represent even more conditions by flags.

Generally, the values of these flags control the behavior of the CPU when it is executing what we term "conditional instructions." (I'll explain this concept more fully later in this chapter.)

The Instruction Pointer

Another special register holds the address in main memory of the instruction currently being executed. Its name, of course, is the *instruction pointer* register (and it is given the designation IP). The value in this register *implies* the location in main memory where the instruction being executed is held; to get the actual location, you must combine this value in a suitable fashion with a value in another register, called a *code segment register*. (You'll learn more about code segment registers later in this chapter when I cover segment registers as a class.)

The value that is held in the instruction register gets changed in one of two ways: One we refer to as the *normal flow* of control and the other as a *branch*.

The Normal Flow of Control

Unless the instruction being executed causes something different to happen, the value in this register, sometimes called the *Program Counter,* is automatically increased by the length of the current instruction each time an instruction is completed. This is done because in most cases the next instruction to be executed is held in main memory right after the current instruction. The complexity of needing to push the pointer up a variable amount comes from the fact that the *x*86 processors are CISC devices, with variable-length instructions. One of the implications of this is that they must handle instructions of different lengths. This variability makes it necessary to be able to push the pointer by alterable amounts.

Branch Instructions

About 10 percent of the time this is not true. In those cases, the current instruction might tell the CPU to fetch its next instruction from some other location. These instructions are called branch instructions, or *jump* instructions, and they come in two types: *unconditional branch* instructions, in which the next location is always different from the normal flow of control, and *conditional branch* instructions, which decide whether to jump to a new location or fall through to the next instruction after this one. These instructions usually base their decision on the value of one of the flag bits. Figure 8.1 shows both the normal flow of control for a program and also both kinds of branch in a graphical manner.

FIGURE 8.1

The normal flow of control and how branch instructions sometimes alter that flow.

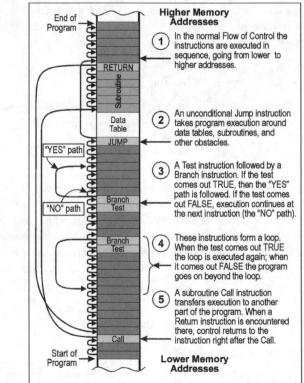

① In the normal Flow of Control the instructions are executed in sequence, going from lower to higher addresses.

② An unconditional Jump instruction takes program execution around data tables, subroutines, and other obstacles.

③ A Test instruction followed by a Branch instruction. If the test comes out TRUE, then the "YES" path is followed. If the test comes out FALSE, execution continues at the next instruction (the "NO" path).

④ These instructions form a loop. When the test comes out TRUE the loop is executed again; when it comes out FALSE the program goes on beyond the loop.

⑤ A subroutine Call instruction transfers execution to another part of the program. When a Return instruction is encountered there, control returns to the instruction right after the Call.

Subroutine Calls

One other way that the flow of control often gets altered is by execution of a subroutine call instruction. This is a way of effectively pausing the program execution briefly and instead invoking another program (or more accurately, a miniprogram that has been embedded in some other place within this program). When that miniprogram is finished with its task, it will execute a return instruction. That will cause the processor to resume execution of the original program at the instruction immediately after the subroutine call instruction.

This strategy of calling a subroutine is one of the ways programmers save themselves work. They can write a subroutine once and then use it from many places within their larger program, without having to copy all the instructions that make up that subroutine into the main program at each place it is going to be used. (Besides saving programmer effort, this also keeps the overall program size down, which can be another significant benefit in some situations.) I'll explain about some other ways programmers save themselves work in Chapter 18.

Other Pointer Registers

Two more of the original 8086's 14 registers are also pointer registers. One is called the *base pointer register* (BP); the other is called the *stack pointer register* (SP). Each of them holds a number that is used as the segment portion of an address if the processor is running in real mode. In protected mode, that number is called a selector, but it serves a similar function. Either way, it is used to point to a region of memory that is used for a stack. I'll explain just what that means later in this chapter.

Index Registers

Two of the registers were designed for use in moving strings of data (many-byte sequences of arbitrary length). One called the *source index register* (SI) might hold the address of the beginning of a string you want to move, for example. The other register in this class, called the *destination index register* (DI), holds the address to which that string will be moved. The number of bytes to be moved is usually held in the CX (Count) register. In addition to their use in moving entire strings of data, these registers can also be used to indicate a location within an array of numerical data or in a number of other ways.

Segment Registers

Finally, the last class is the *segment registers*. In the 8086 there are four of these. These are very special-purpose registers used only in performing address calculations. Later, in the section called "Calculating Addresses," I explain about some of the different ways in which the values in these registers get used in address calculations. Right now, I simply want to tell you the names of the different registers and describe what types of addresses might be pointed to by use of their values.

The first is the *code segment register* (CS). CS holds a value that is combined with the value in the instruction register to point to the next instruction to be executed.

The next register is the *data segment register* (DS). Normally, DS is used to point to a region of memory in which data values are being held. It can be combined with a number in the BX, SI, or DI registers, for example, to specify a particular byte or word of data.

The third register is called the *extra segment register* (ES). It is, as its name suggests, simply an extra segment register provided for whatever purpose the programmer wants, although it most naturally gets used in connection with string operations.

The last register is called the *stack segment register* (SS). The value in this register is combined with the value in the stack pointer (SP) register to point to the word of data currently being processed in the stack (more on the stack later). The SS register can also be used in combination with the BP register for certain instructions.

Calculating Addresses

I mentioned in discussing the instruction pointer (IP) register that the value it contains, taken alone, doesn't indicate where in memory the instruction it points to is located. Every time an *x*86 processor wants to refer to memory, whether to retrieve an instruction or to get or put some data item there, it must go through a more-or-less complex process involving at least two register values to decide where it must go. And often (in protected mode), the CPU must not only use those values from two (or more) registers, it must also access up to three different data tables in memory before it knows what actual, physical memory address is implied.

Going from Abstraction to Reality

There are several reasons for the complexity of address calculations in an *x*86 processor. Perhaps the most fundamental reason is that these processors deal in several different kinds of memory address space.

At the physical level (what actually happens to real, physical objects in your PC), memory locations are addressed by voltages on wires that connect to each memory module or chip. These signals are derived from the voltages on corresponding pins of the CPU. If you look at the voltages on those CPU pins, labeling the ones that are high as 1s and the others as 0s, the binary number you get is what we refer to as the *physical address*.

What Addresses Do Programs Use?

PC programs don't use physical addresses. The *x*86 family of processors doesn't enable them to. Instead, they must use at least one level of indirection. The actual physical address is generated by combining two or more numbers according to one of several strategies. Because of this complexity, you will run across the terms *logical address* (also known as the *virtual address*), *linear address*, and *physical address*. I'll explain each one of these concepts in the following sections.

Technical Note: Some of those CPU address pins have their signals directly routed to the memory modules. (They pass through some other integrated circuits that amplify them, but they go straight through those amplifiers and are not mixed with other signals in the process.)

Others of the CPU address pin signals get combined in circuits called *memory address decoders* whose job it is to decide which, if any, of the different memory chips or modules your PC has should be activated just now. All of those modules (or chips) get all the other signals, and the active module (or chip) uses them to decide which location within itself to access.

Figure 8.2 shows this relationship schematically. In this diagram, I am assuming a PC with just two 32MB modules, each with 64 data lines. This is not as much memory as I use in my PC nor is it what I recommend for yours, necessarily, but it simplifies this diagram. I trust you can imagine readily enough how to extend the figure to allow for a larger number of memory modules, or for ones that hold more than 32MB each.

The CPU, with its 64 data wires, connects to 8 bytes of memory at a time. This means that the three least-significant bits of any address may be ignored in pointing to locations in main memory. They are used only internally by the CPU to decide which of the 8 bytes that it just read is the one it wants to begin working with. Recalling that 2^3 is 8 and 2^{25} is about 32 million, you can see that we need exactly 22 wires (25 − 3) to address each 8-byte location within each 32MB memory module. Furthermore, it is possible (and usual) to make the address pins on the memory modules serve double duty. At one instant they read a row address and at a different instant a column address. That enables the module makers to get away with, in this case, just 11 address pins, plus 1 pin to indicate whether these address lines were reading the first 11 bits of the address (lines A3 through A13) or the remaining 6 bits (A14 through A24). (I have shown all 22 address wires going from CPU to memory modules, even though only half that number of actual wires are used, to make the diagram a bit easier to understand.)

The signal lines on the memory modules labeled *chip enable* are used to turn the integrated circuits in this module on or off. The voltage on this line will either make the module responsive to signals on the rest of its input lines, or make the module go into a sort of stasis in which it ignores all its other inputs and creates no output signals.

The memory address decoder gets all the rest of the address lines—in this case seven lines (A25 through 31). That is enough bits to point to any of 128 different "banks" of memory. This hypothetical computer, however, has only two banks. With 32MB in each bank, that is enough to run almost any one of today's programs (but it certainly is not enough memory to run more than one of the largest of today's programs at once). The memory address decoder must examine the signals on all seven lines in order not to activate those memory modules unless all of those lines except the first one have zero-level signals on them. The level on the first one is then used to decide which of the two memory banks to activate.

FIGURE 8.2
*How the CPU's
physical address
lines are connect-
ed to the banks of
memory modules
in a hypothetical
Pentium-based PC
with 64MB of
memory consisting
of two 32MB
banks.*

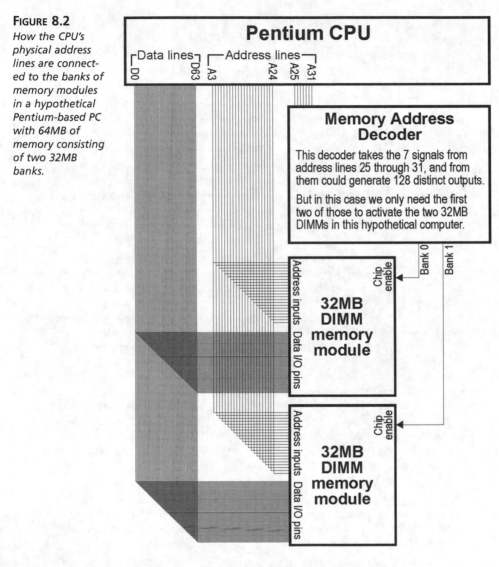

FIGURE 8.2
How the CPU's physical address lines are connected to the banks of memory modules in a hypothetical Pentium-based PC with 64MB of memory consisting of two 32MB banks.

Calculating Physical Addresses in Real Mode

You have already met the simplest of the *x*86 strategies for computing a memory address. In Chapter 6, "Enhancing Your Understanding by Exploring and Tinkering," I told you that memory addresses in real mode are expressed in programs as logical addresses, each of which is composed of a segment value and an offset. Figure 6.2 shows how those two 16-bit numbers are combined to generate one 20-bit number (or in some cases the result might be a 21-bit number) that points to the actual address in physical memory.

To repeat what I said, the segment value is multiplied by 16 (in hexadecimal that means simply shoved to the left one space) and then added to the offset value to get the physical address value. There are 65,536 possible values for the segment number and an equal number of possibilities for the offset. This means that a particular value for the segment portion of the address indicates a particular 64KB region of memory. The offset value indicates a particular one of those locations. The upper portion of Figure 8.3, later in this chapter, shows this algorithm.

Technical Note: An important point to realize is that in real mode there are many different logical addresses (by which I mean a pair of 16-bit numbers, one for segment and one for offset) that point to each physical memory address. If I simply increase the segment value by 1 and decrease the offset value by 16, the physical address remains unchanged. Thus, the logical address 01A0:4C67h is exactly the same as the logical address 01A1:4C57h. (I have put the lowercase letter *h* behind each address to remind you that these are hexadecimal numbers.) Normally, just having two four-digit numbers connected by a colon implies this, but I want to make this point very clear. That should also make it clear to you that the offset value 4C57h is exactly 16 less than the offset value 4C67h, because the two numbers differ by only one in the "sixteens" place. As you will learn shortly, in what we term *protected mode,* there can be even more logical addresses all pointing to the same physical address. (If you are a bit foggy about hexadecimal numbers, please refresh your understanding by looking in Chapter 3, "Understanding Bits, Nybbles, and Bytes.")

Calculating Physical Addresses in Protected Mode

All but the earliest members of the *x*86 family of processors have more than one mode in which they can operate. They all "wake up" in real mode, and in that mode they use exactly the strategy just described for calculating physical addresses.

After several special and necessary data tables have been built in memory, it is possible for any member of the *x*86 family more advanced than the 80186 to go into some version of protected-mode operation. In these modes (and there are three), the numbers held in the segment registers are not simply multiplied and added to the offset value to point to a memory location. The use of the numbers in the segment registers in any of the protected modes is so different from their use in real mode that we use a different name to refer to those values. They now are called *selectors* instead of segment values.

Unlike a segment value, which points to a particular 64KB region of memory, a selector just points to one line in a data structure called a *descriptor table.* That line contains three different facts about the "selected" memory region. One of them points to the beginning of the region. Another says how long that region is. The last "fact" is really a bunch of numbers that indicate certain special properties (called *access rights*) that region of memory has when it is accessed via that selector value.

The name *segment* still refers to the region of memory pointed to by a particular value in the segment register. But because the process for getting from the selector value to the segment position in memory address space is more convoluted, it is no longer appropriate to use the same name for both.

There are three advantages to this strategy. First, we can have any selector value point to any region of memory we want. (No longer is there any necessary connection between the regions of memory specified by two selector values that differ by some fixed amount.) The second advantage is that the size of the segment referred to by a selector value is not fixed. It can be as short, in some cases, as 1 byte or, in certain other cases, as long as 4GB. Finally, the presence of the access rights in the descriptor table allows the CPU to control the kinds of access to this region of memory that will be permitted when it is accessed via this selector.

The name *logical address* is still attached to the combination of two hexadecimal numbers separated by a colon. The first one (which is always 2 bytes—which is to say, 4 hexadecimal characters—long) is now called the *selector* instead of the segment; the second one (which may be either 4 or 8 bytes long) is still called the *offset,* and indeed it still means the number of bytes into the segment from its beginning, wherever that may be. Figure 8.3 shows the contrast between how one gets from a real-mode logical address to the corresponding physical address in real mode and in protected mode.

I told you there were three different versions of protected mode. The first version was introduced with the 286, so it is called *286-protected mode*. The second and third were introduced with the 386 and they are called *386-protected mode* and *virtual 86 mode*.

The only differences between 286-protected mode (which still is supported on even the latest *x*86 processors, for reasons of backward compatibility) and 386-protected mode (which is what is used almost all the time in modern programs) is merely the size of some of the numbers stored in the descriptors, and as a consequence, the possible size of the memory regions these descriptors "describe" and the number of different access rights that can be specified for those regions. In Figure 8.3, the shaded portion of the descriptor table is filled with zeros in 286-protected mode; in 386-protected mode, it contains meaningful (non-zero) numbers.

Calculating Physical Addresses in Virtual 86 Mode

Virtual 86 mode is a strange sort of beast. In this mode, which is always used in conjunction with 386-protected mode, the running program thinks it is running on an 8086 processor in real mode, while in fact the processor is in protected mode, and the operating system is running in 386-protected mode and serving a role described as a *virtual 86 monitor*.

Figure 8.3

From a logical (a selector:offset pair of numbers) address to a linear address in real mode versus in protected mode.

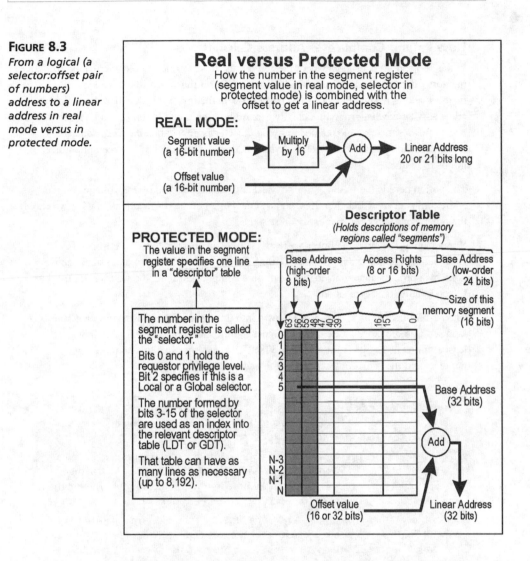

Figure 8.3

From a logical (a selector:offset pair of numbers) address to a linear address in real mode versus in protected mode.

The advantage of this mode of CPU operation is that it enables you to run old DOS programs that were written to run in real mode, while having the advantages of protected mode. (I'll describe a bit of what those advantages are in the next section.) Furthermore, it enables you to run several such programs, each in its own DOS box, without any of them knowing that the others exist. This is what is done when you run an old DOS application in a window (which could be a full-screen window) under Windows 3.*x*, Windows 9*x*, or Windows NT, for example. (Booting in MS-DOS mode allows running the PC in real mode, which is possible in all versions of Windows except NT.)

How Paging Complicates Address Calculations

In the 386 and all later members of the *x*86 family, there is one more complication to memory address calculations. It is called *paging*, and it introduces the third kind of memory address. The selector value combined with the offset is still called the logical address. That is what programs actually use. Adding the offset to the base address in the line of the descriptor table pointed to by the selector is now called the *linear address*. In the 80286, that was the same as the physical address. In the later *x*86 processors, it need not be the same.

The notion here is the following: A physical address is specified by the voltages on the address pins of the CPU chip. It is one of some large number of locations in what we call the processor's *physical memory address space*.

When paging is in use, the linear address is simply an abstract location in some hypothetical memory address space. Getting from a linear address to a physical one is done by a process analogous to, but a bit more complicated than, the way we got from a selector value to a segment address.

The 32-bit linear address gets broken down into three parts. The most significant 10 bits are used as a directory index. The next most significant 10 bits are the table index. The least significant 12 bits are used as the offset. The relationship between these three numbers and the actual physical address is indicated in Figure 8.4.

> **Note:** You're probably used to hearing about *paging* referring to paging to disk. This means that there's not enough physical RAM to contain all the code and data that the computer needs for every application.
>
> By utilizing the processor's operation with an intelligent operating system such as Windows 95/98 or Windows NT, the same constructs that allow logical memory used by a process to be mapped anywhere in physical memory allow memory to be loaded and unloaded from portions of the hard disks on your PC.
>
> This allows more programs to run at one time than there is physical RAM to run them. That's why operating systems that support paging to disk are often called *virtual memory operating systems*—because they can use virtual memory as well as real physical memory.

Enforcing Protections

The name *protected mode* is suggestive. Something is being protected somehow. But what and how? The whole reason for protected mode is to facilitate good multitasking. In any multitasking system (think of a Windows machine running several programs at once), several programs might each think it is the only program in existence, and yet they all are able to run together in the same PC without interfering with one another. Or at least, that is the intention.

FIGURE 8.4

From a linear address to a physical address when paging is active.

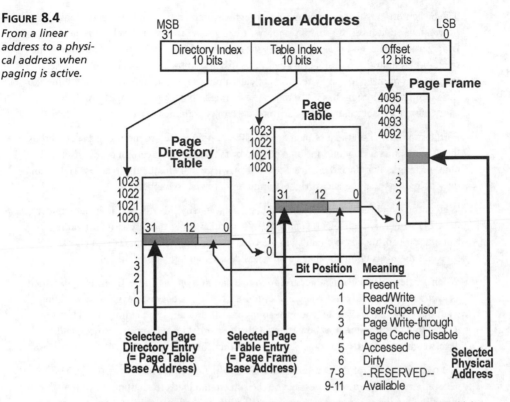

The number in the CPU control register 3 (CR3), rounded down to a multiple of 4K (1000h), points to physical address of base of Page Directory Table.

A Page Directory entry, rounded down the a multiple of 4K, points to the physical address of the base of a Page Table.

A Page Table entry, rounded down to a multiple of 4K, plus the offset (12-least significant bits of linear address) points to an actual physical address.

The "dirty" bit is only meaningful in the Page Table entries. The "page write-through" and "page cache disable" bits aren't used in a 386 CPU.

For this to work, it is necessary for something to keep the various programs from conflicting. Some master program must be in charge. That master program is the operating system (for example, Windows).

That is not enough, however. When an operating system launches an application on a PC, in real mode, the application program can do anything it likes. It can read or write to any portion of memory, can send information out any port, or write all over the screen. There is no certain way for the operating system to prevent this. That is why Intel devised the various protected modes for its *x*86 processors. The idea was not new; it was a direct borrowing from mainframe computer experience (as was the notion of paging), but this was the first time it was applied at the microcomputer level.

The basic notion is that each program is assigned some protection level, and it only can do whatever that level of program is allowed to do. There are four levels of protection, from zero to three, and programs are assigned to one of these four rings. The core of the operating system gets to run at ring zero, and usually, in protected mode only that set of programs is allowed to run there. All application programs normally run in ring three. So far, no operating system has made much use of rings one or two, but they are there in every *x*86 processor, just waiting for some clever programmer to find a use for them.

Furthermore, each segment of memory (recall that now those are the regions specified by the contents of various lines in some descriptor tables) is given certain access rights. Only programs that have the correct level of privilege can change those access rights, and only operations that the access rights permit are allowed to happen.

Who enforces all these rules? The CPU does. That is why this discussion is here, under the CPU's internal architecture, and why in particular under the discussion of address calculations, for the same circuitry in the CPU that computes addresses also checks to be sure that the instruction about to be executed doesn't violate any of the rules.

When a rule violation occurs, it is referred to as an *exception*. These are further classified as *faults, traps,* and *aborts*. When any of these exceptions occurs, the CPU stops doing what the program says to do, and instead it goes off and does something else. (Just how it does this is very similar to how it responds to external or software interrupts, and I describe the mechanism in some detail later in this chapter.)

The most infamous of the exceptions is a *General Protection Fault (of type 13)*. This generally results in an error message on the screen and leads to shutting down the offending application program. You might think that Windows crashes a lot. It does, but not nearly as much as it would without the hardware support that is built into every *x*86 processor for protection enforcement.

> **Technical Note:** This discussion is not complete. I haven't told you about the differences between the global descriptor table (GDT) and the local descriptor table (LDT), nor about the Task State Segment (TSS) and Input-Output Permission Level (IOPL) data structures. Those details are not vital to your general understanding of how the CPU functions and to describe them really *would* make your eyes glaze over.

The Arithmetic-Logic Unit (ALU) and Its Kin

It is convenient, at the level of understanding I'm trying to give you, to lump together another collection of logical subparts of the CPU. These include the Arithmetic-Logic Unit (ALU), and some other portions that do similar things. The ALU is the part that actually adds, subtracts, multiplies, or divides integer values. It also can compare two numbers to determine whether they are identical and, if not, to decide which one is larger.

Some Simple Integer Operations

Besides simple arithmetic (adding, subtracting, multiplying, and dividing) and performing logical comparisons, the ALU can also shift the bits around in a number in any of several different ways. Think of the contents of a 16-bit register as 16 individual bits (think of tiny people) sitting on 16 chairs in a row. The first kind of shift, called an *arithmetic shift*, just makes each bit get up and move one place to the right or left; the end bit that finds itself without a place to "sit down" simply is lost (and a 0 bit is moved in at the opposite end of the register).

Another kind of shift, called a *circular shift*, takes the bit that falls out of one end and stuffs it back in the opposite end. This type of bit shifting comes in very handy when multiplying numbers, and also for certain logic operations. Trust me: Programmers often find this capability vital for their programs.

Dedicated Hardware for More Complex Tasks

I have now told you about all the important elements of an early *x*86 CPU. Later models mostly just have faster (and sometimes more) of these same units. But they also have a few other, specialized hardware units to do some additional tasks.

Floating-Point Operations

Starting with the 486DX, a separate set of circuits is included in every *x*86 CPU to process floating-point numbers. This additional hardware consists of two parts. One is a set of eight very wide (80-bit) registers that are specifically designed to hold floating-point numbers. The other is the set of logic gates (and the special microcode instructions that activate them) that are arranged to do the actual floating-point arithmetic.

The floating-point instructions were added to the instruction set well before the hardware to execute them became a part of the CPU. At first, the CPU would trap those instructions and invoke a special "emulation" program to perform those tasks; later, the CPU would trap them and pass them off to a subsidiary "numeric co-processor" chip. Finally, it was given the power to execute those instructions directly within itself.

Enhancements to the *x*86 Instruction Set: MMX, 3Dnow!, and KNI

The addition of paging and the additional protected modes in the 386 were truly revolutionary. The *x*86 instruction set was augmented with a whole raft of new instructions to take advantage of this new functionality. All later additions to the hardware have had a much less profound impact on the instruction set.

Up until very recently, all the further additions to the *x*86 instruction set (for example, those for the 486 and early Pentium and Pentium Pro) CPUs were only minor tweaks on the previous set. But in the past couple of years, there were two significant new developments in the *x*86 instruction set—and we are looking forward to another, similar improvement scheduled to make its debut in 1999. Interestingly, while some of these additions to the *x*86 instruction set were introduced by Intel, others appeared first in clone *x*86 processors—showing the growing confidence of the clone CPU makers that their customers would respect them for new models that were "better" than Intel's, and not merely cheaper.

The first of these improvements was the addition of the so-called "multimedia extensions." Intel gave these the shorthand name MMX. These are a group of *single instruction, multiple data* (SIMD) instructions. The idea is that in a Pentium MMX, Pentium II, or any later Intel *x*86 processor, you can load *multiple integer* data items into the registers normally used for floating-point computation and then perform some operation on all of those data items simultaneously.

Specifically, an MMX instruction can use 64 of the 80 bits in a floating-point register to hold eight byte-wide numbers, or four 16-bit numbers, or two 32-bit numbers, and then it can act on all of them at once (for example, adding each one to the corresponding number stored in another of the floating-point registers).

This can be quite powerful. In many multimedia programs and certain kinds of business programs, precisely this sort of repetition of the same action on multiple, related data items is required. With MMX capabilities, these jobs can be speeded up very significantly. Examples include digital signal processing (for example, a "Windows modem" program) and certain kinds of two-dimensional graphics processing (for example, "texture mapping").

One inconvenience to all this is that one cannot be using the floating-point registers to do floating-point and MMX calculations at the same time. (Ordinarily, in almost any modern *x*86 processor, there are integer-instruction processing units and a floating-point unit working in parallel to speed the overall processing of your programs.)

AMD worked out a variation on this idea that they called 3DNow!. This involves both an augmentation of the *x*86 instruction set with some SIMD instructions performed in the floating-point registers, just like MMX, but now including ones for both integer and floating-point operations and some alterations to the actual registers to allow for more parallelism of computation. The particular instructions included in the 3DNow! set were chosen, as the name suggests, to speed calculation of 3D images, and also to speed the computations involved in advanced sound and video presentations.

All the recent CPU chips from AMD, Cyrix (a division of National Semiconductor), and Centaur (a division of IDT) include support for both 3DNow! and MMX.

Intel had to respond to 3DNow!, and rather than merely include what might be regarded as "me-too" support for that technology, they decided to enhance the MMX capabilities in future Intel *x*86 CPUs. At first called MMX2, this initiative is now referred to as the *Pentium III New Instructions* (KNI), getting its name from the code name for the CPU model in which Intel will first debut these new instructions and the associated new internal CPU hardware.

KNI refers to improvements in three aspects of the CPU design: new instructions, new registers, and new ways to control accesses to memory.

The new SIMD instructions now include floating-point as well as integer operations. The instructions use some new, dedicated registers which are even wider than the old floating-point registers. This allows working with 128 bits (which could be eight double-byte integer values, or four single-precision floating-point values) at once. Furthermore, the new instructions include some things programmers told Intel they wanted, such as the ability to do averaging with rounding down (used in video decompression for motion compensation), summing absolute differences (used in video encoding for motion estimation), and some other instructions proven useful in speech recognition applications.

All previous x86 processors would first fetch an instruction, then execute it, and finally store the results. It was not possible to begin fetching a new instruction until the storing of the previous instructions' results was underway.

The new "streaming memory architecture" is a strategy incorporated into the Pentium III processor that permits a programmer to specify the fetching of several instructions in advance of their execution, then have them executed, and finally store all the results as soon as possible, but without holding up the execution of additional instructions. This helps keeps the CPU from waiting for the delivery of data or instructions to or from memory. And that boosts overall CPU performance.

The advantages of all these new instructions accrue only to programs that are written to take advantage of them. The same thing applied to the floating-point hardware enhancements when they were new. Only programs that are aware of these processor enhancements, and have been redesigned to use them, will run faster. And only certain kinds of programs benefit from that sort of redesign.

In time, many programs have come to use the floating-point hardware. Running these programs on a 486SX- or 386-based PC, which doesn't have the floating-point hardware built in, is horribly painful! The programs must invoke emulation programs to accomplish the effect of the missing special-purpose hardware, and those emulation programs are always tremendously slow compared to the dedicated hardware.

Even though MMX technology has been out for more than a year, it is still not used extensively in commercial programs other than games. The 3DNow! instructions are better supported, at least for Windows users, because Microsoft has included extensive use of them in the latest version of its DirectX driver program. Any program that uses the DirectX API to activate the hardware will benefit from this whenever that program is run on a CPU with 3DNow! support.

Presumably, Microsoft will support the KNI instructions equally in future releases of their driver and other system software. If so, and if the memory streaming architecture delivers the benefits Intel offers, their Pentium III CPU may leapfrog the competition once more. We can certainly hope so, for all our sakes.

The Level 1 Cache

There is one more key functional group in the CPU: cache memory. Some version of this idea has been an integral part of all Intel and clone *x*86 CPUs starting with the 486.

> **Technical Note:** Actually, a form of caching (for addresses) was used even earlier in the translation look-aside buffers (TLBs) in the 386—and that form is also present in all later members of the *x*86 family. However, this caching is mostly hidden from view in a way that the data and instruction caching I am speaking about here is not.

The reason a memory cache makes sense is that modern CPUs are so very fast they can easily outrun the speed of main memory. So, by putting a small amount of very fast memory—fast enough that it can keep up with the CPU—actually inside the CPU (on the same integrated circuit chip), that cache memory can be used and reused as a temporary holding place for data and instructions on their way into the CPU and for results on their way back out to main memory. (Cache memory is also exceptionally expensive, because of its speed, which is why the two memory types—cache and main—coexist.)

This so-called *Level 1 cache* boosts performance in two ways. The first is when writes from the CPU to main memory are cached. The other way applies when reads are cached.

When information is to be written to main memory, the cache can accept that information and then let the CPU get on with its work immediately. The cache controller circuitry is then responsible for seeing that this information is later transferred to its proper place in main memory.

The second way a cache can speed things up is when the information in a given memory location is read by the CPU more than once. The first time there is no speedup. The second time (and any later times) the CPU asks for that same location's value, if that value is still in the cache memory, the cache controller can serve it up almost instantaneously.

The principal limitation on the effectiveness of cache memory comes from the fact that it is only a tiny fraction of the size of main memory. So only some small fraction of the most recently accessed locations in main memory will have their values still in the cache memory.

Memory Caching Didn't Always Make Sense

When PCs were new, building any cache memory into the CPU wouldn't have been worth it. That was true for two reasons. First, it adds complexity, and the manufacturing processes of the time could barely make chips complex enough to serve as CPUs. And second, those CPU chips ran so slowly that main memory could easily keep up with them. Now, however, the CPU chips can run several times as fast as the memory chips on even the fastest motherboards, and the needed additional complexity for at least a small amount of memory cache inside the CPU is easily affordable.

Careful study of actual everyday computer programs has shown that they very often reuse the same instructions, and even the same data items, over and over. They do so because it often is very helpful to the programmer to use loops in the program in which some task is done over and over until some desired result is achieved. If the loop is small enough that all its instructions and all the data referred to within the loop fit inside the cache memory, during the execution of that loop the CPU can run at its top speed without having to wait for a relatively slow access to main memory.

In any case, if the running program wants to write some information to memory, it can simply hand it off to the cache unit and then continue its work. The cache unit will take care of getting that information to main memory eventually, as soon as the much slower external circuitry allows it to do so.

Making Cache Memory More Effective

A small pool of cache memory can be organized and utilized in several ways. Each of these techniques has different implications, both for how expensive the cache memory is to build and for how effective it is in operation.

Naturally, a lot of jargon is used to describe all the variations. Some of the names you will run across include *read caching, read-ahead caching, write-through caching, deferred write and read caching, fully associative caches, direct mapped caches,* and *set associative caches*. The set associative caches also come in two-way, four-way, and other subdesignations. Finally, the latest wrinkle is to separate the cache into two pieces: one dedicated to caching instructions and the other dedicated to caching data.

You can be pretty sure that the CPU makers are building in what their research says is the most effective kind and amount of cache they can include and still permit them to make the chips using today's technology.

I'll return to memory caching in just a moment because it also shows up in the architecture that goes around the CPU. And that is my next topic. At that time, I will also mention how some of what used to be called *external cache memory* has been included inside the latest CPU designs.

The Architecture That Goes Around the CPU

At this point, you should have a pretty good idea of what the functional parts of the CPU are and how they work together. To complete this discussion of the PC architecture, you still need to examine how the external parts of the PC are arranged. The most important of these is main memory. The next most important are the input/output ports. Everything else communicates with the CPU via one of these two structures.

Memory

Main memory and the CPU are the places in a PC where all the computing action takes place. This is true because data and programs must be in some portion of the main memory before the CPU can do anything with them. Some of the programs and a little bit of data may live there perpetually. Most of them are just brought into that space when they are needed and then either discarded (in the case of programs) or saved to a permanent storage location (in the case of data), after which the memory space they had occupied is once more available to be used by new programs and data.

Main memory in a PC is a mixture of RAM, ROM, and vacant potentiality. That is, your PC's CPU chip can address a physical memory address space of fixed size. At some of the locations in that space are random-access, read-or-write memory chips (RAM). At some other locations are read-only (or read-mostly) memory chips (ROM or non-volatile RAM, called NVRAM). And (usually) for most of the memory address space, nothing is there.

This hasn't always been so. When PCs were new, memory was a lot more expensive per byte than it is now, but the early PCs couldn't address more than a total of 1MB. Many owners of these early PCs had their machine's memory address space at least filled mostly with RAM or ROM.

The Maximum Size of Physical Memory

Modern PCs can address *many* more memory locations. Starting with the 386, they could potentially use up to 4GB of memory, and the Pentium Pro and Pentium II chips can, in theory, use up to 64GB of memory. Even at today's relatively low cost for memory, I know of very few folks who are pushing those limits very closely—yet.

Modern members of the *x*86 processor family have two other address spaces, referred to as virtual (or logical) memory and linear memory. Linear memory address space is usually the same size as physical memory address space. The virtual memory address space, on the other hand, is enormously larger. I will explain just why this is so in Chapter 11, "Giving Your PC's CPU Enough Elbow Room—PC Memory."

The potential size of the CPU's physical memory address space is not the same as the maximum memory you can add to your PC, because PC makers don't connect all the address lines (either directly or via memory address decoders) to sockets. They don't need to, because none of their customers want to put in as much memory as the CPU can address. (Even if they did, no current operating systems could use all that memory. Windows, for example, in all its flavors is, except for Windows NT, limited to using a maximum of 2GB of memory.)

Level 2 (or Level 3) Cache

At the end of the discussion of the CPU architecture, I described the Level 1 (L1) memory cache that is included in all recent *x*86 family members. The idea of using a memory cache in a PC actually goes back even farther than the 486DX, which was the earliest of those L1-memory-cache–enabled *x*86 processors. When the CPU chips became significantly faster than the fastest reasonably affordable DRAM chips, people started to be interested in having some cache memory, but at that point it still wasn't feasible for the CPU makers to put it on their CPU chips.

The first PC implementations of this idea were on 386-based machines. The motherboard in these PCs included some additional, extra-high-speed (and extra costly) RAM chips, plus a specialized integrated circuit called a cache controller. For those PCs, this was the one and only memory cache it could have.

The size of this memory cache is mainly limited by how much money the motherboard maker thinks its customers want to spend for the performance gain which that much added memory will provide, rather than being limited, as the L1 cache is even today, by the amount of room and "spare" complexity available on the CPU chip. (The more cache the better, but after some point, the improvement in performance grows only slightly for even rather large additions to the size of the memory cache.) This meant that even when Intel and the other CPU makers started putting a small amount of cache RAM inside the CPU, motherboard makers found it helped their sales to include a second level of memory cache on the motherboard—provided that this Level 2 (L2) cache was considerably larger than the L1 cache inside the CPU.

A given amount of memory in an L2 cache is not nearly as effective as the same amount of L1 cache for the simple reason that the external clock frequency on modern CPUs is only a fraction of the internal clock frequency. Still, it can be a useful addition to a motherboard, because it normally can deliver data or accept data in a single clock cycle, and often the DRAM that makes up the bulk of main memory requires two or more clock cycles to do those same things.

Intel's latest CPUs, starting with the Pentium Pro, have had two chips in the CPU module. One is the CPU itself, with its L1 memory cache onboard. The other chip is separate, L2 memory cache. This cache is connected to the CPU by a different bus than the one that connects the CPU to the outside world. Intel refers to this as its Dual Independent Bus (DIB) architecture.

There are two advantages to this strategy. First, the fact that transactions with this L2 cache are not taking up bandwidth on the main CPU-to-system ("front-side") bus means that bus can carry other traffic. Second, the CPU-to-L2 bus can run as fast as the L2 cache can support, and that has been, in various models, either half or all of the CPU core speed (in either case, much faster than the front-side bus). In a current Xeon system, for example, you might have the Pentium II CPU and its L2 cache both running at 450MHz while the front-side bus runs at a "mere" 100MHz. (See the discussion in Chapter 7, "Understanding PC Processors," for the details of which Pentium models have full-speed L2 caches and which do not.)

Intel has announced plans to go one step further. In some upcoming CPU modules, they will incorporate both the L1 and L2 caches on the CPU chip and then put in an additional L3 cache on another chip in the CPU module. To minimize confusion (one must suppose), they also propose renumbering these memory caches so the smallest one, closest to the CPU, will be called L0 (Level Zero), the other, larger one on the CPU chip will be called L1, and the largest one (now probably several megabytes in size) co-located in the CPU module and connected via the DIB will be, once again, known as the L2 cache.

For those who want the ultimate in memory caching, a PC with a CPU module that incorporates both L1 and L2 memory caches could have a third level of caching (an L3 cache) on the motherboard. Each lower level of cache would be larger, in part to make up for its being slightly slower to access than the next higher level. The combination of all three levels of memory cache is the ultimate today in this technology.

The only way to buy that combination today is to get a so-called Super Socket 7 motherboard (which almost certainly will include some cache memory on the motherboard) and plug into it an AMD K6-3 processor with its L1 and L2 cache modules included in the CPU package.

Cache Coherency Problems

The whole notion of cache memory is that the local, small-but-fast memory contains an accurate copy of whatever is being held in some portion of the larger, more remote, slower main memory. This way, the CPU can deal with the cache copy as if it were the one in main memory.

That works well most of the time, but there are two situations in which it might not. First is if the information in the cache has not yet made its way to main memory before some other device in the PC attempts to read that information from its supposed location in main memory. The second case happens when the CPU wants to use some information from main memory but doesn't realize that because it was read into the cache, some other device has changed it out in main memory.

Every PC ever built, other than IBM's PC Jr., has had a feature called direct memory access, or DMA. (I'll explain more about why this can be wonderful—or not, depending on the particular kind of PC you have—in the section, "Why DMA Fell from Favor," later in this chapter.) DMA means having a specialized microcontroller that is capable of accepting a command from the CPU to move some data from one place in memory to another—or to or from an input/output port. The DMA microcontroller does this task while the CPU goes on about its business. Furthermore, large PCs that work as servers (and some particularly powerful desktop workstations) boast multiple CPUs, all sharing a common pool of main memory.

Either way, whether because you have multiple CPU chips or because your PC is using the DMA strategy (or perhaps some other "bus mastering" device such as a high-speed

SCSI host adapter), it is entirely possible that at times the contents of main memory will be changed by something other than the CPU's cache controller (or the motherboard L2 or L3 cache controller if your PC has one of those devices). Whenever this happens, a cache controller that is connected to this memory must know about this fact and at the minimum, it must "invalidate" the image of those memory values that it is holding in its cache memory until it can replace them with a freshly read copy of the new values.

The only way that this *cache coherency* can be maintained is for the cache controller that is connected directly to the main memory pool to watch every access to that pool by whatever other device may be doing it. This enables the cache controller to see whether any address that is being accessed is one that is currently being imaged in the cache memory this cache controller is managing. So, every cache controller is, in fact, built to do this sort of *bus snooping* to see who else might be writing to memory besides itself.

The other type of cache coherency problem that can arise is, in a way, more subtle. If the CPU tries to write to a memory address where there is some ROM or one where there is nothing at all, it clearly cannot make that location hold the value it sends out. If, however, the cache controller doesn't know that, it may hold the information written out by the CPU as though it were a valid image of what is actually in main memory at that address. As long as that image stays in the cache memory, the CPU will get that value any time it tries to read it back. If it waits long enough that the cache contents are completely replaced, however, the CPU will discover the real value (if any) that is being held in that location.

The only way to avoid this problem is to tell the cache controller up front which areas of physical memory address space are *cacheable* (meaning they have actual RAM there) and which are not cacheable (meaning either they have nothing there or they have ROM there). It can be—indeed it almost always is—very useful to do read-caching for ROMs, but it is *never* good to allow write-caching of memory locations that are occupied by ROMs.

Technical Note: Actually, a form of caching (for addresses) was used even earlier in the translation look-aside buffers (TLBs) in the 386—and that form is also present in all later members of the *x*86 family. However, this caching is mostly hidden from view in a way that the data and instruction caching I am speaking about here is not.

Warning: Modern PC BIOS setup programs often include a section in which you can inform the cache controller which regions of memory you want it to cache. If that section is initialized properly, nothing will go amiss for this reason. But if you mess with those settings and get them wrong, you could be in for some nasty surprises somewhere down the road.

Stacks

I pointed out earlier that the CPU must have some temporary holding places for information it is processing. That is why it has registers. Sometimes, however, it doesn't have nearly enough registers to hold all the information it must have temporarily stashed somewhere.

This is especially true for a PC that is doing multitasking. This simulation of doing more than one thing at a time is accomplished by doing a little bit on one task, then switching to another task and doing a little on it, then switching to a third task, and so on.

Each time the CPU switches from working on one task to working on another one, it must save the values that are contained in every register for the first task and load those registers with the values it last had for the next task it is going to work on. The CPU accomplishes this by using stacks. This is not the only time stacks are used, by any means, but it is one of the most dramatic uses for them.

A stack is a simple concept. Think of a stack of dishes. When you want to put away freshly washed dishes, you stack them in a cupboard. When you want to take out some dishes, you take them off the top of the stack. The last dish you put on the stack becomes the first one you will take off.

In a computer, a stack is implemented simply as a region of memory plus a register that holds an address pointer. When an item is to be "pushed" onto the stack through an instruction understandably referred to as PUSH, the item gets written to the location indicated by the address pointer; then the value of the address pointer is reduced by one. That makes the next item to be pushed onto the stack go into the next lower memory address. Alternatively, when an item is "popped" off the stack, through an instruction with a similarly clever name, POP, it is read from the location pointed to by the register's contents, after which that register's contents are increased by one. Figure 8.5 shows how this concept is implemented in PCs.

The maximum size of a stack is set first by the size of numbers the relevant register can hold, and second by the initial value of the stack pointer (which normally is the same as the size of the memory "segment" that has been set aside for that stack). Almost always, the latter limit is far more restrictive than the former, although it is possible to make a very large stack that would use almost the entire possible range of the relevant register.

If a program ever attempts to push more information onto the stack than it can hold, that stack pointer value will have to go negative, the CPU will notice this, and before it can happen, the CPU will cause an exception.

A PC must always have some stack ready for use. The CPU holds the pointer to the current location in the stack in its stack pointer (SP) register. That value is an offset into the segment pointed to or indicated by the value held in the stack segment (SS) register.

Figure 8.5

How a PC's stack works.

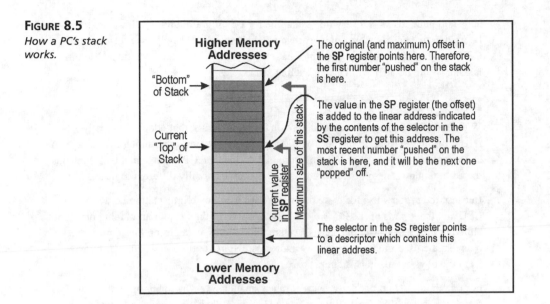

Any well-written program will create and use a private stack as one of its first actions. The reason for this is that the programmer cannot know how much space is left on the preexisting stack. Creating a private stack is done simply by allocating some memory for the private stack, then pushing the value presently in the stack pointer and stack segment registers onto the preexisting stack, and then loading the SP and SS registers with new values pointing to this newly allocated memory region. At the end of its work, the program will pop the old value off the stack and the CPU will be restored to its prior state. (It also is necessary to push onto the stack the contents of any register that the program will be altering and then pop them back off at the end.)

Any number of stacks can be defined in a PC at any moment, but only one of them will be the *current* stack. That is the one pointed to by the logical address [SP]:[SS] (this is the customary notation and you should read it as the hexadecimal numbers held in the two registers whose names appear inside the pairs of square brackets, and with those numbers being joined by a colon as is the usual way to indicate a logical address).

Technical Note: As an aside, note that there is another stack in all recent *x*86 processors. That is a special stack of eight 80-bit registers inside the CPU that are used in connection with floating-point number manipulation and—in the Pentium MMX and Pentium II—when executing MMX instructions. This special, hardware stack is normally used only by MMX (and 3DNow! on clone *x*86 processors) and floating-point math instructions, and it is entirely different from the "regular" software stack created out of a portion of main memory and used by POP and PUSH instructions.

This notion of stacks is a very important one for PC programming. It allows programs to be written that are far more complex than would be possible if only the registers in the CPU could be used as temporary information-holding places. The whole idea of multitasking would be utterly infeasible without stacks.

Ports

When the CPU forms a physical address on its address pins, that address normally refers to some location in memory address space. But by simply changing the voltage on another pin (the Memory or I/O pin) from high to low, the CPU can signal that it intends the address pin value to be interpreted as a location in a totally different logical space.

Because the primary use for these other locations is to move information between the CPU and other parts of the PC, we call this the space of the PC's input/output ports. And although the addresses in this new space are indicated by voltages on the same address pins that are used to indicate memory addresses, the I/O port space is quite different from the physical memory address space.

For one thing, I/O port address space is much smaller. Every member of the x86 family, from the earliest 8086 or 8088 to the latest Pentium II, has the same size I/O port address space, namely 64K (65,536) byte-wide locations. This is because when it is doing an I/O operation, the CPU uses only the bottom 16 address lines.

Furthermore, there are none of the complexities of selectors or paging associated with I/O port addresses. Because there are only 64K port addresses (each 1 byte wide), only a single 16-bit number is needed to point to a desired port. That number can be loaded into any of the general-purpose registers in the CPU, although some instructions assume that the port address will be loaded into the DX register.

Because all the x86 processors except the 8088 can read and write 2 or more (up to 8) bytes of information from memory at a time, they can also read or write the same number of successive port locations in one operation. And, as with memory locations, the processor can address only locations in the port address space with a resolution equal to the width of its data bus. (That is, the Pentium can address only ports in blocks of eight, although it can send information in or out any single-byte-wide port if that is desired.)

What Makes I/O Ports Different from Memory Locations?

The main distinction between an I/O port and a location in memory is what happens to data that is sent there. When you send a succession of bytes to a port, usually each of them will go on to some receiving hardware. When you read from a port, you might get a different value each time you read it (and none of them need be any of the values you sent out to that port), because what you see is whatever was last sent in to that location from the outside. This behavior is in stark contrast to that of a true memory location, where what is there is whatever you last wrote to that place, and that is what you will get if you read from that place.

That is not to say that it is impossible to put memory chips at I/O port locations. That is simply not done very often.

Memory-Mapped I/O as an Alternative to Using Ports

What about the opposite "misuse" of an address, in which some I/O gadget is placed at a location in the memory address space instead of in I/O port address space? This not only can be done, it often has proven to be quite useful. No difficult trick is involved in making the port-like hardware respond as if it were memory. You just invert the signal on the MEM/IO# line and the port hardware will think all memory accesses are port accesses and vice versa.

The reason this can be useful has to do with the very different speeds at which the ISA I/O bus and the memory bus operate. To get maximum speed out an I/O device, it used to be necessary to make it *memory-mapped,* which is making it appear in the CPU's memory address space. The most recent example of this is the Advanced Graphics Port (AGP) used for the highest-speed PC video display adapters.

Unfortunately, this also leads to some considerable complexity that is automatically avoided when the hardware is connected to a real port address. Because of the many ways in which linear memory addresses can be shifted around in physical memory address space both by the selector/descriptor table strategy and by paging, it can all too easily happen that the port hardware will seem to bounce around all over the linear memory map—or it might even disappear. This is not at all what you want an I/O device to do, because the programs that intend to talk to it must know where to find it before they can function successfully. You can see a good example of just how many hoops the hardware must jump through to make this work in Chapter 16, "Faster Ways to Get Information Into and Out of Your PC," where I detail how the AGP card creates and uses its Graphics Address Remapping Table (GART) in order to work properly in the face of the constant swapping of pages of information into and out of main memory.

Fortunately, now that we have fast I/O possible via the PCI bus, there is no longer enough gain in using this memory-mapped I/O strategy to make up for the complexity. Now, almost all the I/O hardware that needs real speed is put on the PCI bus.

Speed Issues for Ports

Originally, the ports were connected to the CPU data and address pins in exactly the same manner as memory chips. But later on, as CPU and memory speeds increased, the paths for data flow to memory and to I/O were made quite separate. They join in the motherboard chip set, but away from that point they operate independently and at quite different speeds.

For example, a modern high-end PC uses a memory bus that currently runs at 100MHz (and an internal CPU clock of up to 500MHz), but the PCI bus runs at speeds up to 66MHz, and every PC that still supports the Industry Standard Architecture (ISA) input/output bus must run it at the same, sedate 8.33MHz or less. These speed limits are necessary to ensure that plug-in cards will be capable of operating properly in even the newest and fastest PCs.

I'll explain all the details of these different buses and how they interconnect more fully in Chapter 16.

Interrupts: The Driving Force

At this point, you have seen all the essential parts that make up a PC. Thus, you have seen its basic architecture, at least in a static sense. What you haven't heard about yet are some of the key dynamic aspects to its architecture. In the rest of this chapter, I explain what these dynamic aspects are and how they work. The first of these, and in some ways the most important, is the concept of interrupts.

Polling Versus Interrupts

Imagine a small flower shop in a mall. The proprietor of this shop must serve the customers when they visit, but between customers she must go back into the back room and take care of paperwork. How does she know when to stop doing paperwork and come out to serve a customer?

The owner can use two fundamental strategies. One is to stop her work at regular intervals, get up from her desk and go out front to see whether there might be some customers desiring service. This is called *polling*. This strategy works, but it is terribly inefficient for two reasons. First, when a customer walks in, he or she must wait until the next time the owner happens to stop the paperwork and comes out to discover the customer. Second, when there are no customers, the owner cannot work steadily on the paperwork, but instead must waste time every few minutes coming out to look and notice that there aren't any customers waiting for help.

The obvious solution, in the case of a flower shop, is to put in a sensor that will be triggered each time a customer walks through the door. One common way this is done is by a light and photocell on opposite sides of the door. The light beam is broken by an entering (or exiting) customer, and that causes a bell to ring, alerting the owner in the back room that it is time to come out and help the customer. This costs more initially than the polling method. The shop owner must buy and install the sensor and bell, but it saves money in the long run by enabling the shop owner to work more efficiently.

Intel included something very much like this in the first 8086 processor and in every *x*86 processor since then. The details of how it implemented this idea are particularly clever.

Interrupt Vector Table

Intel built the *x*86 processors so that when they are operating in real mode and any one of 256 different kinds of event occurs, the CPU will finish the present instruction it is executing, stop what it is doing, save a marker so it can pick up where it left off, and then start doing some specified task that is appropriate to the kind of interrupting event that just occurred.

Intel did this by making the CPU, when it is interrupted, first discern what type of interrupt has happened and then go to a specific address very low in the memory address space. From that location, it picks up a pointer to another location, and at that second location it finds a program that directs it in the proper handling of this kind of interrupting event.

Notice the indirection: Intel could have said, if an interruption of type 75 occurs, go to this specific address and do whatever the program there dictates. Instead, it said, pick up the pointer value in slot 75 of a special interrupt vector table (IVT) and execute the program to which that pointer points.

This indirection has several advantages, not the least of which is that it enables you to change how the CPU will respond to a given type of interrupt on-the-fly. All you must do is change the pointer value for that kind of interrupt from one that points to program A to one that points to program B, and the CPU will alter its behavior accordingly.

Figure 8.6 shows schematically how an interrupt is processed by reference to the IVT. By Intel's mandate, the IVT occupies the first 1,024 bytes of main memory address space. That size means that each of the 256 interrupt types gets a 4-byte number, which is just what we need to specify a logical address (in segment:offset form).

Figure 8.6

The interrupt vector table and how it is used in real mode.

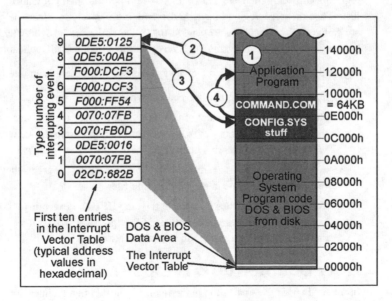

This location for the IVT is, in real mode, the first 1KB of the CPU's actual, physical memory address space. In virtual 86 mode, it is the first 1KB of the CPU's linear memory address space, which may be some very different region of the actual, physical memory. And in 286- or 386-protected mode, it is replaced by a similar structure called the interrupt descriptor table (IDT) that may be located wherever in memory the operating system wishes to put it. (For practical reasons, the IDT must never be put in a portion of physical memory that might get mapped out of the CPU's view. But other than this limitation, it can be anywhere.)

The details of how interrupts are handled in protected mode can get quite complicated, involving concepts such as "interrupt gates," "trap gates," "task state segments," and more. Fortunately, you can get a pretty good feel for how the overall process functions by focusing only on the way real-mode interrupts work. Then just trust that the designers of the CPU and the operating system did the appropriate more-complicated things to make the same ideas work in the more complex environment that occurs in protected-mode operation.

In Figure 8.6, you see on the left the first 10 slots (4 bytes each) of the real-mode interrupt vector table with the actual logical addresses they held on a particular PC when I was creating this figure. On the right, you see a memory map for that PC. On the memory map I have indicated not only the location of the interrupt vector table, but also where the DOS and BIOS data area is, just above the IVT. And above that you see the region occupied by the DOS and BIOS program portions that got loaded off the boot disk. Then there is a region I have shaded a bit more darkly in which the programs that are called for by the CONFIG.SYS and AUTOEXEC.BAT files are loaded. After all that has been assembled in memory, the PC is ready to run a real, useful application program.

Figure 8.6 shows the four steps that always happen when there is an interrupt:

1. The application program is executing when it is interrupted by a keystroke.

2. Because this is an interrupt of type 9, the CPU first saves its place, then goes to the IVT (slot 9) and retrieves the address of an interrupt service routine (ISR) that will be able to handle this interrupt.

3. As it happens, in this example, that ISR is one of the programs that was loaded in response to some line in the PC's startup files.

4. When that ISR finishes its work, it tells the CPU (by executing a special instruction called return from interrupt [IRET]) to go back to what it was doing before, and the CPU resumes executing the application program.

How Do Interrupts Happen?

In my analogy of the small shop in the mall, I indicated that an interrupt might be used to signal some external event (in that case, the arrival of a customer). In PCs, some interrupts happen because of an external event. Others happen because a program says they happen. Yet others happen because the CPU says they should happen.

Hardware Interrupts

The first kind of interrupts, called *hardware interrupts*, is the principal means by which anything outside the CPU can get its attention. For example, each time you type a key on the keyboard, it sends a signal to the PC system unit. Special circuitry inside the system unit (called the *keyboard controller*) notices that signal, and in turn it alerts the CPU to the arrival of a keystroke.

There are only two pins on the CPU by which a hardware interrupt may be signaled: the normal interrupt input (whose pin name is INTR) and the nonmaskable interrupt (with a pin name of NMI). However, many more than that number of different kinds of hardware events might need CPU attention. This seems like a problem. Fortunately, the standard PC design (PC architecture) includes a solution to this problem.

A standard part of the motherboard circuitry that surrounds every PC's CPU is a subsystem we call the *interrupt controller*. In the original PCs and PC/XTs, it could accept signals from any of eight input lines and send an interrupt signal to the CPU. Then, when the CPU acknowledged receipt of that signal, the interrupt controller would tell it from which of the eight possible sources that particular interrupt signal had come. In the IBM PC/AT and all later PC designs, the number of inputs to the interrupt controller has been increased from 8 to 15 or 16. I say 15 *or* 16 because one of the interrupt inputs is used to collect eight of the others, but in some situations it can also be used in its own right.

The input/output bus carries within it 9 of these 16 interrupt request (IRQ) lines. Any device plugged into a slot on the I/O bus can inform the CPU of its need for attention via one of these lines. The rest of these IRQ lines are reserved for use on the motherboard by, for example, the keyboard controller.

Cards plugged into the ISA bus slots cannot normally share an IRQ line. Each IRQ line must be used for only one card. Cards plugged into the PCI slots, or into a CardBus slot, on the other hand, usually can share interrupts with other cards also plugged into these more modern buses. Any of the interrupts caused by a signal on an IRQ line ultimately arrives at the CPU on its INTR pin. The nonmaskable interrupt (NMI) pin is normally used only for the PC's reset circuitry.

The difference between nonmaskable and normal interrupts is this: When a maskable interrupt is asserted, the processor can ignore it if it has been told to ignore interrupts. The fact that an interrupt is pending is remembered until the processor is ready to act on the request. This is much like an adult who says to the child tugging on her sleeve, "Not now, dear. I will talk to you as soon as I finish talking on the phone."

The nonmaskable interrupt is used when no delay can be tolerated. This is more like a fire alarm. The reset circuitry uses this means of interrupting the processor because it is sure to work, even if the processor gets totally confused and would otherwise stay in an "I don't wish to respond to interrupts right now" state indefinitely.

Software Interrupts

Intel decided it would also be a very good thing if a program could, in the course of its operation, cause an interrupt to happen. This would interrupt the running program and invoke another, special program to handle the type of event corresponding to the type of interrupt the running program had asserted.

The advantage of this approach is easy to demonstrate. The writer of an application program can know that at a certain point his or her program must send some information to the screen. But the program (and the programmer) need not know in detail just how to do that. All the program must do is assert the proper type of interrupt, with the correct values in the certain registers to indicate what is to be sent to the screen, and the program invoked by that interrupt will then do the job. This is just one simple example of a much larger principle we will meet again in Chapter 18, namely a sort of divide-and-conquer strategy.

The programmer who writes the program that must write something to the screen need not understand anything about how that will be done. The programmer who writes the program that does that job needn't know anything about why this particular bit of information must be written to the screen at this time.

CPU Exceptions

After it had this mechanism in place, Intel found it convenient to use that mechanism to handle problems the CPU might detect on its own. For example, if a program attempts to access some memory it isn't entitled to access (often referred to as a *general protection fault* or a *page fault*), it will trigger a suitable interrupt. The corresponding program that is invoked can then put up a dialog box telling the PC user what has gone wrong, and it can terminate the program that ran amok.

Interrupt Service Routines

The programs that respond when an interrupt happens are called, quite naturally, interrupt service routines (ISRs). One ISR must be designated for each of the 256 possible interrupts, or at least there must be one for any of them that might happen. However, nothing says these 256 programs all must be different programs. Usually, a great many of them are the same, single, simple ISR.

As I indicated in Figure 8.6, when an ISR is invoked, it runs until it is finished, at which point it executes a special RET instruction (which stands for return from interrupt). The CPU understands that instruction to mean, "Please resume doing whatever you were doing before."

The simplest ISR consists of nothing more than just one RET instruction. That is a "do nothing" ISR. After you have one such instruction in memory somewhere, you can simply make the IVT entries for any interrupts you want to ignore point to that RET instruction.

When Interrupts Interrupt an ISR

Nothing in what I have written so far indicates that ISRs are immune to being interrupted themselves. Sometimes they must not be interrupted for a very short time after they start executing, and in that case they can simply turn on the mask that inhibits interrupts. However, it is considered very bad PC programming practice to let that PC run in this state any longer than absolutely necessary.

As a result, it is quite common for an ISR to be interrupted. When that happens, it is suspended in just the same fashion as the original application program was suspended when that original ISR was invoked, and now a new ISR gets invoked. When it finishes its work and executes an RET instruction, the CPU will pick up what it was doing when it last was interrupted, which in this case means resuming what the first ISR was doing. Only when that one finishes its work will the CPU be able to go back to the application program.

Layers upon Layers of ISR

Not only can interrupts interrupt an interrupt service routine, it is also quite common for one ISR to call another one, which calls yet another one, and so forth. When each ISR is loaded into memory, it replaces the address in certain slots in the IVT with its own address. If it has written properly, it first copies the address that was once there into some holding place within itself. Then, if later another ISR is loaded into memory that wants to handle that same type of interrupt, it will do all the same things. As long as these ISRs are written correctly, the whole multilayer assemblage of programs operates perfectly well and has the desired effects without the user's being any the wiser about what all is going on deep inside the PC's memory.

BIOS Services in ROM

Where does your PC get its ISRs? Every PC ships from the factory with a motherboard BIOS ROM. This chip (or, often, a pair of chips) contains many different things. Most of what it contains, however, is a collection of ISRs to do the most basic things every PC must be able to do, such as responding to keyboard input and writing to a monochrome (or the now obsolete CGA color) screen. As I will explain in more detail near the end of this chapter, the entries in the interrupt vector table (IVT) are initially set up to point to these ISRs.

Many PCs have some additional BIOS ROMs located on plug-in cards. One common example is a video card, which today almost always includes a fairly hefty BIOS ROM. This ROM contains alternative ISRs to handle screen output using the hardware on that card. A part of what must happen early in the boot process is for this card to place the addresses of its ISRs into the IVT in place of the addresses of the default screen handler ISRs in the motherboard BIOS ROM.

DOS and BIOS Services in RAM

Many additional ISRs are loaded into memory when you load the operating system. From one point of view, almost all of any operating system can be described as just one huge collection of ISRs. Most of the services that the operating system performs for programs are provided either by an ISR within the operating system, or by one that is located in some BIOS ROM.

When you load a terminate-and-stay resident device driver (for example, a mouse driver), that is yet another ISR. In almost every such case, not only is the program loaded into memory in a fashion that ensures it will hang around until it is needed, but also it must stuff its own starting address into the proper slot in the IVT, so that it will be activated at the appropriate moments.

> **Technical Note:** The one common exception to this rule is the class of device drivers known as *block devices*. These are the device drivers that create phantom disks (for example, a RAM disk) or that activate special sorts of disks for use with your PC. They usually link themselves into the operating system both by stuffing some entries in the IVT, but more importantly by also inserting themselves into a *linked list* that is called the *device driver chain*.

Interrupts are one of the most important ways that things are caused to happen in a PC other than by direct action of the CPU. In fact, interrupts are so important that they have become a very precious resource. And there aren't enough different ones—especially of the hardware sort. This often leads to resource conflicts in which you need to find an available interrupt for some new piece of hardware you wish to add to your PC, but there simply aren't any.

Fortunately, as the ISA bus is phased out, and as the USB and Firewire (IEEE 1394) buses are phased in, we will at least be freed from this quandary. Those buses require interrupts to work, but just a couple each, and then they can handle a very large number of peripheral hardware devices with no additional interrupts required.

Another special feature in the standard PC architecture that functions in a somewhat similar manner is the DMA channel. I mentioned this concept earlier in this chapter, in the discussion of cache memory. Now I want to explain it in more detail.

What Is a DMA Channel?

For the most part, each time a byte of information is moved from one place to another within the PC's main memory or between a memory location and an I/O port, it gets there in two steps. The first step is for the CPU to read that byte into some register within itself. The second step is to write that byte back out to its final destination.

This works, but it has two drawbacks. The first is that the CPU cannot be doing anything else while it is moving that byte around. The second is that it takes two distinct steps to make the move. For moving a single byte this is not so bad, but when you have a whole flock of bytes to move, it certainly isn't wonderful.

Several kinds of devices in a PC want to do just that sort of many-byte information transfers. The floppy disk was the first. Sound cards do this a lot—so much so that they often use more than one DMA channel. Likewise, scanners generally use a DMA channel, and who knows what new devices might want to do this as well?

Realizing this, the designers of the original PC decided to incorporate an additional microcontroller dedicated to solving exactly this kind of problem. This is a special-purpose microprocessor built to perform just the one kind of action needed for this job. It is called the Direct Memory Access (DMA) controller. With a DMA controller present, the CPU can hasten its work by telling the DMA controller that it is to move a certain number of bytes from successive memory locations starting at one address to successive memory locations starting at some other address. It also has the option of telling the DMA controller to send out a certain number of bytes from successive memory locations to a particular port address, again starting at some specified memory address.

The final option is that it can tell the DMA controller to receive a designated number of bytes from a particular port address and deposit those values in successive memory addresses, starting at some specified address. Each time the DMA controller sets up one of these transfers, it must do so over what is referred to as a DMA channel. That simply means that a particular portion of the DMA controller is assigned to this transfer task.

The DMA controller, however, doesn't get to pick which part does which transfer. Instead, the requesting device (the CPU or some I/O hardware) must specify the channel that will be used. This means that these channels are a precious resource, and conflicts in requests for them can keep them from being used to their full capacity.

So far, not many devices need DMA channels in a PC, so the issue of running out of DMA channels is not nearly as urgent as that of running out of IRQs. However, that happy situation might not last. As more and more devices that often must move large numbers of bytes are attached to our PCs, we might soon find ourselves wondering where on the DMA controller we can possibly find a channel to hook them up.

Why DMA Fell from Favor

At first, DMA was wonderful. The floppy disk controller in the original PC used it, and it helped even that relatively slow device work more quickly and reliably. When they came along some years later, some hard disk controllers and SCSI host adapters used DMA as well.

Then things began to change. The CPUs got faster, but the ISA I/O bus couldn't speed up. Well, it did speed up a little bit, from the original roughly 4.77MHz to the PC/AT's higher 8.33MHz, but that was it. Any of the clone PC manufacturers who ran their I/O bus at a faster speed (and some did crank up the speed as high as 12MHz) were tempting fate, for surely some of the plug-in cards their customers would try in those slots would fail simply because they couldn't keep up with that higher-than-standard clock rate.

As CPU speeds have increased, so has the speed of main memory, although the latter speed hasn't increased quite as fast or as far. The speed of the bus from CPU to memory has crept up from 4.7MHz to 16MHz and then to 33MHz and finally to 133MHz, with some other steps along the way. The ISA bus, however, still must run at a measly 8.3MHz. This means that the DMA controller (in particular when it is sending information from memory to a port or receiving information into memory from a port over the ISA bus) is constantly and quite thoroughly frustrated by the slow I/O bus speed. Although it could do the job without needing constant attention from the CPU, it can't do the job nearly as quickly as the CPU could by tossing the bytes out to a memory-mapped I/O device. So, a few years ago *programmed I/O* to memory-mapped I/O devices became all the rage. (DMA was still useful for memory-to-memory transfers. These simply weren't needed as often as the memory-to-or-from-port transfers.)

How DMA Made Its Comeback

DMA has bounced back, and it is an even better solution now than it was in the first PCs. The reason is simply that we now have I/O bus technologies (the PCI bus, Universal Serial Bus [USB], and the CardBus) that can transfer data to and from I/O devices at speeds that—although somewhat slower—are more nearly comparable to those on the main memory bus. Now, once more, the DMA strategy is a sound time-saver for the CPU and overall.

DMA also has been improved, so it uses the available bus bandwidth even more efficiently. The newest version, called Ultra DMA, can transfer data to IDE devices at speeds up to a full 33MB per second (MBps)—twice the old maximum speed. It does this quite simply by transferring data on both the rising and falling edges of the (square wave) clock signal, rather than merely on the falling edges, as had been the custom and as is still the standard for most bus data transfers.

For the PC user, this means that DMA channels matter once more. They are once again the preferred way to carry large blocks of data into or out of I/O devices, and more and more we will see those devices using this strategy.

Keeping Up with the Clock

PC clock speeds are mentioned a lot. In fact, for many years one of the most prominent numbers in any PC advertisement was clock speed. ("Buy our nifty new 450MHz Pentium II Xeon dual CPU computer.") Just what is that speed? And what parts of the PC actually run at that speed? Are there other clocks in a PC? If so, what do they do? These are the questions I will answer for you in this section.

Asynchronous Versus Synchronous Computers

Although they are amazingly fast, electronic circuits do need some time to operate. Just how much time each one needs varies from sample to sample. It is possible to make a computer that has no clocks in it. Such a computer would run just as fast as each individual piece within it would let it. Data requested from memory would get used just as soon as it showed up wherever it had been asked to show up. The results of calculations would be stashed back into main memory just as soon as they were available. Never would any part wait unnecessarily long, just because it wasn't yet time to move on according to some central clock.

Such an asynchronous computer is *possible* to design and build, but it sure isn't easy. A far simpler way to design a computer is to synchronize each of the parts to some central clock or "heartbeat." As long as this clock ticks slowly enough, you can be quite sure that every part will have completed its assigned tasks before the next tick comes along and tells the parts to move on to their next steps. Synchronous computers are so much easier to design and build that nearly every computer built today is an example of such a design. Certainly every PC is.

Different Clocks for Different Purposes

This doesn't mean that all the parts must march to the beat of the same drum, however. It is perfectly possible, and has now become quite standard, to have a multiplicity of clocks in a PC, each one used for a different purpose. Here is a quick rundown on a few of the most important clocks in PCs. Your PC surely has all of the ones I will mention, and it might also have a several more.

The CPU Clock

The most famous clock is one that "ticks" inside the CPU chip. This is the 450MHz (or 300MHz, 100MHz, or whatever your PC may have) that you hear so much about. It measures how fast the fastest part of your PC runs. Mostly these days, the CPU inner core runs at this speed and nothing else in the PC comes close. Well, if you have a Pentium Pro or a recent Pentium II Xeon CPU, its L2 cache, which is located inside the CPU module, also runs at this speed. In early Pentium IIs, the L2 cache runs at half the CPU clock speed. For all other x86 processors, the external cache runs at the same speed as the main memory bus.

The bus from the CPU to main memory commonly runs at some fraction of the CPU clock speed. Or, to put this more properly, the CPU runs at a multiple of the external bus speed. That is, the actual clock circuit that controls this speed is located outside the CPU and the CPU simply synchronizes its not-very-constant-frequency clock to a fixed multiple of that external clock signal.

For example, a 400MHz Pentium II machine, which is one of the fastest machines widely available as I write this, has a main memory clock speed of 100MHz. This means the internal clock is running at precisely four times the external clock. The somewhat faster 450MHz machines use the same external clock speed, but are designed to run with their internal clock synchronized at precisely four-and-one-half times the external clock speed.

The Main Memory Clock

The same clock that drives the CPU also drives the main memory modules and all the associated circuitry. (Remember, this is a clock that is outside the CPU itself and is running at a small fraction of the speed of the CPU's internal circuits, as I explained in the previous section.) This clock's frequency is that of the front-side bus.

It may be—and commonly was the case in older PCs—that only the external (L2 or L3) memory cache (which is located on the motherboard) actually can keep up with a clock this fast. In that case, the slower DRAM chips that make up the bulk of main memory must be enabled to run more slowly by the insertion of one or more "wait states." These are delays between the clock cycle in which the CPU or external cache controller asks something of a memory chip and the clock cycle in which it expects to find the result of the requested operation. Clever designers have sometimes managed to get around needing wait states for every main memory access by splitting up the memory into "interleaved" banks, or in other ways. Still, if the main memory DRAM chips are simply unable to respond as quickly as the speed of the front-side bus clock would demand, wait states will be required, at least occasionally. This (at least occasional) inability of main memory to keep up with the CPU's demands is why it is useful to have an external memory cache (called Level 2 or Level 3 cache, depending on what is inside the CPU module).

Fortunately, in many recent PCs—especially those designated "performance" PCs—the DRAM chips used in the main memory are able to keep up with the front-side bus clock without any wait states, and for that reason a memory cache on the motherboard is not needed and is not included. (The L1 and L2 caches inside the CPU chip or module in these PCs are still needed and those cache memories run at substantially faster rates than main memory, as I described in the preceding section.)

The Input/Output (I/O) Bus Clocks

As I have mentioned many times now, the ISA input/output bus is required to run no more rapidly than 8.33MHz. This signal is derived from the same clock as the main memory clock by dividing, in the case of our example systems with a 100MHz memory clock frequency, by a factor of twelve. The ISA clock speed is this slow in order to make sure that even very old ISA plug-in cards will function correctly when they are plugged into an ISA slot in even the latest and greatest PC—but because this is so excruciatingly slow, and to avoid the problem of interrupt conflicts, some of the most modern PCs simply don't have any ISA slots.

Thank goodness today's PCs also have one or more additional I/O buses, and these buses typically operate at a faster speed than the ISA bus, although usually not quite as fast as main memory. The PCI bus operates typically at 33MHz and at 266MHz in the AGP slot in the fastest of today's PCs.

Other Clocks in Your PC

Many of the subsystems in your PC must work in synchrony with a clock that runs at some quite different frequency and that is not synchronized with the main memory, CPU, and I/O bus clocks. For example, the video monitor scans the electron beam across and down the face of the display at a frequency set by the desired resolution of the image and the acceptable refresh rate. (If these terms mean nothing to you, see Chapter 13, "Seeing the Results: PC Displays," for a complete explanation of them.)

The disk drives need clocks at special frequencies that are a fixed multiple of the rate at which their disk platters turn. A modem needs a clock that will make it put out or take in bits at the correct speed for the transmission rate it is trying to achieve.

There can be as many different clocks as there are different pieces of hardware with differing speed capabilities and requirements. (You can't make the part go faster than it is capable of running, and in some cases you mustn't let it go either slower or faster than the standard speed for that sort of gadget.)

What Does *Super-Scalar* Mean?

When bragging about how much faster a new PC is than the older ones it has replaced, the manufacturers often point to its *super-scalar* performance. What does that mean? Quite simply, it means that if the clock speed on the new PC is the same as on the old PC, the new one will run programs faster anyway. If the new PC's clock is twice the speed of the old one, the new PC will run programs more than twice as fast as the old one. That is, the performance goes up faster than the clock speed. (If it went up in direct proportion to the clock speed, the performance would be said to scale with the clock speed. Going up faster is, thus, super-scalar.)

There can be many different reasons for super-scalar performance. Usually, it comes from some combination of improvements, such as having more instruction execution units (for integer and/or floating-point instructions); supporting newer, more efficient instructions (such as MMX and 3DNow!); having a bigger instruction pipeline; or having a bigger L1 or L2 memory cache. It may also come from having some part of the CPU "speculatively execute" instructions whose turn hasn't yet come, in the hopes that they will be needed later. At that future time, if those results are needed, they can be stuffed into the flow without waiting for them to execute. Or, perhaps the new PC actually uses more CPU chips than the older one.

Whatever the reason, super-scalar in simple terms just means the new PC works faster than you might have imagined. This is a good thing, but is not nearly as mysterious as the name might make it seem.

How Your PC Wakes Up and Prepares Itself for Work

The last topic I want to cover in this chapter is a brief description of what your PC must go through between the time you flip on the power switch and the time it is ready for you to run your first application program. This process is called *booting* the PC, from the whimsical notion of the impossible task of lifting oneself by one's own bootstraps.

Fortunately, all PCs (as well as modern, larger computers) come with the capability of getting themselves started without all that fuss and effort by a human being. The reason they are able to do so lies in two features of their architecture. One is a portion of how the $x86$ processors are designed. The other is in the contents of a particular program that the motherboard BIOS chips contain.

Just as Intel hard-wired the $x86$ processors to look in the first 1KB of main memory for the interrupt vector table, they also hard-wired the address at which it will look for instructions when it first wakes up. The designated address is exactly 16 bytes below the top of the first megabyte. (An $x86$ processor can access only the first megabyte of memory address space when it first wakes up, because it always does so in real mode.)

So, if only the PC maker will arrange to have the motherboard BIOS ROM show up in the CPU's memory address space in the region just below 1MB, and if it contains an appropriate program starting at that special address, that boot program will automatically run each time the PC is turned on or reset.

Because a PC program normally progresses through memory from lower addresses to higher, and because the starting address is only 16 bytes below the absolute upper end of the first megabyte of memory, it would seem at first glance that the boot program would have to be impossibly short. In fact, one of the very first things the boot program does is an unconditional jump to some address a good deal below this "ceiling" but still somewhere inside the motherboard BIOS ROM.

Next, the boot program begins checking to see whether all the standard parts of the PC are present and seem to be working normally. Before it gets very far into this process, it fills in the first 16 slots in the IVT with pointers to ISRs elsewhere in the motherboard BIOS. After that has been done, the boot program enables the maskable interrupts so the machine can respond to, for example, keystrokes from the keyboard.

Also along the way, the motherboard BIOS program checks to see whether a special video BIOS chip is located on a plug-in video card. If it is, the boot program transfers control of the PC to that program, which uses this opportunity to place its ISR addresses into the correct slots in the IVT. When that has been accomplished, the video card can be used to display information on the screen. That video BIOS program commonly displays a copyright message as the first message on the screen. Then it returns control to the motherboard BIOS boot program.

The boot program now checks main memory to see how much of it there is, and to be sure it all works correctly. (Some PCs do a more thorough job of checking memory at this stage than others, which explains why some PCs can have flaky memory and yet pass this step in the boot process. They may reveal the deficiencies of the memory at a later stage, either when a memory management program loads and does a more careful check of main memory, or perhaps only by failing in the middle of some important task you are doing.)

Around this time, the boot program usually also offers the user a chance to suspend the boot program and enter the BIOS setup program. This enables you to go into a special set of screens that display and enable you to alter configuration settings that are stored in the motherboard CMOS.

> **Tip:** If your PC doesn't display a message telling you how to get into the setup BIOS screens (and you can't remember how to do it), a simple trick might "fool" it into telling you that secret. Just hold down a key on the keyboard while the PC is booting. This will trigger an error and, usually, that will result in a message telling you to press some key to enter the BIOS and some other key to go on. Bingo! You now can enter the BIOS setup screens.

The boot program continues by building some data tables in the DOS and BIOS data area, a region of main memory just above the IVT. This area holds, among other things, a concise record of the number of serial and parallel ports, floppy disks, and other standard pieces of hardware in this PC.

Now the boot program has finished its Power On Self-Test (POST) section, and it is ready to look for an operating system and load it into memory. If it succeeds in doing this, it will then turn over control of the PC to that operating system, and the boot program's job will be done. If the boot program cannot find an operating system, it typically will simply stop with a message saying that you should insert a bootable disk in the A: drive and press any key to restart the boot process.

In all PCs built more than a few years ago, the boot program would always look for the operating system in a standard set of places and always in the same order. That sequence was: First, look on the first floppy disk drive (A:) and then on the first hard drive (C:). If you don't find an operating system in either of those places, give up (or in IBM-brand PCs only, run the BASIC interpreter located in a special motherboard ROM).

Many modern PCs are more flexible, and in their BIOS setup program, you can tell it which devices you want it to check and in what order. The possible boot devices now commonly include the A: and B: floppy disk drives (which could also be the new high-capacity "super"-floppy drives referred to either as a:drives or LS120 drives), the C: hard drive, or a CD-ROM drive attached to either the primary or secondary IDE chain.

Peter's Principle: A Simple Antivirus Safety Net

One way to minimize the likelihood of getting your PC infected by a so-called boot sector virus is to specify that it not try booting from A: or B:. That way, it won't accidentally load a boot virus simply because you forgot to take an infected disk out of the floppy drive before rebooting. When you must boot from a floppy, you can simply first enter the BIOS setup program and reset this choice to allow booting from the floppy disk drive, and then be sure that the disk you use is virus-free.

In the next chapter, I'll explain the various data structures that are to be found on PC disks and hard disks. After you understand that, you will see fairly easily why and how the boot program can load the operating system. The process starts when the boot program loads the first sector (512 bytes long) from the disk and then executes the program it contains. However, before doing that, the boot program checks to see that there is a special "signature" byte sequence 55h AAh at the end of the boot sector. If there is, the boot program assumes that the rest of the sector contains a valid startup program and the other information necessary to continue the search for an operating system on that disk.

Speeding Up Your PC's Waking Up

The boot process can take a long time—or at least it often seems to be longer than your patience will let you accept gracefully. Can you shorten it significantly? Yes, you almost certainly can.

There are several ways to do this. The next sections briefly describe three of them.

Using Your BIOS Options Wisely

The first way to explore speeding your PC's startup process is to find out whether your BIOS offers a setting to disable the memory test during boot, or one to enable "fast booting." The latter is a nickname that indicates not only that the memory check will be skipped, but also some of the other tests of hardware devices that don't often fail.

You don't want to use these settings unless you are pretty sure your PC's memory (and those other devices, such as floppy drives) are working correctly. Otherwise, you are forgoing some valuable checks on their function that might someday save your data. If you have booted many, many times without incident, however, you can select this setting in the BIOS, and from then on, your PC will boot noticeably quicker.

Power-Saving PCs Can Seem to Turn On Faster

Battery-powered portable PCs have led the way in showing how much you might reduce a PC's power consumption. I will talk more about this in Chapter 22, "Why Mobile PCs Must Be Different." But here I want to focus on one pleasant side effect of some of the common power-saving strategies used in those PCs.

The overall notion of power management is to power down all those components that are normally power hungry and that are not at the moment actually being used. Even at their best, modern PCs are not all that smart about how this is done, but some strides have been made toward this goal.

One obvious, and very effective, way to save power is to turn off the video monitor when it isn't being used. This makes the PC look as if it is off. Touch the mouse, or press a key on the keyboard and the monitor wakes up and you discover the PC was on all along.

Another step is to turn off the hard drive. Even more aggressive steps include slowing down or stopping the CPU clock, turning off the modem, and so forth.

These approaches have not proven to be a panacea. If your PC is on, with just the monitor (and perhaps also the hard drive) turned off, it will save some power and look turned off, but it isn't saving as much power as some people want. And a PC in this mode of operation can still be pretty noisy—but it does wake up pretty quickly.

How to Make a PC Hibernate

Portable PC makers have had the strongest motivation to deal with these issues creatively. Saving battery power is crucial. So, they arrange to have as many pieces as possible powered down as much of the time as possible. But they can't just turn off all the pieces and then turn them back on without requiring the PC to start everything all over again—that is to say, without requiring another annoyingly slow reboot.

The problem is that if you turn off power to RAM, it forgets its contents. Similarly, various peripheral parts in a PC are able to remember some important facts about their "current state" only while they are powered up.

So, these PC designers created PCs that can be powered down and back, sometimes a piece at a time, under software control. Then they also made it possible to save the "state" of each piece that might forget its state and to restore that state when those pieces are awakened once more.

In effect, the PC pieces are put into "hibernation," in which state they forget (or don't notice) what is going on around them. Then, when they are "reawakened," they get briefed on whatever they might have missed.

There are several strategies for doing this, perhaps the most common being to write a file to the disk drive with all the required status information just before the PC is put to sleep. Of course, you must also arrange some way to detect that the PC was put to sleep the next time it is started, so it can "merely" awaken all its parts and reload their states before letting you get back to work.

This works pretty well, actually. But it doesn't work instantly. Some substantial amount of time (measured in tens of seconds, typically) is required to awaken all the parts and get them back to their original states. The "suspend file," as it often is called, also takes up a noticeable amount of disk space—over 70MB on one portable I have used.

If this isn't quick enough for you—and it isn't for many folks—don't give up hope just yet. Some of the PC industry leaders (most notably Microsoft) are now pushing something they call the "OnNow initiative."

"OnNow" and "Instantly Available PCs" Promise Instant-On PCs

The premise here is that no PC should ever be turned all the way off. At least none that are to be fully a part of our daily lives as our telephones, microwave ovens, and various other appliances are. Instead these PCs should go into a "sleep" state when they are not in use, and then be able virtually instantly to resume normal operation. (Just think how annoying it would be if you had to "reboot" your telephone every time a call came in or you wanted to place a call.)

Other PCs, for example those in office environments, might really be turned off at the end of the day and then booted up in the ordinary way the next morning. But the choice of which way to make the PC work should be left to the purchaser—or better still, to the actual user of that PC.

These goals can be achieved—or at least Microsoft (promoter of OnNow), Intel (promoter of "Instantly Available PCs"), and their allies think they can be. But it will require a substantial alteration of almost every piece of hardware and software in the PC. Every piece must be made very much aware of the power states of the machine and their impact on its operation. And they must all be able to be commanded by the operating system to turn on or off at a user's option.

An important option will be to set (and easily readjust) the trade-off you are willing to accept between how little power this sort of PC will consume when it is "sleeping" and how quickly it will be able to resume working for you.

Finally, I want to mention a possible very dark side to all of this. Any such never-truly-off PC will consume some amount of electrical power all the time, and as such it will present at least a tiny risk of causing a fire. If there is no one around to notice this, a major disaster could ensue. (This is one reason that early attempts to make television sets that were always on enough to start up nearly instantly were not more of a success. Now most TVs keep just enough circuitry on to sense signals from the remote; they turn the picture tube all the way off—at the cost of a longer wakeup time—just to ensure that no fires get started while they are supposedly turned off.)

If the OnNow initiative succeeds, it will have added some important new layers to an already pretty complex PC architecture. Only time will tell whether the benefits of doing this outweigh its costs.

Some Things to Think About and Try

Look at the screen during the boot process. Also watch the lights indicating disk access. See which parts of the boot process that I just described you can identify. A flashing of the access light for the floppy disk drives or the hard drive might indicate simply that the boot program was checking to see that those drives are responding to commands. If the access light comes on and stays on for several seconds, the boot program might be trying to read information from a disk in that drive. A "ka-thunk" sound from a printer probably means it was reset by a signal sent to it from the CPU at the boot program's behest. Of course, you should see the amount of main memory being counted onscreen as it is being checked (unless you have disabled that check in your PC's setup BIOS).

Explore your PC's setup BIOS screens. You can do this completely safely as long as you never answer Yes to the question Save changes? before you exit from those screens. Find out what options your PC gives you and see what you can discern about its architecture from that set of options.

You Can Never Have Too Much Closet (or Data Storage) Space

Now that you understand how your PC thinks, it's time to talk storage—that's where all the programs your computer uses to think and all the data it thinks about are kept. *Storage* is the collection of places where information is kept, long-term. It is in sharp contrast to *memory*, which is the place where you must put that same information (programs and data) before the CPU can do anything with it.

I pointed out this distinction in Chapter 2, "How (Almost) Any Computer Works," and I can't overstress its importance. This distinction is absolutely the standard industry usage for these two terms, and keeping the concepts clearly separate is vital. (If you find yourself having trouble with this one, you might be reassured to know that nearly all new PC users have that problem, but almost all of them manage to overcome it in a short time.)

This chapter is about the long-term information holding places, *storage*—not about memory. (That is the subject of Chapter 11, "Giving Your PC's CPU Enough Elbow Room—PC Memory") The concept of storage is a broad one. It covers many different kinds of long-term information-holding devices. Because the first storage technology that was commonly used on PCs was the diskette drive, the PC has been designed mostly to view all the rest of these holding devices (including CD-ROMs, Flash memory cards, and tape drives) as though they, too, were disk drives.

In fact, at least if you're using the online tools developed for Windows, this generalization has been taken so far that distant computers you access over a network or over the Internet often appear onscreen as just additional disk drives attached to your local PC. This makes using those diverse resources much simpler.

Traditional PC Disk Drives

Before going into non-disks that look like disks to a PC, you should first understand actual PC disk drives. The first drives were diskette drives. Later came hard drives, and then removable drives of various types. In the next section, I'll explain a little bit about the floppy diskette technologies used in PCs, followed by a section discussing hard disks.

Standards: You might have noticed that I use the term *diskette* whenever I refer to a floppy, and *disk* only when I refer to a hard disk. This usage is common, although not totally standard. I use it to help you distinguish the differences between these different technologies.

Diskette Drives for PCs

The essence of any magnetic disk storage device is that it contains one or more circular disks. These disks are coated with a material that responds to magnetic fields to enable information to be stored there. The disks are mounted on a spindle and they turn under a head (or heads) that can move radially in toward the axis of rotation or out toward the edge of the disk. Normally in PC disk drives, the head is moved to a suitable position and it sits still while the disk spins past it and the information is written to or read from the surface in bursts. Figure 9.1 shows this arrangement, albeit with a much exaggerated scale. Normally, the head is tiny, and the bursts of magnetic data recorded in the surface, even if they were visible (which they aren't) would be so tiny and close together that they wouldn't be clearly distinguishable in this figure.

FIGURE 9.1

As the disk turns under the stationary read-write head, that head passes along a track past sectors of recorded information on the surface of the disk.

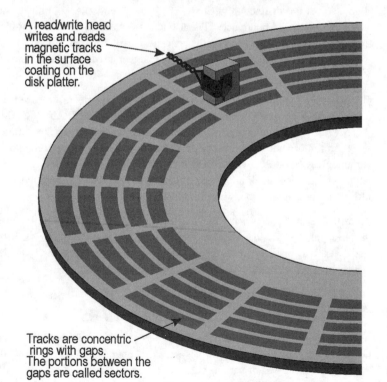

A read/write head writes and reads magnetic tracks in the surface coating on the disk platter.

Tracks are concentric rings with gaps. The portions between the gaps are called sectors.

Getting a diskette drive was an extra-cost option for buyers of the first PCs (and hard disks simply weren't available at all). Having a floppy diskette drive (or even two of them) became standard quickly. Not only did these devices provide a means for storing programs and data for the long haul, they also proved to be a very convenient way to exchange information with other people.

The original PC diskette drives are physically larger than the ones that most of us use today (5 1/4-inch instead of 3 1/2-inch) and yet they could hold only a small fraction of what modern diskettes can. What you see when you pick one up and remove it from its protective paper jacket is a stiff, square paper folder with a large hole in the middle and several small notches on some of the edges.

Inside the square paper folder is a thin disc of clear plastic (usually mylar) that has been coated on both sides with a very thin layer of magnetic iron oxide. This magnetic coating is very similar to the coating on an audio tape. The disc actually is floppy—it's very flexible. But when it is in its sleeve, the whole assembly is moderately rigid. The diskette drive spindle grabs the disc through the large, round center hole. The read-write head actually slides on the surface of the disc as it moves toward the center or away from it, along the length of the oblong hole you see at the bottom of the sleeve. (The details of how data gets stored on a diskette, in terms of tracks and sectors, are quite similar to how it gets stored on a hard disk. I will explain both in the section "DOS Disk Overview," later in this chapter.)

The original PC diskette drives could read and write data to only one side of a diskette, and they didn't use the available surface area as efficiently as later models. This meant those drives could store at most 160KB on a diskette.

We've come a long way since then. The most common diskettes today use 3 1/2-inch diameter discs that are much better protected in hard plastic housings, with a metal shutter to cover the hole where the read-write head contacts the vulnerable surface of the disc, and with a metal hub bonded to the disc to let the drive hold and turn it more precisely.

One result of these improvements is that these 3 1/2-inch diskettes can hold either 720KB or 1.44MB of information per diskette. Indeed, with simply an alteration in how the data is recorded, Microsoft and IBM each came up with (different) ways to push that capacity to something closer to 2MB per diskette, while still using standard diskettes and standard diskette drives. (Microsoft calls its format MDF, for Microsoft Distribution Format, and intends that it be used only for its distribution of programs to save the cost of more diskettes. IBM calls its new format XDF, for Extended Diskette Format, and also uses it only for software distribution.)

A few manufacturers introduced a higher-density standard diskette that held 2.88MB per diskette. Unfortunately, a special drive was needed to use them, because the magnetic coating on these special diskettes requires stronger magnetic fields for writing, and special circuitry was required to understand their different read-head signals as well.

This specialness was fatal. Very few people wanted to replace their floppy drives just to double the capacity. Furthermore, if they did start using those special extra-high-density diskettes, then their diskettes wouldn't be useful for giving files to other folks who didn't have those special drives in their PCs. This theme, "we don't want it if it isn't compatible with everything that has gone before" has been a resounding chorus from the PC user community to the manufacturers. It took them awhile, but now most of the manufacturers know the folly of trying to give people something that isn't fully backward compatible. I'll explain about the latest attempt, the LS120 drive, later.

Hard Disks for PCs

Hard disks are like floppies, except that the media are, well, hard. Called a *platter*, these rigid disks are made of aluminum or glass. They are much thicker than a floppy's disc, but the coating of magnetic material is comparably thin. Some hard disks have just one platter. Some have several, all mounted on the same spindle and spun together.

The huge significance of the rigidity of a hard disk's platters is that after you have recorded some information on it, it's relatively easy to find your way back to the same spot to read the information. Floppies stretch and swell with changes in temperature and humidity. Hard disk platters don't—or at least they don't do so nearly as much. This fact has allowed the makers of hard disks to use read-write heads that are much smaller than those in a floppy diskette drive, and that allows them to pack the information on the disk surface much more densely than is feasible on a floppy.

When PCs were new, adding a hard disk wasn't an option. Hard disks existed and were sometimes installed on small business computers, but only the priciest of those pre-PC machines sported one. Adding a 5MB hard disk to a PC could easily double its cost. By the time the PC/XT came along, IBM realized that the larger capacity and greater speed of hard disks were becoming a necessity.

The earliest PC hard disks were two-part contraptions. The drive itself, with an attached printed circuit card, sat in the disk drive bay. It connected via two data cables to a controller card that was plugged into one of the I/O slots on the motherboard. In its earliest form, these drives and the drive-controller interface were often described by the acronym for the data-encoding technology, MFM (Modified Frequency Modulation), which is the same data-encoding strategy that was used then, and is still used for diskettes.

Technical Note: You might have a picture in your head of how magnetic data recording is done that is overly simple. You might think that the bits of data are recorded directly in the surface of the medium with 1s represented by little regions of north magnetization and 0s represented by little regions of south magnetization.

Unfortunately, disk heads excel at seeing changes in the state of the medium, but aren't so good at noticing the state itself. Thus, any time you pass the head of a disk drive over a spot where the magnetization changes in direction or strength, the circuitry gets a signal that is easy to spot and to which it can then respond. But if you try recording a long field of magnetic 0s (or of magnetic 1s, the data detection apparatus has no change signals to notice, and would likely get lost at least in terms of how many 0s in a row (or 1s in a row) it had seen. It might even get confused about whether it was currently looking at a 0 or a 1.

The right way to record digital data is to first encode it. This means replacing long, unchanging patters of 0s and 1s with patterns that do change regularly, thus better compensating for the disk head's inherent limitations.

Many encoding schemes have been used over the years. They sported monikers such as *MFM* and *RLL* (*run-length-limited*). Each scheme was better than the ones before it, in terms of how much data it could cram into a given space on the disk.

All floppy diskette drives use MFM encoding exclusively. Hard-disk makers have now pretty well settled on some form of RLL, with 2,7 RLL being the most popular.

The next generation of PC drives used an improved data-encoding method called *RLL* (*Run-Length-Limited encoding*), and those drives required new controller cards as well. Although some further improvements in data encoding were made after that generation, essentially all modern hard disks use a version of RLL data encoding.

Drives were improved in other ways. The MFM and RLL drives were followed by *ESDI* (*Enhanced Small Device Interface*) and *SCSI* (*Small Computer System Interface*) hard drives. ESDI is much like the MFM or RLL interface, but with some improvements that make it possible for these drives to have larger capacity and greater speed.

ESDI was popular for a short time, but it died quickly when IDE (Integrated Device Electronics) drives appeared on the market. This trend was greatly accelerated when the improved EIDE (Enhanced Integrated Device Electronics) drives came along. These drives have the matching controller electronics moved from the plug-in I/O card to the circuit card on the side of the drive itself.

The initial IDE interface was merely a subset of IBM's original 16-bit Input/Output bus for its PC/AT model computers. This subset had just those signal wires that were needed to service a hard disk. Soon, with all the clone PC makers using the same design, IBM PC/AT's I/O bus became known as the *ISA* (*Industry Standard Architecture*) bus. And in a similar manner (but with the formal blessing of an official standards committee), that original IDE interface was declared an industry standard called the *AT Attachment* (*ATA*). A later, improved version of that standard is what we now call the *EIDE* interface.

Another enhancement, known by the name *ATAPI* (*AT Attachment Packet Interface*) extended the workings of the EIDE interface to accommodate other sorts of devices than just hard disks (for example, CD-ROMs).

SCSI is not so much a way of interfacing to a hard drive as it is a tiny, one-computer local area network. Attaching a SCSI device of any type (and hard disks are only one of the many kinds of devices that can have a SCSI interface) to a PC requires the use of a *SCSI Host Adapter*. This is a plug-in card that mediates between the activity on the SCSI bus and that on the PC's I/O bus. Generally, if you want only one or two hard drives in your PC, and you don't have any other use for any SCSI-interface devices, the easiest solution will be to use EIDE hard drives. But using SCSI hard drives can give you even greater performance, and it can allow you to add many more drives as well as other peripheral devices.

Both EIDE and SCSI have certain advantages, and so both will probably be around for a long while. (One possible replacement for either may be drives that we shall see in the next couple of years that will work with the new IEEE 1382 Firewire bus standard.) I'll tell you more about all of these interface standards in Chapter 16, "Faster Ways to Get Information Into and Out of Your PC."

Understanding the DOS Perspective (and Why This Still Matters)

The first PCs came with a choice of operating systems, but the hands-down winner of consumer preference turned out to be PC DOS. IBM and Microsoft jointly created DOS and worked together on improvements for all the versions up to 5.0. Only since then have MS-DOS and IBM's PC DOS become somewhat different.

Why am I talking about DOS? Isn't Windows all the new thing, now? As you will learn in more detail in Chapter 17, "Understanding PC Operating Systems," in many ways plain old DOS, Windows on top of DOS, and Windows 95 or 98 (with DOS hidden inside) are the same type of beast. At their core, and in particular, in their view of disks, they are just different flavors of DOS. However, beginning with the version of Windows 95 known as OSR2 (Operating System Release 2) and continuing with Windows 98, Microsoft has introduced a significant variation in how DOS works with hard disks—even though an improved version of DOS is still the underlying operating system.

Windows 95 and 98 each include what amounts to three distinct operating systems. There is the real-mode DOS with which they get started, and that is what one uses in MS-DOS mode or at a command prompt accessed directly from the startup menu. Then there is the Windows 9x graphical interface and its corresponding 32-bit protected-mode operating system. Finally, there is the simulated DOS that one sees in a DOS window (either full-screen or in a smaller window) that can be accessed from within the Windows 9x graphical user interface. All three of these operating systems must be able to deal with the files and disk drives, and in many respects they do so in the same way. However, while the Windows 95 (or 98) GUI and the virtual DOS it presents in a DOS window both understand long filenames, the real-mode DOS does not.

In the OSR2 version of Windows 95 (also known as Windows 95B) and in Windows 98, all three of these DOSs have had their view of disk drives extended to include those for-matted using the FAT32 strategy. But even with that extension, the Windows 98 real-mode DOS still doesn't understand long filenames.

Other operating systems such as Windows NT, OS/2, and Linux look at disks differently. But simply because there are so many DOS-based PCs and therefore such a huge number of DOS-formatted disks, all of these alternative operating systems have been designed to be capable of reading and writing standard 12- and 16-bit FAT DOS disks as well as ones that are formatted in their own special ways. Therefore, understanding how DOS views a disk is very important. And it is going to continue to be important for a long time.

When I refer to DOS, I am referring not only to what a purist might consider the actual DOS portion of the operating system, but also to those files that come on a DOS system disk and act as a portion of an operating system for your PC, plus the portions of the motherboard BIOS that deal with disks. These include the BIOS, the DOS kernel, the DOS file system, the DOS command interpreter, and—in DOS versions starting with 6, in which data compression was a built-in feature—the DOS data compression engine. (I do not include the external DOS commands, which are the many separate applet pro-grams also shipped on a DOS disk, for example FORMAT.COM.) In a Windows 95 or 98 machine, this refers to all the layers of system software from the motherboard BIOS on the bottom all the way up to the GUI (graphical user interface) on the top, or at least to the portions of these layers that have anything to do with handling disk drives.

DOS Disk Overview

The *Disk Operating System* (DOS) is an operating system whose special focus is manag-ing disk drives. To DOS, the most fundamental unit of information storage is a *sector*. A sector is a clump of 512 bytes of information. Other sizes of sector are certainly conceiv-able. Indeed, some people have used other sector sizes (usually some power of 2 times 512 bytes), but without help from an add-on device driver, DOS cannot utilize any disk that uses a non-standard sector size. (To be strictly correct, each sector is actually 571 bytes in length, but only 512 bytes of this total are usable for user data. The remaining space is used to store a header and trailer, or footer, if you like, for each sector. Among other things, these contain checksum information that helps your PC automatically verify that the data in the main part of the sector has been stored properly.

Physical Structure of a Disk Drive

Look back at Figure 9.1, and then also look at Figure 9.2. In each of these figures, the short arcs of darker gray on the disk represent individual sectors. All the sectors around a disk at a given distance from the center form a *track*. The number of sectors in a track varies from one disk capacity to another, but every DOS disk has its information stored as some number of concentric tracks, each made up of a different number of sectors. (This is almost, but not quite, like the grooves on a record. The difference is that record grooves spiral inward, while tracks on a floppy or hard disk are concentric rings.)

FIGURE 9.2

The location and numbering of disk heads (surfaces) and cylinders on a logical hard disk.

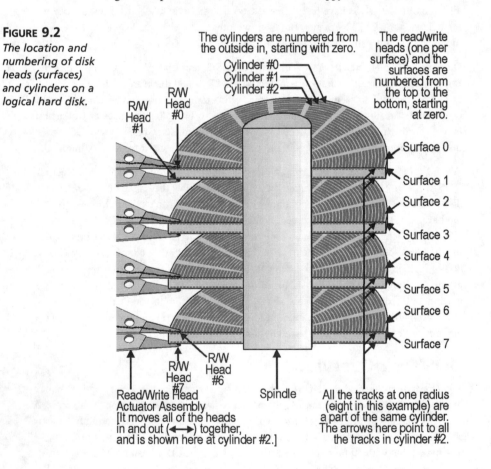

Most diskettes have information recorded on both sides. Most hard disks have more than two recordable surfaces because they usually have multiple platters mounted on the same spindle with two recordable surfaces on at least most of those platters. (Sometimes, the outermost surfaces, the top side of the top platter and the bottom side of the bottom platter, are reserved for special purposes and cannot be used to store the user's information.) The collection of all the tracks at the same distance from the spindle on all the recordable surfaces is called a *cylinder*.

Technical Note: DOS and the PC BIOS were designed from the outset with the notion that the various disks they would manage might have differing numbers of heads, differing numbers of sectors per track, and differing numbers of cylinders. What DOS and the BIOS can't comprehend is a disk that has a different number of sectors on different tracks. And yet that is, in fact, just how most modern hard disks are built.

In these disks, because the outer tracks are longer than the inner ones, it's possible to put more sectors on those longer, outer tracks than on the shorter, inner tracks without crowding the individual bits together too closely in either place. Manufacturers commonly divide the tracks into two or more zones and put the same number of sectors on all the tracks within a zone, but a different number on the tracks in neighboring zones.

There are two ways in which such a disk can be made to work with DOS, and therefore with PCs. One is by making the disk somehow seem to be constructed differently than it really is. The other, more modern method, is to use *Logical Block Addressing* (LBA) to connect it to the PC.

In the first strategy, the disk controller electronics first organize into one long chain all the locations on the disk at which information can be stored. It assigns a logical block number (starting with 0) to each of those locations. Next, the drive electronics create a fictitious drive geometry. This fictitious drive has an almost arbitrary set of numbers representing its supposed number of heads, sectors per track, and cylinders. Each and every logical block number is converted into an equivalent location on the fictitious drive, and that is the pseudo-physical address used for that information when dealing with DOS.

In the second strategy, an extra layer called the INT13H Extensions is added to the BIOS to let it deal directly with a disk that is organized as a one-dimensional chain of logical blocks. That avoids all the messiness of fictitious drive geometries and, more importantly, it allows one to use much larger disks than DOS and the original-style PC motherboard BIOS can natively understand.

One way to add those INT13H extensions to an older PC is to upgrade that PC's motherboard BIOS. Most modern PCs are built with that sort of enhanced BIOS as a standard item.

Another way to use this approach on an older PC is to use a special software product, such as Drive Rocket or EZ-IDE that are often shipped with large hard disks. These products alter the master boot record of the hard disk so that it loads the INT13H extensions to the BIOS into memory before any serious work gets done with the hard disk. I'll explain what a master boot record is in Chapter 10, "Digging Deeper Into Disks."

Now let's focus on how this lowest-level information structure of tracks, sectors, and cylinders gets imposed on a disk, and how it's further organized into logical subsections by DOS.

Physical Versus Logical Formatting of Disks

This section deals with a sometimes confusing distinction between what is called the *physical* or *low-level* formatting and the *logical* or *high-level* formatting of a disk. Both processes consist simply of storing some special information on the disk, but the two processes store information that's used for very different purposes.

A freshly made diskette or hard disk has nothing stored on it. In that state, DOS can't use the disk at all. Two (or in the case of hard disks, three) steps must be taken first. The first step is the physical formatting of the medium. The second step for diskettes, and the third step for hard disks, is the logical formatting. Hard disks add a step in between these two called *partitioning*. (I'll explain partitioning in Chapter 10.)

None of the information that gets put on a disk during the physical or DOS logical formatting is anything you can read or use as a program or data in your PC. Instead, the disk drive needs this information to store your data in an orderly manner, and thus to be able to retrieve your data when it's needed. I like to think of a disk as being like a parking lot for information. If you attempted to store only your data there, you would get, if anything, a complete mess. Likewise, if you let people park their cars in a large, freshly paved, and unmarked lot, they will likely jam them in and later be unable to either find their cars or get them out.

How the Physical Format Information Is Used

So, the first step you must take with a new parking lot or disk drive is to define where, precisely, the parking places (for cars or information) are going to be. In a parking lot, this is accomplished by painting stripes to mark all the individual parking places, and to organize them into rows. On a disk, it's accomplished by recording empty sectors of information in each of the places where information is to go. This level of organization is called the *physical formatting* of the drive.

After the physical formatting is complete, every single sector in which information might ultimately get stored is written to the disk surface. Each sector has a header region that includes numbers indicating where on the disk this sector is located. Each sector has a data section comprising 512 placeholder bytes. And each sector has a section at the tail end for either a CRC value or a few bytes of ECC. (Just what those jargon terms mean and why we must place those numbers there are things I'll explain in the later sections dealing with defects on a disk. Bear with me for now.)

How the DOS Logical Format Information Is Used

The second step in preparing a floppy (and third for a hard disk) is imposing the logical format. That means simply putting some special information that DOS needs to manage that disk into some of those sectors that were created in the first step—sectors that are now empty but available for information storage. In terms of our parking lot analogy, this is like building a valet parking system. A valet parking enterprise needs some way to find where in the lot each car has been parked so it can be quickly returned to its owner upon demand. Similarly, DOS must keep track of every file it stores on the disk so it can get that file's contents back whenever you, or a program you run, wants it.

DOS (or Windows) does this job by putting a special program at the start of the disk and then building some special data tables both there and elsewhere on the disk. The special program and the associated data table located at the very start are called the *boot record*. The system uses this program and its data table to learn about the size of this disk and some of its other properties, and also to facilitate loading of the operating system from this disk, should that be desired.

The next special table is called the *file allocation table* or FAT. On most disks DOS (or Windows) also creates a backup FAT to be used if the first FAT gets damaged. The last of the special data tables that must be created is the *root directory*.

How Each Kind of Format Gets Installed

Diskettes are supplied from the factory either with no formatting, or with both low- and high-level formatting already in place. In either case, you can redo both levels of formatting quite simply by running the DOS FORMAT command. Hard disks are different. It used to be that they came from the factory completely unformatted, which was necessary because the low-level format had to be whatever was needed by the electronics in the hard disk controller to which the disk would be attached.

Now, with all the disk controller electronics integrated onto each hard disk drive, hard disks have the low-level formatting already in place. After a hard disk is installed in a PC, and before it can have the DOS formatting installed, it must be *partitioned*. This is true even if the whole disk will be used as a single partition. (You'll learn why this is true and more about partitioning in the next chapter.)

Because hard disk makers aren't sure how you will be using their disks with DOS, and in particular don't know how you want them partitioned, they rarely do either the partitioning or the DOS-level, logical formatting for you. (Of course, if you buy your PC with both the disks and a bunch of software installed, then that system maker has had to do the partitioning, DOS-level formatting, and software loading.)

When the partitioning information is in place, the DOS logical format can be put on the disk, one partition at a time (if it has more than one) using the DOS FORMAT command. Because the low-level formatting has already been done, the FORMAT command need only insert the DOS-specific data into the defined sectors.

Dealing with Defects on a Disk

No physical systems that people build, and certainly none as complex as a disk drive, turn out exactly as planned. There are always some defects inherent in the device. But PC users demand total perfection in the performance of their disk drives. When you store information there, you want it to come back 100 percent accurate, right down to the very last bit. Anything less, and some—perhaps a vital—part of your PC's operating system may fail, or you might lose some critical document. How can this gap be bridged? A part of the answer is what makes digital computers so special.

Why Digital Equals Apparently Perfect

As I said in Chapter 3, "Understanding Bits, Nybbles, and Bytes," at every stage of digital circuits, the numerical values they handle are represented by voltages that inevitably will vary somewhat from their ideal values. That variation is what we call *noise*. But when those values are sensed by each digital portion of the circuit simple, black-and-white, go-no go decisions are made about what the values are. Each portion also re-creates those voltage values as close to their ideal levels as possible.

This means that you can copy digital data any number of times and be reasonably sure that it still has exactly the same information content that it had when you started out—the noise is totally eliminated, leaving, ordinarily, a perfect copy of the original.

The Two Tricks Used in Disk Data Storage to Ensure Integrity

In terms of disk storage, the same notions apply, with some special considerations. Not only do the digital circuits essentially guarantee that the data you send through them gets to its destination unchanged, disk drives also have special provisions to ensure that when information is stored and then later read back, it can be checked to ensure its integrity.

Disk drives do this in two ways. First, the manufacturers of disk drives check all the information-holding places on each disk during the low-level formatting (and you would be checking it again if you were ever able to force a repetition of that step—which is something you do only by use of certain, specialized data recovery programs) to be sure that each sector will hold and return information faithfully. Any sectors incapable of doing this are marked as bad and are never used. Second, some extra, redundant information (called *error correction codes* or, on diskettes, *error detection codes*) is stored along with your real information. When your data is read back from the disk, the drive checks it against the extra information to be sure that what it thinks it saw stored there is valid.

How Bad Sectors Are Tracked

There are several important differences in the ways that these things are done on diskettes and on hard disks. On a diskette, any bad sectors are simply marked as bad and the diskette's actual capacity is reduced by the number of bad sectors.

Modern hard disks, however, almost always appear to be perfect. They accomplish this by having more sectors for information storage than they tell you about. Some spare sectors are held in reserve, and whenever the disk controller detects a bad sector, it can replace that sector, in a functional sense, with one of the spare sectors. Different disks and different disk controllers use slightly different strategies. Some, for example, have a few spare sectors at the end of each track. Others just have a pool of spare sectors at the end of the entire chain of logical block addresses. Either way, the disk controllers usually manage to hide the defective sectors completely.

In fact, the only way you're likely to see any bad sectors on a hard drive is if it's a very old one, or if a sector goes bad while it's holding some of your data. A very old hard disk might not have been built with all the modern hardware for hiding defects, and if a sector goes bad while it's holding some data, the drive might not be capable of substituting another sector for it without losing the data that had been stored in the failed sector.

I said just a moment ago that, on modern drives, disk controllers usually manage to remap bad sectors, hiding them completely. Actually, that isn't quite true. *Completely* implies that you'll never notice the difference. But if you work with streaming data of any kind—sound, music, or, especially, video—you'll very likely discover quickly that remapping defective sectors can wreak havoc on your throughput performance. (Actually, you may notice a difference even with data that isn't of a streaming type, but less dramatically). You can probably intuit why this is so. For much streaming content, the tolerances between what is being required of your PC's performance and the best it can give are very small. In the amount of time required to move a drive's read/write heads to the spare sectors where your data has been relocated, your video and audio could get completely out of sync. To compensate, your PC will start either dropping frames or skipping audio content, and the video will either look or sound (or both) dreadful.

Fortunately, there's a solution to this problem, assuming you have enough free space on the defective drive to manage it. High-end disk defragmentation tools like Norton Speed Disk will effectively undo this time-consuming sector remap. The sectors that are known to be bad will, of course, remain marked bad, and no new data will be placed there. In the meantime, the defragger will collect all the data in the remapped file and reorganize it—we say it *optimizes* the data—into contiguous sectors. In a worst-case scenario, where the bad sectors fall right in the middle of the space required by a large file, Speed Disk separates the data as unobtrusively as possible, so that only the slightest of head movements is required to jump to the sector where the file continues.

As a rule of thumb, if you're working with data that might be impacted by the remapping of bad sectors, get that data off the drive with the bad sectors. If that's not doable, strict disk defragmentation can give you the best of an imperfect world.

Integrity Maintenance

The beginning of each sector on a floppy diskette contains a few bytes of data for the sole use of the disk drive. These include the address of the sector, plus an indication of whether the sector is bad. Then come 512 bytes of space for your information. Finally, two bytes make up a special, extra number, called the *cyclical redundancy check* (CRC) number. Each time your information is written, this extra number is added.

Each time your information is read, the disk controller first checks the lead-in bytes to be sure it's reading the correct sector. Then it reads the data and recomputes what the CRC value should be. Finally, it looks at the actual CRC value on the disk. If the two numbers are equal, the controller concludes that it read that sector correctly.

If the CRC the drive reads doesn't equal the CRC it computes from the data it read, it may try re-reading that sector. But after doing that a few times and still getting the same mismatch, the only thing the disk controller and operating system can do is announce their failure and prevent you from using the damaged data. That's what has happened when you see the dreaded message, `Error reading drive A: Abort, Retry, or Fail`.

Hard disks handle much more data than diskettes, both because hard disks can store so much more, and also because they can move information onto and off of their disks much more rapidly. They also encounter many more errors than diskettes, but if a hard drive just gave up whenever it misread data, it wouldn't be a useful device at all. Fortunately, our PC hard drives hide at least 99 percent of all mistakes they make.

Instead of merely calculating a CRC value for each sector, hard disks compute a short string of *error correction codes* (ECC). When a read error occurs, the most likely cause is a pinpoint defect on the disk's surface. That defect will mess up just a few bits in the 4,096 bits that make up a sector's 512 bytes. More importantly, the bad bits will all be close together. Some very clever mathematicians and engineers worked out a scheme for ECC that would allow them to not only detect when a mistake is made, but to know exactly what and where the error is. Each bit must be either a 1 or a 0; if you know exactly which bits are wrong, you can compensate for them just by reversing those individual values.

This is why it seems as if our hard disks work perfectly almost all the time. Errors actually occur several times a day, typically, but they're are fixed automatically and transparently. On an average PC, no more than a few times per year does a real error get through and actually cause some problem.

Figure 9.3 shows the anatomy of a hard disk sector. This picture is also a good representation of the anatomy of a sector on a diskette, except that the region that's labeled in this figure as containing ECC numbers is a little shorter on a diskette and holds only a CRC number.

The Logical Structure of a DOS Disk

Now you know how sectors get on disks in the first place. You know something about the internal structure of each sector. What you haven't learned yet, though, is how DOS manages to keep track of all the files you have loaded into all those sectors. I told you the names of the structures it builds a few pages ago (the boot record, FAT, and root directory). In the next several sections of this chapter, I will explain just what each one is and how DOS uses it.

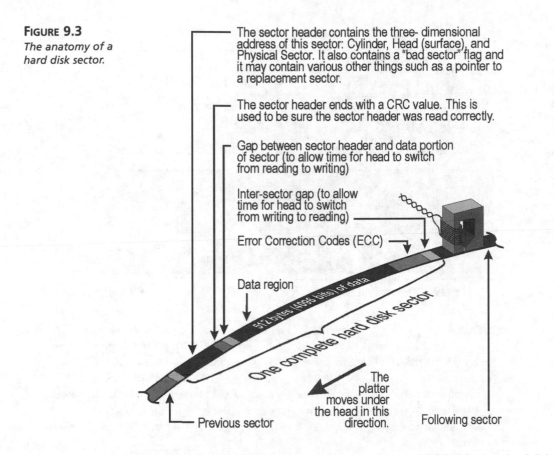

FIGURE 9.3
The anatomy of a hard disk sector.

The sector header contains the three- dimensional address of this sector: Cylinder, Head (surface), and Physical Sector. It also contains a "bad sector" flag and it may contain various other things such as a pointer to a replacement sector.

The sector header ends with a CRC value. This is used to be sure the sector header was read correctly.

Gap between sector header and data portion of sector (to allow time for head to switch from reading to writing)

Inter-sector gap (to allow time for head to switch from writing to reading)

Error Correction Codes (ECC)

Data region

512 bytes (4096 bits) of data

One complete hard disk sector

The platter moves under the head in this direction.

Previous sector

Following sector

Figure 9.4 shows the logical structure that every formatted DOS diskette or hard disk contains. The FAT12 structure is the complete description of what is on a DOS-formatted diskette. A hard disk drive can be logically divided—partitioned—in such a way that it appears to actually contain several hard disks, each of which may have either the FAT12/FAT16 structure or the FAT32 structure. Thus, your C: drive and your D: drive could both exist inside the same physical hard disk case. I'll talk more about partitioning in the next chapter.

The Boot Record

The very first sector on any DOS floppy, and the very first sector in each logical drive on a hard disk is where DOS (or any other PC operating system) puts the *boot record*. (Or, more precisely, that is where it puts at least the beginning of the boot record.)

Every boot record written by any given version of DOS or Windows to a FAT12 or FAT16 disk is precisely the same, except for the contents of a small data table. (Because that table holds information on the size of that drive, and some other things, that part of the boot record must be different on different drives.) With that one exception, a diskette's boot record is the same as that on a hard drive. (All standard diskettes use the FAT12 format.)

FIGURE 9.4

The essential regions within any DOS-formatted logical disk drive. The upper portion of this figure shows the layout used on the older FAT12 and FAT16 formats. The lower figure shows the corresponding information for the newer, FAT32 format.

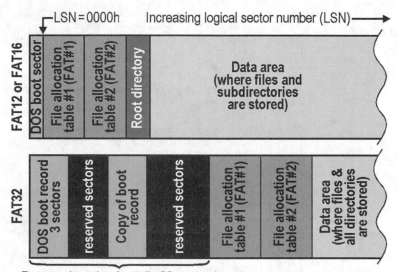

The FAT32 disk format may be applied only to a partition on a hard disk (and then only if the logical drive that partition contains is larger than 512MB). So, if you use Windows 98 (or 95B) and have formatted some or all of your hard disk partitions with the FAT32 structure, the boot record on any diskette you format will be different from those hard disk boot records, because the diskette is always a FAT12 formatted medium. The boot record on a floppy diskette will, however, be identical (except for the data in its data table) to the boot record on any FAT16 partitions (logical disk drives) you may also have in such a system.

Because this boot record for FAT12 and FAT16 is exactly 512 bytes long, it also is sometimes called the *boot sector*—or, to distinguish it from the *master boot record* (MBR), it might be called the *DOS boot sector*. (You'll meet the MBR in detail in Chapter 10.) The boot record on FAT32 disks is quite a bit different from that on a FAT12 or FAT16 disk, and is much larger, and so cannot properly be called a boot sector.

Most of the boot record is a program used to help start up your computer, assuming we're talking about the disk you're booting it from. That's why it carries the name *boot record*. If the disk doesn't have the operating system on it, and if you try to start up from it anyway, the program will display the message: "Non-System disk or disk error. Replace and strike any key when ready."

Figure 9.5 shows how this boot record's information is displayed by Norton Disk Editor (NDE) for a hard disk partition formatted using the FAT32 structure. Here you see just the contents of the data table for the DOS boot record, displayed in an easily readable form, for the C drive of the primary hard disk of our sample desktop system. (I did have to cheat in one sense. The table is too big to see all at once on a normal 25-line display.

If you were using NDE on this hard disk and went into this display, you would have to scroll down in order to see all the lines. I wanted to show you the entire table's contents in this figure, and so I did some cutting and pasting.)

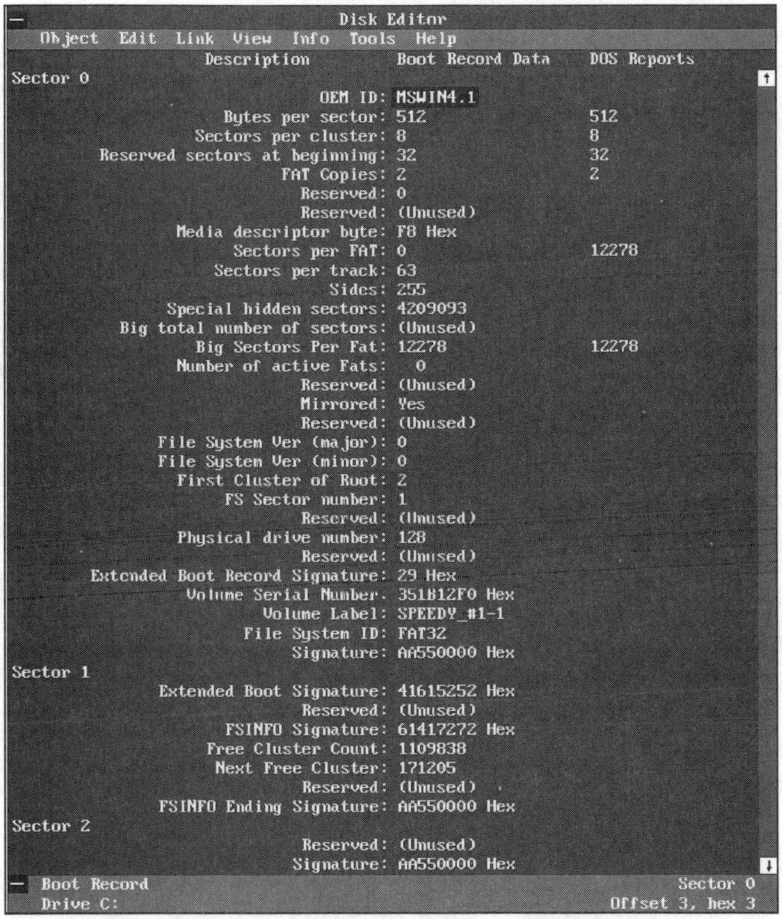

FIGURE 9.5

The DOS Boot Record from the primary hard disk's C partition on our sample desktop system as it is displayed by the Norton Disk Editor. (Note that the large number of hidden sectors indicates that this drive has been configured to support multiple operating systems and boot environments.)

```
───                     Disk Editor
  Object   Edit   Link   View   Info   Tools   Help
             Description            Boot Record Data     DOS Reports
Sector 0                                                              ↑
                        OEM ID: MSWIN4.1
                Bytes per sector: 512                 512
             Sectors per cluster: 8                   8
    Reserved sectors at beginning: 32                 32
                    FAT Copies: 2                      2
                      Reserved: 0
                      Reserved: (Unused)
          Media descriptor byte: F8 Hex
                Sectors per FAT: 0                    12278
              Sectors per track: 63
                         Sides: 255
          Special hidden sectors: 4209093
    Big total number of sectors: (Unused)
             Big Sectors Per Fat: 12278               12278
          Number of active Fats: 0
                      Reserved: (Unused)
                      Mirrored: Yes
                      Reserved: (Unused)
         File System Ver (major): 0
         File System Ver (minor): 0
           First Cluster of Root: 2
              FS Sector number: 1
                      Reserved: (Unused)
          Physical drive number: 128
                      Reserved: (Unused)
    Extended Boot Record Signature: 29 Hex
            Volume Serial Number: 351B12F0 Hex
                  Volume Label: SPEEDY_#1-1
                File System ID: FAT32
                     Signature: AA550000 Hex
Sector 1
          Extended Boot Signature: 41615252 Hex
                      Reserved: (Unused)
              FSINFO Signature: 61417272 Hex
            Free Cluster Count: 1109838
             Next Free Cluster: 171205
                      Reserved: (Unused)
       FSINFO Ending Signature: AA550000 Hex
Sector 2
                      Reserved: (Unused)
                     Signature: AA550000 Hex                         ↓
─── Boot Record                                      Sector 0
    Drive C:                                         Offset 3, hex 3
```

The data table in the DOS boot record, which is called the *BIOS parameter block* (BPB), records some essential numbers that DOS must know about this disk. This is the data that you see displayed by Norton Disk Editor in Figure 9.5. It includes the number of bytes per sector, the total number of sectors on the disk, the number of copies of the FAT, the type of FAT (12-, 16-, or 32-bit), the number of sectors per FAT, the number of sectors in the root directory, plus a few miscellaneous other facts about this disk. In the FAT32 form of the BPB, there are many additional fields. Some are there to increase the reliability of your PC (for example, the fields that specify where to find the root directory and where to find a backup copy of this boot record). Others are included to increase its performance (for example, the fields that show the Free Cluster Count and the Next Free Cluster number). As you can see, this data table is mostly telling DOS where on the disk to find its special data structures, and how much other space there is in which to store your data.

> **Technical Note:** One of the numbers in the BPB that often confuses people is the number of reserved sectors. This is the number of sectors at the beginning of this logical volume that are reserved for the boot program.
>
> For all versions of DOS or Windows prior to the introduction of the FAT32 format for disks, the boot program was only one sector long. On those disks, there's usually just one reserved sector (which contains the boot record)—rarely, if ever, will there be more than one, but the existence of this entry in the BPB shows that having more than one is a possibility, even if it never has been used.
>
> Beginning with the OSR2 release of Windows 95, Microsoft has given us a new way to format disks, called FAT32. Any disk formatted this way has a DOS boot record that takes up the first three sectors on the disk (or partition). It also usually stores a backup copy of that boot record (most often in the seventh through ninth sectors), and the format has been redesigned to allow for possible future extensions. For these reasons, on FAT32 disks you'll normally (but not always) find 32 reserved sectors.
>
> The hidden sectors number may also seem strange. This is the number of sectors on the disk before the first logical volume, and is something I will discuss more in the section "Master Boot Record and Partitions," in Chapter 10.

The Data Area

The next area of the disk I must explain is actually the last area in sequence, and by far the largest one. But until you understand this area's function and structure, my description of the other two areas won't make much sense. The Data Area is where DOS stores your data. In fact, it includes all the space in the logical disk drive that isn't taken up in one of the system structures (the boot record, FAT, and root directory).

Sectors Versus Clusters on a Disk Drive

Your PC's hardware can send data to, or retrieve it from a disk, only one sector at a time. (Well, sometimes it may handle multiple, consecutive sectors in a single operation, but at the very lowest hardware level, the disk drive itself is only capable of handling individual sectors, neither more nor less.) DOS and Windows use logical sector numbers to address everything on the disk (including the system information in the boot record, FAT, and root directory). This numbering starts at zero for the first logical sector (which, on a hard drive, contains the partition's boot record) in a physical disk drive.

Technical Note: A block and a sector are each 512-byte units of information. However, the DOS logical sector numbers are not to be confused with the disk drive's logical block numbers. The difference is this: The disk drive tracks the logical block numbers for the entire drive. So, this is ultimately the unit in which the BIOS must talk to the disk drive if it is using the LBA access strategy. (If it uses the fictitious geometry strategy, the BIOS uses a combination of three numbers, representing the cylinder, head, and sector (CHS) on that fictitious drive while the disk drive itself always uses the logical block number.)

DOS, on the other hand, tracks the logical sector number within a DOS partition (which is usually the same as a logical disk drive—in other words, something that gets its own drive letter). That partition takes up some portion of a disk, but not necessarily all the disk. Thus, DOS's logical sector numbers and the drive's logical block numbers will be somewhat offset from one another. The only time the two are the same is on a diskette, or some other medium that is mimicking a diskette.

In the system areas of the drive—those reserved for the partition table, master boot record, and so on—the drive is capable of reading data one sector at a time. At another level, when it comes to keeping track of the files stored on the main or data portion of a disk, DOS uses a different strategy. This entails using what is usually a considerably larger unit of data called a *cluster* or an *allocation unit*. A cluster is a collection of adjacent sectors of data (and the sectors do, in fact, contain successive blocks of data in a particular file). A cluster is the minimum amount of space that can be allocated to a file by DOS. Therefore, a file's data will use as many complete clusters as are needed to store the file. Consequently, if a cluster on a certain drive is 4KB, and a file's data is 3KB long, the file will still occupy a full 4KB cluster. The unused 1KB portion of the cluster is commonly referred to as *slack space*. If the file later grows to use this 1k of space, it will fill the entire cluster. However, if the file later grows to 6KB, it will then require two full clusters—or 8KB, on our sample disk—because it cannot share a partial cluster with another file.

So, in the DOS view, a logical disk drive consists of the system areas (boot record, FAT, and root directory) followed by some number of identical-size clusters into which it can store data. The purpose of the FAT and root directory is simply to hold the records that let DOS keep track of the information stored in the disk's data area clusters.

The File Allocation Table (FAT)

The *File Allocation Table* (FAT) is the principal structure by which DOS keeps track of what is using which portions of a logical disk. Every DOS logical disk drive (that is, each thing to which DOS assigns a drive letter designation) has a FAT. In fact, each such drive usually has two copies of that FAT. All FAT12 and FAT16 disks have two copies of the FAT. Most FAT32 disks also have two copies, but they are used somewhat differently and it's quite permissible to have only one or have more than two of them.

Technical Note: Having two copies of the FAT protects you against certain types of possible problems that might lead to data loss. Every time DOS or Windows must access a file on a FAT12 or FAT16 disk, it checks the entries in the first FAT to see where to go. If it's writing data onto the disk, it updates both the first FAT and the second FAT.

However, if DOS gets an error reading the first FAT, it will automatically try to get the information it needs from the second FAT. Because it never reads the second FAT until it really needs it, DOS might not notice if the second FAT itself gets damaged until it's too late to do anything about it.

The only ways you can learn about a problem with reading or writing the first FAT is if there's also an error in reading the second FAT—in which case the problems are very serious and you may well never recover your data—or if you run a utility like Microsoft ScanDisk or Norton Disk Doctor to diagnose possible problems with your disk.

If there are any problems with reading either FAT, or if they aren't identical, the program will alert you to this problem. Depending on which tool you use—and assuming that only one of the FATs has been corrupted—you might be able to repair the FAT with the incorrect contents and thus make the two copies identical (and correct) once more.

It is prudent to check for problems on your disk drives on a regular basis, and the Norton Utilities and Windows 98 both allow you to have your PC do this automatically at intervals you establish. If problems are fixed shortly after they occur, your data might never be endangered. If you never check for trouble, you still might not be totally out of luck—but it will require a lot of time and some skill using a tool like Norton Disk Editor to try to recover your data.

This story is slightly altered for FAT32 disks. While normally things work exactly as I described above, it is possible for a program to change some values in the BPB inside the boot record, and thereby change how the FATs are used on that disk. (There is no major piece of software that works in the way you're about to read, but the capability exists, nevertheless.)

One change that is possible is to designate one of the FATs different from the first one as the *primary* or *active* one, which then is the one that will be used for all file accesses as long as that FAT is readable. Another change is to turn off mirroring of the FATs. If you do this, all updates to the FAT will be written only to the primary FAT.

These additional possibilities were included to help deal with damaged disks. By default, these new features are turned off and there are two FATs that are treated (in these respects) exactly like the FATs on a FAT12 or FAT16 disk.

But if a problem develops with the first (and therefore, by default, the primary) FAT, mirroring can be turned off and the system directed to use only the other FAT. A utility program that utilized these features may permit one to recover the data from such a disk quite easily in situations which otherwise would present major difficulties for data recovery. Then, after you have copied off all the valuable data, the disk could simply be reformatted. That will usually fix the problems and you may then resume using the disk normally.

The FAT is simply a huge table of numbers, each of which, in most cases, is simply the address of another cluster. These address numbers are assigned consecutively, starting at 2 as the address number for the first cluster after the root directory on a FAT12 or FAT16 disk, and for the first cluster after the last FAT on a FAT32 disk. The FAT has an entry for each cluster from that beginning point to the end of the disk, and inspecting their contents tells DOS or Windows the status of all those clusters.

On a FAT12 disk, each of these cluster numbers is twelve bits (one and one-half bytes) long. On a FAT16 disk they are each sixteen bits (two bytes) long. On a FAT32 disk, they are each thirty-two (four bytes) long. This means that on a FAT12 disk (for example, a diskette) each three bytes in the FAT holds two cluster numbers. That can make reading them from a hexadecimal display of the disk contents (such as DEBUG might present) quite challenging. Fortunately, the Norton Disk Editor displays them as decimal values, each cleanly separated from its neighbors, no matter which format (FAT12, FAT16, or FAT32) is in use.

The number contained in each location in the FAT normally is the address of another cluster, and it is this linkage that lets DOS or Windows find all the pieces of a file stored on the disk. But the number stored in a cluster location can also have one of several special values. If the value is 0, the cluster is currently unused and available. An End of File (EOF) value means that this cluster is in use, and the file using it has either all or the last portion of its information stored here. A third special number signals to DOS that this cluster is bad—meaning it cannot safely be used to store information. Any other number in the FAT is a signal that the cluster is in use, storing information from a file, and that the information for that file continues in another cluster—specifically, the one whose address number is stored at this location in the FAT. (On a FAT32 disk, the bad cluster number is 0FFFFFF7h, but that number may also be used as a valid cluster number in a cluster chain. The only ways to tell for sure if a cluster with this value is bad are these: First, if there is some other cluster entry in this FAT that points to this one, then this is not a bad cluster. Second, if this number is too large for the size of this disk, then it must be a bad cluster.)

Figure 9.6 shows a portion of a FAT table with some typical values in it. (This display is another screen capture from Norton Disk Editor and it also was taken from the FAT32 formatted C drive on our sample desktop system.)

Here you see two numbers for each entry in the FAT. The first number (which is always a zero in this figure) is enclosed in square brackets. This is the high-order portion of the cluster contents. The low-order portion is to the right of that, not enclosed in brackets.

FIGURE 9.6

A portion of a typical FAT—one showing high levels of file fragmentation—is displayed by the Norton Disk Editor program.

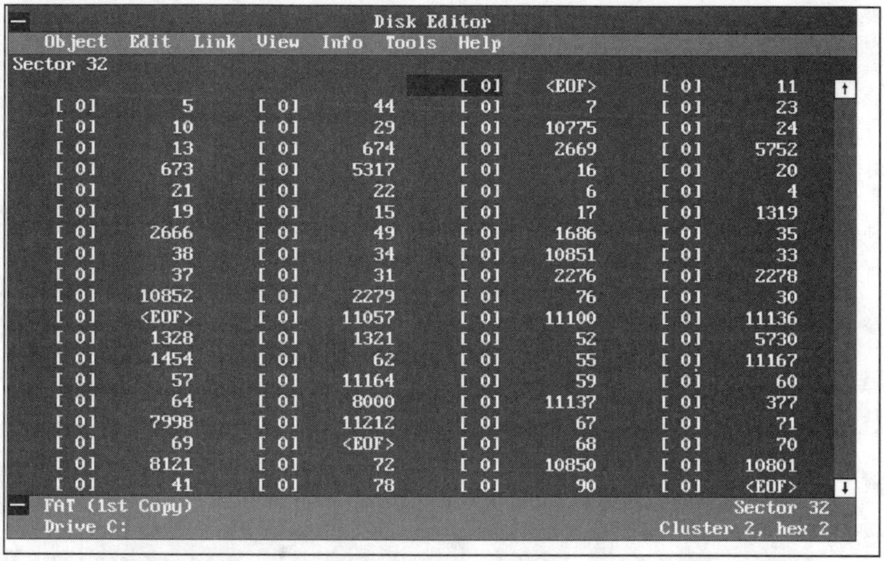

```
─                          Disk Editor
   Object   Edit   Link   View   Info   Tools   Help
Sector 32
                                      [ 0]    <EOF>      [ 0]      11    ↑
   [ 0]      5    [ 0]     44     [ 0]      7      [ 0]      23
   [ 0]     10    [ 0]     29     [ 0]   10775     [ 0]      24
   [ 0]     13    [ 0]    674     [ 0]    2669     [ 0]    5752
   [ 0]    673    [ 0]   5317     [ 0]     16      [ 0]      20
   [ 0]     21    [ 0]     22     [ 0]      6      [ 0]       4
   [ 0]     19    [ 0]     15     [ 0]     17      [ 0]    1319
   [ 0]   2666    [ 0]     49     [ 0]    1686     [ 0]      35
   [ 0]     38    [ 0]     34     [ 0]   10851     [ 0]      33
   [ 0]     37    [ 0]     31     [ 0]    2276     [ 0]    2278
   [ 0]  10852    [ 0]   2279     [ 0]     76      [ 0]      30
   [ 0]   <EOF>   [ 0]  11057     [ 0]   11100     [ 0]   11136
   [ 0]   1328    [ 0]   1321     [ 0]     52      [ 0]    5730
   [ 0]   1454    [ 0]     62     [ 0]     55      [ 0]   11167
   [ 0]     57    [ 0]  11164     [ 0]     59      [ 0]      60
   [ 0]     64    [ 0]   8000     [ 0]   11137     [ 0]     377
   [ 0]   7998    [ 0]  11212     [ 0]     67      [ 0]      71
   [ 0]     69    [ 0]   <EOF>    [ 0]     68      [ 0]      70
   [ 0]   8121    [ 0]     72     [ 0]   10850     [ 0]   10801
   [ 0]     41    [ 0]     78     [ 0]     90      [ 0]   <EOF>    ↓
─  FAT (1st Copy)                                      Sector 32
   Drive C:                                      Cluster 2, hex 2
```

The black highlight surrounding the first entry in brackets shows that we are now looking at the most significant half of the very first cluster number in the FAT. The information at the bottom of the screen shows that we are looking at the first copy of the FAT table, and in particular, at cluster number 2, which is the address of the first entry in that table. From Figure 9.5 you can see that this is the root directory for this disk. Also from the fact that <EOF> appears in the rest of this cluster entry (just to the right of the highlight), you can see that the root directory for this disk is, so far, limited to a single cluster.

That the root directory appears in the FAT as just another file is one of the major differences between a FAT32 formatted disk and FAT12 or FAT16 formatted disks. On a FAT32 disk, if the area that would normally be used for the root directory gets damaged, it is perfectly possible to relocate the root directory to some undamaged area. Of perhaps more importance, there is now no strict limit on the size of the root directory. This is in stark contrast to the situation on all FAT12 and FAT16 disks, where the root directory size must be specified when it is formatted, and is usually held to a rather small number (commonly 512 filename or folder entries, or fewer). This number is further reduced if you use long filenames, as each long filename uses up multiple directory entries.

You may have wondered why the first line of numbers starts in the middle. The blank region at the left represents where you would find the cluster values for cluster addresses zero and one—but because there are no such clusters, this region is blank.

Technical Note: Why do cluster numbers start at two? The more usual choice for counting is to start at one or—if you are a mathematician or computer engineer—perhaps at zero. We can't start at zero, because the entry value must point to a cluster address, and zero is disallowed, because a zero entry value for a cluster means that cluster is available for data storage. But we could start with one. Why not do so?

The answer is that DOS wants to see a very special signature byte at the beginning of a FAT to let it know that this is a FAT, and what kind of FAT it is. The designers of DOS decided to use up the first two cluster-entry-sized places in the FAT for this purpose. (If the cluster entry size is 1 1/2 bytes, they add a hexadecimal value FFFFh to the end of the signature byte. If the cluster entries each occupy 2 full bytes, the signature byte is augmented by FFFFFFh, and for four-byte cluster entries the first two cluster locations are filled with the signature byte plus FFFFFFFFFFFFFh.) Now, when you take the cluster address value times the cluster size, you get the position within the FAT where that cluster's entry starts.

If you now turn your attention to the entry in Figure 9.6 for cluster number three, you can begin to trace out the spaces on this disk used by a particular file. In this case, the number in cluster 3's location in the FAT is 11. That means that the file that starts in cluster number 3 continues in cluster number 11. Checking the table, you will see that in cluster number 11 (two lines below cluster number 3) is the value 24. Thus, the file goes on from here in cluster 24. If you continue this process, you can figure out that this file has its data spread over thirteen clusters in this order: 3-11-24-19-20-21-22-6-7-23-4-5-44. Looking at which groups of these numbers are in numerical order, you can also see that the file is broken into eight fragments (3, 11, 24, 19-20-21-22, 6-7, 23, 4-5, and 44).

Another file you can trace out in its entirety in this figure starts in cluster number 66 (third column, fourth entry from the bottom). This file is spread over six clusters (comprising four fragments) in this order: 66-67-71-70-68-69. All the other files represented by entries in this figure are contained only partially in the first 80 clusters, which is all you can see represented here.

If your head seemed to spin while you were reading the last couple of paragraphs, you may be assured that the disk drive's heads also have to do quite a dance when they are asked to retrieve fragmented files like those I've shown you here—a severely fragmented hard disk can force the drive head to zip back and forth repeatedly to read or write a file. Head movements use a comparatively huge amount of time, and a badly fragmented disk will definitely reduce your system's performance.

How Big Is Your PC's FAT?

I have told you already that there are three kinds of FAT (FAT12, FAT16, and FAT32). What I haven't yet told you is how you or DOS decides which kind to use on a specific disk, and how large those disks and their FATs can be.

The Original and Still Common FAT12

The original DOS FATs used 12-bit numbers for each cluster entry, and DOS still uses 12-bit FATs for all floppy diskettes. (This is crucial, for it lets you read even very old floppies that might have data stored on them from the early days of DOS.) Furthermore, DOS also uses 12-bit FATs for any hard disk volume of less than 16MB.

A number with 12 bits suffices for storing values from zero to 4095. Several of these values are reserved, so all cluster addresses must be in the range from 2 to 4086. If DOS tried to keep track of every sector of data individually, this limit would mean that it could manage data only on a disk whose data capacity was quite small. You can get the actual value by multiplying 512 bytes (the amount in one sector) times 4085 (the maximum number of clusters)—and the answer comes out to be just a little more than 2MB. That's larger than most diskettes, but a lot smaller than any hard disk.

So, DOS can keep track of every single sector of data on a diskette. But on a hard disk it must clump the data together into larger blocks (clusters). For simplicity, on hard disks of any size up to about 16MB capacity, DOS uses a cluster size of 4KB (eight sectors per cluster). Notice that 16MB is about the largest disk that DOS can track with 12-bit FAT entries and this size of cluster. That was fine when hard disks were commonly no larger than 16MB. Now, with hard disk capacity measured in GB, this strategy would mean using ridiculously large clusters.

Upping the Ante: FAT16

Starting around DOS version 3, a second style of FAT was introduced. (The exact point in the development of DOS varied with the many different clone-specific versions introduced around that time, which is why I use this wording here.) These FATs use 16-bit numbers for cluster entries. DOS versions and Windows 95 and 98 still use 12-bit FATs on diskettes. For any disk volume that can hold more than 16MB—but less than 2GB—of data, DOS versions up through 7.0 and Windows 95 use 16-bit FATs . (I'll cover the newer FAT32 option in a moment.)

The DOS designers decided to use clusters with at least four sectors in them (thus, a cluster size of at least 2KB) for all FAT16 hard disks. That size suffices for any hard disk with less than a 128MB total capacity. After that, every time the total capacity doubles, DOS doubles the cluster size. The largest logical disk drives that DOS can handle comfortably have capacities of up to 2GB. For such a large volume, the cluster size is 32KB. This means that even if a file contains only a single byte of data, writing it to the disk uses one entire 32KB region of the disk, making that area unavailable for any other file's data storage.

Some Non-FAT Improvements to Disk Space Accounting

The ever-increasing size of hard disks has caused PC operating system designers to face the limits imposed by the 16-bit FAT structure. The first solution to these problems was introduced by IBM in OS/2's High Performance File System (HPFS). Another solution was introduced by Microsoft with the Windows NT File System (NTFS). Both systems perform FAT-like tasks in completely new ways. As such, they make disks formatted with those file systems largely inaccessible to DOS or Windows 95 programs.

The Newest, FAT32 Way to Go

The most recent solution to these large-disk problems was introduced by Microsoft in its OSR2 release of Windows 95—and it was named FAT32. As the name suggests, FAT32 is pretty much like the earlier 12-bit and 16-bit FAT structures, expanded to accommodate larger cluster entry values (each using 32 bits, or 4 bytes, of space in the FAT) and with many new features (some of which I have described above) that make this quite an exciting new way to format disks. Windows 98 also supports FAT32, and we are promised that Windows NT users will gain this option once they upgrade to the coming Windows 2000.

Windows 9x won't format logical drives with this new 32-bit FAT format unless you choose to have it do so, although any new PC you purchase with a larger-than-2GB drive will almost surely be preformatted with FAT32. When you first run FDISK, if your hard disk has any potential capacity larger than 512MB, you will have a chance to turn on this feature. If you select to use FAT32, FDISK will format all larger-than-512MB logical volumes you create during that FDISK session with a 32-bit FAT structure. The default format is still the 16-bit format, because after you format a disk volume with FAT32, it will no longer be accessible by antiquated versions of DOS or any older version of Windows. But Windows 95 (in its OSR2 version) and Windows 98 can and do work fine with all three FAT-structured logical disk drives.

The minimum size for a FAT32 volume is 512MB. What about the maximum size? Before you start calculating, you need to know that Microsoft has reserved the top four bits of every cluster number in a FAT32 file allocation table. That means that there are only 28 bits for the cluster number, so the maximum cluster number possible is 268,435,456.

If you work it out, this means that a FAT32 FAT table can, itself, grow to a maximum size of 1GB and at that size it contains just barely enough entries to represent all the locations on a 2048GB hard disk—assuming that standard sector size of 512 bytes. That is, for now, the maximum size disk volume (single drive letter) that you can have on a PC. Other limitations exist elsewhere in your system, however. For example, even today's newest BIOSes are only capable of working with single volumes of up to 137GB. This is because the 28-bit LBA scheme currently used won't support larger volume sizes.

The Root Directory

The final part of the system area on a DOS logical disk drive is the *root directory*. The root directory is a part of the system area for FAT12 and FAT16 disks, but not for a FAT32-formatted disk. As I noted previously, a FAT32 disk treats the root directory just like a subdirectory (with some minor exceptions).

The root directory serves much the same purpose for file access on a disk as the directory board that you can find in the lobby of most large office buildings for locating offices. The directory board tells you the office number to use to enter a specific suite of offices. It doesn't mean that this room is the only one that a company uses, but that this is the company's reception area or entry point. Similarly, the root directory entries in a DOS file system point to the beginnings of several files. In addition to those pointers, the root directory entries also hold the names of those files, their sizes, and some additional information about them.

What the root directory doesn't do is tell you the details about all the places on this disk drive where a given file's information may be stored. That is the purpose of the FAT. There can be several kinds of entries in a directory. I'll describe all of them in a moment, but I want first to focus on one special kind: the subdirectory.

Subdirectories

Large hard disks hold lots of files—far too many to keep track of sensibly if all their names were listed in a single place. The designers of DOS allowed for this by including (starting with DOS version 3) the notion of subdirectories. These are files that are pointed to by entries in the root directory (or in some other subdirectory), but their contents are treated as an additional file directory listing.

In almost all respects, the contents of these subdirectory files have a form that's identical to that of the contents of the root directory. But there are a few key differences. One difference is that only the root directory can have an entry for the logical volume's name (the volume label entry). Another is that every subdirectory (other than the root directory under FAT32) contains two special pseudo-directory entries.

The names of these pseudo-directory entries are very odd. One has the name "."—by which I mean its full name is simply a single period. The other has the name ".."—two periods. These are not like the periods you see between the name and extension of a file. If you look at a directory's contents with the DOS DIR command or with the Norton Disk Editor, you won't see the file-delimiter periods, but you will see the pseudo-directory period references.

The single-period entry is a synonym for the subdirectory in which it's found. The double-period entry is a pointer to the directory (root or sub-) that is the parent of this directory—that is, the directory that contains an entry pointing to the file whose contents are this subdirectory. Figure 9.7 graphically shows this relationship. Shown in the root directory are a volume label (whose starting cluster number has the unreal value of zero), and one subdirectory entry (SUBDIR1). On the right, you see a portion of the contents of SUBDIR1, including its two special pseudo-directory names and another subdirectory entry (SUBDIR2). Finally, you see that SUBDIR2 also contains a similar set of two pseudo-directory entries. The arrows show you where each directory entry points—that is, it indicates where each of the starting cluster numbers shown in this figure actually points.

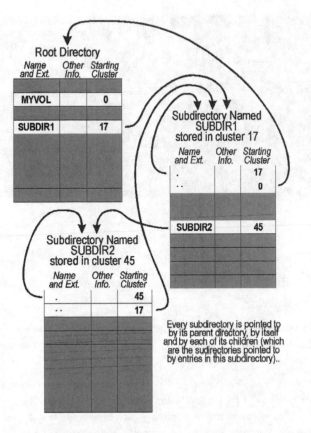

Figure 9.7
How subdirectories are pointed to by their parents and by their children.

The Different Types of DOS Directory Entries and What They Contain

You probably are quite familiar with at least one view of a directory. If you use Windows 9x, you might have seen only the view shown by Windows Explorer. If you use DOS (by itself or in a DOS windows within Windows 3.x or Windows 9x) you will have seen a directory's contents in the form shown by the DOS DIR command.

But whether you use Windows Explorer or the DOS DIR command, you aren't seeing all that's contained in those directory entries. And you certainly aren't seeing how that information is arranged.

The information in a subdirectory is stored in exactly the same format as is used in the root directory. Figure 9.8 shows a subdirectory's contents using the DOS DIR command, but using a command prompt in a DOS Window within Windows 95 or 98 (sometimes called a *DOS box*). This figure shows the contents of a full-screen DOS box directory command in a special subdirectory on my G drive.

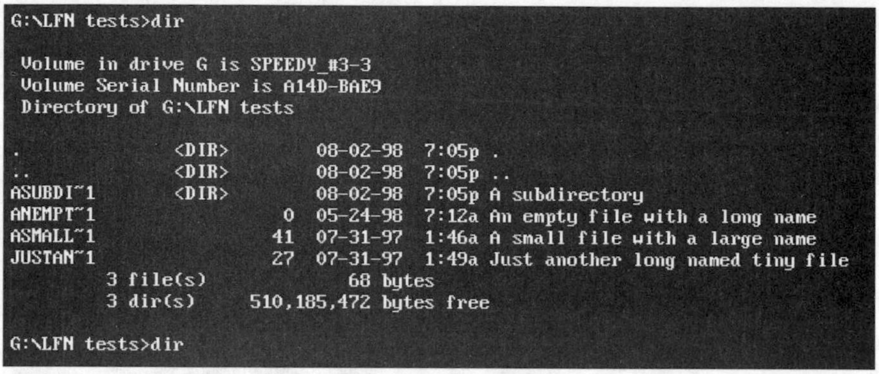

Figure 9.8

The DOS DIR *command issued inside a DOS Window also shows the long filenames (in the right-hand column), but still much information is invisible. The same* DIR *command issued in real-mode DOS (in MS-DOS mode) on this disk would show everything exactly as it is here except for the long filenames.*

```
G:\LFN tests>dir

 Volume in drive G is SPEEDY_#3-3
 Volume Serial Number is A14D-BAE9
 Directory of G:\LFN tests

.              <DIR>         08-02-98   7:05p .
..             <DIR>         08-02-98   7:05p ..
ASUBDI~1       <DIR>         08-02-98   7:05p A subdirectory
ANEMPT~1              0      05-24-98   7:12a An empty file with a long name
ASMALL~1             41      07-31-97   1:46a A small file with a large name
JUSTAN~1             27      07-31-97   1:49a Just another long named tiny file
         3 file(s)                 68 bytes
         3 dir(s)         510,185,472 bytes free

G:\LFN tests>dir
```

The directory listing in Figure 9.8 shows the names of the files and subdirectories in this directory (including the two, special pseudo-directory entries with the names "." and "..") and a size for each item, plus a time and date on which each was last modified.

Notice that there is no size shown for the directory entries. That is not actually true, but it is what the designers of DOS and Windows decided to show you when presenting this information. Subdirectories are files and they each have some length, but that length just isn't shown here. You can figure out their lengths by looking in the FAT to see how many clusters each directory occupies.

Figure 9.9 shows the same subdirectory shown in Figure 9.8, but this time you see its contents displayed in as human-readable a form as possible. This is the default way that Norton Disk Editor shows directory listings.

Here you can see that the directory entry contains more than just the name and extension, the file size, and the date and time of last modification that you could see in the DIR listing. In particular, the NDE display shows that each directory entry also contains some file attributes and a cluster address where this file's contents begin on the disk. In fact, because these are FAT32 format directory entries, they have even more information in them than is shown here. The More> you see on the menu bar at the top of the figure shows how you would access additional views of these directory entries from within NDE. I'll tell you in a moment the rest of what these directory entries specify about the files they represent.

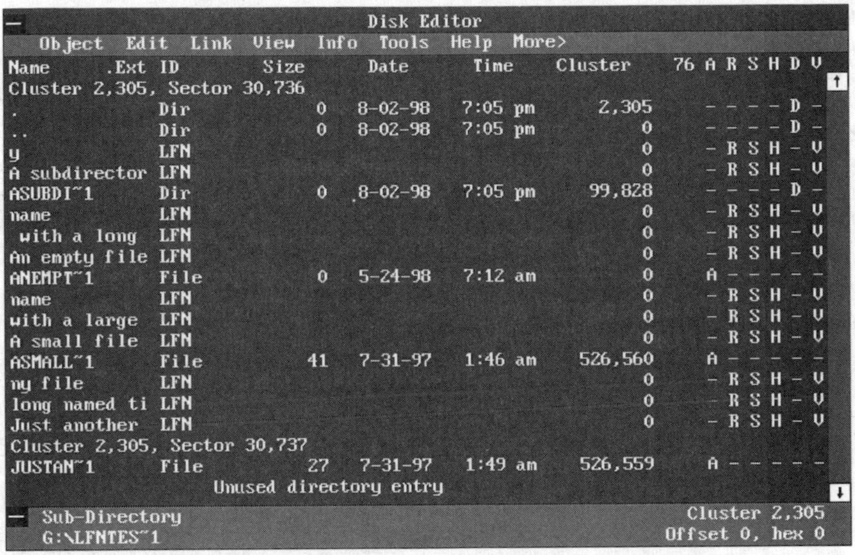

Figure 9.9

Norton Disk Editor can display the information in this same subdirectory in a readily human-readable form.

```
─                              Disk Editor
   Object  Edit  Link  View  Info  Tools  Help  More>
Name      .Ext ID       Size       Date     Time    Cluster     76 A R S H D V
Cluster 2,305, Sector 30,736                                                 ↑
.              Dir         0    8-02-98   7:05 pm      2,305     - - - - D -
..             Dir         0    8-02-98   7:05 pm          0     - - - - D -
y              LFN                                         0     - R S H - V
A subdirector  LFN                                         0     - R S H - V
ASUBDI~1       Dir         0    .8-02-98  7:05 pm     99,828     - - - - D -
name           LFN                                         0     - R S H - V
 with a long   LFN                                         0     - R S H - V
An empty file  LFN                                         0     - R S H - V
ANEMPT~1       File        0    5-24-98   7:12 am          0     A - - - - -
name           LFN                                         0     - R S H - V
with a large   LFN                                         0     - R S H - V
A small file   LFN                                         0     - R S H - V
ASMALL~1       File       41    7-31-97   1:46 am    526,560     A - - - - -
my file        LFN                                         0     - R S H - V
long named ti  LFN                                         0     - R S H - V
Just another   LFN                                         0     - R S H - V
Cluster 2,305, Sector 30,737
JUSTAN~1       File       27    7-31-97   1:49 am    526,559     A - - - - -
                    Unused directory entry                                   ↓
─  Sub-Directory                                         Cluster 2,305
   G:\LFNTES~1                                            Offset 0, hex 0
```

Notice that the entry with a single period as its name points to cluster 2,305, and that this directory entry is in cluster 2,305. Also notice that the entry with the double period as its name points to cluster number 0. In reality, there is no such cluster, but this means that the parent directory for this directory is in the root directory. For a FAT32 disk (such as this one) the root directory is located in an addressable cluster (in this example, and most commonly, in cluster 2). However, because on a FAT12 or FAT16 disk the root directory is not in any numbered cluster, the designers of DOS decided to show the root directory location as cluster zero in all of the different FAT disk formats.

Also notice that here the sizes of the subdirectories are all shown as zero. The explanation for this is the same as for the missing lengths in the previous figure. The actual lengths of the subdirectory files simply isn't recorded in these directory entries. The DIR command omits showing any value; NDE shows them as a zero value.

Directory Entry Structure and File Attributes

Now you've seen a subdirectory in different ways, and it's time to look at the contents of a single entry in detail. Each entry in the root directory, and each entry in any subdirectory, is exactly 32 bytes long in all three FAT formats. Some of those entries hold filenames and information DOS needs to find that file's content, plus other information about the file. Some entries hold similar information about subdirectories. And some entries serve other purposes (including, in Windows 95 and 98, storing pieces of the long filename that belongs to a file pointed to by some other entry in this directory). I will explain first the entries that are used to point to files and then those for long filenames. Figure 9.10 shows schematically the three variations on what a directory entry can hold, depending on which FAT system is in use, and on whether the entry is for a *short filename* (SFN) or a *long filename* (LFN).

FIGURE 9.10

*The three forms
of a directory
entry on a
DOS/Windows FAT
disk.*

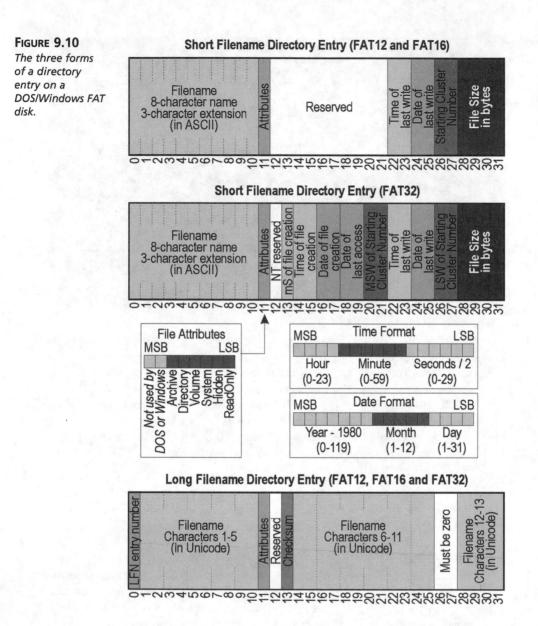

In this figure, the top chart shows all the different fields in a short filename directory
entry on a FAT12 or a FAT16 formatted disk. The next chart shows the same information
for a FAT32 formatted disk. Below that are charts showing the bit-by-bit details of how
the file attributes are stored as well as how the date and time entries are stored. At the
bottom is a chart showing how a long filename entry is stored. This format is identical
for all three versions of the FAT file system (but, of course, applies only to systems

running Windows 98, or Windows 95 with the OSR2 upgrade). Below each of the charts you see numbers running from zero to 31. These are the byte-offset values telling how far into the directory entry a given field will be found. This shows that the locations closest to the start of the disk are at the left in this diagram.

Short Filenames in the FAT12, FAT16, and FAT32 Disk Formats

The first 11 bytes of this type of DOS directory entry are used to store what we term the *short filename* of the file to which this entry points. This SFN is precisely the same concept as what used to be called simply *the* filename before DOS and Windows were given the capability of handling long filenames.

Each SFN is segmented by DOS into two parts. The first eight bytes holds eight characters (letters, numerals, or certain symbols) that form the name itself. The next three bytes hold a three-character extension of that name. The DOS file-naming rules require the name to have at least one non-space character, and they permit a maximum of eight characters. If the name is less than eight characters long, it gets padded with space characters to fill out the eight locations in the directory entry. Similarly, the extension can have anywhere from zero to three characters. The remaining locations, if any, in the directory entry are simply filled with space characters. Because all the 11 spaces are accounted for, there's no need to show the period that one conventionally types between the filename and the extension. It is merely implied in the directory entry.

The 12th byte in the directory entry stores the file attributes. Of these eight bits, six are used by DOS. (Some network operating systems, such as Novell, use one or both of the extra two attribute bits.) The DOS attributes include

- Archive attribute —This indicates a file that has been opened by a program in a fashion that enabled the program to change the file's contents. DOS sets this archive bit to ON when the file is opened. Backup programs frequently turn it OFF when they back up the file. If you use this strategy, then only the files with this bit ON must be a part of your next incremental backup.

- Directory attribute —This indicates that this directory entry points to a subdirectory rather than to a file.

- Volume attribute —This is used on just one directory entry in the root directory. That one holds the name of this disk volume. (This attribute also gets used for long filenames, as you will learn in the next section.)

- System attribute —This indicates a file that is a part of the operating system (DOS) or it can be a file that has been flagged in this manner by an application program (for example, this is often done as a part of a copy-protection scheme).

- Hidden attribute —These files (and those with the S bit set ON) are not to be displayed in a normal DIR listing.

- Read-only attribute —This indicates to DOS that this file is not to be modified. Of course, because this is only a bit in a byte stored on the disk, any program could change this bit, and then DOS will freely let it modify this file. This is mostly used to protect against human error—that is, to help keep you from inadvertently erasing or altering key files.

Notice that having a file labeled with one or more of these attributes can make perfect sense. For example, most files that are tagged as system files are also tagged with the hidden and read-only flags. But it makes less sense (or so it would seem) to make the volume label have any other attributes, except perhaps the read-only attribute. In fact, just such an implausible combination of attributes (RSHV) is used by Windows 9x to flag directory entries that are part of a long filename.

On a FAT12 or FAT16 disk, the next 10 bytes are unused. They ordinarily will be filled with zeros, and they are considered reserved values. On a FAT32 disk, these 10 bytes hold quite a variety of information about the file. The byte marked NT reserved is, as the name suggests, a field not used in DOS or Windows 9x, but used by Windows NT.

For compatibility reasons, the fields that occur in FAT12 or FAT16 short filename directory entries are also found in the same places in the FAT32 short filename directory entries. The remaining fields that occur only in FAT32 short filename directory entries fall within what was a 10-byte-long reserved region in FAT12 and FAT16 short filename directory entries.

The fields labeled LSW of Starting Cluster Number and MSW of Starting Cluster Number contain the least significant word and the most significant word of the double-word (four byte) cluster number that is required to point to a location on a FAT32 formatted disk volume.

The byte at offset 13 (the fourteenth byte in the directory entry) holds what Microsoft terms the "millisecond stamp at file creation time." It can be used to determine to a rather high degree of accuracy which of two versions of a file was created first. The other time fields hold the time to an accuracy of only two seconds, as is shown in the Time Format details chart in Figure 9.10. The time and date formats are referred to as *packed binary* because in each case they fit several different binary numbers into a single sixteen-bit location, simply putting each of those binary numbers into a specified group of adjacent bit locations within that sixteen-bit word.

The last four bytes of each directory entry hold a 32-bit binary number saying how long this file is in bytes. That would seem to suggest that DOS can handle files that are up to 4GB long.

On a FAT32-formatted disk you can actually have individual files with sizes up to just four bytes less than 4GB. Furthermore, because the maximum disk size is 2048GB, you can even have a lot of these maximum size files on a single disk.

On a FAT12-formatted disk, in contrast, the total disk size is limited to around 16MB maximum total disk capacity, and some of it must be used for the boot sector, FATs, and root directory that constitute the disk's system area. Clearly, the maximum size for any one file is somewhat less than 16MB.

Similarly, a FAT16 formatted logical drive cannot be any larger than 2GB, so the maximum size for any one file is somewhat less than that. And you cannot have more than one nearly maximum size file on such a disk.

In addition to the directory entries that point to files and those that point to subdirectories, there can be just one directory entry, and only in the root directory, of the third type: a *volume label*. In this directory entry, the name is used as the volume name (without a period inserted between the eighth and ninth characters, as is done for filenames and subdirectory names). The rest of the fields in this entry are not used.

Starting with Windows 95, there is a fourth kind of directory entry. This is one that holds a portion of a long filename.

How Long Filenames Have Altered Things

Before Windows 95, both DOS and Windows 3.*x* limited all filenames to the old *8.3 standard*. That is, they could have up to eight characters in the filename itself, plus up to three characters for the extension. Windows 95, in contrast, finally allowed filenames to be anything you like, up to 255 characters long. This file naming scheme was first introduced in Windows NT, version 3.1, for NTFS disk volumes and in Windows NT, version 3.5, for FAT volumes. The Windows 9*x* implementation of long filenames is essentially identical to that used for FAT volumes in Windows NT, version 3.5 or greater.

The old DOS standard lets you use only uppercase letters, A–Z, numerals, 0–9, and any of the following symbols:

$ % ' - _ @ ~ ` ! { } ^# &

Any time you entered a lowercase letter in a filename, DOS would simply convert it to uppercase. It was possible to use a space within a DOS filename or extension (as well as at the end of the name or at the end of the extension), but many DOS programs are unable to deal with the resulting filename appropriately. (Certain other ASCII and extended ASCII characters can also be used without causing DOS any problems, but many programs fail to recognize those names and might do unpredictable things to the corresponding files. Understandably, Microsoft recommends against trying these tricks with filenames.)

The new standard for long filenames adds the following symbols to the list of allowable characters:

+ , ; = [ ]

Furthermore, in a long filename you are allowed to mix upper- and lowercase letters freely, embed spaces wherever you like, and use as many periods as you like. (It is important that you realize, however, that when Windows looks at those long filenames it ignores case in deciding whether a given filename matches some other filename.) Microsoft continues to recommend not using extended ASCII characters in long file-names. Figure 9.10 indicates that the short filename is stored in ASCII. This is true as long as the filename (and the extension) contain no extended-ASCII characters. If the name does include some of these high-bit set characters, they will be interpreted in terms of what is called the *OEM code page* currently in effect. Because it's possible to change code pages, the effective names of files could also change in that process. This is just one more reason to avoid using any high-bit set characters in a short filename.

Windows 95 was made capable of working with long filenames by a rather clever strate-gy. For every file with a long name (LFN), it automatically creates an alias, which is also called the *generated short filename* (SFN). That short filename conforms to the old DOS file naming rules, with the additional constraint that it may not contain any embedded space characters.

Then when DOS is creating that file, it makes a principal directory entry for that file whose name field is filled with this generated short name. That directory entry is preceded by one or more special directory entries that hold pieces of the long filename.

Each 32-byte LFN directory entry can hold at most 13 characters of the long filename. This is because those entries store the filename in a 2-byte Unicode format (see Chapter 3 for more on Unicode), and because some of the 32 bytes are used for other purposes, as you can see from the chart in Figure 9.10.

The first byte of the directory entry has a number that is the counting number of the pieces of this particular long filename. (That is, the LFN directory entry that comes just before the SFN entry carries a value of 1 in this location.) The last entry for each LFN has the ordinal number you would expect (one more than the one just below it), but with 128 added to its value. (This just means the most significant bit is set to 1 instead of 0.) Windows 9x uses this fact to help it find the end of a LFN.

The attribute byte in an LFN entry (the 12th byte in the directory entry) now holds the special combination of attributes RSHV, and the 13th byte (now called the *type* byte) always contains a 0. This last statement is true for now, but Microsoft has firmly declared that there will be other types of LFN in the future, for which this value will not be zero. So far it has not hinted at what those other types of LFN might be.

The 14th byte carries a checksum based upon the SFN. This is another tool Windows 9x uses to help keep LFNs associated with the right SFN.

The 27th and 28th bytes of the directory entry in an SFN entry hold the starting cluster in the data area where this file's content is stored (or the least significant sixteen bits of that starting cluster number on a FAT32 disk). In the LFN entries, this field is always set to 0.

The remaining 26 bytes in the directory entry are used to store the LFN in Unicode, 2 bytes per character. This is the only place in the directory where you will see Unicode characters.

How Short Filenames Are Generated

You learned that Windows 9*x* and Windows NT create a short filename (SFN) alias for each file with a long filename (LFN). But how Windows does this isn't so obvious, and certainly can cause you some grief if you don't understand it.

If the file's long name is short enough that it fits in the old-style 8.3 naming scheme, then Windows 95 just uses that name as its SFN, changing any lowercase letters to uppercase in the process. If the name is longer, or if it includes spaces or multiple periods, then the SFN gets more complex.

There absolutely must not be two files in the same directory with the same short filename or the same long filename. And in fact, there cannot be a short filename that matches a long filename in the same directory. If there were, Windows wouldn't know which one you meant to use when you wanted to access one of them. This rule forces Windows to do some pretty odd things with the SFNs.

Windows 9*x* starts with the long filename. It first strips out the spaces, underscores what remains, and then uses the first eight characters of the name and three characters of the extension to form the SFN. For these purposes, if a name has only one period and that one is the very first character—which is a legal LFN—then Windows treats it as having a name with no extension. The SFN is, therefore, built from the first eight characters of the long filename after that initial period. If the filename has one or more periods after the first character position, then Windows 95 treats all the long name after the last period as the extension, and forms the SFN extension from the first three characters of whatever follows that last period.

If the SFN it generates is not unique in this directory, then Windows forces it to be so by lopping off two or more of the final characters of the name and substituting a tilde character followed by a one, two, or multidigit number. The number chosen is as small as possible while forcing the SFN to be unique. So, for example, the long filename Program File List.DOC might have a corresponding SFN of PROGRA~1.DOC. Letter to Mother on 9-11-95.DOC might SFN as LETTER~1.DOC. In this second example, you can see that if you have several letters to mother, and you name them all the same, except for the date, you would have difficulty telling the files apart if you did a directory listing of this disk using an earlier version of DOS (or using a Windows 9*x* MS-DOS mode command prompt). All of the first nine long filenames in this directory will be given short filenames of the form LETTER~*x*.DOC, where *x* is the number of LETTER files in the directory. (If you have more than nine such files, subsequent SFNs appear as LETTE~*xx*.DOC, where *xx* is a two-digit number, and so on.)

The most subtle, and in some ways most confusing, aspect of the way Windows generates short filenames is that it will not necessarily generate the same name for a given file in two different locations. So, when you copy a file from one directory to another, its long filename will go across unchanged, but its short filename might change, depending on what other files are already in the target directory.

Following all these new rules requires Windows to do a lot more writing and rewriting of the directories. In the past, when a program altered one file, the operating system needed only rewrite the one disk sector in which the directory entry for that file resided. Now it might have to rewrite the entire directory, depending on just what changes have been made to the file in question. Normally, however, once the directory has been created with its short and long filenames, any subsequent renaming that doesn't extend the length of the long filenames will very likely be accomplished with no more sectors needing to be written than was the case under earlier versions of DOS and Windows.

To see how confusing this might get, consider what must happen the first time you access a diskette formatted and loaded with files on a computer that was using an earlier version of DOS or Windows that didn't support long filenames. If you do this, you'll find that the disk drive does a lot of thrashing about as the directory gets converted to the long filename format. After this is finished, you'll find approximately twice as many directory entries have been used (which could present a problem if the root directory were already close to full).

Similarly, many programs, such as word processors, open a temporary file, work in it, close it, and after deleting the original file, then rename the temporary file to the original file's name. That was pretty simple when each file involved only one directory entry. Now, if the file in question has a long filename, lots of entries might have to be rewritten, potentially involving more than a single cluster on the disk.

The DOS DIR Command as a Rosetta Stone

Figure 9.8 shows that the DIR command, when it is issued inside a DOS box in Windows 9x, displays both the short and long filenames associated with each file. If you are using Windows 9x, are a committed hacker, and like your old, DOS-based programming tools, you can use this fact to your advantage.

Simply shell out of your old-style program and have the DIR command redirect its output to a file. Then, once back inside your program, read that file and you can match up all the long filenames with the short filenames that happen to be in this particular directory. In a way, this is similar to the way linguists used the famous Rosetta stone to learn the translations from Egyptian hieroglyphics to Greek.

Sorting and Searching with Long Filenames

The somewhat arbitrary and variable SFNs associated with long filenames also lead to some oddities in sorting files or searching for them. The DOS command DIR /O:N, for example, is supposed to list the files in a directory in alphabetical order. It does so, but it uses the short filenames in deciding what that order should be. This can be, and often is, different from what you would get if you looked at the long filename.

And, a search for a wildcard name such as *1.* will match all files with a numeral one as the last non-space character in their short filename as well as any that have a numeral one followed by a period in their long filename. So you must be attentive to these and similar details if you want to understand why programs that search for short filenames under Windows 9x produce the results they do.

What DOS Does When You Delete a File

When you delete a file, DOS doesn't erase it from your hard disk. Instead, it does two simple things. First, it sets to 0 the value in all the cluster locations in the FAT that belong to that file. Second, it changes the very first entry in the (SFN) directory entry for this file from the ASCII value representing the letter, number, or symbol in the filename to the special value E5h. In decimal, this value is 229, and it is the extended ASCII value for the Greek lowercase sigma (Σ) in the most commonly used code page.

These two steps tell DOS or Windows that this directory entry and those clusters in the data area are now available for reuse. But until they are reused, almost all the directory information and all the file's contents are still in place on your disk.

So, if only you could replace the first character of the filename, and then guess correctly which clusters used to belong to this file, you could make it appear once more. Starting with version 6, DOS let you set up either *deletion tracking* or *deletion sentry*. These are two different strategies for protecting you from losing an important file by an accidental deletion.

Delete tracking simply records what clusters it was using and what the first character of its filename was for each file you delete. Then, if you want to undelete the file, you can—provided no other file's content has been written into any of those clusters and nothing has overwritten this directory entry in the meantime.

Delete sentry actually moves files you think you are deleting to a special, hidden directory. Then, if you want to undelete them, it simply moves them back. (Moving a file doesn't actually involve any moving of the file's contents. It just means creating a new directory entry in the target directory that points to the original file's chain of clusters, and then deleting the original directory entry.)

At first it looks like everyone should always use the delete sentry strategy. In fact, Windows 9x does essentially this. (Windows 9x no longer supports the delete tracking strategy.) Any file you delete from within Windows 9x will simply be moved into the Recycle Bin. Any file you delete at a DOS prompt (either in a DOS window under Windows 9x, or using the MS-DOS mode command prompt) is deleted in the manner I described in the first paragraph of this section. The Recycle Bin is just a new, fancy name for the hidden directory that delete sentry used in DOS 6.x. But there is a downside to this strategy: When you delete a file, you aren't actually freeing up any space on your disk. To do that, you must also empty the Recycle Bin (or empty the delete sentry's hidden directory).

Peter's Principle: Undelete Difficulties

The only time you are likely to have trouble undeleting a file is when you try to do it just after deleting a whole bunch of files, and then only if the file you want was fragmented—or, of course, if you have written something else to the disk in the places formerly occupied by the file you want to undelete. You can make your computer run faster and also make it easier to undelete files whenever you want no matter what deletion protection strategy you're using (if any), simply by periodically defragmenting all the files on your hard disk.

DOS and Windows 9*x* include a tool to do this called DEFRAG. The Norton Utilities includes an even more capable version of the same program called Speed Disk. Whatever tool you use, if you are running Windows 95 or 98 you must use a defragmenter that was designed to retain your long filenames, or they may be deleted during the defragmenting process.

This might also be a good place to point out another good idea regarding these or any other third-party utility programs you may have that support either long filenames or FAT32: Upgrade them to their latest versions. Often, when such radical new features are added to an operating system the third-party vendors take a few upgrades to get everything working just right. Fortunately, the Norton Utilities come with a LiveUpdate feature that makes this process quite painless. Just be sure you use it.

Learning About File Formats

Files store your data, but not every file stores just what you think it does. In this section, I am going to explain some of the variety of file formats, and suggest some ways you might explore them on your own.

ASCII Text Files

The simplest files contain almost exactly what you might expect them to. These are what we call *pure ASCII text files*. Examples include your PC's startup files, CONFIG.SYS, AUTOEXEC.BAT (both found in the root directory of your boot disk), and if you have Windows 3.*x*, WIN.INI and SYSTEM.INI (both in your Windows directory). If you have Windows 95 or 98, you might have any or all of these files, or you might not. But you certainly have one called MSDOS.SYS (in the root directory of the boot disk) that is also a pure ASCII text file. (DOS and Windows 3.*x* users also have a file called MSDOS.SYS, but it's a hidden, system file and it is most certainly *not* a pure ASCII text file.)

Other ASCII text files are the various INI files used by many Windows (and some other) programs to store their initialization data. The distinguishing mark of these files is that, in addition to being pure ASCII files, they have a structure very much like that of WIN.INI and SYSTEM.INI. They are composed of blocks of text with each block beginning with a title enclosed in square brackets.

You can see what is in a pure ASCII text file if you're running Windows by loading it into Notepad (or, if you are using Windows 9x, and the file is too large for Notepad, by loading it into WordPad). And even if you are not in Windows, but are in MS-DOS mode or at a command prompt for an earlier version of DOS, you can show the contents of this sort of file by using the DOS command TYPE. For example, this command displays the contents of your CONFIG.SYS file (if you have one):

```
TYPE C:\CONFIG.SYS
```

If your CONFIG.SYS file is large, the first lines may scroll off the screen. To prevent that, you can add a pipe command and the DOS command MORE. Now the command line reads like the following, which will show you the contents of that file one screenful at a time:

```
TYPE C:\CONFIG.SYS ¦ MORE
```

You can apply this technique to any pure ASCII text file and you will find the screen image easy to read. (It may be a bit harder to understand, but that's another story altogether.)

Warning: If you are using WordPad to look at and edit a pure ASCII file, you must be very careful when you save it to choose the File Type as a text document. If you save it in some word processor format, it will have a lot of formatting information added that you really don't want in what is supposed to be a pure ASCII text file.

Although this strategy for viewing an ASCII text file works, it's not as easy as using a program built specially for the purpose. In the next section I discuss the LIST program, which is my favorite tool for this use.

Displaying ASCII text files works so well because they contain almost nothing but simple, displayable text characters taken from the ASCII character set. (If you don't recall just what an ASCII character is, refer to Chapter 3.)

Although these files contain almost only ASCII-displayable text characters, there are some exceptions. They almost always include some special control characters to indicate the end of a line of text. In text files prepared for PCs, that usually means the lines are terminated by a pair of control characters, one to say "move back to the left margin" and one to say "move down a line." These are termed the *carriage return* (CR) and *line feed* (LF) control characters and they have the ASCII values of 13 and 10, respectively (which are Dh and Ah in case you're looking inside the file with a snooping tool that displays the contents in hexadecimal).

Many text files also contain tab characters that have an ASCII value of 9. These characters stand for a variable number of space characters—whatever is needed to move the next character in the file to a column just past the next tab stop. Not all programs that use ASCII text files interpret these tab characters in the same way. The DOS TYPE command and many programming languages, for example, assume that the tab stops should be at multiples of eight columns. Many word processors assume a default spacing of five characters, and most of them also let you set the tabs wherever you want.

One other control character that is often used in text files is the *end-of-page character*. Another name for this is *form feed* (meaning that it signals a printer when to eject a page and start a new one), which carries the abbreviation FF. Its ASCII value is 12.

It used to be universal that all text files would end with a special end-of-file character. That is the Ctrl+Z (Control+Z) character, which has the ASCII value of 26 (1Ah). Before DOS, in CP/M machines there was no other way to know where the end of a file was. Now that the DOS directory entry keeps track of the file length right down to the byte, it isn't necessary to include a Ctrl+Z character. But, if that character is present, the DOS TYPE command will assume that it is an end-of-file mark and stop processing the file there.

ASCII text files also vary as to how they represent paragraphs. Some put all of a paragraph on a single line, then put a single pair of CR and LF control characters after it to indicate the beginning of the next paragraph. Others use a CR-LF pair to signal the end of a line within a paragraph and a pair of CR-LF pairs to signal a new paragraph. Still others may use tabs to indent paragraphs or lines. All of these still qualify for the name *pure ASCII text files*, but they also may go by names such as MS-DOS text, DOS text with layout, or some other variation.

Non-ASCII (Binary) Files

In the universe of files on PCs, ASCII text files are a very small minority. All the rest are called *binary files*. They contain at least some non-ASCII characters (they have bytes of data whose most significant bit is set to one, and thus they represent an extended ASCII character) or they contain some control characters other than the simple CR, LF, TAB, and FF. You could use the DOS TYPE command on them, but if you do, the results may startle you. Quite literally.

Your computer may display some of what you expect, plus a lot of other strange characters. Also, it might beep at you many times. And it might stop displaying information before it reaches the end of the file.

If a binary file contains only ASCII characters and extended ASCII characters (and the usual control characters CR, LF, TAB and perhaps FF), it's possible to display their contents with the TYPE command. But what you will see might not be what you would expect. This is because there are many different definitions for the extended ASCII characters. If the file was prepared using one definition and if the TYPE command uses another, then you might be surprised by what shows up on the screen.

The cause of the beeps, huge blank areas, and perhaps a sudden termination of the output is likely to be the presence of some other control characters. The Bell code (ASCII value 7) causes your PC to beep. The Vertical Tab character (VT) with ASCII value 11 (Bh) may jump the cursor vertically on the screen. And, if the TYPE command encounters a Ctrl+Z (EOF) character (ASCII value 26, or 1Ah), it will stop right there.

All those things are perfectly normal. They just mean that the TYPE command is not the optimal way to look at the contents of those files.

Sometimes, you will know something about how the file was created. For example, if it is a Word for Windows document file, it most likely will have an extension of .DOC. The best tool to use to look at this or any other word processing document file is the word processor that created it. Spreadsheet files are best looked at in the spreadsheet program that created them, and so on.

Because of this more-or-less constant association of file extensions and the application programs that created them, Windows 9x implements a set of File Associations so that you can simply click (or double-click) on a filename in Windows Explorer and that file will be loaded into the appropriate application program. Naturally, this works only for file extensions that Windows 9x knows about. Each time you install an application program, it will ordinarily register all the extensions it understands with Windows; thereafter, you can use this convenient means of accessing the files it understands.

Not every program that creates a binary file uses a unique file extension in its name. Often these programs insert a signature of some sort near the beginning of the file to indicate the kind of file it is, what application created it, and in a few cases, even which version of that application is required to load it. Many programs depend upon that signature to validate the files they are about to load, even if the extension might have told them. DOS and Windows do this with executable files. If the file's first two characters are MZ, then it is regarded as a valid executable file, no matter what the file extension might be, and DOS or Windows will happily attempt to load this file and run it as if it were an executable program.

Peter's Principle: File Snooping

What if you don't know what program created the file, or don't have that program? Is there a universal file-snooping tool you can use? My favorite such program is Vern Buerg's fine LIST program. It began as a simple shareware file-viewing program. It now has grown into a full-fledged file-viewing and management program with two versions called LIST Plus and LIST Enhanced. You can learn more about it (and about Vern Buerg) at:

`http://www.buerg.com/software.html`

Why Binary Files Are Different

Binary files aren't like ASCII files for the simple reason that they hold something other than just text. Even the word processing files, for which text is the main point, also hold other things.

Word Processing Files

Why aren't word processing document files just what I typed into the document? A word processing document file must contain not only the textual content, but also the formatting information. And many modern word processors go further by including pictures, drawings, outline headings, and summary information.

Database and Spreadsheet Files

Database files must keep information in records. That can be done in any of several ways. Some special ASCII control characters seem to have been designed for just this purpose. They bear names such as *record separator* and *group separator*. But the fact remains that most PC database programs don't use them. Some database programs format the records into fixed length blocks. Others separate the records with special characters—just not the ones the ASCII code says they should.

Spreadsheet files are simply special-purpose database files. Their records are displayed differently, but the essential file storage ideas are very similar. Of course, the format particulars vary with the particular spreadsheet program you use. (One reason so many programs use their own file formats is to try to inhibit competitors from decoding their file formats and thus being able to use those data files with a competing product.)

If you have a database file you want to snoop inside, use LIST (or DEBUG, or whatever tool you choose) and look for things you recognize. If you find blocks of recognizable text items separated by regions of garbage, and if the distance from one recognizable block to the next is constant, then most likely you are looking at a fixed-length record database (or spreadsheet) file. The apparent garbage is actually numbers stored as binary values rather than as the ASCII representation of the numerals.

Program Files

Another important type of binary file you will encounter is a program file. Program files contain instructions to the PC in the language it understands: machine language instructions. So, of course, it is not readily readable by humans. One easy thing to look for is the first couple of characters. If they are MZ, then this is likely an MS-DOS EXE file, which is to say either a DOS program or a Windows program. (If a short distance into the file you see a message that reads either This program requires Microsoft Windows or This program cannot be run in DOS mode, then you are looking at a Windows executable program.)

Some of these program files have the extension .EXE. Others are .DLL files or .OVR files or some other extension. But all of them are programs. (Files with extension .COM are a simpler kind of program file. They don't have the MZ signature at the start, and they are supposed to be no larger than 64KB. They are, in fact, simply images of the bytes that are deposited into the RAM when you run them. EXE files, on the other hand, have a relocation header at the beginning that specifies which parts of their content go where in memory when they are loaded.)

Other Binary Files

There are still other kinds of files that are essentially binary. These include image files, sound files, and more. In Chapter 20, "How to 'Wow' a Human," I will tell you more about several kinds of sound and image files.

> **Note:** The essential thing to know about all these binary files is that their precise content matters. You must not alter even one byte or they may become unusable. (This is in sharp contrast to a pure ASCII text file, for which in most cases a minor alteration is no big deal.)
>
> So, feel free to snoop around your PC's disk drives, looking inside all manner of files, but to save yourself much grief, please use a tool that won't alter their contents. Or else be *very* careful!

Summary

In this chapter, we've begun an extensive exploration of how your PC meets the task of reliably storing and retrieving the millions of bytes of data that you require of it. I hope you've begun to understand the various structures that make this possible, along with their strengths and limitations, and how those structures impact your own productivity. In the next chapter, we'll step back to move forward—applying the knowledge of the disk's data area that you've learned here to the disk's vital system areas. Then we'll go on to examine some of the newest technologies that are making hard disks both more efficient and more reliable. Finally we'll take a good look at the other hardware—CD-ROMs, tape drives, and so on—that has been devised to meet your storage needs.

Digging Deeper Into Disks

Up to this point, almost everything that I have told you about disks applies to every kind of disk that your PC can use, from the oldest floppies to the newest EIDE and SCSI drives, and even to most optical disc (DVD and CD) drives. Now I will discuss what makes hard disks different from those other disk-like devices.

How Hard Disks Are Different

In the preceding chapter, I told you about the physical differences between floppy diskettes and hard disks. I pointed out that hard disks have rigid platters and use feedback servomechanisms to position the read/write heads, which enables you to store data much more densely on them. I also pointed out that although floppy diskettes protect data with a cyclical redundancy check (CRC) value, hard disks go an extra step and use error correction codes (ECC), enabling them to not only detect errors but also to correct those errors on-the-fly.

Now I'll cover the logical differences between floppy diskettes and hard disks as they are seen by the motherboard BIOS and DOS. All other disk-like devices are made to look either like floppies or like hard disks in these respects, so understanding these differences is quite important.

Master Boot Record and Partitions

The most important difference between a floppy diskette and a hard disk, from the perspective of the boot process and how data storage is structured on a disk, is that the BIOS assumes that all disks contain a single logical volume or logical disk drive. But the boot program the BIOS loads from the start of a hard disk is different from that on a floppy diskette. On a hard disk, this boot record is not called the DOS boot record. Instead, it is called the hard disk's Master Boot Record (MBR). This program knows that all PC hard disks are supposed to be divided into one, two, three, or four partitions. Each of those partitions may be a primary logical volume, a hidden partition, or an extended partition. Extended partitions are ones that may contain multiple logical volumes.

If you have more than one primary partition on a single hard disk, only one of them may be designated as active and the remaining ones will be hidden. There can be only one active partition and only one extended partition on a single, physical disk drive.

(A *logical volume* simply means all of the storage space that is referred to by a single drive letter. This might be a fraction of one physical hard disk, or it could even be the aggregate of several hard disks in certain special circumstances.)

It is quite possible for a partition to have zero size, but the MBR assumes they are all defined in a data table (called the *partition table*) located within itself, and it looks first for those definitions before it begins to use any of the volumes.

Figure 10.1 shows Norton Disk Editor's default view of an MBR, which is simply a display of the contents of its partition table in human-readable form. In this case, you see that only two of the four partitions have any size, but all four lines in the data table are present.

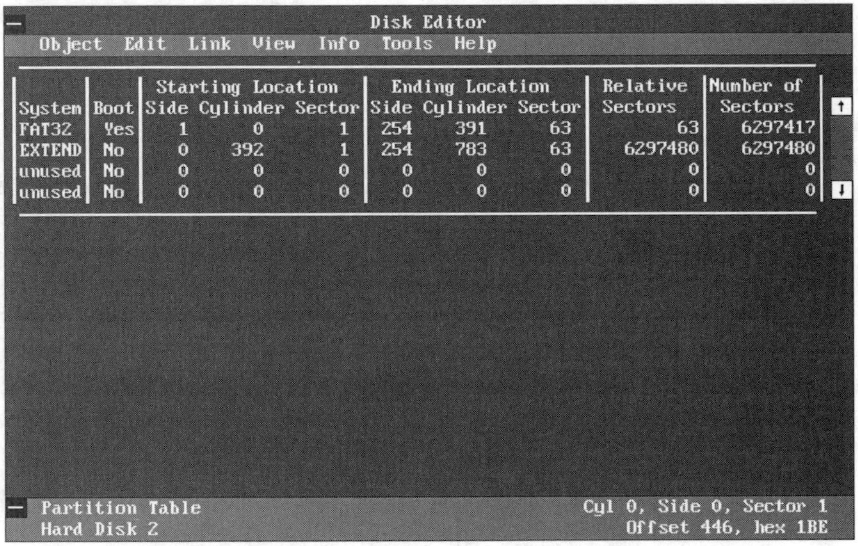

FIGURE 10.1

The partition table in the master boot record of the second physical disk in our example desktop PC, as shown by Norton Disk Editor (NDE).

```
                                    Disk Editor
        Object   Edit   Link   View   Info   Tools   Help

                    Starting Location      Ending Location     Relative  Number of
         System Boot Side Cylinder Sector Side Cylinder Sector  Sectors   Sectors
         FAT32  Yes    1     0       1    254   391      63         63    6297417
         EXTEND No     0    392      1    254   783      63    6297480    6297480
         unused No     0     0       0     0     0        0          0          0
         unused No     0     0       0     0     0        0          0          0


       — Partition Table                          Cyl 0, Side 0, Sector 1
         Hard Disk 2                                  Offset 446, hex 1BE
```

The first column in the following table shows you the type for each partition. This is stored in the actual table as single 8-bit number. Here are the possible values for the type numbers that DOS and Windows 9*x* can understand, and the corresponding permissible sizes those partitions may have. The names I have given for the partitions are Microsoft's; NDE uses slightly different names for these partition types (DOS-12, DOS-16, EXTEND, BIGDOS, FAT32, FAT32X BGDOSx, and EXTNDx, respectively) and NDE also recognizes many other type numbers that are used by other operating systems than DOS or Windows 9*x*. (Another partition type you may encounter on a PC running Windows has a type number of 80h or A0h. This is most likely an Advanced Power Management partition used to store data when that PC goes into a "suspend" power-saving state.)

Partition Type Number	Partition Type	Permissible size
01h	DOS primary partition 12-bit FAT (DOS2)	0MB to 2MB
04h	DOS primary partition 16-bit FAT (DOS3)	32MB
05h	DOS-extended partition	Any size
06h	DOS primary partition 16-bit FAT (DOS4)	32MB up to 2GB
0Bh	DOS primary partition 32-bit FAT (DOS32)	512MB up to 2048GB
0Ch	DOS primary partition 32-bit FAT (DOS32X)	512MB up to 2048GB (Uses INT13h Extensions)
0Eh	DOS primary partition 16-bit FAT (DOSX13)	32MB up to 2GB (Uses INT13h Extensions)
0Fh	DOS extended partition (DOSX13X)	Any size

The partition table always shows the partition boundaries in terms of the cylinder, head, and sector numbers. A newer strategy, particularly for drives larger than 2GB in size, assigns a unique sequential number to every sector, ignoring the cylinder, head, and physical sector numbers. This creates what is in this case—and for all disks for which you are accessing by use of the logical block address (LBA) strategy—a totally artificial equivalent of the actual disk drive. So, it may well turn out that the start of a cylinder in this table has no relationship whatsoever to the actual beginning of a cylinder on the physical hard disk drive.

In Figure 10.1, the disk is assumed to have 255 sides and 63 sectors per track. The maximum cylinder number is then made to be whatever it must be to get the correct total capacity. Partitions other than the first one always start at the beginning of a cylinder (side 0); the first partition always starts at cylinder 0, head 1 which leaves the entire first track (cylinder 0, head 0) for the MBR (and, in this case, 62 unused sectors). (An exception to this scheme is the somewhat specialized circumstance of logical partitions that exist inside an extended partition. In such a case, logical partitions begin on side 1, not size 0.)

This disk—which happens to be the second physical drive on my system—has a total capacity of approximately 6GB. You can see this from the total of the two numbers in the right column (which shows the number of sectors in each partition) multiplied by 512 bytes. Also, by noticing that the two numbers in that column are about equal, you can see that half the disk has been allocated to a FAT32 partition, which makes this region a single logical disk drive (which is D: on this machine). The remainder of the disk has been allocated to an extended partition, which could potentially contain many different logical disk drives.

The second column shows that only the first of the four partitions is flagged as *bootable* (which is a synonym for *active*). This is the partition in which the PC BIOS looks for a boot sector and operating system files to boot your PC. If you were to mark more than one of the four partitions as active, the MBR program wouldn't know which one you meant for it to use. (In fact, it would simply use the first one that was marked active and ignore the active mark on any other partition.) If you don't mark any of them as active, the MBR program won't attempt to boot the PC from this hard disk.

Most PC BIOSes can boot only from the first hard disk, from a floppy or, in some cases, from a CD-ROM. A major exception to this are PCs that use SCSI hard disks, either alone or in conjunction with IDE drives. In that case, a special BIOS on the SCSI host adapter can be enabled that allows the PC to boot from one of the SCSI devices. In the past, a PC that contained both IDE and SCSI drives most commonly could boot only from an IDE device or floppy—the PC's internal BIOS wouldn't give up control to the SCSI BIOS if it saw that any IDE hard drive was available. If none of the IDE drives was bootable and no system floppy diskette was present, the PC would not boot at all. Today, many system BIOSes enable the user to select whether the system should boot from an IDE or, if present, SCSI drive.

A few of the most recent PCs have an even more flexible set of choices for which device to boot from. Our example desktop system, for example, enables you to choose the order in which you want to attempt to boot—with my choices being from a fixed disk, a removable disk, an ATAPI CD-ROM drive, or from a network connection. Then, it enables you to choose which of the selected class of devices will be the one it attempts to boot from when it tries that category of device.

DOS (or Windows 9*x*) will allow you to create a single primary DOS partition only on a given physical hard drive. Third-party utilities can create additional primary DOS partitions; however, all but one will be hidden. Other operating systems also can create primary partitions, but still only one (DOS or other OS) primary partition can be active. An inactive DOS partition will be totally inaccessible until you change it to the active partition and reboot your PC.

Fortunately, DOS can also understand and access exactly one additional partition of the type DOS-extended (either type 05h or 0Fh). That partition can contain within it any number of logical disk volumes—limited only by the number of letters in the alphabet— which are in fact a kind of partition within a partition. Figure 10.2 illustrates this and shows how a hypothetical hard disk might be divided into three partitions, and how it might get a total of seven drive letters assigned to it by DOS or Windows. (This figure shows only the portions of the disk that are assigned each drive letter, or in the case of the first and last blocks, are reserved for the master boot record or for use by an operating system other than DOS or Windows. The details of how this subdivision can be accomplished is explained more fully in the next section.)

In this figure, the first partition is the DOS primary partition. The second partition is the DOS extended partition, which contains six logical disk drives. The third partition shown is a UNIX partition, which cannot be seen by DOS at all. If it is marked as bootable, the DOS primary partition will disappear and the PC will boot into UNIX. Some operating systems can see—and use—DOS partitions. OS/2, Windows NT, Linux, and some other versions of UNIX all have their own native file systems, but each of them has also been designed to work with most DOS partitions as well—although not FAT32 partitions.

FIGURE 10.2

A hypothetical hard drive, show-ing multiple DOS logical drives, plus a UNIX partition.

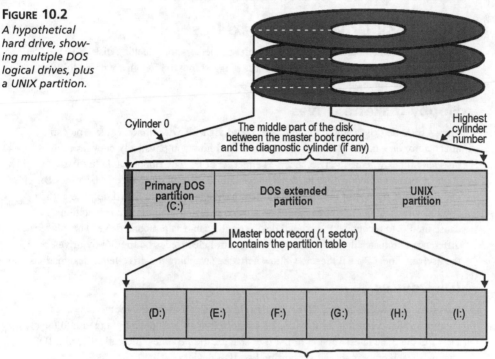

DOS-Extended Partition Tables

I said that you could divide a DOS-extended partition into multiple logical disk drives. How is this done? Simply by extending the notion of partitioning.

The first sector in a DOS-extended partition is a special sector called an extended partition table. This is similar to the MBR, with some significant differences. For example, there is no boot program in an extended partition table. Also, although its partition table has four entries (just like the table in the MBR), only the first one or two entries are ever used. The first entry describes a logical drive; the second one (if it is used) points to another extended partition table (still within the same DOS extended partition) in which an additional logical disk drive is defined.

Managing Multiple PC Disk Drives

Modern PCs can support multiple disk drives or disk-like devices. How this is done is the subject of this section. I won't explain the intricacies of all of the different kinds of disk attachments, but I will tell you how DOS handles each one.

How Disk Drives Attach to PCs

Modern PC motherboards have several special connectors for attaching disk drives. They also can have one or more option cards plugged into the I/O bus, with additional connectors for some other kinds of disk drives.

Floppy Diskette Drives

Floppy diskette drives attach to the motherboard via a 34-wire ribbon cable. You can attach zero, one, or two floppy diskette drives, and how you physically connect each one determines whether a drive becomes either A: or B:. The ribbon cable has two connectors, and a floppy diskette drive hooked up to the middle connector becomes B:, and the one at the end of the cable is A:. This little feat is accomplished because certain control wires within the ribbon cable, when reversed from their normal orientation, cause the PC to recognize the second device on the cable as a second drive. This physical difference eliminates the need for expensive control electronics on the floppy drives themselves. Some PC BIOSes now allow software swapping the drive-letter designations.

IDE Devices

Integrated device electronics (IDE) devices are connected to the PC motherboard via another special connector, or they can be connected to an option card plugged into the PC's I/O bus. The latest version of the IDE specification enables, theoretically, four IDE channels, each one capable of supporting two IDE devices.

Most modern PCs support two EIDE channels on the motherboard. They also usually have one or more IDE or EIDE internal hard drives. A jumper on each drive's circuit board determines whether the drive functions as a *master* or as a *slave*. The first hard drive you install on each of the IDE channels must always be set as that channel's master. It is important that only one device acts as master and one as slave on each IDE channel, so you must pay careful attention to the settings of these jumpers.

The cable that connects hard drives to the motherboard is similar to a floppy drive cable without a twist. Additionally, hard drive cables contain more wires and are thus wider than floppy drive cables. A hard drive cable will have either two or three connectors (one for the motherboard and either one or two for drives), and most are keyed to prevent plugging it in backward. If no key-tab is present, one of the wires of the cable will be marked with a color—usually red. As you have likely already read, on the motherboard and the drives, one end of the connection socket will be marked 1, 2 or with a small triangle; the red side of the cable always connects closest to the marked side of the socket. Unlike floppies, however, each hard drive's jumper settings identify it, and it doesn't matter whether a drive is plugged into the end or the middle of the cable. Figure 4.1 in Chapter 4, "Understanding Your PC's Parts," in the section "Keeping Track of Changes— and Reversing Them Correctly," shows the motherboard end of such a cable and the motherboard connector into which it plugs.

In some PCs, the primary and secondary IDE channels are nearly equivalent. You may put any device you want on either cable, making sure you have only one master and one slave on each one.

In other PCs, the two IDE channels have very different properties. The primary one is set up as a fast EIDE channel; the secondary one is merely an older-style IDE channel. If yours is like this, you should put the hard drives on the primary channel and the CD-ROM drive or other slow devices on the secondary channel.

Even if your PC treats each IDE channel nearly the same, you may still want to put fast devices on one IDE cable and slower ones on the other cable. Some PCs can send messages only as fast as the slowest device on any one channel (cable). Thus, if you put your fast hard drive and your slow CD-ROM on the same IDE channel, you may find your hard drive crawling along, slowed down by the CD-ROM's inability to keep up.

SCSI Devices

The other popular way to attach a disk drive to a PC is via a SCSI interface. You can find all the details on this interface in Chapter 16, "Faster Ways to Get Information Into and Out of Your PC," but here I want to show you a few essentials about how this interface connects disk drives and PCs.

SCSI devices have all their controller electronics on board the device itself. In addition, they have special hardware that can operate over a SCSI bus with a SCSI host adapter. Macintosh computers have a SCSI host adapter built into them. A few PCs have SCSI host adapters built into their motherboards, but a much more common strategy is to put that optional circuitry on a plug-in card. Because the SCSI host adapter may potentially be transferring data rapidly to or from a hard drive, you'll do well to plug it into the fastest input-output bus you can. Currently, the most popular choice is the PCI bus.

A typical PCI SCSI host adapter card, such as the Adaptec 2940W/UW, has a connector on the rear panel for external SCSI devices and two connectors on the upper edge of the card for internal SCSI devices. Only one of the two internal connectors may be used at a time, however. The reason for having two separate internal connectors is to make it easy to connect to either Narrow or Ultra-Wide internal SCSI devices. (The rear-panel connector follows the Ultra-Wide standard, but a suitable cable can adapt that connection down to the narrow SCSI standards.)

A SCSI host adapter can communicate simultaneously with up to seven 16-bit SCSI devices, or up to 15 Wide- or Ultra-Wide devices. Each device must be assigned a unique SCSI identification number between 0 and 7 (or 15). Traditionally, ID number 7 is reserved for the host adapter (except on the Macintosh, where the host adapter uses 0). All the rest are up for grabs by the attached devices.

Making Sense Out of Chaos

Now you know how to physically connect lots of disk drives to a PC, but how are these all managed? What happens to the drive letters? Can you boot from any of those disk drives? These are serious questions without obvious answers. Fortunately, they are not difficult to answer.

How DOS Assigns Drive Letters

Floppy disk drives normally show up as drives A: and B:. This is unalterable in most PCs (although a few enable you to select which floppy will be A:). Hard disks and other disk drives get drive letters beginning with C:. DOS will assign C: to whichever drive it determines is going to be the boot device according to the specification in the BIOS. (That is, it will do this for anything other than a floppy diskette drive.) If your BIOS doesn't have an option for boot device order, DOS will assign C: to the first hard disk it finds. As I mentioned above, because it looks first at the primary IDE or EIDE channel for a master device, that is where you ordinarily will want to put your main internal IDE or EIDE hard disk.

DOS will assign D: to the primary DOS partition of the next physical hard disk, if it finds more than one. This includes both other hard drives on the IDE chains and SCSI hard disks. DOS keeps this up for as many physical hard disks with active (and thus not hidden) primary DOS partitions as it can find. DOS then assigns the next drive letter to the first logical drive inside any DOS-extended partition it finds on the first hard drive. The next letters go to any other logical disk drives in that same partition. Then DOS goes through the logical disk drives inside the DOS-extended partition on the second hard disk, then on to the third hard disk, and so on.

Only after it has assigned drive letters to all the hard disk volumes it can find will DOS allow the assignment of a drive letter to any other disk-like devices. These include super-floppy drives that attach via the IDE chains, CD-ROM drives, and so on. Drives with compressed data (using DriveSpace or some equivalent product) are assigned drive letters in a special fashion. I'll cover those rules later in this chapter in the section called "Data Compression."

Peter's Principle: Why Not Make It O for Optical?

If you are using Windows 9*x*, you can alter the drive letter assignments for any disk-like devices other than hard drives. Just go into the Device Manager tab of the System applet in Control Panel. Then click on the device whose drive letter you'd like to change, select Properties and then click the Settings tab. There you'll see the current drive letter assignment and can set the lowest and highest letter you want Windows to use for this device the next time you boot. If you set those two letters to the same value, that will be the drive letter Windows will use. But it won't let you choose a drive letter that is currently assigned to a hard disk. I often find it useful to use this feature to set the drive letter for my DVD, CD-ROM, and other such devices to something past the last hard disk I have installed. That way, if I want to install more hard drives, the optical disc drive letters won't change.

One oddity I have noted may bear mentioning here. I added a Hitachi DVD-RAM drive to our example desktop system. When I did so, it showed up right away as a CD-ROM (or DVD-ROM) drive in Windows 98. The drive letter for that version of this device is alterable in the manner I have just described. But when I also loaded up the special software that came with the drive, it showed up a second time, as some sort of generic disk drive. And that appearance of this device is one of those that Windows 98 assigns a drive letter to (before all optical drives), and it won't let you change it. This isn't a problem, but it was disconcerting at first, until I realized just what was going on. When the DVD-RAM is being used just as if it were another magnetic disk drive, Windows treats it exactly like all the other floppy and hard drives in the system. But when it is reading read-only optical media in that drive, it is treated just like any other optical drive. (You'll learn why later in this chapter, in the section titled "How DOS and Windows See Optical Discs."

How Big Should My C: Drive Be?

Many people wonder how large to make the C: drive and whether to create additional logical disk drives (logical volumes) on the first physical hard drive. Many PC vendors ship their products with just a single partition (C:) on the installed hard drive.

Keep several important considerations in mind when you are looking at this issue. None of them are simple decisions. You will have to make some judgment calls. This is okay because there are no really right or wrong answers.

First, having too many files and directories on one disk can make finding things much harder than necessary. If you partition your disk drives and put similar files together in each partition or logical disk drive, they will have a level of organization one higher than the subdirectories off the root directory. You might think of this as putting file cabinets that contain material on different subjects or purposes into different rooms.

Next is the matter of cluster size and the resulting inefficiencies in use of the disk space. This is less of an issue with FAT32-formatted disks than it used to be for the older, FAT16-formatted disks, but it still can matter if you have many files and a very large hard drive.

With all DOS (or Windows 9x) hard disks, the minimum cluster size is normally 2KB (four sectors). On a FAT-16 disk, this will only work for logical volume sizes up to slightly less than 64MB. Each time you double the size of a disk beyond either of these, the FAT16 format requires doubling the cluster size. Thus, on a FAT16 disk with just slight more than 1GB capacity, the cluster size must be at least 32KB, while on a FAT32 logical volume of the same size, the clusters would be only 4KB.

What about the option of making each volume very small and using a lot of volumes? This might be a good idea, but there are some drawbacks. First, remember that nearly every Windows application will put some data onto the drive that holds your Windows directory, even if you install the application to some other drive letter. Second, enlarging a logical volume after you realize you've made it too small can be tough. Be sure you allow enough room for growth in every volume, and especially in the one where you install Windows. Additionally, you could easily end up running out of letters for your disk drives! DOS can assign letters only to a maximum of 26 drives, including the floppies, which get A: and B:. (Adding even more pressure, if you want to map some network drives to local drive letters, you have to reserve some portion of the alphabet for that use.)

What about the opposite extreme? Suppose your files are, on the average, really large, so you don't worry much about cluster size. Can you make a single volume as large as you like? DOS and the original release of Windows 95 will not work well with any volume over about 2GB. Nor will Windows NT4 or earlier work with any DOS volume that is larger than 2GB. In both cases, the cause is the same: None of these operating systems can recognize the larger volumes that can be created under FAT32. Windows 95 OSR2, in which FAT32 was introduced, and Windows 98 have no such limitations.

SMART Drives and RAID Are Other Good Ideas

Before leaving the topic of hard disks, I will mention two fairly recent developments that are technologies to watch for on your next PC. SMART hard drives are first. RAID arrays are second.

SMART Hard Disks Tell You When to Fix Them

SMART is an acronym for Self-Monitoring And Reporting Technology. Most hard drive manufacturers now build this feature into at least some of their drives. These SMART drives constantly monitor their internal "health" and set some internal flags whenever they detect some incipient failure. Some BIOSes can read those flags during the boot process and report on what they find. External utility programs, such as the Norton

System Doctor component of the Norton Utilities can check these flags and advise you to act accordingly— enabling you to save your data before one of your disks actually dies.

RAID Finally Makes Sense for Some of Us

Redundant arrays of inexpensive disks (RAID) enhances the reliability of a PC by having it store data on more than one disk, in a fashion that enables you to avoid or minimize downtime and the risk of data loss when one of those disks fails.

At least nine levels of RAID are formally defined. They range in complexity and in the degree of safety they offer. The highest level stores data and ECCs across several disks in a way that enables you to replace any disk at any time with almost no chance of losing any of your data. (I discuss the most popular levels in Chapter 25, "PCs That Think They Are Mainframes.")

Some RAID implementations enable you to exchange, or *hot swap*, disk drives or power supplies whenever they seem about to fail or have failed, all without shutting off your PC system. This is especially critical for large companies that are running their mission-critical applications on such a PC.

Formerly, RAID was used only on mainframe computers and large servers for networks because, despite the name, implementing RAID is more expensive than just buying a hard drive or a set of hard drives with the same total capacity. Now, with hard drive prices plummeting and inexpensive RAID controllers available for desktop systems, it might be time for you to consider adding RAID to your desktop PC.

Peter's Principle: Manual Mirroring of Key Files Can Also Be Useful

Even without implementing a true RAID subsystem, you can give yourself a welcome margin of safety and convenience by manually mirroring your most critical files. That is, in addition to making (and periodically testing) backup copies of all your valuable data, you can simply copy those files to another hard disk, either on the same PC or on another PC you access over a network. This can be done both easily and quickly. And it supplies you with handy copies of those files in case they become damaged (most likely through human error, although hardware failures and software glitches may also cause problems).

It used to be that you could count on hard disks dying, and that was why backups on other media were absolutely crucial. Now, however, hard disks are so much more reliable and have so much mean time between failures (MTBF) that you are more likely to decide that the disk has become obsolete before it actually dies. Thus, a safety copy of your critical files on another hard disk will provide almost as much safety as backup copies on other media outside your PC. Of course, if you experience a fire or even a really virulent computer virus that races through all the hard drives attached to your PC, those disasters may render any sort of mirror copies useless. In those cases, only offsite storage of verified backups will save your data.

Variations on the Theme of PC Storage

Until fairly recently, floppy diskette drives and hard disks were the only widely used data storage hardware for a PC. It doesn't appear likely that either floppies or hard disks will totally disappear from PCs any time soon, but a plethora of new products for PC storage have become quite popular. These products use many different technologies—some new, some new versions of old. I would like to give you a broad overview and enough depth on the most important of these products so that you can understand where each one fits into the picture. This understanding will be critical in guiding your future PC storage purchase decisions, and my emphasis upon the basics will stand you in very good stead when you are confronted with even newer storage options (which you can be quite sure will almost constantly be introduced).

The Multiple Dimensions of PC Storage Technologies

All PC storage technologies can be classified in one of several dimensions: speed (performance), capacity, whether a device can write as well as read data, and the technology behind the technology (or, what makes it go). Keep these dimensions in mind as you read what follows. I will organize my presentation around the last dimension I named: the technology behind the technology. Thus, I will talk first about magnetic data storage devices (other than the hard disks and floppies that I have already discussed), followed by optical, magneto-optical (MO), and electronic PC data storage devices, respectively.

Primary Versus Secondary Data Storage

Almost all of these devices are used most often for what we call secondary data storage—as opposed to primary data storage, which is perhaps best exemplified by your PC's hard disk. When you use your PC, the programs you run usually come from your hard disk. The data comes from your hard disk also, and the data that is generated goes to your hard disk—almost always. Thus, hard disks are our primary storage devices.

Secondary storage devices are the ones to which you copy data from the primary device (or from which you copy it onto the primary device). A floppy diskette is one of the most common secondary storage devices. A tape drive, ZIP drive, or almost any other data storage device you can name is most often treated as a secondary storage device.

DVD, CD-ROM, CD-R, or CD-RW are good examples of PC storage devices that are most often used as secondary storage, with some exceptions. You probably use CD-ROMs to install programs, but you may also use them to run those programs if you don't want to give up the hard disk space the program would require. Most of us, for example, use DVDs and CD-ROMs as primary data storage when we use a reference disc (an encyclopedia, atlas, and so on) that comes on one of those media.

Going the other way, some people actually use hard disks as secondary data storage. They'll remove a hard disk from one PC and carry it to another, or store one that is loaded with archival data in a closet. Such things are (or were) common for large companies, but less so for individual users.

Alternative Magnetic PC Data Storage Devices

The same basic magnetic recording technology used in hard drives has also been used in several alternative PC data storage devices. The most common are tape drives. Others include removable hard disks, hard disk drives with interchangeable media, and various types of super floppy diskette drives.

Tape Drives

Besides floppy and hard disks the one magnetic storage device that has been used for PCs from the beginning—actually, from before the beginning—is the magnetic tape drive. One option with the earliest PCs was to hook up an audio cassette tape drive and use it to store data. Audio cassette recorders were designed to record audible sound—analog signals. In order to make them suitable for digital data recording, the data must be encoded as tones. (This is what is done by a modem to encode data for transmission over the voice telephone network, for the same reason.) This worked, but not well. It was slow beyond belief, and not much data would fit on a standard audio cassette.

Soon those tape drives were supplanted by special-purpose drives meant just for digital data recording, which worked much better. They used another form of data encoding, storing the information as magnetized regions on the tape and reading that information back as the tape passed over the read head. These drives have gone through many generations of improvements, with special Digital Audio Tape (DAT) drives representing the present state of the art. Many manufacturers, including Sony, make this kind of tape drive for PCs, and tape capacities go up to 24GB or so per cartridge.

One thing is constant here. All the different types of tape drives are sequential access devices. This means that to read something from a tape, all of the tape must pass over the read head from the beginning of the reel or cassette to wherever the data is that you want to read. When you want to write to a tape, you must again scroll past all the previously recorded information before you can start recording more (unless, of course, you want to tape over the previously recorded information with the new data).

Because tape drives are sequential devices, they are best suited for situations in which you want to read or write a great deal of information at once but won't need to retrieve it repeatedly or instantly. Backing up your hard drive's data is a perfect example. If the tape controller, tape drive, and PC are all matched properly, data can flow continuously, or *stream*, off the hard drive and onto the tape without you ever having to stop the tape movement until the entire task is complete.

If, however, the whole system isn't properly tuned, you might have to move the tape a short distance, and then stop it while you wait for more data to be prepared for writing. To keep from having a gap in the tape, you might even have to back up the tape and let it make a running start before resuming recording where you left off. Such a lack of streaming performance can make an otherwise relatively speedy tape drive into a real sluggard.

Peter's Principle: Cheap, But Not Realiable

Generally, tape is the cheapest form of data storage available for your PC, but it's also the slowest. Unfortunately, it is not always as reliable as you might want. Every good tape system comes with software that includes an option to verify the tape. Whatever that option does, it doesn't catch all the mistakes the tape drives make. So my recommendation to you is this: If you use tape as a critical backup medium, please verify your backups on your own by restoring a sample backup set to a different drive letter and checking that every file flawlessly made that round trip (hard disk to tape and back to hard disk). Then repeat this test occasionally on at least a random sampling of your backed-up files.

The software that operated tape drives initially was totally different from that used for disk drives, because their operating characteristics are so different. More recently, some manufacturers have created device drivers (the software that handles talking to the tape drive) for their products that make them emulate disk drives. If you use one of these products, you might think you are performing random access to some DOS logical drive that acts just like all the others in your PC—except that it will be horribly slow.

The largest PC installations, with many dozens of gigabytes of storage attached, are most commonly backed up to tape libraries. These are devices that have multiple tape cartridges and one or more drives, plus robotic devices to load and unload the tapes as needed. With these systems, you can readily store many terabytes of data. Indeed, there are few viable alternative options today for storing these huge quantities of data.

Removable Hard Disks

At the opposite extreme from a tape drive, in terms of speed and cost, is a removable hard disk. You could, of course, use any ordinary IDE or SCSI hard disk, remove it (after turning off your PC) and take it to another PC or store it away as archival storage. It is much more convenient, however, to add a docking bay to your PC. This is a box that goes into a space in a PC that is meant for a floppy diskette drive, with an opening in the front into which you may plug suitably designed swappable drives. The docking bay connects internally to the PC's power supply, and also to either an IDE channel or a SCSI host adapter.

With this type of device, you can swap drives in the bay while the PC is turned on, although you might have to reboot the PC before it will recognize what you have done. A PC with full plug-and-play support, on the other hand, may be able to see that the device has been swapped and immediately recognize it and use it properly.

Aside from the mechanics of the docking bay, these devices are just like a normal hard disk you might install inside your PC or via an external SCSI cable.

An alternative approach is to make a hard drive subsystem that can be attached to a PC's parallel port. This works, but it has an inherently lower performance than a drive that is attached directly to the PC's I/O bus either via an IDE channel or a SCSI host adapter.

A new possibility just now entering the market are external hard disks that attach to a PC via either a USB or an IEEE 1394 (FireWire) port. On PCs running Windows 98, these devices will be automatically recognized when they are plugged in. You do have to make sure that any disk cache you use with them is flushed before you unplug them, but as long as you take care of that matter, you may also unplug them without powering down your PC. The USB port is not really fast enough to support hard disks as satisfactorily as a direct SCSI or EIDE connection, but the IEEE 1394 ports (when they are commonly available) will be amply fast.

Hard Disks with Interchangeable Media

You can gain most of the benefits of a removable hard disk at a much lower cost by using a special kind of hard drive that can accept interchangeable platters. It isn't easy to make this approach work well—primarily because even tiny dust particles can foul up a hard drive, and keeping a removable cartridge clean is hard—but with good design, it can be done. The most popular example of this approach is the Jaz drive from Iomega, which stores either 1GB or 2GB per cartridge.

These devices most commonly attach to your PC via a SCSI bus, and they provide a performance level (rate of data transfer and speed of initial access to randomly chosen data) that approaches or equals that of a good internal hard drive, while offering the potential for unlimited amounts of storage.

Super-Floppy Diskette Drives

The super-floppy diskette category can cover several different technologies. All of them differ from the simpler technologies used in standard floppy diskette drives. Ordinary floppy diskette drives position the head using a stepper motor. Any system that aspires to store a much greater amount of data cannot afford to do this because the stepper motor cannot be made to support the necessarily higher data density. Thus, all super-floppies use the same type of advanced head positioning mechanism as is used in hard drives.

Another difference is in how the head is positioned relative to the surface of the medium. A normal floppy diskette drive presses its two heads against one another, with the floppy's disc in between. This means that these drives are actually dragging the heads across the surfaces of the disc. To keep wear to an acceptably low level, the drives cannot turn the disc quickly. Again, to get high capacity and higher performance out of a super-floppy, these issues must be addressed.

Other Manufacturers' Floppy Drive Replacements

A number of other manufacturers have brought out drives that are competitive with the ZIP technology. Perhaps the most successful at this time are the LS-120 Superdisk drives and disks.

These Superdisks are actual magnetic and optical hybrids, but not in the same sense as magneto-optical discs. In the LS-120, the recording is done magnetically in quite the same way as on an ordinary floppy (but at a reduced scale), but the head positioning is done by the same optical method as is used in an audio CD player (even using some of the same parts as in an ordinary CD drive). To make this optical positioning work, the diskettes have an optical track impressed on them at the factory. The head positioning mechanism uses this to locate the head, and then the reading and writing are done in exactly the same manner as any normal magnetic disk drive. (I'll explain the different way in which MO disc drives work later in this chapter.)

The LS-120 drive's ability to work with normal floppy diskettes as well is explained by its having two heads. One is an absolutely ordinary floppy diskette read/write head. The other is the much smaller read/write head needed to work with the more densely packed data on the Superdisk's 120MB format.

The LS-120 drive acts very much like a floppy diskette drive, except that when it is used with its special diskettes, it can store much more information and it can deliver the data to and from the special LS-120 diskettes much faster than is possible with normal floppy diskettes. This previous point implies that one must attach the LS-120 drive to the PC in a different way than the way in which floppy diskette drives are normally attached, because the standard floppy interface just works too slowly to keep up with these drives.

Most internal LS-120 drives are connected as IDE drives, just like a CD-ROM drive. This presents a possible problem for folks who want to use an LS-120 drive as a replacement for their PC's floppy diskette drive. This is the problem of how to boot from a standard floppy diskette. Until very recently, hardly any PCs could boot from a CD-ROM drive or any other IDE devices. Now, partly in response to the need to support the LS-120 drive and partly to allow booting a PC with a freshly formatted hard disk directly from a distribution software CD-ROM, most new PCs permit selecting any suitable ATAPI-compliant IDE device as the boot device. And if your PC's BIOS is LS-120–aware, it may even explicitly allow you to make that drive your A: drive.

Hooked up in this manner, an LS120 drive can serve as your PC's main floppy disk for booting from a safety boot disk (or from a system disk, in case your hard disk dies), and it can be used to install programs that expect to be loaded from the A: or B: logical drive. It also can be used for backups; with 120MB per diskette, it won't take too many of them to back up all the files you have changed recently for all but the most active PC user. However, be aware that an LS-120 drive, although much faster than a normal floppy diskette drive, is slower than a ZIP drive or many of the other alternatives on the market.

The LS-120 drive makers have had some success in convincing some PC makers to include them as an option in lieu of a normal floppy diskette drive. But they still don't have nearly as much market presence as the Iomega ZIP drives, which also can be purchased as an internal option in many new PCs (but in addition to, rather than in lieu of, a normal floppy diskette drive).

Even newer than the LS-120, and in some ways even more interesting, are Sony's new HiFD floppy diskette and drive designs. This is really a magnetic floppy diskette—the exact same size as the standard 1.44MB floppy—yet it holds an amazing 200MB. Sony accomplishes this feat by having these diskettes turn at 3600 rpm—the same speed as most hard disks (at least the older models) and ten times as fast as the fastest floppy diskette. Furthermore, by equipping the HiFD drives with a dual read/write head it—like an LS-120 drive—will read and write the older 1.44MB floppies as well as its own special disks. (Naturally, the ordinary floppy diskettes are made to turn at only the usual sedate rate.) The HiFD is too new to know how the market will accept it—but it shows that innovation continues I'd guess that this is one of the newcomers with more than a fighting chance of earning a significant market share.

Iomega's ZIP Drives

Currently, the most popular of the floppy-diskette-like technologies is the ZIP disk from Iomega. This is just slightly larger than the now-standard 3 1/2-inch floppy diskette, and it comes in both 100MB and 250MB capacities. Naturally, because the physical size of the disks is different from a standard floppy diskette, a ZIP drive will read and write only ZIP disks. So if you have a PC with a ZIP drive, you will probably also want to have a normal floppy diskette drive.

ZIP drives come in both internal and external SCSI interface models for both PCs and Macs, as well as external models that attach to any PC's parallel port and an internal model that connects to a PC's IDE bus. When a device driver program is run on that PC, or when the drive is attached to a PC running Windows 95 or Windows 98—which natively support ZIP drives—the ZIP drive will appear as an additional DOS logical drive. This is a great way to carry small amounts of data from PC to PC when a LAN is not available. The latest addition to this product line is an external ZIP drive that attaches to a USB port on either a PC or a Mac.

The performance of a ZIP drive over a parallel port is not very high. Over a SCSI port, however, it approaches the performance of a (slow) hard drive.

PC Card Hard Disks, Magnetic Stripe Cards, and Other Similar Devices

There is a constant push from consumers for smaller devices for their PCs. In part, this trend is driven by the increasing power of portable PCs and folks' natural reluctance to lug along lots of heavy add-on gadgets for what is getting to be a rather light and compact computer.

The removable magnetic data storage industry continues to create more and better gadgets to serve this market. In addition to creating adapters that let PCs read magnetic stripe credit cards, there are devices that read special-purpose cards. These cards have magnetic stripes that hold more data than a normal credit card.

The memory suppliers to both the PC and the game machine world created a standard some years ago for small cards to carry add-on RAM. This was first called the PCMCIA card (for PC Memory Card International Association, the name of the trade group that published the standard). Now we call them PC Cards. They come in one size but three thicknesses, and they're called Type I, Type II, and Type III, depending on how thick they are. Type III PC Cards are thick enough that some clever manufacturers managed to fit tiny hard drives inside them—a good trick, but not one that has proven terribly popular. So the PC card became another technically interesting product that failed to meet market requirements, and is now just a historical footnote.

That doesn't mean that there are no magnetic data storage options for miniature computers. There are many. For example, Iomega offers a super-small storage device they call Clik!, which is just slightly larger than a mounted 35mm slide (about 2×2×1/2 inches). Each of these minidisks will hold 40MB of data. Initially targeted for use in digital cameras, personal digital assistants (PDAs), and the like, they may well end up in many other devices as well. Iomega also offers a small external Clik! drive that enables you to transfer files to or from a PC.

IBM has recently announced what they call their Microdrive. This is a hard drive with eight times the capacity of the Iomega Clik! drive, and yet it is quite a bit smaller, physically. This technology will likely be a hot contender for inclusion in the next generation of digital cameras, and it may also find a place in PDAs, electronic books, and other small, portable devices that need a lot of high-speed storage capacity.

Other miniature magnetic recording options include magnetic strip cards. These are similar in size to credit cards, but they can have a larger data storage capacity than is typical of a credit card with a single magnetic stripe on one side. This greater capacity is achieved by using more of the card's area for recording data. At this point, these are hardly mainstream products, but they do exist. If you really want a small, rugged, magnetic data storage device, this is one candidate. A variation on this theme is the laser data card. These are like the optical disks I discuss in the next couple of sections, but in a flat form—just as magnetic stripe cards are like magnetic disks, but in a flat form. In both cases, specialized reader/writer devices are needed to use these cards.

Optical PC Data Storage Devices

The most common optical PC data storage device is the CD-ROM (Compact Disc, Read-Only Memory). As the name suggests, this is a form of read-only storage. That is, a CD-ROM comes from the factory with its content already in place; you cannot alter that content later.

CD-ROMs are, however, far from the only kind of optical data storage available for PCs. We also have the recordable (write once) and rewritable versions, called CD-R and CD-RW, plus the new DVD (also available in read-only, recordable, and rewritable versions). Some companies with very large archival data storage requirements have been using larger laser discs (LD) and magneto-optical (MO) discs for many years, and these too are now being used with PCs, but only in selected applications.

To explain how a CD-ROM drive works, and also to explain the many alternatives to them that arenow on the market, I must start the story where it actually began: with music CDs. Or in a sense, even earlier: with vinyl records.

Music CDs Set the Standard

In "the old days," when someone made a new audio recording, the electrical signal from a microphone was used to vibrate a needle while it dug a spiral groove into a master vinyl record. (In the *very* old days, the microphone's diaphragm was simply connected mechanically to the needle—no electronics were involved at all!) Next, this master record was duplicated in two steps. The first step was to cast a mold of the master. The next step was to stamp out huge numbers of identical copies of the master using this mold.

CDs Are Made Almost the Way Vinyl Records Were

The process for making music CDs shares much in common vinyl records, with one tremendous difference. The master discs for music CDs are made in a different way.

The first step in making a music CD is to convert the analog signals from the microphone (or from synthesizers and other sources), which represent the audio information to be recorded, into a string of numbers. This analog-to-digital conversion captures the music in a form that can be reproduced over and over again without any alteration (which is very much *unlike* analog music recordings on tape or vinyl records).

The binary digital data is recorded on the master disc in a manner I will describe in a moment. From this master, molds are made and multiple copies are stamped out much in the manner in which vinyl records are made. The differences are these: Only one side of a CD is available for use, and the opposite side is silk-screened with the disc's identifying label. Additionally, the binary data is read optically instead of mechanically (by passing the data under a beam of light instead of dragging a needle across it), and the data bits are stored more densely on the CD's surface than the wiggles in the grooves of a vinyl record.

Because of the second difference, the surface of the CD that has the data impressed into it is coated with a mirror-like metal film (aluminum or gold). That surface is then protected by an overcoating of clear plastic. Because of the third difference, that mirror-like surface is broken up with tiny spots that might appear to be imperfections but are actually the data, arranged in a spiral. This spiral has its turns so closely wound that the resulting disc acts like a diffraction grating, breaking white light into a rainbow.

How CDs Store Digital Information

The way in which music CDs store information digitally is both simple and stunningly clever. It uses the fact that lasers produce highly directional light beams of a single, pure wavelength. You can focus such a beam onto a small spot. If that spot has a mirror-like surface, the beam will bounce back essentially unchanged. If, however, that spot has a pit of exactly—or almost exactly—the right size and depth in the mirror, the light bouncing from the bottom of the pit will be out of phase with the light bouncing off the surface around the pit. These two out-of-phase components will interfere with each other, and the resulting reflected beam of light will be noticeably different from the original.

Manufacturers have developed a way to use a moderately high-powered laser to burn these pits in a spiral on the master disc. Your CD player has a (relatively low-powered) diode laser that tracks this spiral as the disc turns, shining a tiny spot of infrared light on the spiral to detect the data stored there. It then converts the digital information it reads into analog signals that can drive your headphones or be routed to your stereo system.

The pits serve two purposes in this scheme. First, of course, they encode the digital data. Second, their presence signals where the spiral track goes. The read head follows the pits like a trail of bread crumbs and reads the data encoded in the exact placement of those pits.

Technical Note: In the previous chapter, I mentioned that in magnetic data storage it is necessary to encode the digital zeros and ones into patterns of zeros and ones to be able to read them back reliably. The same thing is true for optical digital data storage, for essentially the same reasons.

CD-ROMs Aren't So Different; CD-ROM Drives Are

The data CD-ROM emerged when someone realized that if an audio CD player *didn't* convert the information it read from digital-to-analog form, this could be a wonderful way to store huge amounts of digital information.

Data CD-ROMs are made in the same way as music CDs. That is, they are stamped out as exact copies of a master disc (which are subsequently coated with metal and then protected with a plastic overcoat), and they contain purely digital information. The only difference is that the CD-ROM drives don't convert that information to another form; it remains digital. These drives simply present the data they read to your computer and let it decide what to do from there. (CD-ROM drives can also play music CDs, and for that purpose they have the digital-to-analog conversion circuits built in. But now, with fully digital sound systems in some PCs, it has become possible to play audio CDs in a wholly new and better way, avoiding the digital-to-analog conversion step until the very last possible moment, when the information reaches the speakers.)

Partly because of the demands of the huge music industry for music CD players, manufacturers have learned how to make CD-ROM drives inexpensively. (This same technology is also used as a part of the new super-floppy drive technology known originally as a floptical drive, and now called the LS-120 Superdisk drive.)

Key to this success is the fact that all CDs—including audio CDs, CD-ROMs, and the CD-R and CD-RW discs I will describe next—and their drives are built to a set of exacting specifications. These standards (variously called Red, Orange, Yellow, Green, White, and Blue Book) guarantee that these different styles of discs share many properties in common. This enables the sharing of designs and even some parts between the different kinds of CD drive.

Having a CD-ROM drive, or more than one, is a great boon to the PC user, and an even bigger boon for software companies. With a maximum storage capacity of around 650MB per CD, it is possible to provide huge amounts of data and some large programs on a single disc. This disc can be used directly at modest access speeds, or the PC user can load those programs (and perhaps some or all of the data) onto their PC's hard drive for even quicker subsequent accesses.

However, there is still one major limitation to CD-ROMs: They can't be used to store data, but only to read data that was stored on them by the manufacturer.

Recordable CDs (CD-R) Are Really Different

Naturally, so inviting a prospect as a CD to which you could write was a challenge to inventors. After some missteps, the inventors have come through. The resulting device is now called a Compact Disc, Recordable (or CD-R for short). Expensive at first, at the time of this writing these blank disks cost only about half a dollar for 650MB of storage, in quantity. Incomparable! (Well, except for digital tape cartridges.)

A CD-R disc looks largely like a CD. Although all pressed CDs are silver, CD-R discs are gold or silver on their label side and a deep green or cyan on the recordable side. The silver/cyan CD-Rs, known as Type II, were created because the green dye used in the original CD-R design does not reflect the shorter-wavelength red lasers used in new DVD drives. The cyan dye used in the Type II format will allow complete compatibility with DVD drives. Either way, CD-Rs act like a CD-ROM (in that you can read the contents of a CD-R in any normal CD-ROM drive). Put one in a special CD-R drive, however, and you can also write to it.

This trick is achieved by making both the CD-R disc (blank) and the CD-R drives a little more complicated than their ancestors. The CD-R disc has four layers instead of three for a CD (see Figure 10.3). The CD-R drive's laser operates at three or more power levels. At the lowest level, the laser light suffices to detect the presence or absence of pits or marks on the recording surface—to read the disc. At the higher level, it can actually burn marks into that surface.

FIGURE 10.3
A CD-R disc has one special extra layer and a slightly wobbly spiral pregroove.

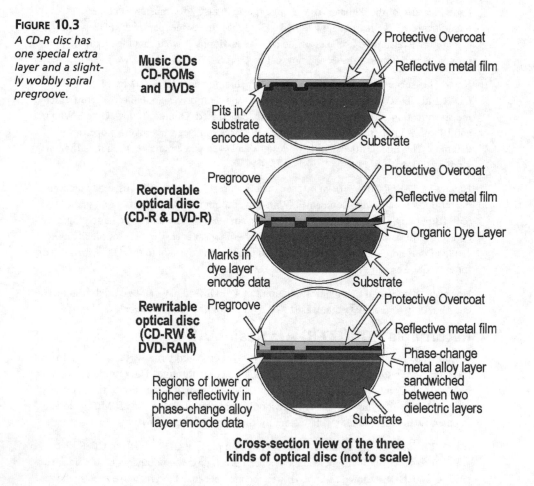

Cross-section view of the three kinds of optical disc (not to scale)

You might not have thought about it, but the that are machines used to make a master CD (for an audio CD or a CD-ROM) must have one complexity that the corresponding players don't need. The recorders must be capable of creating—not merely tracking—the spiral pit pattern. They do this by having a carefully machined mechanism that moves the burning head out away from the center by a fixed amount each time the disc makes one revolution.

To keep from having to build that type of mechanical complexity into all CD-R drives, the designers of this new medium added a slightly wobbly spiral pregroove to the disks. The laser light that will be used to read or write information to this disc can sense this groove and follow it. The wobbly bit around that groove means that the light reflected from it will vary in time, giving the tracking mechanism an always-changing signal to grab hold of and lock onto. This helps not only with following the pregroove, it also helps keep the disc turning at just the right speed. (Some disks have information modulated onto that pregroove signal to tell the drive about the optimal power level for recording, and so on.)

Technical Note: Until recently, most CD drives turned theirdisks at a speed that varied depending on how far the portion of the spiral they are currently reading was from the center. The purpose for doing that was to keep the head moving over the surface at a constant linear velocity (CLV). This is in contrast to the way a hard disk turns at a constant angular velocity (CAV)—a behavior that is also referred to as a constant number of revolutions per minute (rpm).

The newest high-speed CD-ROM drives (above 12X) use a mix of CAV and CLV, but so far there are no new standards for doing this,.

The main way this affects users today is that manufacturers are free to call a CD drive (of any variety) a 12X drive (for example, if, at its peak speed, it passes the head over the surface 12 times faster than is standard for music CDs). If the disc turns with CAV, that means its top linear velocity occurs only for the outermost turns of its spiral track. Because CDs record from the inside out, only a full CD will completely benefit from the advertised speed of the drive, and then only when reading from its outermost portion of the spiral track.

By the nature of the process used to record data on a CD-R, recordable discs are write-once objects. You can burn marks into the surface, but you cannot remove them later. This makes a CD-R best suited for archival storage of information. It is not a candidate for day-to-day temporary and reusable storage, like a floppy diskette. The fact is, however, that most floppies are recorded on once, most paper is written on just once, and there are many situations in which a CD-R is an almost ideal recording medium.

CD-RW Adds Erasability and Reusability

As nice as CD-R disks are, you can't reuse them. Folks value reusability in a disk, so inventors and engineers have toiled and come up with a still more complex version of the CD. A CD-RW disc contains two more layers than a CD-R. What really matters is that the recordable layer is made of a special material, an alloy of several metals. When it comes from the factory, this layer is formed of some highly reflective crystals (refer to Figure 10.3).

Instead of burning marks into the disc with a high-powered laser, a CD-RW drive uses its highest power to melt a small region of the recording layer. After it is melted, the material freezes into an amorphous form that doesn't reflect light nearly as well as its crystalline form. The laser's middle power level is used to warm the layer to something less than its melting point, but a high enough temperature to anneal those spots back from the amorphous form to the highly reflective crystalline form.

This strategy allows the CD-RW media to be written to and erased many thousands of times. The erasing can happen as new data is written, unlike the earlier rewritable optical disc technology we now call MO (magneto-optical). One downside to this technology is that the marks created on a CD-RW disc are not quite as good at light-scattering as the marks on a CD-R disc or the pits on a CD or CD-ROM, so they are not readable in all CD drives. Only drives with automatic gain control circuitry can handle them correctly, and so far this feature is far from ubiquitous.

CD-RW is a relatively new technology, but it has been gaining market share quite rapidly. The drives now cost little more than CD-R drives, which makes them a good purchase because they can be used to play audio CDs and CD-ROMs as well as playing and recording CD-RW discs. Sales of the CD-RW media have also been quite healthy; apparently a great many people are willing to pay around three times as much per disk to get the reusability of the CD-RW media, rather than the less expensive but nonreusable CD-R media.

There are four types of CDs: audio CD, CD-ROM, CD-R, and CD-RW. But there are a number of additional types of optical discs that matter to PC users. The newest, and soon probably, the most important, are the various flavors of DVD discs.

Digital Versatile Disc (DVD) Ups the Ante—And How!

Essentially, a DVD is a higher-capacity version of a CD, but this difference has made quite an impact. DVD technology is, in some ways, different from that used for CDs; in other ways, it's very similar. DVDs, like CDs, are optical discs, which are read by a laser. But the DVD laser, unlike the traditional CD laser, produces a visible beam and is tuned to the red band of the visible light spectrum (635 or 650nm). If you have a red laser pointer, it operates at this same wavelength. Consequently, its operating wavelength is considerably shorter than the infrared lasers used for CDs. This shorter wavelength makes it possible to read the far more densely packed data on a DVD disc. As you've already read, the different laser frequency also mandated the creation of CD-R Type II discs. Some DVD systems, notably from Sony as of this writing, employ two lasers: an infrared laser (790nm) for CDs and CD-R discs, and the shorter-wavelength laser for DVDs. Most DVD drives also contain two lens systems, one for CDs and one for DVDs.

Besides a significantly shorter wavelength laser, DVD data points, or pits, are a good deal smaller than are those of CDs. These pits are packed together tighter and also span a slightly larger area of the disc than do their CD cousins. Major improvements in error-correction methods have made all of these other improvements practical. Finally,

DVD disks can—unlike CDs of any variety—be double-sided, with up to two recordable "layers" per side. By simply refocusing the laser's lens, data from either layer may be read. (Actually, in some systems it's more complex than that, but at its simplest, refocusing is all that's necessary.) A double-sided, double-layered DVD designed under today's specifications has a capacity in excess of 17GB.

What's the Rush About?

Why is this so exciting to so many people? Audio CDs were first devised to record music. DVDs started out as Digital Video Display, and their primary claim to fame was that their data capacity was sufficient to permit recording an entire feature movie (in MPEG2 compressed form) on one side of these high-density optical discs. That got Hollywood (and the rest of the movie and television industries) excited. And the plans didn't stop there.

You've already read that formats exist for DVDs with as many as four "sides" (two layers of data on each of two physical sides). One proposed standard would make the spiral of pits go from the inside to the outside on one of those two layers and in the reverse direction on the other. This could enable playing a movie (or other streaming content) nearly continuously from inside to outside and back to the inside again. That's why moviemakers got excited about DVD. But before they could formulate a standard that met only their needs, the computer industry weighed in to be sure that the needs for digital data storage would be equally well-served. Soon what had been the "digital video disk" became the "digital versatile disk," capable of holding either computer data or a movie. More recently, the name changed yet again—this time simply to DVD.

Incidentally, the player used to show a DVD movie need not be different from the drive you would use to "play" digital data into a computer, but several other factors must be met before a PC DVD-ROM drive can play DVD-Video movies. Among other things, a DVD-ROM drive must have either internal or external hardware support for decoding the MPEG2 combined video and audio data stream. Additionally, your hardware will have to contain the copy-protection circuitry that is part of the DVD-Video standard.

Movies aside, with this much capacity and with backward compatibility ensured, it was almost a given that PC-makers would rapidly adopt the DVD drive (in a read-only version for DVD-ROMs) as the thing to include in at least their best models, in place of the CD-ROM drive that had become ubiquitous. During the past year, exactly that has taken place. You can still get a CD-ROM drive, but why would you want to when you can get the more capable DVD drive for nearly the same price and it will play all the discs the CD-ROM drive will and also the newer, more capacious DVDs? (Actually, you need to be aware that while DVD drives are fast, they won't read a CD-ROM as quickly as some of the fastest CD-ROM-only drives now on the market. DVD drives deliver data really quickly only when they are reading DVD discs with their much higher data density.) Overall, these developments were so exciting that many manufacturers didn't even wait for the standards committees to finish their work. Thus, you can not only buy

DVDs with movies on them or DVD-ROM discs, you also can buy DVD-RAM discs—which is quite amazing, because there is still a major argument going on between some pretty powerful interest groups about how to make the recordable and rewritable formats for DVDs. There are, in fact, three different versions of the rewritable format under discussion—only one of them has been accepted by the relevant forum, but the other two aren't yet ruled out. Still, the one that has been accepted (DVD-RAM) is now on the market. Our example desktop system has one of these drives, and I'm using it for backups today. It acts just like a humongous floppy diskette—one with 2.6GB per side of storage capacity! DVD-RAM drives capable of supporting a full 3.0GB per side are now available.

Are We There Yet?

I should caution you that things aren't quite as rosy as the account I just gave might have made you think. For one thing, video DVDs and DVD-ROMs come in jewel cases, and you take them out to put them into a drive just as you do for audio CDs and CD-ROMs. On the other hand, the DVD-RAM discs come only in sealed cartridges, because they get recorded on both sides and their recordable surfaces are quite vulnerable. So you can play them back only in DVD-RAM drives at this time. All the DVD read-only drives are meant for use with bare discs, which means either video DVDs or DVD-ROMs. Still, you can also play bare DVDs and CDs in the DVD-RAM drive, if you want.

The standard for audio DVDs is still being debated. Because there is much less pressure for a version of the audio CD that can hold that much data, the industry is waiting for that standard to be adopted before bringing any products to market. The recordable (nonrewritable) DVD (called DVD-R) is likewise yet to appear. Most industry experts expect that it never will. Rewritability seems to be the name of the game.

Magneto-Optical PC Data Storage Devices

In addition to devices that use either a purely magnetic or a purely optical technology for data storage, there is one more important hybrid of the two. This is the magneto-optical (MO) disc mentioned previously. These were first developed many years ago in large platter formats, and they are still the best understood of all the recordable optical disc types.

The only reason that they haven't made more of a splash in the PC world is that the drives are quite expensive. The media are not all that different in construction or price from CD-RW discs, but a MO drive costs a lot more than a CD-RW drive.

On the other hand, MO drives don't have to conform to any standards that describe other optical discs. This freedom has led to a small speed advantage for MO drives, especially for reading data. That and their long familiarity are reason enough for many companies that have already committed to the technology to stay with it for many years to come.

Basics of Magneto-Optical Data Storage

When I wrote about how hard disks work, I skipped over many of the more arcane details. You must understand one, in particular, in order to realize how MO recording is both almost the same and at the same time, different from all the other magnetic data recording technologies.

What you must understand is how the physical characteristics of the magnetic recording medium dictate the design of the recording device. Three properties of the magnetic recording medium are used in MO recording: two for recording and another one for reading back the recorded data.

MO Recording

All magnetic storage devices, and this includes MO, use as their medium a material that can be permanently magnetized in either of two directions. The material is never *not* magnetized—at every place in the medium it merely is sometimes magnetized in one direction and sometimes in the opposite direction. There are several key properties of any such magnetizable medium. The most important one, for our purposes, is how easily you can switch the magnetization from one orientation to the other. The name for this property is the medium's *coercivity*.

If the material's coercivity is low, magnetizing it is easy. This helps when you are trying to design a tiny write head for a miniature disk drive. The small head can generate only a fairly modest level of magnetic field. However, a low value for coercivity also means that it is relatively easy for the magnetization of the medium to get reversed accidentally. If you have ever damaged data on a floppy diskette by inadvertently passing it near a magnet, you have seen a vivid demonstration that the coercivity of the magnetic material used in floppy diskettes (and, as it happens, also that used in most hard disks) is not very high.

Magneto-optical disks, in contrast, use a medium whose coercivity is over 10 times higher. This means that after you record something on an MO disk, it is almost completely invulnerable to any stray magnetic fields. That higher coercivity also means that MO disks require recording magnets that can generate fields that are over 10 times stronger than those used in other magnetic data storage devices. Those fields just can't practically be made in the tiny sizes needed to pack lots of data into a small space.

The solution to this dilemma is a clever one. It takes advantage of a second important physical characteristic of the magnetic recording medium. This time, the property to focus on is called the Curie temperature. All permanently magnetizable materials have a coercivity that falls as the temperature rises. In fact, after a critical temperature is reached (called, as you might now have guessed, the Curie temperature), the material stops being a permanent magnet. After you cool it off to below that critical temperature, however, its permanent magnetic properties return.

So, if you use a laser to heat the surface of an MO disk hot enough, you can easily set the orientation of its magnetization with a small magnetic field from the write head. A blast of light from a focused laser of a suitable power quickly heats the magnetizable material in just one tiny spot almost to its Curie temperature. Simultaneously, the write head generates the field necessary to change the magnetization of this spot. Soon after, as the spot cools off, that new magnetization will be locked in place. The laser spot can be very small—smaller even than the magnetic recording head, which means MO discs can hold more than a magnetic disc of a comparable size.

Reading Data from an MO Disk

Reading back data from an MO disk uses the third curious property of the magnetic recording medium: its capability of twisting the polarization of light. A laser beam consists of light of a single wavelength, moving in a single direction. It also is strongly polarized, which means that the magnetic fields for each quantum of light (each photon) are parallel to one another (and at right angles to the direction the beam is traveling). Bounce such a beam off a magnetized surface, and the angle of all those photons' magnetic fields will rotate a small amount in a direction that depends on which way the magnetic field points in the surface from which the light beam bounced.

The returning light beam is passed through a linear polarizer. (You can think of this device as a comb that passes only photons whose magnetic fields are aligned so that they can slip through the teeth of the comb.) If the polarizer is set just right, it will pass many or most of the photons bouncing off places on the surface that are magnetized in one orientation and almost none of the ones bouncing off places where the magnetization is oppositely oriented. Detect this change in light amplitude, and you have, in effect, read the orientation of the magnetic field on the surface of the medium.

There are now two standard sizes for modern MO media: approximately 5 1/4-inch and approximately 3 1/2-inch. The larger ones can hold about as much as a CD-ROM. MO disks come permanently housed in much thicker and sturdier cartridges than even the smaller floppy diskettes. This is important because they are often used to store valuable data, and keeping the surface of the media clean and undamaged can be key to giving data a long life.

Electronic PC Data Storage Devices

One other group of electronic data storage devices is used in or with PCs. This group uses totally electronic means for data storage. They look like disk drives, but they really aren't. Therein lies both their strengths and weaknesses. Ordinarily, electronic memory is volatile, but there are several ways to make nonvolatile electronic data storage devices.

RAMDRIVE and Its Cousins

In the past, it wasn't at all uncommon to use physical RAM to emulate the existence of additional hard drives. In fact, if you've ever started up your PC using a Windows 98

Startup diskette, you know that RAM disks are still around in limited circumstances. In the case of the startup diskette, several Windows 98 utilities are stored on the diskette in compressed form. When you boot with the diskette, possibly because your hard drive has ceased to function, these utilities are expanded and copied into RAM. By use of a DOS utility known as RAMDRIVE, an electronic disk simulator, Windows simulates the existence of another hard drive on your PC. By switching to that "drive's" letter, you can run the utilities stored there, allowing you, ideally, to fix your hard drive problems. Essentially, RAMDRIVE adds a block device driver to DOS, and thereby creates the illusion of a disk drive. Whenever DOS (or Windows) writes information to that "drive," the RAMDRIVE block device places the information into a region of RAM that it has set aside for its exclusive use. Whenever you read from that disk, the block driver retrieves the information as it would from any other kind of disk drive. Although access to this pseudo-disk is phenomenally fast, this type of electronic drive is still volatile; turn off your PC and the contents of its RAM get zapped.

Outside of this sort of specialized context, however, you'll want to think carefully before creating a RAM disk for other purposes. Holding RAM aside for a pseudo-disk is really quite antiquated. Physical storage today is so fast and so inexpensive and RAM is still so precious in most systems, you're far better off using your disks as disks and your RAM as RAM. Indeed, in almost any circumstance, you'll be best off if you allow Windows 9*x* to use physical RAM for cache, at its own discretion.

PC Card Flash RAM

Portable computers need storage, just as much as desktop PCs, but they can't always accommodate the same kinds of storage devices. One solution to this need is to use PC Card Non-volatile RAM. These are devices roughly the size of a credit card, but somewhat thicker (approximately 86×54×5 millimeters, which is about 3.4×2.1×0.2 inches in English units).

These PC Cards, formerly known as PCMCIA cards, have some non-volatile RAM chips inside them. This memory could be made of erasable electrically programmable read-only memory chips (EEPROMs), ferro-electric random access memory chips (FRAMs), or simple DRAMs with a small battery attached to preserve their contents. The latest models use what is termed *flash memory,* which is a kind of inherently non-volatile electronic memory similar to EEPROMs. These devices don't ever lose their contents because their battery died.

Whatever their technology, PC Cards enable you to permanently (or close to permanently) store information rapidly, and you can read it back even more quickly. The only drawbacks they have are that their capacity is small and their cost is high. Still, if you have a PDA, you might find that PC Card flash memory is your best option. This is especially so if you treat your PDA roughly, because a flash memory card with its lack of moving parts is inherently more rugged than any kind of hard drive, and even more rugged than most floppies.

CompactFlash and SmartMedia cards

It can never be too small, can it? PC Cards are nice and fairly small, but not small enough for some folks. So, we now have two more formats that have become quite popular with the digital camera makers. One is called CompactFlash. The other is SmartMedia.

Both of these are essentially the same flash memory you get in a PC Card, but because they are smaller you get less space in which to store images or whatever it is you are storing. The CompactFlash cards are about one-third the area of a PC Card and two-thirds as thick. The SmartMedia cards are about the same area as a CompactFlash card, but much thinner. If you have a digital camera or other device that uses one of these, you'll need to get whichever kind your device uses, because they are not interchangeable. You can also easily get a reader that plugs into your PC for either of these types of flash memory cards to allow speedy transfers of data from the flash card to your PC.

If you've got a notebook, you can purchase a simple adapter for CompactFlash memory that enables it to be inserted in a PC Card (PCMCIA) slot. Windows 9x will automatically install the card as another drive on your system.

The main reason that the CompactFlash card is so much thicker than the SmartMedia card is that CompactFlash includes the electronics to manage the process of recording images to the NVRAM chips and of making this device appear to be a disk drive. The SmartMedia cards depend on having that controller electronics built into the camera or other devices into which these cards may be inserted.

Figure 10.4 shows the Lexar Media SmartMedia reader and a SmartMedia card. This particular SmartMedia card is the one that came with the Olympus camera I described in Chapter 12, "Getting Your PC's Attention: Input Devices," and that I used to take most of the pictures in this book. This card holds 4MB of data and operates at 3.3 volts. Other cards in this format are available that hold several times this much data. All SmartMedia flash memory cards are only about 45×37×0.8 millimeters thick. (That's about 1.8×1.5×0.03 inches in English units.) What you see in the figure is about 80 percent of actual size.

Flash memory is convenient, but it does have some drawbacks. When taking pictures with the Olympus camera, I found that it takes about 10 seconds after I snap a picture for the camera to finish writing the image to the flash memory card. If I download that image to my PC via a serial cable connected directly to the camera, it will take me around a minute per picture.

One way to speed this process is to remove the SmartMedia card from the camera and put it in the Lexar Reader (which is connected to the PC's parallel port with a printer pass-through connector). When I do that, I get access to the contents of the SmartMedia card as if it were an additional disk drive. It shows up in Windows Explorer within just a few seconds, and copying image files off that "drive" takes a lot less time than the camera took to write them in the first place.

It is perfectly okay to put the SmartMedia card into the Lexar reader or to remove it from the reader without shutting off the PC first. (Just don't do it while your PC is writing data to the card!) Windows 98 and the special driver that comes with the reader simply recognizes the card when it is present and adds a disk drive to the system. And it automatically "disappears" that drive when I take the card out of the reader.

For these reasons, I believe that the Lexar (or any equivalent) reader would be a very handy accessory to have for any digital camera that uses flash memory. Naturally, you'll need to get the model that supports the type of flash memory card that your camera uses. You can learn more about PC Card memory, CompactFlash cards, SmartMedia cards, and the Lexar readers for SmartMedia and CompactFlash at this Web site:

`http://www.digitalfilm.com/`

How DOS and Windows See Optical Discs—The Origin and Value of ISO9660 and UDF

DOS was designed to work with floppy and hard magnetic disks—only. That means that "bare" DOS cannot do anything with any optical discs. Fortunately, the designers of DOS included the possibility of what are termed *installable file systems*. Originally, they did this to support the use of networked drives as if they were local hard drives, but they also did this in order to allow possible future extensions of the types of (local) drives that might be attached to your PC.

When CD-ROMs came on the scene, Microsoft created another extension to DOS (and later to Windows 9x) to support what are, in fact, rather differently formatted collections of files. CD-ROMs arrived with a format that was not like that for a DOS disk. It also wasn't standardized across platforms or operating systems. Most CD-ROM titles worked either on a PC or on a Macintosh, but not both. (A large part of the reason for this was that the Macintosh supported long filenames, but DOS was limited to one-to-eight-character names plus extensions of up to three characters—the so-called *8.3 file-naming convention.*)

Soon we began to see titles that had been made with two versions of the same material on the same disc so that these discs could be used on either a PC or a Mac. (These hybrid discs stored the names of all the files in two ways: once in what was to become the ISO9660 format for PCs, and once in Hierarchical File System [HFS] format for Macs.) Although this served the needs of CD creators for the moment, the industry realized that this nonsense couldn't be allowed to persist.

A meeting was held at a place high in the Sierra mountains. At this meeting, a compromise was reached and a new standard was born. Thereafter, CD-ROMs made to the new High Sierra standard worked with both PCs and Macs. This new standard was later blessed with official status by the International Organization for Standardization (ISO) as ISO9660. This standard worked well for several years. Then CDs started to change, with the introduction of Photo-CDs, CD-R, and then CD-RW. The standard needed to grow along with the times.

Even before we had these new types of CDs, there were folks who were unhappy with the ISO9660 limitations on CD formats. In particular, the strict ISO9660 format includes a limitation on the filenames to something very much like what DOS supported. In particular, ISO9660 specifies all filenames shall have no more than eight characters and no more than three in the associated file extension. It even proscribes use of some of the characters that are allowed for DOS filenames.

UNIX users wanted a way to record CDs with UNIX-style long filenames. So they devised a supplement to the ISO9660 standard called the Rock Ridge extensions for this purpose.

When Windows 95 came along with its support for long filenames, people wanted to use that type of long filename, with its Unicode support, on CDs. This was the inspiration behind the Joliet supplement to the ISO9660 standard. This permits the use of Windows 9*x* long filenames, complete with Unicode support, up to a maximum of 64 characters including spaces. It specifies that the "ordinary," DOS-like 8.3-style names will also be recorded, so these discs are readable from any version of DOS or Windows, although this rarely works in practice.

Not everyone wanted Unicode support in the filenames (and early Windows NT users wanted to read CDs without the difficulties the Joliet format created). So, yet another extension to the ISO9660 standard was created, this time called Romeo. This system uses long filenames consisting only of ASCII characters (up to 128 characters if the disc is only for use on a PC) that are readable by Windows 9*x* and Windows NT, and also are readable (if all the filenames are no longer than 31 characters) on a Macintosh.

This was, and is, a rather confusing state of affairs. The authors of CDs who use these approaches must know what machines and operating systems are going to be used to read the CDs they create. Otherwise, they might make them in a form that would be readable by only some of their target audience. Also, the ISO9660 standard with, perhaps, its Rock Ridge, Joliet, or Romeo extensions (all of which are mutually incompatible) doesn't deal well with discs that are to be written to in multiple sessions or those that are going to be erased and rerecorded. So with the emergence of CD-RW, and then of DVD, it was clear that some unifying generalization of these standards was needed.

What we got next, and have now, is the Universal Disk Format (UDF) specification, currently in version 2.00. This was promulgated by the Optical Storage Technology Association. This defines a new file system (that is a subset and expansion upon an earlier definition) for optical storage media. It explicitly addresses the special needs that arise when you are using a write-once medium, including the possibilities that occur when you can write only once to each location, but can write many times to the disc as a whole. It also provides a proper foundation for read/write optical storage organization and, of course, covers the manufactured all-at-once ROM discs.

Further, the UDF standard has been upgraded to cover how each of these issues changes when one considers DVDs as well as CDs. In particular, it allows for the many different types of data storage you might want to store on a DVD and their differing needs for access. One particularly interesting addition is that of *named streams*. These are a generalization of the notion of a file's attributes to allow any amount of information of any kind. Each named stream is associated with one file, through its extended file entry. Thus, you will see only one file, but you can access either its actual contents or the named stream associated with it that contains supplementary information about the file.

The big advantage to UDF is that it is explicitly a platform-neutral, operating system-neutral way of addressing files on a storage device. Thus, a UDF-formatted disc can be read quite nicely, thank you, on a Macintosh, a PC, a RISC machine, or a mainframe, and so forth—and these machines may be running the Mac-OS, DOS, Windows (most any flavor), UNIX, Linux, OS/2, MVS, or whatever you might want. All you need is a driver (installable file system) that understands UDF.

You don't have to go this route. Many CD writers still support the ISO9660 standard, with or without one of its extensions. Or, you can (with the use of appropriate drivers) treat most writable optical media as if they were simply additional hard drives, putting on them a FAT-style file organization. That mostly won't serve you very well. The UDF standard is the "proper" way to go for optical media—and using it is crucial if you want to be able to share the discs you create with others, or even to read them on a different machine's CD drive (where a UDF disc is what the most modern software will expect and the only kind it will accept).

Disk Utilities

What a wonderful and wild world of PC data storage devices we have, and what a terri-
fyingly diverse set of technologies on which to manage our data. There are two saving
graces in this situation. First, the manufacturers of most of these devices—and certainly
of all those that have been blessed with market success—have managed to design them
in a way that lets them appear to be normal rotating hard or floppy disks. Second, there
are many quite useful (and some wonderful) tools you can use to manage your data on
all these diverse devices.

The disk emulations provided for some of these devices are nearly perfect. The RAMdisk
is a good example of this. Others, hampered by what is inherently a different technology,
manage only a halting emulation of a hard disk, and using them as if they were a disk
drive turns into an exercise in patience. Certain brands of tape drives are a good example
of this. The utilities you can use on these devices include some that are shipped with
DOS or Windows and some that are sold separately.

Disk Utilities That Come with DOS Versus Third-Party Programs

Unless you have given it some thought, you might not be aware that DOS and Windows
95 and 98—the products—are much more than just operating systems. The essential
operating system in DOS is contained in just three files: two have hidden and system
attributes (usually called either IO.SYS and MSDOS.SYS or IBMBIO.COM and IBMDOS.COM),
and the third has a familiar command interpreter called COMMAND.COM. The essential real-
mode (DOS) operating system in Windows 95 and 98 is contained in just two files:
IO.SYS and COMMAND.COM. (Windows 9*x*'s most essential file for the full 32-bit GUI is
VMM32.VXD, but a number of other files are required as well.)

I mean by these claims that you can boot a PC to either DOS or Windows 9*x* with a floppy diskette that contains only the files I listed previously (and a DOS boot record that
will load them). If you prepare a DOS system diskette (using, for example, the DOS SYS
command), you will get a disk with either of just those essential files. If you prepare a
startup diskette under Windows 9*x*, you are actually creating an emergency startup disk,
and Windows puts nearly a score of files on that diskette, hopefully providing you with
tools to emerge from an emergency situation. However, only the two files I mentioned
previously are truly essential to booting to a real-mode MS-DOS 7.*x* command prompt.

At the resulting DOS or Windows 9*x* command prompt, you can issue any DOS
command you like. However, only the DOS commands that are "internal" commands
(and thus whose programs are built into COMMAND.COM) will work. All the other commands
you normally are able to use depend on the presence of additional components, many of
which are the files you will find stored on a Windows 9*x* emergency startup diskette.

So what are the several dozens of files that come in DOS or Windows 95, the product? Why do these products come either on a CD-ROM or on a whole stack of diskettes?

There are two answers. First, some of the files you get in either of those products are modules you can use to extend the basic operating system. These include the data compression driver (DBLSPACE.BIN or DRVSPACE.BIN) and various device drivers and terminate-and-stay resident (TSR) programs that augment what the OS can do. For Windows 9x, these modules also include device drivers to enable Windows 95 and 98 to support a vast array of diverse hardware, plus the 32-bit operating system essential components and its GUI interface. The second answer is that both DOS and Windows 9x come with a lot of utility programs—small, but very useful tools to accomplish some specific tasks.

I will talk more about the whole subject of data compression in just a moment. First, I want to look briefly at some of those other parts of DOS (or Windows 9x) that you might want to use to help you manage the files you have stored on your disk drives.

The DOS (or Windows 95) Disk Utilities

All the files included in the DOS and Windows product packages that are not needed to run your PC are add-on utility programs. These programs are, as far as the operating system is concerned, just like any other DOS or Windows application program. They are loaded and executed to accomplish some specific task. The FORMAT command is a good example. You run it only when you want to format a disk. Other important DOS commands for dealing with storage devices include FDISK (which is used to partition disks), SYS (which is used to copy the operating system to a formatted disk), and SCAN-DISK (which is used to check the integrity of the file system—which is to say, the consistency between the information stored in the FAT and the various directory entries).

If you want to learn more about what each of these DOS commands does and how to use it, you can ask the program in question. That is, issue the command FORMAT /? at the command prompt and the FORMAT program will tell you, very concisely, what it can do and how to get it to do each of those things. Every other DOS command will provide you with similar additional help.

If you want more help than you can get from DOS or Windows Help, refer to *Peter Norton's Complete Guide to Windows 98* or *Peter Norton's Guide to DOS 6.22*, both from Sams Publishing. These books will tell you all that you want to know about each of these operating system's commands. Space limitations prevent me from going into any more detail about those commands in this book.

Third-Party Disk Utilities

I've already mentioned the Norton Utilities several times, and in particular, the Norton Disk Editor. You can use it in its read-only mode to learn about disks, and when you are ready, you can turn on its capability of changing things, and then actually use it to alter a disk's contents.

The Norton Utilities also include several other utility programs that can help you deal with PC storage devices. Perhaps the most important is Norton Disk Doctor. This program can diagnose many disk drive ailments (and often those in disk-like devices as well). For most of those ailments, the Norton Disk Doctor has a solution.

Norton Disk Doctor is also capable of undoing whatever it does. So if you ask it to fix some problem, and then you change your mind, you can usually get NDD to reverse its actions.

Another type of disk utility program is known as a disk *defragmenter*. In the Norton Utilities suite, this is called Norton SpeedDisk; in Windows 95 and 98 it is creatively called, Disk Defragmenter. I'll tell you about these next.

Optimizing (Defragmenting) Your Disk Drives

You might be saying to yourself, "All this sounds great. But what, exactly, is this disk defragmentation all about?" I told you earlier in this and the previous chapter how DOS allocates units of space in the disk's data area (called clusters), and how it links them by entries in the File Allocation Table (FAT). I also pointed out in that discussion that if you add information to an existing file, after some other file have been written to the disk, you will almost certainly end up with a fragmented file.

DOS (and Windows 95) usually do a splendid job of hiding all this from you, and of getting your data for you whenever you want it. But they can sometimes get confused by a disk with too many fragmented files, especially when it comes to undeleting ones you have inadvertently deleted. Also, very fragmented files can trash your PC's performance.

Peter's Principle: Defragment Regularly

Maintaining the integrity of your existing data is one of the most important tasks you'll ever perform on your PC. I strongly recommend that you defragment the files on your hard disks regularly. How often you do it is a personal decision, resting a lot on the type of work you do. Your PC is, after all, your *personal* computer. In general, however, I'd certainly defragment *at least* once a month. Some folks do it daily.

There are many ways to optimize the placement of files on a disk. Having them unfragmented is only the beginning. You also can choose to put the files that contain programs you use a lot near the beginning. That will let DOS find and load them just a tad faster. You might want to put frequently referenced data files relatively near the front as well. Most disk optimizers (including Microsoft's Disk Defragmenter and Norton Speed Disk) suggest that the ultimate in disk optimization is achieved when all your files are unfragmented and pushed up as close to the beginning of the disk as possible. Under Windows 98 and the Norton Utilities for Windows 95, v.3, you can have your PC automatically track which files you use the most. With that information, your drives can be optimized for you, personally, and not merely in accordance with what "most optimizers" suggest.

> **Warning:** Whenever you use a utility tool to make alterations on a disk drive, you are putting your data at risk. You can minimize this risk by making sure that your tool has been designed with a full knowledge of the operating system version you are using.
>
> Check with the vendor to be sure the version you have is the correct one for your operating system version and also see whether there are any patches or upgrades available. Some software—the Norton Utilities, for example—comes with a feature that you can configure to automatically go online and check for new versions at regular intervals. Additionally, each time you upgrade your operating system, double-check with the makers of all your utility programs to see whether you should also upgrade them. There is not much that will make you unhappier than learning that you just damaged your files unnecessarily simply because your tools were out of date.

Data Compression

One of the most confusing areas in disk management is the notion of compressed disks. This name, for one thing, is a total misnomer. Disks aren't compressed—data is.

The compression being referred to in this context can also be called "squeezing out redundancy." Chapter 3, "Understanding Bits, Nybbles, and Bytes," discusses that ordinary speech contains a lot of redundancy, so do most PC program and data files. If you could create from one file another, smaller file that contained the same information as the source, and from which the source could be exactly reproduced, you could store only the nonredundant form of that file and save space on your disk drive. In fact, you can do this.

There are two complementary strategies for doing this. One uses a utility program to compress individual files or groups of files whenever you choose. The other strategy builds the data compression (and decompression) engine into the PC's operating system so that every file is compressed when it goes to the disk and decompressed when it returns from the disk. This way takes no thought on your part, and so is much more convenient.

A downside to using a separate compression utility program is that you must consciously use it twice on each file or group of files for which you want to save disk space. You use it once to compress the file and another time to decompress it back to its original form. If you don't do the second step, you will find that the nonredundant form of your file looks like gibberish. The advantages of this approach include these: You can compress only certain files that you know will compress well. You can combine compressed versions of multiple files into one file called an *archive*. That file can then be sent over a modem in less time than the collection of uncompressed files, and you have the advantage that all the different, related pieces can be kept together.

The downside to using operating system compression is that when you have your PC compress or decompress a file, some time is required for the PC to do that work. If you do this for every file going to or from a disk drive, you may well slow down your computer.

On the other hand, after the file is compressed there are fewer bytes to be written to or read from the disk drive, so perhaps you'll actually see a speedup. What you see on your PC will depend critically on the balance between the speed of the processor and the speed of the disk drive.

Generally, the decompression is much quicker than the compression, so almost always you will see a speedup of your PC for reading files that have been compressed.

The advantage to the integrated OS approach is simply that you don't have to think about it. It works automatically for every file you copy to the compressed drive, and it works just as automatically to decompress those files when you read them from that drive. So, there is a place in our world for both programs to do compression of files on demand, and also for an operating system-level data compression engine. Fortunately, both kinds of data compression are available for our PCs. Even more fortunately, the plummeting cost of long-term storage is making compression all but unnecessary in terms of saving space on your hard disk. (It is still very useful to reduce the size of files you want to move over the Internet, or even those you want to put on a floppy or other removable disk to give to someone else.)

Standalone PC File Compression Programs

Many programs that can scrunch files down to a fraction of their original size are now available. These programs come in two basic flavors. One flavor is the loss-less compression program. The other is the lossy compression programs.

Lossy Compression

Lossy compression programs are useful for making an approximate representation of an original file. That is fine if the file was an image and you don't mind a slight degradation of the image when you reconstitute it from the compressed file. Lossy compression programs usually can be made to compress files by differing amounts, depending on how you want to trade off degradation versus space saved on the disk. Often, you can compress an image (or a video clip and so on) by a factor of 10 without much noticeable degradation. But if you compress it by a factor of 100, you almost certainly will notice that the reconstituted images are not the same as the originals. Examples of this type of compression are used to create JPEG image files, RealAudio/RealVideo streams, and MPEG movie files.

Loss-Less Compression

The more interesting programs for most uses are those that can create a nonredundant version of a file and then, upon demand, can re-create the original file *exactly*—that is, *loss-less compression programs.* Make no mistake: When you are compressing a program file, you must be able to get it back again exactly as it was, right down to the very last bit. Otherwise, it is worse than useless. A program that is incorrectly reconstituted might simply not run—but it also might do something horribly different from what the original would have done.

Typical compression ratios achievable with program files are a little less than two to one. That is, the nonredundant form of the file may be only a little more than half the size of the original. Some spreadsheet and other data files can be compressed by much more than that, with the nonredundant copy sometimes taking only a tenth of the space needed for the original file.

A couple of the most popular DOS-based loss-less compression programs are Phil Katz' PKZIP (and its companion PKUNZIP), and Haruyasu Yoshizaki's LHA. PKZIP is a shareware program. LHA is freeware. You can get more information on PKZIP and the other PKWare products at:

`http://www.pkware.com`

You can also download either PKZIP or LHA from many shareware program Web sites or local electronic bulletin boards.

If you're running Windows 98 and have the Plus! Pack installed, you already have a new feature called Compressed Folders. Essentially, Compressed Folders makes support for zipped files a native part of Windows. With no additional software, you can simply double-click any `.ZIP` file and it will open like a regular Windows folder. You can compress or decompress files by simply dragging and dropping them in or out, respectively. To create a new empty Compressed Folder, you only right-click on the desktop or in any Windows Explorer window and select New, Compressed Folder. It's extremely handy.

Data Compression Integrated into the Operating System

If all that mess about compressing and decompressing files sounds like too much to think about, perhaps you'd prefer to use the hands-off way to do data compression. This is the notion behind the DoubleSpace and DriveSpace programs offered by Microsoft as a part of DOS 6.*x* and Windows 9*x*.

If you choose to use this type of automatic data compression, the operating system will load at boot time an extra device driver that does the data compression and decompression. This driver works in such a way that what appears to be the space on the compressed drive is actually the contents of a huge file on your hard drive. (That file will have the hidden and read-only bits set, so you won't normally see it if you do a DIR on the disk, and you won't be likely to erase it inadvertently.)

This means that if you choose to create a compressed drive E: (and I remind you that the drive isn't what is getting compressed—the data that you store there is), the compression engine will create a large file on, perhaps, your C drive. When you think you are writing information to the E drive, you actually are sending it to the compression engine, which compresses it and stores it away inside that special file on the C drive. When you look at E: (for example, with Windows Explorer), you will see what appears to be the uncompressed files. When you copy them off of E:, they will come out just as you sent them in. What really happens, though, is that the nonredundant form of that information is read from within that special file on your C drive, decompressed, and then handed to you as if it came from the phantom E drive.

> **Warning:** These on-the-fly, integrated data compression schemes have been developed and tested over several years and by lots of people. Still, things happen. Nonredundant files leave no room for mistakes. (This is not to say that the disk drives that store those files don't still use ECC to protect the information. They do, but even with that, things happen.) So test your system before you trust your data to it, and, in any event, keep good backups—periodically tested backups—of all your valuable files. Then when things happen you can just say, "Oh, well," and head for your backups to restore the glitched files.

Some Things to Think About and Try

How many disk drives do you have in your PC? How many logical volumes? Do you know which drives have been partitioned and which logical drive letters are located in each partition? Do you know whether there is any space on any of your PC's hard drives that hasn't been allocated to any logical drive letter?

You may be surprised when you learn the answers to these questions. If you are running short of space, and if you see some unallocated space when you run the command I suggest next, you may want to alter the partitions to make that space available for data storage. But be careful; figure out why that space is currently unallocated. Just be sure nothing else needs it left that way, and that your PC's hardware and software can accommodate accessing that additional space. Many PCs aren't able to use more than about 8GB of any given hard disk—but if that is true of yours, you can get a BIOS extension program that will enable you to surmount that limit.

Go to a DOS command prompt. It may either be an MS-DOS mode command prompt, or it may be one in a DOS box within Windows 9x. Now enter this command:

```
FDISK /STATUS
```

This undocumented command-line switch to FDISK has been valid since version DOS 4.0, and it is the quickest way to see what drive letters have been assigned to which logical drives in what partitions. This is the only thing you can do totally safely with the FDISK command from within Windows 9x. For any other use of this program you must be at an MS-DOS mode (real mode DOS) command prompt.

If you have the Norton Utilities, there are several ways in which it can help you explore your system. Its System Information component will tell you a lot about the drives (and about many other features of your system).

The Speed Disk degfragmenter can give you a fragmentation report showing which files are fragmented and which are not.

The Norton System Doctor has many sensors that will reveal various facts about your system on an ongoing basis. One is the Disk SMART status sensor. If you run this, you will find out right away whether any of your hard drives support this feature, and if so you'll also learn whether any of them has experienced problems of the sort that might indicate an imminent failure.

Windows 9x also has some powerful reporting utilities. The first place to start is with the Device Manager tab on the System applet in Control Panel. First, click on the radio button labeled View devices by type. Then click in the device tree on the Disk drives, CDROM, and Hard disk controllers and Floppy disk controllers items. In each case, click on Properties and then see what you can learn from the various tabs on the dialog box that pops up.

Next, click on the View devices by connection radio button. Now try to find the disk drives! Eventually, you will discover each of them, but only after you expand the portion of the tree of devices that includes the controller that is managing that particular drive.

Another tool that will tell you a great deal about how Windows accesses and controls your PC's disk drives—if you understand what you are seeing there—is the Microsoft System Information applet. You'll find this program on the Start Menu under Programs, Accessories, System Tools. When you run it, open the portion of the tree labeled Components and then click on Storage. Scroll down the list of information presented there and study it. You'll find a lot of details, including the I/O addresses, DMA channels, and IRQ lines that are used.

Peter Norton

Giving Your CPU Enough Elbow Room—PC Memory

In the last two chapters, you read about storage in a PC. This chapter focuses on PC memory, which is where all of the required elements are temporarily held while the actual computing happens.

Understanding PC Memory

Many new PC users become very confused by the difference between storage and memory. And keeping these two things clearly separate in your mind is crucial to developing a sound picture of how a PC is built and how it works. So I will say it for you once more: *Memory and storage are two entirely different things.* Here's the difference in a nutshell: Memory is the collection of all the fast-information holding places (made up of RAM and ROM). Storage is the collection of all the long-term information-holding places (often made up of magnetic or optical disks or tapes).

If you find analogies helpful, you might think of your entire computer as an office. The memory in your computer is like a desk, providing space where all of the work can be performed. The storage in your computer is like a filing cabinet where information is kept for the long haul. As that information is needed, it can be placed on the desk (into memory), worked on, manipulated, changed, or used to create new information, and then all of that can be placed back in the filing cabinet (into storage) when you're finished with it for the time being.

Typically, a PC will have tens or hundreds of times as much capacity in storage as in memory. For example, a pretty good system these days might have between 64 and 256 megabytes (MB) of RAM (Random Access Memory), and it might have up to tens of gigabytes (GB) of disk storage. 1GB is the same as 1024MB.

The CPU's Essential Playground

The PC's main memory is the collection of all the fast information-holding places in a PC that can be seen by the CPU. That is, it's those places into which the CPU can place information—or from which it can retrieve information—directly, without needing to have that information pass through any other holding places along the way. It is only in these places that programs can execute or data can be processed.

> **Note:** Well, if your PC has a memory cache, that is a temporary holding place for information on its way into or out of the CPU. We normally don't think much about this memory area when discussing PC memory because it is basically a part of the CPU subsystem. I discuss this topic in more detail in Chapter 7, "Understanding PC Processors," and Chapter 8, "How Your PC 'Thinks.'" Your video card also probably contains its own dedicated memory.

Most of these fast information-holding places are contained in the memory modules (DIMMs or SIMMs) that are most likely plugged into special slots on the motherboard. These memory modules are small printed circuit cards that carry several integrated circuit (IC) memory chips, which are the actual holding places for information. You can see the DIMMs that are used for most of the RAM in our example desktop system in Figure 4.4, in the section "A Platform to Build Upon: The Motherboard" in Chapter 4, "Understanding Your PC's Parts." In that figure, they are referred to as PC-100 SDRAM DIMMs. I'll explain exactly what that jargon means later in this chapter.

It is important to realize that the physical locations of these holding places is not important to your understanding of how your PC knows their logical locations. They are all logically located at some range of addresses in the CPU's memory address space. (The CPU's memory address space is discussed in some detail in Chapter 7.)

Why Memory Is "Where the Action Is"

The reason why storage is where information is kept and memory is where it is processed is quite simple: Storage devices are good for holding information for a very long time. Most are capable of accepting alterations to their contents, yet they hold those contents very well between alterations. This is unlike the behavior of memory chips, which usually "forget" whatever they are holding the instant the power fails or your PC is reset.

Almost every type of storage device is much slower than the memory chips used in a PC's main memory. And this speed difference is why the memory, and only the memory, is the CPU's essential playground. It must have all the information it is going to use readily available at electronic speeds.

It would be extremely impractical to have the CPU constantly fetch all its information from a disk drive and store intermediate values there while it was computing some result. The only practical approach is to bring your information (both the data and the programs that specify how that data is to be processed) into the PC's main memory. Then, and only then, can the CPU be asked to process it.

The difference in speed between memory and storage devices such as hard drives becomes obvious when you take a glance at the numbers. Hard drive access time is commonly measured in milliseconds (ms)—that is, thousandths of a second. A typical hard drive has an access time of between 9–12ms. Memory, on the other hand, has access times measured in nanoseconds (ns)—that is, millionths of a second. Memory access times are typically around 50ns. In other words, memory access is commonly about 180 times faster than storage access. Would you rather walk across the country at 1 mph or fly at 180 mph?

What You Must Know About Memory Chips and Modules

There are at least three reasons you should know some details about memory chips and modules. One is simple intellectual curiosity. After all, memory chips and modules are among the most intricate devices ever designed and built by human beings. There are probably more memory *bit cells* manufactured and sold each year than any other computer product. (This is virtually guaranteed by the fact that most current memory modules contain millions of bit cells. And many millions of those modules are sold annually.)

A second reason is that understanding memory at the chip level and the module level helps you understand the overall design of a PC. This includes such key ideas as banks of memory and parity memory and error correction.

Third, you must know the key parameters that describe memory chips or modules if you are going to buy more and insert them into your PC. And knowing what they look like is also handy when it comes to finding them, and perhaps removing or inserting them, if appropriate.

First I'll tell you a little bit about the many ways that memory has been packaged for use in PCs. Then I'll go into some of the different "flavors" of RAM now available and describe which kinds you might be using in your PC.

Recognizing the Different Ways Memory Is Packaged

Electronic memory is made in integrated circuit (IC) chips. These are tiny, tremendously complex devices crafted from very pure silicon, some trace impurities, and a little bit of metal, built in super-clean (and super-expensive) factories.

Each chip can hold up to tens of millions of bit cells, and each bit cell can hold one bit of information. These chips are made on large, hyper-pure, single-crystal silicon wafers. Each wafer holds one dozen to 100 chips. Only after all the chips on the wafer have been completely manufactured and tested are the chips cut apart. The good ones are used and the bad ones are discarded.

IC memory chips come in two main types, with many flavors within each type. The two types are read-only (or non-volatile) memory chips, also known as ROM, and random-access (or volatile) memory chips, also known as RAM.

The ROM memory chips either have data placed on them permanently or are rarely reprogrammed with new data (non-volatile random-access memory, or NVRAM). In either case, they hold any data that's put on them essentially forever, even when you turn off your PC.

The RAM memory chips—which are by far the more numerous in almost every PC—are meant only for holding information temporarily. They can be written to as easily as they can be read from, but they forget any information they were holding when power is turned off. These integrated circuits are mounted and packaged in a variety of ways. In one of these cases, groups of chips are mounted on tiny printed circuit boards that can be plugged into a socket. The earliest of these were the *Single Inline Memory Modules*, or *SIMMs*. These were common when PCs used a 32-bit-wide memory bus, because each SIMM normally has 32 or 36 data lines (the larger number refers to SIMMs that support parity, which is discussed in the next section). A variant of this same form were the SIPPs, which resembled SIMMs but connected with motherboards using pins (like those on the back of your hard drives or on the underside of your CPU) instead of the card-connector used for the SIMMs.

Currently, the most common memory module is the *Dual Inline Memory Module (DIMM)*. The physical difference between a SIMM and a DIMM is an obvious one: a DIMM has a separate set of leads on the back surface of its connector, and a SIMM either has no contacts there or contacts that are merely duplicates of the ones on the front.

I'll just briefly mention the next version of memory module that we are sure to see in PCs, which will be described in much more detail later. This is the *Rambus Inline Memory Module (RIMM)*. It looks almost the same as a DIMM, but which differs in some very subtle and enormously important ways. For example, a RIMM has its notches in different places than a DIMM to keep you from inserting the wrong module into a memory module socket.

What Is Parity?

IBM's original specification for the PC indicated that all RAM used in the main memory would have a *parity bit*. This means that in addition to storing the 8 bits' values (1s or 0s), a ninth bit is also stored. The value of this bit is chosen so that counting all nine locations there will add up to an odd number of 1 bits.

According to this strategy, each time a PC writes to memory, a special circuit on the motherboard will calculate the correct parity bit value for that byte and then all nine bits will be sent to the main memory location. Correspondingly, whenever such a PC reads a memory location, it again computes what the parity bit should be from the eight data bits it finds there, and then it compares that to the parity bit it also read. The PC will let you go on only if these two are the same value (1 or 0). Otherwise, it comes to a complete halt and a message is displayed announcing this parity error.

IBM's decision to use parity bit protection for all data stored in a PC's main memory reflects its belief that data integrity is of the highest importance. IBM felt it was the best plan to prevent you from computing with any incorrect data.

Modern RAM is very reliable. This is particularly true in light of the next significant development in memory error-protection: ECC.

What Is ECC?

Although parity RAM is still in use, its successor, Error Checking and Correcting (ECC) has widely pushed it out of use for a variety of reasons. (ECC is sometimes wrongly called Error Correction Codes, not that it matters in the least.) ECC RAM is generally less costly than parity RAM. Functionally, ECC RAM just does more. Although parity RAM can detect errors, that's all it can do, and it generally halts the system when errors are encountered. ECC RAM can correct errors without ever interrupting your work. This difference is absolutely vital in mission-critical applications such as network servers, which simply cannot go down. Let's look quickly at how ECC does what it does.

There are a number of different ways in which errors in RAM can occur, and there are several different types of these RAM errors. At the simplest level, individual bits get "flipped" and store a 0 when they should be storing a 1, or vice versa. As you can probably guess, even a 1-bit error can be fatal to your system (and multi-bit errors certainly occur, too).

ECC memory uses a set of extra bits to store a special code, known as a *checksum*. This is an encrypted version of the actual data you store in memory. For each binary word of data, there is a corresponding ECC code. The number of bits required to produce this ECC code depends on the length of the binary word your system is using. For example, 32-bit words require an ECC code seven bits in length; 64-bit words require eight bits of ECC. When data is requested from memory, the actual data *and* its ECC code are retrieved and quickly compared. If everything is in order, the actual data is passed on to the CPU. If the code and the actual data don't match, the structure of the ECC code allows for the errant bit (or bits) to be identified. The error is then corrected as the data is sent on to the CPU. The errant bit (or bits) in memory isn't changed. If the same data is requested again, the error is simply corrected again.

Of course, in practice, the contents of memory are overwritten again and again. Unless there is truly a physical flaw in one of the RAM chips, the error will simply disappear. ECC corrections can be logged for review by a system administrator, who will check for errors happening repeatedly in the same parts of memory. This generally indicates hardware in need of replacement.

> **Peter's Principle:** Not Worth Cost
>
> Do I recommend that you pay extra to get parity memory in your PC? No. It's a good thing to have, but it's not worth what it will cost you, particularly with the existence of ECC. The deciding factors will probably be how much memory your PC has (the more it has, the more likely you are to encounter errors) and how critical your application is. The more costly your PC and the more RAM that's installed, the more likely it is that you'll want ECC protection.

How Memory Chips Are Organized Internally

Many ROM chips and some NVRAM chips have their bit cells arranged in groups of eight. These groups are always accessed as a unit. This means that each chip must have eight wires for data to flow out of those locations in parallel (and for an NVRAM chip that can be reprogrammed, another eight wires for data to flow into them). In addition, each chip must have several *address wires* so the chip can be told which of its many groups of eight bits is being accessed at that time. This type of a chip is called a *byte-wide memory chip*.

This strategy is not commonly used for RAM memory chips, which usually have a much larger capacity, simply because this large capacity means more address wires are needed to point to the desired memory location. The chip designers would rather have a single pair of data in/out wires than 16 of them, so RAM chips most often have their bit cells individually addressed. At most, you can address groups of four bits at a time. The former kind of chip is called a *bit-wide memory chip*, and the latter is a *nybble-wide memory chip*.

How might these chips be combined into a usable amount of RAM? That depends on the number of parallel data wires in the memory bus from the CPU to the main memory. If your PC has 16 bidirectional data wires, you'd need to use 16 bit-wide memory chips (or 18 if you want to also hold parity information), or else you might use four nybble-wide memory chips plus a pair of bit-wide chips for parity. Each of those memory chips would hold its 1 (or 4) bit of information for each of a large number of locations—and for the same number of locations in each chip, of course. This collection of memory chips is referred to as a *bank* of memory for that PC.

Modern PCs have many more data wires, and so their memory banks must be correspondingly wider. A Pentium, for example, has 64 data wires. Its banks of memory must store 64 bits of data (and perhaps also eight bits of parity information) for each of a large number of locations.

If you use memory chips that are all bit-wide and that each can hold 1MB (1,048,576 bits), you could hold a total of 64MB of data in one memory bank in a Pentium-class PC. This arrangement of 64 or 72 chips would take up a lot of room, and changing those chips would be quite an arduous task.

Fortunately, we now have a better way to do this. As I mentioned earlier, the first memory modules used in PCs were called SIMMs. A SIMM was a small printed circuit card with anywhere from three to nine memory chips soldered in place on one side. The complete module typically was organized as a byte-wide memory module. That is, it had enough contacts on it to enable you to load or recall one byte (all eight bits, plus perhaps a parity bit) at once. These contacts were located along one edge of the card, which slipped into a socket at an angle and was then tipped upright to lock into place.

You could plug one of these SIMMs into a socket much more easily than you could plug in all of the chips it contained, and the manufacturer could guarantee that the memory chips on a SIMM were compatible with one another. These features accounted for the great popularity enjoyed by SIMMs from almost the moment they were introduced, and for the near-total disappearance of individual plug-in memory chips from modern PCs.

SIMMs proved very popular, but they have been replaced by DIMMs for the most part. The reasons for this are not hard to find.

As I explained earlier, a bank of memory contains enough memory chips or modules to hold or supply in parallel as many data bits as there are data lines on the PC's CPU. It's important that all the memory chips in a single bank are fairly well matched. In particular, they must all be able to hold the same number of bits of information. Furthermore, they should all respond to requests to hold or recall data within about the same time, and should need similar signals to do so. These things can be readily guaranteed if you use identical memory chips or modules in all the sockets that make up one bank. But doing that with multiple chips or modules per bank takes conscious action on your part of whoever puts in those memory chips or modules.

> **Note:** It isn't obvious, but many PC motherboards let you fill up each bank of memory sockets with several different sizes of memory modules or chips. All the chips or modules in one bank must hold the same number of bits as every other chip or module in that bank, but the ones in the next bank over might hold a different amount.

One simple way to guarantee that each bank will be properly filled with matched memory chips is to make up larger memory modules. These will have 64 data lines, and so a single one of them will serve as an entire bank of memory. Of course, such a memory will need to have many more contacts than a byte-wide SIMM where it plugs into its socket. To fit all of those contacts without making the module unduly large, the manufacturers have put contacts on both sides of the printed circuit card that carries the memory modules. (They also can put the memory chips themselves on both sides.) These modules are called DIMMs.

Plug in a DIMM and you've plugged in an entire bank of memory for your PC. Everything in that bank is automatically matched, with no further effort required on your part. Furthermore, these modules come with notches that "key" them, preventing you from plugging a DIMM that's designed to work at 3.3 volts into a socket meant for a 5-volt DIMM, and vice versa. Also, DIMMs have many more ground wires than a SIMM, which is becoming crucial as memory modules run at ever higher speeds.

> **Warning:** Every PC motherboard or system comes with a manual that specifies just which types of memory chips or modules it can accept. Please read this document carefully before you go out and buy additional memory for your PC. You must follow the manufacturer's recommendations or your PC might malfunction.
>
> This also means that there might be some pretty severe limits on how much (or how little) RAM memory any particular PC can have. If you want to upgrade your PC, you might be able to plug in a new DIMM, or you might end up having to remove and replace all the memory chips or modules it now contains with new, more capacious ones. The course you must follow will naturally affect the cost of the upgrade.
>
> Another aspect of this is the question of parity memory versus nonparity memory. If your PC requires parity memory, you must supply it with memory chips in groups that store nine bits at each location. Similarly, if it uses memory modules, you must have memory chips that store and return that ninth bit for every byte location. (Some PCs enable you to specify whether you're using parity or nonparity memory modules by adjusting a jumper setting on the motherboard. You must make that jumper setting agree with the kind of memory modules you use, of course, and you must use all the same kind in every bank.)
>
> You cannot change this aspect of your PC's design without replacing the motherboard. Again, you need to know what kind of PC you have and what it uses. Then, if you want to upgrade your PC's RAM, you will know what to buy.

Well, things aren't always quite as simple as I might have made it sound so far. You might also have a choice between different flavors of RAM modules. I discuss that choice and the reasons for it in the next few pages, explaining what RIMMs are and why they are going to be common in PCs in the very near future.

Various Flavors of RAM

Ordinary, volatile RAM comes in a variety of types, but there are two main groups. One group is called static RAM (SRAM), and the other is called dynamic RAM (DRAM). The DRAM group is further broken down into several additional categories.

Static RAM (SRAM)

The earliest electronic memory chips used at least two (and sometimes as many as four) transistors per bit cell. In this design, one transistor—let's call it transistor A—is on (carrying current) when the cell holds a 1, and another transistor—let's call it transistor B—is on when the cell holds a 0. The circuit is arranged so that when one of these two transistors is on, the other one is forced to be off. This arrangement has two stable states: A on and B off, or A off and B on. The additional transistors, if they are used, are there to help you switch the circuit from one of its stable states to the other.

This works very well, and SRAM chips can be very fast. This isn't the best way to make really massive amounts of memory, however—dynamic RAM (DRAM) chips can have up to four times as many bit cells packed into a given amount of silicon. By the economics of IC manufacturing, that means DRAM can be about one-fourth as expensive for a given data-holding capacity.

Still, when you need the fastest possible RAM—for example, in a PC's L2 memory cache—or you need only a modest amount of RAM, SRAM is the way to go.

Dynamic RAM

A constant pressure is on the makers of RAM chips to come up with newer designs that will hold more information. One way to do this is to reduce the number of transistors required to hold each bit.

In dynamic RAM chips, only a single transistor is used to hold each bit. This must be a field effect transistor, and its gate electrode must be enlarged a little in order to serve as a *capacitor*, which is an electrical device that can hold an electrical charge. Because a field effect transistor needs no input current to control its output, it is possible for this capacitor to control whether the transistor is on or off for a (relatively) long time. Using techniques similar to those used in EEPROMs, it is possible to put charges onto those gate capacitors or remove charges from them whenever you want.

There is only one fly in this ointment: The capacitor that's formed on the gate of the field effect transistor isn't perfect. Over time, it will leak away its charge. Does this mean DRAMs can't be made to work? Clearly not. The computer I'm using to write this has hundreds of millions of bits of DRAM information storage, and it works very well.

I can best explain how this happens by using an analogy. Suppose you have a team of people who are going to help you remember some numbers. You arrange these people into an array with a certain number of rows and columns (also known as ranks and files—which is the source of the term *rank and file*). Now tell each person what number he or she is to remember. If you don't let these people write down their numbers and you engage them all in small talk, within just a few minutes many of them will have forgotten their numbers. However, if you do one special thing, they'll all be able to remember their numbers essentially forever.

Here is what you do: Have a helper go to each row and call out just to that row, "All right, people. Listen up. Get ready to tell my buddy your special number if he asks." And have another helper go to one of the columns and call down that column, "Okay, if you're in the active row, tell me your number." Only one person will call out his number. But every person in that row will bring it into the forefront of his mind and thus "refresh" his memory. Do this to every row often enough, and no one will forget the number he was told to remember.

This is a very good analogy for how a DRAM chip works. If it contains one megabit of information, for example, those 1,048,576 bit cells are arranged into 1,024 rows with 1,024 cells in each row. When you read from this chip, you tell it which cell to read by activating one *row address* and one *column address*. (This could take 20 wires, but more often it is done by using the same 10 wires in two steps.) Every cell on the selected row is activated. Doing this means that if the cell's voltage is high, it becomes even higher. If its voltage is low, it becomes even lower. In that way, all the information on these cells is refreshed, and they place that output value on the corresponding column output line. Only the value of the one selected column line is reported to the data-out line of the chip.

If you remember to read one cell from each row in every DRAM chip often enough, your PC's DRAM memory will work. But if you fail to do this for too long (more than about a thousandth of a second), some of those bit cells drift to a voltage somewhere between high and low, and thus they cannot be refreshed accurately.

You say you don't remember doing this with your PC? You might not even touch the keyboard for several minutes, and yet it keeps remembering information in its RAM. How does it do this? It has a special *DRAM refresh* process going on all the time in the background. This happens no matter what else the PC is doing. In fact, it is the highest-priority task performed by your PC because keeping those DRAM cells working properly is crucial to everything else it will be asked to do.

This DRAM refresh process takes some time and effort. If you had only a small number of DRAM bit cells to refresh, it wouldn't be worth all the overhead. This is one reason why SRAM is often used instead of DRAM for a small amount of memory (as in an L2 cache, for example). The other reason is that SRAM is often faster than DRAM, and its premium price can be affordable if you use only a little bit of it.

If you have hundreds of millions of bit cells to refresh (as is the case in a modern PC with tens of millions of bytes of RAM), it is most assuredly worth the time and the cost of special circuitry for the savings in the cost of all that RAM. This is why DRAM is used exclusively in the main memory of PCs.

The DRAM Alphabet Soup: From FPM and EDO Through VRAM to SDRAM

Now for the confusing part: all the different subflavors of DRAMs. This is where the alphabet soup comes in. In an effort to make DRAM chips that work faster, manufacturers have enhanced them in many ways. Each one carries its own fancy name and some special advantages. The only types of DRAM you are likely to encounter in a modern PC are EDO, SDRAM, DDRAM, and Direct Rambus. But before I explain these types, let's look at how we got to where we are today.

One early way that manufacturers sped up DRAM, called *fast page mode DRAM*, was possible because DRAM chips normally have only half the address lines they need. They use the same wires for row and column addresses, distinguishing between the different values by when those values are placed there. If the processor is accessing several memory locations in successive locations, or even nearly adjacent ones, it need only give one of these chips a row address once. Then it can access all the columns it wants. Only when it must move to a new row will it have to reissue the new row address. This speeds things up.

Another strategy, used in EDO DRAM, is to cause the data produced by the chip to linger awhile on the output. With this *extended data out* design, while you are still reading the information you just accessed, the chip is getting ready to supply the next bit of data. This approach is no longer the best one for desktop PCs, but for various reasons involving both the history of the DRAM manufacturing processes and the marketing history of various flavors of DRAM, EDO DRAM is still the predominant form of DRAM in large servers.

Dual-ported DRAM chips enable you to access two locations at once because they have two complete sets of circuitry for reading data from locations in the bit-cell array. When millions of bit cells are on a single chip, this additional overhead can be included for a minor additional cost. These devices are not symmetrical. That is, whereas one of the input-output ports enables you to access any place you like at random (and it also has the input circuitry for writing data to those locations), the other port is used just for reading data out, and then only an entire row at a time. These dual-ported DRAM chips, also sometimes called *video RAM (VRAM)*, are especially useful for video frame buffers because they're inherently used for random-access writing and reading by the CPU and linear readout by the video display circuitry. I'll tell you more about this in Chapter 13, "Seeing the Results: PC Displays."

Windows RAM (WRAM) is a special version of VRAM that is optimized for the types of access that are common in PCs running Windows and Windows applications. These include such things as filling in all of a region's bits that are devoted to a single color with a constant value, as well as easy ways to move a block of data from one region to another (*bit blitting*).

Synchronous DRAM (SDRAM) is currently the most popular kind of DRAM for use in desktop PCs. These chips can operate in lockstep with the clock signals on the memory bus. Thus, they can accept or retrieve information in a single clock cycle.

The original SDRAM modules were designed to work with systems whose memory bus (front-side bus) clock ran at 66MHz. Now, the most common performance PCs all use a 100MHz front-side bus, and there are SDRAM modules that can keep up with that faster rate as well. These DIMMs are labeled *PC100 SDRAM*. Usually, this is indicated by a paper label that is stuck on an otherwise ordinary SDRAM DIMM. Figure 11.1 shows one of these PC100 SDRAM DIMMs.

FIGURE 11.1
*Today's newest
desktop PCs use
PC100 SDRAM
memory modules
that can keep up
with the 100MHz
memory bus clock.*

Soon, we will be able to buy systems with a 133MHz front-side bus. These will come
with PC133-labeled SDRAM DIMMs. The good news is that these faster DIMMs
will not cost any more because the industry has learned to make them in volume as
inexpensively as they used to make the PC100 SDRAM modules.

What's a Serial Presence Detect?

You may have seen a message when your PC boots up, telling you something about the
Serial Presence Detect data it has found. If you have, no doubt you have wondered what
that might be.

With all the variations in memory modules, many of which fit into the same standard
DIMM sockets, the industry has developed an automatic method for a PC to ask each
memory module what kind it is and what speed ratings it has. The method it has come up
with involves another special-purpose bus.

This is yet another use for a new but little-known serial bus inside your PC: the *I2C bus*
(Inter-Integrated Circuit bus). Because it is a serial bus, it conveys information one bit at
a time. It is a very low-speed bus in computer terms, although it's pretty speedy in
human terms. The clock speed of this bus is less than one-thousandth the speed of the
memory bus—yet this is still fast enough to perform every task it is asked to handle
within a fraction of a second.

The particular I2C bus connection that is relevant for the Serial Presence Detect function
is between the motherboard chip set (and in particular the Northbridge chip) and the
memory modules. The chipset can send commands across this bus. When it uses this bus
for Serial Presence Detect business, it is usually interrogating the DIMMs to learn what
memory capacity each has, what technology it uses (for example, EDO, or SDRAM, or
RDRAM), and how fast it may safely be clocked. When it knows these things about all
the modules you've installed, it can choose a compatible means for sending data to or
retrieving it from the RAM. For example, if you have some slower DIMMs installed, the
chipset may need to insert wait states. Whereas if all the DIMMs are speedy SDRAM, it
can dispense with those time-wasters altogether.

Not all DIMMs have the Serial Presence Detect circuitry. If you've installed some that
don't, the chipset cannot learn about those DIMMs and will simply have to make some
assumptions. Often, you can specify those assumptions by setting some jumpers on the
motherboard or choosing some settings in the motherboard BIOS setup screens.

Various Flavors of ROM and NVRAM

Like RAM, all ROM chips are simply arrays of transistors that are wired together in a particular pattern to do a specified job. This wiring is created by etching the pattern into the last few metal layers on the chip.

When a CPU or another part of a PC reads data from a ROM chip or collection of memory chips, it supplies an address and then waits for the binary values to show up on the data pins. Internally, the chip activates a particular subcircuit specified by the address values on its input address lines, and then sends the output from that subcircuit to the data output lines.

Mask Programmed ROM

The earliest read-only memory chips, called *mask programmed ROM*, were manufactured in a way that forced them to produce the binary data corresponding to the information they were supposed to contain. This hard-wired information content is clearly permanent. It was a simple and effective means of making ROMs, and it is still used whenever you need many chips that all contain exactly the same information.

The Oxymoron Chips: EPROMs

The makers of mask-programmed ROM chips knew that some of their customers wanted to have different information permanently held in different chips, and they wanted to have relatively few chips with each set of information. This is not something that is economically feasible through the mask-programming method because creating the mask used in the fabrication process typically costs thousands of dollars, which is affordable only if you need several thousand chips.

The first solution to this problem took advantage of one of the ways a ROM chip can fail. The wiring that connects the circuits is composed of extremely fine traces of metal. If you run too much current through one of them, it will melt or vaporize. Someone realized that if you put the points of failure in predictable places by thinning the traces, you'll have a circuit with a manufactured set of data, but you can alter that data simply by overloading selected points. In essence, these chips are manufactured to hold data that consists of all 1 bits. You can "blow out a fuse" to convert a 1 to a 0 wherever you need it in a particular chip. Manufacturing the 1 bits is done at the factory. Converting some of them to 0s can be done anywhere and anytime you like.

Thus was born the *electrically programmable read-only memory (EPROM)* chip. This name is surely an oxymoron. Think about it: If you can program it, in effect you're writing data to it. So how can it be read-only? But it is true that most of the time you can only read data from these chips. You must use a special over-voltage circuit in a special fashion to program these chips.

Battery Backed-Up RAM

When PCs were young, you could easily buy mask-programmed ROM (and even EPROMs) or RAM. You couldn't buy any simple, inexpensive devices that would act like ROMs most of the time, yet would enable you to change the contents occasionally. This is exactly what PC makers wanted for one special role in their machines.

In the IBM PC and PC/XT (and their clones), switches on the motherboard were used to store configuration information. This was awkward and required you to open up the PC and alter some switch settings to change the PC's configuration.

IBM decided to include more configuration information in its PC/AT than in the XT, some of which might change at times when you didn't otherwise want to open up the case. IBM also wanted to include a *real-time clock* circuit so you wouldn't have to tell your PC the time and date each time you turned it on.

IBM's solution was to include in the PC/AT's motherboard a special integrated circuit chip that held both a clock circuit and some RAM to store the current time and the configuration data. This circuit had a battery to keep it working even when the rest of the PC was turned off. To reduce the demand for power from the battery, IBM used then-expensive CMOS technology for that chip.

This soon got the name *BIOS Setup CMOS,* or simply *the PC's CMOS*. Now, even though virtually all the circuits in our PCs are made using the CMOS technology, we still often refer to the subsystem of the CMOS chip plus the battery used for the real-time clock and configuration storage as the PC's CMOS. (Recently, some manufacturers have begun calling this the PC's *NVRAM,* which stands for *non-volatile RAM*.)

This is such an attractive combination that some manufacturers now sell modules that look just like any other integrated circuit packages, but that actually have long-life batteries built into them along with the semiconductor integrated circuit chips.

EEPROMs, Flash RAM, FERAM, and other NVRAM Technologies

Now we have some better solutions to these problems. Clever engineers have found several ways to make a chip that acts like a ROM most of the time, yet that can be altered on demand. Generally, these chips can have any specified collection of 1 bits changed to 0s, but they can have the 0s changed back to 1s only in a mass operation that affects all locations on the chip, or all of the locations in one block on the chip.

These chips carry many different names. *Electrically Erasable Programmable Read-Only Memory (EEPROM)* was an early name that was accurate, but cumbersome. (It's usually pronounced *double-e-prom*) These chips use a newer strategy than the fusible-link EPROMs. In an EEPROM, each bit cell stores its data as an electric charge on a capacitor. By one of several methods, the manufacturer makes it possible to alter that charge with a suitable electrical signal. A newer design uses a ferro-electric effect bit-cell. These *FERAM (or FEROM)* chips act pretty much just like RAM, except that they don't forget the information they hold when you turn off the power.

All of these devices can accurately be called *non-volatile random access memory (NVRAM)* chips. Because the average PC user doesn't care which technology is used, this name is coming to refer to the function and not the technology by which it is created.

What's Rambus, and Why All the Fuss About It?

Up to now, all our PCs have used clock signals in the same way. The clock for some portion of the PC's circuitry "clicks," and that signal is sent to all the relevant circuits. They do whatever they're supposed to do when that happens, and the results of those actions are sent wherever they're supposed to go. Then everything settles down before the next clock tick occurs. But PC clocks are getting faster and faster. Soon we will have no choice but to do things in a rather different manner. After all, electrical signals cannot travel any faster than light, and even at that speed, signals can barely make it from the CPU to the other side of the PC system unit within much less than a clock cycle.

The Rambus Solution

Rambus offers a solution to this problem. The whole idea of Rambus is to use memory chips that are fast, but not all that much faster than the best SDRAM chips we are using today. Yet, they'll act as if they were much faster. This may increase the memory bus clock speed from its present level of 100MHz all the way to 800MHz, which is an enormous step up. (Later on, it may be increased even further.)

The key idea behind Rambus is that it isn't necessary to wait for all the effects of one clock tick to die out before launching the next one. All we need to do is ensure that there are never two clock ticks passing through any given circuitry at once. Each circuit sees a steady procession of clock ticks and responds to them as it should. The results of those actions make their way back to the rest of the PC as they should, following alongside the clock tick signal that triggered them.

Conventional PC Memory Architecture—How It Used to Be, and Mostly Still Is

Figure 11.2 shows this architectural difference in a simplified form. In the top panel you see the essential pieces of the main memory system in all modern PCs, prior to Rambus. The CPU communicates with the DIMMs that make up the system RAM via the Northbridge chip. The CPU-to-Northbridge bus is 64 bits wide, as is the bus from the Northbridge chip to the DIMM sockets. The Northbridge chip also connects the CPU to the rest of the PC, mainly over a 32-bit wide PCI bus. (You'll learn more about the Northbridge chip, as well as several ways in which this diagram might become more complex—most significantly by the addition of an AGP bus—in Chapter 16, "Faster Ways to Get Information Into and Out of Your PC." You'll also learn all about the PCI bus and the AGP bus.)

FIGURE 11.2

The most common memory architecture for current PCs, contrasted with the new Rambus memory architecture.

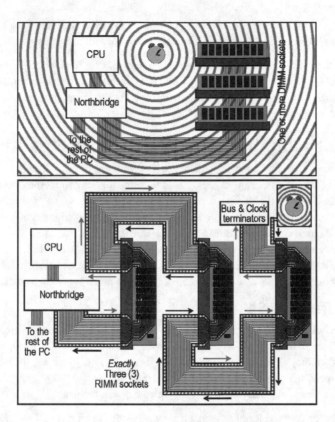

The memory system clock, which also provides the timing signals for the front-side bus between the CPU and the Northbridge chip, simply broadcasts its signal for all to hear. The delay between when the signals are sent out and when they are received must be small compared to the time between those signals. Mainly for this reason, system clock frequency is now topping out at 100 to 133MHz.

There are three DIMM sockets in Figure 11.2, but there could be more or fewer of them. Because the Northbridge-to-memory bus serves all those DIMM sockets in parallel, it doesn't matter to the PC how many sockets there are, nor if they are filled or empty. All that matters is that there is enough total RAM on all the DIMMs that are plugged in, and that those RAM chips work speedily enough.

The Coming New World of Rambus Memory Architecture

In the lower panel of Figure 11.2, you see the new world of PC memory systems according to Rambus and its partners, the most prominent of whom is Intel. Here, the memory system clock is trapped inside a box. The only way any circuits can "hear" the ticks of the clock is via the signals that flow out of the box through the indicated pipe. (I've shown the clock signals themselves in both panels as wavefront segments in gray.)

Notice that this pipe travels through each of the *Rambus Inline Memory Module (RIMM)* sockets in turn before arriving at the Northbridge chip. It then returns through each of the RIMM chips again, ending finally in the Bus & Clock terminators box. The clock will initially run at either 600 or 800MHz, and the front-side bus will run at one-sixth of that speed (100 or 133MHz). At this high speed, the time it takes for the clock signals to traverse the entire path from clock to terminator is likely to be much longer than the time between clock signals. Because every trace in the clock and data lines is closely matched in length, width, capacitance, and loading, the data signals and clock signals will travel alongside one another at exactly the same speed.

When the Northbridge chip (the Rambus Master) wants to write data to RAM, it can send out the data and the addresses where it will be stored in parallel whenever a clock tick passes through the Northbridge chip. When the data arrives at the correct RAM chips on the RIMMs, it is stored. In the meantime, the Northbridge chip may be furiously writing other data to different addresses, and those commands will already be traveling toward the RIMMs.

When the Northbridge chip wants to read from memory, it sends out the signals indicating which addresses it wants to read. It can send out new addresses each time it sees a clock tick, even though it hasn't yet heard the answers from the previous requests. When the requests arrive at the appropriate DRAM chips on the RIMMs, the RAM chips serve up the requested data, which then flows back along the data bus to the Northbridge chip.

The Rambus data path is broken into four byte-wide paths, so four independent transactions can be going on at once, accessing different portions of the DRAM on the RIMMs. The DRAM on each RIMM is actually broken down into 16 blocks to further facilitate nearly simultaneous accesses to locations in adjacent blocks.

It's important to understand that, although there can be almost any number of SIMM or DIMM sockets in a conventional memory architecture, in the Rambus architecture there are exactly three. And whereas in the conventional architecture you need not fill all the sockets, with Rambus you absolutely must fill every one of them.

What if you don't need that much memory? Then you must at least put a special *continuity module* or *C-RIMM* in any RIMM socket that isn't going be carrying DRAM. A C-RIMM is simply a RIMM without the DRAM chips. Its purpose is to carry the clock and data signals just as if it had DRAM chips.

In principle, the Rambus solution is a wonderful breakthrough. No longer does it matter how long it takes for electrical signals to propagate through your PC. The clock speed can go arbitrarily high, without regard to those time delays. In practice, things are just a little bit different.

Mostly, the designers and manufacturers of all the pieces have to be incredibly careful to match every single wire that is going to carry data or clock signals with every other wire.

Otherwise, these signals can get out of step with one another. Holding the very tight required tolerances is just barely doable with modern manufacturing techniques.

When two signals propagate on parallel wires and get a little bit out of step, we say they are *skewed*. Controlling clock skew (or clock-to-data skew) is therefore the key to making Rambus work. The folks who developed this technology claim that soon we will be able to run the clock at 1.6GHz (1600MHz) or even faster. But before we can try that, the whole industry will have to get the kinks out of running the Rambus clock at considerably slower speeds.

By the way, the small black rectangle near the bottom of each RIMM in Figure 11.2 represents the tiny EPROM memory chip that stores the Serial Presence Detect data. You can look for this on all your DIMMs as well. If you see such a small chip, you may assume that DIMM (or RIMM) has an SPD device. Otherwise, it probably does not.

What's Next?

In another few years, it's likely that a new memory chip landscape will confront us. All we can be sure of is that there will be larger, faster capacity and cheaper memory, which will make our PCs all the more delightful to use. Of course, the programs of the future will demand all the additional space and speed we can possibly give them.

Addressing Memory: Intel's Segments

I mentioned earlier that the contents of memory chips are addressed by voltages on the wires that attach to them. That is the physical level at which the circuitry actually works. From the programmer's point of view, the important issue is how memory is addressed from a logical perspective. In Chapter 8, in the section titled "Calculating Addresses," you learned that in real mode (which is how every PC starts working when it is first turned on), memory is addressed in a peculiar way called `segment:offset` addressing. (Refer to that chapter, if you are unclear on the difference between real mode and the several protected modes that PCs can use.)

The `segment:offset` addressing strategy simply means that every reference to a memory location in a program uses two 16-bit numbers. One is called the *segment value* and the other the *offset*. The segment number, multiplied by 16, is added to the offset to get the actual physical address.

One consequence of this design is that a PC in real mode can address only about 1MB of memory. That is the size of its real-mode memory address space. When the design was created, this seemed like a generous amount of space compared to the mere 64KB address space in previous microcomputers. Now it is positively stifling. Of course, our PCs are now programmed to go into protected mode early in their boot process, in which they can access as much RAM (and ROM) as you have installed.

Technical Note: There's a trick for addressing one-sixteenth of a megabyte in every PC that has some extended memory. This extra 64KB is what we call the High Memory Area. But for most purposes, a PC can address only 1MB in real mode.

There is one other trick that can be used to give PCs with a 286 or 386 CPU access to up to 32GB of memory—the full amount it can access in protected mode—even in real mode. This involves cheating, because it uses an undocumented command to manipulate the contents of the page descriptors in a way that Intel never intended and does not sanction. This isn't often done, but for completeness (and only for the very techy among my readers) I thought I should mention it here.

In the late 1970s, Intel chose to make its first *x*86 CPUs access memory in this two-step fashion, using segments and offsets, to simplify the conversion of programs originally written for the previous generation of microprocessors for the newer CPUs. And we have been stuck with this design ever since.

In protected mode, conversion of a logical address to a physical one is more complicated. Several steps are required to combine the selector value (which is the protected-mode name for what was the segment value in real mode) with the offset and pass that address through the page translation tables before finally coming out with a physical address. You'll find all the messy details described in Chapter 8, but I will recap them briefly in just a moment.

The important point is that when any PC starts booting, it has only about 1MB of memory address space. This implies some things that are critical to memory design and usage in PCs, even when they aren't running in real mode.

IBM's and Intel's Limiting Choices

Intel made some other choices that force the hand of any PC designer. It made all its *x*86 family of CPUs automatically go to a particular address, FFFF0h, immediately after they "wake up." This is just 16 bytes shy of 1MB above the bottom of memory address space. Whatever number the CPU finds there is presumed to be the first instruction it is to execute (see Figure 11.3). This means that you absolutely need ROM located at this defined FFFF0h address and at least a few addresses beyond that. If you don't, the CPU won't find any instructions and it won't be able to start the boot process.

FIGURE 11.3
The special memory addresses for every Intel x86 CPU.

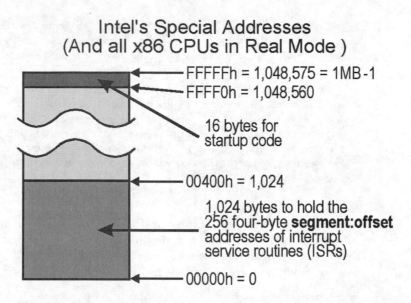

Intel's Special Addresses
(And all x86 CPUs in Real Mode)

FFFFFh = 1,048,575 = 1MB - 1
FFFF0h = 1,048,560

16 bytes for
startup code

00400h = 1,024

1,024 bytes to hold the
256 four-byte **segment:offset**
addresses of interrupt
service routines (ISRs)

00000h = 0

At the other end of the memory address space, Intel put in the interrupt vector table. Again, this is only a real-mode issue, but because all PCs start out in real mode, it affects memory design for every one of them.

In this case, RAM is required. This enables the PC to store numbers that point to interrupt service routines, and to change those numbers when new ISRs are loaded. (If you aren't clear on these concepts, please refer to the discussion in the section titled "Interrupts: The Driving Force" in Chapter 8.)

ROM at the top, RAM at the bottom; it's actually a pretty simple picture. Then IBM went on to make some more decisions that slightly complicated this picture. In IBM's previous mainframe computers, it had reserved half of the memory address space for system uses and left the other half for users to utilize however they wanted. That is, the operating system and hardware had the exclusive use of half the memory address space. Any application program could use some portion of the other half.

IBM apparently realized that Intel's 1MB of memory address space wasn't all that generous, so it reserved only 3/8 of it for system use and left the remainder for application programs to use. Five-eighths of 1MB is 640KB, which is where the infamous *640KB barrier* comes from —which I will discuss at the end of this chapter.

Figure 11.4 shows how the real-mode memory address space of a PC is divided according to these choices made by Intel and IBM. This figure shows some of the details of how the system space was to be used according to IBM's initial plans.

FIGURE 11.4

IBM's plan for PC real-mode memory usage.

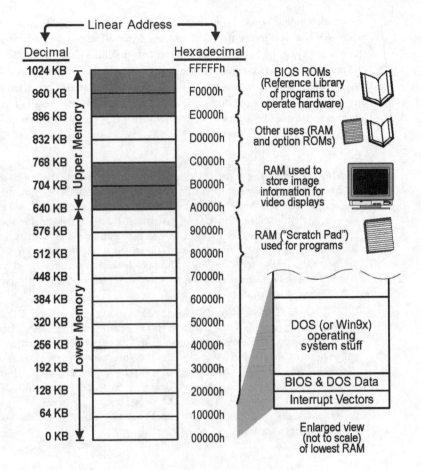

The Newer, Flatter Memory Model

You have probably run into the phrases "32-bit access" and "32-bit program," and you might have wondered just what these phrases mean. Unfortunately, their meanings are not always the same. You also might recall running across some reference to a "flat memory model" and wondered what that is. This section explains all these things.

When a PC is running in real mode, it can access only about 1MB of memory address locations. This means it needs only a 20-bit address to point to any place in its memory address space. (It actually needs 21 bits if you include access to the High Memory Area.) This is true even for the latest and greatest Pentium III machine—when it's operating in real mode.

Although Windows 98 is a protected-mode environment, the DOS operating system that is used to start up Windows 98 operates in real mode. This has two important implications. First, to maintain backward-compatibility with outdated hardware, PC operating systems (including Windows) must retain the capability of switching back into real mode. When in real mode, the PC can access memory only in the first megabyte, so that space is always going to be special and precious (until the next generation of hardware and operating systems completely passes and no one needs to worry about real mode any longer). Second, while in real mode, all the protections that give protected mode its name aren't there. Whichever old driver or piece of hardware has temporarily forced you back into real mode must be a very trusted one if your PC is not to be vulnerable to all sorts of unexpected crashes.

> **Technical Note:** There is one exception to this last problem. One of the several protected modes of operation of an x86 CPU is called *virtual 86 mode (v86)*, and another one that's found in the most recent models is called *extended virtual 86 mode (Ev86)*. In these modes, the CPU acts as though it is in real mode for most purposes, but actually it remains in protected mode with all of that mode's, well, protections. If the program running in this mode attempts to do something that's prohibited, the CPU automatically transfers control back to a portion of the operating system called the *v86 monitor program*, and that program decides what to do next.
>
> This is how a "DOS box" (or DOS window) inside Windows 3.*x* or Windows 9*x* works. For a program that can run in this environment, the mechanism offers a lot of protection between that program and all the others running on that PC at the same time. Unfortunately, not all real-mode programs can run in virtual 86 mode, which is why Windows 9*x* provides its MS-DOS mode. In that mode, the CPU really *is* operating in real mode with no protections at all. (Of course, the real-mode program can't access extended memory and no other programs are multitasking, so at worst you'll simply have to reboot your PC to recover from whatever crashes may occur.)

PC operating system designers have been eager to move us past DOS and on to something better. The most common shorthand for this newer, better, protected-mode world is *32-bit*. When a PC is running in protected mode (provided it has a CPU that is at least 386-compatible), it has access to a full 4GB of memory address space, for which 32 bits of address are a necessity.

At the beginning of the section "Addressing Memory: Intel's Segments" earlier in this chapter, I pointed out that in real mode, a program refers to an address in segment:offset form. In protected mode, the same form is used; the segment number (still a 16-bit number) is called a *selector*, and the offset now is expanded from a 16-bit number to a 32-bit number.

The selector's value is not itself a part of the memory address. It is instead a pointer to a data table called a *segment descriptor table*. (There is one of these for all the programs running in the PC at a given moment, called the Global Descriptor Table or GDT, and there is another one for each program, called its Local Descriptor Table or LDT.) Part of the information in that descriptor table is the base address for this segment, which can be anywhere in the CPU's 4GB memory address range.

Another part of the segment descriptor specifies its size, and this includes a bit called the *granularity bit*. If that bit is turned off, the maximum segment size is 1MB. If this bit is turned on, the size number (which is 20 bits long) is multiplied by 4,096. In this case, the maximum segment size is equal to the total memory address space (4GB), and the size must be some integer multiple of 4KB.

It is possible, but by no means necessary, for a protected-mode operating system to set the granularity bit to 1 and the segment base address to 0 for all segments. If this is done, every program sees the full 32-bit address space. This is the ultimate in what a programmer would call a *flat address model*. In this case, only the 32-bit offset portion of the address would have any significance.

However, PC operating systems don't do this, and for some very good reasons. The best way to protect one program from another is simply to ensure that neither one can see the other's memory address space. This requires each program to use segments that are smaller than the total memory address space. (There are other considerations as well, but you get the idea.)

Not All Memory Is Equal

When you hear a reference to memory in a PC, it usually refers to some portion of the main memory that is in view of the CPU. But not always. In this section, I want to remind you about some memory areas that are not a part of main memory, and also about some of the jargon used in reference to memory.

Even before that, I will remind you about another very important fact: Not every physical memory address has memory. Some addresses are locations in ROM. More are locations in RAM. But in almost every modern PC, most of the memory addresses the CPU can address simply point to nothingness. Not even to an empty socket where you could plug in a memory module. Just to nowhere at all.

This means, of course, that the CPU better not address those locations. And it doesn't. It still gets to use the full range of memory address in its internal workings, however, because of the magic of page mapping.

Logical, Segmented, Virtual, Linear, and Physical Memory Addresses

I want to bring together some concepts I have scattered around in various other places in this book and flesh them out a little more. Four terms are used to describe a memory address, and they mean quite different things:

- Logical memory addresses
- Segmented memory addresses
- Virtual memory addresses
- Linear memory addresses

Logical Memory Addresses

Logical memory addresses are the addresses used in programs. This term can be applied whether the program is running in real or protected mode. It simply means the numbers that specify where a program is pointing in the PC's main memory.

Segmented Memory Addresses

A *segmented memory address* means an address in a real-mode program. It is specified by a pair of 16-bit numbers joined by a colon, such as 1A35:0043. (Whenever you see an address written in this way, both numbers are assumed to be in hexadecimal notation even though there is no trailing h or leading 0x in either number.) The first number is the segment, and its value multiplied by 16 is added to the second number (called the *offset*) to get the physical memory address.

Virtual Memory Addresses

In protected mode, what was called a segmented address is now referred to as a *virtual memory address*. This is still a pair of hexadecimal numbers separated by a colon. Now, however, the first one (still a 16-bit number) is called the *selector*, and it points out which segment is to be used by referencing a segment descriptor table. The second number is the offset and now can be up to a 32-bit number. If you want to see the details of the descriptor table elements, please refer to Figure 8.4 in the section "Calculating Addresses" in Chapter 8.

Linear Memory Addresses

Both segmented and virtual memory addresses are translated from two numbers into one. This single memory pointer is called the *linear memory address*. So far, its maximum size in PCs is also a 32-bit number. (Well, in the Pentium Pro and Pentium II it could be a 36-bit number, but so far that possibility has not been supported in any PC's operating system.)

Physical Memory Addresses

Beginning with the 386, all of Intel's x86 processors and clone CPU chips have had a built-in memory paging mechanism. This paging mechanism can either be enabled or disabled, under software control. If it is disabled, the linear address is put on the CPU's address lines, and as such it becomes the *physical memory address*.

If paging is enabled, on the other hand, the linear memory address is further translated into a generally different physical memory address by referencing a pair of tables in main memory. These tables are called the *page directory table* and the *page table*.

The most significant 10 bits of the linear address, bits 22-31, pick out a line in the page directory table. That line contains a number that points to the location in RAM where the relevant page table can be found. The next 10 bits in the linear address, bits 12-21, select a row in the page table. A number found there points to a page frame, which is a 4KB region of physical memory address space. The bottom 12 bits of the linear address, bits 0-11, point to an actual memory location within that page frame. The page table and page directory table entries also hold some additional information the CPU must know about the page frame and page table to which they point. If you find this confusing, you might want to refer to Figure 8.5 in the section "Calculating Addresses" in Chapter 8, which shows this process graphically.

Some Ways the CPU Saves Time When It Does Memory Address Calculations

All this translation from segmented or virtual addresses to linear addresses, and linear addresses to physical addresses, could take up a lot of the CPU's time. This is especially so because each translation requires a reference to some table or tables in RAM. However, starting with the 386, Intel has included some special hidden registers inside the CPU to cache the relevant information.

Each time a new selector is loaded into a segment register, the segment descriptor information from the corresponding Global or Local Descriptor Table (GDT or LDT) is loaded into an invisible portion of the segment register called the *descriptor cache register*. That enables the CPU to use it for address validation and translation without repeatedly rereading the GDT or LDT.

Similarly, whenever a page table is read, its contents are cached in the *Translation Lookaside Buffer (TLB)* in the CPU. Therefore, linear-to-physical memory translations can also be accomplished without a constant need to reread that table from RAM.t

> **Note:** All this caching for the purpose of speeding up memory address calculations is in addition to the L1 (and perhaps L2) memory caching that is being used to speed up access to data and instructions. This combination of techniques is a substantial part of the much faster operation of PCs using 386- or-better CPUs over their predecessors, even when the CPU clock speeds are comparable.

Finally, when the CPU wants to send data out or pull data in, it puts the physical memory address on its address lines as low and high voltages, which stand for the 0s and 1s of the binary number that is the physical memory address value. From there, the external circuitry must route this memory reference to the correct memory chips or module (see Figure 8.2 in the section "Calculating Addresses" in Chapter 8.)

Memory the CPU Can't See (At Least, Not Always)

Not all memory in your PC is a part of its main memory. The following is a quick rundown of some of the other kinds of memory you can have in a PC.

Cache Memory

In effect, the CPU doesn't "see" the memory that is actually closest to it physically. That is, it doesn't really see the cache memory. It uses it, looking through the cache to see the main memory beyond. (If you want to review what the Level 1 and Level 2 cache memory are all about, look them up in Chapters 7 and 8.)

Video Memory

The video subsystem needs some memory in which to build the images it will display on your monitor. This memory is referred to as the *video frame buffer*. (If you have two monitors, each will likely have its own frame buffer.) Because memory always comes in powers of two, and because most frame buffers need some different amount of memory, it is quite common for the video subsystem to have some other memory under its control in addition to the frame buffer.

When PCs were young and their video displays were primitive, the entire video frame buffer showed up in the CPU's memory address space. That was fine for a 16KB, 32KB, or even 128KB video frame buffer in a 1MB PC. But now, with high resolution and large color depth displays, a 16MB frame buffer is common, and even larger ones are being used in high-end machines. In real mode in particular, it just isn't possible to fit all that frame buffer into the CPU's meager 1MB of memory address space. This is solved by making no more than 128KB of it show up at once. The CPU can command the video subsystem, via some I/O ports, to reveal whichever portion of the frame buffer the CPU must access. The rest of the time, that memory is kept out of the CPU's direct field of view.

This means that different portions of the very large frame buffer will occupy the same region of the CPU's memory address space, but at different times. When such a portion is not occupying that portion of the CPU's memory address space, it is simply nonexistent as far as the CPU is concerned.

In protected mode, with the full 4GB of memory address space available, this no longer need be a problem. It is perfectly possible to have the full 4MB or more of frame buffer show up somewhere in the CPU's 4GB memory address space. But often this is not done, for simplicity and compatibility with the real-mode way of doing things.

Finally, the video subsystem might have some uses for memory that don't involve the CPU. The video subsystem's main uses of the frame buffer are simply to store the image that is currently on the screen and to pump out the pixels to the monitor repeatedly so it will continue to redraw that image. But it also might need to have some font bit-patterns cached somewhere, or might need some scratchpad space for doing graphics acceleration. Often, that space is taken from the portion of the frame buffer memory that isn't being used for the actual frame image.

Expanded Memory

This isn't common anymore, but if you have a very old PC, it might have an expanded memory card in it. This was a way to make a relatively large amount of memory available even in a mere PC or PC/XT. Up to 32MB of RAM on a special add-in card could be made to show up in the CPU's memory address space just 64KB at a time (in four groupings of 16KB each), in a manner analogous to that used by modern video subsystems to reveal just a portion of the frame buffer at a time.

This EMS strategy was very valuable in its day, but it is completely obsolete now. With recent models of the x86 CPU family and modern software, we can give even DOS programs all the memory they could possibly want by using a so-called DOS extender program to enable them to access extended memory. Windows programs can inherently access all the extended memory in your PC, and thus they don't need any EMS memory either. Still, there are some of the old, EMS-using DOS programs doing useful work today. Some folks need what those programs can do, and they don't want (or perhaps cannot get) those services from a more modern program.

Today, if you have a program that wants to use some EMS memory, that resource is simulated by the operating system. DOS users know the programs that do this by the names HIMEM.SYS and EMM386.EXE. These are device drivers that augment what DOS alone can do. HIMEM.SYS takes some or all of the *extended memory* in the PC (anything at addresses above 1MB) and converts it into something called *XMS memory*. EMM386 then converts as much of that XMS memory into what appears to a program to be EMS memory as that program requests.

XMS memory is not a special new kind of memory. It's simply extended memory that is under the control of a special protected mode program called a *memory manager,* and that is accessible via that memory manager by a protocol described by the *Extended Memory Specification (XMS)*. Microsoft's version of this memory manager is called HIMEM.SYS, and it has included a version of this memory manager in every version of DOS and Windows 9x since the introduction of MS-DOS 5.0 in 1991.

After we had the Intel 386 (and later x86) CPUs in our PCs, it became possible for software programs to remap 16KB "pages" of memory from the extended region into portions of the first megabyte. That is the essential trick performed by EMM386 and similar memory management programs that simulate EMS memory by using extended memory (usually in the form of XMS memory). That meant it was possible to go on using DOS applications that were programmed to assume the presence of EMS memory even on a PC without an EMS memory card.

With the decreasing popularity of DOS programs in general, and those that assume the presence of EMS memory in particular, even the EMS-simulator programs are becoming obsolete. Instead, all our modern software uses the XMS protocol or a Windows memory allocation request API to get the memory it needs to do its work. Even when the occasional program does need EMS memory, it can now get the effect of that memory from Windows 9x without any user intervention at all. At least this is true if those programs are run inside a "DOS box." Only if you run one of them from the MS-DOS prompt might you have to include EMM386.EXE in your startup files (CONFIG.SYS and AUTOEXEC.BAT).

Disk Controller Card Memory

Some hard disk controllers have cache memory built onto them. This is a way to speed disk accesses that doesn't use any of your PC's main memory. The only advantage of this method over a disk caching program, which uses a portion of main RAM to do the same thing, is that you relieve your CPU of the burden of managing your disk cache. Particularly with the clock speeds of today's CPUs, this usually isn't compelling enough to justify the added cost. Again, this is a relatively rare kind of CPU-invisible memory, but you might have some of it in your PC.

Network Interface Card Memory

Some network interface cards (NICs) use a small amount of on-board memory to cache information on its way into or out of your PC via the network. This is another kind of memory your PC's CPU knows nothing about and cannot directly access.

Memory on an Add-In Slave PC Board

These days you can buy a PC in many forms. One form is an entire PC on a plug-in card meant to be inserted into another PC. That way you can have multiple keyboard, mouse, and screen setups attached to your PC. Each one has its own CPU, and each CPU has its own main memory. Naturally, the host CPU can't see any of this. It just communicates with the slave PCs through input-output ports via its input-output bus.

Printer Memory

You might have as much as several megabytes of memory in your printer. If it's a page printer (such as a laser printer), it probably has an internal buffer that enables it to compose most of a page image before it begins printing that page. This is also memory that the CPU doesn't see.

External RAM Disk Memory

You can create a fictitious RAM disk inside your PC by running a program that uses a portion of your PC's main RAM to emulate a disk drive. This RAM is fully in view of the CPU, and indeed, under the direction of the RAMdisk program, the CPU causes that RAM to act like a disk drive.

But you can also buy external RAM disks, boxes that contain a large amount of RAM, a power supply (probably with battery backup to keep them running when power fails), and a small computer that causes your PC to see this RAM just like any other disk drive.

Your PC's Memory Needs to Be Managed

Memory is one of a PC's main resources, and it must be managed along with all of the PC's other resources (input-output ports, DMA channels, IRQ lines, drives, and so on). In fact, resource management is one of the defining characteristics of any computer's operating system. It's a means of scheduling and managing the PC's resources for the benefit of its users and its programs.

DOS and Windows are mainly systems for managing a PC's resources. They make these resources available to your programs as those programs require, and they arbitrate between competing requests for resources. DOS and Windows don't exist in a vacuum, however, and you might find it beneficial to actively help the operating system manage your PC's memory.

How DOS and Windows 9x Allocate Memory

First, you must understand how memory is assigned for various uses in a PC. I have already told you most of the story for protected mode. Now I will tell you the real-mode portion of the story, and then finish the story for protected mode.

Real-Mode Memory Allocation

In real mode, DOS manages memory by using a chain of *memory allocation blocks (MCBs)*, also known as *memory arena headers*. Because no protections are operative in real mode, DOS cannot really manage memory in the same aggressive fashion that is possible in protected mode. At best, it can control which programs are loaded where, and then trust that each of them will do only safe things. Each program can do anything it wants after it is loaded and given control of the machine.

How the OS Core Gains Control of Physical Memory

When a PC boots up, the BIOS POST program has absolute control over everything. At that point, no memory is allocated for any use—except that, by Intel's fiat, the first 1KB is reserved for the interrupt vector table (IVT) and the top of the first megabyte must contain a ROM with some suitable boot program code in it.

During the POST process, some IVT entries are filled in with pointers to interrupt service routines (ISRs) located in the motherboard BIOS. Also, some data is placed in the BIOS and DOS data area, which is a .75KB region immediately following the IVT.

When the BIOS POST completes its work, it loads the operating system. Well, actually, it loads the boot sector program from the boot disk. That program is loaded into memory at physical address 700h, immediately after the BIOS and DOS data area. Control is then passed to that program to do whatever it was written to do.

If it's a DOS boot sector, it contains a program that can load the operating system files and enable them to prepare the in-RAM, ready-to-run version of the operating system. (And both DOS and Windows 9x use what amounts to a standard DOS boot sector— except for hard disks formatted with a FAT32 file system under Windows 98 or Windows 95B or 95C, and even then the rest of the preceding sentence still applies.) It takes some initialization steps, and the program code to do those steps is discarded when they have been done. At the end of that process, more of the IVT is filled in and the operating system core is loaded into RAM, also starting at 700h (overlaying the boot sector program).

How the OS Core Builds the Memory Arena Chain

Now the operating system core starts to process the startup files (CONFIG.SYS and AUTOEXEC.BAT, or the Windows 9x registry and then those files). At this point, some memory management becomes both possible and necessary.

Deep inside the operating system's core, at a location that is officially undocumented but quite widely known (and that has been very stable from version to version of DOS) lies a special table of pointers called the *list of lists*. One entry in this table points to the beginning of the first MCB, which is located just above the operating system core. Each MCB is "owned" by some program. The first one is owned by DOS, and so is every other block that controls an unallocated region of memory.

Any memory region (also known as a memory arena) that contains a program is owned by that program. Any other memory regions that are used by that program for data are also owned by that program. (One program might end up owning half a dozen MCBs— or only one, if that's all it needs.)

The first MCB that DOS creates starts out including all the rest of lower memory (from its location up to the infamous 640KB boundary). DOS loads programs into an empty memory arena (the area controlled by an MCB that belongs to DOS). Ordinarily, it will load any program into the first such block that is large enough to accommodate that program. Then, control of the PC is passed to that program.

Some programs (all application programs, for example) will do their thing and then exit, returning to DOS all the memory they were using. DOS then reuses that memory to load the next program.

Some programs (device drivers, for example) will do some initialization work and then return control of the PC to DOS, but will ask to keep some portion of the memory they were using. As mentioned previously, such a program is also known as one that terminates and stays resident (often referred to as a TSR program). In those cases, DOS shrinks the memory arena to whatever size that program declares it must keep and creates a new MCB to control the memory that it reclaimed from that program.

After this process goes on for awhile, a chain of MCBs will develop. Each one says how large the memory arena it controls is, and figuring out where that arena ends is pretty easy because it always starts right after the MCB. The next MCB in the chain comes right after that.

This is a fairly straightforward process, and it allows you to do some illuminating "snooping" inside your PC. I suggest that you look at just how the first megabyte of memory is allocated in your PC when you are running several programs and yet have a command prompt. You can do this in three different ways. The first is to load DOS (and not Windows), load some device drivers and TSR programs (perhaps by using lines in the CONFIG.SYS and/or AUTOEXEC.BAT file), and then work at the DOS command prompt that results from all that. Second, you can do the same thing, but also run an application program that permits you to *shell out to DOS*. When you have shelled out to DOS, you will again get a DOS command prompt at which you can do this exploration. Finally, if you are running Windows, you can open a DOS box (also known as an MS-DOS command prompt) either in a window on the desktop or in full-screen mode. Here, too, you will have a DOS command prompt at which you can begin to explore memory allocation.

After you learn how to decode the contents of an MCB, stepping through the MCB chain yourself is pretty easy. Just use the DEBUG program to display the contents of one MCB. Now figure out the length of the memory arena it controls and add that length to the address of this MCB using hexadecimal arithmetic (and don't forget to add in the length of the MCB itself). This will give you the address of the next MCB in the chain. Use DEBUG to display its contents. Repeat this until you find a chain with a block type of Z, which indicates the end of the chain.

You can get much of the same information, without seeing the form in which it is held in memory, by using the MEM command with its optional /d command-line switch. I describe this a little more later in this chapter.

Secondary Chains of MCBs

One main chain of MCBs starts with the first one just above the operating system core, and typically ends just below 640KB. There can be one or several secondary chains. One type of secondary chain is more commonly called a *subchain*. This is a chain of MCBs within one memory arena controlled by another MCB. Figure 11.5 in the next section shows two examples of this.

The other type of secondary chain is found in upper memory, at a physical memory address above 640KB but below 1MB. Such a chain can be formed by a third-party memory manager, by any XMS-aware program, or by DOS if you use its memory managers and declare DOS=UMB in your CONFIG.SYS file.

Structure of a Memory Control Block

A memory control block occupies exactly 16 bytes. It always starts at a physical memory address that is an integer multiple of 16.

Table 11.1 shows the structure of an MCB. Figure 11.5 shows a typical chain of MCBs on a PC running Windows 95 (in this case, a Dell Latitude XPi CD M166ST portable). I created this figure by running a small DOS program I created to "walk the MCB chain" inside a DOS window running under Windows 95. This program doesn't report the Process ID field of the MCBs directly. Instead, it attempts to give the name of the program that owns each one.

Table 11.1 The Structure of a Memory Control Block (MCB)

Byte Position	Contents
0	Block type[*]
1 and 2	Process ID[**]
3 and 4	Size/16
5 to 7	Reserved
8 to 15	Owner name[***]

[*]   Z for end of chain, M for all others except in device subchain, where

D = Device driver (from Device= line in CONFIG.SYS)

E = Device driver appendage

I = Installable file system (not currently used)

F = Storage area (if FILES > 5 in CONFIG.SYS)

X = File Control Blocks (FCBS) storage area

B = Buffers (from BUFFERS= line in CONFIG.SYS)

L = Drive information table (from LASTDRIVE= line in CONFIG.SYS)

S = Code and data area for DOS stacks (from STACKS= line in CONFIG.SYS)

[**]   The Process ID is 0000 for free space, 0008 for blocks owned by the operating system, and the segment value of the Program Segment Prefix of the owning program for all other MCBs.

[***]   Only for those MCBs whose Process ID is one greater than the segment value of that MCB (and thus is a block controlling the PSP of its owner), and only for DOS versions 4.0 or later, this area may contain the name of the owning program, either null-terminated or padded with spaces.

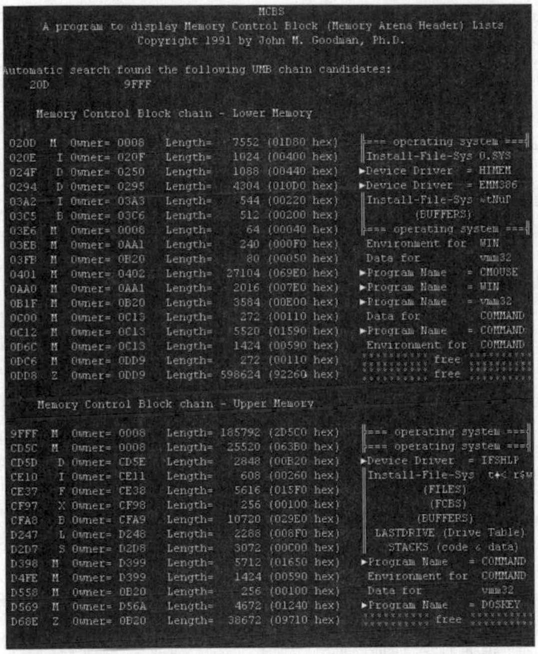

FIGURE 11.5
Sample MCB chain on a Windows 95 machine.

This particular PC has a small CONFIG.SYS and AUTOEXEC.BAT file in which I load the necessary real-mode device drivers to support memory management and a contour design mouse. The program that's used to display this particular list of MCBs is one I wrote a few years ago for another project. You can get the same information for yourself by stepping through the chain, using DEBUG, and manually doing all the translations from the numbers you find.

In Figure 11.5, notice that installable file system devices (which are block devices) have very odd names. Typically, the name field in the MCB is nonsense. Ordinarily, this only occurs for block device drivers. All the other MCBs that control a region in which there is a program will have a sensible name.

If you use a third-party memory manager, you might find that some of the MCBs will have very odd Process ID values. These programs use their own proprietary values in that location to signal something special to themselves. They typically don't tell users what those special values are or what they mean.

IBM's PC DOS 7 also has added some new block types for the device subchains. IBM also has declined to publish what these additional block types mean.

What Real-Mode Memory Management Is—And Isn't

Remember, in real mode there is no way for the operating system to force a program to stay within any particular memory boundaries. (Nor can it prevent that program from doing anything it likes at any of the input-output port addresses.) After control of the PC is passed to a program, that program reigns supreme. It can do anything at all. So memory management in real mode can be more accurately described as "cooperative memory allocation and use." Everything is on the honor system. Protected-mode memory management is altogether different from this.

Protected-Mode Memory Allocation

I have already told you a lot about how memory addresses are specified in protected mode. You know that the segment portion of a logical address is replaced by something called a selector in a virtual address (which is what a logical address becomes in protected-mode programs). You also know that selectors designate one segment descriptor either in the global descriptor table or in a local descriptor table. That descriptor contains an actual linear memory address for the beginning of the specified segment, and it also contains a length for that segment.

I haven't yet told you about the protection mechanisms that are involved in all this. There are several, so please bear with me.

Actually, the entire story is too long to tell here, so I'll just give you the short version. That should be enough to show you roughly how memory is allocated and protected in protected mode, and what that means for programs running in that mode.

Intel's Rings

Intel has defined four levels of privilege for programs running on any *x*86 CPU in protected mode. It demonstrates this with a diagram that looks like an archery target. Ring zero is at the center, surrounded by rings one and two, with ring three on the outside.

Programs running at ring zero have full access to the entire machine. They are every bit as powerful as real-mode programs. In fact, they are a little more powerful because they can set the boundaries on what programs running at lower permission levels can do.

In each ring outside ring zero, programs have increasingly less access to the hardware and increasingly more restrictions on their behavior. Programs in ring three are the least powerful. Still, even a ring-three program can accomplish any task, provided that some ring-zero program is willing to handle the hardware accesses for it.

This model is splendid. In principle, you would have a very small operating system core, consisting only of modules that have been extensively tested and are highly trustworthy, running in ring zero. Ring one would contain other parts of the operating system. Ring two might contain helper programs—applets, that sort of thing. Ring three would be reserved for your application programs.

As it happens, all the mainstream PC operating systems use only rings zero and three, which turns out to be sufficient. More than that is too much sophistication and complexity, and using too many levels would cost too much in terms of performance because it takes at least a little bit of time to switch operating levels.

Therefore, most of the operating system runs in ring zero, as do portions of many third-party device drivers and certain other kinds of modules. Everything else runs in ring three. This works, but it also helps explain why even after extensive testing, Windows and Windows applications manage to crash every once in awhile.

Protected-Mode Segments Are Special

In real mode, any segment is just a region of memory that is exactly 64KB in size and starts at some memory address that is an integer multiple of 16. That's all it is. Protected-mode segments are much more than this. A protected-mode segment can start at any memory address. It can have any length, and ordinarily it won't be any larger than it must be. But most importantly, protected-mode segments have *properties*.

There are two main types of segments, and one of these has some subtypes. The main two types are *code segments* and *data segments*. These names suggest something about their purposes and imply some of their properties. Data segments can be further subdivided into *stack segments* (which can be identified as either 16-bit or 32-bit) and other data segments.

Code segments are meant to hold pieces of a program, which is necessarily held there in the form of machine code so it can be directly used by the CPU. Because of this, these are the segments from which the CPU is permitted to withdraw its instructions—and only these segments. It is not possible to alter the contents of a code segment. (Well, if you define another segment of a different type that just happens to cover the same stretch of linear memory, you can modify its contents, which are the same contents as those in the code segment. This sounds convoluted, but it's exactly how you must go about modifying a program in memory and also executing it.)

Stack segments are places that hold information temporarily. A program normally directs the CPU to "push" the contents of some or all of its registers onto the stack before beginning a new task. At the end of that task, those values can be "popped" back from the stack into the registers from which they came. (This must be done in just the right way. Otherwise, a value might be put back into the wrong register, and that could lead to much trouble.)

Therefore, a stack segment must be a region in which it is possible to both write and read information. But it won't be used to hold instructions, so being able to execute the information held there as CPU instructions is not necessary. These rules are enforced by the CPU after it discerns that a particular segment is of the type stack segment.

Stack segments also come in two sizes, but in this context "size" doesn't refer to how large a region of memory is in the segment, but rather to the assumption the CPU will make about which size numbers it is to push on and pop off the stack. As you might have guessed, the two sizes are 16-bit and 32-bit.

Data segments are the remaining segments. These can be given a variety of properties. Like stack segments, data segments cannot have their contents executed as instructions. (Unless, of course, a code segment is defined that just happens to contain those same contents, because its memory region happens to coincide with or overlap that of this particular data segment.) But they can be set to be read-only segments, write-only segments, or read-write segments.

Segment Descriptor Table Entries

In Chapter 8, I told you about selectors and the segment descriptors to which they point. Each descriptor contains a linear address that indicates where the segment starts, another number that specifies how large a region of memory this segment contains, several more fields that specify what kind of segment it is, and more.

In the "Calculating Addresses" section of Chapter 8, Figure 8.3 shows the access rights portion of a segment descriptor and the requestor privilege level bits in the selector. Figure 8.4 shows the details, but I didn't discuss them there. Nor will I discuss them here any more than I just have. You can get a sense of what they do from what I just told you and by studying those figures. If you *really* want to know more, I suggest you refer to any of the many books on the subject. One of my favorites is Robert L. Hummel's *The Processor and Coprocessor*, (Ziff-Davis Press, 1992).

The main thing you need to know is that a combination of the requestor privilege level of the selector and the access rights bits in the segment descriptor pointed to by that selector determine most of what a program can do with the contents of that segment. These descriptors are entries in either the GDT or an LDT.

The contents of the GDT (of which there is only one for the entire PC) and of the particular LDT that a particular program accesses totally control which portions of memory that program can see and use. (There are also similar ways in which the operating system and CPU cooperate to protect the other resources, such as interrupts and ports, from misuse by errant programs, but those topics are outside the scope of this chapter.)

The CPU contains some special registers that point to the GDT and the LDT. Normally, only the operating system is allowed to change the contents of these registers, which is another aspect of how it can keep control over different tasks.

When One Program Calls Another

Things get really complicated when one program asks another program to do something. This happens all the time. If the calling program and the called program both reside in the ring of privilege, there is no special problem. But if they're in different rings, special care must be taken to ensure that the more privileged program isn't conned into doing something it shouldn't, and that in the process it doesn't confer more privileges on the calling program when it returns control.

These matters have been taken care of by some very clever and intricate features of the x86 processors. To understand them, you must learn all about Task Switch Segments (TSSs) and gates. This is all very arcane stuff, and too much off-track for this discussion. Just know that Intel's engineers figured all this out correctly. So if the operating system is also crafted correctly (as seems to be the case with all the popular PC protected-mode operating systems), the right things will happen and the wrong ones will be prevented.

The Bottom Line

Protected-mode memory management enables the operating system to rigidly enforce limits on programs, with a lot of help from the CPU's protection hardware. It can keep programs completely separate, or it can enable them to share some resources but not others. The particular decisions differ from operating system to operating system, and are in fact the source of some of the most critical differences between Windows 9x and Windows NT, for example.

Understanding the MEM Command

Both DOS and Windows 95 provide the MEM command, which enables you to look at how memory is being used on your PC. This isn't a book about DOS commands, so I won't go into any detail about how the MEM command works. But I wanted to point out that it is there, and it will enable you to see much of what I have just been discussing.

If you just execute the command, you'll get only a summary of the types of memory your PC has and how much of each type is in use. If you add a command-line switch of /?, you'll get a help screen that shows you the other switches you could use.

The /c switch is very useful for seeing which programs are loaded into lower or upper memory and how much memory each one uses. The /d switch essentially presents the information you can get by walking the MCB chain. The form of this display has changed with different versions of DOS and Windows. Earlier versions used only hexadecimal values in the /d display, which discouraged most folks from using it (although it was wonderful for programmers). The latest versions use only decimal values except for the segment addresses in the left column. This is more user-friendly, but it does mean you might have to do some translations from decimal to hexadecimal if you wanted to add the size of one memory arena to its address to get the address for the next one, for example. (See Chapter 3, "Understanding Bits, Nybbles, and Bytes," if you need a refresher on how to do this translation.)

The Infamous 640KB Barrier and How to Break Through It

Let's return for a moment to the relatively simple (if uncontrolled) world of real-mode PC operation. Here is where memory management all began, in the sense of something a PC's user could do to make it work better.

I have told you about how DOS loads one program after another and lets each one keep some or all of its memory if it needs to. After awhile, you can accumulate quite a stack of programs in your PC. Normally, you want to do this because those programs extend the operating system so you can access your CD-ROM drive, a network, a mouse, and other things that you must use. It is also very possible that these programs will use up so much memory that there isn't enough room left over for that big application program you must run. That's when memory management comes into play.

The first 640KB of physical memory is what IBM decreed that programs could use. IBM reserved the rest of the 1MB of real-mode memory address space for system uses. In most PCs, only a fairly small part of that reserved space is actually being used by the video adapter and motherboard BIOS ROM. This suggests an opportunity: If only you could use some of that extra, unused space in lieu of a portion of the lower memory region, you might leave enough room down there for your big DOS program.

I won't go over the many ways folks have devised to take advantage of this unused space, but I will tell you briefly about the one we mostly use today.

By putting a 386 CPU (or later model x86-compatible) into its virtual 86 (v86 or Ev86) operating mode, you can make it act as though it is in real mode and yet take advantage of extended memory and the CPU's paging mechanism. This is precisely what HIMEM.SYS and EMM386.EXE do, and what Windows 95 and 98 do for DOS applications. They take control of the PC, put it into protected mode, and remap some of the extended memory so it appears to be located at physical addresses in upper memory (between 640KB and 1024KB). Then they run your DOS programs in v86 mode so they think they are running in real mode. They don't actually move the memory to a new physical address, but any program running in v86 mode thinks that the linear addresses it generates are actually physical ones. The paging mechanism can make any correspondence between the two that it has been told to make.

This creates some available RAM in upper memory. The next step is to move some of the real-mode programs cluttering up lower memory into this newly available RAM. Starting with version 5, DOS enables you to do this quite easily. Just put the line DOS=UMB in your CONFIG.SYS file and then use the LOADHIGH, DEVICEHIGH, and (in DOS 6.x) INSTALLHIGH directives to put your resident programs up there. (The DOS=HIGH directive also helps because it moves some of the core of the OS up into the High Memory Area, just past the end of the first megabyte.)

If you find yourself needing to run lots of TSR programs and real-mode device drivers, and if you then run low on available lower memory, this is the best approach to use to get more free lower memory.

If you are running Windows 9x, it will take care of much of this problem. Mainly, it does this by substituting protected-mode drivers for most of those real-mode drivers and TSR programs. Also, it solves some memory usage problems that Windows 3.x has, which was another reason many folks had to use DOS-level memory management on their PCs.

Understanding Windows Memory Use

DOS plus Windows 3.*x*, or Windows 9*x*, is in many ways just DOS in a pretty dress. So whatever DOS does with memory before Windows is started is something that Windows simply must deal with. Then Windows goes on to do more with memory on its own.

Most of the time, Windows does an admirable job of using memory for its needs and those of the programs it runs. But when it doesn't, you will get an Out of Memory message. This doesn't mean that all your PC's RAM is in use. It just means Windows needs more RAM than it can get right now. This is when memory management makes sense for Windows users.

The most important point to remember is that Windows (either version 3.*x* or Windows 9*x*) is a protected-mode environment. This means that after you start Windows, your PC is running in protected mode until you shut Windows down. Well, it will revert to real mode from time to time to do some low-level DOS system actions, but then it immediately springs back into protected mode. (Windows 9*x* goes back to real mode much less often than Windows 3.*x*, but it still goes back many times each second.) This means that Windows will allocate memory for programs from the entire pool of RAM on your PC. It can access all the RAM you can give it. (And it would probably benefit from having more!) It uses memory from every range of available addresses, both in the first megabyte and beyond.

Some of its uses are for system-level things, such as a disk cache to speed up access to your disk drives. Other uses are for pieces of programs and portions of the data with which they are working. Windows is quite clever about swapping out chunks of data to disk and overlaying chunks of programs with other program chunks whenever it starts to run low on free memory. But it still isn't always capable of running programs you'd think it could. Sometimes the reason is that Windows is running low on some specialized pool of memory it needs.

Windows Has Some Special Memory Needs

Whenever Windows loads a Windows application (or a Windows applet—any program that is a Windows program), it must use a small amount of the first 1MB of real, physical RAM to hold some information about that program. This special region, which is normally called *lower memory plus upper memory* or *conventional memory* when we are talking just about DOS, is now called *global DOS memory*. This is one of the precious memory regions Windows must use. Windows might find it doesn't have enough room there for its needs, especially if you have a lot of TSR programs and device drivers cluttering up your global DOS memory. In that case, you will get a "not enough memory, close some applications and try again" message.

Windows also uses some much smaller special memory regions called *heaps*. These are places in which Windows stores the elements of the dialog boxes, windows, and other things you see on the screen. These also are places that Windows programs store some of the many small data structures they use. They are most often described as the GDI and User resource heaps, but in fact, several heaps are being referred to by each label.

Different versions of Windows use different numbers of heaps, and their sizes can also differ between versions. Under Windows 3.*x*, there were clearly too few heaps and they were too small. If you ran out of heap space (which in Windows jargon became running out of *Windows resources*), you'd find yourself simply unable to run the programs you wanted to run.

Windows 9*x* has mostly solved this problem. You still can run out of resources, but it is much less likely. The most common situation in which it might occur is when you run programs that have *resource leaks*. Some programs ask for portions of the heap space and then, when they are finished with it, forget to tell Windows it's okay to take that memory back. Run enough of these programs, and you're sure to run out of resources.

DOS Virtual Machines Under Windows

Whenever you run a DOS program under Windows 3.*x* or Windows 9*x*, you are actually running it in a special environment called a *DOS Virtual Machine (DVM)*. Another name for this is the DOS box or DOS window, as mentioned previously. This is true whether you see the DOS application running in a window smaller than your whole screen or in full-screen mode.

The only exception to this rule is that if you run a DOS application under Windows 9*x* that must run in MS-DOS mode, Windows 9*x* will first shut down all the other programs that are running, shut itself down, and then run your DOS program in real mode. (If you want, you may run that program from a batch file that loads a memory manager and then runs your DOS program in something other than real mode, but this isn't commonly done. The point of MS-DOS mode is to enable you to run DOS programs that just can't tolerate the protected-mode environment created by Windows.)

Under Windows 3.*x* and Windows 9*x*, you can have as many DVMs running at once as you want. Well, almost: Each one of them can use up just a little more than 1MB of your RAM, so how much RAM your PC has will limit the number of DVMs you can have running at once. Don't forget that Windows still needs some memory for itself.

Each DVM is actually an instance of v86 protected mode. It gets what it sees as a megabyte (or with the HMA, 17/16 of a megabyte) of what it thinks is physical memory address space, starting at address zero. Indeed, the interrupt vector table appears at the bottom of this space and the BIOS ROM near the top. Actually, this is some remapped RAM (courtesy of the CPU's paging mechanism) into which Windows has copied these portions of the real first megabyte's contents. This allows each DOS program to do what- ever it likes in that megabyte of memory with utterly no impact on any other program running on the PC at the same time, whether it's a Windows program or another DOS program in a different DVM.

Anytime this DOS program tries to access the screen, keyboard, or some I/O port, or tries to do other similar action, the Windows v86 monitor program will intervene. It "virtualizes" the screen memory (the frame buffer) so the DOS program thinks it is writing to the real screen. Windows then copies over a portion of the frame buffer's contents to make the appropriate window appear on the screen to show you what that DOS program is doing. (Of course, if the DOS program is minimized, Windows won't show you any of its frame buffer.)

Similarly, the DOS program gets to see only the real keystrokes when that DVM has the focus. The rest of the time, Windows gets the keystrokes and uses them for itself or passes them to some other program.

Almost all DOS programs can be run this way, and this is the best way to run them on a Windows machine because they are protected from one another in this fashion. This is *real* memory management.

The Windows Virtual Machine

Curiously, Windows 3.x and 9x don't do nearly as good a job of protecting Windows programs from one another, for a simple reason. Only one Windows virtual machine exists. All Windows programs share that one simulated PC.

Windows NT is different in this regard, or at least it *can* be. You can decide whether to run 16-bit Windows programs, such as those written for Windows 3.x, in a single Windows virtual machine (WVM), or to run certain of them, or all of them, each in its own virtual machine.

Another way in which Windows fails to fully protect one application from another is that it uses a message-passing model that enables one ill-behaved program to stop all the rest from working. If such a program doesn't properly receive and respond to messages sent to it by the operating system, that program is likely to "hang" or "freeze." Windows 3.11 and 9x partially solves this problem by making it relatively easy to use a local reboot (Ctrl+Alt+Delete) to force that errant program to quit.

Some Ways to Help Windows Manage Memory

You can do several things to help Windows use memory more successfully. Undoubtedly, the most important one is to buy and install all the RAM you possibly can. You can do some other things as well. If you are getting any Out of Memory messages from Windows, the first thing you must do is figure out which kind of memory is in short supply. The most probable kinds are global DOS memory and heap space (resources).

The first stop should be the information that Windows itself offers on the topic. Look at the Help/About dialog box in Windows Explorer (Windows 9x) or File Manager (Windows 3.x), or in almost any other Microsoft program. They all will tell you something about the program, but they also will tell you about the available memory and resources. Just one number for each one.

That might be enough. If the free resource percentage gets low, that may well be the problem. Sometimes, something as simple as not loading a huge wallpaper image will free up enough of the heap space to enable you to get on with your work. If that doesn't do the trick, however, you might have to dig a little deeper.

Another way to find out what is going on is to use a system monitor program. There's one built into Windows 9x, and Windows 3.x has one included in the resource kits you can buy. These Microsoft tools require resources of their own, and they don't quite do the job when it comes to finding out about the amount of free global DOS memory.

The Norton Utilities for Windows 9x includes Norton System Doctor among its many tools. Among the many "sensors" this provides are those for (global) DOS memory and separate ones for User and GDI memory. In NSD, you can configure various gauges or sensors to display many details about your system.

If you determine that you are running low on global DOS memory, go back to the section in this chapter titled "The Infamous 640KB Barrier and How to Break Through It." When you have done what you can at the DOS level, there will be at least one more thing you can do.

> **Tip:** If you're running Windows 9x, make sure you aren't loading any real-mode device drivers that you can avoid using. (This is a good idea in any case, because the protected-mode drivers that come with Windows 9x generally work better and faster than their real-mode counterparts.)

So, How Much RAM Do I Need, Really?

I'd like to close this chapter with the one question I get asked most about memory in PCs: "How much RAM do I need, really?" My favorite answer is, "It depends."

And it does. You must look at what you are doing with your PC, or perhaps what you are attempting to do, if low RAM is preventing you. Also look at how much RAM your PC can accept and what it now has in it. You might also look into the capabilities of your PC's L2 cache system. Certain motherboards support L2 caching of memory only up to a specified maximum. This maximum cacheable memory is less than the maximum amount of RAM the board will support. With more memory installed than can be cached, the performance of your PC will be seriously degraded. Finally, look at your budget and think about your plans for possibly getting a newer, bigger, better PC someday soon. After you have looked at all those issues, you'll be ready to address the question of how much RAM to have.

Let me make a few remarks about some of those questions. First, let's talk about what you are trying to do. If you want to run several large Windows applications at once, and especially if you will be manipulating large graphic files or video presentations, you almost can't have too much RAM. For Windows 3.*x,* I'd start with 32MB. For Windows 9*x,* start with 64MB. For Windows NT, start with 128MB. If these sound like impossibly large numbers, your understanding is outdated. Fortunately, RAM prices have been coming down recently. Adding lots of RAM to your PC has never been less costly. (Memory for portables is sometimes still pretty pricey, however.)

When you are considering the cost of adding RAM, also remember to think about what *not* adding it is costing you. Every time your PC must use the swap file (also known as virtual memory), it slows things down. Add more RAM and that won't happen nearly as often.

Of course, if all you want to do is run one rather modest-sized Windows application, or if you are running only DOS applications and don't use Windows at all, you can get away with a lot less memory in your PC. In that case, you might settle for as little as 8MB if you *never* use Windows, and 32MB if you use Windows moderately. But no less—there just isn't any good reason not to have that much.

Indeed, if you are buying a new machine, you probably cannot get one with less than this much RAM. If you are building a PC from scratch and are using a motherboard with multiple banks of memory (multiple DIMM sockets or pairs of SIMM sockets), be sure to get all the memory you get in a single DIMM or pair of SIMMs, if possible, so you can later add more RAM without having to discard what you just bought.

Some Things to Think About and Try

Use the MEM command, first without any command-line switches and then with the /c and /d switches. (You might also want to use the /p switch to keep from having the output scroll off the screen.) You can capture the output to a file with redirection by putting the greater-than symbol and a filename after the command.

Now use DEBUG to explore memory. See the discussion in Chapter 6, "Enhancing Your Understanding by Messing Around," for some suggestions on how to do this. Try to find the MCBs in your PC. Use the segment address information you get from the output of the MEM command with the /d option to guide you.

Use any system monitoring tools you have to learn about what kinds of memory you have and how it is being used. If you have Microsoft Word or any of a number of other large Windows applications, you may find a System Information button in the Help/About dialog box. Try it out and see what it tells you. These and similar methods are among the very best ways to learn about your PC in particular, and in the process about how PCs work in general.

Getting Your PC's Attention: Input Devices

Your PC is valuable only because it does what you want it to do. And it can do that only if you *tell* it what you want it to do. So having a means of sending messages to your PC is vital. Furthermore, you want to be able to enter data for the PC to work on. For example, right now I am doing that by typing on a keyboard the words I want the PC to put into this chapter.

The keyboard is the means of information input that we use with our PCs most often, but it is hardly the only one. In this chapter, I explain how keyboards work, and also discuss many of the other technologies used for information input on PCs.

> **Note:** You don't actually need to have a keyboard or a mouse attached to a PC. It can run quite happily without either—if the BIOS is set up appropriately. Of course, this isn't something you are likely to do unless the PC is being used essentially as an embedded computer (running a fixed program) or you have attached to it some alternative input devices, such as a touch screen.

The focus here is on the devices that capture information from external sources (people or other things), and not on the means by which that information is conveyed from the input devices into the PC. That latter topic is just one aspect of a more general question that I treat in great detail in Chapter 15, "Understanding Standard PC Input and Output," and Chapter 16, "Faster Ways to Get Information Into and Out of Your PC."

There is one other aspect of PC input I feel is important to cover, at least briefly. I'd hate to see you hurt yourself—especially unnecessarily. Although most things about PCs are quite harmless, some of the things we often do when putting information into them can do real damage to our bodies. I call this topic the "dark side" of PC computing. PCs have empowered many office workers in unprecedented ways. They also have helped make office work into much more of a hazardous occupation than ever before.

One name for these problems is repetitive stress injury (RSI). This is not just a PC-specific problem. It also strikes many musicians, meat packers, and even grocery clerks (now that package scanners have become ubiquitous). We PC users can thank our lucky stars that we aren't the only group of affected workers. Because these problems have been around and recognized in other industries for many years, there is a body of research on RSI. The results of this research have been applied to PC-caused RSI, and now we have both an understanding of the problem and several useful aids for solving it.

RSI is not something to make light of. Ignoring the symptoms is never the cure. Fortunately, an awareness of the problem, and of some of the ways to prevent or mitigate that problem, can go a long way toward preventing a minor case of RSI from becoming a truly disabling injury, with repercussions far beyond working with a PC. In my discussion of keyboards, mice, and other pointing devices, I will mention a few specialized versions of these devices that have proven useful, either for minimizing the risk of developing a repetitive stress injury or for making the use of a PC more practical and less painful if you already have an RSI condition. I close this chapter with some pointers to resources where you can learn more about this very serious problem, as well as about how you can minimize your likelihood of being damaged in this way (or how to find help if you already have experienced some damage to your body).

The Keyboard Is "Key"

PCs began as character-manipulating devices. Now, of course, we also routinely use our PCs to create and modify images. And even when we use them for "simple" character-oriented tasks, such as letter writing, we concern ourselves with much more than just which letters, numerals, or symbols our documents contain. But before you can think about fonts, formatting, and fancy file manipulations, you must first enter the words themselves. For that, the keyboard is so far the unequaled champion.

Keyboard Basics

Computer keyboards descended from typewriters, which is the reason for the placement of the keys (including the QWERTY key layout). This way, people who have learned to "type" (in the olden days we used to refer to it this way) now can "keyboard" (which is what perverters of language call this action these days) equally easily. Of course, computer keyboards must do more than typewriter keyboards. So your PC keyboard has more keys than most typewriters do. Also, there quite probably are more keys on the keyboard you are using than there were on earlier PC keyboard models.

The extra keys on a PC's keyboard that aren't found on any typewriter are there to enable you to perform some control functions. These include navigation keys (up, down, left, and right arrow keys, Page Up, Page Down, Home, and End), the Delete and Insert keys, two Control (Ctrl) keys, and two Alternate (Alt) keys. The Ctrl and Alt keys are used in conjunction with other keys, pressed simultaneously, to modify the meaning of a keystroke. Many keyboards now also have a key bearing the trademarked flying Windows logo, which, when pressed, automatically opens the Windows 9x Start menu. Of course, like any typewriter, a PC keyboard has two Shift keys.

These facts apply to almost every PC keyboard, but PC keyboards are quite a diverse lot in many other ways. Next, I'll tell you some of the details about how keyboards work. Then I'll tell you how they sometimes differ in how they convey information to (and, in many cases, receive information from) the PC to which they are attached.

Different Keyboard Technologies

The purpose of a PC keyboard at its lowest level is to tell the PC each time a key is pressed or released. Knowing about the key releases is just as important as knowing about the key presses. This is especially so for the Shift keys (which modify the meanings of other key presses for as long as the Shift keys are held down), but it also can matter for keys that can be used together in sets (called *chords*).

Some Different Kinds of Keyboard Key Switches

Any way in which the keyboard can sense when the person using it presses or stops pressing a key will do. Many different ways have been tried for keyboards intended for different uses.

Snap-Action Key Switches

The initial IBM keyboards used special, miniature snap-action switches. If you press the key very gradually, the key presses back with a force that increases as you press it down farther and farther. But at some point (the *break-over point*), the force with which the key stops pushing back ceases for an instant. Instead, the key lunges down a short distance, after which it resumes pressing back on your finger. Shortly after that, you will reach a point at which the key simply cannot be moved any farther, no matter how hard you push.

As you then slowly reduce the pressure of your finger on the key, at first the key moves slowly back up. Then, at some point the pressure on your finger falls briefly to almost nothing, and the key lunges upward. After that, it continues to follow your finger until it returns to the full-up position. The break-over points on the push and release occur at different points in the key's motion—which is called *hysteresis*.

Hysteresis is built into many electric switches. This is especially true for those that carry substantial electric currents, such as the toggle switch you might use to turn on and off your room lights. The snap action in these switches guarantees that their contacts will snap together rapidly and decisively when they are turned on, and also snap apart very rapidly when they are turned off. This helps keep the switches from burning out because of arcing that otherwise would happen for as long as the switch contacts were nearly but not quite, closed.

This is a non-issue for switches used in PC keyboards, and making switches this way generally costs much more than almost any alternative method. So why did IBM choose to use this type of switch in the original PC keyboards? For a very good and important reason. The keys on a keyboard can do more than just make and break contact when you press and release them.

When you press a key on the keyboard, your purpose is to send a message to the computer. A good typist will also expect and depend on getting a message back from the keyboard when it has noticed that the key has been pressed (and has, therefore, passed that message along to the computer). Knowing when the keyboard and computer have "heard" your key press, you will know when you can stop pressing harder. Also, knowing when the key-release signal goes to the computer tells you know when to stop lifting your finger.

You might think that you could simply watch the screen and see whenever the computer noticed you pressing a key. That sometimes works, but not always. The computer might not do anything you can see for some time after it has noticed a key press or release—if it ever does. And in any event, there are better and more direct ways to learn when the keyboard notices those events.

When you press a key whose force-distance curve includes substantial hysteresis, you will feel the key lunge down and, on release, pop back up. This gives you valuable tactile feedback. At the same instant that the key is lunging up or down, you will hear a click. That gives you auditory feedback. For the snap-action type of key switch, these three events (the computer sensing the key action, the feeling of the key lunging, and the noise) occur at precisely the same time. They must, by the very nature of the switch.

IBM did tests and discovered that typists were more accurate when they got both tactile and auditory feedback for every keystroke. Therefore, they chose to use these more expensive, but, better quality, snap-action switches in their initial PC keyboard.

Snap-action is important for the key switches on a keyboard that's being used for a lot of typing. For some applications with a keyboard in which only a few keystrokes need to be entered at a time, this tactile feedback is not nearly as important as certain other keyboard characteristics (such as cost, durability, or resistance to liquid spills).

Inexpensive "Dry-Contact" Key Switches

The most common alternative way to build switches for a PC keyboard is what is sometimes called a *dry-contact switch*. This is a switch designed for use in circuits that carry very little electrical current. Because they don't carry much current, these switches will never arc. Therefore, their contacts don't have to snap together and snap apart.

At its simplest, a dry-contact switch might be just a spring wire that the key presses against another wire. When they touch, the switch is closed. When they come apart, the switch is opened. Nothing snaps, no sudden movements occur, and there is no noise. Nothing about this type of switch actually lets you know when the computer senses your key press or release.

Some PC makers include in their BIOS setup an option to have the PC beep or click every time you press a key. That feature is included in case you are using a keyboard with no other means of giving you feedback.

Membrane Key Switches

PC keyboards that are intended for use in hazardous environments often are sealed and use a membrane or simple capacitive switch. The latter is a switch similar to those often used on microwave ovens. Instead of keys that move, these keyboards have sensitive regions called keypads. Push on one, and the computer notices it.

Again, you get no direct feedback from the switch when it closes or opens. Even if you have your PC beep or click for each keystroke, you'll find that you simply cannot type as quickly, nor will your typing be as accurate, with this type of keyboard as with either of the preceding two. But these keyboards last far longer in places where they are likely to be abused, or where the environment is too hostile for an ordinary keyboard.

Domed Elastomer Key Switches

Perhaps the most common key switch design in use today is one made with a sheet of an elastomeric substance (an artificial rubber) placed between the keys and a printed circuit board. This rubber sheet has a dome formed in it directly beneath each key. When you press a key, it pushes down on the dome. When it is pushed far enough, the dome buckles and the key pushes the rubber sheet into contact with the circuit board below. A conductive spot on the inside of the dome completes a circuit on the printed circuit board, signaling to the computer that the key has been pressed.

Correctly designed, this type of keyboard has an action very much like the "good" snap-action key switch designs, and it can be made at a much lower cost. These two facts are why this is now a very popular way to make PC keyboards.

Key Matrices and the Keyboard's Own Computer

When you press and release a key, that action generally closes and opens only one electrical contact (and perhaps makes some noise and gives you some tactile feedback). By itself, this action doesn't cause any messages to go to the PC. Those messages come from some electronics that are built into the keyboard. In fact, an entire computer exists within every PC keyboard. This is an example of what we term an *embedded computer*. It runs a single program all the time. This program causes this keyboard computer to watch all the keys to see which are pressed or released and to send appropriate messages to the PC to inform it about those events.

Ordinarily, the keys on a PC keyboard are arranged in five or six rows. The keys in each row are offset to the right from the ones in the row just above. Internally, the keyboard has a wire that goes to each row of keys and other wires that go to each (angled) column of keys. This forms a matrix, with each key at the intersection of one row and one column wire. The keyboard electronics activate one column at a time and look briefly at the signal on each of the row wires (or vice versa). In that way it can examine the state of each switch in the entire matrix. It does this scanning so rapidly that it can examine every switch on the keyboard many times each second.

Besides noticing the switch closings and openings, the keyboard's computer creates and sends appropriate messages to the PC. Also, it turns on and off the lights that indicate whether or not the Scroll Lock, Num Lock, or Caps Lock states are in effect.

Many Designs, One Language, and Two Dialects

Despite all the different forms in which keyboards for PCs have been built, they all speak the same language in their conversations with a PC. There are two dialects of this language. However, all recent PC keyboards use only the more modern of the two.

Historical Aside

The 83-key keyboards used with the original IBM PC and PC/XT (and all clones of those two computer models) were output-only keyboards. The language they used was just slightly different from that used by all subsequent PC keyboards. Starting with the IBM PC/AT, the PC keyboard gained the capability of listening as well as speaking to its host PC. The language for its messages back and forth was changed to accommodate that fact.

Some clone PCs know both the XT and AT keyboard languages, and they detect which kind of keyboard is attached each time they boot up. Some clone PC keyboards know both languages, and you can tell them which one to use by flipping a small switch on the back or bottom of the keyboard. But today, we only have and use the newer, AT-style keyboards (which speak and listen), and our PCs assume that this is the kind of keyboard that is attached to them.

Details of What the Keyboard Computer Does

The conversations between keyboard and PC are simple and boring. At the time of boot, the PC tells the keyboard to reset itself, thus restarting its internal program from the beginning. (The older-style, XT keyboards only reset themselves when power is first applied or is reapplied to them.) Later, the keyboard sends a message to the PC every time any key is pressed and every time any key is released. The PC tells the keyboard anytime a program wants to change the state of Caps Lock, Scroll Lock, or Num Lock (so it can update the little lights on the keyboard). The PC also tells the keyboard computer what time delay and repetition rate to use for its *typematic action*.

The typematic action is what happens when you hold down any key other than a Shift key. The keyboard's internal computer notices when you first press a particular key, and sends a corresponding message to the PC. Later, if it notices that you have been holding down that key for more than a set time—which by default is one-half second—the keyboard computer will start spitting out multiple messages to the PC—10 times each second by default—each saying that this key has just been pressed again. When you finally release the key, the keyboard computer sends a final message saying that key has been released (and, of course, it stops its typematic action with respect to that key).

> **Tip:** What to do if the default typematic rate isn't to your liking? You've no troubles if you're using Windows 9*x*. The Keyboard control panel applet enables you to easily adjust the typematic rate and the typematic delay at will.

Scan Codes and the System Unit's Keyboard Controller

The messages from the keyboard enter the PC's system unit through a special dedicated keyboard serial port. For more details on just what that means, please see Chapter 15. From there, the messages go to what we term the *keyboard controller*. The PC system unit's keyboard controller can be another tiny embedded computer with its own microprocessor, ROM with a fixed program, and some RAM. Or, that functionality can be included as a part of the motherboard chip set.

From the keyboard, the keyboard controller gets messages about which keys have been pressed or released. Every time it gets such a message, the keyboard controller takes two actions. Its first action is to place into a buffer (a small region of RAM), which is normally located at a very low address in main memory, a scan code that stands for the keystroke. The second step is to issue a hardware interrupt request (IRQ) on interrupt level 2. (Interrupts are discussed in detail in Chapter 8, "How Your PC 'Thinks.'")

One very important fact to understand is that the scan codes indicate which key has been pressed rather than which symbol you intended to type. Thus, the scan code for *a* and that for *A* are identical. The scan code must be interpreted in light of the present state of each of the three kinds of keystroke modifying or shift (letter and numbers, control, and alternate) and the three kinds of shift-lock (caps, numbers, and scroll) to determine what the person typing intended that keystroke to mean.

The original PC keyboards sent out 1-byte scan code. All modern PC keyboards do that for the keys they have in common with those earlier keyboards, and they send modified forms of some of them (indicated by a prefix byte or bytes) for keys that have been added to that layout. This includes, for example, the second Ctrl and Alt keys. The scan code for a key release is identical to the scan code for that key being pressed, except that the most significant bit is turned on. This is equivalent to adding 80h to the scan code value.

The interrupt handler for interrupt 9 retrieves the scan code from the buffer, and also the state of the shift and shift-locks from location 0417h and 0418h in the BIOS data area. It then converts this information into an ASCII or extended ASCII character code, or if the key pressed was a shift or shift-lock key, it alters the data on them stored in locations 0417h and 0418h in the BIOS data area.

How Application Programs Learn About Keystrokes

I hope by now that you have been thoroughly disabused of the notion many people have that whenever they press a key on the PC's keyboard, that directly causes a character to appear on their PC's screen. Clearly, things are much more indirect than that. Indeed, many times you will be typing away and nothing appears on the screen for awhile. Then suddenly a burst of characters appears. Other times, the keystrokes get swallowed up or sent somewhere else, and you never see them on the screen.

The only way any program finds out that a keystroke has arrived at the keyboard is by "hooking interrupt 9" if it is a DOS program or by looking for an appropriate message from the Windows kernel if it is a Windows application. These concepts are described in more detail in Chapter 8 and in Chapter 17, "Understanding PC Operating Systems." For now, though, I just want to make the point that when keystrokes happen, two embedded computers (one each in the keyboard and the system unit) have a conversation, and then one of the PC's CPU interrupts is triggered. What happens from there is strictly determined not by the hardware, but by whatever software is running in the PC at the time. For example, the keystroke might result in a character appearing on the PC's screen, but often it does not.

A Trip to the Keyboard "Zoo"

Keyboards for PCs come in a variety of sizes and styles. Before we look at some of them, you'll benefit from understanding a little bit about keyboard history.

When the first modern typewriter keyboards were developed in 1860, they were a major advancement after over 40 years of attempts to produce a practical typing machine. With many earlier typewriting machines, typists could easily jam the machine by typing too quickly. A man named Chris Sholes determined that typists could be forced to type slower—thereby avoiding jamming the machines and making them more marketable—if the most commonly used letters were placed far apart from each other on the keyboard. This "we can only make our machine work right by making people less efficient" methodology is what gave us the QWERTY-style keyboard (named for the six letters at its upper-left corner) that most of us still use today.

In this century, several other keyboard layout styles were developed with the aim of reducing repetitive stress injuries and allowing truly fast typists to type truly fast—electric typewriters and computer keyboards not being subject to the limitations of one hundred years earlier. Chief among these is the Dvorak keyboard layout.

Here's a brief description of some common, and some not nearly so common, keyboard designs.

Ergonomic Keyboards

Figure 12.1 shows the original Microsoft Natural Keyboard. This is a popular ergonomic design. Instead of a flat keyboard or one that slopes up toward the top row, this design actually places the top row of keys slightly closer to the desktop than the bottom row, and it includes a flap you can raise to tilt the front of the keyboard up even more. Furthermore, the keys are arranged in three groups. The left and center groups where your left and right hands spend most of their time, are turned slightly in toward one another. The right group has the dedicated navigation keys and the numeric keypad, and it is oriented in the same way as a nonergonomic keyboard.

FIGURE 12.1
The Microsoft Natural Keyboard is a popular ergonomic PC keyboard design.

Front edge of keyboard is raised
to ergonomically correct angle

This is referred to as an ergonomic design because research has shown that using this type of keyboard keeps our hands in a more neutral position, which reduces the likelihood that you will develop a repetitive stress injury.

Microsoft now makes what it calls its Elite model of the Natural Keyboard. You can see this keyboard in Figure 22.6, which is in the section titled "Mobile PCs at Home and in the Office," in Chapter 22, "Why Mobile PCs Must Be Different."

Cirque makes a variation of this design that it calls its "Smooth Cat Keyboard." It looks very much like the Microsoft Natural Keyboard, but it also has a Cirque GlidePoint touchpad and a two small buttons associated with that touchpad embedded in it, just below the navigation keys. This provides an alternative way to point that many people find preferable to using a mouse. I'll cover what touchpads are and how they work in just a moment. But first I want to describe a few of the more unusual keyboards that have been developed, mainly in an attempt to make it easier for people to use a keyboard—especially people who have some injury that makes normal keyboards unbearably difficult to use.

Figure 12.2 shows three different keyboard designs. All three manufacturers make strong claims that theirs is the best ergonomic keyboard on the market.

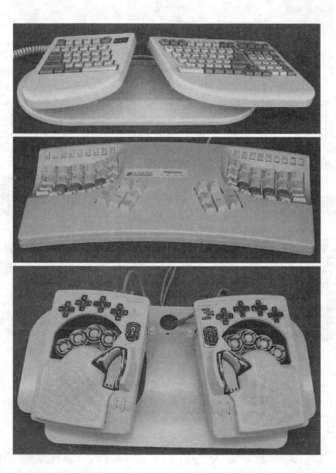

All three of these keyboard designs begin by dividing the keys that you press with your left hand from those for which you use your right hand. The difference between them is how they position those keys.

The Pace keyboard (at the top of this figure) puts those two sets of keys on different platforms and then connects the platforms to the base in a flexible manner. You can tilt each platform quite a bit off of level in just about any way that feels good to you. And you can even change the angles if you want to make the keyboard feel different for a change.

There are a few other PC keyboards on the market that do something similar, including one design that allows you to tilt the two halves of the keyboard until they are almost vertical, so you can end up typing with the palms of your hands facing each other. In all these models, the manufacturer claims that their adjustability is a desirable feature.

The Kinesis design is quite different in this regard. They have done research and convinced themselves that they know the "right" way to position the keys. That, they say, is in two dished shapes in a rigid keyboard. They also put a few keys that are used less often outside these two bowl shapes on the flat portion of the keyboard. An optional footswitch is also available to modify the actions of some of the keys.

At the bottom in this figure is the most different PC keyboard design I have yet encountered. This is the Datahand keyboard. There are two roughened surfaces for the palms of your two hands. Then your thumbs and fingers reach down into pockets, and each pocket has multiple paddles surrounding it, as well as a button at the bottom. These paddles are very easy to move, and their motion is detected when they break a light beam. Thus, this keyboard is particularly helpful for the many people whose RSI damage has left them very weak and unable to press strongly, or unable to do so without great pain.

You type on this keyboard by pressing those buttons, or by moving your fingertip or thumb sideways, forward, or back. Each finger has five actions it can perform. The thumbs each have four. This is only 48 independent actions, which is fewer than the number of keys on an ordinary PC keyboard. Datahand gets around this limitation in two ways. Some of the key switches act as shift keys that modify the meanings of other key switches, just as on an ordinary keyboard. In addition, you can switch the keyboard into any of three different modes: one for typing letters, one for typing numbers, and a special mode to facilitate simulating mouse actions.

The Datahand keyboard requires a serious commitment of effort. Most users need at least 40–50 hours to become proficient with it. Once you know how to use it, you can type, mouse, and otherwise do anything a normal PC user would need to do without ever moving the palms of your hands off their rests. (You also can supplement the Datahand keyboard with a foot switch to make changing modes even easier.) As a consequence, this rather expensive keyboard is the preferred choice for some of the most severely injured or physically limited PC users.

In Figure 12.2, you see the Datahand's two hand input platforms connected to a base. This base is heavily padded for use on your lap. Alternatively, you can readily detach the two platforms and place them wherever you want, or secure them to, for example, the arms of a wheelchair. This may be the only PC keyboard that can be modified easily in this way.

Keyboards and Laptops

Laptop computers present many design challenges, not least of which is how to include a full-size keyboard. Most present laptops use a compromise keyboard. It isn't quite full size, nor does it have all the keys you will find on a normal PC keyboard. But it is still large enough for touch typing and has some means for simulating all the missing keys. You will learn more about the special challenges faced by laptop designers in Chapter 22.

Keyboards for Handheld PCs and PDAs

When a PC is too small, there simply isn't room for a normal keyboard. Still, that functionality has proven to be important for many applications of these devices. The Palm Pilot and some similar devices use a touch screen and handwritten, stylus-based system for most of their input. In one mode, however, that screen displays a miniaturized keyboard, and you can point at keys there with its stylus, one at a time. The fact that the designers of this popular personal digital assistant felt it necessary to include some type of keyboard shows how vital an input device can be.

Alternatives to Typing

For those among us who aren't touch-typists or who might find even the most ergonomic of these keyboard styles to be unusable for whatever reason, voice recognition is a pathway to efficient data entry. Eventually, voice recognition, which you can read more about in Chapter 19, "Some PCs Can Understand Speech and Talk to Us," will very likely replace keyboards—at least partially—for all of us.

The Point Is Pointing (Mousing Around)

Your mother might have taught you that it is impolite to point. And it is, for humans in public. But when you're running a Windows program on a PC, you almost can't avoid having to point at and select various items on the screen. My "point" is that some type of pointing device has now become an essential complement to a keyboard. The most common pointing device is, of course, the mouse. Whatever pointing device you use, remember that its only function is to indicate (by pointing at) some item and then to select or act upon that item (usually by clicking or double-clicking a button on the mouse).

Many Kinds of Mouse

Compared to a keyboard, a mouse is a simple device—as it should be, for it has a very much simpler job to do. Essentially, a mouse is an object that you move around on your desktop (or some other surface). As you do so, it reports to the PC its motion. The mouse software in the PC uses these signals to move a pointer around the screen. When that *mouse cursor* points to some object of interest to you, one way you can signal your interest is by pressing one of the buttons on the mouse.

Mechanical Mice

The original mouse was a box with a small rubber ball sticking out of the bottom. Pushing the box around on the desk caused the ball to roll, and that in turn made some shafts turn and switches close to indicate the amount of motion in each of two perpendicular directions. This mouse design has been copied and refined in many ways.

Figure 12.3 shows four designs for a mouse. All of them are considerable improvements on the original mouse design, each in its own way. All of these mice are shown with the end that goes closest to your body at the bottom of the figure.

FIGURE 12.3

Four PC mice, showing some of the differences in design for what is functionally the same in all four devices.

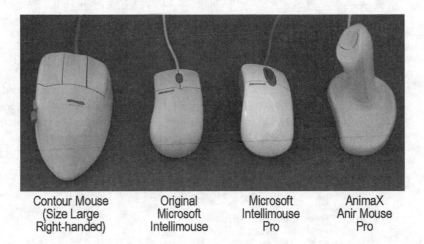

| Contour Mouse (Size Large Right-handed) | Original Microsoft Intellimouse | Microsoft Intellimouse Pro | AnimaX Anir Mouse Pro |

The mouse at the far-left side of this figure is a large, right-hander's mouse from Contour Design. (They affectionately call it "the big rat.") This mouse slopes down to the right and toward the front (the end with the cord coming out of it, where the buttons are), and it has a rest for your thumb on the side. It also has three buttons, which is one more than many PC mice offer.

The intention of this mouse design is to almost force you to grasp the mouse with your entire hand, and to move the mouse with your hand and lower arm all as a unit. This is in contrast to how most of use mice: we may flex our fingers to move the mouse small distances, and only move our arms for larger mouse movements. The slope also rotates the hand into a more normal position than is common for the majority of mouse users. (Think of how you hold your hand when you reach out to shake hands, or when your arms are hanging at your sides. The palms of your hands are facing in, toward your body. Any rotation from that position is stressful on your wrist.)

Contour Design is the only company I know of that makes mice in both left-handed and right-handed models. They also make their right-hand models in three sizes. Every other company makes mice mainly for right-handers, or without a handedness, and expects lefties to simply accommodate themselves to one of those designs.

The mouse just to the right of the Contour mouse is Microsoft's original Intellimouse with wheel. I will discuss the wheel and the number of buttons in some depth in a later section of this chapter. This mouse was Microsoft's first asymmetrical mouse, and like most, it is better suited to right-hand use than to left-hand use, although it can be used with either hand. (Microsoft suggests that you change hands from time to time in order to rest your dominant mousing hand for a while.)

Next is Microsoft's latest mouse design. This Intellimouse Pro is not only asymmetrical, it is also sloped to one side somewhat as the Contour mouse is. But it is much smaller and so lends itself to being gripped lightly with a thumb and one or two fingers. This grip enables you to move the mouse in a very controlled fashion with the fingers rather than from the shoulder as you must move the Contour mouse. I find that this delicacy is vital for serious graphics work—but it does put a lot more stress on one's fingers and wrist.

The rightmost mouse in this figure is the Anir Mouse Pro from AnimaX. This Norwegian company has created what I find to be the most comfortable mouse to hold and use, but not one with which I can easily do the most precise mousing tasks. You grip the shaft with your right hand, wrapping your fingers around it. Then you put your thumb on the top of the shaft, resting on the rocker switch. A slight upward pressure by your thumb presses the "right mouse button." A slight downward pressure presses the "left mouse button." There is also a third switch in the handle for use as a third mouse button.

You can learn more about the Contour Design mouse at this URL:

`http://www.contourdes.com/`

and about the Anir mouse at this URL:

`http://www.animax.no/anirmouse.html`

All these mouse designs work the same way internally. They all have a ball that rolls on the table top (or on a mouse pad), and that ball transfers its motion to two rollers inside the mouse. These rollers measure the motion of the mouse in two, perpendicular directions (referred to as the X and Y directions, which you might also refer to as side-to-side and forward-and-back, respectively).

Figure 12.4 shows the Microsoft Intellimouse turned on its back, with the ball removed. The ring that you see beside the ball is what holds that ball in place normally. You can just barely see the two black rods that serve as rollers in this design to sense the motion of the ball.

All these mice open up in some similar way. This is important because you must be able to clean out dust and hairs that get caught on the ball and rollers. Otherwise, the mouse will not accurately sense and report its motions to the PC.

Purely Optical Mice

Perhaps the worst problem with mechanical mice is how much they tend to pick up dirt and hairs. This interferes with the mechanism that converts the ball's rolling motion into X- and Y-displacement signals. An early solution to this problem was a design for a ball-less mouse that shines light of two colors downward. You move this optical mouse over a smooth, reflective pad that has many parallel lines printed on it, one color going in the X direction and a different color going in the Y direction. The mouse detects its passage over these lines by changes in the light that reflects back into it from the pad. This design worked well, but it was too limited, requiring you to use only a special mouse pad. That design has fallen from favor.

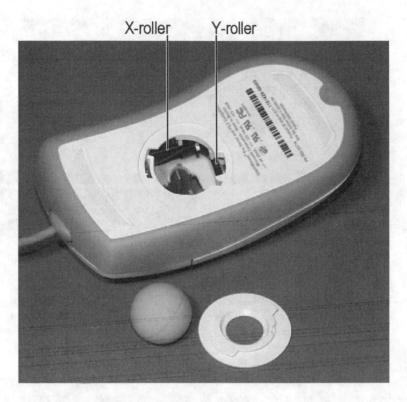

X-roller   Y-roller

FIGURE **12.4**
*A Microsoft
Intellimouse Pro
from the bottom,
with its ball
removed to reveal
the shafts that
sense its motion.*

Opto-Mechanical Mice

The best mouse designs today use a combination of optical and mechanical devices. Most of them have a ball that rolls on two shafts, which turn optical shaft-angle encoders, which convert those motions into electrical signals for the PC. These mice get dirty, but they are much easier to clean than the original, purely mechanical models.

Key Tronic sells a different type of opto-mechanical mouse. This one, originally developed by Honeywell, has small plastic wheels attached directly to the two optical shaft-angle encoders. When you move this mouse on the desktop, these wheels roll directly on the mouse pad or desktop, converting the mouse's X and Y motions into signals for the PC. These mice work very well, and they aren't nearly as prone to problems when they are used in a dirty environment.

Other Ergonomic Alternative Mouse Designs

Ingenious people have designed what can only be termed alternative PC mice, because they function like mice but with some very different ways of being used. Figure 12.5 shows three of these different approaches.

At the top you see an ordinary Dell keyboard. In fact, it is the standard keyboard shipped with our example desktop PC. But in front of it and extending to the left is a narrow platform that can serve as a wrist rest.

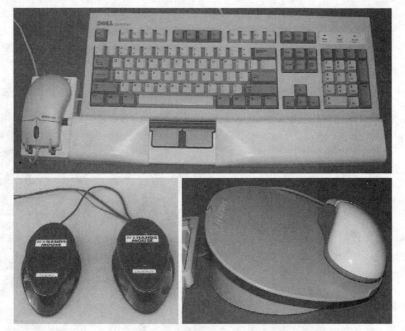

In the middle of this platform, just below the spacebar on the keyboard, you see two paddles that you can operate with your thumbs while your hands are still in their normal positions on the keyboard. Just above those paddles you can see a dark, round shaft. This you can roll with your thumbs forward and back, or you can shove it left or right. At the far-left you see a standard Microsoft mouse sitting in a "trap."

Pressing on one of the paddles causes the corresponding mouse button to be pressed. Moving or rolling the rod causes the mouse ball to roll. So in effect, you are mousing with the industry-standard Microsoft mouse, but you are doing it without ever moving your hands from the keyboard. (Well, if you want to use the mouse wheel, you will have to move your hand over to it for that action.) The Swedish manufacturer of this device has named it a Mouse Trapper. I have found this to be the most comfortable and best design of any alternative to the ordinary mouse—particularly when I have to do precision graphics work requiring very subtle mouse movements.

At the lower-left corner of Figure 12.5, you see a No-Hands Mouse. This is a pair of foot pedals. One is used to move the mouse cursor, the other for clicking its buttons. In both cases, you just wobble one of your feet to activate the appropriate function. The maker of this mouse alternative says that many graphic designers find it useful to trade off between using this and using an ordinary mouse with their hands. This enables them to rest their hands for a while, yet still return to the normal mouse-in-their hand actions for maximum precision whenever that is necessary.

At the lower-right corner of the figure, you see an X-O Genous mouse platform with, in this case, a Microsoft Intellimouse Pro. This tilted platform helps you keep your wrist closer to its natural position, with the palm more nearly vertical than is common for mousing on a flat table. There is a lip on the platform at the right that keeps the mouse from sliding off. This device can be used by lefties simply by rotating it 180 degrees and placing it at the left side of the keyboard. Also, the tilt is adjustable up to the amount shown here.

You can learn more about these mice alternatives at the following URLs. The Mouse Trapper is described at

http://www.swedentrade.com/ergoexpo/sns.htm

and

http://www.ascentient.com/

You can learn about the No-Hands Mouse at

http://www.hunterdigital.com/

and you'll find information on the X-O Genous mouse platform at

http://www.spacestar.net/users/xogenous/

Before leaving this topic, I want to mention a software program that you may find useful. Some people can move the mouse cursor around easily enough, but the act of clicking on a mouse button is just too painful. The solution for this problem, and a possibly interesting option even for people who don't have this problem, is the program MouseTool. With this program installed, when you hold the mouse cursor over an onscreen button, the program will press the mouse button of your choice for you (or even double-click it). You can learn more about this novel program at this URL:

http://www.mousetool.com/index.html

Force Feedback Mice

A new variation on the traditional PC mouse is the FEELit mouse, developed by the Immersion Corporation and being brought to market by Logitech. This is a fairly conventional-looking mouse, but when you use it you will immediately notice that it gives you forcible feedback. Thus, if you click and drag on an object or a window corner to resize the window, you will feel some resistance to that action. If you try to mouse past the edge of the screen, you'll feel as if you have hit something. Even crossing over a window edge will give you small sensation of going over a bump. Pushing an onscreen button can produce tactile feedback similar to what you get when you press a key on a typical PC keyboard.

This technology works by putting more than just motion sensors inside the mouse. There are also multiple motors that can move the mouse in various directions under computer control.

This all depends, of course, on there being suitable software running in the PC to support this novel hardware device. The makers provide software to enable force feedback from common Windows elements (such as window boundaries and resizing operations), as well as a programming interface for developers to use to add force feedback to their programs.

This may sound to you like just a gimmick. But because tactile feedback has proven to be so useful on keyboards, I suspect that it will also prove very useful in this instance as well. However, we will have to wait to make that judgment until these mice have been around awhile, and until there are more programs that use special capabilities.

Mice That "Fly"

The Logitech Magellan 3D Controller is the first mouse for a PC that provides complete information about motion in three-dimensional space. Not only does this device signal movement in the X, Y, and Z directions, it also signals rotations around three mutually perpendicular axes (usually referred to as *yaw, pitch,* and *roll*). You can learn more about this device, which is also marketed under the name Space Mouse by the company that originated the technology, at this URL:

```
http://www.spacemouse.com/
```

Mice That Lie on Their Backs

What? Is that a mouse lying on its back? It isn't a dead mouse or one that wants to be tickled. It could be a mouse you are about to clean (as shown in Figure 12.4), but it's a device we use like a mouse but that goes by the name *trackball*. With a trackball, you roll the ball with your fingers or hand. That means you don't need to have an open space on your desk for a mouse to roam. And it can provide much more precise pointing than is possible with an ordinary mouse.

Many different companies have made a variety of trackballs. The balls themselves range in size from less than half an inch in diameter to four inches in diameter. Figure 12.6 shows two examples of this type of pointing device. Near the end of Chapter 19, in the section "Speech Recognition," Figure 19.1 shows a Philips Speech Mike. This is a combination of a tiny trackball with two buttons, a microphone, and a speaker. Trackballs similar to the one in the Speech Mike are included in many laptop computers.

The trackball at the left in Figure 12.6 is an Evolution Trackball from ITAC Systems. This device has six symmetrically placed switches and an internal microprocessor that can be programmed by the user just by pressing various switch combinations. It will operate as a standard Microsoft mouse, but you can make it left- or right-handed and change its functions in other ways, all without nedding a specialized mouse software driver in your PC. It also has some well-supported claims to a very high degree of ergonomic effectiveness. In my experience, your hand must be the right size (neither too large nor too small) for this to work well, but it can be wonderful. ITAC also makes a variety of other trackballs for both desktop and industrial uses.

FIGURE 12.6
It's a good thing mice aren't turtles.

On the right, you see Microsoft's EasyBall. This is trackball has the largest ball of any I have seen. Although Microsoft intended it for children, I find it one of the most comfortable trackballs I've ever used. Unfortunately, it has only one button, and many PC applications require the use of more than a single button.

Mice That Don't Look or Work at All Like Ordinary Mice

Touchpads and pointing sticks are some of the most widely accepted innovations in the pointing device marketplace. I already mentioned the Cirque Smooth Cat Keyboard with its embedded touchpad. This looks like a small gray window, just over two inches wide. You merely slide your fingertip across the window and the mouse cursor moves. You tap the window and it reacts as if you had clicked the primary mouse button. Tap and then slide your finger, and it interprets this as you're pressing and holding the primary mouse button and then dragging the mouse, thus enabling you to resize a window or drag an icon or other object around on the screen. Our sample laptop PC, shown in Chapter 22, is one of many portable PCs that comes with a Alps touchpad (which uses Cirque's GlidePoint touchpad technology) as its primary pointing device.

Cirque also makes several standalone versions of its touchpad, including a larger one it calls the Power Cat. Figure 12.7 shows the Power Cat and its optional special stylus (with a flexible foot that you drag across or tap on the touchpad surface). The "window" on this device is about three inches wide. It has a special region on it (in the upper-right corner, shaded a different color from the rest) where a finger-tap produces the effect of a secondary mouse button-click and some regions along the edges of the window that you can use to scroll up, down, left, or right in a document. It also has two places for triggering the effect of the Forward and Back buttons in a Web browser. (Cirque also includes two actual buttons in case the user prefers pressing them to learning the necessary touch for accomplishing button-clicks by finger tapping.)

Most of its recent models incorporate some, but not all, of these extra actions. You can check the Cirque Web site to learn more about the features included in each model:

```
http://www.glidepoint.com/
```

Figure 12.7
*The Cirque Power
Cat touchpad and
its optional stylus.*

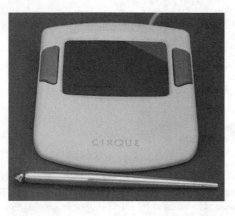

The technology behind the Cirque touchpads is called the GlidePoint Control. It works by sensing the mutual electrical capacitances between two sets of parallel electrodes embedded in the pad at right angles to each other. These mutual capacitances will vary whenever any conducting object (which is a fair description of one's fingertip) passes close to the surface. Specialized electronics inside the touchpad detect these changes and interpret them as pointing actions. Or, if you tap the touchpad, it treats that as a mouse button-click.

The Cirque GlidePoint technology is not the only one used in touchpads. Also common are semiconductive or resistive pads that sense the location and pressure of one's touch. Common to all of these is that they need little if any cleaning and stand up well to most environments, including many that would be intolerable for an ordinary mouse. They also take up much less room and, with no moving parts, last longer than an ordinary mouse in the relatively hostile conditions often encountered by portable PC users.

Some people with severe RSI damage to their hands are simply unable to use any mice, or even most touchpads. One person has reported learning to use a Power Cat with a stylus held between his toes as an alternative.

The pointing stick, which is the other principal pointing device that is built into many laptop computers, is a force transducer. It was developed by IBM, which gave it the name TrackPoint, and first appeared on that company's line of ThinkPad notebook computers. It is a small post on a keyboard that usually sticks up between the F and G keys. When you push on it with your fingertip, it doesn't bend appreciably, but it does signal the computer as to the direction and pressure with which you are pushing. That gets translated by software into the equivalent of a mouse motion, with more pressure corresponding to higher speed. In addition to the stick, there must be a couple of buttons somewhere nearby that you can press to get the effect of mouse button-clicks.

Absolute (Versus Relative) Pointing

You use a mouse to indicate displacement—but from what? That is, by intent, not clearly determined. The purpose is to move the mouse cursor from wherever it is in your chosen direction and at your chosen speed. Alternative pointing devices exist in which one points to a place, not just a displacement from wherever one happens to have been. Many of these devices can also be used in a *mouse mode*, in which they send displacement information to the PC just like a mouse, rather than their usual practice of telling the PC an absolute location.

Graphics Tablets

A graphics tablet is a flat, rectangular device. Each point within a defined inner rectangle corresponds directly to a point on the PC's screen. It comes with a stylus, a puck, or both. The stylus is like a pen with one or two buttons on the side and a pressure switch in the tip. The puck looks a lot like a mouse, but it might have a paddle sticking out with crosshairs engraved on it for very precise following of a drawing or map placed on top of the tablet. The puck may have from 2 to as many as 16 buttons.

Point to a spot on the tablet with a puck or stylus and, without even a button press, the mouse cursor immediately jumps from wherever it was to the corresponding place on the PC's screen. This is what is meant by absolute coordinate pointing. Pressing down with the stylus is like pressing the primary mouse button (which is usually the left one, except for left-handed mice or any mouse that has been reprogrammed to act as a left-handed one).

Graphics tablets use any of several different technologies. Most have a grid of wires buried in the surface of the tablet. The tablet's electronics sends signals through those wires, and the stylus or puck acts as an antenna to receive them. The signal returned by the stylus or puck to tablet electronics enables it to determine over which intersection of wires the pointer was positioned. Alternatively, the pen may emit signals that the tablet picks up.

Some graphics tablet pens are connected to the base by a wire, just as most mice are tethered to the PC with a cord. Some graphics tablets now come with battery-powered cordless pens. Many of the recent designs for graphics tablets enable the user to enter more than just a position and a switch-closure (button-click). By pressing down on the pen with more or less force, you can enter a continuously variable value that is converted to a digital value and then transferred to the PC. Suitable drawing programs might draw a line whose width was proportional to the pressure, to give just one example of a use for this capability.

Other graphics tablet technologies include ones based on sonic and magneto-strictive effects. To keep this discussion reasonably brief, I won't describe those in detail here.

Graphics tablets are made in many different sizes, ranging from small handheld ones up to ones as large as a drafting table. One primary use for a tablet is to allow tracing over an existing drawing, photograph, or other two-dimensional piece of artwork. Naturally, you are best served by a tablet that is just a little larger than the largest such art you must trace.

Other Digitizers

There are many other two-dimensional and even three-dimensional digitizers made for use with PCs. These devices come in a variety of forms, but in all cases their purpose is to facilitate entering absolute 2D or 3D coordinates into a computer.

What Mice (and Other Pointing Devices) Say to PCs

Most mice, trackballs, touchpads, pointing sticks, and graphics tablets connect to a PC via either a standard serial port or a special bus mouse or PS/2 mouse port. Some of the more recent models are available in USB-enabled versions.

The messages these devices send into the PC are received and acted upon by a software program called a *mouse driver*. (You can learn all about standard serial and USB ports in Chapter 15. You can learn more about device drivers in Chapter 8.)

What do mice say to a PC? Ordinary mice, trackballs, and the like, or graphics tablets operating in mouse mode, send a message every time the user moves them by a specified unit of distance in either the X or Y direction. (I'm going to limit my discussion to the more common 2D mice and graphics tablets.) The jargon for this minimum unit of displacement is the *Mickey*. Originally, a Mickey was 0.01 inch. Now it can be whatever the maker of the device wants it to be, and often is as small as one-third to one-quarter the original size. The only other thing a mouse must tell the PC is whenever one of its buttons is pressed or released.

Graphics tablets can act as if they were mice. If they do, their conversations with the PC are just like those of a mouse. But when they are operating in their native, absolute position mode, they do something different. In this mode, they send messages at regular intervals, saying either the pointer (stylus or puck) is out of range or at which coordinates it is now pointing—and, of course, information about any button presses or releases.

There are a variety of protocols (languages) in which these conversations can take place. But the industry-standard methods are those that Microsoft developed for its mouse, or the ones that were developed by Calcomp, Summagraphics, or Wacom for their graphic digitizers.

One Button, Two Button, Three Button, Wheel

"One Button, Two Button, Three Button, Wheel"—this sounds like the start of a child's rhyme. It also describes the number of buttons you are likely to find on a PC's mouse or other pointing device. (Well, graphics tablet pucks sometimes have as many as 16 buttons, but that is a special case.)

Usually, one-button mice (or other pointing devices) are used on Apple Macintosh computers, and not on PCs. One exception is the EasyBall trackball shown in Figure 12.6. When there are two buttons, one (usually the left button) is designated as the primary button, and the other is the secondary button. This is the most common arrangement (see the two Microsoft mice in Figure 12.3).

Other mice have three buttons. Because most PC mice have only two buttons, most PC software ignores the third button. However, the mouse driver software that comes with three-button mice almost always can be programmed so that pressing the third mouse button activates some user-defined feature. In the absence of such special drivers, a software package responding to the third button often is also capable of responding in the same way to a chording of both buttons on a two-button mouse. (*Chording* means pressing more than one button or key at a time.)

Microsoft's Intellimouse is different. It includes a wheel located between its two buttons. This can be rolled forward or back, and you will feel it click from position to position as you do so. If you are using a software program that supports this new mouse, this wheel motion can scroll a document, file list, or some other window's contents up or down the screen. (This is different from moving your insertion point or selection cursor up or down within the document or list, which is what the arrow keys do.) The wheel also has a switch that is activated when you press on it. This serves as a normal third mouse button, or, with software that is specially programmed to use this feature, it can activate an automatic scrolling mode.

Windows 98 supports the wheel feature natively, including its scrolling actions, and many modern Windows programs take advantage of this support. The Intellimouse driver software will also allow the wheel to be supported under Windows 95. There are now several competitive mouse makers that include wheels in their products, with the same functionality as that introduced by Microsoft in its Intellimouse products. Additionally, IBM has produced the ScrollPoint mouse, on which the wheel has been replaced by a TrackPoint stick that controls the scrolling feature.

The Pointing Device of the Future?

When you point at something with your finger—or touch it, press it, or grab it—you don't think about *how* you are going to do that. You just think of where you want your finger or hand to go and what it is to do when it gets there—and it simply does what you intend. But you weren't born with this ability. You had to learn to control your body in these ways.

The early months of all human beings' lives are spent learning to voluntarily control all the different parts of their bodies. That sort of learning can go on for a lifetime. All that is needed is a good feedback loop and some determination to learn.

Biofeedback is now an accepted alternative medical practice. You can learn to relax the muscles that cause a migraine headache, or to lower your blood pressure. Could you, with a small amount of augmenting electronics, also learn to move a PC's mouse cursor simply by willing it? This is very possible—and I believe it is quite likely to become commonplace within a surprisingly short time.

All you need is some apparatus that can consistently sense some aspect of what your body does and have that external apparatus move the mouse cursor (and click the virtual mouse buttons) in response to those actions, whatever they might be. They could be subliminal muscular motions, or brain waves—anything we can sense reliably from outside the body. Then you need to take the time and devote the attention necessary to learn how to make the desired actions happen.

You might think I am merely speculating or spinning science fiction here. Not at all. To learn just how far along this path some experimenters have come, and to see one commercial product you can buy today that uses this approach, go to this URL:

http://www.brainfingers.com/

There, you will learn about the Cyberlink. This is a headband that detects up to 12 distinct signals and uses them to cause the effects of mouse motion, button-clicks, and so forth. This device uses a combination of EMG (muscle electrical signals) and EEG (brain waves); the user can at first use subtle motions of the eyes and eyebrows, and later on learn how to use mere intentions of motion to cause the mouse cursor to move or the button-clicks to happen.

Naturally, this technology is primarily being used at this time by people who have little in the way of alternatives. Severely disabled people have been given new hope for communication and control over their lives. But that is only a beginning.

So far, the price for the Cyberlink is a great deal more than for a simple mouse, and the achievable control isn't nearly as good—even after one climbs up the rather substantial learning curve this technology requires. That it works at all shows something of what is possible. And if history is any guide, the power of this computer-enabled technology will increase quickly and dramatically, and as these devices become more broadly capable, their price will also plummet. I think this could well be how many of us will "point and click" on our PCs within the next couple of decades, if not much sooner.

Some Other PC Input Devices

A keyboard and a pointing device are the most commonly used PC input devices. Many others sometimes are just the ticket for what you must do.

Scanners

Perhaps the most common other input device is a scanner. These come in several forms. Originally, most were black-and-white-only devices, just capable of seeing lightness or darkness at each point on the scanned document or object. Now, however, color scanners are available for very little more money, and they are fast becoming the most common kind. After all, you can still scan black-and-white objects or documents with a color scanner.

The other big difference in the types of scanners has to do with whether they can scan only flat sheets of paper or film (called *sheet-fed scanners* or *drum scanners*) or if they can scan bulkier objects, such as a page in a book (called *flatbed scanners*). Then there is the size issue. Many scanners accommodate full letter (8 1/2×11-inch) or legal (8 1/2×14-inch) pages. Others can scan objects no larger than a business card or a snapshot, and there are scanners that can accept much larger objects. Finally, some scanners are designed to be held in your hand and rolled across a document manually. Most will either move the document through for you, or they will scan a document or object while it sits stationary on a window. (This last type resembles a full-size office copier and works in a similar manner, except that it produces a digital data file as output instead of creating a printed copy of the source document.)

In all cases, the output of the scanner and its associated software is a bitmapped image file representing the appearance of the document or object that was scanned. This later can be converted in any of several ways, but this is the essential form that scanner output always comes in first.

Figure 12.8 shows an inexpensive yet very capable flatbed USB-enabled scanner made by Acer. This scanner is typical of most flatbed scanners, because it uses a moving mirror and some focusing optics to image a line of the document lying on its window onto a linear array of light sensors called a *charge-coupled device* (CCD). A bright white light inside the scanner illuminates a band on the window that moves along with the mirror's motion, thus permitting the scanner to read the contents of the object (sheet, book, or whatever) that is placed on top of the window, under the cover you see in the figure.

An alternative flatbed scanner design uses what is termed a *contact image sensor* (CIS). This is an array of light sensors that can be moved along the underside of the window (alongside a linear light source) and receive reflected light from the document directly, without focusing optics. That design is simpler and makes for thinner scanners, but so far, those units are not able to give as much resolution, image quality, or color fidelity as the CCD-based scanners.

The two essential numbers that describe a scanner (besides its type and the maximum size of the objects it can scan) are the resolution of the images it captures (in dots per inch) and the color depth (in bits per pixel) of those images. As you might guess, these numbers are often quoted by the manufacturers in ways that may mislead you, rather than explaining the capabilities of their products.

Common scanners meant for use with pages of text and illustrations are likely to have a resolution of at least 300 dots per inch, up to perhaps as much as 1200 dots per inch. This is the *optical resolution,* which measures the fineness of the actual process of capturing information from the page or other scanned object. Many scanners have a different resolution in the direction across the page (which is based on the spacing of the light sensors in its CCD or CIS array) than along the page length (which depends on how often the unit "takes a picture" as it moves the sensing array or imaging point down the scanned object).

Most scanner makers also brag about what is called the *interpolated resolution.* The software can be directed to generate images with many more pixels than the scanning hardware has actually seen. The extra pixels are merely given values between the values at the seen pixel locations. (In an alternative methodology, the scanner *oversamples,* reading each pixel more than once and averaging the values. Either method is of dubious benefit in most applications of these devices.)

Scanners meant for scanning 35mm slides must have a very high resolution (in dots per inch), but only over a relatively short distance (across a normal slide's width). This can be accomplished either by having a very high-resolution scanner that can actually see all the detail in the slide directly, or by optically throwing a magnified image of the slide onto a larger area that will be scanned by a lower-resolution scanner.

The color depth is another slippery term in scanner descriptions. Scanners convert the analog light values falling on their light sensors into binary numbers. The more bits in those numbers, the more sensitively the scanner can discriminate between nearly similar colors. Often, scanner makers will boast that their units convert the images at 30-bit or even 36-bit color depth. But when you read more carefully, you see that they may send out only a 24-bit color value to the PC. This might be adequate, especially if the hardware in the scanner makes an intelligent choice about which 24-bit numbers to send, depending on the overall brightness and range of brightness in the object being scanned. The best scanners not only convert the analog light into 36-bit numbers, they also provide the PC software with every one of those bits.

Optical Character Recognition

The output of a scanner is a bitmapped image file, usually in a TIF, PCX, or JPG format. When you scan a page of text, it would be nice if the output were an editable text file (either pure ASCII text or a formatted word processor document).

Converting scanned text into editable text is the job of *optical character recognition* (OCR) software. Several OCR packages now on the market do a very creditable job. Some will even recognize columns of text and ignore figures, and will create fully formatted word processing documents in approximately the right fonts and sizes to match the original.

As with all artificial intelligence computer applications, OCR programs require human supervision. They make mistakes, and you must go in and fix up the file after they finish. Still, if you have many pages of text to enter, this can be the fastest way to get the job done. It certainly is less stressful than typing all that text yourself.

Facsimile (Fax) Modems and All-in-One Machines

Two standard pieces of office equipment today are the copier and the facsimile (fax) machine. With the developments in PCs, more and more of us are moving away from having these as separate objects. Instead, we use our PCs to perform the same tasks, or we have them as just two of several tasks that are performed by a single peripheral device attached to our PCs. To understand how this is possible, I need to discuss briefly how each of these technologies used to work and how that job is done today.

Standard office copiers used to work by forming an analog image of a source document on a photosensitive drum or belt. Then they would use ink (toner) particles to place that latent image onto the copy. If you wanted multiple copies, the copier would simply do that same process over and over again, as many times as you wanted.

Facsimile machines work differently. They have always incorporated two fully digital devices. One scans the source document and generates a digital image description. This information is commonly compressed (to reduce redundancy and thus speed up the process) and then is sent over a phone line by a modem. (I explain how modems work in Chapter 23, "The PC Reaches Out, Part One: Modems and More.") The other device in every fax machine is a digital printer. It receives the image information, decompresses it, and then prints it to create the received fax document.

There were two main reasons why these two devices remained separate for so long. First, fax machines scanned and printed digital images at a much lower quality than the analog images printed by copy machines. Second, the cost of memory and processing power was too high to justify including much of it, if any, in either copiers or fax machines.

Now, however, things have changed—a lot. Copiers now are commonly all-digital devices. They capture a high-quality digital image of the source document, then they hold that image in some internal memory. While it is there and before it gets printed, the copier may do a substantial amount of processing that image—to optimize contrast, for example. Finally, they print the image out on the copy or copies. Notice that making multiple copies by this approach requires scanning the input document only once—in sharp contrast to what was required with the fully analog approach common only a few years ago.

Fax machines have also changed. Now they have a lot of internal memory, too. This means they can scan a source document and hold its image for later transmission. They also can send it multiple places with successive phone calls. Likewise, they can receive multiple pages of faxed image information and hold that for later printing. The quality of fax images has been improved as well. Now the limiting factor in the quality of a facsimile image is the fax communication protocol standard, and not necessarily the hardware for scanning or printing that is built into the fax machine.

It was a short step from this point to putting those machines together. You now can buy rather inexpensive all-in-one machines. These combine a fairly high-quality digital scanner (such as you might use in a copier), a digital printer (usually one capable of printing better images than a typical fax machine printer can), some memory, a fax modem, and a bidirectional parallel port for communicating with a PC. They also have some built-in "intelligence" (processing power).

Figure 12.9 shows one of these machines. This particular example is a Canon MultiPASS C3000. Its printer uses inkjet technology and can do either monochrome or color printing. The scanner in this particular model is limited to monochrome scans (appropriate for faxing), but other models include color scanning as well. Typically, these machines have only a sheet-fed scanner for the input documents, although building in a flatbed scanner is certainly possible. (Of course, flatbed scanners with automatic document feeders have been around for almost a decade. This format has recently been combined with fax machine hardware by several manufacturers, including Hewlett-Packard.)

Because this machine is connected to a PC, it not only can be used to scan documents to be printed as copies by its internal printer or for facsimile transmission, but it also can be used to scan documents whose images you want to input into your PC. Likewise, the printer portion can be used for PC output as well as to print incoming faxes or copies of scanned documents.

There is also another way in which you can get away from the dedicated standalone copier and dedicated standalone facsimile machine. You can put a fax modem into your PC (or attach an external modem) and then attach a standalone scanner and a standalone printer to the PC. Now you have all the pieces, and your PC will enable them all to work together.

Whether you have a fax modem in your PC or an external all-in-one machine attached to your PC, either one enables any fax machine (or other computer with a fax modem) anywhere on the planet to become an input device to your PC. Just save the files incoming fax messages to your hard disk.

FIGURE 12.9
An all-in-one machine can scan, print, and fax.

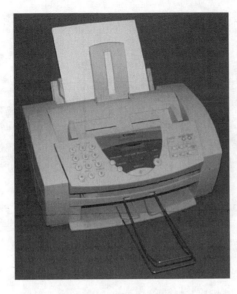

Digital Cameras

Image capture is not solely the province of scanners and fax machines. Cameras do this job, also. Just as the typical office copier has changed from an analog device to a fully digital one, still-image cameras that are fully digital devices are beginning to replace their analog cousins. All motion picture cameras used to be analog devices, capturing images on film. Then came television, and we had semidigital cameras for motion pictures. (A TV image is generally captured, transmitted, and displayed as an analog signal representing the brightness of the pixels, but it is displayed on well-defined lines that could be thought of as a digitally defined location within the image.) Now we are beginning to see fully digital television cameras (with digitized brightness values as well as digitally precise pixel locations) and fully digital television broadcast transmissions as well.

Digital Still Cameras for Use with PCs

Until recently, if you wanted a good photograph—one with high image quality, color fidelity, and resolution—you had to use an analog still-image camera. But if all you wanted was a low-resolution, snapshot image, you could get a digital camera. This market is changing rapidly, and at last we can get reasonably priced, all-digital cameras that produce quite acceptable quality images for many uses.

Figure 12.10 shows the Olympus D600-L digital still-image camera that I used to take almost all the photographs you see in this book (including this one). This camera has a 3:1 zoom lens, and it takes images in either of two resolutions: 640×480 pixels or 1280×1024 pixels. In either case, it captures them in 24-bit color. Unlike earlier generations of consumer-level digital cameras, this camera can be set to do very little image compression, or it can be set to do quite a bit.

The resulting images are amazingly good. Being able to produce really good images requires two things, and only recently have both been available in affordable digital still image cameras. First, you need a good lens system. Without that, you'll get only mediocre images no matter what else the camera offers. The second requirement is enough memory and processing power built into the camera.

An uncompressed 1280×1024×24-bit image file would occupy 3.75MB. Several of these would quickly exceed the storage capacity in almost any camera. Fortunately, images can be compressed in well-understood ways without losing much visible quality—provided the camera has enough processing power built in, plus an adequate amount of data storage to hold the resulting image files.

The highest-quality images this camera generates are JPEG files that are typically just under 1MB in final size, but that show little evident image degradation. The medium-quality images are around a quarter that size and still look better than the best ones from many earlier digital still-image cameras. (Those earlier-generation consumer digital cameras would produce images that were typically less than 50KB—with a correspondingly poor image quality.)

There are three ways to use this particular digital still image camera with a PC. The images it captures are stored on a SmartMedia memory card that is inserted into the camera. (The camera is supplied with a 4MB card, and additional SmartMedia memory cards are available with capacities up to 16MB.)

You can leave that memory card in its place within the camera and connect a serial cable between the camera and a PC. Using suitable software on your PC, you can download pictures from the camera, and you can also command the camera to do various other things. (I used this feature—and a pair of mirrors—to get it to take a picture of itself without my hands showing in the picture.)

Alternatively, you can remove the SmartMedia card from the camera and place it into an adapter, and then transfer the images to the PC. Olympus offers an adapter that uses the floppy diskette drive on your PC to do image transfers. Lexar Media offers a different kind of adapter that uses the parallel port and achieves faster image transfers as a result.

The first kind of adapter is a very clever device called a FlashPath floppy diskette adapter. It is actually an all solid-state, no-moving-parts device that simulates a floppy diskette. You place the SmartMedia card within this device and place it in a standard floppy diskette drive in your PC, and it appears to the PC as if you had inserted a multimegabyte floppy diskette.

The other adapter you can use is a memory card reader made by Lexar Media. This is a gadget that connects to your PC's parallel port. After you have loaded its special device driver, whenever you insert a memory card, that card shows up as a new hard disk on your PC. You also may remove the memory card, and that new drive will simply disappear. You can do this without having to reboot your PC or restart Windows. I find this to be the fastest and most convenient way to transfer images from this camera and into a PC. You can see the Lexar reader and a SmartMedia card in Figure 10.4, in the section "Electronic PC Data Storage Devices," in Chapter 10, "Digging Deeper Into Disks."

Some other digital cameras use CompactFlash memory cards, which are essentially the same as SmartMedia cards except that they have some controller electronics built into them. In fact, CompactFlash cards are really nothing more than PC Cards in a reduced format. Still other camera models use full-size PC Cards, or even standard floppy diskettes. In the future, we may see digital still-image cameras with built-in hard disks.

The range of available digital cameras includes some with other, different, and possibly quite valuable features. For example, some cameras—while primarily intended for still-image photography—can also take short video clips, or capture a brief audio recording to associate with each still image. This is one of the fastest-moving areas of PC-related, consumer- and business-oriented technology today.

Digital Video Cameras for Use with PCs

Digital video cameras for PCs are also popular. Here, one of the main applications is to augment email or Internet chat conversations with short video clips.

Figure 12.11 shows a Zoom digital video camera and the Zoom interface card it uses to connect to a PC. In this case, the card is a data and fax modem as well as a video input card, and as it happens, it plugs into one of the PC's ISA bus slots. This camera can display only relatively low-resolution video images (from 128×96 pixels up to 352×288 pixels). This is suitable for limited video conferencing, chat sessions, and enhanced email, but not for much more than that. This camera comes with software for those applications. Other digital video cameras are also available from companies such as Sony and JVC (so far, at a much higher price) that can capture full-motion video at a higher quality than most other home videocams. These newest devices often sport an IEEE-1394 (sometimes called FireWire) port that can be connected to proprietary video capture cards. This connection allows digital video to be transferred to a PC, possibly for editing, with no loss of quality.

Biometric Devices

Another category of PC input devices that is just now becoming common are biometric ID systems. These include fingerprint scanners, auditory speaker identification systems, retinal scanners, iris scanners, face recognizers, and more. The purpose of these devices is not primarily to accomplish data input into your PC. Rather, they are used to ensure that only an authorized person will be able to use that PC.

All these devices are useful only in connection with a sophisticated software program and perhaps some hardware security add-ons to one's PC. With all those pieces in place, any of these can make it virtually impossible for anyone other than the authorized user to use that PC. And they end the problem of the authorized users forgetting their passwords.

The technologies behind these devices vary. Fingerprint, retinal, and iris scanners are basically image-scanning devices, similar to the page scanners that I discussed in a previous section of this chapter—but adapted for use in a particular, specialized way. Auditory speaker identification systems are simply a specialized application of the voice recognition technology I discuss in Chapter 19.

Less Common PC Input Devices

Anything that can generate digital information and supply it to a PC is potentially a PC input device. These include video capture cards, touch screens, and GPS (Global Positioning Satellite) receivers, among others. In Chapter 19, I tell you about the state of the art in voice input to PCs. In Chapter 21, "Immersive PC Experiences," I tell you about some additional input devices, including ones that you push on and that can push back on you.

Joysticks and Other Game Port Devices

The *game port* is meant for use with a joystick (or a pair of joysticks) to let one or two players control a game on the PC. A *joystick,* in its original form, was a post that could be wobbled in any direction, plus one or two buttons that could be pressed. The stick was supported with springs to make it pop back straight up when you released it. The joystick innards sense the amount and direction in which the joystick has been moved from the straight up position, and they indicate this to the PC via the game port. Of course, they also indicate when each of the buttons is pressed.

Why would you want such a device when you already have a pointing device in your mouse? Because joysticks are designed for games in which you may want, or need, to point in a particular direction for a long period of time. That makes a mouse impractical.

Today, we have much more complex game controller devices. Some of them can still be connected to a PC via the game port, but others must be hooked to a USB port. (I will tell you much more about USB ports and devices in Chapter 15.)

Microsoft's Human Interface Device (HID) Classification

You may have read something about the HID class of objects and wondered just what this was all about. Microsoft has defined what it terms the Human Interface Device class of objects. These are all the input devices for a PC, plus all the output devices that require a human response. Thus, everything I have discussed in this chapter falls into this category.

The HID class definitions are special because after appropriate software is written to describe each member, it can be recognized and worked with appropriately by a PC. In particular, if the device attaches to the PC via a USB connection, it will be recognized immediately and any necessary drivers will be loaded so it can be used right away. This is what the plug-and-play initiative promised, and in this case we are seeing the full fruits of that promise today.

I will tell you more about USB input devices and my experiences with them in Chapter 23. You also will see a couple of them pictured there.

The "Dark Side" of PC Input

The worst thing about PC input devices is that using them can hurt you—sometimes very badly. Every PC user must be aware of this danger and learn how to minimize it. If you ignore the problem, you can end up disabled in a way that prevents you not only from using your PC normally, but that also affects the rest of your life. Many sad stories abound of people who no longer can even hold a knife and fork to eat their meals, all because they ignored the warning pain and let a full-blown case of RSI develop.

This is hardly a new topic. Historians have noted that telegraph operators over a century ago were complaining of something they called "glass arm." (This was a condition with symptoms very similar to those of some RSI sufferers today.) I also want to point out that the hand position and muscle actions used by those telegraph operators were very similar to those used by most of us when we operate a PC mouse.) Furthermore, many of these telegraph operators complained that their employers wouldn't buy them the newest telegraph keys that were easier on their hands and arms, and so many of them would buy their own and take them with them from job to job. Sounds a lot like what some PC users are going through today!

Before I leave this topic, I want to make sure you don't get the wrong idea. I've told you about a lot of ergonomic keyboards and pointing devices. You might think you must rush out and get one or more of them. This is not necessarily correct. If you already have a fairly serious RSI condition, I would encourage you to seek out whatever devices alleviate that condition. I hope you also will seek out help in other ways.

However, if you are in good health now, a more important lesson from all of this is that you need to learn how to use your PC safely. If you start to hurt when you are using your PC's keyboard or mouse, pay attention to that sign. Pain is a message from your body to your brain, and it doesn't pay to ignore those messages—especially when possible RSI damage is involved.

There Is Light on the Other Side

The good news in all of this is that we now understand the RSI problem quite well. The sequence that causes RSI generally goes like this: An environmental stress (such as using a non-optimally configured workstation too many hours at a time) combined with bad habits leads to tension in your body, which over time leads to injury. One way to address this is to make sure your workstation is as ergonomically correct as possible. Another is to become aware of your bad habits (incorrect posture, for example). It helps a lot to know that "working hard" can be a euphemism for being tense as you work—which almost certainly will lead to pain and eventually injury. To help you avoid inadvertently building up intolerable stress, you might like to use a program that reminds you from time-to-time to stop and stretch. There are many of these programs available. Here is one place to look:

http://www.stretchware.com/

I cannot go into much more detail about RSI and its prevention in this book. Instead, I suggest that you look at the following Internet Web sites (plus the links you will find at each). I particularly like the approach you will find at the first URL. It speaks to what you can and must do to yourself, apart from whatever you can do to make your workstation more ergonomic, to protect yourself from RSI:

http://www.somatic.com/

http://www.engr.unl.edu/eeshop/rsi.html

http://www.engr.unl.edu/ee/eeshop/findadoc.html

```
http://www.eecs.harvard.edu/RSI/
```

```
http://www-engr.sjsu.edu/~svei/tifaq/
```

The following pages offer information on some products that might be of interest as well:

```
http://www.ergodyne.com/
```

```
http://www.bambach.com.au/
```

```
http://saturn.vision.net.au/~macsol/equip.htm
```

```
http://www.mousetrak.com/
```

Summary

In this chapter, I told you about some of the most common PC input device technologies. Far more could be said about these, not to mention the many I had to omit. Still, with the information you've found here, you should now know pretty much what any PC input device does, in a general sense, and you have a fairly solid knowledge about the most important characteristics of several "key" devices (not to make a pun—unless that's what you want).

Seeing the Results: PC Displays

One of the five key parts of any computer is its mechanism for information output. In almost all PCs, the principal means of information output is the *video display,* also known as the *monitor* or the *screen.* This chapter introduces you to most of the technologies that now are in use, or might soon become important, in PC display subsystems. Although my goal is primarily to help you understand these different technologies, you will find that such an understanding will come in very handy when you evaluate different options for the display on your next PC, or if you are considering upgrading the display on your present PC. You can find a more in-depth look at some of these issues in Part V (Chapters 20–21), "Splendiferous Multimedia PCs."

It's Just No Good If You Can't Get the Information Out

What good is a computer that can process information, but cannot display the results of that processing? Not much, which is why your PC has a video display screen, or monitor, attached to it. And that's why, while you are using your PC, you spend most of your time looking at that screen.

What Is the Display Subsystem?

Every PC's display subsystem consists of three parts. One part creates and holds the image information; this is the video display *adapter.* Another part displays that information; this is the *monitor.* The remaining part is the *cable* that runs between the other two parts.

The video adapter can be either some specialized circuitry on the motherboard, or a plug-in card. In the latter case, it is often referred to as the PC's *video card.* The monitor consists of a display device (the hardware that actually creates the image you see) and some electronics that activate that display. Often, though, people use the terms *monitor* and *display* interchangeably.

You can change your video subsystem's capabilities by changing the video hardware. Mainly, this means changing your video card. However, the monitor to which that card is attached (and the cable used for the attachment) must meet the minimum requirements of the video card or it will not be capable of displaying the images the video card creates. Some video monitors can, however, display images produced by any of several video cards, and even a single video card often is capable of forming images with a variety of resolutions, thus requiring a monitor with flexible capabilities.

Fundamental Notions to Keep in Mind

There are several extremely fundamental notions about images and how humans see, plus some critical jargon, all of which you must understand in order to make sense of any discussion of PC image display technologies. I'll define each one here briefly, then go back and describe some of them in more detail as I tell you more about how they are used.

Pixels

Digital computers make images one "picture element" (or *pixel*) at a time. These pixels are simply small regions of the overall picture. The color and brightness in each one are fixed. The neighboring pixels can have some other values of color and brightness, but each of them also will have a constant color and brightness throughout its portion of the image. The assemblage of some very large number of pixels, placed so close together that we see them as touching, makes up the image we see.

The computer computes and holds in its memory somewhere a number, or a small group of numbers, that specifies the color and brightness of each pixel in the image. Said another way, it is clear that the number of pixels in an image is fixed by the program that creates that image (and might be limited by the amount of video image memory in the PC). It is not set by the hardware used to display it. A related concept, which I will cover in just a moment, describes the minimum size of adjacent, visibly different parts of the picture. That size is a property of the display hardware, and it commonly goes by the name *dot pitch*.

Resolution

The *resolution* of a computer-generated image refers to the minimum distance over which the color (or brightness) of the image changes. This is the distance from one pixel to the next. Image resolution is often described as some number of pixels per inch. For example, a typical PC monitor displays screen images with a resolution of somewhere between about 25 pixels per inch and 80 pixels per inch.

The most fundamental meaning to image resolution is this question of pixel spacing, but often the term in used in another way. In this alternative version, the resolution of an image refers to the total number of pixels in the entire width or height of the image. Thus, we often speak of images that have a resolution of 1024×768 pixels.

The pixel spacing gives you the *image resolution*. The monitor also has an *inherent resolution*. This is the minimum distance between points at which it could display dots with different colors or brightness. This is not the same thing as the image resolution.

Don't feel bad if you find this all a bit confusing. You'd hardly be the first person to be confused. One way to help straighten out the confusion is to limit the use of the term *resolution* to the properties of the image—that is, compute the resolution from the spacing of the pixels. Instead of speaking of the inherent resolution limit of the monitor, we usually speak about its minimum dot pitch and perhaps also its beam spot size.

Dot Pitch and Beam Spot Size

Dot pitch and *spot size* are properties of the monitor hardware. You can change the resolution of the image you are asking it to display, but these physical properties of the display device won't change.

Imagine that you want the monitor to display an isolated dot of light surrounded by blackness. How small a dot can it create? This depends wholly upon how the monitor causes dots to appear. The most common type of monitor, a cathode ray tube (CRT), squirts a beam of electrons at a phosphor. Wherever the electrons hit the phosphor, light is emitted. So, the minimum size spot the monitor can create is set by the diameter of the beam of electrons.

Typically, a CRT's spot size is smaller in the center of the screen than it is near the corners or edges. Often, we care a great deal about the details of our screen images in every part of the screen. This means that what matters to a PC user is not the smallest spot the monitor can create in any one place, but rather the smallest spot that it can create in all parts of the screen.

Now imagine that you ask the monitor to create two dots, side by side, with different colors. How closely can they be spaced and still be seen as two distinct dots with different colors? (You are allowed to use a magnifying glass for this test. This is not a test of your eyes.) There are two different ways to look at this question. If you try to place the dots closer together than the diameter of either one, they will end up overlapping and you won't really have two distinct dots. This means that the minimum space between distinguishable dots must be at least as large as the beam spot size.

This is not, however, the whole story, in particular for color monitors. All modern computer color monitors cheat. They don't really make spots of arbitrary colors. Instead, the monitor makes triplets of what I will call "subpel spots," each of which glows with a single pure color (red, green, or blue). By controlling the relative brightness of the different-colored subpel spots, the computer is capable of creating what to our eyes appears as a small spot of almost any color you want. This trick works only if the minimum size spot of color you want to create is at least large enough to include one each of all three colors of subpel spots.

Standards: Like pixel, *pel* is a shorthand name for a picture element. The term pel is used exclusively to refer to the minimum-size dot of full color that a particular display device can produce. (This usage began with printers, but I find it very useful for any display device.) In color monitors (both CRTs and LCD panels), each pel will have three subpels—one each for emitting red, green, and blue light. By using this term, I can now reserve the word *pixel* for exclusive use as the name for the minimum-size chunk of an image.

The distance from a red subpel spot to the next red subpel spot (or green to green, or blue to blue) is, therefore, another important limitation on the minimum spacing of distinguishable spots in the image. This one we call the dot pitch of the monitor. A monitor's dot pitch is commonly quoted as some decimal fraction of a millimeter. (A pretty good 14-inch [diagonal measurement] monitor can have a dot pitch of 0.25mm.)

No necessary connection exists between the beam spot size and the dot pitch for a CRT monitor. In an effort to make computer monitors that are capable of displaying images with the maximum possible detail and with the maximum possible brightness, manufacturers typically try to make the dot pitch and the beam spot size about the same. Because the dot pitch is clearly set by how the monitor is manufactured, that number is usually what is quoted. You just expect and hope that the beam spot size is not much larger than that.

Most of this discussion has assumed that the monitor uses a CRT as its display device. What about liquid crystal display (LCD) panels? They also are built with triplets of single-color subpel spots that can each glow with an adjustable brightness. So, the concept of dot pitch is exactly the same for them as for CRTs. The difference is that LCD panels activate each subpel individually. So, in effect, they have a beam spot size exactly equal to the dot pitch, and this is true in every part of the screen.

Image Resolution Versus Dot Pitch

What happens if the image resolution is different from the inherent resolution of the display device? There are two cases to consider. If you try to display an image that has many more pixels than there are pels on the screen, each pel will show a color and brightness that are an average of several adjacent pixels. The effective resolution of the image will be reduced to what the monitor is capable of displaying.

Because what matters to us most of the time is the content of our images, clearly the second situation is preferable. Don't try to display a 1024×768 pixel image on a monitor that has only about 700 pels per line. The image will look blurry, and you'll lose some of the information that it is supposed to be showing you. Naturally, when the number of pels and pixels per line is identical, the image is displayed perfectly, and the monitor is being used to its maximum capacity.

Most of the time, you can get away with displaying images that have fewer pixels almost as well as ones with the optimum number of pixels for a given monitor. The only case in which this really doesn't work out well is when you try to display an image on an LCD display with just the wrong number of pixels. Some pixels will be properly displayed, and others will fall in the cracks between pels and will appear drastically fainter than they should. This is one reason why you are normally better off using an LCD display panel to display images that match its nominal resolution, or ones that have half as many pixels per line, but not two-thirds as many (just to name one example where trouble might arise).

Color Models

I said each pixel in an image has a particular color and brightness. We use several different *color models* to describe the visual appearance of the pixels. This topic may seem unnecessarily complex and arcane. However, it turns out to be a very important one to understand some of the difficulties in getting good color images on screen and is even more important in understanding why it is so hard to transfer those images to a printed page without having the colors change appreciably.

The most common model for PC video displays is referred to as the *Red-Green-Blue* (RGB) model. This says that you can describe any color of light coming from a spot within an image by saying how much red, green, and blue light it contains. This is an *additive color model*, because the total light that hits your eye from that spot is the sum of the amounts of red, green, and blue light. Because of the way in which most PC displays create their images, this is the most natural way to describe them.

In the RGB model, you can specify a pixel's color by giving three numbers representing the amount of R, G, and B light the screen emits on some suitable scale. Thus, a color of (0, 0, 0) would be black (no light of any color is emitted). A color of (255, 0, 0) would be a pure red at maximum brightness (assuming a scale of 0 to 255, which is the most commonly used scale). A color of (255, 0, 101) turns out to be a lovely rose, the color (162, 240, 0) is a vivid new-leaf green, and (0, 142, 61) is a dark forest green.

However, certain types of display, in particular LCD panels, don't emit light at all. Instead, they modify the light that is reflected from them or that passes through them. Some make color images by passing light through a clear liquid crystal that is covered with an array of colored dots. This results in an effect very much like the three-color emitting dot groups on a color CRT. Other LCD panels pass light through three layers of colored liquid crystals. Each layer subtracts an adjustable portion of only one color of the light that falls on it.

This latter behavior is very nearly the same as what happens when you look at a printed image on paper. Colored images are formed from layers of color-absorbing dyes. The color you see is determined by what other colors are absorbed by those dyes. From this description you will understand why this is referred to as a *subtractive* color model. The primary colors—normally red, blue, and yellow—get slightly skewed in this model into cyan, magenta, and yellow, so this model is called the *CMY model*. When black is added, we call this the *CMYK model* (the *K* standing for blac*k* to avoid using *B*, which might imply blue). This is the model used by every modern desktop PC inkjet printer and some color laser printers. (A few inkjet printers that are designed for portability and use on the road have eliminated the presence of actual black ink from their color cartridges, and they produce a composite black [actually, a very dark brown] by combining the yellow, magenta, and cyan inks in high densities.)

A third model for expressing color is termed the *Hue-Saturation-Brightness* (HSB) color model. This model forms the basis for understanding color television signals. That means that if you want to display a television image on your PC monitor, the PC is going to have to do a "color space conversion" to get what is basically an HSB image (or a variant of that called YUV), into RGB. Conversely, if you want to display your PC's output on a large-screen TV, then the PC must do the reverse color-space conversion to go from the RGB image it normally generates to the YUV image it must send to a normal television set. Near the end of this chapter, I discuss some of the ways in which PC images and television signals are being combined today, and also tell you about an exciting new possibility that is just beginning to appear.

Figure 13.1 shows these three color models. In all cases, the left portion of the model shows a range of colors, and the bar on the right indicates the brightness. In each drawing, the circled numbers 1 through 4 show where the colors I mentioned previously would appear on those schematic color solids. Number 1 is the pure, bright red, number 2 is the rose, number 3 is the new-leaf green, and number 4 is the forest green.

FIGURE 13.1
Three common color models.

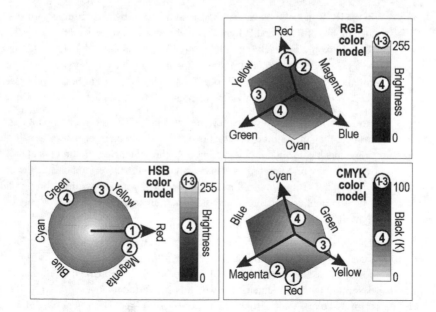

How Images Are Painted on the Screen (Overview)

The pixels that make up an image are "painted" on the screen. I think you'll find that the following analogy to this process will make some important facts about this process clearer.

Imagine that you are holding a hose and directing a stream of water at the side of a building. The wall surface is rough, and it reflects a lot of sunlight. But where the water hits the wall, the reflectivity of the wall drops markedly. This means that you can "paint" darkness on a region of the wall simply by directing your stream of water there. As long as any place on the wall stays wet, it will also stay dark, and you'll be able to see that you had pointed your hose there. But suppose that it is a very hot day and the water evaporates quickly. Now you can see only the places where you have most recently played your stream of water. Finally, suppose that you modulate the amount of water that is flowing out of the hose as you sweep it across the building. This makes some places that it passes get very wet whereas others hardly get wet at all.

This method of "painting" water on a wall is very much like the way most PC display technologies make images. In CRTs, the water stream is replaced by a beam of electrons hitting a phosphor. Wherever the beam is intense, with many electrons hitting the phosphor each microsecond, the spot will glow brightly. Wherever the beam is weaker, it will produce less light. In an LCD panel, the pixels are addressed one after another, each one being set to the appropriate color and brightness in its turn, thus achieving a similar effect.

What does the notion that each spot on the wall will dry up shortly after the water stream leaves it say about PC displays? Two things. First, CRTs and some other display technologies have images that naturally die after some short period of time. These devices need the PC to "refresh" the images many times per second. If they aren't refreshed often enough, you'll experience a flickering image, and it might also be too dim to see clearly. The number of times each second that the image gets refreshed is called the *refresh rate*. Typical PC CRT-based displays have their images refreshed at least 60 times each second and sometimes more than 100 times per second.

LCD panels, on the other hand, are capable of holding images indefinitely. Their weakness has traditionally been that they cannot arbitrarily change those images rapidly. (In our analogy, the humidity isn't low enough, and so the water doesn't evaporate quickly enough.) This makes these displays fine for static images, but unsuitable for video clips (movies). If you try to refresh (and alter) an image on a passive LCD screen too quickly, either you see a smeared version of the image (which we call an *artifact*), or you might not see an image at all. In the former case, it is as if the wall got wet all over, and until it dries up, you won't be able to see the image. In the latter case, you are trying to turn on pixels and then turn them back off again so fast that they never really get turned on at all. (In our analogy, the stream of water is so weak the wall doesn't have time to get properly wetted.) However, the newest active-matrix (TFT) displays—and several enhanced-technology versions of the older, passive displays—do, in fact, display motion video remarkably well. (One person working on this book, Scott, has a new Silicon Graphics 1600SW digital flat panel monitor that is breathtaking. This seventeen-inch monitor is truly artifact-free and rivals a traditional CRT for brightness and color clarity.)

Raster-Scan Versus Vector Displays

How do you move the water stream to paint an image on a building? If the image is a circle, for example, you could just swing the hose in a circle, painting only those parts of the wall that needed to be painted. Some CRT displays do something very similar. They move their electron beam across the screen in a pattern similar to how one might move a pen or pencil over a piece of paper. In effect, they print each character and symbol by drawing it as a number of curves or lines. This is called a *vector-scan* display. This type of technology has found some niche applications (laser light shows and some classic video games such as Tempest, for example), but it is not commonly used for PC displays.

The alternative to a vector-scan display, and the one used in virtually every PC display subsystem, is a *raster-scan display*. Some raster-scan displays use a CRT; others use an LCD panel. I will describe the details of how each type is built later in the "Raster-Scan CRT Images" and "LCD Panel Images" sections. For now, I just want to focus on the nature of the images being displayed.

This applies to a CRT display because the electron beam is played across the screen from left to right in essentially a straight, horizontal line. Then it is moved back to the left edge and down a little, after which it again is moved smoothly across the screen. This continues until the lines have been painted in succession all the way down the screen. (Actually, the beam drifts slowly downward the whole time, so each line is very slightly tilted down to the right. The right end of each line is essentially at the same level as the left end of the next line.)

In a vector-scan display, the path of the beam forms the image, one stroke at a time. (When the beam must be moved from the end of one stroke to the beginning of the next, the intensity is simply turned down to zero.) Raster-scan displays, in contrast, use an unchanging pattern of sweeping the beam to draw any image. The image is drawn while the beam sweeps by modulating the beam intensity very rapidly in an appropriate pattern.

Figure 13.2 shows how both types of display might draw a triangle. The top of the figure (a) shows the strokes that make up the triangle using the vector-scan approach. The bottom-left portion (b) shows how a raster scan can accomplish the same thing. The bottom-right section (c) shows graphs of the raster-scan beam's horizontal and vertical position, each as a function of time.

FIGURE 13.2

How vector-scan and raster-scan displays form images.

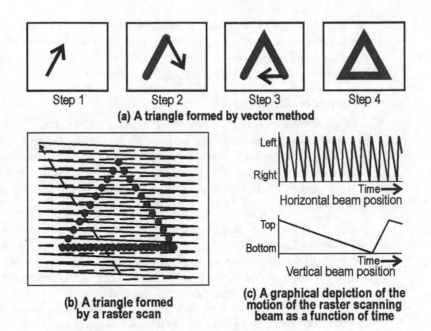

Step 1   **Step 2**   **Step 3**   **Step 4**

(a) A triangle formed by vector method

(b) A triangle formed by a raster scan

(c) A graphical depiction of the motion of the raster scanning beam as a function of time

Scanning Frequencies and Refresh Rates

Your PC display subsystem draws and redraws the screen image constantly, and at very frequent intervals. It must do this. If it didn't, you wouldn't know it when the information to be displayed changed.

How often must it redraw the screen image? That depends on what type of image it is. In all cases, you want to have the feeling that you aren't waiting to see the new information. That requirement alone means that you must have the screen refreshed at least 10 times per second. If you are looking at a movie, it will appear jumpy unless you see at least 24–30 new images each second. If the scene has any objects that change their brightness significantly from one screen image to the next, those images better be painted on the screen at a rate of at least 60 per second. Otherwise, you will see a flickering, and soon you will get a headache.

To be sure that your PC display works well for all purposes, manufacturers usually try for a refresh rate of at least 60 times per second. Indeed, many of the better video cards and CRT monitors are capable of operating at refresh rates in excess of 60Hz, all the way up to 120Hz in a few cases.

Here, I'll point out some of the requirements that this imposes on the display mechanisms. First, I'll treat the case of the CRT displays and then that for LCD displays. Most other display technologies will closely resemble either one or the other of these two principal categories.

To simplify this discussion, I will go through just one example numerically. You can generalize this to any other case you might want to consider. The case I'm going to use is a graphic screen image with a resolution of 1024×768. That means an image with 768 lines of information, each line containing 1024 pixels.

Raster-Scan CRT Images

A raster-scan image on a CRT is painted one pixel at a time, and the display must paint all those pixels 60 or more times per second. This implies some pretty tough requirements on the speed of the display system. PC displays form raster-scan images in what is called a *progressive* manner. That means they sweep down the screen from top to bottom once per image. They must do this in 1/60 of a second or less, so the minimum *vertical sweep rate* is 60Hz.

To get all 768 lines of pixels drawn 60 times each second, the lines must be drawn at a rate of 46,080 lines per second. Actually, the required rate is a little bit higher than this, because there must be some time equivalent to that required to draw several lines for what is called the *vertical retrace blanking interval*. During this time, the electron beam is shut off and the beam steering mechanism moves it up from the bottom of the screen to the top. So, the actual rate at which lines are drawn horizontally is probably at least 48KHz (48,000 lines per second). We call this the *horizontal sweep rate*.

As it is drawing a single line, the display mechanism in a CRT must be capable of turning the electron beam on or off (or to some intermediate level) rapidly enough to set the correct brightness for each pixel, independently of the brightness for its neighbors. Because it is sweeping the lines at least 48,000 times per second and must paint 1024 pixels on each one, it is painting individual pixels at a rate of around 48 million per second. Again, to account for what is termed the *horizontal retrace blanking interval*—the time during which the electron beam is shut off and the beam steering mechanism moves back from the right side of the screen to the left—we must add something to the 1024 before multiplying by 48KHz. When this is taken into account, the actual rate of pixel drawing might be around 50 million per second. This means that the electronics in the monitor (and those on the video display adapter) must have a bandwidth in excess of 50MHz.

The CRT display must, therefore, be capable of synchronizing its electron beam sweeping to the vertical and horizontal drive signals that are, in this case, coming to it at around 60Hz and 48KHz, respectively. Its video bandwidth must be at least 50MHz. These are the numbers to look for if you want to have a CRT that is capable of displaying good, clear, 1024×768 graphic screen images.

After the electron beam has painted an image, that image will immediately start to fade away. In fact, with the type of CRTs used in most PC displays, the pels in any given region of the screen fade essentially to black in a small fraction of the time it takes the system to draw an entire image. (If you photograph a PC display, you'll do well to use an exposure that is at least 1/60 of a second, and preferably 1/30 of a second or longer. If

you attempt to take a very short-exposure picture—for example, 1/1000 of a second—
you will find that some areas of the screen are brightly lit and most of the screen is dark.)
The technical term for this effect is the *persistence* of the phosphor in the CRT, and for
most PC displays it is at most a few milliseconds and perhaps much less than that.

LCD Panel Images

LCD panels come in several types. The different types create their images in different
ways. (I'll describe the principal types in some detail later in this chapter.) All of them
use a raster-scanning procedure, but some allow the individual pixels much more time to
be set to the correct brightness than is the case with the others. That is good, because
LCD panel pixels cannot be turned on or off at anywhere near the rate at which pixels
are painted on a CRT's screen. On the other hand, the pixels (or pels, to be more precise)
in an LCD panel have, effectively, an infinite persistence time. That is, after the pels are
set to some brightness or color, that image tends to remain on the panel as long as power
is applied or until it is replaced by some other image.

Character Versus "APA" (Bitmapped) Images

The original IBM PC display subsystem that most people bought was what IBM called
its Monochrome Display Adapter and Monitor. This monitor was a simple green-screen
cathode ray tube. The video adapter that drove it created images that consisted solely of
letters, numbers, and a few graphic symbols. The screen image was divided into 25 lines
with 80 character positions on each line. Any symbol could be placed in each of those
2,000 character positions, and each of those symbols could be either bright or dim, or it
could blink. This was a pure character display system.

An early alternative to this green-screen character display was the IBM Color Graphics
Adapter (CGA) and its monitor. This display system took quite a different approach to
forming its images. Instead of putting character symbols into character cells on the
screen, the CGA display painted 64,000 individual pixels. Each one could be made to
glow in any one of four colors. Far less detail exists in an image formed this way, but
what detail there is can be specified more arbitrarily. IBM dubbed this type of display an
All-Points-Addressable (APA) display. Today, we usually call it a *bitmapped display,*
because one or more bits in the video image memory are assigned to each pixel on the
screen.

Today, most PC users see only bitmapped screen images almost all the time. If you are
running Windows 95, for example, the only character screens you ever see are those you
get when you first boot the machine, when you go to MS-DOS mode, or work in an MS-
DOS window. If, on the other hand, you are running plain old DOS on your PC, you will
see a character screen whenever you are at the DOS command prompt, and often when
you are in other programs, as well.

Where and How Is the Image Formed and Held?

As just explained, screen images for PCs come in two forms: character images and graphic (APA, or bitmapped) images. Each of these forms requires storing the image information in memory in a different form. For a character image, all you must store in RAM is 2 bytes of information for each character position on the screen. One of these bytes holds the extended ASCII code for the character to be displayed in this position. The other byte holds attribute information. (These attributes specify such things as the color for this character, how bright it is, and whether it should be blinking or underlined.)

If, on the other hand, the image is to be a graphic, much more detail must be stored. The color of every pixel must be described. Just how that is done depends on what color depth this image is to have.

Bit Planes and Color Depth

Color depth refers, indirectly, to the number of possible colors for each pixel in a graphic screen image. If all the pixels are either black or white, you need only 1 bit to specify in which of these two colors a particular pixel is to be shown. If the image allows each pixel to have any one of four colors, you need 2 bits per pixel to define which of those four colors is to be used. By similar reasoning, you can see that 4 bits suffice to select any one of 16 colors. Eight bits can specify any one of 256 colors. The color depth is simply the number of bits needed to specify the color of each pixel.

The most commonly used color depths in PC images have been 2, 4, 8, 15, 16, and 24. Some special-purpose video cards use 32 bits per pixel, but in this case only 24 are used to specify the color. The remaining 8 bits are used for what is called *alpha channel information*. This includes such things as information that specifies a degree of transparency to let an underlying image (perhaps from some external video source) show through.

A *bit plane* is simply an organization of the bits used to store an image in a three-dimensional array. First, you form a planar array of bits, with 1 bit for each pixel on each line of the raster-scan image. Then, you replicate this plane as many times as there are bits per pixel, placing each bit plane behind its predecessor. The result for *N* bits per pixel is a collection of *N* planes.

To put some numbers to this, consider a common VGA graphic display. The resolution of the entire image is 640 pixels per line and 480 lines. This says there are 307,200 total pixels. Normal VGA specifies that each pixel can be given any one of a specified set of 16 colors. That means that the color depth is 4 bits. So, for each pixel you must have 1/2 byte of video image RAM, for a total of 153,600 bytes (exactly 150KB). Because RAM chips always hold a number of bits that is some integer power of 2, normally VGA video cards carry 256KB of video image RAM.

Where Physically and Logically Is the Video Image RAM?

I just said that the video image RAM is typically on the video card. Is that always true? Why? Screen images for a PC must be held in some very special memory locations. These locations must be accessible to the CPU, but they also must be accessible to the video image output circuitry. The CPU needs rapid access to them, but the video output circuitry needs even more rapid access. This dictates where the chips that make up that memory must be placed physically.

If you have a plug-in video card, because the video image output circuitry is on the card, it only makes sense to put the video image RAM there also. If your PC has its video display adapter circuitry located on the motherboard, you will find the video image RAM somewhere very near it. In any event, the video image RAM consists of a set of chips totally separate from those that make up the PC's main memory that is used by the CPU for all other purposes. That is because of the special qualities this memory must possess and to enable it to be placed right next to the video image output circuitry. (There are a few exceptions to this, incidentally. Silicon Graphics, Inc. has developed a Visual Computing architecture for its Visual Workstation systems which enables nearly the entire system's main memory to be used for video-related purposes. Of course, one aspect of how this is achieved is that all memory in these systems must meet the higher performance and tolerance specifications reserved for dedicated video memory in more standard-use PCs.)

Exceptions aside, the newest mainstream PCs separate things even a bit more fully. They use an Advanced Graphics Port into which one plugs an AGP video card. This AGP connector carries the data from the CPU over a different set of wires than those that serve all the other plug-in cards, and it is able to do this both at the same time as other data are going to the other plug-in cards (for example, on the PCI bus) and several times more rapidly than the data flow in the PCI bus.

The video image RAM is located physically on the video card (or in the near vicinity of the video output circuitry). Logically, things seem quite different. From the perspective of the CPU, this block of RAM is just more RAM, like any other it can see in its memory address space. This block of memory in 386-and-higher CPUs can have its physical memory addresses remapped to any location within the CPU's logical address space. (To learn more about the differences between physical and logical memory addresses and about memory mapping, see Chapter 11, "Giving Your PC's CPU Enough Elbow Room—PC Memory.")

Forming PC Images the Old-Fashioned Way

Character-based images are prepared by the CPU. It stores the ASCII values for the characters to be displayed, with an attribute byte for each one, in the display adapter's video RAM. These are the simple images. Much harder to create are graphic images, simply because they have so much more information in them. One way to do this job— and the only way it was done in early PCs—is to again have the CPU compute the correct color value (the number of bits the color depth for this image requires) for each pixel and then store those numbers in the video display adapter's video image RAM. This works, but it uses a lot of the CPU computing power.

Accelerated Video Cards

A better solution for creating complex graphic images is to have a *graphics coprocessor* as part of the video display adapter. This is a small computer within the PC (located on the video display adapter option card, unless your PC has its video circuitry all on the motherboard). Its sole job is computing pixel color values for graphic images. The program that is creating the image can describe that image in fairly broad, high-level terms. For example, it might specify that a triangle is to be drawn and give the coordinates of the corners, the width, and color of the line to be used, and perhaps a color to use to fill the interior of the triangle after it has been drawn. (This sort of sequence of high-level instructions for a graphic image is called a *display list*, as opposed to the detailed pixel image data otherwise required for a graphic image.)

If your PC has a graphics coprocessor, most of the time the CPU won't compute the pixel information for the images to be displayed, but it will instead pass instructions at this high level to the graphics coprocessor. That device will then compute which pixels in the image must be set to the color of the border and which are to be set to the fill color. And it will load all those pixel values into the video image RAM.

Figure 13.3 schematically shows these two approaches to graphic image generation. The upper panel shows a block diagram of how images are created and then displayed when a graphics coprocessor is not involved. The lower panel shows how this changes with a graphics coprocessor. This figure doesn't show any details for the video image readout hardware. (Nor does it show the rest of the PC, with all its complexity!) I will cover shortly the pieces that make up the video image readout hardware.

Perhaps the most significant point to make here is that the speed of data flow from graphics coprocessor to video image RAM and the flow from there to the screen are controlled only by the details of how the video card is built. If you have a high-end video card, it might use a very fast clock speed and a very wide data bus (up to 128 bits flowing in parallel) between the graphics coprocessor and the video image RAM. Furthermore, whenever the images being formed are very detailed (high-image resolution) and have a lot of color depth, the data flow from that RAM to the screen must also be tremendously fast. Naturally, the high-end video cards can support whatever rate they must to handle the images they are designed to create.

FIGURE 13.3

Two ways to generate a graphics image.

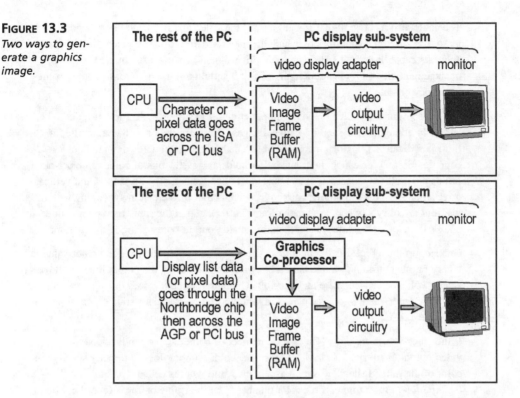

What Paints the Image on the Screen—and How?

I have mentioned many times now, but up to now have not explained, the video output circuitry that makes up one essential part of any video display adapter. Now it is time to explain that.

Modern display adapters can operate in a huge number of different video modes. The particular mode you are using determines three things. First, it specifies whether the image you are creating is composed solely of characters, like a DOS-mode screen, or whether it is a bitmapped graphic. Second, it specifies the resolution of the image (how many pixels per line and how many lines). Third, it specifies the color depth (how many bits per pixel are stored in the video image RAM). The video output circuitry has from one to three separate jobs to perform, and these are determined by the video mode in which the video display adapter is operating.

I am going to limit my discussion here to the most common kinds of video monitor: a VGA-or-better analog display. These monitors connect to the video display adapter through a cable with 15-pin connectors. Inside that cable are three analog signals carrying brightness information in parallel for the three color components of each pixel.

The cable also has two digital signal lines for the video and horizontal drive signals and up to three digital signal lines by which the monitor can inform the video display adapter about its capabilities. (The H-drive and V-drive signals are also used by a PC's power-management circuitry when it determines that it should tell the monitor to go into some lower power state.)

The video modes in which the video output circuitry has the simplest job turn out to be, curiously enough, for the most complex images. These are the ones that are crafted in full-pixel detail in the video image RAM (frame buffer) by the CPU and graphics coprocessor, and for which the frame buffer holds at least 15 bits of color value per pixel. In this case, all the video output circuitry must do is generate the horizontal and vertical drive signals (so the monitor can sweep its beam across the screen in synchrony with the read-out circuitry's sweep through the frame buffer), and at the same time pump out each pixel's three color brightnesses on the three analog output wires going to the monitor.

One step in this process is worth noting. The video output circuitry reads a color value (a binary number) from the frame buffer, but what it must put on the output lines are three analog voltages between zero and one volt. The output circuitry does this by breaking down the color value into three parts and sending each part to a separate digital-to-analog converter (DAC).

If the color values are only 8-bit or 4-bit numbers, another step often is added to the video output circuitry's job. In these cases, the color number doesn't directly specify the color of the pixel. Instead, it is used as a pointer into what is called a *palette* or *color lookup table*. For example, if the color number from the frame buffer is four, the actual amounts of red, green, and blue to be displayed for that pixel will be found at the fourth line of the palette. Figure 13.4 is a block diagram of this circuitry and also a sample palette table showing the default values for 16-color standard VGA images. (A 0 in the table represents none of that color; a value of 63 represents the maximum amount of that color. These numbers are representable in 6 bits, which is how much information is sent from the palette lookup to the DAC circuits.)

A palette mechanism is used for 4-bit or 8-bit color modes because when you have so few colors, you may not like the ones you get. By using a palette, you can still have no less than 16 or more than 256 simultaneous colors, but the particular ones you get on a given image will be determined by the contents of the palette table, which can be altered any time you (or a program you run) want to change it.

For example, GIF images typically use this strategy. They have at most 256 colors in any single image, yet sometimes they look stunningly like a photograph. The reason is that GIF images normally contain a palette that has in it a set of well-chosen colors that best represent whatever image the file contains. Graphics image display programs read that palette out of the GIF file and load that set of colors into the hardware palette in the video display adapter whenever they are displaying a GIF file.

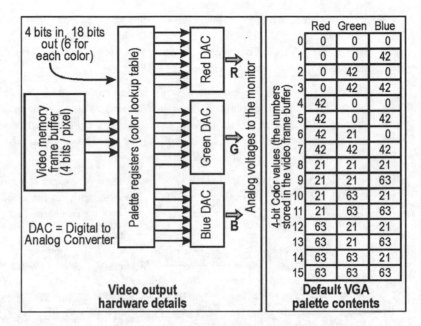

FIGURE 13.4

How a VGA display creates colored pixels through translating numbers from the frame buffer.

	Red	Green	Blue
0	0	0	0
1	0	0	42
2	0	42	0
3	0	42	42
4	42	0	0
5	42	0	42
6	42	21	0
7	42	42	42
8	21	21	21
9	21	21	63
10	21	63	21
11	21	63	63
12	63	21	21
13	63	21	63
14	63	63	21
15	63	63	63

Video output hardware details

Default VGA palette contents

Figure 13.5 shows the video display adapters for our sample desktop system. The top portion of this figure shows a Matrox Productiva G100 quad-PCI accelerated video display adapter. The two larger connectors on the bracket (at the left) connect to special cables, each of which terminates in two standard VGA connectors (to connect to two monitors) plus an RCA jack (for video input from a camera or VCR). The smaller connector in the center of the bracket permits receiving cable TV signals.

You can see that the cable TV signals are brought directly to a metal box at the right side of the card in this figure. That is a TV tuner. The output of that tuner (or the video signal put in on one of the RCA inputs connected to the monitor output jacks) can be mixed with the PC graphic images if suitable software programs are used. This board also includes audio-mixing circuitry to mix the television sound with any other analog audio signals you may have in your PC (for example, from your CD drive).

The four largest chips on this board are the four video display circuits. The other large chips are memory, the video BIOS, and assorted other functions. Because there are two of the indicated 2MB memory chips for each of the four display adapters, these display adapters each have 4MB of video RAM.

The lower-left image shows a Matrox G200 AGP accelerated video display adapter. The large integrated circuit chip on this card is hidden underneath a heatsink, right above the AGP connector. This card comes with 8MB of video image RAM, and it has a socket (the white C-shape on the right-side surrounding the two visible video memory chips) that accepts an additional memory module, shown here at the bottom of the figure, to give a total of 16MB of video image RAM. (The indicated chips each hold 2MB of video information, and on this board, but not on the Productiva, there are identical memory chips located on the back of the board behind each one on the front. That is also true for the plug-in memory card shown below the AGP card.)

The lower-right image is a close-up view of the connector by which the AGP card plugs into the AGP slot, and also of the add-on memory card. Notice that the memory card, like the PCI plug-in card in the upper portion of this figure, has a single row of gold contacts along the edge of the board, where it plugs into the slot connector. (It has another set of similar contacts on the back of the board.)

Notice also that the AGP card has a double row of contacts, stacked above one another. The AGP slot connector is shorter than a PCI connector, but it has more contacts because it has both an upper and a lower set of contacts for both the front and back of the card.

FIGURE 13.5
The video cards from our sample desktop PC.

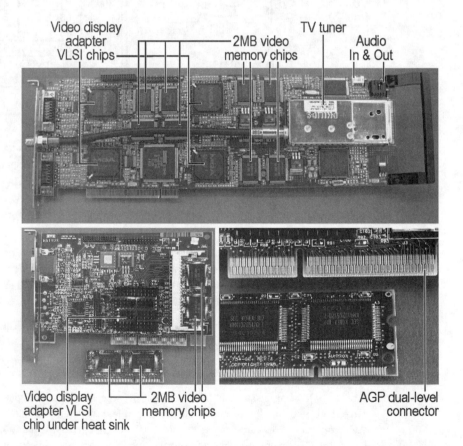

The Matrox G100 can display four independent images, each with a separately settable resolution of up to 1024×758 pixels with photo-realistic color (24 bits per pixel), or up to 1600×1200 pixels with high color (16 bits per pixel), or up to 1800×1440 or 1920×1200 with 256 colors (8 bits per pixel). The DAC modules on this card are capable of running at a pixel clock rate of up to 230MHz, which implies that it can pump out all the pixels in a VGA (640×480-pixel) image quickly enough to refresh the entire screen up to 200 times per second, or at least 60 times per second for even its highest-resolution modes. (The actual speed it uses is set in the driver software.)

The Matrox G200 AGP card with its added memory installed is capable of resolutions up to the same maximum value, 1800×1440 or 1920×1200, and it can do that with the full photo-realistic color (24 bits per pixel). The RAMDACs on this board run at 250MHz, making even faster refresh rates possible.

Getting the Colors (Almost) Right

Including color in an image makes a huge difference. Color displays convey information more compactly than monochrome ones, because colors can be used to convey subtext to various items on the screen. (For example, warning messages often appear inside a red box.) Because color printers now are becoming quite affordable and capable, and thus more commonly found on PC systems, preparing documents in color is becoming more important.

Colors are slippery things, however. People don't see them the same way on paper and on a monitor, nor are all color display devices (monitors or printers) properly adjusted when they come from the factory. These things combine to make it difficult to be sure when you look at a screen image whether its colors are the same as what you will see when you print it.

You can take two approaches to get the colors in an image just right. One is to tweak how the monitor displays colors, and the other is to alter the stored information in the image until the monitor colors look however you want them to.

Adjusting the Monitor

If you plan to print some computer-generated color images, or intend them to be viewed on more than just your PC, you probably will want to adjust your monitor until each color appears at least very nearly correct. That is, white pages should look white, and red should look red.

The first level of accomplishing this is called *aligning the monitor*. This is simply making sure that the electron beam that carries information for the red subpixels in the image is hitting only the dots or stripes of phosphor that glow red (and, of course, doing the same for the other two colors of subpixels). When that is done, any field of pure color will appear to be the same hue and saturation. This color might or might not be right, because of some details of both how humans see color and how display devices create colored images.

You can make some useful adjustments to an image that can make its colors appear more nearly correct. Figure 13.6 shows the Color tab on the Display Properties dialog box from the Windows 95 driver for the Matrox video cards shown in Figure 13.5. Notice the adjustment slider for color temperature at the bottom left. This is used to make a white page seem white rather than bluish or yellowish. At the right are three sliders to adjust individually the "transfer curves" shown at the left for the three color signals. In essence, these enable you to emphasize or deemphasize mid-level brightness pixels for a given color relative to the brightest ones. Normally, you set these sliders until a test image displayed on your monitor looks as much like a printed copy of that image as you can manage.

FIGURE 13.6
The Matrox Display Properties dialog box enables you to tweak images for proper appearance.

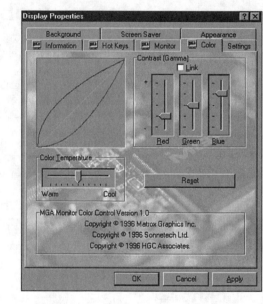

Adjusting the Image Information

The alternative way to adjust the color appearance of images is simply to alter the color values that are stored in the image itself or in its palette table. This is the only way to go if your video display adapter and its driver software don't provide the type of color compensation program I just described. It also is often the best way to go if the images you are creating are to be viewed onscreen only on one PC. It is not the best way to do things if the images you work with must also be displayed on other PCs or will be printed on a color printer.

How to Talk to a Video Display

Now you know pretty well how a PC creates, stores, and outputs a video image. But, in fact, I haven't yet told you the newest wrinkle in how that output step can be done.

The original PC displays sent purely digital data to the display over several wires in parallel. (The signal on each wire was either ON or OFF at every instant.) Monochrome displays used two wires to get four brightness levels. CGA displays used four wires to get potentially sixteen colors. EGA used six wires to get up to 64 colors.

This approach ran out of steam right about there. So, IBM introduced an analog approach with its VGA display (three wires with variable voltages representing variable amounts of red, green, and blue). All PC displays up until very recently used a refinement of that approach.

Now, with LCD digital flat panel displays in particular, and someday in the not-too-distant future with all displays, we will be returning to a truly all-digital interface—but with a big difference from the old way.

We still want to have many levels of brightness for each color subpel in our images, and we cannot have dozens of wires in the cable. So, the industry is moving toward using a very high-speed digital serial bus. The brightness information for each subpel will be digitized and sent as binary numbers over this bus.

What's the advantage to doing this? There are several. First is the usual advantage of all things digital: You can send the information without fearing that any noise will get into it and degrade the signal. As long as the signal is received and regenerated properly, it will be a perfect copy of what was sent. Second, the images on a fully digital display potentially can be better than those on the present generation of analog-brightness-for-each-digital-subpel displays. Certainly, they should be more reproducible, meaning that you won't have to adjust them to get the image to look right, nor will the image differ noticeably from one display to the next. Finally, when the industry has this all worked out, the interface will be cheaper to build than the present all-analog one.

Why aren't we using all digital video interfaces already? For one thing, if you switch to a purely digital flat panel display, you will have to replace your analog output video display adapter. (At the least, you will have to augment your existing analog video card with an all-digital daughtercard, such as the Matrox Millennium 2000, which plugs into the expansion socket of several analog Matrox video cards.) Second, there isn't yet one industry standard for this technology. The most significant two that are competing for dominance are Digital Flat Panel (DFP) and Plug-and-Display (PnD). There is also a standard for the latter protocol called PanelLink. You'll read a bit more about digital flat panels later in this chapter.

Understanding Display Technologies

Up to this point, I have told you a great deal about color vision and color images, but actually not very much about exactly how the display devices we use create images we can see. There are two principal categories of display devices for PCs, and several others that are not yet in common use. The most common for desktop PCs are CRTs. Virtually all laptops use LCD panels of one type or another. Projection display devices (for use in showing PC presentations to large audiences) can be built using either type of technology. Plasma panels, field emission displays, and personal, retinal displays are some of the additional types of display device that you might get; but so far, very few of us have them.

Cathode Ray Tubes (CRTs)

A CRT is a big glass bottle with a vacuum inside. It also contains three electron guns that squirt focused beams of electrons, some deflection apparatus (either magnetic or electrostatic) that deflects these beams both up and down and side to side, and a phosphor screen upon which these beams impinge. The vacuum is necessary to let those electron beams travel across the tube without running into air molecules that could absorb them or scatter them off course.

Color CRTs also have one more essential part, which is termed either a *shadow mask* or an *aperture grill*. In these tubes, the phosphor is not a continuous sheet of material, but instead consists of dots or stripes of three different materials. All three materials glow when they are hit by an electron beam, but each glows in its own color (red, green, or blue).

In the first kind of color CRT, a *shadow mask* is located a short distance away from the phosphor. This mask is simply a metal sheet with a regular array of holes punched in it. The electron guns are arranged in a triangle at the back of the tube, and the phosphor has a triangle of dots of different color phosphors in front of each hole in the shadow mask. Because of this geometrical arrangement, each of the electron guns can "see" only the dots it is supposed to illuminate. The beam deflection apparatus deflects all three beams together to form the raster scan pattern. As the set of three beams sweeps across the shadow mask, the holes guarantee that each beam lights up only phosphor dots that glow in the correct color for that beam.

The alternative arrangement uses an *aperture grill*. In these CRTs, the electron guns are placed side by side, just as you see in Figure 13.7. The aperture grill is simply an array of parallel wires, shown in this figure as the dashes in the dashed line near the phosphor. The gaps between those wires enable the beams from the three electron guns to illuminate three adjacent stripes on the tube surface. At just those locations behind each gap are three stripes of the corresponding phosphors.

Sony patented this technology under the name Trinitron. That patent has now expired, and many manufacturers use it. Figure 13.7 shows a simplified diagram of how such a tube is constructed.

FIGURE 13.7

Color CRTs use three electron guns and a shadow mask or aperture grill to illuminate triplets of phosphor dots or stripes.

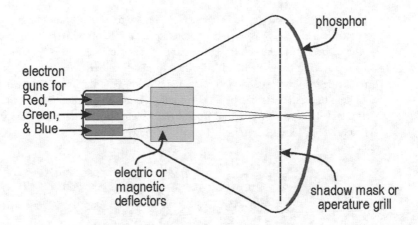

The industry standard for TV sets, and now for monitors as well, is to state as the size the diagonal dimension of the tube. Some portion of the edge of the tube is covered by the case, of course. TV images are normally adjusted so that you don't see the edges of them, but we must be able to see all the way to the edge of our PC images. So, in our system's 20-inch monitor, for example, the actual viewable image size (VIS), or usable portion of the front of the tube, measures only 19 inches from corner to corner. Like most standard TV sets and computer monitors, the height is about three-fourths of the width. Thus, in our case, the image width is about 15 inches and the height is about 11 inches. For a 1024×768 image, this implies the pixel spacing is about 0.37 millimeter (to convert to metric measure, as is commonly used for dot pitch specifications). This monitor has a dot pitch such that it can support images of up to 1600×1200 pixels.

Thinner CRTs

With the advent of Philips' flat screen television and Silicon Graphics' digital flat panel, the amount of desk space taken up by traditional CRT monitors has suddenly started to seem inordinate. I suspect that the "cool" factor has a lot to do with this, but there's certainly no question that CRTs are big, and big CRTs are *really* big. Because LCD panels are still somewhat expensive and plasma panels are incredibly expensive, CRT manufacturers have begun to develop traditional CRT monitors that are not nearly as deep as their predecessors. These "short-neck" models use an advanced deflection mechanism that affords the electron beam a much broader sweep. By extension, the electron gun no longer needs to be the distance from the screen that was required by previous beam-control technology. Because the gun doesn't have to be as far away, the tube can be shorter. Viewsonic, for example, makes an 18-inch-viewable monitor that is no deeper than a 15-inch model.

Liquid Crystal Displays (LCDs)

The other major category of PC display devices is LCD panels. These devices come in many variations, but the fundamental method of operation is the same for all of them.

Figure 13.8 shows a simple LCD panel. Here, a light source shines through a linear polarizer. This sheet passes only photons (quanta of light) with their electric fields aligned parallel to the polarizing direction of that sheet (shown as horizontal). Next, this light travels into a container filled with a special liquid crystal fluid. The property of the molecules in this container will rotate the plane of polarization of the light quanta by an amount that can be altered by an electric field imposed parallel to the path of the light. The last element is another linear polarizer, which will preferentially pass the photons that are aligned in its preferred orientation (shown as vertical).

FIGURE 13.8
A simple LCD panel.

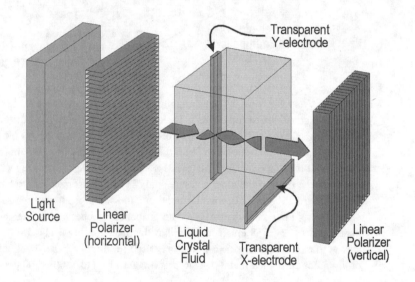

The container of liquid crystal fluid has many, parallel horizontal transparent electrodes on one surface and a similar set of vertical ones on the opposite surface. A voltage applied between one of the x-electrodes and one of the y-electrodes will impose an electric field on the liquid crystal material where they cross, and that will alter the light transmitted through that spot on the panel. By applying a voltage to one x-electrode and driving each y-electrode independently, it is possible to adjust the transparency of each pel on that row at the same time. Repeat this for every row (all the different x-electrodes) and you will have scanned the entire image.

This design is termed a *passive-matrix* LCD panel. That means that each pixel just sits there and responds when you address it, but does not respond at any other time. I'll describe how an *active-matrix* LCD panel differs from this in a moment.

Additive Color Versus Subtractive Color LCDs

There are two ways to modify this design to make a color LCD panel. One way uses three times as many intersections as the number of pels to be formed in the final image. Each subpel is covered with a colored plastic filter. Then the signals applied to each intersection adjust the brightness of each subpel. This creates a color image in a manner essentially identical to that used by color CRTs.

The other way to modify the design is to layer three liquid crystal panels on top of one another. Each one is filled with a colored liquid crystal. Each has its own set of x- and y-electrodes, this time just one intersection per pel. Each layer absorbs an adjustable portion of just one color of the light passing through it. This is similar to the way printed color images are created. The principal advantage to this design is that it enables you to create as many pels as intersections, thus making higher-resolution LCD panels possible. The principal disadvantage is that the light must pass through three layers, and so the resulting image is fainter, unless you use a stronger back light.

Painfully Plodding Panels—And How to Speed Them Up

The main problem with LCD panels is the time it takes to set the brightness of all the pels. A simple LCD panel can be refreshed from only a few times to perhaps a dozen times per second.

Most passive LCD panels paint an image in a manner that is quite analogous to that used with a CRT. The line electrode for the first line is activated. Then the driver proceeds to address each of the column electrodes in turn, causing the pel at the intersection to alter its transparency. After that pixel has been set, the driver moves on to the next pixel. The main way that an LCD panel differs from a CRT is that the effective persistence time is infinite. Each pel "remembers" whatever color or brightness it was set to until it is reset to a different value (or until you turn off power to the LCD panel).

This time required to set a single pel's brightness can be as much as a few hundred microseconds. Spending that much time on each line, for our sample image with 768 lines, means that refreshing the screen more than a few times per second just isn't feasible.

Double-Scan LCDs Are Somewhat Faster

Double-scan LCD panels paint the top and bottom halves of the screen in parallel. They do this by having each of the vertical wires broken at the center, and by having two, independent circuits for driving the upper and lower halves of the display at the same time.

This strategy doubles the effective refresh rate. That helps, but these panels are still too slow to display convincing video, for example, and you'll often "lose" your mouse cursor if you move it too quickly on either a single or dual-scan passive-matrix LCD panel.

Active-Matrix (TFT) LCDs Are Now the Preferred Way to Go

Active-matrix LCD panels differ from the passive-matrix panels in one simple-to-state, but for many years, very hard-to-build way: They have a small circuit (with one or more transistors) located at each pel. (Actually, they use one circuit for each subpel, or three per pel in a color screen.) These circuits are built by a process that carries the name "thin-film transistors" (hence the acronym you commonly will see added to the name: active-matrix/*TFT* LCD panel).

Because these are essentially electronic memory circuits, they respond very quickly to a signal telling them what value to store. Then they drive the appropriate voltage across the cell and hold it there until they are told to change that value.

The raster-scanning mechanism in an active-matrix LCD display goes very rapidly over the whole array, setting brightness values into each transistor on the entire screen. In fact, it scans those displays at the same rate as a CRT.

This analysis explains why LCD panels, other than active-matrix, have trouble displaying movies, yet are quite capable for simple static graphics or text screens. Because an active-matrix display "latches" (remembers) the pel values, it isn't necessary to "refresh" the display rapidly in order to keep from having the image flicker. The only reason you might want to redraw the image very quickly is that you are changing it very frequently (for example, in a simulated 3D display as described in Chapter 21, "Immersive PC Experiences," in the section "'Real' 3D").

Replacing Your CRT with an Active-Matrix LCD Panel

When active-matrix LCD panels became sufficiently close in cost to the passive-matrix panels, most laptop makers moved to using them almost exclusively. This helped power a mass market, and the usual thing happened as a consequence—prices fell even further.

Now we are seeing these very nice flat screen displays showing up in offices, on desktops, at point-of-sale terminals, and elsewhere. They are still more expensive than a CRT of the same size and resolution, but not by a huge factor. The LCD panels are delightfully lightweight—around a quarter of the weight of an equivalent CRT—and they take up very little desktop space (because they don't require the big CRT "bottle" poking out of the back). Those two factors alone have made them highly desirable in many places where there either isn't room for a big CRT or the display needs to be moved often from one place to another. Having one also makes you instantly "cool."

Figure 13.9 shows a 15-inch (diagonal measurement) flat panel LCD display for use as a CRT replacement. It can display photo-realistic (24-bits per pixel) color images at an actual pel resolution of 1024×768. You can use it to display images with lower resolution by using only a portion of the screen. Alternatively, the display can stretch the image to more or less fill the screen. If you try to display a higher-resolution image, the display will simply not show it at all. You can, in that case, reduce the resolution of the image in software and then display it.

This display includes stereo speakers and a microphone, and it comes with the stand you see in the figure; it also has provisions to make it easy to hang on a wall like a picture (with the stand removed).

FIGURE 13.9
A Nokia 500 Xa active-matrix LCD flat panel display.

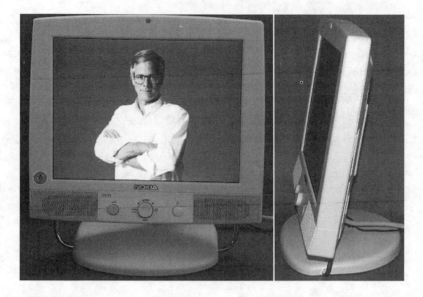

Images whose pixel resolution differs from the pel resolution of the display can be degraded by the stretching process. This will be especially noticeable when the stretching factor is not the ratio of two small integers (for example, 1:2, 2:3, or the like). For example, type may appear odd as some of the strokes get displayed on a double row or column of pels and other strokes get displayed on a single row or column.

When the image fits the screen, the resulting display is wonderful to behold. Someday, when this or some similar technology evolves even further, we'll no doubt have large units hung on our walls to display our choice of art in addition to using them for PC output, for video conferencing, and for watching television shows.

There is, nevertheless, a downside to these first flat panel displays. In order to retain compatibility with mainstream video card systems, these displays are still driven as analog devices. The video signals in your PC are converted from digital to analog by the DACs, just as they are for a CRT, and then are converted in the panel's own circuitry back into the digital data required to drive the flat panels. This conversion from digital to analog and back can cause some very noticeable loss of image quality. In particular, analog flat panels have had problems with color fringing, with clarity, and—even on TFT panels—with artifacts.

Enter the new all-digital flat panels, which I mentioned earlier. The first of these are the Silicon Graphics 1600SW and the Viewsonic VPD150. These monitors are fully digital. They require an all-digital video card, preferably in your PC's AGP slot (although PCI all-digital cards certainly exist). The quality difference in keeping the video signal digital at all times is nothing short of staggering. In a recent article, a prominent computer magazine actually suggested that desktop LCD panels weren't yet good enough for mainstream use—except for the all-digital variety. Surprisingly, premium quality doesn't come at a premium price in this case. The 17-inch silicon graphics panel, bundled with a Number Nine Visual Technology digital AGP card, sells for $600.00 less, at this writing, than the competing analog panel (with no card) from NEC. As prices continue to fall, digital flat panels will likely start replacing CRTs all over the world.

Other Display Technologies

CRT and LCD monitors account for almost all the displays used in and with PCs, but a few other technologies have been tried at one time or another. Perhaps the most important are *plasma displays*. These are essentially a huge collection of neon bulbs with fancy electrodes and internal partitions to effectively form one lamp per pel. You drive them in a manner similar to that used for LCD panels, but the voltages involved are much higher. The result is to cause a small section of the gas inside the panel to form a glowing plasma. If you do it right, this plasma won't spread to neighboring cells, and it will die promptly when you turn off power to that cell. These plasma displays are most often used for very large panels that must be viewable in relatively high-ambient light situations.

Although until very recently no one had figured out how to make color plasma displays, in the past year or so Philips has produced them. These are still quite expensive devices, so they are best used in spaces where you want to have television (or PC) images that can be viewed by large numbers of people at once. They have very stable color and brightness output, making them invaluable in situations where you want to have multiple panels making up a much larger overall image and not have the viewers notice a difference in color or brightness between segments of that overall image.

Three more digital display technologies to watch, but not yet ready for market, are *field emission displays, electroluminescent displays,* and *transparent organic light emitting device displays*. Each of these technologies has been under development for several years (or even several decades), and each has some very interesting properties. But so far, they haven't been crafted as commercial products.

Finally, there is what has been termed *electric paper*. Several laboratories are working on technologies that make something that looks and feels a lot like an ordinary sheet of paper, but that can be driven electrically in a manner resembling the way a digital flat panel display is driven, and in that way can produce "permanent," yet infinitely alterable, text and graphics that you can view as you might a printed page. One sheet of this would stand in for an entire book or magazine. Or, it could be used as a desktop PC's primary output display device. This technology will very likely show up first in so-called *e-books* and then migrate to other uses when the technology has been proven and the production costs brought down sufficiently.

I describe several other special-purpose PC display technologies in the section of Chapter 21, titled "'Real' 3D." That discussion includes mention of head-mounted displays, direct retinal projectors, and other exotic technologies; some of these are only on the drawing board, and others are available now in your local computer store.

This Story Is Incomplete

As you can imagine, more developments in PC displays will occur as time goes on. None of the ones we use now are perfect, so there is ample room for improvements. For now, CRTs and LCDs are the primary display technologies in use. In addition to CRTs and LCD panels meant for direct viewing, there are products that use displays of either of those types in a projection mode. These projectors can fill a large screen with a PC-generated image, and they might seem quite exotic compared to a simple desktop or laptop PC's usual monitor. Actually, though, they are merely the same types of display made superbright and imaged on a screen.

Running the Display System Backward

The PC display system is all about showing you output from your PC. Well, that is mostly true. Sometimes a PC input device uses the display as part of its hardware. One example is a light pen, which is essentially a fast-acting photocell in a pen. You hold it up to the screen of a CRT, and it will "see" the scanning beam go by. Electronics in the PC can detect this pulse and correlate it with the part of the screen being scanned at that moment. In this way, you can point to things on the screen and the PC will know just where you are pointing.

This approach to using a CRT display as an input device has mostly fallen from favor. The main problem is that usually the screen is not placed in a convenient location for pointing. Also, there are now many other ways to point to locations on the screen, and apparently most PC users prefer one or more of those alternatives. Finally, as we move to digital flat panel displays—in which it may not be the case that each pixel is refreshed in a strict raster scan, and in any case the pixels stay glowing at a constant brightness until they are next refreshed—the basic light pen strategy just won't work.

The most common other example of this approach is a touch-screen display. These are monitors (usually CRTs) in a case that add some means of detecting any time someone touches a spot on the screen. One method uses both a horizontal and a vertical grid of invisible light beams and photocells to see your finger approach the screen. Another method uses a transparent sensing membrane applied to the face of the CRT. Whatever the means, the effect is the same: You can point and the PC knows when and where you pointed. These pointing devices aren't suitable for very fine work, but they work well to let a user pick out one among several choices without needing to use a keyboard. This means that the most common application for this type of display system is in information kiosks rather than in general-purpose PCs.

When PC Images and Television Begin to Blend—And Why You'll Probably Watch the New, Digital Television Programs on Your PC

When discussing color models near the beginning of this chapter, I said that if you want to display a television signal on your PC—or conversely, send a PC image to a television set—the PC must do a color-space conversion.

Actually, the job of converting a PC image into a television image can be quite a bit more complex than just doing a color-space conversion. The resolution may have to be altered, and if the output is going to a normal, analog television set, the image will have to be broken down into two *fields* for each *frame*, with the lines in each field *interlaced* between the lines of the other field.

That is, the odd-numbered lines of the image, counting down from the top, are sent out first. Then, the even-numbered lines are sent out. The total time to send out all those lines is, typically, 1/30 of a second, or about as long as the time between the redrawing of all the lines in a typical PC display.

Recall that I told you that PCs normally use what is termed a *progressive* display strategy, just painting the lines one after another, in numerical order, from top to bottom of the screen. The television strategy is referred to as an *interlaced* display to make clear the difference in how those lines are painted.

The resolution conversion has to be done differently to produce the kinds of analog television signals used in different countries. The United States and Japan, for example, use what is termed NTSC format. European countries use either PAL or SECAM. All three are interlaced formats, but they have differing numbers of lines and different field and frame rates. However, for the purposes of this discussion, those are simply details that the PC (or the program it is running) must know about—you, fortunately, don't have to bother yourself with them, other than to know that you want the program to do the correct conversion to make the output playable on your TV set.

You see that it can be quite difficult to create television-type signals from a PC, and correspondingly, it can be quite difficult to accept a standard TV signal and make it show up correctly on a PC's screen. So why would you want to do anything like that?

It used not to be very useful, but with the improvements in PC processing power, and in PC display system capabilities, more and more people are finding that at times they want to put their PC screen images on an external television set, or they want to display television images in a window on their PC's screen (and still be able to see other portions of their PC's normal images at the same time).

I'm going to describe briefly only a couple of these mixed-PC-and-TV image applications, to let you see the kind of thing I mean. But then I want to alert you to the very real possibility that you will want to make your PC your primary system for displaying the new, high-definition digital television (DTV) signals. First, you may want to do a presentation for a large audience and support your talk with slides you created on your PC. If the auditorium you'll be using doesn't have a digital projection system, you may have to use a converter and an analog projection (or large-screen) television set. This works, but you'll find that the image quality is not nearly what you are used to on your PC—so you'd best design your slides with that in mind. Don't use small type or other highly detailed imagery.

Second is a case that goes the other way: bringing a television signal into a PC. Some people like to have a television set going in the background as they work. If you are a stockbroker, for example, you may need to know the "breaking news" in order to anticipate how it may affect prices on your stock exchange. In the past, you would simply get one or more small television sets and have them play off to one side while you worked at your PC. Now, it is quite feasible to pipe the television signals into your PC and have it display them in a window on your PC desktop.

I find it really exciting that we may find that our PCs, with just a simple modification, are actually the best devices to use to watch the new DTV. There are some very good reasons why this is so. PC displays almost always have more resolution than ordinary television sets of any size. A standard television image can have no more than about 500 lines in the image, and often there are no more than about 400 distinguishable pixels on each line. (TV images often look more compelling than most PC displays, but that is because of three things about those TV images. First, they use a very large number of subtly different colors in each image. Second, they are moving images. Third—and this is all too easy to overlook—they are created by professionals who know what they are doing, and who are very good at creating compelling images within the limitations of their medium.)

DTV signals will come in a number of different formats, some barely better than today's analog TV signals, but others with resolutions up to 1280 pixels across and 720 lines high. (This is the new, 16:9 aspect ratio, similar to wide-screen movies—as opposed to the now-standard 4:3 ratio for all analog television sets and most PC displays.)

Any reasonably decent PC today can display at least 800 pixels per line for 600 lines in each image, and it can do this with at least a fairly large number of simultaneous colors. Your PC may very well be able to do a lot better than this.

If you can display PC images with at least 1024 pixels per line (and preferably 1280 pixels per line), your PC is well suited to display digital television signals. You will probably find that the image is not as tall as your screen—so there will be a black band at the top and bottom (or perhaps the program will permit you to use that additional space for supplemental information or for interacting with the broadcaster).

If you were to go out and buy a digital television receiver today, it would cost you a lot of money—probably more than an entire, rather high-end desktop PC with a rather large display. Why does a digital television cost so much? Mainly because it will have a very big screen (perhaps a 72-inch diagonal). And why is that the case? Because, normally, people watch television from at least 10 feet away from the TV screen. If you are going to benefit from the new, higher-definition (higher-resolution) images digital television can send, you'll need either to have a very large screen or to sit uncommonly close.

Ah, but sitting close to a high-resolution image is just what you do with your PC every day. So, if only you could receive and display digital television signals properly on your PC, it would work as well for a single viewer, sitting up close, as the much more costly, much larger digital television set positioned across the room.

Vendors will be introducing DTV adapters for PCs in the very near future for just this reason. They won't cost much more than a good video display adapter, which is to say not more than a few hundred dollars, as opposed to the nearly one hundred times that much that a good digital television set may cost you.

You probably won't want to use your PC to have the whole family watch a DTV movie, but if only one or two people want to see a DTV show, then sitting close to your PC may well be acceptable. Furthermore, some broadcasters are going to be experimenting with interactive broadcasts. These will offer the viewer the opportunity of selecting supplemental information to be displayed alongside the main program, for example. Sitting at your PC's keyboard, or in reach of your mouse, may be just what you need to take advantage of those broadcasts.

Summary

When it comes to PC display subsystems, you have a lot of choices. Many different technologies exist, as well as many implementations of each one. Armed with the information in this chapter (and the additional information in Chapter 21, "Immersive PC Experiences"), you will be able to understand each new PC display product. You will know why it works as it does, and therefore which ones will be of interest to you and which you can quickly pass by.

Now that you understand how PCs display information on a screen, it is time to turn to the other most common method of getting information out of your computer: printers. That is the subject of the next chapter.

Getting It All Down on Paper: Printers

Most PC information input comes via the keyboard (or is loaded in bulk from a disk or over a connection to a remote computer). Most PC output goes to the screen. The second most important information output path is to some type of printer. Screen images can be very rich in information, and when animated or video images are combined with sound, they can be very compelling. However, they are inherently transient displays, and they can't be carried away from the display device.

The Purpose and Power of PC Printers

A page of printed output can display considerably more information than can a single screen image, and it clearly is much more permanent and portable. Thus, PC printers are one of the most-used peripheral devices. As such, they have attracted a lot of development effort, and we now have a wide variety of printer technologies to choose from.

The point of a printer is to make marks on paper or some similar medium. In this chapter, I first explain the five principal mechanisms that are used in PC printers to make those marks. Then I explain the difference between character printers and page printers and give you a brief description of the principle kinds of each. Finally, I mention some of the special issues surrounding printing images in color.

Printing Technologies—An Overview

No PC printers use chisels to carve marks in stone tablets. That is almost the only method of "printing" ever devised that hasn't been adapted to use in a printer for a PC. All the printers in common use with PCs use one of five basic methods to make their marks on the paper or other media on which they print. Each of them comes in many forms, some of which are different enough from one another that I will discuss those details later. First, let's look at an overview of these five ways to "make your mark."

Making an Impression: Impact Printers

The first computer printers were simply computer-controlled typewriters. In these machines, a ribbon soaked with ink is positioned in front of a piece of paper, then banged upon with a shaped hammer. The impact drives ink out of the ribbon and onto the page. Many modern computer printers do much the same thing. We call them *impact printers*.

Impact printers can be further subdivided into two classes: those that use shaped hammers to produce an entire symbol in a single blow (called *character printers*), and those that form images one dot at a time, in a manner reminiscent of the way in which PC displays form their images. These latter devices are commonly called *dot matrix impact printers*. I'll explain these differences among the various impact printers in more detail after I finish going over the alternative ways of putting marks on paper.

Xerographic (Laser, LCS, and LED) Printers

Having a laser printer for your PC has been one of the ultimate status symbols (as well as a very practical thing to do) since Chester Carlson's 1938 invention of xerographic printing—which was turned into the wonderfully convenient Xerox 914 office copiers (in 1959)—was further transformed into the Hewlett-Packard LaserJet family of PC printers (starting in 1984). The correct name for what most folks refer to as a *laser printer* is a *xerographic printer*. That is, its basic process is xerography, the printing process that Chester Carlson invented.

Three physical facts underlie xerographic printing:

- Photoconductive materials exist that are very good electrical insulators as long as they kept in the dark, but which become good electrical conductors whenever light shines on them.

- Materials that have opposite electrostatic charges are attracted to one another.

- You can bond particles of one material to another material by melting and refreezing some bonding agent. If, instead of simply melting the bonding agent, you also produce some chemical cross-linking, the resulting solid bond will be relatively immune to being softened by heat later.

A xerographic printer is built around a photosensitive transfer surface. This surface is usually built either in the form of a rigid cylinder of metal with a thin coating of the photoconductor on its outer surface, or in the form of an electrically conducting closed-loop belt with similar coating on one side. Xerographic printing proceeds in six steps:

1. The photoconductive surface (which is in a darkened space) is cleaned of any residual toner and then charged to a high electrostatic potential.

2. This charge is selectively drained off by shining light onto only selected regions of the photoconductive surface.

3. The surface is flooded with toner particles. These are a mixture of tiny specks of some highly colored material and equally tiny chunks of a plastic bonding material. The toner particles stick only to the portions of the photoconductor that are still carrying a large electrostatic charge.

4. A piece of paper (or other medium on which printing is to occur) with an opposite electrical charge is pressed against the toner-coated photoconductive surface.

5. The paper is then separated from the photoconductive surface. In this step, most of the toner comes along with the paper, held there by electrostatic attraction.

6. The toner-laden paper is heated, thus fusing the ink particles to the paper.

The image being printed is formed at the second step. In a traditional, analog office copier this is accomplished by imaging a document onto the surface. The dark places on the document show up as the regions that don't get discharged on the photoconductor. That means they stay charged electrostatically, and therefore they attract toner, which is later transferred to the paper and fused to make dark places on the copy.

That is how it used to work, when copiers were exclusively analog devices. As I explained in Chapter 12, "Getting Your PC's Attention: Input Devices," most modern office copiers are now fully digital devices. That is, they scan the document to be copied and capture that information as a digital image. They may do some processing on that image—to optimize contrast, for example—then they print that image on a digital printer that is much like any other computer printer.

Computer printers create images that start with information in a file. There is no preexisting dark and light image to be projected onto the photoconductor. So, instead of imaging a preexisting image, a xerographic computer printer builds the image one pel at a time, just as a computer display shows graphic images by building them up one pel at a time on the monitor's screen. We'll continue this discussion, using a laser printer as our example.

Standards: As I did with PC display technologies, I'll call the minimum-size dot you can print a *pel*. This is in contrast to the notion of *pixel*, which is the minimum element you can specify in a computer-generated image file. Pels refer to the smallest printable (or displayable) dot. You can print one pixel to a pel or you can spread a pixel over several adjacent pels, but you cannot print two different pixels within the space of one pel. (At best, you can print an average value for all the pixels that contribute to a pel; but the pel itself is the indivisible unit of what gets printed.)

The computer printers that truly deserve the name "laser printer" (and the HP LaserJet family is an example of this type) have a laser light source inside them. A set of moving mirrors causes the beam to scan across the photoconductive surface in a raster, just like the raster drawn on the screen of your PC's monitor. The major difference is that the laser beam draws a much smaller spot.

Modern laser printers can modulate the beam intensity, from full-on to full-off, in some subtle ways. This modifies the size and sometimes even the location of the spots that get printed within the region described as a single pel.

Xerographic printers are perhaps the most popular of all the printer technologies in use today, at least for general-purpose office use. Among their other virtues are that they are among the fastest printers and the quietest, and their per-copy costs are among the lowest.

The lower initial purchase cost of low-end inkjet printers, and the fact that they often can print in color for little more than the cost of black and white, has made them currently a more popular type of printer for home use—and is making them grow in popularity in offices as well. But as the price of color xerographic printers continues to fall, and their quality improves, I expect to see color xerographic printers achieve preeminence in the office, and eventually corner the market for home use, too.

Squirting Ink Printers

Another traditional way to make marks on a surface is by painting them. That means, in its essence, by putting a colored liquid on the surface and letting it dry. This is the basic technology behind what we term *inkjet printers*. These printers spray a liquid ink onto the page. Most of them are descended from the dot matrix impact printers, and so the design of much of their internal mechanisms is quite similar to those earlier-generation printers. (Most inkjet printers have multiple jets vertically aligned on a carriage that moves horizontally across the page, for example.)

This category of printers covers a large range in terms of both quality and cost. The low-end inkjet printers are among the cheapest available for PCs today. The very high-end inkjet printers cost many times as much and are used for very demanding graphics arts applications. One reason for the range of prices is that the inexpensive printers in this category often rely on the PC's CPU to do much of the work. The trade-off in this is that you save money on the printer, but you may find that you can do very little else with your PC while it is printing—and these are some of the slowest PC printers, so you may find that you are locked out of other productive uses of your PC for longer than you can tolerate. Finally, realize that a lower cost to buy often translates into a higher cost to operate.

Pass the Crayons: Hot Wax Printers

Crayons are sticks of colored wax. Heat a crayon just to where it begins to melt, then touch it briefly to a piece of paper. You will leave a small amount of colored wax stuck to the paper where you touched it. This is the basis of several different kinds of hot wax printers.

One kind of hot wax printer can best be described as an inkjet printer that uses a solid ink that is melted before it enters the inkjets. A very different design uses a ribbon that carries the wax and that is as wide as the paper. Although this ribbon is in close contact with the paper along a line across the page, individual spots (pels) on that line are heated briefly. This melts the wax, which as it cools tends to stick more to the paper than to the slick surface of the ribbon's base material.

In the latter kind of hot wax printer, the individual spots can be heated in any of a really large number of ways. Electric sparks, tiny electrically heated wires, piezo-electric emitters of sound energy, lasers—you name it, somebody has probably used it to build this type of printer.

This category of printer is a strong competitor to color inkjet printers—sometimes achieving better print image quality—but so far, the price for most hot wax printers has kept them from achieving the level of market acceptance enjoyed by the low-end inkjet printers. On the downside, these printers are slower than almost all other ink-based printers, and the finish they leave may not be suitable to all needs or tastes.

The Sublime Printers: Dye Sublimation

Some solid materials don't melt when you heat them. Instead, they turn directly into a gas. (So-called "dry ice," which is solid CO_2, is an example of such a material.) We term this process *sublimation*. In dye-sublimation printers, a ribbon carrying a special colored material that can be sublimed is placed in close proximity to a specially treated paper. A spot on that ribbon is heated briefly. The dye there sublimes, and the resulting tiny gas cloud partially resolidifies on the paper. This is the basic process used in dye-sublimation printers.

An important point to notice is that the amount of dye that is transferred to any one pel can be controlled by regulating how much energy is dumped into the corresponding spot on the ribbon. Thus, this process inherently allows printing in a sort-of grayscale fashion—something many of the other processes are inherently incapable of supporting.

The list of methods that have been used to produce the spot heating of each pel in this class of printers is essentially identical to the list for the hot wax printers that use a pagewide ribbon. In fact, some printers can be used for either hot wax printing or dye-sublimation printing with just a change of ribbons and paper, and perhaps a resetting of some parameters used in the spot-heating mechanism by the driver software.

This category of printers includes some of the best ones for producing photographic quality color images, as well as some of the slowest. Speed notwithstanding, their image quality has made them favorites of graphics arts houses, both in the usual letter-size format and in large-format models capable of printing an entire tabloid page at once.

The superior image quality these printers can achieve at a relatively low cost has made this a popular type of printer in very small formats (4×6 or 5×7 inches, for example), as well. These printers can, in some cases, be driven directly by a digital camera to produce "instant" color snapshots similar in quality and ease of creation to those produced by a Polaroid camera.

Impact Printers for PCs

As I told you earlier, impact printers for PCs can either be formed-character printers or dot matrix printers. That might surprise you, because formed-character printers are rarely used with PCs today. Still, for historical accuracy, I want to mention them. And indeed, if you get a computer-printed paycheck or utility bill, it very possibly was printed by a formed-character printer attached, typically, to a computer that is larger than a PC.

Character Printers

Formed-character impact printers use shaped hammers to drive ink out of a ribbon in the shape of the letter or other symbol you want to print. Their chief advantage is that you can print very complex symbols in this way, without having to specify that shape anywhere inside the computer that is driving the printer. The principal disadvantage of this type of printer is exactly the converse of that statement. Because the shapes of the characters are fixed by the shapes of the hammers, the computer cannot alter them, even when you might want it to.

The only way to change fonts in such a printer, for example, is to remove and replace the entire set of hammers. Ordinarily, this is done by stopping the entire printing process and having some human being open the printer and change an object that carries all the hammers. And that is certainly not something you want to do many times per page of printed output.

Computer-Driven Typewriters (Daisy Wheel and IBM's Selectric Printers)

When PCs were young, the only affordable technology for printing really good-looking text was a computer-driven typewriter. The most common of these used a electromagnetically driven solenoid to pound a shaped hammer tip against the ribbon and drive the ink onto the page. The earliest of these printers were simply converted IBM Selectric typewriters with their "golf ball" typing element that tipped and rotated to bring various points on its surface into contact with the ribbon. But soon the industry settled on another design for the type element, in which the hammer tips were formed out of plastic and placed at the ends of narrow strips of plastic radiating from a central hub. This wheel-like arrangement of spokes around a central hub looks a little like a daisy flower, hence the name *daisy wheel printers*. Before a character can be printed, the computer must turn the daisy wheel to the correct orientation, so the properly shaped hammer tip is in front of the solenoid. The daisy wheel, its electromagnetically driven solenoid, and the ribbon mechanism travel together on a carrier from left to right and back again, and between passes, the paper is advanced vertically by a rolling action of a platen, just as has been standard for typewriters for many years. Naturally, this arrangement prints only one character at a time, just like a typewriter.

The Selectric's golf ball type element or another model's daisy wheel type element can easily be swapped for a different one to change the font. But "easily," here, is a relative term. Even though a person could do it in a few seconds (with practice), it takes long enough and takes enough human effort, that normally it just isn't done. Certainly not several times each page.

Standards: I want to make one thing very clear here. A *font,* in the way I am using the term here (which is the formally correct usage) means a particular *style* of a particular *typeface* in a particular *size.* For example, it might be 12-point Courier bold italic. In this example, Courier is the typeface, bold italic is the style, and 12-point is the size.

Many people incorrectly call *Times Roman* (just to name one common example) a font. But that is incorrect, because the size and style have not been specified. All this name really tells you is the typeface, which is the name for a family of fonts. True enough, when you get a "font file" for your PC, it is a single file that can be used to print any size letters, and often in any one of several styles. But this usage of the term font is actually a misnomer.

The computer-driven typewriters faded away quickly when laser printers got inexpensive enough for offices to use, and when inkjet and impact dot matrix (wire-in-head) printers got good enough to create acceptable-quality typing for home use. There were at least three excellent reasons to stop using computer-driven typewriters. The first was their miserable speed (faster than a human typist, but vastly slower than a page printer). The second was their relative font inflexibility. The third reason was the noise they made.

Line Printers

The other principal kind of formed-character impact printer is the *line printer*. These are still in use in many large computer installations. They have never, however, been very popular as PC printers.

A line printer has a solenoid-driven hammer for each column of type on the page. In one variation, each hammer has a vertical strip of metal raised and lowered between it and the ribbon. On that strip are formed all the different character shapes it can print. When the strip is raised to the correct height, the hammer strikes it and the character is printed. This can be going on simultaneously for every column on the page, and in that fashion, an entire line of type can be printed at once.

An alternative design for a line printer uses a ribbon or chain of hammers. The set of character shapes is repeated on this chain many times. The chain is in continuous motion in a loop around all the hammers for all the columns. Each hammer strikes out at just the right time to imprint the correct character in its column position. In this kind of printer, not all the columns on a line are printed simultaneously, so it is somewhat slower than the design described a moment ago. On the other hand, only one set of hammers is needed, so this can be a somewhat less expensive kind of printer to manufacture.

The principal advantage of either kind of line printer is its speed. The disadvantages are inflexibility (changing fonts in these machines is really hard), noise, cost, weight, and size. These are more than enough reasons for their unpopularity as a printer for PCs. But they are as durable as tanks, which has kept them in use by many large businesses with lots of forms to print.

Noncharacter (Dot Matrix) Impact Printers

The first noncharacter impact printers for PCs were again based on the design of a typewriter. Only the hammer design was changed. Now, instead of a single hammer that drives a formed shape onto the ribbon, these printers have a vertical column of closely spaced round wires that strike the ribbon. Each one is driven by its own solenoid and is capable of printing a single dot on the page with each stroke. By moving the carriage horizontally only about one dot's width and striking the page again and again, this mechanism can use a single wire hammer to "draw" a horizontal line on the page. It is, of course, actually a row of dots, but if they touch one another it will look like a line.

While that is happening for one wire, similar things are happening for all the others above and below it. This means that in one pass across the page this mechanism can print, or not print, all of the dots within a rectangle whose height is the distance from the top wire to the bottom wire and whose width is the width of the page.

> **Note:** The name *dot matrix printer* comes from the notion that these printers form characters out of a rectangular array of dots. That array is called the *matrix*. The particular dots in that array that get printed define the character's shape. A dot matrix printer normally prints an entire row of characters each time it passes the head across the page. Each pass, therefore, corresponds to a line of "type," as was the case with the predecessor technology, the typewriter.

Because there is no need to wait for a character hammer to get into the right position for each character, these printers can be quite a bit faster than daisy wheel printers. However, they are not nearly as fast as laser printers or line printers.

After the hammer finishes its first pass across the page, the printer rolls the paper up just as far as the height of that rectangle, and then the head passes back across the page, again printing as it goes. Repeating this enough times will allow you to print dots on the page anywhere and everywhere you want.

I pointed out in Chapter 13, "Seeing the Results: PC Displays," that if you can control, one by one, all the spots in an image, you can form any image you want. Similarly, a dot matrix printer can print virtually any image you want. With fewer than ten wires, you can make a dot matrix printer that can print readable text with a single pass per line of type. It isn't pretty, but it is legible. That is what the original, inexpensive dot matrix printers were made to do.

They also could operate in a "near–letter-quality" mode in which they would make two passes across each line at slightly different vertical positions to allow putting in more dots for each character. That helped a lot, but it still didn't produce letters nearly as nice looking as those printed by daisy wheel printers. On the other hand, this technology does enable you to change fonts on-the-fly. Because the computer is dictating each and every pel that is to be printed, it can change the shapes or sizes of letters arbitrarily and often arbitrarily within a page.

Modern dot matrix impact printers have many more wires in the print head—24 is today's popular standard. This enables them to print better-quality documents, but still not nearly as nice as almost any laser printer can. Dot matrix impact printers continue to be used, despite their noise and relatively low print quality, because they are fairly cheap and they will print multipart forms. Only impact printers have the latter capability, so as long as there are multipart forms to be printed, impact printers of some kind will continue to be used. (Of course, the alternative to printing on a multipart form is to print each page of that form separately. And that is precisely what more and more businesses are now doing, using a xerographic printer or a high-end inkjet printer.)

Nonimpact Printers for PCs

All nonimpact printers for PCs are, in a sense, dot matrix printers. That is, they all control the printed image, pel by pel. Some of them even do so in groups of pel-rows, just as the stacked-wire impact dot matrix printers do. Others in this class print an entire page one row of pels at a time.

Describing Images to Be Printed

If a page to be printed contains only text, and especially if all of that text is to be printed in a single font, all you must tell the printer is which characters go where. A simple ASCII text file can be used to do this very nicely. If, on the other hand, you want to print highly formatted pages, possibly including some graphic images as well as type in various fonts, you must tell the printer what it is to do in a great deal more detail.

Bitmapped Page Images

The simplest solution is to tell the printer about each and every pel it is to print. This means sending the printer a bitmapped image of the page. In some cases, this is the only available means of telling a particular printer how to do its job.

Pure ASCII Text Pages

A printer that uses a formed-character mechanism obviously must be told only which characters to print in each column of each row. That is, after all, the limit of what it can do. Practically every PC printer in use today is capable of printing bitmapped images; and yet, most of the time we don't give them information in that form.

With the sole exception of some PostScript printers, every PC printer has built into it the necessary capability to convert a stream of ASCII characters into a corresponding stream of printed characters (in some default font) onto successive lines on the page, as if it were a formed character printer. If you don't do something special, it will interpret any arriving ASCII text as something it is to print in just this fashion.

Plotter Languages

Before we had any kind of PC printer other than a computer-driven typewriters, it was possible to make drawings by using a computer-driven plotter. This is a machine that essentially has a robotic arm of some type that holds a pen and can press that pen down or raise it up while moving around on the page in a prescribed manner.

Plotters are like the vector display devices discussed in the section "Raster-Scan Versus Vector Displays" in Chapter 12. Because they draw images one stroke at a time rather than one pel at a time, you must command them in a different way. (Plotters have now been all but replaced by large-page–size inkjet printers.)

Several languages were devised for sending commands to a computer-driven plotter. Hewlett-Packard's HPGL is perhaps the best known. Later, an industry-standard graphic file format was developed for holding descriptions of computer images of all kinds, including those for plotters. This file format is called Computer Graphics Metafile (CGM). These languages are still sometimes used with PCs, but mostly they matter to us now because they led the way to the page description languages used more commonly today.

Page Description Languages

When Hewlett-Packard introduced the LaserJet, it also introduced a new way to specify how a computer-generated page should look. Its new Printer Control Language (PCL) was primarily intended to control the font, size, style, and placement of letters on a page. It had some provisions for other, more graphic elements, but those clearly were not its main focus. (You'll sometimes see this language referred to simply as PCL, but also sometimes as HP-PCL, in recognition of its source.)

Not long after that, Apple Computer introduced its LaserWriter printer. With it, Apple bundled another new page description language, Postscript, which had been developed at Adobe. A major difference between PostScript and PCL is that PostScript is intended to be a totally general-purpose page description language. Indeed, with suitable hardware, a computer running PostScript can become a general-purpose computer. It has provisions for handling disk storage of information and many other things that the makers of PCL apparently never contemplated including in a page description language. (Observers at the time noted that it was ironic that the most powerful computer being marketed by Apple—and it was more powerful by a large margin than the Lisa, which was Apple's best other computer—was the one contained in its LaserWriter.)

> **Historical Aside**
>
> Much has been made of how the Apple Macintosh's graphical user interface and "ease of use" won the hearts and minds of the graphics arts community. Even today, more Macs than PCs are used in that industry, although they are a tiny minority of the personal-scale computers used in most other industries. Likely, the real reason for that bias was first and foremost the great graphic design power that PostScript gave to designers who used the Apple LaserWriter.

Both of these general page description languages (generically abbreviated as PDLs) have been substantially improved and extended over the 15 or so years since their introduction. PostScript, as the more fully fleshed-out concept initially, has needed much less in the way of extension. The current version of PostScript is 3, but many printers that respond only to the older, PostScript 2 are still being sold. (There are also some brands being sold with a "clone PostScript" page description language included. These generally work pretty well, but occasionally they will trip up in processing a PostScript print job, especially if it uses some of the more unusual PostScript operations.) HP's PCL has undergone many more revisions and a much larger expansion of its scope. It now is quite comparable to PostScript in its graphic power, control, and flexibility. The most recent release of PCL is 6 (but again, many of HP's printers, and those from its competitors, are still being shipped with support for only some earlier version of PCL—in some cases, going all the way back to HP-PCL version 2).

> **Warning:** The flexibility you have with a good page description language, combined with the power to control every step of the process of preparing documents—from creating the text to formatting the output—has led some PC users into some very bad habits. They go hog wild putting multiple fonts on a page. This is excusable. After all, they never had any training as typographers or graphic designers. But it is regrettable, nonetheless.
>
> Pages like that look ugly. With modern PC printers, you have even more power to create documents that are absolutely stunningly beautiful or ones that could qualify for the "Document Hall of Shame." Generally, good graphic design rules recommend that you use on any one document at most several sizes of a single typeface (or maybe two faces), and in differing styles (italic or not). In this case, more is definitely not better—at least most of the time.

Smart Page Printers

When HP introduced the LaserJet and when Apple introduced the LaserWriter, the common personal computers of the day to which these printers were to serve as peripherals were simply not very powerful. They were not nearly powerful enough to do all the computing needed to rasterize pages described in PCL or PostScript in a reasonably short time. (To *rasterize* a page is to compute the color for each of the pels on the entire page. The name comes from the notion that those pels can be organized into rows just like the pels on a raster-scan video display.) This is why those companies made their printers with a very powerful computer built into each one. Those computers were dedicated to just the one job of rasterizing pages.

This makes them what I call *smart page printers*. You send such a printer a description of the page in either PCL or PostScript, and it will figure out what the page is to look like and then print it. Not only does that mean that these printers need a lot of computing power, it also means that they must have quite a lot of RAM in which to hold the page image they are computing. Only after the entire file has been processed can they be sure it is safe to begin printing any portion of it. This is so because both PCL and PostScript describe pages in a way that is somewhat like the way a vector art file describes an image. They use the display list concept. That means that the very last item in the file might be telling the printer about a header line that is to go at the very top of the page.

Back when these printers first came on the market, enough RAM for a full page frame buffer could cost a small fortune—more than the rest of the printer's parts put together. So a strategy was devised to enable us to print the page in pieces, called *bands*. In this strategy, one might have a RAM buffer that is only large enough to hold, for example, one-tenth of a page. The computer that is rasterizing the image will pretend that it has a full page buffer to work with. It then merrily rasterizes the entire image and deposits that information into that imaginary frame buffer. Only one-tenth of those locations have actual RAM; in the rest of the locations, the information "written" is actually simply discarded. If that real RAM is located at the top of the page image, that top one-tenth of the page can be printed when the computer has completed rasterizing the entire page. Next, the RAM is cleared, and its addresses reassigned to the next tenth of the frame buffer. The computer then must redo the entire process of rasterizing the file, from the beginning to the end. When it finishes, the next tenth of the page can be printed. This continues, with the paper advancing through the printer in spurts, until the entire page has been printed.

That strategy works, and it saves on the cost of RAM, but it obviously also makes printing pages take much longer. Now that RAM is (relatively) cheap, it makes more sense to be sure your page printer has enough RAM so it can rasterize the entire page image just once and then print it as a whole. (Furthermore, this will ensure that you don't get lines across the page where the bands end, which can happen if the paper-moving mechanism cannot be stopped and restarted gracefully.)

All of these smart page printer ideas have been applied to page printers using each of the principal printing technologies. Thus, you can have an inkjet page printer, a xerographic page printer (using a laser, an array of LEDs or an LCS array), or a hot wax or dye-sublimation page printer. In all cases, the most common way those printers are supplied is with a very powerful computer inside of them to rasterize the page images. Some of these printers come equipped to interpret PCL files; some "understand"

PostScript files; a few can do either; and all of them also can accept a pure bitmapped image of the entire page, or of any portion of a page, if that is what you want to send it.

One advantage to PCL as a language for controlling a printer is that if you just send some ASCII text to a PCL printer, it will print what you send it in some default font. (You must be sure to include the Form Feed character to tell it when to print and eject the page.) A pure PostScript printer can print an ASCII text file only if you first wrap the text inside a short PostScript program.

"Dumb" Page Printers

PCs are much more powerful than they were a dozen years ago. Pages of text or even of images aren't all that much more complex than they were back then. So now our PCs are capable of doing the rasterizing job every bit as well as the computers in our printers.

Some companies have capitalized on this fact. They point out that if you buy a very fast computer, you can then buy (from them) a very inexpensive printer that can print images that are just as good as those from a much more expensive printer. This will work because these inexpensive, "dumb" printers don't have any computer inside. They depend instead on a software program running in your PC to do all that work and then ship out just the pels to be printed to the printer. All it can do is print a bitmapped image from that string of pels.

These companies also point out that the money you are investing in your PC can be put to good use when you are printing and also when you are not, whereas the investment you make in a computer that is built into a printer can do you some good only when you are actually printing something. This argument has merit, and it certainly has convinced some PC owners to get a much more graphically capable printer than they otherwise would have invested in. There is a downside to this approach, of course. If all your PC's power is going to be consumed in the rasterizing task for the next hour, then during that time you aren't going to be doing much of anything else with it. It also means that you must have a lot of free RAM and free disk space on your PC for this strategy to work.

To cite just one example, I have a tabloid (20×12-inch page size) dumb page printer that can use either the hot wax or the dye-sublimation printing process to print page images in full color at 300 dots per inch resolution. This means that there are 20×12×300×300 pels per page. That is 21.6 million pels. For full color, I must store 3 bytes for each pel. This isn't possible unless I can give the software rasterizing program at least 62MB for its frame buffer, in which it will create the image. In practice, the program spools most of that information to a disk file, so I can get away with merely a few megabytes of free RAM. But I find that unless I have a couple of hundred megabytes of free disk space, the printer simply fails to print the page at all!

Getting the Color (Almost) Right

I haven't said much about color printers up to now, but nearly everything I have said applies to them just as much as it does to black-and-white printers.

Color Models

Monochrome (black-and-white, or any single color and white) printed pages require knowing for each pel just how black (or colored) it shall be. Many printers allow each pel to be only fully black or fully white. Some permit gray values as well. To print images in color, first you must understand how we see colors and how we can be fooled by the clever use of just a few colors of ink into thinking we are seeing a much wider range of colors. This is an area of psychophysics and technology that I have already explained in connection with PC displays. So, if you skipped Chapter 13, I suggest you turn to it now and read at least the section on color models.

> **Technical Note:** One problem with all color image reproduction technologies is the issue of the total range of colors that can be reproduced. Human eyes can see an amazing range of colors, considering that we are sensitive to only about one octave (a two-to-one frequency range) of light waves. The technical term for the range of colors we can see, or that a given technology can reproduce, is the *color gamut*. It turns out that the color gamut for RGB (red, green, blue) video displays is markedly less than the total color gamut humans can perceive. Similarly, the color gamut for each printing technology is a subset of all the colors we might want to print—and worse, it is not the same subset as that of a video display.
>
> One way printer manufacturers have dealt with this problem is by using more than three ink colors. Monochrome printers use a single color. Traditional color printing processes for reproducing photographs and the like use the four so-called *process colors* (cyan, magenta, yellow, and black). Recently, some printer manufacturers have introduced models that can print in six or even seven distinct colors. Each added color expands the color gamut that a printer can achieve, albeit by an ever-decreasing amount, so adding still more colors than seven is not likely to help noticeably.

Printed images on paper (or on a transparency for use in an overhead projector) are subtractive images. That is, you shine nominally white light on them and the inks on the page subtract some of that light before it is bounced back to your eyes. To create the appearance of a red pel, for example, you must subtract most of the non-red color in the light that gets reflected from it. That is usually done in printing by the use of a suitable combination of cyan and yellow inks, with possibly some black thrown in to lower the overall brightness of that pel.

> **Note:** There is another way to print colors, called *spot color* in the printing industry. Here, you use inks in each of the colors you care about. This can require the use of up to a dozen separate inks, and it is the only way to print documents with convincing golds and silvers, for example. But all common color printers for PCs do not use this approach. Instead, they use the more common four-color printing model with inks that are cyan (C), magenta (M), yellow (Y), and black (K).

Whichever mark-making technology is used (impact, xerographic, inkjet, hot wax, or dye sublimation) it can be done in color just as well as in black and white. Color printers are more complex, so they generally cost more to make and to buy. Likewise, they use more expensive *consumables*. This is the jargon term for the paper and ink you use when you print documents. In some printers, the ink comes on a ribbon; in others, it comes in another form.

Ribbons or Cartridges

Impact printers normally use a fabric ribbon that is soaked in ink. If they are color printers, commonly that ribbon will have four parallel stripes of different colors (CYMK). You can exchange that ribbon for a single color one when you want to print documents just in black (or any single color) and white. Doing so will save your expensive four-color ribbon for when you must print in color. When any one of the four stripes of color wears out, you must replace the entire four-color ribbon.

Color xerographic printers must have four supplies of *toner* (the "ink" for this type of printer). Some models will have each color in a separate container. Others will combine all four and perhaps even include the photosensitive drum unit as well. How much of the printer you end up replacing when you run out of a single color of ink (and the cost to do so) will vary, depending on which way your printer is constructed.

Inkjet printers can come with a unified ink supply or with separate containers for each color of ink. Naturally, when any one color runs dry in the unified supply version, you must replace (or refill) the entire unit. Hot wax printers that use solid sticks of colored wax are very much like inkjet printers with separate ink reservoirs. They can be reinked one color at a time rather easily. Hot wax printers that use a paper-wide ribbon must have their entire ribbon, with all four colors on it, replaced when it gets used up. This also applies to all dye-sublimation printers.

Color Correction Programs and Printer Profiles

Just as with color displays, color printers won't always print images that look exactly alike. Our eyes can be very sensitive to even minor variations in color in an image. Some companies are extraordinarily concerned that their logos, for example, be printed in exactly the "right" colors.

One way the printing industry has coped with this problem is by the creation of a standard set of color swatches. The most famous of these sets is called the Pantone colors. This trademarked set of colors comes in a special book. If the graphic designer has a copy and the printer also has a copy, when the designer specifies that a certain area shall be printed in Pantone number whatever, the printer can compare the actual, final printed pieces against his copy of the Pantone color set and see whether the color came out right—and if it does not, make suitable adjustments to the printing press and ink supply so that it will.

That is how designers in one place can be sure printers in another place get the printed colors to be "just so." A different problem arises when the designer (or anyone who creates color documents) wants to design the document on a computer screen and then be reasonably assured that it will look the same when it is printed out on paper on a printer attached to that same computer.

The colors you see on a computer monitor come from glowing phosphors. The colors you see on a printed page are created by absorption of a portion of the incident light by the inks on that page. These two very different ways of producing color often lead to the colors appearing quite different. Here is one example: If the incident light changes—for example, from white to yellow—the colors you see on the printed page will change (with every color shifting toward yellow). The colors on the computer monitor will change much less, and whatever changes do occur may seem to be in the opposite direction. This is because when the overall room light changes toward yellow, your brain attempts to compensate and now permits somewhat yellow things to appear to be white. And really white things then look somewhat bluish.

What you want is for the screen and page images to look the same in some specified set of standard conditions of room lighting, kind of paper, particular monitor, and so forth. This can be done, but it takes a bit of special modification of the video driver and/or the printer driver. These modifications go by the name *color correction*.

Color printers, just like the color monitors I described in the previous chapter, often are supplied with a special *printer profile* file. This file contains information on just how much of each of the four colors it must be commanded to print to achieve certain standard, blended colors. Such a profile might be prepared separately for each individual printer, or it might be one that applies, in an average way, to all printers of a given model.

The International Color Consortium (ICC) has worked on this problem extensively. They have crafted a number of color models and color-model transformation strategies. Their work has led to a standardized set of color correction profiles for a wide variety of color image creation devices.

Windows 98 incorporates color management support in what is termed its *Color Management Module* (CMM). The CMM contains ICC profiles for many different monitors and some printers. Printers that qualify for a Windows 98 logo must come with an ICC printer profile that you can add to that collection.

You can load a color correction profile for a monitor by going into the Display applet in Control Panel, selecting the Settings tab, and clicking on the Advanced button. Choose the Color Management tab, and you will see what has been loaded and have the opportunity to change it if you want. Similarly, the printer driver that sends color images to the printer will probably allow installation of a printer color correction profile. This informs that driver how to shade the colors in the image it sends out in order to make the resulting printed colors more nearly accurate representations of the image creator's intentions. Programs to create color images often also incorporate tools to compensate for the characteristics of your particular color printer.

By using some combination of all these tools (printer profile, driver adjustments, and image creation program adjustments), creating images both on your PC's screen and printed on paper that look very nearly alike should be possible, and in the case of ones that reproduce the appearance of some real objects, very nearly like those actual objects. Getting the colors almost right is, in fact, a relatively straightforward process with Windows 98 and its supported output devices. But getting it exactly right—which must include allowing for the slight individual deviations of the output of any given printer or monitor from others of the same brands and model numbers—is a tough job, even now, requiring specialized test equipment. When it is done right, though, the matching can be spectacularly good.

Summary

You now know the five basic mark-making methods used in PC printers. Each of the hundreds of models on the market uses only one or two of these five, and none of them uses anything else. You know that printers often have a default font (and you know that this means a prescribed typeface, style, and size) in which they will print ASCII text. You also know that most are also capable of being commanded to print much more complex page images.

I have explained to you the difference between a formed-character printer and a dot matrix printer, as well as the difference between printers that print a single character at a time, a line at a time, or a page at a time. You have been at least introduced to some of the issues that are special to color printers.

I pointed out that most PC printers have some pretty powerful computers inside, and that those printers that do not contain such a computer will in effect need to borrow the power of your PC in order to get their jobs done. Armed with all this knowledge, you can now analyze any printer you come across. You can understand both what it is likely to be capable of doing and what it will require in the way of support from your PC and from you to get it to keep on doing those things.

Understanding Standard PC Input and Output

Computers are useful only if information can get into them and back out of them. In this chapter, you'll learn about several of the most important technologies used to get information into and out of PCs.

> **Note:** In Chapter 7, "Understanding PC Processors," you learned how the CPU can send data to or receive data from either memory address locations or input/output (I/O) ports. Those ports are the logical interfaces for the CPU to everything external to it (other than memory). In this chapter, you will learn more about input/output ports, but focusing on the interfaces between the PC system unit and the world beyond it. Please try not to let the similarity of name and description confuse you; but if it does, you can be assured that you are hardly the first person to be confused in this way.

Some Special-Purpose I/O Interfaces

The keyboard is one input device that is so much a standard part of a PC that it has, from the beginning, had its own special-purpose interface. Our modern PCs often have several other obviously dedicated, special-purpose input or output interfaces.

In Chapter 12, "Getting Your PC's Attention: Input Devices," you learned how keyboards and mouse devices function as information inputs to your PC. You didn't learn about the hardware interface these devices use at that point because the interfaces used for the keyboard and mouse resemble in many ways one of the multipurpose I/O interfaces (the serial port). Later in this chapter, you'll learn about the serial, parallel, and USB ports. The discussion of the sound inputs and outputs appears in Chapter 20, "How to 'Wow' a Human." You'll learn about the video output interface later in this chapter, and the signals that pass over that interface are discussed in Chapter 13, "Seeing the Results: PC Displays."

Talking Through a Tiny Pipe: Serial Ports

PCs move information around internally, either one byte at a time (on eight parallel wires) or several bytes at a time (using even more wires). This is perfectly practical inside the system unit, and quite valuable because all the bits of a byte arrive at their destination together and the maximum possible number of bytes are transferred each second. This, of course, is precisely how the various internal buses—PCI, ISA, and so on—in your PC work. (For a refresher on buses, take a look at Chapter 15, "Understanding Standard PC Input and Output.")

This is not so practical outside the system unit. At least, it isn't always the best way to go. If you are sending information a relatively short distance—say to your monitor or perhaps even to a printer nearby—you can use a multiwire cable to carry data in many parallel bit paths similar to those inside the system unit. If you want to send information a longer distance, and especially if you aren't concerned with achieving the ultimate in speed of communication, it's often more practical to use a totally different strategy called *serial communication*.

This approach is often used where a parallel cable would work, because there is no pressing need for speed. Your mouse and keyboard are examples of this. Some older printers also used serial connections to a PC. That is still an option on many modern printers, although most printers are now connected to PCs via a parallel port (and usually they need the fastest possible data link). Understand, of course, that there is nothing *inherently* slower about a serial link, relative to a parallel link. It just so happens that, as these methods have been implemented on our PC's ports, parallel data generally moves faster than serial data. (An exception to this is USB, which you'll read about later in this chapter.)

The serial approach becomes much more than just a measure of convenience when you want to send data for many miles. The cost of the wire alone argues against using a parallel cable for such a distance. A modem that connects your PC to the telephone line expects data in serial form, because that's what it must send (and receive) across the phone line—an example of a single-wire pair communications link.

Naturally, sending data a single bit at a time is generally slower than pumping it across a multiwire bus. Choosing a serial link is almost always a compromise between cost and speed. Modern PCs can send and receive data over a serial link at rates of up to 115,200 bits per second (bps).

Later in this chapter, you will learn about a much higher-speed version of the serial bus, called the *Universal Serial Bus (USB)*. In Chapter 13, I described another, even faster serial bus that is beginning to find favor for connecting a PC to a digital flat panel display. And in Chapter 16, "Faster Ways to Get Information Into and Out of Your PC," I discuss the IEEE 1394 super-fast serial bus (also known by the name FireWire). But first you need to understand the basics of serial communication and how it applies to the traditional, not-terribly-fast standard PC serial port.

Serial Communications Basics

The idea behind serial communication is quite simple: Just send 1 bit at a time. To send a byte, send each of its 8 bits, one after another. If you want some insurance that the byte gets where it's going without any of the bits being changed, you can have the serial link also send along a ninth (parity) bit.

In principle, you should need only a single wire—or actually a single pair of wires, because you need a ground wire over which the electric currents you send out can return—for serial communications. In practice, separate wires are normally used for the outbound and the inbound data, making a minimum of three wires in a serial communication cable (send, receive, and ground). Often, several more wires are added. These extra wires are used to signal things such as whether the receivers at each end are ready for incoming data.

Two common connector styles are used for standard serial ports on PCs. One is the DB9 (9-pin) connector; the other is a male DB25, which is essentially the same except that it has 25 pins instead of 9. Adapters are readily available to permit interconnecting devices and cables that have any combination of these two sizes of standard serial port connector.

What's a UART and What Does It Do?

People needed devices to convert data from several parallel wires into a succession of bits on a single wire and back again, long before there were such things as PCs. Several decades ago, engineers designed some integrated circuits to handle this task that are rudimentary by today's standards. The module that does this task is a *Universal Asynchronous Receiver/Transmitter* (*UART*).

There have been several generations of UART. The first popular model was called an 8250. This integrated circuit module could convert a single byte into serial bits and back again, and it could do this at a maximum rate of 9,600bps. (That is the maximum *guaranteed* rate; many individual chips could do much better than this.) This model was soon replaced by a 16450, which could convert a single byte at a maximum (guaranteed) rate of 115Kbps. It also was capable of working reliably with a faster bus on the parallel side, which was necessary as PCs began to run faster than the original 4.77MHz. Because of the overhead inherent in an asynchronous serial link, a data rate of 115Kbps translates to a top data transfer rate of about 11.5KBps.

> **Standards:** Notice that a lowercase letter *b* usually stands for a *bit,* and the capital letter *B* stands for a *byte* in these discussions. (Many folks get confused over this point, especially in connection with data communication speeds.)

An even later model of UART, the 16550, could transfer data at rates up to around 400Kbps, and it had some other even more important advantages. Those added advantages are explained in the section "How the 16550 Buffered UART Saved the Day" later in this chapter.

How Serial Data Is Sent

The serial data-sending process occurs like this: The CPU addresses the UART at one of the CPU's (internal) port addresses. It sends a byte of information to the UART over the system's (internal) I/O data bus. The UART picks up the data and stores it temporarily in a register inside the UART. At that point, the CPU is free to use the system bus for other purposes.

> **Technical Note:** The CPU actually uses eight consecutive I/O port addresses for its conversations with each serial port's circuitry. The first one (with the smallest address) is called the port's *base address*, and is used for the actual data transfers. The other ports are used for various control functions, including the means for setting the *serial communications parameters* for that serial port.

Now the UART serializes the data bits, sending them out one at a time over the serial communications link's outbound data wire. Because this is an asynchronous device, it can start this process at any time. (The other kind of serial communication device is a synchronous link device, which means that it will always operate in lock step to the clock of the receiving system at the other end of the link.)

It is possible to program a UART to send 5, 6, 7, or 8 bits per character. In most PC communications situations, you send either 7 data bits plus a parity bit or 8 data bits and no parity bit. Finally, the UART will wait 1, 1 1/2, or 2 bit-times before it begins to send the next byte. That waiting time is referred to as the *stop bit* (or bits).

The UART incorporates an internal clock that tells it when to send out the next bit of data. One cycle of this clock is a *bit-time*. You can program this clock to run at different rates. When you tell the UART what clock speed to use, how many data bits to send, whether to use parity (and if so which kind), and how many stop bits to use, you are setting the *serial communications parameters*.

It is vital that the UART at each end of the serial link be programmed in the same way. If not, the receiving UART will be unable to make sense of the signals it receives, and the overall link will fail.

Physical Characteristics of Serial Communications Signals

The actual voltages and currents sent on the serial link wires are not the same as the electrical voltages used in the system bus. Inside the PC's system unit, any voltage that is nearly 0 is seen as representing a binary 0 value. Any voltage that is over about 2 volts is seen as representing a binary 1 value.

On the serial link, 0s are represented as Space values, which means by a positive voltage (greater than 3 volts, but less than 12 volts) or a positive current. Binary 1s are represented by a Mark level that is a similar size negative voltage or current. Figure 15.1 shows these details. One advantage to this approach is that a broken wire is readily detectable, because it will result in a lack of voltage or current, which the receiver knows is not legal for either 0s or 1s. Additionally, as you've previously read, serial links support moving data over longer distances.

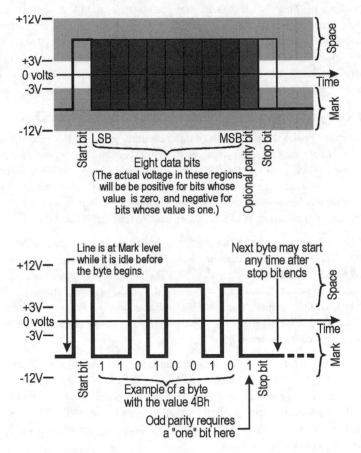

FIGURE 15.1

Asynchronous serial data communications protocol.

How Serial Data Is Received

At the other end of the line is another UART. Its job is to undo what the first UART did. That is, it must notice each incoming packet (which it does when the transition from a Mark level to a Space level occurs, marking the beginning of a start bit). Then, it must look at the right times for each bit of the data byte to arrive and store those values in a register. After it has received the entire byte (plus its parity bit if it has one) and checked the parity (if that is the mode in which it is operating), the UART is ready to present the complete byte on its output port.

When the UART has the data byte ready, it "rings the CPU's doorbell." That is, it asserts an interrupt request. When the CPU acknowledges that interrupt and requests the data from the UART, it sends the data byte onto the system's internal I/O bus, from which the CPU will read it. Notice that the CPU is not required to accept the byte immediately, because this is an asynchronous serial communication. The CPU normally waits at least until it is finished with the current instruction it is processing, and it might wait much longer than that.

Notice something else: If the CPU waits too long, it might lose some of the incoming data. Most of the time, the first few bits of the next byte arriving across the serial link will already be coming into the UART while the UART is waiting for the CPU to pick up the just-received byte. If the CPU fails to pick up that received byte in time, the UART simply discards it and replaces it with the next byte it received. (It also signals the CPU that a byte of received data has been lost—an event referred to as a *data overrun*.)

How the 16550 Buffered UART Saved the Day

Keeping up with the UART can be quite a burden on the CPU, especially at the higher rates of data transmission commonly used in PCs today. Every time a byte is received or a byte has been sent out, the CPU must go through a fairly convoluted process of saving its place in whatever task it is performing, switching to the communications program that handles the data sending and receiving, sending or receiving the next byte, then saving the state of that program and switching back to the original task.

To help reduce this burden, an improved version of the 16450 called the 16550 was created. The most obvious difference—and it is significant—is that this version includes two 16-byte FIFO buffers inside the UART. (The 16550 is also guaranteed to run at data rates faster than what is guaranteed to work on the 16450 or 8250, but in most PC applications it is not called upon to do so.) A *FIFO* buffer is simply a fancy name for a queue. The name stands for First In First Out, meaning that bytes are pushed in one end and pop out the other end in the same order.

Consider what this means for data transmission: It is now possible for the CPU to dump up to 16 bytes of data in a block into the UART for it to send out; then the CPU can go away and do other things until the UART has completed that task. Only then must the CPU stop its other work to dump another 16 bytes in the UART. Thus, even without constant attention from the CPU, the UART will keep busy sending out the bytes (as serialized bits) just as fast as it can.

The effect of buffering is even more important for data reception. Now the UART can accumulate up to 16 bytes of received data before the CPU must get them in order to prevent the UART from losing any of the incoming information. (Normally, you set up the UART so it will signal the CPU after its receive buffer is almost full—typically, when it has 14 bytes in it—to give the CPU some time to respond before that buffer it totally filled. If you experience lots of data overruns when downloading files, you might want to set this number to something less than 14.)

Both for incoming and outgoing data, the buffering of data on the UART saves a lot of overhead time that the CPU would otherwise have to waste as it constantly jumps between servicing the UART and whatever else it was doing. (Incidentally, shortly after the 16550 was released, problems relating to how it handled data in its buffers were detected. These were rectified with the 16550A UART and its subsequent models.)

What You Must Know and Do About Serial Communications

Modern PCs often have the serial port interface electronics included in the motherboard chip set. In today's systems with their large-scale integrated circuits, you probably won't actually have a 16550, or other UART chip, on the motherboard. You will probably have the functionality of one or more such chips hidden away inside a Very Large-Scale Integrated Circuit (VLSI) chip that is part of the motherboard chip set. The UART circuitry is there, but it might not be activated, or might be only partially activated, until you take some specific actions. This statement also applies to many of the plug-in cards you can purchase to add extra serial or parallel ports to your PC.

The motherboard BIOS setup program often includes entries to enable or disable the serial ports. It might also enable you to set the default communications parameters for those ports. Even though the UART circuitry has buffers, they can do nothing unless you explicitly instruct that circuitry to enable buffering. Some BIOS setup programs enable you to do this; most do not. However, Windows 95 handles all this for you.

Serial Links Without the Wires

Serial links usually include a serial port interface on the PC, a cable from the PC to some peripheral device, and a serial port interface on that peripheral device. Sometimes, you can have the effect of all that without using a cable. This is the growing field of wireless connectivity. Several physical technologies are used in lieu of passing an electrical current down a copper wire.

One technique uses infrared light. This is essentially the same technology used in most TV and VCR remote controls. In desktop PCs, this is simply an attachment to a standard serial port that converts the electrical signals into light signals and back again. The form of those light signals is a modulation on a carrier wave imposed on the light beam. This type of wireless serial port is particularly popular on laptop computers.

The Infra-red Data Association (IrDA) has defined a standard called, appropriately, *IrDA*. Devices that are compliant with this standard are capable of linking two standard serial ports at any data rate up to the normal maximum for such ports of 115Kbps. Special high-speed versions of these infrared links can achieve data rates of up to 4Mbps. Those higher-speed devices are used to link network interface adapters instead of normal serial ports. You'll learn more about network interface adapters of all types, this one included, in Chapter 24, "The PC Reaches Out, Part Two: Through the NIC Node."

The Universal Serial Bus (USB)

For about the past two years, most new PCs have come equipped with one or two connectors for a special, new version of the standard serial port. This new version is called the Universal Serial Bus, or USB for short. (I will, at times, refer to "the USB bus." This is, I know, a redundancy, but I find that it is useful—as most of us don't hear the implied word "bus" when we hear just the acronym "USB.")

Until well into 1998, there were only a very limited number of devices on the market that could make use of these ports. Now, however, they are in plentiful supply. So, at last, the delights of USB connectivity are starting to be felt widely.

The USB port is in many respects very much like a traditional PC serial port, but there are also some important differences—ones that have a profound impact on how it feels to use a USB-connected device. It is much simpler to set up and use USB-enabled devices, and using them enables us to avoid all the nightmares associated with IRQ and port address conflicts that plagued us in the past when adding new peripheral devices to a PC.

Key Differences Between USB and a Standard PC Serial Port

A USB cable has only four wires. Two carry data (in both directions), and two carry power (to allow the use of at least some USB peripherals without having to plug them into wall power or run them off batteries). This is in sharp contrast to the 9 or 25 connections required for the older-style serial port.

Despite having fewer wires, a USB can transfer data much faster than the original PC serial port. This is possible because the basic signaling rate on a USB cable is either 1.5Mbps or 12Mbps. Even the lower of these two speeds is over ten times faster than the traditional PC serial port's top speed. The bus switches dynamically between these two speeds as needed to accommodate all the devices that are currently attached to it. If you use only low-speed devices, the cables may be unshielded, and the bus clock will never rise to the upper rate. If you attach any high-speed devices, you probably will need to use shielded cables for all the USB connections in order not to have problems with radiated signals when the bus switches into its higher-speed mode.

The USB cables are designed to be nearly goof-proof. The end that connects to a PC, or to a hub through which it will send data toward the PC (and receive data from the PC), has a flat, rectangular shape. (You can see one of these connectors in Figure 15.3, later in this chapter.) At its other end, a USB cable has a very different, nearly square connector. This marks the end that spits out data to a peripheral device or accepts data back from that device.

A traditional serial port uses one port address range and one IRQ line to support a single peripheral device. A USB port uses just the same amount of the PC's internal resources—one IRQ line and a modest number of adjacent I/O port addresses—but it can support up to 127 external peripheral devices.

USB Hubs

The USB strategy for connectivity permits devices to be connected either directly to the PC, or indirectly through one or more hubs. Each hub has a hub controller, a signal repeater, and multiple inputs for attaching USB devices—called *downstream ports,* plus one output—called the *upstream port*—for connecting back to the PC or to another hub that is closer to the PC on the USB "tree" of hubs and devices.

Each USB-enabled peripheral device may also have a hub built into it, or you can get standalone USB hubs, and you may use as many hubs as you need in order to attach all the USB peripherals you want (up to the limit of 127 USB peripheral devices and hubs). Figure 22.6, in the section "What to Look for in a Multipurpose PC," in Chapter 22, "Why Mobile PCs Must Be Different," shows a laptop PC with an external USB hub and, attached via that hub, a USB-enabled keyboard, a USB-enabled mouse, and a USB-enabled sound system.

> **Standards:** In USB jargon, a USB-enabled device that does something (generates and/or consumes data) is called a *function.* One that includes more than a single function (for example, a keyboard with a built-in pointing device) is called a *compound device,* and it must also have a hub with the several functions it contains acting as nondetachable devices coming off that hub. Simple hubs are ones that serve only to connect other USB devices; they have no other function.

What sorts of peripheral device might have a USB hub built into it? The first, and most obvious, candidates are USB-enabled devices that sit out in front of your PC where you may find it handy to have USB ports. For example, you might have a USB-enabled keyboard with ports into which you could plug a USB mouse and possibly some other USB devices. But any manufacturer can build a hub into any PC peripheral device and thereby enable you to add other USB devices in that vicinity. Unused USB hub inputs are simply ignored by the system, and thus cause no problems.

A PC's monitor needs to get the information it displays over a cable that enables much faster information transfer than the USB bus can accommodate. So, it cannot use just a USB connection. (That is, no PC monitor can be a USB device itself.) Still—just for the convenience it adds—some monitor makers are including a USB hub in their product. This provides another convenient place for you to attach a USB keyboard, mouse, or other device. Eventually, these monitors will be built with just one cable for both video and other services. But that isn't likely to happen until we get to the next higher-speed general-purpose serial bus, the IEEE 1394 bus (also known as FireWire). I will expand on this point in Chapter 16.

The USB port on the back of your PC (or both of them if you have two) is connected to what is termed the *root hub*. Each external hub may run off the power it receives from the root hub over the USB bus, or it may have a power supply that plugs into a wall out-let. The use of external power for a hub is necessary only when you are going to plug into it some USB devices that require a lot of power and that don't have a source for that power.

What You Need to Use USB

You cannot use USB peripherals unless your PC supports the USB. That support means that the PC must have three things.

The first, and most obvious, requirement for USB support is that the PC must have one or more USB ports into which you can plug your USB peripheral devices. But that is not enough. The second requirement is that the PC's motherboard chip set must include a USB host controller. Finally, the PC's operating system must also support USB function-ality, including its plug-and-play aspects.

All recent motherboard chip sets have included the USB host controller function. This host controller must comply with one of these two standards: the Universal Host Controller Interface (UHCI) or the Open Host Controller Interface (OHCI). Windows 98 (and also Windows 95, starting with the OSR 2.1 upgrade) provides the third requirement through its plug-and-play support for USB devices. (Windows NT 4.0 does not support USB.)

If you don't have a PC with these things, you can buy an add-in bracket with the USB ports, but that works only if your motherboard has a place to attach it, as well as chipset and BIOS support for it. Even then, you must also be sure you are using an operating system that supports USB.

Using USB

Most wonderful about USB is how it works when you use it. If you have a PC that sup-ports USB (has the physical ports and hub controller, and is running a suitable operating system), you simply plug in the USB devices and they work—almost instantly. No fuss, no muss, no bother. They just work.

Well, what if they don't just work? What might have gone wrong? Of course, the first thing to check is whether your PC supports USB. Next is to see whether that support has been enabled. Many BIOS setup programs include an option to turn USB support on or off. (You might turn it off if you are short on available IRQs and you don't plan to use USB. When you decide you want to use USB, you will then have to turn it back on.)

And what if that doesn't do the trick? Intel has provided a nice troubleshooting tips document at this URL:

`http://support.intel.com/support/createshare/camerapack/usb/23729.htm`

The best news is that you are quite unlikely to need its help. For most of us, USB simply works on the first try and pretty much every time thereafter.

The USB Communication Protocol

How is it possible for a single IRQ and port address range to serve 127 peripheral devices when, up until now, it sufficed to serve only a single peripheral device? The answer to that lies in how communication is managed over a USB bus, and it also explains why USB is, in certain respects, even more wonderful than I have told you up to this point.

The short answer is that the PC supports only one device via those port addresses and that IRQ level. That one device is the *USB host,* which is the collection of software and hardware inside the PC system unit that supports the USB bus. That host, in turn, supports all the attached peripherals over that bus.

The host is in charge of the USB bus. It is the sole master of this bus. No other USB devices are permitted any real control; they are, therefore, termed *slaves.* When you plug in a USB device, the host notices this fact and then starts a "conversation" with that device to determine what it can do and what software support it requires from the PC. The host then loads any needed device drivers dynamically. Likewise, when you unplug a USB device, the host notices this, unloads any drivers it had loaded, and otherwise notifies the system that this device is no longer available.

Furthermore, when that device wants to send data to the host, it must wait for the host to tell it when to send that data. The host must poll each of the attached devices constantly to be sure it permits any pending data to be sent to it.

The host controller starts a new round of communication every 1/1000 of a second. It sends out a Start of Frame packet and then follows that with other packets as it deems them necessary. If it wants data from a peripheral device, it asks for it by sending an inquiry packet addressed to that target device. If it has data to deliver, it sends it in a packet addressed to that target device.

Messages on a USB bus are always one of four kinds. The first are *control* messages. These are how the host learns about the peripherals and also how the peripherals alert the host to their needs for service. The second are *interrupt* messages. Third are *isochronous* messages. The last are called *bulk* messages.

The essential idea of isochronous and bulk messages is that all the data transfers can be divided into two kinds according to their urgency and their need for accuracy. If you are sending digital information that represents music or conversation to a speaker or telephone, getting the message there in a timely manner is very important. There is little trouble caused if you should lose a few bits now and then. If you are transferring a computer program, however, or a critical data file, accuracy is your primary concern. The transfer can take as long as it must, but the data absolutely has to get through without any lost or altered bits.

Isochronous data transfers are used for the first of these two kinds of data transfer; bulk data transfers are used for the second kind. (The control and interrupt messages are, of course, not a part of this simple, two-way classification. If they were to be included, they would fall in with the bulk transfers as ones that must be transferred without error, but still they must be delivered in a timely manner. So they really are a separate kind from either isochronous or bulk, and the USB specification treats them separately.)

The USB host will set aside a portion of every millisecond-long frame for isochronous communications and use the remainder for any pending bulk transfers. Each device that requires isochronous communications can inform the host how much assured bandwidth it desires. The host will allocate that as a fraction of the total bandwidth by reserving for that device its designated share of each frame.

The host will not allow any more than 90 percent of the entire frame to be used up by isochronous requests. That ensures that bulk transfers will always get at least a little bit of the bandwidth; so those messages may be delayed some, but not forever.

I've just given you a lot of information on USB and how it works, but there is much more that I could have told you. If you want more details, I suggest you look at the actual bus specification, which you will find at the following URL:

http://www.usb.org/developers/docs.htm

For more information, including an Intel white paper on USB and a look at some of the variety of USB-enabled items that are available, check out this URL:

http://www.usbstuff.com/

The Keyboard Interface

The keyboard connects to the PC system unit via a special connector that can be used only for that specific purpose. In fact, it is just another serial interface, much like the more general-purpose serial ports I described in the last section.

The keyboard port's UART is a part of the *keyboard controller*. One key difference between this port and the standard serial port is that the buffer for the keyboard port is located in the PC's main memory, instead of being inside the keyboard controller circuitry. This means, among other things, that its contents are available for any program to pick up in any order that the program needs. The bytes stored there aren't just available in the order they were placed there. Also, that buffer can be relocated and enlarged if it turns out to be too small.

There are two commonly used connectors for keyboards on PCs, and now one new one as well. The most common connector used for older desktop machines is the 5-pin DIN. (The name comes from the acronym for the German standards agency that published the specifications for this connector family.) The male connector (the plug) goes on the keyboard cable; the female connector (the jack) is mounted on the PC's motherboard.

The other common design is a 6-pin mini-DIN connector. IBM pioneered the use of this connector for keyboards and mouse devices in its PS/2 line of computers, and it has become the favored connector for both keyboards and bus mouse devices in most modern PCs. (Bus mouse devices are discussed in the next section.) The 6-pin mini-DIN is virtually the only kind of keyboard connector used on portable or laptop PCs.

The newest variation is the USB connector. I've been using a Microsoft USB-enabled keyboard on one of my machines. It appears to be a standard Microsoft Natural Keyboard (with a PS/2-style, 6-pin mini-DIN connector at the end of its cable), plus a small adapter to enable me to plug it into a USB port. However, if you are using an older system whose BIOS was not designed to natively support USB, you might find that your USB keyboard won't work outside Windows 98—which has drivers to provide its own support. This could be a disaster, theoretically preventing you from having any keyboard access to your computer. However, in my tests on another PC, when a non-USB BIOS is present, the USB keyboard simply isn't recognized. When you try to boot, you'll get the familiar (to some of us) error that indicates that no keyboard is present, and you should press F1 to continue booting. (If anyone ever figures out precisely how to do that—press F1 on a keyboard that isn't present—please email and let me know!) In this circumstance, you'll be forced to plug in a standard PS/2 or DIN-5 keyboard before your system will even start.

Figure 15.2 shows the 6-pin mini-DIN plug on the end of the cable from the keyboard of our sample desktop system. Also in this figure is an adapter that accepts that plug on its far end and has the 5-pin DIN connector on the near end. With such an adapter, you can use a modern keyboard on an older PC. A reversed version of this adapter enables you to use older keyboards with newer systems. Wrapped around that adapter is the USB connector I mentioned in the preceding paragraph.

Figure 15.2

The 6-pin DIN on the left is the most popular connector for modern PC keyboards. The adapter in the middle allows use of such a keyboard with older PCs that have a 5-pin DIN keyboard port. The adapter at the right (and with its tail next to the keyboard cable) permits plugging this keyboard into a USB port.

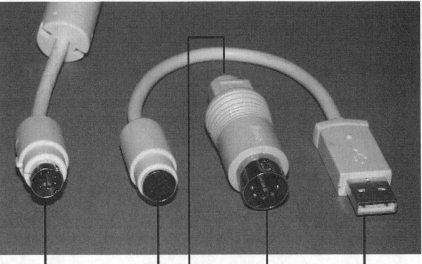

| 6-pin male PS/2-style keyboard cable plug | 6-pin PS/2 female connector accepts cable from keyboard | 5-pin male "DIN"-style keyboard cable plug | USB cable plug |

Bus Mice Versus Serial Mice Versus USB Mice

Mouse devices can come with any of five kinds of plugs at the end of their cables. One kind is the PS/2 6-pin mini-DIN mentioned earlier; another looks similar to the PS/2 6-pin mini-DIN but is electrically and physically different. It is used by a variety called *bus mice*. Two more use female DB9 and DB25 connectors and are called *serial mice*. They are for use with standard serial port connectors on a PC. Finally, we now have USB-enabled mice, and those have (of course) a USB plug on the ends of their cables. Many PCs now come with a PS/2 mouse port. Others can have a bus or PS/2 mouse port added by using a plug-in option card. Most modern PCs now come with one or two USB ports.

Some laptop computers come with a single 6-pin mini-DIN connector that can be used for either an external keyboard or an external mouse, but not for both at once. These computers typically have both a keyboard and a pointing device internally, so you wouldn't need to use this port at all, or you could use it for a keyboard or a pointing device—whichever internal device you most want to replace with an external one.

There are only a few differences between a bus mouse port and a standard serial port. Both work in the same manner. However, commonly the bus mouse ports (the ones with the mini-DIN connector) use an IRQ value in the upper range (8–15), whereas the standard serial ports (with DB9 or DB25 connectors) usually can be set to use only one of the lower IRQ values (most often 3, 4, 5, or 7). The only other difference between the dedicated mouse ports and standard serial ports is in the CPU port addresses over which they communicate with the internal system I/O bus.

> **Tip:** USB mouse devices are also very similar to serial or bus mouse devices. But they do have some significant differences that you may want to keep in mind. Microsoft did not create a USB mouse simply by adding an adapter to a serial mouse. It had to redo its internal parts as well as change the plug on its cable. Furthermore, although a USB mouse is supposed to work just fine on any desktop PC with USB support, it may work a little bit differently on a laptop PC. In particular, the PC99 specification (to which most PCs are built now) says that any desktop PC must have USB support built into its BIOS, and that this support must include activating and using any USB-attached keyboard or mouse, even if those devices are connected to the PC through an external USB hub (but not through more than one hub). But it also permits portable computers that have both a keyboard and a pointing device built in to be manufactured without BIOS support for those external USB devices. So you may find that you must use the built-in keyboard and pointing device for anything you do with such a laptop machine before Windows 9x loads. After Windows 9x is loaded, you will find that the external USB mouse and keyboard are fully supported by Windows (which ignores whatever the BIOS does or does not do in this regard), and you may subsequently plug them in or unplug them as many times as you like— generally without causing any problems.

Mouse devices typically communicate at a fairly low data rate. The most common speed is a mere 1,200bps, but they will adapt to whatever speed the serial port is set to, up to some limit. Even the low default data rate is plenty, because all a mouse must do is tell the PC each time it moves a unit distance (usually 1/100 of an inch) in either the X or Y direction and each time one of its buttons is pressed or released. There's no point in darting your mouse around faster than it can track. Slow down, and you may avoid mouse-related repetitive stress injury.

There are several reasons to be concerned about the difference between serial and bus mouse device. One is that if you have too few serial ports on your PC, using a bus mouse can free up one of the serial ports for some other use. Of course, you can do this only if you have a bus mouse connector available.

The second reason for paying attention to the bus-versus-serial mouse issue is much like the first: If you are running out of available interrupt request lines for your serial ports, switching to a bus (or PS/2) mouse (which usually uses one of the upper-eight IRQ lines) might help. Most serial ports can use only one of the lower-seven IRQs, and mostly those are taken for system uses, so the remaining few can't do all the things you'd like them to do.

Naturally, if your PC has USB support, getting a USB mouse is an even better alternative. It will not only free up an interrupt and the port address range used by a standard serial port, it will also permit you to use multiple other USB devices on the same port address and interrupt line as the USB mouse.

This discussion has described only how the mice connect to your PC. The discussion in Chapter 12 covers what they say to the PC (mouse protocols).

Combining the Keyboard and a Pointing Device

Some keyboards now come with a pointing device built in (usually either a trackpad or pointing stick). Other keyboards sport a mouse port on the side or back, so you can plug in a standard mouse there instead of into your PC's system unit. This is mostly just a matter of packaging. At the end of the cable from such a keyboard you will typically find that it splits into two cables, ending in two separate plugs. One goes into the special keyboard connector on the back of the PC system unit. The other connector goes into either a mouse port or a standard serial port near the keyboard connector. (Again, the exception is if you have a USB keyboard with a pointing device. It can and probably will have only one cable terminating in a USB plug.)

The Faster Output Path That Can Work Both Ways

When IBM introduced the PC, it offered an optional printer interface card and printer. Breaking with what had been customary for small-scale computer makers up to that time, IBM used a parallel interface on its printer port. Such an interface uses a separate wire for each bit of the bytes of data being sent to the printer. Thus, an entire byte can go to the printer at once. This approach enabled IBM's printer adapter to pump characters to the printer much faster than would have been possible with a serial communications link.

We now use parallel ports on our PCs that have far greater capability than the original IBM PC unidirectional printer port—but all of them are built on the same, solid foundation. So, I will first explain that original port in some detail, then go into the several ways in which that original design has been elaborated and improved upon in recent years. All of these versions are now included in an official standard called IEEE 1284, as I will explain in more detail shortly.

The Original IBM PC Unidirectional Printer Port

Clearly, you need at least eight ata wires (one for each bit in a byte) for a parallel port. In fact, many more than just eight wires are needed for this type of parallel-data-transfer interface. In the IBM printer port design, 17 wires are used for signals plus several more ground wires. Why so many signal lines? The printer port sends data to the printer by first putting the data bits on the eight data lines. Then, it sends a pulse called a *strobe* signal on another line to tell the printer that the byte to be sent is ready to go. After it receives the strobe signal, the printer reads that byte and, after it has finished, sends back an *acknowledge* signal on yet another wire to the PC. This tells the printer port circuitry that it's okay to prepare the next byte for transmission. Because of this tightly inter-locked handshaking protocol, the printer port can send data to the printer just as fast as the printer can accept it (and it won't send it any faster than that).

Five status wires enable the printer to ask the PC to wait if it is busy processing the data it has already received; or it can tell the PC when it is out of paper or when some error (such as a paper jam) has occurred. Four control wires enable the PC to tell the printer, for example, to reset itself or to move to the top of the next page.

Bidirectional Printer Ports

The intent of the original IBM PC printer port was simply, as its name suggests, to pump data to a printer. Soon it became clear that there were times when it was highly desirable for the parallel port to be capable of receiving data as well as sending it out. IBM includ-ed this capability in its next-generation computer, the PC/AT, publicizing it aggressively when it introduced the PS/2 line later. In fact, there are two ways to make a standard PC parallel port function in reverse. The method used by IBM in the PS/2 computers is to modify the circuitry so the data wires can be driven either by the port or by the peripher-al device to which it is attached. This method enables data input rates that are compara-ble to those achievable on data output.

Enhanced Printer Ports

Despite the limitations of parallel ports, they have been the fastest standard I/O hardware available on just about any PC. For this reason, lots of additional uses for them have been developed.

There are two classes of use for parallel ports that go beyond its original purpose. Because these two kinds of use involve different patterns of data transmission, they have led to the development of two different, improved standards for parallel ports.

One of these classes involves a fairly well-balanced use of both input and output, with data transfers in both directions needing to go as fast as possible. These uses include hooking up a CD-ROM drive, external hard drive, ZIP drive, or other mass storage medi-um to the parallel port. This strategy always runs slower than if these devices were directly connected to the PC's general-purpose I/O bus via a plug-in card with interface circuitry that has been optimized for that use. On the other hand, it's convenient to be able to hook up such an external peripheral device to a PC parallel port, perhaps load a driver program off a disk, and then use the device. For one example, this makes doing backups a breeze, and it also enables easy transfers of rather substantial amounts of data between PCs that are otherwise not connected. These two possibilities help explain why the ZIP drive has been such a smashing success.

The other class of extended use is for printers that must get much more data for each page they print than just the characters you might see there. (In particular, this describes page printers, especially those printing large bitmapped graphic images.) These printers might occasionally need to send data back to the PC—sometimes even a fairly substantial amount of data—but those occasions are fairly rare compared to the times they need huge amounts of data shipped out to them.

The two new designs for "super parallel ports" have been combined with the two methods for using standard parallel port hardware bidirectionally into an official standard published by the Institute for Electrical and Electronic Engineers (IEEE) in 1994. It named this the IEEE 1284 standard.

Any peripheral device that conforms to the IEEE 1284 standard connected to a parallel port that also conforms to that standard is capable of operating in any of five modes. Of these, the two new, "advanced" modes are referred to as *EPP (Enhanced Parallel Port)* and *ECP (Extended Capability Port)*.

EPP Ports

The EPP super parallel port design was developed to focus on supporting fast data transfers, both in and out of the PC, and also enable easy switching between the two directions of data flow. The initial group of companies supporting this approach soon swelled to around 80 members. That level of industry support was instrumental in getting IEEE to include the EPP design/protocol as a part of its 1284 standard.

The original PC parallel port design was so simple that instead of the eight CPU I/O port addresses needed to operate a serial port, IBM originally used only three. One was for data transfer. The other two were for status and control.

After the parallel port hardware has been told to operate in EPP mode, up to five additional CPU port addresses become active. (All these I/O ports are at the addresses immediately above the nominal "base address" for this parallel port. Using a block of eight addresses in the CPU's I/O port address space is thus identical to the way serial ports use CPU I/O ports.)

If the software driver program that must transfer data over the parallel port accesses only the traditional three CPU I/O ports, the port operates in compatibility mode. If, however, that driver sends the appropriate commands to the other five registers (and if the peripheral hardware attached to the port can respond suitably), the port will function at a much faster rate. The main reason it can do this is because the hardware of the parallel port has been enhanced so it is now able to handle all the separate steps for a single byte transfer by itself. Now the CPU can execute just one command and the byte transfer happens, without it having to be involved in each of the negotiation steps in the interlocked handshaking.

Right away, this means that EPP data transfers can go as much as four times as fast as compatibility mode transfers. If the interface hardware also enables transfers of multiple bytes in one cycle, which is the case for some EPP port hardware designs, this top speed can be boosted to nearly 2MBps. This is over 10 times as fast as the compatibility mode.

Additionally, the EPP design enables block transfers of data as well as arbitrary intermixing of reads and writes (data reception and data transmission) with no additional setup delays. This is the ideal mode for use with a ZIP drive or similar peripheral device.

ECP Ports

Hewlett-Packard and Microsoft were interested in a different kind of parallel port improvement. They focused on speeding up huge block data transfer rates and lowering the demands on the software driver and CPU even below those needed for EPP operation. The result of their work is now a part of the IEEE 1284 standard, and is called the Extended Capability Port (ECP).

Among other features, ECP includes provision for data compression using run length encoding (RLE). This is a data compression scheme that is particularly effective if the data being sent has long runs of a single value. For example, if you are sending a bitmapped image of a page and there are big areas of white, RLE will just say, in effect, "Okay now, white goes here for the next thus-and-so-many pels." That is much more efficient than sending a white pel over and over again. Combining this efficiency improvement with the high data rates (comparable to EPP) yields the highest possible data transfer rates for large blocks of data all going in one direction.

ECP is a more loosely coupled mode of operation than any of the other 1,284 modes. Unlike standard compatibility mode and EPP operation, the handshaking is not tightly interlocked. This makes the ECP protocol suitable for systems with large FIFO buffers at either end and also supports the goal of achieving maximum speed at single-direction data transfers. This capability is even further enhanced—and in particular, the CPU demands dramatically lowered—by ECP's support of direct memory access (DMA) data transfers. This means that the CPU can tell the DMA controller to transfer a block of data via an ECP port with a single command. The DMA controller and the ECP port do the rest.

ECP can accomplish data transfers in either direction, but the channel must be "turned around" before it can be used in a direction opposite to its most recent use. This turnaround requires several steps of time-consuming negotiation. Perhaps the greatest delay involved is that the turnaround cannot happen until after the current DMA transfer is complete and the FIFO buffers have been flushed. This restriction makes ECP port mode less suitable than EPP for external mass storage devices in which reads and writes are often intermixed.

ECP also has the drawback that it requires the exclusive use of a DMA channel. If you have one to spare, go ahead and assign it to this use. But if you are running short of DMA channels (as seems pretty often to be the case in a modern, fully equipped PC), you might have to forgo the advantages of ECP and fall back on EPP operation instead.

Finally, there is one other way in which an ECP port can be used that goes well beyond what is possible with a parallel port used in any other mode. This involves the use of *ECP channels*. In effect, ECP channels are subdevices within the peripheral device attached to the ECP port. By designating different data transfers as going to or from different channels, it is possible to communicate with one channel over an ECP port even when another channel in that same peripheral device is busy. For example, in a combined printer/fax/scanner device, it would be possible to receive a fax while the printer was busy printing a separate document. You'll see this same idea in Chapter 16, when the SCSI interface and its idea of logical units within a SCSI device are discussed.

"Printer" Ports Aren't Just for Printers Any More

As noted before, what were first called printer ports (and now are referred to more generically as parallel ports) are often used for much more than just shoveling data out to a printer. Indeed, these ports have become one of the most-used means of connecting external peripherals to a PC—for some good reasons.

It's so easy to get a peripheral to work when it is plugged into a PC's parallel port that this is now the preferred way to hook up almost any device for which you want a substantial data transfer rate, as long as you are willing to put up with not getting the absolute ultimate in data transfer rates. (With an ECP or even an EPP port, you can approach the maximum possible transfer rates of any other channel available on a PC today.)

Circumventing the Limits on Numbers of Parallel Ports

It's nice that you can hook so many things to a parallel port on a PC. But remember, PCs can have at most only three parallel ports, and most PCs have only one. So, how are all these different devices attached?

One of the answers used to be by the use of printer port switches. You'd hook up several printers and perhaps some other devices to this Hydra-headed box, and simply flip the switch to the one you wanted to use at the moment. Later, electrically switchable boxes were developed that could flip their own switches as needed. These devices enabled the user to have multiple peripheral devices and to send messages to or request messages from any of them. That worked—sort of. But it was at best a clever kludge.

A far better solution is to use an ECP port and have the hardware for each peripheral device set to respond to a different channel. That way, no switching of the parallel port connection is needed. Each device sees all the messages, but it responds only to the ones for its channel. (This is much like an old-fashioned party-line telephone hookup.) Still, this solution leaves something to be desired. It requires modifying all the attached devices to make them respond to only one ECP channel, and then it requires all uses of that parallel port to be made in ECP mode. That is just too much to ask, especially if you want to combine different gadgets from different manufacturers.

Therefore, the stackable parallel port device was invented. In this picture, you connect one device to the parallel port. On its backside are two connectors. One hooks the cable to the PC, and the other is an additional parallel port. You can now plug in a printer here. The first device—for example, a ZIP drive—communicates with its software driver over the parallel port. Whenever the printer driver sends some information to the printer, the ZIP drive is smart enough to know that it must pass that data along to its pass-through port instead of acting on it.

Can you stack up many such devices? Maybe. It depends. (Those are two of my favorite, all-purpose answers to questions in the PC field—and they almost always apply.) If the devices have been built by different manufacturers, you cannot be sure they will work in a stacked fashion. You just have to try them. If they don't work stacked in a certain order, try reversing that order. Don't be surprised if one or both devices fail to work properly. That often happens simply because there is no industry standard for how these pass-through parallel ports function, and in particular no standard way to make several of them cooperate. Will there ever be such a standard? Unlikely. Instead, you'll probably see PCs moving to newer I/O standards, such as USB and IEEE 1394.

Serial and Parallel Port Addresses and Their Names

Parallel ports are addressed by the CPU at certain of its I/O port addresses. The address you mostly see mentioned in descriptions of these ports, or that is displayed by diagnostic programs—such as Microsoft's System Information utility that is included in Windows 9x (MSINFO32.EXE) or the older Microsoft Diagnostics (MSD.EXE) that was bundled with some of the earlier versions of DOS and Windows—are the port's *base address*. The CPU uses this address to send and receive data, and it also uses several additional ports (at the immediately higher port addresses) to read the port's status and send it control commands.

If you have multiple ports (either serial or parallel), it's important that none of them tries to use the same CPU I/O port addresses as any of the others. If you break this rule, the CPU will end up sending messages to one port, and it will be received (and acted upon) by both that port and some other one with a conflicting address. Worse, when the CPU is "listening" for input from that port, it will "hear" what both ports have to say at once, and that will at least be confusing and at worst will damage your PC's port hardware.

So far, what you've learned about a parallel port applies equally to serial ports. But there are some significant differences as well:

Serial ports all use a block of eight consecutive CPU I/O port addresses. Standard parallel ports use only blocks of three port addresses (but enhanced parallel ports use more, and often as many as eight just like the serial ports).

However, while PCs can have up to three parallel ports, called LPT1, LPT2, and LPT3, there is no necessary association between these names and the base port addresses.

When IBM first introduced the PC, it offered printer ports two ways: on a standalone option card or as an additional feature on a monochrome character video display adapter (MDA). The parallel port on a video adapter had the port address 3BCh. The parallel port on a plug-in card of its own could be set to either 378h or 278h.

Later, IBM used the port address 3BCh for the standard parallel port on its PS/2 models with the MCA bus because those machines couldn't accept the MDA video card (so no conflict could occur). Most clone PC makers have simply not used this address for a parallel port, in case you might want to plug in an MDA video card.

The motherboard BIOS program looks for these ports during the PC's Power On Self Test (POST) in the order 3BCh, 378h, and then 278h. The name LPT1 is assigned by the BIOS to the first parallel port it finds, LPT2 to the second one, and LPT3 to the third one. If it finds only one parallel port, that one gets the name LPT1, no matter which port address it might happen to use.

Some Other Ways to Get More Than the Allowed Number of Serial (or Parallel) Ports

The design of PC serial and parallel ports imposes some severe limits on how many ports you can have. You can have up to four serial ports, although finding enough free IRQ values to support all of them is often a problem. You can have up to three parallel ports, but again an IRQ shortage may limit you to fewer than that. How do you get past these limits if you really need more ports? There have been several ways to do so in the past, and soon there should be several more.

Two situations are prevalent in which people needed a lot of ports on their PC: when there was a need to attach a lot of terminals (each terminal having a keyboard, a monitor, and perhaps a mouse), or when there was a need to support a large number of modems (or other serial peripheral devices such as data acquisition stations). A need for many parallel ports on a PC is less common.

The Option Card Solution

The usual solution to the need for many more than four serial ports on one PC has been to fit a plug-in card with a microcontroller that can handle many (up to 64) serial ports in one of the ISA bus slots. This board comes with a specialized software driver that runs in your PC and communicates with the onboard microcontroller to cause it to route messages to and from all these different ports appropriately.

Essentially, that solution involves putting another computer inside your PC. A number of vendors have made cards with this sort of functionality for many years.

Recently, this kind of augmentation of a PC has become much more interesting, as the processing power of the CPU has risen to heights previously available only on main-frame computers. Processing power is right up there, but the input-output capability is not. Thus, several groups are working to devise a new, industry-standard approach that will push PCs into mainframe territory in terms of I/O capabilities as well as processing power.

Intel is now moving this thrust forward in its Next Generation Input-Output (NGIO) ini-tiative. The aim of this is to connect intelligent I/O boards to one another and to external devices in server clusters and storage area networks. The NGIO plan is to move from simple I/O operations to a messaging model that can be made more robust and able to work with a wider diversity of external I/O systems.

IBM, Compaq, and Hewlett-Packard—along with several more partners—are countering Intel's NGIO program with a new one of their own, labeled Future I/O. The details of this plan are just now emerging, but its goals are certainly quite similar to Intel's goals for NGIO.

The outcome of all this is in some doubt—at least in terms of the details—but what is certain is that PCs will gain the capability of doing mainframe level input-output transactions in the very near future.

The LAN Solution

An alternative solution to a shortage of printer or serial ports on a PC is to hook it to one or more other computers. Connect them via a local area network (LAN) of some sort and then use all the serial (or parallel) ports you want as long as you use no more than four serial and three parallel ports per PC on the network. You'll learn more about LANs in Chapter 26.

The Ultimate Solution

We have another way to solve this problem, albeit not with outputs that will work quite as fast as the option cards used in the I2O, NGIO, or Future I/O approach. You can attach to your PC any device or collection of devices for which you would have used serial or parallel ports—and you can attach all of them at once—in a different way that works at least as well as anything I have discussed so far, and that totally solves the problems of limited numbers of serial and parallel ports. This solution requires you to get suitable adapters for your devices and then plug them into one or more USB hubs connected to the USB port on your PC (assuming it has one, as most modern PCs do).

This approach enables you to attach up to 127 of these USB devices (including those hubs) and thereby get all of them to work off no more resources (in terms of port addresses and IRQ lines) than a single device attached to a serial port or parallel port. If you want to learn more about this possibility, please turn to the section "The Universal Serial Bus (USB)" earlier in this chapter.

The Video Output Port

The last of the standard special-purpose ports on a PC is the video output port. If you have a monitor to display images on your PC, you have a video output port to which that monitor is attached. (Some PCs, such as our sample desktop system, have two or more monitors and a matching number of video output ports. For the purposes of this discussion, they just have that number each of all the pieces discussed here.)

The original PC offered two video options: monochrome character display or color graphics display. Both of them used the same female DB9 connector for the video output, so that became the standard video output connector for PCs for the next several generations of video displays.

In this original nine-wire design, all the signals are digital. This worked okay for the early monochrome and color display systems, but as explained in Chapter 13, this didn't allow for the subtlety we expect of modern PC display systems. For that, you need analog signals for the three colors. Only in that way is it possible for the PC to tell the monitor exactly how much red, green, and blue to put into a particular pixel on the screen. The horizontal and vertical signals, on the other hand, can still be essentially digital, because all they must do is signal when a new line or a new scan is to begin.

When IBM introduced VGA video (just one more of the innovations included in its PS/2 offerings), it defined a new video output connector standard. This is a female high-density DB15 connector with three rows of holes to accept the pins of the mating male connector. Three of the pins are used to send the three analog signals telling how much red, blue, and green signal is needed at this time. To keep down noise, there is a special *analog ground* connection for each of them. That accounts for 6 of the 15 pins.

The H-sync and V-sync signals use two more pins, and there are two digital ground pins. The seven pins still not accounted for are used for some different purposes. One is plugged, so you can insert only a male high-density DB15 plug that has the corresponding pin removed. This helps to keep the user from plugging in a cable from something other than a video monitor.

The remaining four pins were initially just "reserved." Now they are used for communications from the monitor to the video display. (Yes, even though this is called a video output connector, it also accepts some input signals.) This enables the monitor to inform the video display what range of frequencies it can handle for the H-sync and V-sync signals, for example, and thus helps to keep the video display adapter from sending inappropriate signals that might harm the monitor. It also enables a monochrome VGA monitor to tell the adapter to send only grayscale signals, because such a monitor cannot display color in any case. The Video Equipment Standards Association (VESA) hammered out several standards that address the proper use of these (digital) signal lines. Those standards have helped ensure that all the different brands of monitor and video display adapters will use the signal lines for the same purposes, and thus can be connected without concern for what those lines mean to a particular brand.

Some video displays are really different. In Chapter 13, I told you about flat panel displays. Some of those use analog inputs and they can be connected to the standard VGA-style video output port on any PC. Others require a totally different kind of output port—one giving out only purely digital signals. There are two competing standards for what this port will look like. The VESA-sponsored standard is called the Plug and Display (PnD) standard. The alternative, sponsored by Compaq and some partners, is called the Digital Flat Panel (DPF) standard. Both use very high-speed serial data communication, but they use different connectors and are different in other ways. Until the industry settles on a single standard, most folks will probably adopt flat panel displays that use analog inputs provided by standard VGA-style output ports on all the standard video display cards.

Some of the best monitors were designed to work with specialized video systems (not necessarily in a PC). They require five separate shielded cables ending in BNC connectors to convey the Red, Green, and Blue analog signals and the Horizontal and Vertical Drive signals. Some monitors can accept input over either a standard VGA connector or these five separate cables. Figure 15.3 shows the rear panel of the monitor for our sample desktop system, which happens to be one that can accept input either over five shielded cables with BNC connectors, or via the standard VGA cable.

FIGURE 15.3

Some video displays accept a VGA cable, and others accept only five separate shielded cables with BNC connectors. This Dell Ultrascan 20TX accepts both.

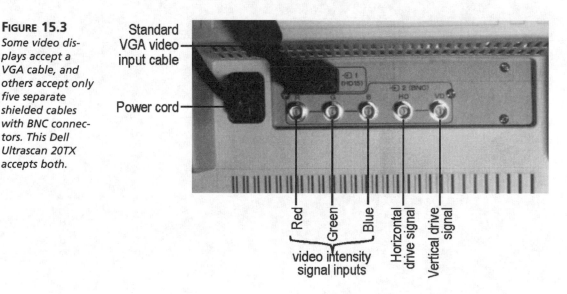

Summary

I've now told you about the basic set of I/O ports (serial, parallel, keyboard, and video) that have been around since the dawn of IBM's PC. You have seen some of the improvements made to each as the PC's design has matured (most notably the USB interface), but there are other, wholly new protocols on the horizon. Chapter 16 covers in detail the standard I/O bus (where option cards are plugged in) and some of the exotic new I/O options appearing on today's systems.

Faster Ways to Get Information Into or Out of Your PC

In Chapter 15, "Understanding Standard PC Input and Output," I told you all about the dedicated-purpose I/O connectors most PCs have for transferring data to and from the keyboard, mouse, or other pointing device, as well as the modem, printer, and so on. This chapter discusses those mysteriously general-purpose input-output slots on the motherboard and the various things that you can plug into them to facilitate faster input and output of information. I will also discuss in this chapter where those standard I/O connectors are hooked into the overall PC architecture.

The Most General I/O Interfaces: The PC Input/Output Bus(es)

In Chapter 4, "Understanding Your PC's Parts," you learned that information is frequently carried within a PC, and also into or out of a PC, on a bus. So most of this chapter is going to be the story of PC buses. As explained in Chapter 4, a *bus* is a definition of how one part of a computer communicates with another. It defines a pathway for signals to flow between functional elements of the computer. If it's a full bus definition, it will be sufficiently detailed and complete for different manufacturers to make those different parts, safe in the assumption that their separately designed and manufactured products will work together properly when they are connected.

The remainder of this chapter is also a description of many of the important standards that have defined PC hardware and architecture. Although the design of the CPU has been the primary driving force in the evolving design of PCs, the bus definitions have played an important supporting role.

The Original (ISA) PC I/O Bus

When IBM introduced the original PC, it used a CPU that had only 8 data lines and 20 address lines. The CPU was connected to every other part of the PC over a common bus that carried those lines (and some other wires for control signals). Data moved on this bus at the speed set by the CPU's internal clock. Everything worked in synchronization, and it was all quite simple.

This simplicity was both intentional and necessary. At that time, it wasn't possible to put all the necessary memory on the motherboard. Often, some of the PC's main memory would end up on plug-in option cards. Most of the other functions that required much in the way of integrated circuit support also had to be put on plug-in cards. This was true of the controllers for the floppy disk drives (and later for the hard drives introduced with the PC/XT). It also was true for the video subsystem and for the serial and parallel ports. Every one of these parts ran initially at a speed of 4.77MHz. Later, with the introduction of the PC/AT, that clock speed was increased first to 6MHz and later to 8MHz. But that is as far as it went.

Before CPUs started running significantly faster than this, the input/output (I/O) bus was separated from the other functions in a PC. Before I explain that development, I want to explain more about the I/O bus in the early models of the IBM PC, and the clones of those computers—and how this design became an industry standard.

An Industry Standard Is Born

IBM not only created the first PCs, but it also published the details of how they were designed. This was done so others could know enough to build plug-in cards that would work with the PC. That was a very wise decision on IBM's part, because it led directly to the huge success of the PC in the marketplace. In the long run, this openness about the design of the PC also led to the development of the clone PC market. That development nearly put IBM out of the PC business altogether.

Because the original PC used a CPU with only 8 data lines, that is all that was needed in the I/O bus. Likewise, the bus needed only 20 address lines in order to address the full 1MB, which was the maximum memory such a PC could use. It was also necessary to add lines to carry power, ground, clock signal, and an assortment of control lines (such as interrupt request lines and so on), giving the total I/O bus in a PC or PC/XT 62 wires.

When IBM introduced the PC/AT, which used the 80286 CPU chip with its 16 data lines and 24-bit addresses, it needed to widen the I/O bus accordingly. It didn't want to make obsolete all the plug-in cards that it and other manufacturers had created for PCs, so it added an extension to the connector behind the original PC I/O 8-bit bus portion of the connector. The original portion of the connector was referred to as the *8-bit section,* and the new part as the *16-bit section* for the overall PC I/O bus. This new section carried the additional 8 data lines, the additional 4 address lines, and some additional control signal, power, and ground lines. This 16-bit section has 36 contacts in it; thus, there were 98 contacts in both connectors together.

Cards designed to plug into only the 8-bit section still worked fine, and the newer cards had an extra tongue on them to plug into the new, 16-bit section and to enable them to access the newly included lines in this expanded PC I/O bus. Figure 16.1 shows how the ISA bus was used to connect the CPU to various PC peripheral devices both inside and outside the system unit. I want to emphasize that this figure shows the initial configuration, before some of the more recent advances in I/O buses for PCs.

FIGURE 16.1
The Industry Standard Architecture (ISA) bus used to be the main means of connecting to PC peripherals.

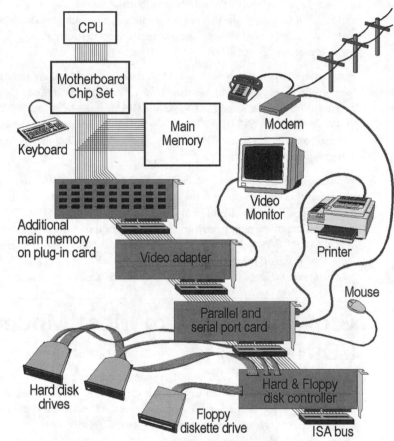

In Figure 16.1, the keyboard is shown connecting directly to the motherboard chipset. In fact, it connects to the keyboard controller. Originally, this was a separate chip (one of perhaps 50 in the original PC). Still, this is a part of the overall motherboard chipset's function, and it now is built into the large-scale integrated circuits (now usually only one or two) that make up your PC's motherboard chipset.

The serial and parallel port interface circuits and the floppy and hard disk controllers are shown as residing on plug-in cards. That is how it was done in early PCs. A more modern PC also includes that functionality as a part of the motherboard chipset.

IBM's decision to augment, rather than replace, the PC I/O bus design was the first sign that this was becoming a real standard—what we now know as the *Industry Standard Architecture (ISA)* I/O bus. This name reflects the market reality that, although IBM created this design, they no longer "owned" it in the sense that even they couldn't ignore it, but needed to respect it in their next generation of PCs.

Only in the very latest generation of PCs are you likely to find a motherboard that does not include at least one of these 16-bit ISA bus slot connectors. (For reasons that I explained in Chapter 4, the ISA bus is now looked on as a regrettable legacy from the early days of PCs, and hardware manufacturers and Microsoft are urging its abandonment just as soon as possible.)

Not only are we still using the original ISA connector (with all the same definitions of the purpose for each contact), we also are using this I/O bus at the original speed, or very nearly so. The first PCs and PC/XTs ran the CPU and the I/O bus at 4.77MHz. The first PC/ATs ran them at 6MHz, and later AT models ran them at 8MHz. Some clone XTs and ATs ran their I/O buses and CPUs at speeds up to 15MHz, but they didn't always work correctly at the highest speeds.

When the industry came out with the Extended Industry Standard Architecture (EISA) version of this bus, the designers of this standard specified that no matter how fast the CPU is, the I/O bus should not be clocked any faster than 8.33MHz. This was done to ensure that all the plug-in cards ever designed for this connector, no matter how antiquated, would work in any PC, no matter how modern and zippy it might be. And indeed, no standard PC that is properly configured will have any signals in these connectors that change more often than 8.33 million times per second.

Growing Up ISA to Meet Modern PC I/O Needs

The ISA bus served the PC/AT well. But soon, clone computers that ran faster came on the market. With their faster CPU speeds came a need for faster input and output capabilities, as well as for faster ways to connect the CPU to the system memory chips. Many different ways of meeting these needs have been tried over the years. IBM had its *MicroChannel*. Many clone makers made machines based on an alternative standard called the *Extended Industry Standard Architecture* (EISA). An industry group called the *Video Equipment Standards Association* (VESA) was formed, initially just to help create new standards for building video display subsystems, but now to promote a variety of standards useful in many parts of a PC. This doesn't even begin to exhaust the list of ways people have tried to improve on the good old ISA standard.

In Chapter 11, "Giving Your PC's CPU Enough Elbow Room—PC Memory," I talked about the modern way to connect the CPU with the system RAM and ROM. In this chapter, I mainly focus on the faster ways that have been devised for carrying signals into or out of a PC.

There are four parts to this story. I'll (briefly) tell you now what those four parts are. Then I will expand on each one of them in its turn:

- The first part tells how people have improved on the ISA bus to allow different and more convenient ways of connecting devices that work in more or less the same manner as the original ISA devices. This part of the story introduces some acronyms you probably have heard, such as IDE, EIDE, ATA, and ATAPI.

- The second part of the story talks about the new, much higher-speed and much more capable input-output bus that is the designated replacement for the ISA bus as a place to plug in option cards. This part of the story talks about the PCI bus and its enhancement, the AGP bus.

- The third part of the story is all about an I/O bus for small computers that actually predates the PC. This is what we now call the SCSI bus. I also will talk a bit about its progeny, most notably USB and IEEE 1394.

- Finally, I will tell you about a way in which the story got a new twist for portable computers (PC Card, CardBus, and Zoomed Video).

ISA Grows Up—The Origin of IDE, EIDE, ATA, ATAPI, and More

If you want to understand, in a general way, what all this IDE, ATA, and ATAPI stuff is about, a simple version of the tale will do. The IDE bus is that part of the ISA bus the is needed to support disk drives and the like, redirected to a special connector to save on the use of ISA slots. The ATA standard describes how to deal with hard disks over this IDE channel. The ATAPI standard extends ATA to enable dealing with CD-ROM and certain other types of devices on that same channel. You say that's too brief? Okay. Then here is a little more detail.

For perspective, note that the IDE channel (to give it the technically correct descriptor) is intended only for use inside a PC's system unit. Any devices hooked to this channel will be internal ones, unlike what is possible with the SCSI expansion bus, the USB and IEEE 1394, or with the PC Card interface (and its elaborations, which include CardBus and Zoomed Video).

The Early Days

When PCs were young, electronics could not be nearly as densely integrated as they can be today. It took a lot of room to hold all the chips one needed to do useful tasks. This meant that hard disks had a lot of electronics built into them, and they still required a controller card plugged into an expansion slot and connected to the drives by multiple ribbon cables.

Electronics evolved. Eventually, all that was needed to operate and interface a PC with a hard drive was put onto the drive itself. The first hardware in which this showed up were products such as the HardCard. That was Plus Development's trademarked name for a hard disk controller card with the hard disk itself actually mounted on the card. These cards were huge. They completely filled one ISA slot and physically obstructed another. But when you plugged one of them into your PC, voila! You had a working hard drive. No having to match up a controller, cables, and a drive. No having to low-level format the drive. You could just add DOS and go.

Early IDE Drives

The next stage was closer to what we have today. The electronics were further reduced in size, to the point they were all put on the hard drive itself. This drive didn't need a separate controller. Because all the electronics were on the drive, this was called an *Integrated Device Electronics* (*IDE*) hard drive, and it was the first of the breed of today's most popular hard drives.

These IDE hard drives didn't need any external controllers, but they did need to connect to the ISA bus. So we got things called *IDE paddle cards, IDE host interface cards,* and so on. These looked a lot like the old hard disk controller cards. They plugged into an ISA slot and had a 40-pin post and header connector that accepted a ribbon cable from the IDE hard drive. Instead of a lot of interface electronics, these cards essentially enabled you to plug a ribbon cable into the ISA bus. Most of the time these cards—like the hard disk controller cards that preceded them—also had a floppy diskette controller, two serial ports, and one parallel port on them, and that meant having at least a little bit of circuitry, including some integrated circuit chips.

The next move was pretty obvious. Makers of motherboards knew their customers were going to want to plug in a floppy diskette drive or two, and also one or two hard drives. So they moved the floppy diskette controller to the motherboard chipset. They connected it to a 34-pin post and header connector for the cable to the floppy diskette drives. Next to that, they put a 40-pin connector that carried all the signals from only those wires in the ISA bus that an IDE hard drive needed to see. Plug in your floppies to one connector, plug in your IDE hard drives to the other, and you were off and running. (But note: This solution enabled you to attach, at most, two floppy diskette drives and two IDE hard drives.)

At first, the IDE channel connectors were more or less directly connected to the CPU, just as was the ISA bus. In later generations of PCs, including those being built today, the ISA bus and the IDE channels each come off of what we now term the Southbridge chip, which you will learn about in a later section of this chapter. This new way of connecting the IDE channels has allowed them to grow up in some ways that would otherwise have been very difficult or impossible.

EIDE, ATA, and ATAPI

Next, motherboard manufacturers started including two IDE connectors. These were connected separately to the ISA bus lines so that each of these connectors could support one or two IDE devices. (Besides adding a second IDE cable connector, accomplishing this required some changes to the motherboard BIOS, both to add the necessary four-drive support and to add the appropriate entries to the Setup program.)

Then they speeded up first one of the IDE channels and then both of the channels by using Fast PIO support. They added logical block addressing, as well as some other extensions, to the Interrupt 13h BIOS calls (the primary way that application programs ask DOS to help them move information on and off a hard disk and to various other parts of DOS). Overall, the result was to enable you to have any mixture of slow CD-ROMs and fast hard drives you liked, with the hard drives being allowed to be as large as you wanted (for now, anyway). This new, faster standard for the IDE interface is termed *Enhanced IDE*, or *EIDE*.

That is where we are today. In Figure 16.2, you see a modern clone PC "baby AT" motherboard. This particular one, made by First International Computers (FIC), has three ISA slot connectors and three PCI slot connectors. (There can be only five cards inserted into these slots, because the ISA connector that is next to the PCI connector shares a common slot in the back of the case with that PCI connector.) This motherboard also has an AGP slot connector. I will explain all about PCI and AGP slots later in this chapter.

FIGURE 16.2
A clone PC "baby AT" motherboard, with its option card slot connectors indicated by type.

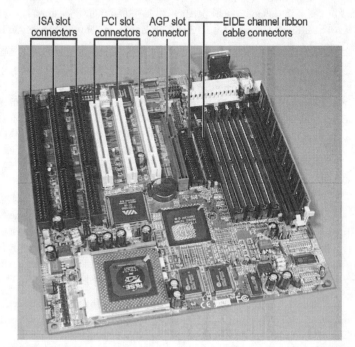

ISA slot connectors   PCI slot connectors   AGP slot connector   EIDE channel ribbon cable connectors

This figure shows the motherboard from a position above and to the left of the front of the case. The slots in the case where cables connect to option cards are at the rear, near the edge of the motherboard that is farthest from the camera in this view.

The long black connectors at the left in this figure are the ISA slot connectors. There is a gap in the slot that you can see. This separates the original, 8-bit portion (nearest to the back of the motherboard) from the additional portion for 16-bit communication. The two EIDE channel connectors are just to the right of the AGP slot connector.

You may want to compare this figure with Figure 4.4 in the section "A Platform to Build Upon: The Motherboard," in Chapter 4. That motherboard is an ATX design, which arranges the parts differently. On it you can see not only the connectors I have pointed out here, but also the floppy diskette ribbon cable connector that is hidden from view in Figure 16.2. The motherboard in Figure 4.4 has one more PCI slot connector and one fewer ISA slot connector, but it is otherwise quite similar to the one in Figure 16.2 as far as its input-output capabilities are concerned.

Better I/O for Better (Faster) Devices

Modern EIDE interfaces enable much faster communication than the original ISA interface, even though the bus clock is still stuck at 8.33MHz. The speed increase is due to the improvements in the protocol that describes how the clock cycles will be used to address devices and transfer data.

Appropriately, modern EIDE hard drives—and in particular those termed Ultra DMA hard drives—are indeed much speedier devices than their ancestors. (I explain what DMA is, and how Ultra DMA is better, in the section "How DMA Made Its Comeback," in Chapter 8, "How Your PC 'Thinks'.")

The *AT Attachment* (ATA) standard is the formal specification for how IDE and EIDE interfaces are supposed to work with hard drives. The *ATA Packet Interface* (ATAPI) is an extension to this standard that describes how the interface works with non-hard drive IDE devices, such as CD-ROM drives. These ATAPI devices use an almost completely different set of commands, but they function just like the ATA devices electrically and in terms of the timing for those commands. The ATA and ATAPI standards are published by the Small Form Factor (SFF) Committee.

Details About Speed Issues and EIDE

The typical use for the IDE channel, in all its variant forms, is to transfer a block of data between a peripheral device and some location in the main memory address space of the CPU. There are several ways to make these transfers. Some of these ways require a lot of attention by the CPU, essentially involving it in each transfer of one or a small group of bytes. Other methods permit transferring larger blocks of data as a single transaction.

Every transaction requires some setup before it can begin. The source and destination addresses must be specified, and the nature of the transfer must be defined. Only then can the actual data transfer proceed. Clearly, the highest data transfer rates will occur when this overhead is incurred as rarely as possible. To accomplish this, most IDE channel data transfers now are done in what is termed "burst mode," which uses one setup phase followed by the transfer of many bytes of data in succession.

Even though this is the most-efficient possible way of using the channel (according to the original protocols), it still takes two clock cycles to transfer each pair of bytes. (Because the channel has sixteen data wires, it can transfer 2 bytes at the same time.)

A more efficient protocol was then introduced in which each 2-byte data transfer can be accomplished in only a single clock cycle. Because there are 8.33 million clock cycles per second and on each one 2 bytes are transferred, this protocol allows a maximum of 16.6 million bytes to be transferred each second. Until very recently, this was the fastest at which one could transfer data across any EIDE channel.

ATA33 (Also Known as UDMA)

When hard disks were relatively slow, the 16MB/sec maximum data transfer rate was ample. Now, with larger and faster hard disks becoming common, this data transfer rate is a serious bottleneck to the smooth flow of data inside PCs. The industry's first response was the introduction of yet another variation on the data transfer protocol.

One key to understanding this shift is to know that the clock signal is ordinarily a square wave. That means that the voltage on the clock signal line spends half of the time in the high-voltage state and the other half in the low-voltage state. Ordinarily, the only significant moment in each clock cycle is when that voltage makes the transition from the high state to the low state. In the so-called Ultra ATA or Ultra DMA transfer protocol, data transfers take place on both "edges" of the clock signal. This means that 2 bytes of data can be transferred when the clock transitions from high to low, and another 2 when it goes from low to high.

This doubling of the number of data transfers from 8.33 million per second to 16.7 million, combined with the fact that each data transfer carries 2 bytes of data, means that the new maximum data transfer rate is now 33.3 million bytes per second, normally written as 33MB/s. The name for this new protocol is, not surprisingly, ATA33. To ensure reliability, ATA33 also incorporates a cyclical redundancy check (CRC) verification per burst of data transferred.

Virtually all hard drives being made today conform to the requirements of this new protocol, as do the EIDE channel controllers on all modern PC motherboards. Thus, this is now the standard (maximum) speed of EIDE channel data transfers.

ATA66

The industry has not stopped there. And it shouldn't, because hard disk speeds are fast becoming capable of clogging even this high-speed of channel.

The National Committee on Information Technology Standards (NCITS) is the organization formally charged by the American National Standards Institute (ANSI) with developing and maintaining this sort of standard. NCITS has a Technical Committee called T13 that deals only in ATA-related standards. You can learn more about this committee and its work at this URL:

```
http://fission.dt.edc.com/x3t13/t13.htm
```

The latest of the standards being developed by the T13 committee is termed ATA66. This new standard is the first that actually requires a change in the EIDE channel hardware. To meet the requirements of this new standard, the cable connecting the EIDE devices to the host controller (the PC motherboard) must have 80 wires instead of the normal 40. Curiously, the connector on each end of this cable (and in the middle, if there are two EIDE devices to be connected to this channel) still has only 40 contacts.

The original cable had 16 data wires, 16 control wires, one unconnected wire (at the "key" position where there is a missing pin in the motherboard or device connector and a plugged-up hole in the cable connector), and 7 ground wires.

The new cable has those same 40 wires, but between them are 40 additional wires. These added wires (all the odd numbers or all the even numbers) are connected to the 7 ground wires at each connector. This means, in effect, that each data- or control signal- carrying wire is shielded by an adjacent ground wire.

There are also some changes necessary in the host controller electronics and in the device electronics. When all these changes are in place, the channel clock frequency is doubled to 16.7MHz. This, combined with the Ultra ATA data transfer protocol, enables up to 66.7 million bytes of data to be transferred each second—hence the name ATA66.

This can work only if all the devices on the channel (the host controller and up to two EIDE devices) and the cable connecting them are capable of operating at the higher clock speed. The definition of ATA66 includes provisions to ensure that this is the case. If you plug an older EIDE device into an ATA66-capable EIDE channel, the host controller will detect this and will simply not switch the clock to the higher rate. In that case, the channel will function only as an ATA33 channel. Similarly, if you plug an ATA66-capable EIDE device into a channel with only an ATA33-capable host controller, the device will function as if it were only an ordinary ATA33 device.

Nothing is lost, but nothing is gained, either by having ATA66 capabilities in only some of the devices on a specific EIDE channel. The only real gain comes when all are ATA66-compliant, and at that point the gain is a very significant one—a doubling of the maximum speed at which the channel can convey information.

Tip: ATA66-capable devices are now coming into the marketplace. If you buy a new PC with ATA66-compliant EIDE host controllers on its motherboard, and you also buy one or two ATA66-compliant hard drives, be sure to hook up these hard drives to an EIDE channel with only that sort of device. Don't mix them with the older ATA33-compliant devices (such as most CD-ROM drives). Instead, put those slower devices on the second EIDE channel by themselves.

Also, if you have only one ATA66 device connected to the new 80-wire cable, be sure to connect it at the end. Use the middle connector (if there is one) only for a second ATA66 device attached to this channel. This precaution—which is not necessary on ATA33 channels and devices—is required for ATA66 in order to prevent signal reflections that could mess up the data transfers at the new, higher clock speed.

Hooking Up Multiple IDE or EIDE Devices

There is one detail about IDE and EIDE devices that probably deserves a little more careful discussion. Each IDE channel can have one master device and one slave. As mentioned in Chapter 10, "Digging Deeper Into Disks," when you install these devices, you must take care to have only one of them set to be a master device and the second one, if it is present, set to be a slave. It doesn't matter which one (master or slave) is at the end of the ribbon cable (and thank goodness you don't have to worry about terminating this cable).

If you are particularly lucky, you might have a BIOS that supports the Cable Select setting of the master/slave role for each drive. In that case, the system will make that assignment on its own during its plug-and-play setup. Of course, if it does something unexpected, you could find your nominal C: drive suddenly becoming your D: drive. But if your system is set up appropriately, that shouldn't happen.

You once had to put only fast IDE devices on the primary IDE channel and all your slower IDE devices on the secondary channel, or everything would run at the speed of the slowest device. Improvements in the ATA and ATAPI specifications have made that worry mainly of historical interest now, but it is still good practice to put your fast devices on one channel and the much slower ones on the other. (If you have some of the newest, ATA66-compliant devices and an ATA66-compliant motherboard, this precaution is once again essential and will remain so until all EIDE devices in your PC are ATA66-compliant.)

Furthermore, the current version of the ATA standard enables you to have up to four EIDE channels. No commercial motherboards support more than two, but you can add plug-in cards to support one or both of the others. Promise Technology's FloppyMAX card is an example of this. It is an ISA bus card that can be used to put one or two LS-120 drives on the fourth ("quarternary") EIDE channel, for example.

The PCI Bus

Now we are ready for the second part of our story of faster PC input and output. This is the part about the *Peripheral Component Interconnect* (*PCI*) bus. This mostly Intel-sponsored new way to connect the parts of a PC started as just a way to make mother-boards more efficient. Later, it was extended to become a way to attach outside components as well.

An important point in the PCI design is that it can be adapted for use in many different kinds of computers or other high-tech hardware. It is by no means limited to replacing the ISA bus, nor to working only in an IBM-compatible PC.

As I shall explain in a moment, the PCI bus is no longer a singular thing. There are several important variations. CompactPCI, for example, is a variant form of PCI that is used widely in industrial control and instrumentation. And the basic PCI bus is used as the main I/O bus for computers using many different CPUs (x86, Alpha, PowerPC, and others). Finally, there are now four different flavors of PCI for the PC, involving different data bus widths and different clock speeds. I'll explain all of these flavors, but for simplicity, I shall not give you any details on the CompactPCI standard, nor on the uses of the PCI bus with other than x86-based PCs.

PCI Basics

Fundamentally, PCI is a rethinking of the way the parts of a PC are interconnected. Initially, this included only those parts that were internal to the system unit, but later versions of the PCI design also encompass ways of connecting to pieces that are outside that box.

PCI began as a means of interconnecting the chips that surround the CPU more efficiently, and to make those interconnections less dependent upon just which CPU chip one might be using. Later, once Intel explicitly added a PCI bus connector, this became a viable replacement for (and vast improvement upon) the ISA bus.

Because it was a fresh rethinking of the problems that the ISA bus had been designed to solve, (and some that the ISA bus was not equipped to solve) the PCI bus could be made as good as the technology of that time would enable, without having to carry along all the baggage that the ISA bus carries even to this day. However, when the PCI bus was defined and widely adopted, it quickly acquired new baggage of its own. Still, it is proving to be a remarkably robust and flexible bus definition—as shown by the variety of forms it takes and the widely different applications in which it is being used.

PCI Is an Efficient Bus

A PCI bus has only about half as many active lines as the ISA bus, yet these include twice as many data lines and can operate four times faster. To make the PCI bus work reliably at this speed, the connectors have a few more connections (124), with most of them being connected either to ground or to one of the power supply voltages. The main way that the PCI bus gets away with fewer lines is by using one set of them for both address and data information (at different times).

Also to enhance reliability, both address values and data are supplied with a parity bit. The PCI bus will notice whether either addresses or data get messed up. If that happens, the bus controller will notify the devices involved in the transfer, but leaves it up to those devices just what type of error recovery procedure to take.

The PCI bus is designed to operate without termination (unlike a SCSI bus). This makes it easier for users because they don't have to think about termination issues. And it is designed to use the reflected signals that an unterminated bus implies. But these design choices also limit the length of a PCI bus segment to just a few inches, and limit the number of PCI cards or other components on a single segment of PCI bus to no more than 10. (However, you can extend the PCI bus's reach a lot by using bridge chips between segments.)

PCI Supports Plug-and-Play Automation

The PCI bus definition was crafted with automatic (plug-and-play) system configuration in mind. Each board that's plugged into a PCI slot (and each device connected to the bus on the motherboard) is required to have a local configuration data storage unit. The system reads and writes the data stored in these units as it configures the system.

PCI Supports Multiple Masters and Shares Interrupts Gracefully

There are two challenges for a bus that ISA is simply not sufficient to meet. One is having multiple devices on the bus that, at different times, may want to take control of communication across that bus. The second is having multiple devices that all share the same few interrupt lines when they need to call for the CPU's attention. The PCI way of handling multiple masters is to have an arbitration unit as a required part of the host system. Its way of handling interrupt conflicts is to let every device that wants to tug on an interrupt line do so, figure out which ones those are during an acknowledgement conversation, and then serve each of those requesters in turn.

The PCI Bus Is Called a Mezzanine Bus—What's That?

PCI was designed to replace the ISA bus, but it is in fact a little different. Like the ISA bus, it routes signals between the CPU, various other chips on the motherboard, and cards that are plugged into its bus slot connectors. To do this, it must buffer those signals and, in some cases, alter their timing.

Unlike the ISA bus, the PCI bus definition is not tied to any particular CPU chip or even to a chip family. The advantage to having a bus (or as Intel prefers to call it, an interconnection standard) that is processor-independent is that now many manufacturers can build PCI cards and potentially have them be usable in a much wider variety of microcomputer-based systems. A larger market almost always means lower price products, as well as more variety of products—both desirable outcomes, from any consumer's perspective.

Furthermore, the PCI bus standard explicitly includes support for bridges. These can be bridges between PCI buses, or between a PCI bus and some other standard buses, such as the memory bus and ISA buses in a PC, or a VME bus in an industrial application.

PCI Is a Flexible Bus—Speed and Data Width Issues

The PCI bus was designed to run at what was, at the time, the full motherboard system bus's speed, and to support what was then the full motherboard system bus-width parallel data transfers. Given the year it was introduced, this means that PCI is clocked at 33MHz and has 32 data lines. That makes this bus four times faster and twice as wide as the ISA bus it replaces.

PCI was widely adopted very soon after its introduction. It was such a better idea than its predecessors in the PC bus arena that all the PC makers wanted to include it in their new products, and their customers were happy to buy these new products. Many companies started making PCI cards to go into these new slot connectors. (Most of them were video cards, hard disk interface cards, and network interface cards because those are the only kinds of card in most PCs for which the higher speed of PCI is really crucial.)

When motherboard speeds jumped to 66MHz, the PCI bus stayed at 33MHz. And when CPUs starting handling data 64 bits at a time, the PCI bus stayed with 32 bits. Finally, just in the past year, the PCI standard has been extended to encompass both a 64-bit version and operation at 66MHz. And even better, these extensions have been made fully backward- and forward-compatible. That is, you can use an old 32-bit, 33MHz PCI card in a new 64-bit, 66MHz PCI slot or vice versa (with some resulting limitations on performance). This two-way compatibility is really quite rare in standards-extension history.

This magic has been accomplished quite simply. The wider 64-bit PCI bus definition simply adds an extra section to the PCI connector, much as the 16-bit ISA definition extended the older 8-bit IBM PC I/O channel connector. Now, however, not only can you plug a 32-bit PCI card into one of these new connectors, but you even can plug in a new wider (64-bit) PCI card into one of the older-style 32-bit PCI connectors—and both ways work just fine. The trick is that the "wide PCI" (64-bit) card must configure itself to operate as if it were only a "narrow PCI" (32-bit) card when it is in a "narrow PCI" slot.

Similarly, the 66MHz definition for the bus works with older PCI cards because the PCI controller for a given segment will recognize whenever a slow PCI card is plugged into its bus segment, and then it will slow down that segment to 33MHz. In the other direction, any fast PCI card can run slower. The PCI definition generally supports cards or buses that run at any rate you want, down to 0Hz—but of course, mostly all of them run at the maximum permissible rate for the version of the standard they have been built to support. Otherwise, they wouldn't get as much accomplished in any given interval of time.

One exception to this generality would be in a system that was configured to do power saving when it was not being used to its maximum performance. It could, slow down the PCI bus and save some power. Not many of today's PCs do this, but they could be designed to do so if the power savings to be achieved were deemed sufficiently worthwhile.

Thus, while mixing and matching PCI cards and slots between all four flavors is permissible, it will limit the bus performance a lot. So we can expect to see PCs sporting the new, faster PCI buses on one segment and still having a different PCI bus segment that runs at the older, slower rate. If the PC supports the new, wider PCI bus (probably on the fast segment), the user of that PC will be advised to plug all the narrow PCI cards into the other, slower segment and reserve the wider and faster segment for only those cards that truly need that extra speed.

Finally, I'll mention that PCI cards can come in two different voltage ratings. The older ones are all 5-volt cards. The newer ones are 3.3-volt cards, meaning that their internal circuitry runs at a lower voltage. This enables them to run cooler and helps make the faster PCI cards possible. There are differences in the places in the slot connector where the gaps are (and thus where the notches must be in the cards) to keep you from plugging in a wrong-voltage card for a given slot—and there is a provision in the specification for making slots and/or cards that can run in a universal manner, indifferent to the voltage supplied in the slot.

The Next Version, PCI-X

The new, 64-bit wide and fast (66MHz) PCI bus is four times as fast as the original PCI bus. That is still not fast enough for some purposes. To help push up this technology yet another notch, the PCI Special Interest Group (PCI-SIG) is considering and is expected to approve a variant form of the PCI protocol, named PCI-X.

This new and very clever protocol was developed jointly by Compaq, Hewlett-Packard, and IBM, with the goal of making it possible to continue using a PCI-style connection in PCs where the amount of data flow would overwhelm even the fastest, widest PCI bus permitted by the previous standards. Most impressive is the fact that this new, higher data speed is fully compatible with existing 64-bit-wide-by-66MHz-clock-speed PCI hardware. The key observation these developers made was that the original PCI protocol was limited from going to higher speeds by a bottleneck that could be removed rather simply.

This speed-limiting bottleneck in conventional PCI systems is that within each clock cycle, each device is expected to notice what is passing over the bus, decide whether information is intended for it, and then latch (grab) the data if it is. As the clock speed has risen from 33MHz to 66MHz, designers have found it difficult, but possible, to ensure that this can be done. A further doubling of the clock speed would simply have made this impossible with existing electronics.

The proposed solution to this bottleneck is very simple. Every device is modified by adding a register (a temporary electronic data holding place) that grabs the data off the PCI bus every clock cycle, whether it is intended for that device or not. Before the next clock cycle occurs, the device examines the data and decides what, if any, action it is supposed to take. This doubles the time it has to "make up its mind" and act. It also means that the responses come not one, but rather two, clock cycles after the stimulus— thus adding one clock cycle to the overall transaction.

This permits doubling the clock speed to 166MHz. The added clock cycle cuts performance by only about 10 percent because most PCI transactions take at least 9 clock cycles, and now will take 10. Overall, the gain is not quite a doubling of the speed, but it comes very close.

> **Technical Note:** The designers of PCI-X took the opportunity of a new protocol definition to add something else. This is a new "attribute phase" in which 36 bits of attribute data are sent along with the rest of the transaction's data load. These attributes specify such things as how large the overall data load is, whether cache snooping is required, what reordering of transactions is permitted, and the identity of the transaction initiator. (If you don't understand all of this jargon, don't worry. That isn't necessary to a general understanding of the benefits of PCI-X.)

To implement PCI-X, each device on the bus must be PCI-X–compliant. An important part of the PCI-X definition is the capability of sensing whether this is the case. Just as with the ATA66 enhancement to EIDE, PCI-X permits increased speed of operation only when all the pieces that are connected are capable of reliably operating at that higher speed. Because the physical connectors are not changed, nor are the electrical and logical aspects of the interface definition, you can plug older PCI cards into a PCI-X bus slot, or you can plug a newer, PCI-X card into an older PCI slot. Either way, if you do this these devices will operate only with the older PCI capabilities.

PCI as the "North-South" Axis in a PC

Precisely because PCI is a mezzanine bus—and thus is intended to link between different types of buses—it is a wonderful means of interconnecting different parts of a PC, both within the system unit and outside that box. Intel took advantage of this to separate the different functions of its motherboard chipsets into two groups—and now the PC industry generally is supporting this separation in all the newer chipsets. This design innovation integrates one group of functions into a chip that is called the *Northbridge* chip. The other group of functions are integrated into what is called a *Southbridge* chip. The connection between the two chips is made using PCI. This (and a lot more) is shown in Figure 16.3.

FIGURE 16.3

A rather fully fleshed out example of the architecture in today's best PCs.

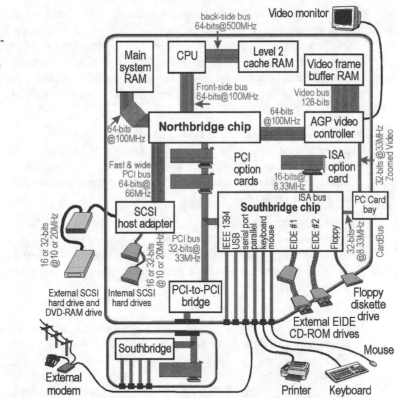

Figure 16.3 is complex—and it contains perhaps the most information of any single figure in this book. It summarizes a lot of what I have been explaining up to now—plus many things I will be explaining later in this chapter—and it adds to this function of the Northbridge and Southbridge chips. Careful study of this figure will give you a deeper understanding of the architecture that is developing for modern PCs. I suggest you mark

this page so you can easily return here again and again as you continue in this chapter, and perhaps while you are reading other portions of this book.

This figure, I must add, shows the architecture for a hypothetical PC. One that is at the state of the art (or just beyond). It could be a desktop PC, or it could be a laptop computer connected to a docking station. The notion behind this last item is that when the docking station is disconnected, the PC is a perfectly usable machine, but when it is docked, the PC becomes potentially much more powerful. I'll give you a guided tour of all the things the figure contains, starting with a description of the Northbridge chip and of the newest way to hook up the video subsystem to the CPU.

The Northbridge Chip

The CPU in all modern PCs connects to main memory via a faster and wider data path than it uses to connect to the PCI bus. This faster bus is what we term the *front-side*, *system,* or *host* bus. The CPU is not capable of connecting directly to the memory modules. Some buffers and some memory address decoders are needed, at the least. Likewise, it cannot connect directly to the wires in the PCI bus. Thus, one of the jobs of the Northbridge chip is to buffer (strengthen) the signals from the CPU and then connect to the several places they must go.

The CPU "talks" with external I/O devices and with memory over the same set of wires. It just changes the voltage level on one of the associated control wires to indicate whether a memory or an I/O device access is happening. The Northbridge chip uses this control signal to separate messages to and from the memory modules from those going to and from the I/O devices.

The needed interface electronics to do these tasks (sometimes called a part of the *motherboard glue logic*) has been integrated into one very large integrated circuit chip (nearly as complex as the CPU), and this is what we now call the Northbridge chip. While they were at it, they also threw in support for another special-purpose, very high-speed data bus. They called this the Advanced Graphics Port.

Note: What I am describing here is primarily based on Intel's latest designs for a PC motherboard chipset. There are a number of other makers of motherboard chipsets, and they make some that are comparable to the Intel offerings, plus others that are quite different. Furthermore, Intel offers many different chipsets, each one optimized for a different set of uses. In this discussion, though, I am going to gloss over these differences and describe a hypothetical chipset that includes pretty much all the latest and greatest features—even though there might never be any single chipset that does all of these things.

AGP: The Side Trip to Better Video

The Advanced Graphics Peripheral bus (AGP) is fundamentally a specialized application of the PCI bus, with a number of improvements that are focused on what you need for a good PCI video display subsystem. That video display subsystem will, of course, have a good video accelerator as its controller. (You can learn more about video accelerators in Chapter 13, "Seeing the Results: PC Displays.") Also, the video display system will doubtlessly have a large frame buffer in which to build the potentially high-resolution and large color-depth images it displays on the screen. Such a video display subsystem needs two things from this new bus: a speedy connection to the CPU, and a direct connection to some portions of main system RAM so it can move information into or out of locations there without having to involve the CPU. The AGP bus provides both of these capabilities.

An AGP video accelerator could be mounted on the motherboard, or it could be mounted on a plug-in card to go into a special AGP connector. Most common today are designs that use an AGP slot connector, because this enables the manufacturer or user to choose a different video card for different purposes (trading off, to name just one example, cost versus performance for 3D rendering).

When you have an AGP slot, it will always replace one of the PCI slots—and in particular, the one that is nearest to the CPU.

AGP 1X, 2X, 4X, and Pro

Like the PCI bus from which it was derived, the AGP bus has now evolved into many related standards. The original bus standard supported single-speed (AGP 1X) and double-speed (AGP 2X) processing. The fastest version so far defined is termed AGP 4X. Most AGP video cards today support the 2X standard, as do most motherboards built today. However, very soon we can expect to see many more motherboards and video cards supporting the higher-speed 4X AGP standard.

The differences between these standards have to do partly with the voltage levels at which they work, and partly with how the clock signals are handled to make sure they stay in sync with the data signals. Many of the same ideas that I described in Chapter 11, in connection with the new Rambus way of creating very fast system memory, are also used in connection with the fastest of the AGP definitions. Also, the slot connectors for the various types of AGP cards use the same strategies that all PCI buses use for working with different voltage cards.

Speed of communication with the AGP video card or subsystem is important, but it is not the only thing that matters. Also important is the processing power of that system. With today's levels of integration, it just isn't possible to put all the power and local RAM that you might want onto a card as small as a PCI or AGP card. If you did put that much processing power and RAM on an ordinary AGP card, it would overheat, or at least it would draw more power from the slot connector than the AGP standard permits.

The way around these limitations is yet another variation on the AGP standard, this time called AGP Pro. This standard proposes AGP cards that will be so "fat" (have so many components on them, and perhaps also have one or more daughterboards or other attached modules) that they cannot fit into the 0.8-inch space between PCI connectors.

An AGP Pro card is permitted to be thick enough to take up two slot spaces (the AGP slot and the nearest PCI slot), or three slot spaces. In either case, the manufacturer of the AGP Pro card is permitted to make it plug into just the AGP slot connector, or also into the PCI slot connector it spans. Having the card plug into more than one slot connector can give several advantages, including access to more power and to some of the PCI bus connections that are not replicated in the AGP bus slot definition.

So far, we have the initial AGP Pro standard definition and some statements from manufacturers who intend to introduce AGP Pro video cards, but no actual AGP Pro products are yet on the market. When they are, we can see just how much more powerful a PC can be when it is equipped with the absolute maximum in video processing and display power yet created for workstations or any other kind of standalone computer.

What's a GART?

I told you that one of the design goals of AGP was to give the video card direct access to the main, system memory. But it wouldn't make sense to have it able to access all of that memory. After all, the system RAM is partially used by each of the several programs that typically are running at once for their program code plus for data—and only a tiny fraction is likely to be used for anything the video display adapter itself actually needs to see. The main use for this feature is to enable the AGP video card to store graphical texture maps in system RAM, thus enabling it to use nearly all of its local frame buffer for the actual image it is constructing and displaying. When it needs a texture map, it can reach out and grab it, and then apply it to the relevant portions of the image.

Thus, in the definition of the AGP bus, there is the notion that the video display adapter will have access to only a portion of main memory. That portion is what it can see through a special AGP window. Which portion shall it be? Here is where something called the *Graphics Address Remapping Table* (*GART*) comes into play.

The GART is a table, built either in some local memory on the AGP card or in main memory, that specifies which regions of main memory are directly accessible to the AGP card. Just by changing the contents of this table, you can alter which portion of main memory is being made available by the AGP card. There is specialized hardware on the AGP card to point to this table and to use its contents when accessing main memory through the Northbridge chip.

You Can Have Many PCI Buses in One PC

I just told you that the AGP bus is a PCI bus in disguise. It's also a totally separate bus from the PCI bus. That is, the AGP card can carry on a "conversation" with the CPU, or access main memory, independently of whatever the PCI bus may be doing.

Furthermore, it is perfectly possible to design a Northbridge chip with more than just an AGP bus and one PCI bus. There's no reason it couldn't have multiple PCI buses. After all, the functions of the Northbridge chip include being a bridge between the PCI (and AGP) bus and the front-side bus—and it could just as well bridge several PCI buses, plus the AGP bus, to that front-side bus.

The main reason to expect this to be included in future PC designs is to enable you to have a standard, 32-bit wide, 33MHz PCI bus plus another 64-bit wide, 66MHz PCI bus. That way, as I explained previously, you can put in both older, slower, and/or narrower PCI cards and newer, faster, and/or wider PCI cards and each of them will perform up to their maximum capabilities. (You may someday have a PCI-X bus coming off the Northbridge chip in addition to one or more PCI buses.)

Alternatively, you could have a fast and wide PCI bus (or a PCI-X bus) come off the Northbridge chip and, after passing some fast-and-wide PCI (or PCI-X) slots, end in a PCI-to-PCI bridge chip that spawned another PCI segment, this time of the more traditional, narrower, and slower sort.

Another reason for including multiple PCI buses coming directly off the Northbridge chip is to support more PCI slots than a single bus can have. Normally, by the time the loads on the bus represented by various parts of the motherboard circuitry are taken into account, a single PCI bus segment in a PC can have no more than four slots. The main place I'd expect to see more than this many PCI slots is in PCs that are intended for use as servers or otherwise emulating a mini- or mainframe computer.

Finally, there is yet another way to have multiple PC buses in one PC. That is to bridge from one PCI bus to another. Our example desktop PC does this in its quad video display adapter. That card has a PCI-to-PCI bridge chip on it, and the four video display adapters on that card are all located, logically, on the secondary PCI bus, across that bridge from the motherboard PCI bus.

In Figure 16.3, I show a PCI-to-PCI bridge chip as one way to support a docking station. Here, the docking station can have up to half a dozen PCI loads, and it only looks like a single load to the motherboard PCI bus.

The Southbridge

At the "south" end of the PCI bus is a Southbridge chip. This chip contains all the rest of what normally comprises the *motherboard glue logic* or *motherboard chipset*, other than what is in the Northbridge chip. This is to say that the Southbridge chip has the needed interface logic to convey the signals from the PCI bus to the much slower ISA bus and all the other interfaces that a PC may have. The ISA bus shown here has just a couple of slots, partly because so many of the things that once were done with plug-in ISA cards are now done with dedicated ports or with PCI cards.

The floppy diskette drives connect to the Southbridge chip. That chip usually supports two Enhanced IDE channels (primary and secondary) with up to two EIDE devices on each one, but it can support up to four EIDE channels. And it has a separate bus for a keyboard, a bus mouse, a standard (possibly ECP or EPP) parallel port, and one or more standard serial ports. Plus, it can have yet another bus interface for some Universal Serial Bus (USB) connectors as well as some IEEE 1394 (Firewire) connectors. Finally, the Southbridge chip will probably have an interface for a PC Card bay, in this case shown as a Card Bus (32-bit) interface with a Zoomed Video bus connecting directly to the video subsystem.

If there is more than one PCI bus in a particular PC, it is perfectly possible to put one or more Southbridge chips on each of them. But that is not necessary. If there are going to be any slots for ISA cards provided in this PC, the slot connectors for them will connect to a Southbridge chip. Thus, the ISA bus in this architecture is appended to the PCI bus, rather than being connected more or less directly to the CPU, as was the case with the original ISA bus.

The ISA, IDE, and PC Card interfaces run at 8.33MHz (exactly one-quarter of the original PCI bus rate). The only exception to this is if you have an ATA66 EIDE channel, in which case it would use a 16.7MHz clock, but only if the devices attached to it and the cable interconnecting them are all ATA66-compliant. The other ports connected to the Southbridge chip run at various slower speeds. (The Zoomed Video connection from the PC Card bay to the video controller runs at 33MHz, even though the connection from a PC Card bay to a Southbridge runs at only 8.33MHz.)

What We Gain from This North-South Division

By establishing a standard way to divide the electronics needed in a PC between what it calls the Northbridge and the Southbridge, Intel made it possible to do many interesting things. One is, as shown in Figure 16.3, to have a docking station to which a (perhaps portable) PC could be connected. That docking station has its own set of peripheral devices that can augment the functionality contained in the PC.

Another possibility is that the Southbridge chip can be made by a different vendor than the Northbridge chip. As long as each one properly interfaces with a PCI bus, they will work together flawlessly.

Finally, by having multiple Southbridge chips in a PC (and only one Northbridge chip) it would be possible to have multiple pointing devices, each supported by its own port, and multiple other ports as well. Of course, supporting all that hardware in one PC could be a software nightmare, but I won't get into that just now.

The Really Good Bus with the Really Bad Name (SCSI)

The small computer system interface (SCSI) bus, pronounced *scuzzy,* is a relative old-timer in the industry. But it didn't achieve much popularity in PCs until fairly recently. There were several good reasons for this, among them the perceived difficulty in setting up a SCSI bus on a PC and making it work correctly.

In contrast, a SCSI bus has always been built into every Macintosh computer, so Apple aficionados have enjoyed the advantages of this bus available to them for much longer. Now, after some years of struggle, the SCSI bus host adapters and supporting software for PCs are all in place and well-tested. So for those situations in which the SCSI bus outperforms all the alternatives, PC owners can take advantage of it easily.

The SCSI bus is the preferred way to connect hard disk drives with the largest capacity and highest data transfer rates (although this preeminence is constantly being challenged by developments in EIDE drives). It also provides a convenient way to attach several different types of external PC peripherals (such as CD-ROM, ZIP, and other removable media storage devices, scanners, video cameras, and so forth) and get maximum performance from them. These advantages are offset to a degree by a slightly higher price for SCSI-enabled versions of all these devices, and by some added complexity in the setup of your PC.

The SCSI Architecture

Fundamentally, the SCSI architecture is simply two buses connected by a bridge. I have included this detail in Figure 16.3. The SCSI host adapter sits on the PCI bus (or it could sit on the ISA bus, at some substantial cost in terms of its performance), and the host adapter connects on its other side to the SCSI bus, extending both inward toward an internal hard drive (as an example) and outward to external SCSI devices.

In a sense, you can think of a SCSI bus as a small local area network. The main difference between the SCSI bus and an ordinary LAN is that rather than being a means of communications between multiple PCs (and perhaps a file server), the PC to which the SCSI bus is attached is the only general-purpose computer on this bus. Each SCSI device has, in fact, a small special-purpose computer in its SCSI interface portion. That computer has only one task to perform, and that is to manage communications on behalf of the peripheral device to which it is attached with the host adapter, and perhaps with other devices on the SCSI bus.

The term "the SCSI bus architecture" has been used in this discussion as if it were a singular thing. But as with most standards that have been around for a while, it has grown and changed over time. So there are in fact several versions of what SCSI means. By now it has evolved into several distinct flavors of buses. The overall architecture has not changed, but the details of the bus design have, and along with those changes have come a range of performance possibilities.

The Several Flavors of SCSI

The original source of the SCSI standard was a proprietary protocol developed by Shugart Associates (an early maker of hard drives) and the NCR Corporation at just about the same time as IBM's introduction of the first PC. They called it the *Shugart Associates Computer Interface* (*SASI*). A short time later this standard was adopted (and somewhat modified) by the American National Standards Committee, giving it at that time the name *Small Computer Systems Interface* (*SCSI*).

SCSI-1

The original version of SCSI, now called SCSI-1, called for a cable with 8 data wires (or 16 pairs in the preferred, differential signaling mode) plus 1 for parity. This cable was to be connected from the host adapter to any SCSI peripherals inside the system unit in parallel, and to SCSI devices outside the system unit in a *daisy-chain* fashion. (You can see such a daisy chain of cables in Figure 16.3. On the internal cable, you see the hard disk at the end of the cable and an extra connector in the middle that could be connected to a second internal SCSI device.)

The SCSI bus operates as a synchronous bus. All the SCSI devices attached to that bus operate independently. Each has its own unique SCSI ID number (from 0 to 7). Any of them can put a message on the bus requesting permission to transfer data from itself to a specified other device on that bus, or to receive data from a specified other device. If the bus is not otherwise occupied, these two devices "have a conversation" all on their own, without any intervention on the part of the SCSI host adapter. The host adapter is involved only when it is the target (or source) of such a conversation.

It is vital that each device on the SCSI bus has its own unique ID, because that is the only way it knows when it is being "spoken to." Normally, the host adapter is given the SCSI ID of 7. The other devices can usually have their ID set by the user. There are two common ways this is done.

Most external SCSI devices have a switch of some kind on their back panels to enable you to set their SCSI ID. Some will enable you to choose any value you like; others will enable you to choose from among only a few preselected options. One common design for such a switch has a number showing in a window and two tiny buttons above and below that window. If you press in the button above the window with a piece of wire (an unrolled paper clip works nicely), the switch will move to the next higher number. Pushing on the other button lowers the number. A different kind of switch that is also popular for SCSI ID settings is one that looks like a miniature clock face, with a pointer you turn with a small screwdriver. The proper way to connect SCSI devices outside a PC is by daisy-chaining them. This means that each device must have two SCSI ports on it. The first device is connected to the host adapter directly. The second device is connected to the first device. The last device on the external chain has its second SCSI port filled with a terminator (or else it must terminate the SCSI bus internally).

Internal SCSI devices normally are connected slightly differently, and their SCSI IDs are also set differently. All the internal SCSI devices are simply plugged into a common ribbon cable. The last one on the cable (the one physically farthest from the host adapter) must itself terminate the bus or be followed by a separate internal SCSI terminator.

It takes 3 bits to designate a number between 0 and 7, so the usual way to designate an internal device's SCSI ID is to use three jumpers. Putting shorting plugs on just the appropriate jumpers will set the SCSI ID for that device. (Think of the shorted jumper pairs as representing 1 bits and the open ones representing 0 bits.)

The original version of the SCSI bus allowed data transfers at rates of up to 5MBps (1 byte on each clock cycle, with a 5MHz clock frequency). That is faster than the ISA bus could support, and so was thought to be amply fast for the time when it was introduced. The cables and connectors used with this standard are discussed in more detail in the "SCSI Cables and Connectors" section, later in this chapter.

SCSI-2 and Wide SCSI

In 1991, ANSI came out with an update called SCSI-2. This newer version of SCSI included everything in the older version, with some additions. First, it endorsed a new, more compact cable-end connector. Second, it enabled the use of multiple cables to support 16- or even 32-bit data transfers in parallel. Third, it established a complete software-control system for SCSI, called the Common Command Set (CCS).

SCSI-2 also provided support for doubling the clock speed on the SCSI bus. This variation was called Fast SCSI. With Fast SCSI and later Wide SCSI (which meant 16 bits in parallel over two separate cables), it became possible to carry out data transfers at rates up to 20MB per second.

SCSI-3

As soon as SCSI-2 was officially approved, the committee began work on SCSI-3. This update made several significant changes in the standard. First, it decoupled the CSS (software) definition from the hardware definition. That means it is now possible to have several different hardware connection schemes that are all a form of SCSI simply because they use the same command set.

In fact, the SCSI-3 standard is a whole collection of standards documents, each covering one layer of the interface. The lowest level is called the *physical layer* and defines the cables and connectors to be used. The next layer, referred to as the *protocol layer*, describes how the signals are organized to send packets of information. The third layer is called the *architecture layer*, and it covers how command requests are organized, queued, and responded to. Primary commands are the top-level set of commands that all SCSI devices must support. Device-specific commands are optional ones used by particular classes of devices (for example, CD-ROMs or hard drives).

The second major change in SCSI-3 is the formal endorsement of a new kind of cable-end connector, this time with more contacts to enable support for 16-bit data transfers over a single cable. Today, this style of cable is referred to as a Wide-SCSI connection.

Third, SCSI-3 adds 1 bit to the SCSI ID, thus allowing up to 16 devices on a SCSI bus. The host adapter is still given the SCSI ID of 7 by default, but now other devices may be given any ID from 0 to 15.

Finally, SCSI-3 enables the use of a variety of physical layer media. These can be anything from a serial link (sending only a single bit at a time) all the way up to a parallel link that conveys data 32 or even 64 bits at a time, and the link can use wire, infrared beams, or optical fibers. Along with this new catholicity about what type of hardware link is used there is the capability of supporting even more rapid data transfers than any previous version of SCSI. With Fast-Wide SCSI, it is possible to transfer 40MB of data per second on a single SCSI (wire) cable. Use of special proprietary extensions or an optical fiber link enables even higher data rates.

The serial SCSI link became the basis of what is now called the IEEE 1394 standard. You'll learn more about that topic in the section "The Wonderful, New, High-Speed Serial PC Bus (IEEE 1349)" near the end of this chapter.

SCSI Devices

What, exactly, is a SCSI device? It can be almost anything: hard disks, CD-ROM drives, ZIP drives, recordable CD drives, printers, mice, tape drives, image scanners, and graphics tablets. Really, just about any PC peripheral device can be given a SCSI interface. The defining characteristic of all SCSI devices is that they have a SCSI interface. This is a small computer that "speaks SCSI" out of one side of itself (across the SCSI bus) and that understands how to operate the peripheral device to which it is attached out of the other side of itself.

Because of this "intelligent" aspect of SCSI devices, and because the SCSI standard allows multiple independent conversations between SCSI devices to happen simultaneously across a single SCSI bus, it is possible to have a high degree of multiprocessing in a PC with a SCSI bus and a suitable array of SCSI devices. This won't happen automatically, but it can happen with suitable software support.

SCSI Logical Units

The SCSI standard contemplated only up to eight devices (including the host adapter) on a single SCSI bus prior to the advent of SCSI-3, and 16 on a SCSI-3 bus. However, as mentioned previously, you can have more than one SCSI bus in a single PC by installing more than one SCSI host adapter. This works, but it uses up IRQ lines (each host adapter will need its own IRQ).

Another solution is to put more than just 7 devices, plus 1 host adapter, on a single SCSI bus. Although you can have only 7 (or 15) SCSI devices on the bus (in addition to the host adapter), it is perfectly possible for each of them to be a minimanager of multiple (up to 8 or 16) logical units.

This a very complex process, and it is not something that you should try at home—but it is perfectly possible, and it is supported in the SCSI standard. Many custom systems houses have built such systems for their customers.

The SCSI Host Adapter

The SCSI *host adapter* is interface circuitry that sits between the internal system bus of the PC and the SCSI bus. Its job is to send and receive messages in the SCSI fashion on the SCSI bus and simultaneously to send and receive messages on the PC system I/O bus in its native protocol.

Some PCs have a SCSI host adapter built onto the motherboard (as has been the case for all Macintosh computers), but most use a separate plug-in host adapter. If it's on a plug-in card, the host adapter could be on an ISA card, a VESA VL bus card, or a PCI card. To get the highest performance out of SCSI devices, it is important that the data transfers not be limited by the slow ISA bus. Most of the good SCSI host adapters sold today are PCI cards.

Because SCSI functionality has not been built into PCs from the beginning, the motherboard BIOS does not contain software support for that function. This means that to operate a SCSI bus, either the host adapter must have an on-board BIOS ROM chip or you must load a suitable software driver from a non-SCSI hard disk before using the SCSI bus at all.

Furthermore, the software in the BIOS ROM on a SCSI card (or in the lowest-level software driver that might have been provided on a disk with the host adapter) is probably only barely adequate to set up the SCSI host adapter for minimal operation. To get the full benefit of the SCSI bus, and in particular to support multiple devices hooked to it, you probably must load at least one more driver program. This might be a CAM (Common Access Method) driver, or it might be an ASPI (Advanced SCSI Programming Interface) driver. You must use whatever is required by your SCSI host adapter and the devices attached to it.

You can have more than one SCSI host adapter in your PC. However, if you have many of them, you likely will find yourself running out of IRQ levels to assign to them. The practical limit is probably two.

> **Tip:** Another job of the host adapter is to check at powerup and see which SCSI devices are at which SCSI IDs on the SCSI bus. For this to work, all those devices must be powered on when you boot your PC. If you plug everything into one power strip or power controller, you can easily turn on the entire system with one switch. Otherwise, just get in the habit of turning on the external SCSI devices before you power up your PC.

Some SCSI Host Adapters to Avoid (or Use Sparingly)

Some SCSI host adapters have been built onto sound cards. Others are shipped with external removable media drives (for example, ZIP drives). Most of these host adapters support only 8-bit data transfers, and they usually use an ISA bus or IDE interface, neither of which is capable of the highest data transfer rates. The intent of these interfaces, typically, is to support just a slow SCSI device, not to also support a hard disk. For these reasons, I don't recommend that you attach a SCSI hard drive to such a host adapter. In practice, many such adapters will not function properly if any other SCSI device (other than the one they came with) is attached to them.

Any host adapter sold today that is intended for use with SCSI hard drives will likely be a PCI card, and it probably will have a BIOS ROM on it to enable you to boot your PC from a SCSI hard disk if there is one attached to that SCSI bus (and if that disk is suitably formatted and has an operating system installed). If you don't have one of these and you want to use a SCSI hard disk, then get one. It's are worth the cost.

SCSI Cables and Connectors

Many of the problems involved in SCSI installations originate with the necessary cables and connectors. Knowing the differences between SCSI cable and connector types and the factors involved in proper termination can keep a simple SCSI installation job from turning into a challenge to your patience.

External SCSI Device Connectors and Cables

Most SCSI-1 devices use a 50-pin Centronics-style connector. This has enough wires to support eight pairs of data wires plus all the needed control, status, and ground wires. That means it is possible to do differential data transfers over this sort of cable and connector. A *differential mode* of operation simply means that when the signal on a data wire goes up, the voltage on its paired companion wire goes down. The receiver doesn't actually care what voltage is on either wire; it looks only at the difference between the two voltages. This strategy is very useful for canceling out inevitable noise signals that will be picked up on any long cables, because adjacent wires commonly pick up approximately equal noise voltages.

However, the SCSI-1 standard also permits the use of single-ended cable with only a single wire per data or parity bit, and with receivers that simply compare the voltage on those wires with ground. This reduces the needed number of wires enough that a 25-pin connector can be used, but it limits the length of the SCSI cables attached to such an interface to about 20 feet. (With differential signals, it is possible to extend a SCSI bus to around 80 feet from the PC.)

> **Warning:** Macintosh computers use female DB25 connectors on their SCSI bus interfaces. This is the same connector used on PCs for the parallel port (printer) interface.
>
> Until PCs had SCSI host adapters, this was not a problem. Now it can be. If you have a SCSI host adapter that uses the Macintosh-style female DB25 connector for the SCSI bus, you might inadvertently plug your printer into it. Not only would this not work, it likely would burn out some of the interface circuitry in the printer and could damage the SCSI host adapter as well. The reverse is also true of plugging a SCSI device into a printer parallel port. If your PC has both kinds of female DB25 on it, look carefully for the SCSI logo on the cable connectors (it looks like a diamond with a short line segment projecting through one of the diamond's corner points). You'll usually find the logo embossed on good-quality SCSI cables. If your cables aren't already marked, please mark them yourself so you never make this mistake.
>
> Also, you should realize that a SCSI cable with a 25-pin connector on one or both ends is likely to be quite different internally than a printer cable or a serial port extension cable (which also has the same sorts of connectors on its ends). So don't confuse them. The SCSI cable is likely to be better shielded, and because its several uses put data on different pins on the 25-pin connector, these three kinds of cables will protect the signals on the wires more carefully for the application for which they are intended. Finally, some printer cables simply don't connect all the pins at one end to all of them at the other end. Label your cables so you know what each is good for, and then use them only for their proper function, please.

If your PC SCSI host adapter has the more conventional 50-pin connector, you won't have that problem. But there are other issues to attend to.

You can get a SCSI cable with any of several different combinations of connectors on its ends. The original standard cable has a 50-pin Centronics-style male connector at both ends. And many SCSI devices have two female Centronics 50-pin connectors. But some have 25-pin female DB connectors instead. You can buy adapter cables that have a 50-pin connector on one end and a 25-pin connector on the other. If you do this, and if your SCSI host adapter has a 50-pin connector, be sure to put all the SCSI devices with 50-pin connectors closer to the host adapter than any of the 25-pin ones. You do this because after you make the transition from 50-pin down to 25-pin (going out across the SCSI bus from the host adapter.

And, it gets worse. There are two other kinds of connectors to be concerned with. The SCSI-2 standard introduced a miniature 50-pin DB connector, which has its pins spaced 1/20-inch apart (instead of the 1/10-inch used in the DB25 connector and a somewhat larger spacing in the Centronics-style connectors). Except for the style of the connector and the fact that it is small enough to fit on the rear panel of a PC plug-in card, this is electrically the same as the 50-pin Centronics connector.

The really different connector is the *P connector* introduced with SCSI-3. This 68-pin connector has enough pins to support differential data transfers 16 bits at a time. If you have any SCSI devices with this type of connector, you'd better have a host adapter with one, also.

You must have a full 16-bit data path from a 16-bit SCSI device to a 16-bit SCSI host adapter. That can be done only with a single 68-wire cable, or with two 50-wire (or 25-wire) cables. At any point on the SCSI bus you may convert from a 16-bit connection to an 8-bit connection (using a single 50-wire or 25-wire cable with a special 68-pin connector on one end). But you won't be able to support a 16-bit SCSI device at any point beyond there (going away from the host adapter) on the SCSI bus.

Internal SCSI Device Cables and Connectors

On the SCSI host adapter card, in addition to the external data cable connector mounted on the rear panel, you will likely find one or two post and header connectors. If there is only one, it will probably have 50 pins. If there are two, one will have 50 pins and the other will have 68 pins. The 50-pin header is for 8-bit data transfers, and the 68-pin header is for 16-bit transfers.

From either of these connectors, you will run a ribbon cable (with the correct number of conductors) from the host adapter to the SCSI devices that are mounted inside your PC's system unit. If you have only one, be sure to put it at the end of that cable, even if some connectors are on that cable midway. Those other connectors are only for use when you have more than one internal SCSI device to hook up.

The Issue of SCSI Terminations

If you have a cable and you launch a rapidly changing signal onto it, that signal moves down the cable as a wave traveling at very nearly the speed of light from where you launched it to both ends of the cable. (If you are launching it from one end, you will only notice the wave going away from you to the other end.) At either end of the cable, unless something absorbs the energy in this wave, it will bounce and return back toward its source.

If this is a SCSI bus and a device is monitoring its signals, it will see two waves go by instead of just one. If this is a hard disk that is recording data, it might record too many instances of the data. Worse, if a new chunk of data follows the first (as is usually the case), the bounced copy of the first batch of data can overlap the new data and confuse the hard drive about what data value it is to record. Follow this reasoning even a little bit, and you can see why signals that bounce back and forth on a cable can cause data loss.

So, how can you stop this from happening? The obvious solution is to absorb all the wave's energy at the end of the cable. That is precisely what a *cable terminator* does. It takes away the signal's energy so nothing is left to bounce. However, if you do this in the wrong place—like in the middle of the cable—you could keep the signal from ever reaching some of the devices on the cable. So, it is necessary to properly terminate cables that carry fast signals over any distances greater than a few inches.

On a SCSI cable, the usual practice is to terminate the cable at both ends, and nowhere else. This means one of two things: Either the devices at the ends of the cable must incorporate some suitable termination network (some resistors going between each data wire and either a power source or ground), or a terminator must be added to the end of the cable. The power source may be supplied locally by the SCSI device, or the terminator may depend upon power that is supplied along the SCSI bus on what is called the TERM PWR line. The former strategy is called *active termination*; the latter is *passive termination*.

Both internal and plug-in terminators are used for external SCSI devices. If the device has two SCSI connectors, one will be used for the cable going toward the host adapter. The other will be used either for a cable going to another SCSI device, or else it may have a special terminator plug plugged into it.

Alternatively, there might be a switch on the device to terminate the cable internally. If it has such a switch, that is generally a preferable way to do SCSI cable termination. Just be sure you don't have the internal termination turned on in any devices before the end of the cable, and use only the internal terminator or the external terminator on the device at the end of the cable. Two termination devices at the end of a SCSI chain can cause erratic operation of the devices attached to it. You may also purchase active termination devices that will sense the presence or absence of proper termination on a SCSI bus and provide only what is necessary.

What about the other end of the cable, back at the host adapter? Some host adapters are clever enough to always provide the right termination at that point. Others are not. If you have both an internal and an external SCSI cable attached to the SCSI host adapter, depending on exactly how its internal circuitry is built, the host adapter might have to provide termination to the cables going out in both directions, or it might have to avoid terminating what amounts to one long cable that passes through the host adapter. You must consult the manual that comes with your host adapter to know which way it is built.

Finally, for the ribbon cable that extends inside the system unit, you have only one option. Turn off (or remove) the terminator resistor packs or other termination means on each SCSI device before the end of the ribbon cable and be sure the cable ends on a device that has a terminator.

Some Special Considerations for SCSI Hard Disks

The SCSI host adapter "lies" to the PC about any hard disks it has attached to it across the SCSI bus. It must lie because SCSI has no concept of a three-dimensional disk drive (with some number of heads, cylinders, and sectors per track). On the other hand, the PC BIOS is built assuming that all disk drives have that type of structure.

So most, if not all, SCSI host adapters do something like this: They treat the actual hard disk simply as a long string of logical blocks. Then they turn those block addresses into head, cylinder, and sector numbers on some fictitious 3D hard drive, and they tell the

BIOS about the data's location in those terms. (Conversely, when the BIOS asks the SCSI host adapter to put or retrieve some data at a particular head, cylinder, and sector location, the host adapter converts that set of numbers to a single logical block address and puts or gets the data from that block.)

> **Warning:** All this works very well. That is, right up until you change which brand of SCSI host adapter a particular hard drive is attached to. You can freely move many kinds of SCSI devices from host adapter to host adapter and never have a problem, but if you move a formatted hard disk with data on it, you stand a very good chance of finding that the new system you attach it to sees this hard disk as unformatted and without any data at all. You haven't really lost anything—yet. But if you actually go ahead and use this hard disk on the new system you will be destroying the data it contains as you reformat it to the new system's view of how it should have its logical blocks arranged.
>
> Removable hard disks (such as a SyQuest disk or an Iomega Jaz disk) and CD-ROMs or CD-R discs don't have this problem. The device driver software that supports their use handles all these geometrical conversions in a universal manner—or it doesn't do them at all.
>
> Bottom line: Don't move a hard disk from one SCSI host adapter to another unless you plan to reformat it and start over as if it were a brand new disk immediately after you move it. If you must move it while it is full of important data (say, if your SCSI host adapter dies), be sure to use a new host adapter of the same brand, preferably the same model, and even the same firmware revision as the original one. Even within the same model of adapter, significant changes to functionality may be implemented from one revision (firmware change) to the next; these could render your drive useless. It's probably always a good idea to consult the manufacturer's technical support department to inquire about such changes before you get burned.

Mixing IDE and SCSI Disk Drives

The most common kind of hard disk in a modern PC is one that connects to an IDE bus. You can have up to four IDE devices (hard disks, CD-ROM drives, and so on) in most PCs, and with the use of special plug-in cards, you can add up to four additional IDE devices.

You also can use SCSI hard disks in a PC. There are two advantages to using SCSI hard disks. One is that at least the best of them are capable of higher data transfer rates than even the best of the IDE drives, and the other is that you can have more SCSI hard disks than you can have IDE drives. (You can easily put in 7 hard disks (or 15 on a SCSI-3 host adapter), and with the use of logical units you can push that as high as 56 (or 240 with SCSI-3). This latter advantage might be of little interest to you unless the operating system you are running is capable of supporting that many hard disks—which certainly rules out DOS and Windows 95 or 98—or at least as many hard disks as you want to use, which could be well less than those higher numbers, yet more than 4. SCSI also has other performance benefits for operating systems such as NetWare, Windows NT, and most flavors of UNIX, which can take advantage of them.

What if you want to use both IDE and SCSI hard disks in your PC? In that case, you must know some special things. First, some older motherboard BIOSes will require that you boot your PC from one of the IDE devices. (This could be a hard drive or an EIDE CD-ROM.) The only other alternative supported by most PCs is to boot from a floppy disk. Most newer BIOSes incorporate support for booting from any EIDE or SCSI drive.

Less standard is which drive will show up with which drive letter. The boot drive will always be C:, but from there things get much murkier. The most common BIOS strategy puts the primary EIDE channel's master as the first hard drive, then the primary EIDE channel's slave, then the secondary EIDE channel's master, then its slave, and then the SCSI hard drives, if any. But I have seen many variations on this. The BIOS, during POST, assigns a numerical physical address to each hard drive. Later, DOS or Windows 9x will assign a drive letter to each hard drive in numerical order, with C: being associated with drive number 80h, D: with 81h, and so forth (assuming each hard drive has a primary DOS partition on it). You can learn more about how DOS and Windows 9x assign drive letters in Chapter 10.

PCMCIA Becomes PC Card, and Now We Have the Card Bus and Zoomed Video

Now we are ready for the last of the four parts to our story of faster PC I/O connectivity. This part is all about a means that could be used in any PC, but in fact is common only in laptop PCs, plus in some personal digital assistants (PDAs) and a few digital still-image cameras. This is the PC Card and its related technologies.

It All Began as Memory, and Not Just for PCs

Memory chips (RAM and ROM) are useful in many devices. We may focus on PCs, but the makers of these chips are well aware that automobiles, game machines, and other products also use up lots and lots of their output. Several of the major memory chip makers got together and decided to create a standard specification for how to package some small add-on memory modules for use in game machines and other applications. Because they were interested in memory cards and were an international group of companies (and because PCs are one of the major target uses of the products they met to discuss), it is perhaps not surprising that they named their group the PC Memory Card International Association (PCMCIA).

They settled on a form factor (size and shape) for these modules that is roughly that of a calling card (business card) and a third of a centimeter thick (about an eighth of an inch). They published a standards document (which is a lot fatter than the cards it describes) detailing many arcane details about these cards.

Broadening the Range of Uses

One especially important group that adopted this new standard module for memory add-ons was the laptop PC makers. They received this new form factor gratefully, because it fit well with their goal of making laptop computers ever smaller while still providing the amount of memory that their customers wanted.

Type I cards are the original size, about 85×54×3.3mm (which is about 3.3×2.1×0.13 inches). Type II cards are 5mm thick. Type III cards are 10.5mm thick. Allowing for the space between cards, this you can build a card bay that will hold one Type II or one Type I card, or a larger card bay that will hold one Type III or two of any mix of Type I and Type II cards.

The thinnest cards (Type I) work well for RAM or ROM (or Flash RAM), and very clever manufacturers have even managed to put a modem or a network interface card into this PC Card. The thickest (Type III) cards have been used for such relatively bulky items as a miniature hard disk.

Many different kinds of PC Cards are now available, including the original use for RAM or Flash RAM, as well as modems, network interface cards, GPS (Global Positioning Satellite) receivers, and various combinations of these functions.

Connecting PCMCIA Cards to a PC

To use these cards, it is necessary to provide a bay in which they will fit, and appropriate additional connection circuitry and software. What the committee evolved was a standard that essentially specifies that the socket for a PCMCIA card shall present what amounts to an ISA slot in a smaller space. This enables those cards to do anything functionally, that an ISA card can do—provided one is clever enough to fit that functionality into such a tiny space.

Originally, whatever was on a PCMCIA Card was supposed to show up in the CPU's memory address space in a single 64KB region of upper memory (between 640KB and 1MB). Soon this restriction was relaxed to accommodate the wide range of devices being put on these cards. And, ultimately, the PCMCIA Card jawbreaker of a name was shortened to PC Card.

What's a Card Bus and What Is Zoomed Video?

The original PC Card interface was, like the ISA bus, a 16-bit interface. As PCs evolved, it became clear that it would have been nice if the interface had been designed to support 32-bit data transfers and direct memory access (DMA). So the committee went back to the drawing board and came up with just such a variation on the original plan. It named this new interface design the *Card Bus*, mainly to distinguish it from the earlier PC Card (just 16-bit) interface. Having twice the number of data lines meant, of course, that the new Card Bus interface could transfer data twice as fast as the original PC Card interface.

Even that wasn't fast enough for some. So the committee came up with one more innovation. This is a special new system bus that goes directly from a Card Bus slot to the video subsystem. This enables the video accelerator to use the memory (or other resources) on a PC Card without the delays of going through the slow ISA bus. The folks at PCMCIA gave this new bus the fancy name of *Zoomed Video Port*. (This apparently refers more to the zippy way data can move from PC Card to video frame buffer, rather than anything about actually "zooming" a video image. So far, the MPEG decoder PC Card is one of the few kinds of PC Cards that actually uses the Zoomed Video connection.)

The Card Information Structure (CIS), Card Services, Socket Services, and More

Every PC Card carries some information on it in a standard location and format, to identify just what type of card it is and what it can do. This *metaformat* information is contained in something called the Card Information Structure (CIS).

The software support for PC Cards includes some additions to the operating system. At the lowest level, these pieces are called the *Socket Services*. These deal directly with talking to the socket in which the PC Card sits. The logically next-higher-level operating system enhancements are called the *Card Services*. They include the software that responds to calls from application programs that need to use the capabilities offered by the PC Cards plugged into a given PC. Some varieties of Card and Socket Services software use the CIS information to decide how the PC Card should be connected to and serviced by the operating system.

Other parts of the evolving standard that describes PC Cards include the *Media Storage Formats* (describing how a Flash RAM card can be made to look as if it were a hard disk, among other things), the *PC Card ATA* (details on how to use the now-customary ATA protocol to access hard disks, and how to modify it for use with PC Cards), and the *eXecute in Place (Xip)* standard for running programs stored in ROM on a PC Card without first having to load them into the PC's main RAM.

This is a vital and fast-developing area of PC technology. It is being pressed by developments in storage devices such as the CompactFlash and SmartMedia memory cards, as well as by some very tiny hard drives. But for things such as adding a modem, network interface card, or GPS receiver to your laptop PC, the PC Card is about the only way to go—and I expect we will see more developments in this area in the future.

The Future of PC-to-Peripheral Interconnections

There have been several major trends in the PC world in the past decade. If they keep going as they have been, there will be a collision between them. The rest of this chapter is about what folks who've noticed this are doing to avoid that collision.

Learning from the Past

Certainly, the major story about PCs in the past decade has been how rapidly they have become more powerful, more complex, and less costly for what they do. One obvious consequence of this is that as these little boxes have become more capable and more affordable, more and more people want to have them. That is why PCs are now a mass-market item. It is very much in the interests of all of us in this industry for PCs to become even more of a mass-market commodity, used by even more people for more of what they do.

But a problem is brewing. Right now, PCs sport close to a dozen special-purpose I/O interfaces. Each one is different from all the rest, and you must have most, if not all, of them on your PC to hook up all the pieces of hardware you want to have connected to your PC.

It appears that it is going to get worse before it gets better. We are beginning to see the much-touted convergence of PCs with telephones and other commodity appliances, such as VCRs, televisions, radios, washing machines, ovens, toasters—you name it. Probably in the not-distant future, you will be able to buy one that is ready to be controlled by your PC or to report to your PC. We can't go on adding special-purpose interfaces for each and every one of these gadgets. Nor can we hook them all up to the I/O interfaces we have today. Something radically different is needed.

We must make PCs simpler: simpler to buy, simpler to set up and use, simpler to maintain, and simpler to upgrade. Their cost must be reduced as much as possible. Only then can they reach their true potential as ubiquitous computing devices, helping out in nearly every area of daily life.

The New Direction for PC Input and Output

The solution, some very clever people have decided, is to replace all the present-day special-purpose I/O interfaces with just one or two truly general-purpose ones. Well, that is, one or two *types* of truly general-purpose interfaces. You might need more than one of a given type to get enough data transfer bandwidth for all your needs.

These interfaces must be simple to set up and dirt cheap. This argues for an interface that uses a small, simple, and inexpensive connector with a thin, highly flexible cable. You'd like to be able simply to plug in a gadget and have your PC notice it, recognize it, and respond appropriately. No powering down the PC. No opening up the box. No setting jumpers, switches, or even software options to select an IRQ level, a DMA channel, an I/O port address, or a memory address. No fussing with terminators.

But is such a dream interface workable? Could it possibly be fast enough if it were so simple and easy to use? Surprisingly, the answer seems to be "Yes"—or at least that is the message we are hearing from the development laboratories and the meeting rooms of some of our industry standards committees. We will need two types of interfaces—but only two. And they will be just as simple and elegant as I have described.

The Wonderful New High-Speed Serial Buses (USB and IEEE 1394)

The groundwork for these developments was laid some time ago. As I told you earlier in this chapter, the SCSI bus has many of the properties we want. The PCI bus has some others. Combining the best of each and using what they've learned, engineers have come up with some better-than-ever options. These are new developments, just now coming into the marketplace.

I have already described one of them, the Universal Serial Bus (USB), in Chapter 15. The other is a similar standard, but optimized for faster data transfers, currently called by its standard committee's name, IEEE 1394. (Apple Computer helped develop this latter standard and it gave its implementation of it the much more mellifluous name Firewire, but it has trademarked that name and so far is not allowing anyone else to use it.)

I'll remind you now of some of the salient features of the USB bus—in particular, those that are similar to features of the IEEE 1394 bus, or where the contrast is an important distinction between the two—and then go on to describe the IEEE 1394 bus's special features in some detail.

They Have More in Common Than Not

There are probably more ways in which these two standards resemble one another than there are differences. So first I'll describe those common features. Then I'll point out some of the differences.

First, both are serial standards. That is, they send data over a link just 1 bit at a time. That sounds slow, until you realize that at the very slowest, 1 1/2 million bits move over the link every second. At the fastest, more than 1,000 million bits will pass each second. Even though it takes approximately 10 of those bits to send each byte, these are some pretty seriously impressive data transfer rates.

Next, each bus can accept a whole flock of different peripheral devices, ranging from a keyboard, a mouse, a "smart" loudspeaker, or a "smart" microphone all the way up to video camera, DVD player, or a hard disk. In fact, you can hook up all those things at once.

Here is where we first come to a difference between these buses. The USB is specifically designed for low- and medium-speed peripherals. A keyboard, for example, must send very few bits per second to the PC, and it receives even fewer of them back. This is a typical low-speed device. A *smart* loudspeaker (and by that I mean a device that can receive digital data and convert it into sounds) will need to receive a lot more bits per second, but a few hundred thousand would be enough. This is a typical medium-speed peripheral device.

The USB can handle these devices in two modes. In low-speed mode, it enables communication at a rate of 1.5Mbps (1 1/2 million bits per second). At medium speed, it goes eight times as fast 12Mbps. Converting these into bytes per second you come up with something like 150–200KBps (which is around the top speed of a standard serial port) up to a little more than 1MBps (close to the maximum speed of an EPP parallel port).

In contrast, an IEEE 1394 connection is meant for high-speed, serious-capacity data transfer work. The starting speed for this bus is around eight times faster than the top speed of a USB bus. Projected developments (still in the laboratory, but likely to reach the desktop in the next few years) will stretch up past the speed of the fastest SCSI bus.

Back to something these buses have in common: They handle bandwidth intelligently. That is, they will enable any device to have as much data transfer capacity as it can use—up to a point. But they will reserve enough of their overall capacity to enable them to also service the other devices on the bus. A device like a video camera, which *must* have all its data passed down the bus because it has nowhere to store it, can request and be assured of receiving enough data transfer capacity to keep the frames of the image flowing down the wire as they are taken. Other devices that can afford to wait might be forced to do so, but their data transfer needs will ultimately be accommodated as long as the total bandwidth (bits per second) of the bus is sufficient.

Transfers like those needed for a video camera are called *isochronous*, meaning that uniform amounts of data must be transferred every second, and fixed amounts of that data must be transferred in chunks on a regular schedule. In this type of data transfer, late data is useless, and if there is some error, there is no point in trying to resend the data because then it would be late (and thus of no value).

The other kind of data transfer these buses support is called *asynchronous*. This type of transfer emphasizes reliability. The data *will* get through eventually, and retries are not only permissible but are mandated if errors occur. The host PC and the software running on it has the job of managing the available bandwidth and parceling it out to all the requesting devices, keeping a good balance between the needs of all of them. Only when there simply isn't enough total bandwidth will a problem occur, and then some device must be denied its request for bandwidth. (In that case, the PC might direct you to unplug that device and plug it into another bus that has some available bandwidth.)

Both USB and IEEE 1394 can support multiple devices, because each of them assigns an address to each device. These addresses function very much like SCSI IDs, but with the very important difference that they aren't set by hardware switches on the devices, but rather are assigned by the host when the device is plugged into the bus.

Also, both buses enable devices to talk to one another without to involving the host in the conversation. That is, after the host has assigned addresses to everyone on the cable, any device can ask the host about who else is on the cable, and subsequently can address messages directly to a desired target device. The host might be carrying on a separate conversation at the same time with some other device. (In fact, the packets of data are interleaved. Only one voltage can be on a wire at a single instant, but it will appear to all the devices as if the conversations are simultaneous.)

The commands supported on these buses are modeled after those used in the SCSI-3 standard. This is explicitly so for IEEE 1394, and certainly the lessons learned in the SCSI development have influenced how USB's commands work.

Furthermore, both buses enable power to travel alongside data. Each cable design (and USB and IEEE 1394 use different cables) includes power wires separate from the data wires. That enables devices that need only a little bit of power, such as a keyboard or mouse, to get it from the data cable just as they do in present-day PCs. Any device that needs massive amounts of power (for example, a big loudspeaker) must have a local power supply, but again this is no different from our present situation.

With both USB and IEEE 1394, a device may serve as a link to other devices. The details differ somewhat, but in essence, it will be possible to plug in some devices to the PC and then plug other devices into the ones you connected first. In this way, you can extend the cable reach for either bus as far as you are likely to want to extend it. (Not surprisingly, the faster IEEE 1394 bus is limited to shorter distances than the slower USB bus—especially if the IEEE1394 bus is running at one of its higher data rates.)

The resulting chain of cables may branch at some devices and may just be extended at others. But logically, the system will treat all the devices on the chain, no matter which branch they may be on, as equals. It is as if they were all connected in series or all were connected directly at the PC host.

The Many "Flavors" of the IEEE 1394 Bus

If you are interested in getting an adapter to add IEEE 1394 connectivity to your PC, you will need to be aware of the several variations on that standard that are now being developed. Whatever you get in the way of IEEE 1394 devices and an adapter must, of course, be able to work with one another gracefully.

Here we come to one more place where USB and IEEE 1394 are different. USB is a completed standard. That is not to say it won't be extended and modified, but an adopted standard is out there for manufacturers to use, and every major PC manufacturer is already using it, shipping PCs with USB ports in them.

The state of IEEE 1394 is a bit more confusing. The IEEE organization has approved a version of this standard (1394-1995) and is considering several extensions to it (called things like P1394.1, P1394.2, P1394A, and P1394B). The reason for these different, in effect competing, "standards" is that different groups of would-be users of this bus have different needs. Hard disk vendors want one thing. Video camera makers are concerned with something else, and each group wants the standard "bent" toward their concerns.

We are clearly well on the way to having a real, usable 1394 standard. With all the advantages it offers, we can expect to see at least one of the competing versions of IEEE 1394 get approved and compliant hardware get built and sold. Just not right away.

What Is Device Bay?

The IEEE 1394 standard permits hot-plugging of high-speed peripheral devices outside the PC system unit, but it might be nice if you didn't have to have all those devices in their own separate boxes. This is where Device Bay comes into the picture.

The notion is that a Device Bay will be a place into which you can plug a peripheral device and connect it to the IEEE 1394 bus as you do so. That means you could hot-swap hard disk drives, for example, or exchange a hard disk drive for an optical disc drive.

Because Device Bay presumes the presence of an IEEE 1394 bus, we probably won't be seeing Device Bays commonly included in PCs until the IEEE 1394 bus is fully established. That may be longer in coming than was once thought.

One reason for the delay is that Apple has recently become quite aggressive in defending what it feels are its proprietary rights to the underlying technologies used in FireWire, which is Apple's implementation of what the IEEE has described in its 1394 bus standard. This could mean higher costs for IEEE 1394 hardware, and that could make it less desirable for PC makers to include this capability.

Another reason for delaying IEEE 1394 is that the emergence of PCI-X and improvements in SCSI and Fibre Channel are providing alternative ways to get most of the benefits of IEEE 1394 in many setups without having to include an IEEE 1394 interface.

Eventually, I expect we will see both IEEE 1394 and Device Bay on many PCs. It just makes sense in the long run as a means of further simplifying the experience of using a PC while enhancing its performance of which those PCs will be capable.

There *Will* Be More I/O Bus Standards

This has been a long and involved story covering many different I/O standards. It ended with what appears to be a new and wonderfully simple age that is dawning. Is this story then about to end? No way.

As experience is gained with USB and IEEE 1394, we can expect those standards to go through additional generations. As PCs move further into convergence with all the other electronics in your life, new needs are likely to pop up. Some of those might necessitate the devising of wholly new standards. Finally, some of the old warhorses aren't likely to die any time soon. We will have EIDE interfaces inside our PCs for quite some time to come. Parallel cable SCSI buses might last even longer. USB and IEEE 1394 aren't *that* much better than everything that went before.

Next Generation I/O (NGIO) and Future I/O

As the CPU speeds in PCs have increased, so have the aspirations of their users. Now PCs are being expected to do jobs formerly only possible on minicomputers and mainframe computers. CPU speed is not all that is required to do those jobs successfully, however.

In particular, we need to be able to do massive amounts of data input and output. We also must be able to transfer data reliably between several processors and many storage devices.

The most efficient ways of doing this are what are termed *point-to-point switched fabric* interconnections. These are a means of transferring data between any pair of a large number of storage devices and processors in a cluster. Many such transactions may be going on in parallel. This somewhat resembles all the telephone interconnections and parallel voice conversations that are typical of a telephone company's local exchange. Indeed, the concepts behind each are very similar.

First to be added to PCs should be the capability of doing very fast I/O transactions. That has been addressed in part already, and will be more fully addressed with the other coming technologies I have already discussed (such as PCI-X, the latest SCSI developments, Fibre Channel, and IEEE 1394).

Something more is also needed. We must be able to send information in messages that can be switched across the connecting fabric in ways that can be altered as necessary to accommodate the presence of other data conversations and of failures of some components, or the addition of others. All this adds complexity, but it permits much higher total data traffic rates, and it also allows sending data over much longer distances between components of the cluster.

Naturally, some new protocols and standards must be developed to support this new approach. Many companies have been hard at work on this problem. Intel is the principal sponsor of what it calls Next Generation I/O (NGIO). Compaq, Hewlett-Packard, and IBM are the principal sponsors of a competing approach they have termed Future I/O. How these two competing plans will develop, and whether or not they will be combined, cannot yet be predicted. It will have to be determined in the course of 1999 and 2000. Some such newer, better way of interconnecting PCs is going to come, and with it much higher capacities for data transfer, leading to more ambitious applications for PCs.

Keeping Up with Tomorrow

So you can rest assured that the I/O bus standards committees will have plenty of work to do for a very long time to come. You'll just have to stay tuned if you want to know how all those future buses will function. The basics I have given you here should stand you in very good stead as you attempt to understand whatever innovations the future may bring.

Understanding PC Operating Systems

The topics covered in this chapter are a substantial departure from those in the other chapters in this part of the book. Those emphasized hardware. This one is all about software. But it's not about all kinds of PC software—just one very special kind that all of us use every day.

In fact, this chapter is about the most popular computer program ever created—and one that most of its users normally don't even think about as a software program. I am referring here to the *operating system*. Until recently, in nearly all PCs ever made, the operating system underlying everything was called DOS. If your PC is turned on right now, it probably is running DOS, and you might not even know it. In the near future, many of these same PCs will be upgraded to the forthcoming Microsoft Windows 2000 operating system, and DOS will become a thing of the past. That notwithstanding, understanding the past is an important aspect of understanding the present. For that reason, you'll learn about past, present, and future as we discuss operating systems in this chapter.

Most people who use PCs think of the software they use in terms of the application programs: Word, Excel, and Netscape Communicator. But you couldn't run any of those programs unless you first ran the program that creates the environment in which they are designed to operate. For the three programs I just mentioned, that program environment creator is some version of Windows. And Windows cannot run unless DOS is loaded first. This is still true even if you are running Windows 95 or 98. Although most of DOS is, in effect, "put to sleep" when Windows 9*x* gets up and running fully, DOS must run before Windows 9*x* can start up.

Of course, you might be running some other PC operating system. If so, you probably know it. Popular choices include Windows NT, Linux, or one of several versions of UNIX. I'll discuss these in the section of this chapter near the end titled "Understanding Your Choices for Your PC's Operating System."

What Is an Operating System and Why Do I Need One?

For something that has been used by so many people, DOS is very much misunderstood. It is a computer operating system. But that sentence may not mean a lot to you. What is a computer operating system and why must you have one? Those are important questions with less than obvious answers. I will make the answers to those questions clear.

The formal definition of a computer operating system is something that "manages and schedules the resources" of the computer. Unless you are different from most people I have talked to, reading that doesn't help increase your understanding very much at all.

Let me put it this way: Think of your computer as a business, and you are the owner. You have tasks you want accomplished. You hire workers who have specialized skills to do some of those tasks, but they need a good work environment. When they pick up the phones on their desks, they need to hear a dial tone.

When supplies are needed, they should be in stock and be deliverable. In an office, these tasks are done by the office manager and sometimes a whole staff of helpers. That is very much like what an operating system is. It is a manager of the environment in which other programs work, and it also is a bunch of grunt laborers ready to do particular subtasks whenever they are directed to do them.

How You Can Avoid Having an OS—And Why That Is a Bad Idea

It is perfectly possible to avoid having an operating system for your PC, in the sense of a separate program you run first before you run your application programs. But doing that would be a very bad idea.

The way to avoid having a separate OS is simply to build into each application program all the instruction code necessary to accomplish all the things an operating system normally does.

That is, if you are going to be doing some word processing, your word processor program also would have in it the necessary detailed instructions to accomplish reading characters from the keyboard (and knowing when to do so). It would also need to know how to write them to the video display and access the disk drives to store your work in files and manage those files appropriately.

One reason doing this is a terrible idea is that it requires the authors of all application programs to know intimately how your particular PC's hardware works and is configured. That's really not their job. They must know how to write the word processor (or other application) and shouldn't be bothered with the nitty-gritty details of making a PC work.

The second reason this is a terrible idea is that each application would be very much larger than it now is, because each one would have to incorporate much of the same set of instructions for operating the PC hardware. Putting those common instructions into a separate program you run first (and that keeps on running "underneath" your application programs) is a much better plan.

Finally, if you did put all that operating stuff into each application, the only way you could shift from one task to another would be to reboot your PC with a new boot disk containing the next application you wanted to run. Major awkwardness! And what about multitasking? Under this scenario, the only answer would have to be "forget it."

This is not a viable solution. There are just too many compelling reasons to have and use an operating system. For most PCs to date, that has meant using DOS.

What Is DOS? Hasn't It Gone Bye-Bye?

DOS stands for *disk operating system*. This means that DOS is an operating system that is particularly concerned with how to deal with disk drives.

In Chapter 5, "How to Get Your PC to Understand You," I told you that the motherboard BIOS ROM contained some small programs to activate the normal PC hardware pieces. Those mostly are interrupt service routines to deal with the keyboard, the original PC video display options, the floppy disk drive, and some elemental actions on the hard disk drive. An operating system, like DOS, uses all these programs, but it also does much more. (If you are unclear about what an *interrupt service routine* is, please review Chapter 8, "How Your PC 'Thinks.'")

DOS is mainly concerned with how the disk drives are used at a higher *logical* level. DOS manages files and how you store and access them. The BIOS routines, by contrast, deal only with the physical reading and writing of data at some absolute address (specified by a head number, cylinder number, and sector number within the single track at that head and cylinder location).

DOS is, however, concerned with much more than just disk management. It has had the job of allocating memory (RAM), scheduling tasks, and resolving competing demands for the PC's other resources. Thus, DOS launches programs, which in turn use DOS to access various features of your PC. Today, although DOS certainly can still perform these functions, most of the jobs traditionally performed by DOS are performed by Windows 9x. As you've already read, DOS enables Windows 9x to load. In this regard, Windows starts out like just another program, as far as DOS is concerned. After loading, however, Windows manages almost all PC resources and devices. In fact, the forthcoming Windows 2000 Professional will do away with DOS altogether. You'll read about why this is advantageous in the section, "Microsoft Windows Takes Over," later in this chapter. For the time being, let's explore how DOS interacts with PCs; from this, you'll have a strong foundation for understanding how most any operating system works.

How Does an Operating System Such As DOS Work?

Operating systems provide an environment for the user and for other programs. Their job is to keep track of what—application or data—is using what portions of memory, which spaces on the disk drives, and so on. They also have the job of coordinating the work of all those lower-level programs that respond to interrupts. These include the ones in the motherboard BIOS ROM, ones that come bundled with DOS, and ones added to your system by various device driver or TSR (terminate-and-stay resident) programs.

What Are the Essential Pieces of an Operating System?

An OS such as DOS comes on several disks or on a CD-ROM. (Of course, it may also be preinstalled on a new PC's hard drive by the manufacturer). It contains a huge number of modules, each of which generally resides in its own file. This collection is a great deal more than what I would consider the essence of an operating system. The essence of DOS, for example, is a *kernel* and perhaps a *shell program* (which also is often called the *command processor*). Most of the remaining files function as *device drivers*, each of which integrates with the rest of the operating system to provide a specific type of functionality or access to installed hardware. Although these integrate seamlessly with the operating system and may be distributed by the operating system manufacturer, they are, strictly speaking, external components. (In the specific case of DOS, there are additional files included with the OS that are actually independent utility programs that function as if they were internal to DOS. These are known as *external commands*.)

The DOS Kernel

The kernel is the fundamental, central part of the operating system. (Think of a nut, such as a walnut or cashew, that has a shell on the outside and a kernel in the center.) For DOS, this kernel consists of two or—in recent versions if you are using OS-level (on-the-fly) data compression—three components, each of which comes in its own file.

Microsoft's names for the DOS kernel files were IO.SYS, MSDOS.SYS, and DBLSPACE.BIN or DRVSPACE.BIN. These are all files with the file attributes of *hidden, system,* and *read-only.* (Please do not confuse these DOS files with the Windows 95 files of the same names. Those are different, though IO.SYS in Windows 9*x* contains most of the functionality of both the files IO.SYS and MSDOS.SYS in MS-DOS version 6.22. The Windows 9*x* MSDOS.SYS file is entirely different from its DOS cousin and isn't really part of the kernel.)

The DOS Command Processor

The only visible (not hidden) file on a DOS disk that might qualify for the description "an essential part of DOS" is the command processor, or shell program. This is the file called COMMAND.COM (in virtually all versions of DOS).

I mentioned previously that you can think of the kernel of DOS as being like the kernel of a nut, namely the portion at the core that is hidden from view but which carries most of the value of the nut. This analogy is why the only visible-to-the-user portion of the operating system, the command processor, often is referred to as the "shell" program for the operating system. (This usage is universal in references to UNIX, and it is not uncommon in discussions of DOS written for programmers.)

The Essential Parts of an Operating System

The kernel, as its name suggests, is at the core of the operating system, and as such it is involved in nearly everything DOS does and much of what is done by other non-Windows programs running on your PC. The kernel presents a uniform *application program interface* (API) by which other programs can ask it for services. It also supports the rest of the programs (including other parts of DOS) in doing their jobs. (In the case of Windows 9x and later, the Windows API performs these same tasks after Windows is running.)

Generally, a program that wants some help from DOS will cause a *software interrupt*. This causes the CPU to stop what it is doing within that program and go instead to an external program called an *interrupt service routine* (ISR). In the case I am describing here, that ISR program will be somewhere within the operating system. That program does whatever it was designed to do, and then it returns from the interrupt. At that point, the CPU resumes executing the instructions in the original program. All of this happens very rapidly, and normally it does so totally without the PC user's awareness.

The command processor, or shell, is not only the only essential part that is contained in a visible disk file; it also is the most visible portion of the operating system when you are running it. This program presents the user interface—the command prompt in the case of DOS, the Windows environment in the case of Windows 9x and later—and it accepts and processes commands for you. As you can doubtless see, both parts of the operating system—its kernel and its shell—are required. While the kernel provides underlying services, the shell (command processor) enables the user and the user's applications to interact with and benefit from those services.

In the case of DOS, the command processor also includes several useful built-in command functions. These include the DIR command to display a directory listing, the VER command to report the DOS version, and several others, referred to collectively as "the DOS internal commands." Most of what you know as DOS commands, such as FORMAT and FDISK, are not among them. Those are the external DOS commands, which I mentioned previously.

What Does the Operating System Do for Me?

An operating system such as DOS works for you in several ways. Some of these are apparent to you; others are fully hidden from you. In the next section, I'll use DOS as an example—one which almost all of us have already encountered regularly—of how the operating system, and particularly its command processor shell, functions.

What COMMAND.COM Does for You

Have you ever booted your computer directly to the command prompt or instructed Windows to shut down and restart in MS-DOS mode? If you have, you've doubtless seen the familiar DOS prompt, which usually looks something like this:

```
C:\>
```

When you access the command prompt in one of these two ways, you are using DOS directly to control what your PC does. You type a command and press the Enter key; you expect your PC to do what you just told it to do.

It sounds simple, doesn't it? Let me assure you, it is not nearly as simple as it appears. (If you run programs by clicking on their names or icons in Windows, or run them inside Windows DOS boxes, you are causing a similar chain of events, with differences that I will go into later.)

The first thing for which the DOS component called the command processor (COMMAND.COM) is responsible is presenting you with this DOS command prompt and then watching the keyboard and noticing every keystroke you type. As you type each one, COMMAND.COM takes that keystroke, converts it to the appropriate ASCII character, and sends that character to the screen for display. If it didn't do this, you'd never see what you typed. COMMAND.COM also keeps track in an internal buffer of all the keystrokes you have pressed so far in the current command (and, in a separate buffer, of the last command you issued).

If you type a backspace, COMMAND.COM has a more complex job to do. First, it must send a backspace to the screen. That moves the cursor back one space (unless it is already back as far as it can go). Then COMMAND.COM sends a space character to wipe out the character that was at that position on the screen. As is the case with any other character it "prints" on the screen, this moves the cursor forward one space. Then COMMAND.COM sends a second backspace to the screen to move the cursor back again. Finally, it must adjust back one space the pointer in its internal buffer that tells it where to store the next character you type.

If you press one of the function keys F1 through F6, COMMAND.COM must take some other special actions. These usually involve copying one or more characters from the last command buffer into the current command buffer and putting them on the screen.

All of this activity's complexity pales by comparison to what COMMAND.COM must do when you press the Enter key. Now it must switch roles from assisting you in typing a command to trying to figure out what your command means, and then doing that job.

First, COMMAND.COM must *parse* your command. Parse is a fancy word that means to figure out where the "words" are that make up this "sentence." Any valid DOS command must begin with a verb (an action word), and it then can go on to add an object, or a subject plus an object, or some qualifying adjectives or adverbs.

COMMAND.COM is mainly concerned with finding out what the verb is, and it assumes that will be the first "word" on the command line. After it has found the verb, it checks this word against its list of DOS internal commands. If there is a match, COMMAND.COM launches the miniprogram of that name that it contains as a part of itself, and as a part of that process it sends the rest of the command line to that program. This is, for example, how the program that does the work of the DIR command gets to run and do its job.

If the verb doesn't match any of the entries in COMMAND.COM's list of internal DOS commands, it will assume that this verb is the name of a program that you want to run. It now turns to the task of finding that program.

COMMAND.COM will look first for that program in what is referred to as the *current directory* on the current disk drive. DOS, in a portion of the kernel, maintains a pointer to the current disk drive and another pointer to the current directory on that disk drive. (What Windows 9x calls a *folder,* incidentally, is the same as what DOS calls a *directory*.)

COMMAND.COM will assume that the name specified by the verb is to be followed by .COM, .EXE, or .BAT unless it already has an explicit extension attached. It looks for files with the verb name as the filename and with one of these three extensions in the current directory.

If it finds such a file, it uses DOS kernel services to open the file and read it into memory. If it is a COM file, the contents of the file are simply copied into a region of RAM. If it is an EXE file, just the first 256 bytes of the file are read into memory initially. COMMAND.COM examines the contents of that "EXE header" to determine where in memory to put which portions of the rest of that file's contents. Finally, if the file is a BAT file, COMMAND.COM reads in just one line of that file at a time, each time treating that line as if it were typed at a new DOS command prompt.

When COMMAND.COM loads a COM or EXE program into memory, it also puts the remainder of the command line you typed (or that it found in a batch file) into a small block of memory it provides for the program's use located just below the program in memory (RAM). Then it passes control of the PC to that program. While the program is running, it interacts directly with the DOS kernel to obtain the resources that it requires.

As that program quits, it will ask the kernel to turn control of the PC back to COMMAND.COM, deallocating the memory that program was using (unless that program asks for some of its memory not to be deallocated, as device drivers and TSR programs do). This completed, COMMAND.COM presents another DOS command prompt and goes back into the mode in which it helps you compose the next command.

If COMMAND.COM doesn't find a matching file in the current directory (with an appropriate filename extension), it must look elsewhere. To do this, COMMAND.COM refers to a region of memory called the DOS environment and from that region reads an ASCII character string called the *PATH*. This is a collection of locations on your PC's disk drives that are specified in terms of disk volume letters and subdirectory names separated by semicolons. It parses this path statement into its elements. For each of those locations, COMMAND.COM repeats the search it performed in the current directory until it finds a program to run, or until it runs out of places to look. In the latter case, it will put up the message Bad command or filename and again present you with a new DOS command prompt.

What Does DOS Do for My Programs?

I have given you a summary of the things DOS does for you, the PC user, more or less directly. But DOS is much more important to you than even that rather lengthy description suggests, because virtually every non-Windows program you run will call upon DOS for the help it needs to do whatever it was designed to do.

In particular, every non-Windows program that must use some of the memory in your computer will ask DOS for it. (As I explained in Chapter 11, "Giving Your PC's CPU Enough Elbow Room—PC Memory," DOS allocates all the memory blocks in the first 640KB and often in upper memory as well. I also pointed out that there are other memory managers that can be called upon to allocate memory in the upper memory region—640KB to 1MB—or beyond that in the High Memory Area or Extended Memory.) Likewise, if an application program must access a data file, it must have DOS help it find the file and then either open the file and read the contents of it or put new or additional contents into it. And there are a whole bunch of other things that DOS can do for a program, ranging from the relatively trivial, such as telling it the time of day or the date, to fairly complex actions, such as launching another program and then returning control to the original program after that program has completed its work.

Of course, after Windows 9x is running, it provides all memory and resource allocation services for Windows programs and DOS programs that are run in a Windows DOS box. Disk access, too, has come under the purview of Windows 9x and later, as you'll read later.

Does DOS Have a Future?

You might be getting the idea that DOS is still a pretty important part of our PC landscape. That is correct today, because Windows 9x still requires DOS to load. But it will likely not be true tomorrow. First, DOS has some serious Y2K-related limitations that make it a far-from-suitable operating system for the future. Additionally, as you'll read later, Windows 9x has already stripped DOS of most of its functionality for most users. Finally, the question of DOS's future seems settled with the advent of Windows 2000 Professional. Although the Windows 9x kernel will continue to exist a little while longer (in a version rumored to be called Windows 2000 Personal Edition), Windows 2000 Professional (and higher versions) will be entirely DOS-free.

Microsoft Windows Takes Over

Windows has put DOS out to pasture. Although it's true that DOS is still used to start up Windows 9*x*, nearly all the DOS functionality that users relied on in Windows 3.*x* and earlier DOS-based environments has been usurped.

Originally, Windows was designed and marketed not as a replacement for DOS, but as an add-on "operating environment." That phrase was supposed to clarify its relationship to the underlying operating system. The earliest versions of Windows used DOS to manage most of the resources in the machine; the only job for Windows was to manage the appearance that the user saw and the appearance that Windows applications "saw." Users got a graphical user interface (GUI); programs got a new and much richer collection of application program interface (API) calls they could issue to ask Windows, or DOS, to do something for them.

As Windows has evolved, each new version has redefined the boundary between Windows and DOS down a little. With Windows 9*x*, particularly with Windows 98, nearly everything that DOS once did—from memory management, to displaying data onscreen, to providing access to external devices—is now done with 32-bit (protected-mode) modules within Windows. These modules are, generally, faster, more efficient, and more adaptable to the needs of specific devices and nascent technologies than was possible under DOS. With the exception of loading it when you boot your PC, Windows 9*x* hardly needs DOS for anything today. Windows 2000 Professional doesn't need DOS at all.

> **Note:** Another way to look at this is that Windows 9*x* (95 or 98) has really been two operating systems in one. At startup, and at some other times, the real-mode DOS operating system is the dominant member of the team. The rest of the time—which is nearly all of the time—protected-mode Windows 9*x* is running the show. Windows 2000 Professional will unify everything. Even though the Windows 9*x* kernel will still be around for another year or so, the jury has come back. DOS is dead.

On the application front, nearly all commonly used programs run under Windows. Indeed, even in the vertical markets of legal and financial software—long some of the most staunch holdouts for conversion from DOS to Windows—usability and training issues have forced widespread change. The latest versions of some of the most popular DOS legal applications, for example, are now Windows programs.

Variations on Windows Now in Common Use

Windows is not a singular thing. Microsoft has brought out many versions of it, and even some third-party versions have achieved a significant market share. The earliest versions of Microsoft Windows are of only historical interest at this point. They were very limited functionally, and they have been rendered almost totally obsolete by the later versions.

So, for this book I shall just recap briefly the different versions of Windows that are still being used in significant quantities on PCs. (Certainly, if you haven't yet upgraded at least to Windows 95—and preferably to a later version—now is an excellent time to do so. You won't be sorry you did.)

Windows 95

Windows went through many successful incarnations—known variously as Windows 3.*x*, Windows for Workgroups 3.11, and so on. After a long period of development, Microsoft introduced Windows 95. This version was meant for ordinary desktop PC users, and it was a direct upgrade from Windows 3.11. (If you look deeply inside Windows 95, it will identify itself as Windows version 4.*x*.)

Microsoft intended that everyone using Windows 3.*x* and almost all new PC users would use Windows 95. Windows 95 was different from Windows 3.*x* in many ways; at least, it certainly *looked* different. More accurately, Windows 95 represented two things. One is that it exemplified a very substantial rethinking of the user interface. The other is that Windows 95 was nearly the end product of the process of moving all the operating system support functions that could be moved from real mode (DOS) to protected mode. Now, ideally, almost nothing a Windows-specific application needs is likely to require switching the machine from protected mode to real mode and back again. (The only substantial exception to this is the case of antiquated external devices, which continue to require real-mode drivers.)

These issues notwithstanding, Windows 95 is generally a more stable operating environment than Windows 3.*x*. And it has support for a very wide range of hardware and software, which goes a long way to explain why it was the desktop PC operating system of choice for a very sizable number of PC users.

Even though Windows 95 took over most of DOS's functionality, DOS did still exist, operating in two different ways, underneath Windows 95. One version of DOS under Windows 95 was the actual real-mode operating system that loads before Windows starts. This is what you got when you booted to the Startup menu and selected the Command Prompt option. It is also what you got when you used a "Windows 95 startup diskette" (for example, if you have a problem that prevents you from booting Windows from the hard disk). And it is very nearly what you got if you selected Restart in MS-DOS mode from the Shut Down menu. (This real-mode DOS was augmented by its HIMEM.SYS memory manager program, so in fact it ran in a version of protected mode after HIMEM was loaded. But this was a very limited sort of protected-mode operation. All of the DOS real-mode API was available, and very little else.)

The other version of DOS you got under Windows 95 was what is provided in a so-called "DOS box" or "DOS command window" running while Windows 95 is also running. This could be a full-screen DOS window or it could be a smaller window running on top of the Windows 95 desktop. This is actually a simulated DOS, provided as an aspect of the protected-mode Windows operating system. It is created by the VMM32.VXD program, which also "virtualizes" all the hardware aspects of the PC so that DOS programs running in this mode cannot do any damage either to Windows or to other DOS or Windows programs that may be running at the same time. I'll discuss this point a little more fully later in this chapter.

One way you could see that this protected-mode simulated DOS was different from the real-mode DOS you got at the "bare" Command Prompt you get from the Startup menu or from working in MS-DOS Mode was to notice that this windowed DOS had a somewhat different functionality. In particular, it supported Windows 95 long filenames, and some of the DOS commands (such as XCOPY) had several added command-line switches (revealed if you ran the program with the command-line switch /?).

Both of these Windows 95 "DOSes" had many of their external commands (in particular those that pose some danger to data when run in a multitasking environment such as FORMAT) removed. That functionality was moved into protected-mode (32-bit code) modules within Windows 95.

I'll describe Windows 95's inner working in some detail shortly. First, though, I want to mention some of the other versions of Windows on the market.

Windows NT

Before Windows 95 came on the scene, Microsoft came out with a version of Windows that was a really different animal. It was never intended to be anything less. This was Windows NT, and it was Microsoft's answer to IBM's newly improved OS/2. It also was Microsoft's attempt to displace Novell and Netware as the de facto industry standard of PC networking.

Windows NT truly is a different operating system, built from scratch rather than built on top of an earlier combination of DOS and Windows 3.*x*. Compatibility was much *less* of an issue for its developers, and stability was much *more* of one. As a result, Windows NT is among the most reliable of PC operating systems. It is fully 32-bit code, and although it makes some attempt to be able to run older 16-bit Windows applications and DOS applications, it has some very stringent requirements on those it will accept. Some of the older programs just won't run on NT at all—certainly none that attempt to access the PC hardware directly (as many did to improve their performance). But then, that is the price of its far greater stability and security.

> **Note:** The change from 16 bits to 32 bits may seem like a subtle difference, but it has a profound impact on the complexity of the program that a programmer must write. The 32-bit code does away with the segmented memory architecture that we discussed in Chapter 8. It also enables the CPU to run in protected mode, thus protecting the operating system from poorly written applications.

Windows NT comes in two flavors (and several versions) at the time of this writing. The two flavors are NT Server and NT Workstation. (The current version is 4. As you've already read, the next version, once called Windows NT 5, has been renamed to Windows 2000 and is still under development as I write this.)

Microsoft's original notion was that Windows NT would be the high-end, "commercial" version of Windows, and Windows 3.x or 9x would be the "consumer" version. In fact, Windows NT's greater stability has caused many companies (and not a few individuals) to adopt Windows NT for their desktop machines. With the coming of Windows 2000, Windows NT was slated to "take over" as the operating system for all Windows-based PCs. That is, the next version of Windows NT *and* the next version of Windows 9x were to be a version of Windows 2000. (Windows 2000 will be available in Professional, Server, Advanced Server, and Datacenter Server editions to meet the needs of different classes of users.)

The latest news however, is that the Windows 9x kernel (and its underlying DOS) will remain for at least one more revision (perhaps to be known as the Windows 2000 Personal Edition).

Windows 98

With the release of Windows 98, Microsoft originally hoped that most consumers would opt to upgrade from Windows 95 (or Windows 3.x, for those stragglers), and that large corporations would upgrade, instead, to Windows NT 5. Windows 98 addressed, in particular, the growing need for the operating system to support the many new types of hardware—particularly multimedia hardware—that were beginning to appear in households and small offices. Many corporations have, in fact, decided to upgrade to Windows 98.

What is different about Windows 98? First, this version of Windows (and its underlying real-mode DOS) is capable of working with the new FAT32 formatted partitions. In fact, this capability was introduced before Windows 98, in the OSR 2 release of Windows 95, also known as Windows 95B or version 4.00.950B or 4.00.1111). Real-mode DOS *must* have the capability of accessing and storing files on a FAT32 volume in order to enable you to boot from a FAT32 disk and then access any other disk volumes formatted in that manner. (You read about FAT32 at length in Chapter 10, "Digging Deeper into Disks.")

Many of the functional changes from Windows 95 to Windows 98 were anticipated in the steady stream of updates and upgrades to Windows 95 that Microsoft made available on its Internet Web site. Many of those upgrades were also bundled into the Windows 95A Service Pack upgrade and later into the Windows 95B (or OSR2) version it supplied to original equipment manufacturers (OEMs) for installation on new PCs. Some functional changes were not available however; the integration of DirectX technologies into the OS (which you'll read about in Chapter 20, "How to 'Wow' a Human") was first made with Windows 98.

Note: OSR2 and the FAT32 support it provided were never available as an installable upgrade for end users. Therefore, for most of us, Windows 98 was an important upgrade, enabling us to reap the benefits of implementing FAT32 on our existing PCs.

One area in which there is an obvious difference in Windows 98 is in its level of integration of the Internet. This integration enables users to use the Internet Explorer Web browser as their default shell program for Windows 98. In this way, working with Web-based content and working with files on your local drives require only that the user learn one set of skills. However, this integration is not mandatory. Many users prefer to retain the familiar Windows 95 appearance and launch a Web browser when they wish to access some remote computer, either over the Internet, or over some other link. This change in integration merely reflects the growing importance of the Internet. Microsoft realized that to keep its dominant position, it essentially had to expand its next-generation operating systems in a manner that would make the Internet appear to be a part of the OS, built in seamlessly (or apparently so). The idea is that all resources you want to access—whether they are on a drive on your PC, on another PC across the room connected to yours via a LAN, or on some PC clear across the globe connected via the Internet—should look to you just like more folders on your PC. So, the distinction between the Windows Explorer and the Internet Explorer is now meant to seem trivial. Of course, there is a much *nontrivial* difference between what you have on your own PC's hard disk or on a disk attached to a PC on your local area network and what you might be able to access on some remote computer halfway around the globe. After all, you can count on the integrity and safety of files on your hard disk in ways you simply cannot trust files on some distant machine belonging to a total stranger. With the blurring of the line between what is local and what is remote, it is important to keep those different levels of trustworthiness in mind.

One of the "coolest" features of Windows 98 is its capability of working with up to nine PCI or AGP video display adapters attached to a like number of monitors. You can spread the Windows desktop over all the attached monitors, and then you can put an application's window in whichever visible portion of the overall desktop you want. You might think of this as the "Windows 98 video wall" concept. Look back to Figure 4.1. There I have shown a desktop system with multiple monitors running under Windows 98.

This unquestionably "cool" feature is actually useful—for some users. To give just one example, if you are doing a lot of Web work, having the capability of putting a browser on one screen and an email program, an editor, and perhaps a database program on other screens can make transferring information among them a lot simpler. Each program running can use all the available space on one of those screens. Although far from flawless, this multimonitor capability has brought many professionals—particularly graphic designers and artists who rely on multiple monitors daily—into the Windows-based fold. (Previously, only Apple Macintosh PCs supported multiple monitors in any truly useful way.)

Windows CE

Windows on your washing machine? Maybe so, in just a few years. Microsoft's ideal is to have Windows become the ubiquitous computing interface.

Windows CE is the version of Windows that Microsoft created for use on smaller, less capable hardware. Initially targeted at the handheld PC (HPC) and the personal digital assistant (PDA), it may also be made a part of many other consumer electronic devices and eventually of other appliances. So, yes, you may use a Windows GUI to set your washing machine clothes cleaning cycle someday. Or, better, you might be able to schedule it to run at a predetermined time and use your choice of cycles, with all this being set from your desktop PC, which will be linked to the washing machine over a Universal Serial Bus (USB) link. Indeed, there is a growing interest in home automation today, with many proprietary, incompatible technologies vying for dominance. The establishment of a standard, automation operating system would enable you to connect all of your automated devices together and control them centrally—or from anywhere in the world, via a modem or an Internet connection.

The current Windows CE, version 2.0, supports a color display and a wide variety of microprocessors. (Neither was true of version 1.0.) As a result, it is showing up in an increasing number of handheld calculators, personal digital assistants, and even some cellular phones. The first generation of Windows CE devices wasn't very popular, but Windows 1.0 wasn't either. Will Windows CE become a standard part of every electrical device you own? Currently, this seems unlikely, but all bets are off until we are a bit farther down the road.

(Incidentally, Windows CE is available only to device manufacturers; it's not something that can be installed retroactively or as a user alternative to some proprietary OS.)

The Future of Windows

What can we expect in the future? Well, you've already read briefly about Windows 2000 replacing Windows NT. There will also be one more generation of Windows in the model of Windows 95 and Windows 9x. After that, the next step for the desktop PC user will be the same for the corporate networking user. All roads—except, perhaps, those used by Windows CE—lead to Windows 2000 and its successors.

Windows Is an Event-Driven Environment

So far in this chapter, I have pointed out that DOS and Windows are the dominant operating systems for PCs. And I have described the various versions of Windows that are in common use today, or are forthcoming. I also told you a little bit about how DOS works, both in terms of what you see it do for you, and what it is doing behind the scenes both directly for you and also for the benefit of the application programs you choose to run.

Now I want to go into one of the most important ways that Windows as a programming environment differs from DOS. Understanding this is crucial to understanding how any Windows program works.

When a programmer sits down to write a DOS program, he or she will start with a procedure it is to perform. Then the programmer writes instructions that follow each step of the desired procedure. This is called, not surprisingly, *procedural programming*.

Windows is different. The programmer first must think about the appearance of the program. The next concern is to define all the events that might occur—for example, a mouse pointer being moved across a certain region or a mouse button being pressed while that pointer was at that location. Then, for each event, a separate procedure is written. The collection of all these event-handlers is the Windows application.

Windows must send notice of all these events to all the programs that might need to react to them. After all, only one mouse pointer is on the screen, and many programs can be running. So, the underlying Windows program will notice where the mouse moves, when the mouse's buttons are clicked, when keystrokes occur, and so on. For each such event, Windows sends out a message. This is routed to every Windows program much in the manner of a magazine making the rounds at a company with a checklist of readers stapled to the front cover.

Each Windows program must receive the message, decide whether it is supposed to act on it, and if not (or perhaps anyway), pass it along to the next program.

If any one of the Windows programs becomes stuck, messages can't be passed around this loop—and that can stop Windows as a whole. There are, however, usually several loops going, and some of them might still continue to work. This is why often even when your PC seems to be, and in fact is, quite solidly stuck, you still are able to move the mouse pointer all around the screen as freely as you like.

For these reasons, Windows programming is not referred to generally as being procedural in character (even though Windows programs are full of procedures). Instead, it is called *event-driven* or *message-based*.

Cooperative Versus Preemptive Multitasking

Now I have set the stage so that you are ready to learn one more important aspect of how Windows works, and also how this aspect of Windows has evolved. I am referring here to what is called cooperative multitasking versus preemptive multitasking.

Multitasking means running several programs at once. In fact, it means having the CPU spend some time running one program, stop that and spend some time running another program, stop that and go on running a third program, and so on. If all those times add up to a very short time, so that the CPU gets back to each program many times each second, it will seem to the user as though all the programs are running simultaneously. But actually they are simply doing what is called *time sharing, time slicing,* or *time domain multiplexing*.

There are two ways this can be accomplished. In both cases, you need some supervisor program that handles the context switching for the CPU from one program to the next. (Each time a context switch is about to occur, the CPU must be instructed to save enough information about the task it has been doing to be able to resume that work later on, and then it must reload the previously saved information about the task on which it is about to resume its work.)

The two strategies for multitasking differ in how they figure out when it is time to make a switch to the next program. *Preemptive multitasking* means having the supervisor program set strict time limits on each program. At the end of its *time slice*, that program simply gets cut off, no matter where it was in its process. This is okay, because the CPU will complete the current instruction, and it will save enough information for it to be able to resume exactly where it left off, as soon as it gets to return to running this program.

Cooperative multitasking, on the other hand, means that each program is asked to relinquish control on its own. Windows programming guidelines suggest a maximum time that any Windows program should be allowed to hold control before it relinquishes it, but it is up to the programmer who writes that program to be sure that those guidelines are not violated. Microsoft specified that Windows programs include code that would let them relinquish control to Windows, and thus to other Windows programs, on a regular basis. But this is simply not always done.

Anyone who has run any number of Windows programs in the past has seen many of them share the machine most of the time, yet on occasions grab the machine in a viselike grip and not let go until they are good and ready. Worse yet, sometimes a Windows program will get "hung" and be unable to let go of control, at which point you have no choice but to reboot your PC. Microsoft has noticed this behavior, as is obvious from how later versions of Windows handle things. Whereas Windows 3.*x* used only cooperative multitasking for all Windows applications (and preemptive multitasking for DOS applications), Windows 95 uses cooperative multitasking only for the older, "legacy" 16-bit Windows applications. All newer, 32-bit programs are preemptively multitasked, as are all DOS applications.

Windows NT goes even further, using only a preemptive multitasking model. That prevents any one program, no matter how badly (or maliciously) written, from taking control of your PC and not letting go.

Windows 9x Internal Details and Boot Process

Let's change tracks now and look in depth at how Windows 9*x* works. The preceding sections laid out the feature sets and some of the trade-offs in various versions of Windows; here, I will tell you how the pieces that make up Windows 9*x*, in particular, fit together and work.

I told you earlier that Windows 9x is really two operating systems in one. The first is real-mode DOS. This loads first and then when it loads the second, protected-mode operating system (Windows itself), that operating system essentially puts the real-mode DOS "to sleep"—and wakes it up again only for the rare occasions when Windows needs to use one of the DOS real-mode services.

Figure 17.1 shows graphically this division between the two operating systems, and it also reveals several other important points about the structure of Windows 9x. Like most operating systems, Windows 9x loads itself in stages, and this diagram shows some of the most important phases of that process.

FIGURE 17.1
Windows 95 and 98 key component groups.

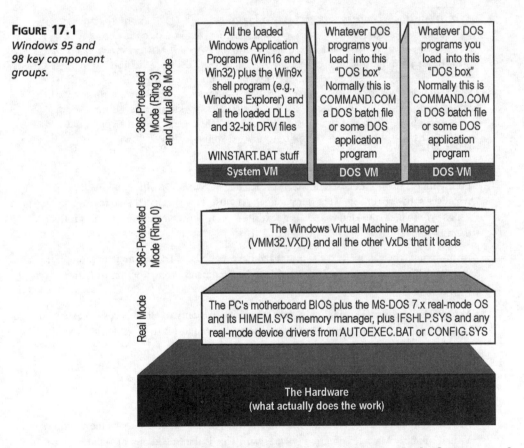

Hardware Does the Actual Work (of Course)

At the bottom of my diagram, and ultimately fundamental to the operation of your PC is, of course, its hardware components. They are the only part that can possibly *do* anything physical. The role of all software is merely to direct the actions of those physical parts.

Laying a Real-Mode Floor

The essential kernel of the operating system is shown—or, because we are talking about Windows 9x here, the two operating systems it includes are shown—in the next two layers. The layer just above the hardware is shown as containing the PC motherboard BIOS (which is all real-mode code) plus DOS. The motherboard BIOS is invoked first, during the Power On Self Test (POST) phase of booting the PC. Then it loads IO.SYS which, in Windows 9x, includes all the kernel of DOS. The IO.SYS code, in turn, loads HIMEM.SYS and IFSHLP.SYS.

> **Technical Note:** HIMEM.SYS is, as you may know, the DOS memory manager that converts extended memory into XMS memory and takes control of any upper-memory RAM blocks and the High Memory Area (HMA). A version of this program has shipped with every version of MS-DOS since version 5.0 in 1991. IFSHLP.SYS is the *installable file system helper* program. This first showed up in Windows for Workgroups. As its name suggests, it provides the necessary hooks for installing alternative file systems. These include the file system used to access optical discs and those used to access computers across a network. As it happens, this support is required before you can load the Windows GUI.

Furthermore, IO.SYS processes the CONFIG.SYS and AUTOEXEC.BAT files and loads whatever software (or sets whatever parameters) those files specify. It also reads MSDOS.SYS (which, in Windows 9x, is a text file) and follows whatever directions it finds there.

At this point, you can load COMMAND.COM and have a good old DOS command prompt, if you want. That is what happens if you select the Command Prompt option from the Startup menu.

Your PC is, at this point, running in protected mode, but only to allow access to extended memory, and then only to programs that know how to request it from HIMEM.SYS. No Windows applications can be run yet.

Hiding That Floor with Protected-Mode Windows

Next, if you are booting Windows 9x normally, the program WIN.COM loads the Windows Virtual Memory Manager program (VMM32.VXD). This is the true kernel of Windows 9x's full, protected-mode operating system. After it loads, the DOS code resident in memory and the PC's motherboard BIOS with its real-mode programs are ignored—at least most of the time.

Of Rings and Descriptor Tables

Notice that I have shown the second layer as the real-mode layer and the third layer as the 386-protected mode, Ring 0 layer. Everything above this layer is shown as the 386-protected mode, Ring 3 and Virtual 86 mode layer. There are profound differences between these three portions of the Windows environment. (If you don't recall what the Rings in an x86 CPU are, you can read about them in Chapter 11.)

VMM32.VXD loads all the most essential helper programs (device drivers and the like) into Ring 0 with itself. These are all programs with the extension .VXD, and they are, generically, referred to as *virtual (anything) drivers,* or in a sort of acronym form as VxDs. That is *all* that gets loaded into Ring 0. These programs are responsible for *virtualizing* all of the hardware. (This means that they hide the actual hardware and intercept any attempts by a program to touch that hardware and then decide whether or not, and how, to do whatever that program requested). These programs also are responsible for creating the simulated DOS that you see in a DOS box, and that programs can access when they want to have DOS services.

> **Technical Note:** Remember, only the programs loaded into the Ring 0 state have the full run of the hardware. All the other programs must pass messages to one of the Ring 0 programs asking it to access real hardware on their behalf. If all these kernel programs are perfect, it shouldn't be possible to crash the hardware, no matter how much you might mess up the software running on top of it.
>
> But that state of grace is not a plausible one. Not only do programmers make the occasional mistake, the design of Windows 9x enables any other third-party programmer to create VxD files that will be loaded along with that programmer's application program. This means the stability of our Windows machines are dependent in part on having *every* programmer for *all* our programs do their jobs perfectly. That, as you may imagine, just doesn't happen.

The System Virtual Machine

VMM32.VXD now loads more of Windows into a special "virtual machine" (or VM) called the *System VM*. What does this mean? It means that all of these programs share one local descriptor table (LDT) as well as the always-shared global descriptor table (GDT). This means that they are all, in essence, "playing on the same field." This is convenient when one of these programs wishes to talk to another of them. But it also is one of the major sources of instability in Windows, because it means that it is possible for an errant program to trash another program on that playing field, including even some of the essential Windows pieces. (If you've forgotten what the GDT and LDT are, you'll find them discussed in Chapter 11.)

Which programs get loaded into the System Virtual Machine? Well, first come the dynamic link libraries and the protected-mode device drivers. (Usually, these will be programs contained in files with extensions .DLL or .DRV, but some are EXE files such as KRNL386.EXE, USER.EXE, and GDI.EXE, and a few others have yet another extension, such as .CPL.

Some of these programs are what are termed 16-bit protected-mode programs. Some are full 32-bit programs. They collectively create two Windows APIs: one for 16-bit (old, Windows 3.x-style) application programs and the other for more modern, 32-bit (Windows 9x-style) application programs.

Finally, a Windows shell program is loaded into this layer. This creates the Windows GUI, and is what the user sees and what accepts user input. There are many possible programs you could use for this task, but the default ones for Windows 9x are Windows Explorer or Internet Explorer.

Now you have a full Windows 9x environment, loaded up and ready to use. Any application programs you run will now have the things they need to do their jobs, and you will be able to control all that goes on with your keyboard and mouse input. The various programs "talk" to one another (send and respond to messages) up and down the layers I have shown as they accomplish their assigned tasks.

DOS Virtual Machines

Any time you start up an MS-DOS prompt from within Windows 9x (by invoking that item on the Start or Start[hr]|[hr]Programs menu, for example), the Windows Virtual Memory Manager sets up a new LDT just for that one task. The only difference between running any old DOS program and starting a DOS command prompt is that in the latter case, the DOS program you are running is COMMAND.COM.

You also can run a DOS batch file in a virtual machine in the same way. Double-clicking on a BAT file in Windows Explorer, for example, starts a new DOS VM and loads COM-MAND.COM into it with the batch filename as a command-line parameter to COMMAND.COM.

This approach does a marvelous job of protecting DOS programs from Windows programs and vice versa. Because they are using different LDTs, they simply cannot see one another. This strong protection is the reason why we often refer to the process as running a DOS program "in a DOS box."

You should notice that the DOS program in a DOS VM can see and communicate with the VMM layer (and potentially with the layers below that). But it cannot see the DLLs and other pieces of the Windows environment in the System VM any more than it can see or mess with the Windows applications programs that may be running there.

However, because the VMM is running in the Ring 0 state and serving as a Virtual 86 monitor program, whereas the DOS program is in Ring 3 and is running in Virtual 86 mode, the DOS program can really only interact with the simulated DOS API presented by the VMM layer's VxD programs, or with such hardware as the VMM layer programs permit it to see and talk to (if any).

This is in sharp contrast to what DOS programs are able to do in actual real mode. There, they can do anything to anything any time they want. Some old DOS programs depend on that, and those are the programs that cannot be run inside a DOS VM, but must instead be run in "MS-DOS mode."

Waking the Sleeping DOS

If the picture I have painted so far were complete, it would seem that Windows 9x really doesn't use DOS any time that the Windows GUI is running. But that isn't so. In order to achieve the high level of backward compatibility that was Microsoft's primary focus for Windows 9x, it found that it was necessary at times to let the VMM layer reach down into the DOS and BIOS layer and utilize some of the real-mode code that resides there. Because this layer is below the VMM, it cannot run that code in Virtual 86 mode, but must instead actually switch the entire PC into real mode briefly, run that code, then switch it back again. These mode switches are happening many, many times each second—and most Windows users are simply unaware that they are.

There is a second way to wake DOS from within Windows 9x. That is to restart your machine in MS-DOS Mode. This is only necessary, however, for particularly "ill-behaved" DOS applications, and it means that you have to stop running all your other Windows programs for as long as you are running your PC in MS-DOS mode.

Understanding Your Choices for Your PC's Operating System

For most of this book, I have acted as though you are running DOS, DOS plus Windows 3.x, or Windows 95 or 98. I have done this because, statistically speaking, you are. Of course, you might not be. You aren't, after all, a statistic.

And there are many fine choices for your PC operating system. This section briefly lists some of the more popular options and tells you a little about why you might want to choose each one.

Sticking with DOS

DOS has worked fine for many purposes. If you have an older computer, and especially if you do some not-very-demanding things with it, DOS may still be a viable choice for its operating system. You don't need Windows unless you must run some Windows application, want to multitask DOS applications, or want support for a hardware device for which only Windows drivers are available (a circumstance that is increasingly common).

DOS Plus Windows 3.x

Many PC users have decided that DOS plus Windows 3.x is the way to go. They value its capability of using all the RAM they can give it. They also like it for enabling them to run many DOS applications at once (and, with version 3.1, being able to use the local reboot feature to end one errant DOS application without having to shut down and restart the machine).

Windows 95 and Windows 98

When Windows 95 came out, it was the focus of an enormous amount of media coverage. It was the hot new thing, but moving up to it often meant having to add to or upgrade your hardware. It does, however, give developers some new features to exploit for users' benefit, so the very latest versions of all the top-of-the-line PC products have been rewritten to run on Windows 95 or 98, or in some cases on Windows 9x or NT.

Windows 98 supports more hardware options, most notably USB support. This means you need to use Windows 98 if you want to use peripheral devices that connect to a PC via a USB port. (Or, at least that will be the easiest way to accomplish that end—and the method I recommend.)

Both these versions of Windows are all about compatibility: compatibility with the past and with the present cutting edge of technology. They support nearly any DOS or Windows program ever written, including some pretty funky game programs. They also support the latest efforts from the major PC software publishers and offer built-in support for more oddball hardware than any other PC operating system. Occasionally, you still must go to the hardware gadget's manufacturer for a suitable device driver, but out of the box, Windows 95 and Windows 98 support so much stuff—and with their plug-and-play aspects even recognize the stuff—that many people never need to concern themselves with a search for or the process of installing third-party drivers.

I will say for Windows 98 that you should not starve it for RAM. Give Windows 95 machines 32MB of RAM or more, and preferably 64MB for Windows 98. If you are running Windows 9x on a laptop, you might have to settle for less RAM than this, but these figures represent reasonable lower limits for ideal performance. Additionally, if you are running a lower-end Pentium machine (as opposed to a Pentium II), more than 64MB of RAM installed can actually *decrease* your performance. This is because those machines were not designed to provide L2 cache support for any memory above 64MB. You've read elsewhere how the L2 cache can dramatically increase overall system perfor-mance, so 64MB of RAM should be considered an upper limit for these older processors.

Windows NT and (When It Arrives) Windows 2000

Windows NT is Microsoft's crown jewel. Windows NT is stable and it is secure, so it is a safe choice even for large corporations with vast amounts of critical data to manage. But

Windows NT is also the most finicky Windows version. You simply will be unable to run that old DOS game program. And you might be surprised to discover that some other, seemingly ordinary, Windows or DOS programs also have problems under NT. Before you commit to this operating system, be sure it will support programs and hardware devices that you simply *must* be able to use. (Alternatively, check out the last part of this section where I explain how you can have your cake and eat it too, running your PC both with and without Windows NT.)

At the time of this writing, the successor to Windows NT, Windows 2000, is seriously behind schedule. There has been a variety of news—at various levels of reliability—accounting for the delays in different ways. When Windows 2000 does arrive, users with any kind of mission-critical tasks will likely wait until Windows 2000 has been in wide use for several months at least. Whether Windows 2000 adoption is right for you or your company, only you can determine.

Linux

Linux is a marvelous program and an unbeatable value. It is free! Linux is a version of UNIX that first was crafted as a work of love by one programmer and then augmented by many others. You can get the whole operating system, source code and all, plus a variety of Linux-compatible software, for nothing more than the price of a download. Or, you can buy it on a CD-ROM for the cost of the disc.

Maintenance and improvement of Linux are being carried on by an even larger, international team of programmers than Microsoft can field. Although they aren't working under anyone's central direction, Linus Torvalds (the originator of Linux) is still working to maintain some sanity in terms of what new features get included in successive versions of Linux.

The existence of this body of far-flung, and knowledgeable, advocates of Linux means that if you run into a problem using it you very likely can get some free help fairly rapidly from the Internet—at least if you are familiar with the use of usenet news groups. Or, you can buy versions of Linux that are supported by several companies (Red Hat and Caldera being a couple of them). This may be a better option if you aren't a hacker at heart and would rather ask questions than work things out independently.

Given its heritage (UNIX), it is not surprising that Linux is a suitable choice for a PC operating system for a PC that is to serve as a Web server. In fact, this or some other flavor of UNIX is the best choice for any system that must be extremely reliable and flexible or any that must do a lot of *real-time* work—that is, where the PC must respond in a time-critical fashion to events in the outside world.

Most computers that host World Wide Web sites are UNIX-based machines. Among the other computers that make up the Internet, probably there are more Macintosh computers than PCs running Windows, but PCs running Linux might well have the Macs on the run.

QNX or Some Other UNIX

If your task is to set up a PC to do a critical real-time job (for example, a numerical controller for a machine tool), where it simply must keep working at all times and must be able to respond in a timely manner to even a lot of very fast external events, DOS is a bad choice of OS; so is Windows 9*x*. Windows NT might do the job, but almost any flavor of UNIX will work better.

QNX Software is one of the leading contenders for this task. Its real-time optimized UNIX clone has one of the smallest kernels (under 32KB). All the other modules in this system run at a lower level of privilege than the kernel, and thus PCs running QNX are protected against even the programming errors in the operating system (outside the kernel) by the CPU's built-in protection features.

As a demonstration of the tiny size and great power of its product, QNX has released a combination of its x86 operating system plus a full Web browser that fits on a single 1.44MB floppy diskette! The look and feel of the system are very much like that of many larger UNIX systems, and its performance is exemplary.

QNX also offers a rich assortment of modules and programmers' tools. With it, you can build a highly sophisticated, full-featured GUI-based system to do almost anything. If buying is more your style than programming, a lot of companies specialize in building custom or semicustom QNX systems.

Furthermore, QNX offers a module that will enable you to run DOS programs on top of QNX. This might let you have the best of both the DOS and UNIX worlds.

How You Can Avoid Making a Choice

Finally, I must point out that you really don't have to choose. You can have them all. Yes, really, you can run one PC with all the operating systems I have mentioned loaded onto it. Naturally, you will be running only one of these operating systems at a time, but you will be able to change which one is running simply by rebooting your PC.

Several strategies exist for doing this. Windows 95 and Windows NT come with a version of *multibooting* built in. This strategy enables you to choose between their native operation or booting to another OS, usually DOS. Usually, this involves some batch files that replace critical system files for one operating system with the corresponding files for the other system.

Warning: I'd be remiss if I didn't end this discussion with a cautionary note. Some of these PC operating system choices use the old DOS FAT12 and FAT16 formats for their file systems. All of them are able to read those file systems (and almost all of them can write to them). But many of these operating systems also support some alternative file systems.

Windows 95B and Windows 98 support the FAT32 file system, but none of the other operating systems can make any sense out of disks formatted in that way. Windows NT also supports a file system that only it can access, called NTFS.

Linux normally uses several different disk volumes, some with their own proprietary format and others with a DOS-like format. Many other UNIX flavors do something similar.

If you choose to load several different operating systems on your PC, you must have enough disk space for all of them. Each one wants some space for its files—and in modern versions, those are some pretty substantial amounts. The only shared spaces will be those that use a commonly accessible file system. Any nonshared spaces are in addition to that. Thus, you'll need a pretty large hard drive to make this strategy practical. (Fortunately, these days, that doesn't have to cost you very much money.)

Therefore, the bottom line is this: If you want to be able to boot your PC into any of a number of different operating systems, you will have to give some careful thought to what file systems you will be using under each one. Be sure that each OS will be able to access the files you want it to see (and perhaps also assure yourself that it won't be able to access the files you want it *not* to touch). You can do this, with sufficient care, but it does take some careful thought and planning.

Summary

This chapter told you a lot about a topic you might never have realized you would want to understand. I hope you found it interesting and illuminating reading. After you make your decision as to which operating system to use, you will be able to go back to ignoring your PC's operating system much of the time. Still, knowing what you now do about how it works will serve you well whenever you find that your PC's OS isn't working quite the way you want it to work.

This chapter completed the task I set for myself in this part of the book—namely, explaining how all the basic hardware and the fundamental (operating system) software in an isolated PC function. Armed with that understanding, you now are ready to learn how people program PCs to do useful things. That is the focus of the next part of the book.

Peter Norton

PART IV

PC Programs: From Machine Language Bytes to Human Speech

Understanding How Humans Instruct PCs

This chapter is all about the many ways in which we can tell our PCs what to do. That covers a broad range of subjects, from the careful crafting of assembly-language programs and the ins and outs of object-oriented computer languages to simple macro definitions that customize how some application works. Chapter 19, "Some PCs Can Understand Speech and Talk to Us," continues the story with how you can instruct some PCs simply by talking to them, as well as how those and other PCs are now sometimes talking back to us.

Harnessing the PC's Power to Help Mere Humans

The first digital computers were programmed in a very laborious manner. The only "language" they understood was an appropriate collection of binary numbers, so their human makers had to insert these numbers by hand. In those days, every time a computer operator turned on a computer for the first time (or had to restart it for some reason), he or she would have to set a group of switches to represent the 1s and 0s of a binary instruction word, then press another switch to enter that instruction. This process had to be repeated many times until an entire short program was entered. Finally, pressing yet another switch would start that program, which would prepare the computer to read and then run a longer program from punched cards or a tape drive.

Fortunately, we no longer have to worry about all that. Our PCs know how to start themselves, and modern methods of program generation enable us to create computer programs in a much easier way. There are, in fact, several quite different ways people program computers. The rest of this chapter describes the most popular ones.

Assembly Language Saves Mental Effort

People are good at different things than computers are good at. Computers excel at keeping track of details. People excel at seeing the big picture or, in general, at seeing patterns.

Using assembly language is a strategy for using the computer to do what it does well, in ways that make it easier for humans to do the work of building computer programs. This strategy is the closest to the original method of computer programming of all the ones I will describe for you. It also was the first strategy devised. But it still is extremely useful, because it is in certain ways the most powerful way to program a computer. Because it shows most of the characteristics of all the other ways to program computers, I will spend more time describing this kind of language than on any of the others.

The General Characteristics of All Computer Programs

A computer program is simply a long list of instructions, perhaps with some data values mixed in. The CPU reads the instructions and performs the indicated actions. If some data is mixed into the program, there must be some instructions in that program that tell the CPU when and how to use those data values. There also must be some other instructions that will cause it to skip over the data values as it is reading the program so it can find the next instruction it is to perform.

Some instructions contain data within themselves. Others reference data the CPU will find in a specified register or at some designated memory location. Some instructions are simple, taking only 1 byte to state. Others are much more complicated, and expressing them might require more than a dozen bytes of program code.

That means that a list of the binary numbers that make up a computer program will almost certainly make little sense at a glance to any human. We see the meaning a whole lot more easily when the program is broken down into its individual instructions. If each instruction is further broken down into the action to be done and the data to be acted upon (or an indication of where that data may be found), the intent of those instructions is much easier to see.

The next section goes into an example in great detail. If you already know how an assembly-language program is structured and how it corresponds to the machine-language program it represents, or if you simply can't be bothered, you can skip the next section. However, if you want to understand how assembly language works, in at least this very simple case, please take some time to study this example.

A Very Simple Sample Program

Figure 18.1 shows a very short (15-byte) program as the CPU would see it. You and I see numbers here. The CPU sees this as what we term *code,* which means that these numbers *encode* the actions we want the CPU to perform. Every pair of hexadecimal values in this figure specifies the value of 1 byte of the program code. So, for example, the hexadecimal values 8E (for the fourth byte) imply a byte whose binary content is 10001110 (8h = 1000b, Eh = 1110b—where the trailing *h* implies a hexadecimal number, and the trailing *b* implies a binary number). Go back and review the section in Chapter 3, "Understanding Bits, Nybbles, and Bytes," on hexadecimal numbers, and especially Figure 3.3, if you are confused by any of this.

Figure 18.1

A very short pro-gram as it is seen by the CPU.

```
BA 00 00 8E C2 26 80 36-17 04 20 B4 4C CD 21
```

Now I will show you how that short program would look as an assembly-language program (see Figure 18.2). All the numbers in this figure are, like those in Figure 18.1, hexadecimal values, even though I didn't put a letter *h* after each one. That is simply the assumption you must make whenever you read any assembly-language program, at least in the forms in which they usually are presented.

Note: Sometimes, authors put a suffix letter *b* for binary numbers, *o* for octal, *h* for hexadecimal, and *t* or *d* for tens for decimal. Other times, you are simply expected to know from context the number base that is being used.

Figure 18.2

That same information expressed in assembly language.

```
MOV        DX,0000
MOV        ES,DX
ES:
XOR        BYTE PTR [0417],20
MOV        AH,4C
INT        21
```

This is, as it happens, a small real-mode program. You could run it at the DOS prompt. But before you do, it would be nice to know what it would do to your PC if you did. I will explain that in some detail right now.

The first instruction (MOV DX,0000) "moves" (copies) the explicitly stated value of 0 into the 16-bit wide data register (DX). The second instruction (MOV ES,DX) copies the contents of the DX register (which we now know is 0) into the extra segment register (ES).

Note: Situations like this, where two instructions are needed to accomplish a single goal—moving 0 into ES—are necessary because the CPU doesn't allow you to directly move a 0 into the ES register. Issues like these are why programming can become so complicated.

Notice that the structure (syntax) for a line of assembly code such as this is that the first "word" is the verb, specifying the action to be taken. The next word is the destination, and the last word is the source of the data to be used in this action—or, in the case of the first line, it is the actual data value to be used in the action.

Then comes a line that asserts that the currently active segment (for purposes of reaching out into main memory) will now be the extra segment. This assertion applies until it is countermanded by another, similar assertion, or until the program ends.

The line that begins with XOR (XOR BYTE PTR [0417],20) is an *exclusive or* statement that determines whether the values of 2 bytes are the same. Just what this statement tells the CPU to do takes a little explaining.

First, you must know what an exclusive or (XOR) of 2 *bits* means. If either of the bits is a 1, but not both of them, the result is a 1; otherwise, it is a 0.

Another way to look at this is to notice that if one of the bits is a 0, the result is going to be the same as the value of the other bit being compared. But if the first bit is a 1, the resulting bit will be the exact opposite of the other bit you are comparing.

When you do an XOR of 2 *bytes,* you just go through each position in the 2 bytes. First, you compare the least significant bit in each byte and put the XOR result into the least significant bit of the result byte. Next, you move to the second bit in each byte, and then on to the third, fourth, and finally the eighth, or most-significant, bit in each byte.

The part of the assembly-language line that says BYTE PTR [0417] indicates that one of the bytes to be compared is whatever number is located at address 0:0417—and here I am giving the address in the usual *segment:offset* form—which always means that one implying hexadecimal numbers before and after the colon. (You might wonder why I put the number 0 before the colon. Remember, the segment value was set to be whatever value is in ES in the line just before this one, and we just loaded it with a 0 value in the lines before that.)

The final portion of this assembly-language line gives an explicit value to the other byte in our comparison. That value is 20h, which is the same as the binary number 00100000b.

There is one more not-so-obvious thing you must know about this assembly-language instruction: The result of the comparison of the 2 bytes will be put into the memory location from which the first byte value being compared was taken. That means that this instruction reads into the CPU the value that was stored at 0:0417 in main memory, XORs that 8-bit value with the 8-bit value 20h, and then puts the resulting byte back into main memory location 0:0417.

Now, from what I just told you about what the XOR operation does and the fact that one of the bytes being compared is 20h, you can now see that this instruction just reverses the value of the sixth bit in the byte at main memory location 0:0417, leaving all the other bits in that byte unchanged.

As it happens, this particular memory location has a special significance. It is the byte in which the BIOS stores the current state of the shift keys on the keyboard as well as the *shift state* of the system corresponding to each Shift key. The first (least-significant) bit has the binary value 1 if—and only if—the right-hand Shift key is depressed. The next bit is a 1 if—and only if—the left-hand Shift key is depressed. The next bit tells whether either Ctrl key is depressed (1 = yes; 0 = no), and the fourth bit does the same for the Alt keys.

The upper 4 bits show whether the system is in the Scroll Lock, Num Lock, Caps Lock, or Insert states. That is, a 1 in any of these positions corresponds to that state being on.

Aha! Remember that our program is going to change only 1 bit, the bit in the sixth position. Now you know enough to see that when you run this program, it will reverse the value of the bit that says whether the Num Lock state is on. Thus, running this program will set the Num Lock state off if it is on, and on if it is off. That is just what pressing the Num Lock key does. So, this program is a way to press the Num Lock key without touching the keyboard.

But the program does something more. The next line (MOV AH,4C) says that it moves the byte value 4Ch into the upper half of the AX register (which is also known as the AH register, meaning the higher portion of the A register). The last line (INT 21) produces a software interrupt of type 21h. This is perhaps the most commonly used DOS interrupt service. It handles a significant portion of the calls a program will make to DOS. The value of AH tells DOS that this program is finished with its work and that DOS should return control to whatever program had it before this program got loaded. Normally, that means to let COMMAND.COM put up another DOS prompt and wait for you to tell it what you want to have your PC do next.

This was just a simple program. It is actually a useful one (in case you want a way to achieve the effect of pushing the Num Lock key in a batch file), but by no means does it show you the range of things you can do with an assembly-language program.

In particular, many assembly-language programs enable the programmer to refer to locations in memory or locations within the program by symbolic names. The assembler keeps track of where these locations are (actual RAM address or offset from the beginning of the code segment and actual line of code). The programmer then can use meaningful names for each block of code, based on what it is supposed to do. When an instruction tells the computer to jump to a new block of code to do some new task, that instruction will read something like JMP CloseFile instead of JMP 0A35 or some other arbitrary numerical address.

The Power of Assembly-Language Programs

You can see from this example how detailed and "close to the hardware" an assembly-language program really is. It actually must specify each and every byte of *machine-language code* (the binary numbers the CPU will read) that is going to become a part of the final program. That is in marked contrast to what a programmer does when using what we call a high-level programming language, as I will explain in more detail in a moment.

This low-level characteristic of assembly-language programming means that a person who writes a program in assembly language has total control over what the PC will do. It is logically exactly equivalent to writing down the exact bytes of machine code the program is to contain. But writing assembly language instead of machine language code is much easier for humans to do.

The main reason to write in assembly language instead of in actual machine language bytes is that it is so much more *mnemonic* (which means suggestive and memorable) to write MOV DX instead of writing simply BAh, which is the actual byte that means that action to the CPU. If there were only a few instructions that you had to remember, memorizing them all might not be too tough. But when there are as many instructions as there are for a modern x86 processor, plus a large number of possible modifications to those instructions, it all becomes a bit much for mere humans to memorize.

After an assembly-language program is completed, the programmer will *assemble* it. This means running a special "assembler" program that takes the assembly-language statements as input data and generates the actual machine-language bytes that the CPU must see in order to know what it is supposed to do as its output.

Let me repeat that thought in several sentences: A programmer writes assembly-language statements. An assembler program converts them into machine-language bytes with a nearly one-to-one relationship between the programmer's assembly-language commands and the final machine-language code. It stores the result in a file. That file is the final program the programmer set out to create. When it is run, the CPU reads those bytes and does what they direct it to do.

The Problem with Assembly-Language Programs

The power of assembly-language programming is the ability you have to specify *exactly* everything that is going to happen and *exactly* where and how it will happen. This is also the problem with assembly-language programming.

It is a problem simply because humans are not very good at keeping huge amounts of detail in their minds at once. You can keep track of which numbers are where in a short program, but when the program becomes really large, there simply is too much to keep track of. Or, at least, doing so without making mistakes from time to time becomes very hard.

It would be so much nicer if you could somehow let the computer keep track of the details and just focus your attention on the bigger picture. So, for example, you might want not to have to decide which numbers would be put into which registers, or when to put a number into a memory location instead of into a register. And when writing information to a disk, you certainly don't want to have to be concerned with all the things DOS must do to manage files. That's why we have DOS.

Indeed, we can let the computer do more of the work, but as always, there is a price to be paid when we do so. Still, most programmers, most of the time, are more than happy to pay that price in exchange for what they get from using a higher-level programming language.

Working at a Higher Level: Letting the PC Do More of the Work

A popular piece of advice to managers is "Don't micromanage." That means, tell your workers what results you want, but don't tell them exactly how to do their jobs. Assume they know what they are doing, unless you have a pretty good reason to think that they don't.

The Notion of a High(er)-Level Language

This also describes the goal of higher-level programming languages, which embody a lot of detailed programming knowledge. They are like workers who know how to do a job. We call them tools, because they help us do jobs with less effort.

The programmer who uses one of these tools is acting like a manager, specifying a desired result without having to go into the details of just how that result will be achieved. The program then figures out a means of accomplishing the specified result and generates a machine-language code sequence that will do that.

In effect, this notion enables you to break up the work of writing a complex computer program into two steps. One is the step of deciding what overall actions are to be performed, in what order, and so on. That is the job of the programmer at the higher level. The other job is deciding how each of the specified actions will be carried out. That is the job of the author of the programming tool that the first programmer is going to use.

After a program is completed, if it is going to be used a lot, a good programmer will examine how the tool did its job in at least those areas of the program that are used most extensively. Then, depending on the programmer's judgment about how well the tool constructed that portion, he or she may redo it using a lower-level tool that gives the programmer more control over just how that task is carried out. In this way, the portions of the program that get executed most often can be made as efficient and speedy as possible, without the programmer having to spend an equal amount of effort on all the other parts of the program that only rarely get invoked.

Higher- and Lower-Level Programming Languages

Many different "higher-level" programming tools have been constructed. They differ in a number of ways. Some are barely higher-level than machine language. That is, they make it pretty easy to specify almost exactly what the machine is going to do at every step of the way, yet they manage to take off the programmer's hands at least a little of the grunt work.

Other high-level programming tools are much farther away from what actually will happen. They enable the programmer who uses them to specify actions in much more general terms, and then they do those specified actions in whatever way the author of the tool deemed best. Using one of these tools makes writing complex programs easier, but it also makes those programs less predictable in terms of exactly how they will do whatever it is they are to do. Generally, even the best of the programs written using the higher-level languages are less efficient and run more slowly than equivalent programs with equivalent functionality that have been carefully crafted in a lower-level language. There is at least one major exception to this: Programs written in high-level languages need only be recompiled with a compiler that supports a new processor's extensions to take advantage of those instructions, whereas assembly-level programs must be rewritten.

Classifying Computer Languages by Generations

Observers of the industry have come up with a classification of computer languages according to how low- or high-level they are. These levels are called *generations* (which partly reflects the fact that it was not very feasible to develop a yet higher-level language until the immediately preceding generation of programming tools was available). Many different computer languages exist in each generation, each optimized for a certain kind of programming task.

The lowest-level, or *first-generation,* languages are simply the actual binary machine languages "understood" by the various CPUs. Each different kind (or model) of CPU has its own machine language. (The machine languages used for all the models in Intel's x86 family of CPUs are sufficiently similar to one another that rather than refer to each one as a completely new language, you can think of them as simply different dialects of a common tongue.)

The *second-generation* languages are assemblers. This includes both the very basic assemblers, such as the one built into the program DEBUG (which is a utility program that has been bundled with nearly every version of DOS and Windows—and that I described briefly in Chapter 6, "Enhancing Your Understanding by Exploring and Tinkering") and much more powerful macro assemblers that enable you to use symbolic names and also to name whole blocks of code as macros and invoke them simply by using their names. Generally, you need a different assembler for each new kind of CPU with its own new machine language. Each assembler typically is upgraded when new *models* of that kind of CPU come out; then it can understand and assemble correctly the new dialect of machine language understood by the newest model of the target CPU and still be able to handle assembly-language programs written for earlier models in that CPU family.

The *third-generation* languages enable a programmer to create programs without having to know much about the details of how the particular computer on which it will run is constructed. In particular, you don't have to know how many registers the CPU has (let alone their specific names or sizes), whether there is a memory cache, and so on.

Typically, each of these languages is available in several dialects, each dialect being designed for use in generating machine language code for a particular kind of machine. The programmer may well be able to write the program once and then compile it several times, using different dialects of the same programming language to create versions of the program to run on each of several different kinds of computer.

An enormous number of third-generation computer programming languages has been created. Some that are commonly used on PCs include FORTRAN (*Formula Trans*lator), COBOL (*Common Business Oriented Language*), BASIC (*Beginners All-purpose Symbolic Instruction Code*, to give it the original full name), Pascal, Lisp, APL, C, Ada, C++, and so forth. (I have listed these names roughly in the historical order in which these languages were developed.)

The most popular third-generation languages for writing commercial software today are probably C, COBOL, BASIC, and FORTRAN in descending order of popularity. There are so many different languages and so many in widespread use because each different language has its own strengths and limitations.

FORTRAN was originally created to help scientists program computers for technical calculations.

COBOL was developed by a committee as the best all-purpose computer language for business programs. It is widely used for accounting programs and other financial applications in large corporations.

BASIC was developed as an instructional language for students at Dartmouth University, so it stresses ease of program crafting with minimal need to remember arcane details.

C is intended as a very powerful language for writing operating systems and other incredibly complex software. Because it is intended for use mainly by professional programmers, you must master a lot of arcane detail to become an expert C programmer. Also, it has enough low-level manipulation possibilities that it almost could be described as both a third- and a second-generation computer language bundled together.

A variant form of C that has had many object-oriented features added to the base language is called C++ and it is now one of the dominant languages used to craft commercial programs. (I'll explain just what *object-oriented* means a bit later in this chapter.)

Closely related to C++—and one of the newest programming languages in common use—is Java. It has become quite popular for Web site programming. I'll describe Java and some of its kin briefly in Chapter 26, "You Can Touch the World, and It May Touch You, Too!"

The *fourth-generation* computer languages are designed to minimize the effort necessary to create a program. Often, these are intended for use by nonprofessional programmers. Examples of fourth-generation languages (or 4GL languages as they are sometimes denoted) include dBASE, Forth, Perl, Clipper, and Visual Basic.

Finally, a *fifth-generation* computer language incorporates knowledge-based expert systems, inference engines, natural language processors, or other kinds of *artificial intelligence* (AI). These are only now being developed, and therefore there aren't yet many good ones in widespread use on PCs.

Choosing a Computer Language Requires Compromise

From all this diversity, you might be getting a notion that there are some trade-offs you must make—and that would be exactly right. Sometimes, a programmer wants nearly total control. Other times, programmers must relinquish some of their control in order to focus their attentions on larger issues and leave the lower-level work to others. Some applications involve lots of higher mathematics. Others simply do an enormous amount of simple arithmetic. Still others are primarily concerned with organizing and managing large databases. Choosing the right programming language for a particular task is, therefore, an exercise in balance and compromise.

Sometimes, the right choice is to first work in some very high-level language to get a working program no matter how inefficient it may be. Then you can go in and redo portions of that program using a lower-level tool to create greater efficiency. This sort of strategy is closely related to the reasons why there are both interpreters and compilers for many of the higher-level programming languages. But to explain that, I must first tell you what those things are.

Interpreters

I have told you that, after you have written a program in a higher-level language (anything above the first generation), it must be translated into actual machine language (binary) code before the CPU can understand and use it. This translation step can be done in any of several ways.

One way that has a lot of utility is to run a program that will translate one line of the program and then ask the CPU to execute that line (in its translated form, of course). Only after that step is done will it go on to translate the next line. Such a program is called an *interpreter*.

The advantage to this approach is simplicity for the user. I write a program and then run it immediately and see exactly what each line of the program causes the computer to do. If I must alter a line or two, I can do so and immediately rerun the program, reinterpreting it each time I do so. But when I finally finish the program and then intend to run it many, many times, this is not the optimum way to do the translation.

Compilers

Think of the human language parallel: I am writing this book in English. Suppose the publisher wants to sell many copies in certain foreign countries; the sensible plan for the publisher is to hire interpreters to translate the whole book one time into each target language, and then print and sell copies of each translation.

The alternative, which would resemble the use of a computer language interpreter, would be to let customers rent only the English language book accompanied by a skilled human translator and have that translator read it to the foreign language–speaking customer. Obviously, this isn't the least expensive or most efficient way for the publisher to distribute the work.

So people have crafted *compiler* programs. After a program is completely written out in the high-level language, the compiler reads it, generates a machine-language program, and saves it in a file. Then, as a totally independent step, that file (the executable program) can be run once or as many times as you want.

Almost all commercial programs are created this way, and usually only the executable (translated) program is shipped to the customer. The programmer and publishing company keep the *source code* (the high-level language version of the program) to themselves, in part to keep others from seeing just how they wrote it and perhaps writing a competing program more easily.

The advantages of doing this are clear. The disadvantage to this approach is also clear: If you must alter even 1 byte of the higher-level language program, you must recompile the entire program before you can test it.

P-Code

In an attempt to get the best of both worlds, some tool builders came up with what they term *p-code* (or *pseudo-code*). In this approach, you write the program in a high-level language, and it is immediately processed into an intermediate form that is close to machine language, but not actually machine language. (The particular form the p-code takes is one that can be generated relatively quickly, and that in turn can be very rapidly interpreted into actual machine code.) Then, when you want to run the program (to test it, for example), the corresponding p-code interpreter is invoked to do that final step in the translation.

The advantage to this approach is that the p-code translator has a relatively simple job to do, and thus it can be much faster than a full interpreter. But it can enable you to alter just a portion of the program (and recompile just that portion to its p-code equivalent) and then quickly test the whole program once more.

This approach was used for Pascal when it was first introduced for the PC as one of the initial programming languages offered by IBM. BASIC was introduced for the PC only in a fully interpreted (and relatively slow) version. Later, various companies (including Microsoft) came out with compilers for BASIC. Eventually, Microsoft introduced QuickBasic, which is a p-code interpreter and editing/compiling environment for BASIC that functions in much the way the early Pascal tools did.

Visual Basic is a direct descendent of QuickBasic because it also provides an editing and debugging environment (and includes a p-code compiler and interpreter) for generating a variant form of the Basic computer language. It differs because it was designed to create programs to run under Windows, and to facilitate this job it enables you to see the program under construction in a graphical user interface and to construct it in a more directly graphical manner than was possible before. Furthermore, because Windows programs operate primarily in response to "messages," Visual Basic programs—like all other Windows programs—are written in a more sophisticated modular fashion than was customary for earlier versions of Basic.

Virtual Machines

In another variation on this theme, some high-level language developers have built special-purpose computers whose machine language instructions are essentially identical to the constructs in their particular high-level language. Then the programmer can write the program and directly execute it on this special kind of computer. No interpretation or compilation is needed.

This special kind of computer (one that has as its basic instruction set the instructions that form a particular high-level computer language) can be, and occasionally is, actually built in a hardware form. A recent example of this is Sun Microelectronics' microJava 701. This is a CPU chip that has a dialect of Java as its native language.

More commonly this type of special computer is merely simulated by running a special program on a more general-purpose computer. For example, you can run a program called Pick on a PC or on a mainframe computer. Either way, the result is to make the computer act as though it were built in some different way as a "Pick machine." Then you run Pick programs on this "virtual Pick machine." Pick machines are special database engines, and they are optimized for that task. Pick programs access databases, using the special qualities of a virtual Pick machine. An important point to notice is that this strategy enables a user to run the same program on any virtual Pick machine, no matter what kind of computer hardware is actually doing the work.

Similarly, although it now is possible to build a computer with a CPU that executes Java directly, the more common approach—and what is now universally done in PCs—is simply to simulate the Java virtual machine in software running on the PC's normal CPU. I have more to say about this language in my discussion of the Internet in Chapter 26, but for now I want to point out that Java is meant to be run on either a virtual (simulated) Java machine or on an actual hardware Java computer. And the main virtue of Java is precisely the relative hardware independence which this approach provides. Supposedly, a 100 percent pure Java program will run in exactly the same way (although at perhaps different speeds) on any computer—a Macintosh, a PC, or Sun workstation. It won't need to be rewritten or recompiled for each different type of computer.

This approach is especially powerful when writing programs for use over the Internet, because the program author need not be aware of which types of computers the users of his or her program might be using. Anything Java permits is okay, as long as the user's computer has a Java virtual machine inside it.

Dividing Up the Work

I have mentioned several times the notion that programming a computer can be quite complex, and that often the best strategy to follow is to divide the overall task into several subtasks, letting specialists work on each separate subtask. Now I want to go back over that notion in a little more detail and explain the distinction between BIOS programs, the operating system, application programs, and applets.

BIOS-Level Programming

BIOS (basic input/output system) is the name given to the programs in your PC that are designed to activate the various pieces of hardware. Someone must know exactly how each chunk of hardware works and therefore exactly what instructions the CPU must process in order to get that chunk of hardware to do some useful task. There is no need for everyone who writes any other type of PC program to have this detailed knowledge.

Instead, we let BIOS programmers write those very low-level, right-next-to-the-hardware programs to activate each gadget within our PCs. No matter how this particular keyboard (or video screen, modem, or whatever) operates, any other program can ask for it to be operated by using a standardized protocol called an Application Program Interface (API).

The motherboard BIOS includes hardware driver programs for all the standard pieces of PC hardware. Any added, nonstandard, hardware must either have as a part of itself another BIOS ROM containing its driver programs, or you must load the appropriate programs off a disk into memory before the PC can utilize that nonstandard hardware.

No matter how nonstandard the hardware may be, the application programmers don't need to know anything about how it really works. They can just write their programs to ask for standard "services" from that hardware and trust the BIOS driver to handle the details.

On the other hand, many modern operating systems (notably Windows NT and most variants of UNIX) tend not to use the BIOS programs for much of anything. One major reason for this is concern about security coupled with a need to make sure the operating system works in the same way, independent of the machine on which it is running.

Application Programs

Application programs do whatever it is you bought your PC to do. At least I don't know of many people who bought a PC just to watch the DOS prompt or read directory listings. Most of us want to write things, keep track of our money, or communicate using our PCs. And we need application programs to accomplish those tasks.

The Operating System as Middleware

Between the BIOS and the application programs is the realm of the operating system. In a way, it could be termed *middleware*. (There is another use for this term that I will explain in Chapter 24, "The PC Reaches Out, Part Two: Through the NIC Node," when I discuss what is termed *client/server* computing.)

The operating system does many things, including, as I mentioned previously, scheduling application programs, resolving conflicts among applications that want access to the same resources, and so on. It also has the task of handing off service requests from the application programs to the hardware device drivers in the BIOS that do the actual work.

Sometimes in the handing off, the operating system also must amplify those requests for service. For example, an application program can ask the operating system to open a file named C:\MyDocs\Alice and leave the task of finding that file up to the operating system. But the BIOS can't do that task, described in that way. It must know the exact head, cylinder, and sector numbers where the contents of that file are stored. So the intervening layers of the operating system have to do some work to prepare the request for the BIOS routines.

In this example, the operating system must ask the BIOS to do several subtasks before it can proceed to the main task. The OS must find out, by using the services of the BIOS, which files are stored in which locations so it can figure out from which locations to ask the BIOS to retrieve the required data.

There are many other instances in which the API used by the application program is stated in more general terms than the API understood by the BIOS routines. Each time, the operating system must do any necessary translation and amplification in order to get the BIOS routines to do whatever is needed to satisfy the application program's requests.

I have stated all this in very general terms. I didn't say whether the operating system I was talking about was DOS or Windows, or perhaps Linux. It doesn't matter. All of them work in conceptually the same fashion, which is the point I want you to understand.

How Not to Keep On Reinventing the Wheel

Programming is detailed, hard work. Programmers love efficiency as much as the rest of us, so they have devised some clever ways to avoid the avoidable portions of the task of designing software. This section describes briefly some of those strategies. In the process, I also will help you understand one of the most misunderstood jargon terms of our time: object-oriented programming.

Programming Libraries

Almost all application programs must handle the same jobs, such as getting input from the keyboard and mouse, putting information on the screen, and opening files. By the division of labor described earlier, all the picky details of these tasks are handled by low-level driver programs. Even with that help, the application program must have at least a few lines of code to ask for that help, and those lines will be repeated over and over in program after program.

To save time and effort, the obvious thing to do is save those lines of code in some form that lets them be reused as needed. This is the essential idea behind a *programming library*.

Such a library can be as simple as a single file that contains many lines of code, with the idea that the programmer will cut and paste sections from this file into the program currently under construction. Or, it can be somewhat more sophisticated, with a directory portion that describes all the blocks of code it contains so that the cutting and pasting can be automated.

Program Linkages and Modular Programs

The next step beyond this is to build a mechanism for assembling programs out of building blocks. Those building blocks are pretested blocks of code in a library. But now, instead of cutting out each little program fragment he or she wishes to use and then pasting it into your main program, the programmer can simply include in the main program a pointer to that block. Then when the program is compiled, the compiler can know enough to open the library file, read the relevant blocks, and act as though they were a part of the main program.

This action is called *linking*. The compiler translates the main program into machine code (putting it in a file called an *object module*), with a description included of where routines from the library must be inserted. Then a separate program, called a *linker*, will read the object module and extract from the library the appropriate machine-language routines to complete the program. Notice that now the library will not contain blocks of high-level language code. Instead, each of those blocks must have been precompiled and ready for use.

There is another way to use a library of this type. You don't have to have the compiler actually include the machine language code fragments inside the compiled application program. Instead, you can have the program reach out and execute those code fragments from within the library program each time it needs them whenever that application program is itself executed. In order for this to work, of course, the library in question must be available to that running application program. Such a memory-loaded, instantly available, runtime library of code fragments is called a *dynamic link library* (DLL).

Object-Oriented Programming

Finally, we come to that wonderful and frustrating buzzword phrase, object-oriented programming (OOP). This once meant something very precise. Now, however, it sometimes seems to mean whatever the speaker wants it to mean. If a company says its tools support OOP, it means the tools support what the company wants you to think OOP is. And each company's tools are likely to do slightly (or, sometimes, dramatically) different things.

I won't go into all the variations on this idea that are currently in use. Instead, I will try to give you a sense of the overall concept. It is a very powerful concept, even though the tools to put it into practice are still being refined in an attempt to make all the promise of this approach at last become real.

Before I can define OOP, I must describe the old style of programming in a slightly different way than I have up to now. In most older programming languages, the programmer crafts some lines of code designed to perform a procedure on some data. The data is thought of as being the object acted upon by the program—something that is outside the procedure.

If you were to create a new program based on an existing program, you would read over the details of the existing program, copy unchanged what you wanted to use, and write the new parts from scratch. Then, after compiling it, you would introduce this program to the data on which it is to work.

The essence of OOP is to create new kinds of programs. They are functional blocks that contain procedures and even some data, and you are supposed to view these blocks as being black or *opaque*. That is, you can activate a block (have it do one of the things it "knows" how to do) and yet have utterly no notion of how it works or what it contains.

This all sounds quite abstract, and it is. So let me get a little more explicit, and in the process introduce you to some of the OOP jargon.

Objects, Classes, Instances, and Libraries

In OOP programming, a key concept is a *class*. A class is a type of something. For example, you might define a class as a button in a dialog box on a computer screen. You can do something with this button (in particular, you can "press it" by clicking on it with your mouse or other pointing device), and it will react somehow. The class in this case would be simply all possible buttons that you can make appear on a computer screen and that could then be pressed.

When you have a class, you can define *subclasses* with some additional particulars. For example, you might define a subclass of buttons called rectangular buttons. Or green ones. Or ones with labels. Each of these is a particular subset of all possible buttons. Of course, you could have among the rectangular buttons a subclass of buttons that also have labels, and within them a subclass of buttons that are red but turn green when pressed.

A particular button is an *instance* of a particular subclass of the class of all buttons. An instance of a button is also referred to as an *object*.

The definitions of various classes of objects (and also of some subclasses) can be referred to in the aggregate as a *class library*.

Attributes, Behaviors, and Methods

Each class (or subclass) will have some set of *properties*. Some of these are best called *attributes*. For example, a particular instance of the button class will have a particular size, shape, color, and value (content) for its label.

The attributes are stored in *variables*. The values in those variables are the attributes for this particular instance of this class; the variables themselves are the attributes of the class.

Other properties tell how the button behaves. For example, when it is pressed (by a mouse click) it will do something. Perhaps it will send a particular message to some other object. Behaviors are defined by *methods*. That is, you write a procedure to spell out just what a certain behavior shall be, and that procedure is now one of the methods for this class of object.

Notice that methods within a class can act upon objects outside that class. Thus, in our example, the button can send a message to some other kind of object (perhaps a window that is supposed to open or close when that button is pressed). This behavior is specified by a method within this class definition, even though it implies an action on an outside object.

Inheritance, Interfaces, and Packages

The payoff to all this begins with the concept of *inheritance*. After you have defined some classes, you can define a new subclass by naming the class of which it is a subclass and then spelling out only those attributes and methods that this subclass has but its parent class doesn't have.

By the act of saying that a new object is an instance of a subclass of a certain class, you automatically imply that it has all the attributes and methods that characterize the objects in that class, plus the new ones that you are explicitly defining for this subclass. (If you don't want some subset of the attributes and methods in the class of objects you referred to, you can simply redefine those attributes or those methods in your new subclass definition.)

The jargon language for this goes thus: A subclass *inherits* the attributes and behaviors of its parent class of objects. This helps because you don't now have to copy the sections of older programs that you like. Just name your new objects as subclasses of those older program's classes (with specified differences), and you will get the full attribute and behavior set you want. The older program is in a sense included by reference. (And you must build into your OOP program a pointer to that older program, which is to say to its class library.)

The *interface* to an object is just a list of the methods it contains (without the details of what those methods actually do). This list doesn't include the methods that are defined in the parent classes above this one in the hierarchy; only the ones defined in this class definition are listed in its interface.

Finally, *packages* are groups of related classes and interfaces that are bundled together, so you can imply all of them by referring to the package name, or some of them by referring to the package name and the class name within that package. This lets different objects have the same name and yet be different, simply by being contained in different packages.

Putting It All Together

Whew. That was a quick one. Let me try to recap everything. Object-oriented programming simply is a formally defined way to access the capabilities of previously written programs within a new program. This strategy means that when you have a useful package of classes and interfaces, you can use it without needing to know the details of its contents. And yet you can override any of the attributes or behaviors of any of the individual classes within that package any time you need to do so.

There is nothing magic about OOP, nor is it necessarily a "better" way to program than the older style with its libraries and linking. Modular programming in some manner is almost a necessity, and certainly adds efficiency to the programming task. Which kind of modularity one uses is less critical.

Helping Ordinary People "Program" Their PCs Easily

Now for the last section of this chapter, the one that tells you how you, whoever you are, can and probably do engage in programming your PC. Often it is so easy that you won't even be aware that what you are doing is programming—but it is.

If you have ever written a DOS batch file, which is a list of commands you don't want to have to type over and over at the DOS prompt, you were programming. You put those commands into a file with each one on a separate line, gave the file a name (with the extension .BAT), and thereafter you could simply type its name at the DOS prompt and COMMAND.COM would do the rest. COMMAND.COM is, in this instance, acting as an interpreter of the DOS batch programming language.

If you use a spreadsheet program and write some macros to perform useful calculations for you, you are programming. The spreadsheet program is interpreting them, which is to say that, among other things, it is an interpreter for that macro programming language.

Early versions of Microsoft Word had a macro language (Word Basic). That was modeled upon QuickBasic, which is one of the older computer programming languages (well, at least in its earlier, interpreted form, usually referred to as BASIC). With this language, you could write macros to do all manner of things within Word. More recently, Microsoft has phased out Word Basic, but that functionality has been transferred to a more general language, subsets of which are available in all of the MS Office applications. This universal language is now based on the more GUI-oriented version of Basic known as

Visual Basic, and the form in which it appears in Office is known as Visual Basic for Applications (VBA).

> **Warning:** A side observation is in order here. Anyone can put a Word Basic or Visual Basic for Applications macro into a Word document file. If that macro is given the proper form and name, it will automatically be executed each time that document is opened in Word.
>
> This means that if you download such a document from the Internet (or load it off a floppy disk given you by a friend) and then open it up in Word, you may activate one or more macros within that document. These are potentially powerful enough to do great mischief.
>
> We call such rogue macros embedded in a Word document (or any similar file from a macro-enabled application program such as Excel) a *macro virus*. Before you open any such document from a source not well known to you, it's a very good idea to scan it with a virus scanner such as Norton AntiVirus.

With the growth of the power of these batch and macro languages, many people who never thought they would be programmers are writing some pretty serious PC programs. Now we have yet another kind of programming that "ordinary" folks may find themselves doing: HTML programming for Web or intranet publishing. If you run a Web page editor or word processor that can save your work as hypertext, you will seem only to be typing and formatting a page of text. Then you will highlight some phrases or words and indicate that they are links to some other pages. The program you are running will use that information to construct for you a Hypertext Markup Language (HTML) document, which is a kind of program. You can see this when someone viewing that page clicks on a link, and some *action* results (the display of a new link usually, but it also could be the downloading and running of a Java applet or a JavaScript program). In this context, your word processor or Web page editor is actually a fourth-generation computer language programming tool.

Summary

In this chapter, I explained a wide variety of ways that people write programs for PCs. I also showed you some of the distinguishing features of different generations of computer programming languages and of different ways that these high-level language programs can be translated into machine-language instructions that the PC's CPU can understand and act upon.

Finally, I explained what OOP means (and a lot of associated jargon), what Java applets are, and how creating a Web page—which is some serious programming—can be done as easily as writing a letter.

In the next chapter, I carry this story on to the next stage: how PCs can literally talk to you, and how you may be able to fix up your PC so that when you talk to it, it will understand you and act on what you tell it to do.

Some PCs Can Understand Speech and Talk to Us

For many years after the invention of the digital electronic computer, virtually all the information that was put into computers came via a keyboard. And virtually all human-understandable computer output took the form of characters printed on paper—or, later on, characters printed on terminal screens.

Historical Aside

In the very early days, those keyboards were mostly on *keypunch* machines, and they caused holes to be punched in *Holerith* punched cards. Decks of those cards were then submitted to the computer operator as a *batch job*. Starting around 1960, people began using terminals attached to mainframe computers. Although there were a few terminals that could display graphical images, almost all the work done on these terminals was, like the work done with punched cards previously, a matter of characters typed in and characters printed out, either on screen or on paper.

The era of mainly characters-in-and-characters-out computing persisted until after the PC was introduced in 1981. In the mid 1980s, computer interactivity took on a new aspect. We became concerned for the first time with the *graphical form* of the information being put into and coming out of our computers.

Most input was still done by means of characters typed on a keyboard, but we supplemented that with the use of a mouse, trackball, or graphics tablet. The output, on screen or on paper, began to take on a much richer graphical form. Letters were set in various fonts, and pictures were often added. (Color had been an option for screen output for a long time. Soon, adding color to output printed on paper became another common option.) All of this input and output, of course, involved things we could see.

More recently, another new dimension has been added to computer input and output. This time it involves a different human sense: hearing. The new dimension is that of sounds—both sounds generated by our PCs and sounds we make that it "hears" and responds to.

This and the next several chapters tell you the story of how sound has been added to the PC's repertoire. This chapter focuses on the ways in which sounds are used to enter information that otherwise would have to be typed on a keyboard or input by using a mouse, and as an alternative means of output for information that in the past could only have been printed (on screen or paper).

Making Conversational PCs: Breaking Down the Overall Job

The notion of being able to converse with a computer is not new. *Star Trek* is famous for having used this idea very effectively for over 30 years. But when manufacturers tried actually making a computer that was capable of conversing with users, they found that the task was much, much harder than they had expected. (I can recall reading the predictions of many "experts" in the field that speech recognition would be common to computers "within the next five to ten years"—and this same phrase kept popping up time after time for more than 25 years.) It seems that even the experts couldn't believe that this task would turn out to be as hard as it really is. Even today, I know of a thirty-year-old engineer who says she expects to be able to "ride the speech-recognition gravy train all the way to retirement." It's one of the most complex tasks we have ever asked of computers.

You can divide the things a PC must do in order to converse with a user into four subtasks. It was obvious to researchers early on that these were the tasks to be performed, although just how each one could be performed by a computer turned out to be not quite so obvious.

First—and by far the easiest—the PC must speak. By this I mean it must be able to produce sounds that resemble what one human might say to another.

Second, the PC must be able to listen and to recognize what it hears. By this I mean that if you speak into a microphone, the PC must be able to convert the electronic signals from the microphone into a stream of data that it can manipulate. This has proven to be one of the most difficult parts of the overall job.

Third, the PC must be able to understand the speech it has heard. This means taking the sentences it recognizes and figuring out how to respond. The sentences might be commands it is to perform, or they might be data it is to process. Combinations of these two are also possible—even likely. You might say to your computer "Find Joe Jones' phone number." The PC must understand that this sentence is both a command (find a phone number and display it, recite it, or perhaps offer to dial it) and data (the name of the person whose number is being sought).

Finally, the PC must be able to compose relevant responses, in a human language form. Then it can use its speaking capability to deliver that response.

Making PCs Speak

Most natural human languages are expressed in two ways: orally and in writing. Either way, an expression in a language can be broken down into its constituent parts. There is a virtually unlimited number of possible expressions, but only a limited number of basic elements are needed to construct these.

For written language, we all know the rules: Anything we write will be composed of paragraphs, each containing sentences, with each sentence containing words, and each word being written as a string of letters. Letters are the basic symbols; words, sentences, and paragraphs are larger units in which those basic symbols are organized.

Spoken languages have a similar, yet different, structure. You can think of a spoken sentence as being composed of words, but if you consider it in terms of the sounds that make it up, it pretty clearly isn't made up of words—or at least not of clearly separated chunks that can easily be recognized as words. Realizing this was the first step to making PCs that could speak (or hear).

Phonemes

The actual building blocks of speech are called *phonemes*. These are the elemental sounds any human being can make. You can utter only some fairly limited number of possible sounds.

The sounds that any particular person learns to utter are determined largely by the language spoken around that person early in life. You normally learn to speak as your parents and others near you speak. So if you grew up in Japan hearing only Japanese, you learned a different set of common sounds than if you grew up in France hearing only French.

Anyone who has learned a foreign language as an adult can testify to the difficulty of learning the sounds that are used in that language but not in any you learned early in life. Still, it is possible to learn to utter just about any sounds that any other human can utter. And the whole collection of those sounds makes up the universe of human phonemes.

After you understand the relationship between phonemes and speech, the next step is to relate the strings of characters we call words in the written form of a language to the corresponding phonemes as those words are spoken by a native speaker of that language. If we can make that connection, we can teach a computer to speak. This isn't, as it turns out, a trivially easy task. But doing a pretty good job is possible.

Pronouncing Dictionaries Are Necessary, but Not Enough

The first step in the association of text and sound is simple. Associate a most commonly used phoneme or set of phonemes with each letter used in the language you want the computer to speak. Next, consider all the special-case combinations. In English, the combination *ph* carries the same pronunciation as the letter *f* (most of the time). Similarly, the letter combination *tion* usually is pronounced like the English word *shun*.

Some words are special cases in themselves. They simply don't have the pronunciation you would expect from the way they are spelled. For these, you must have a dictionary that spells out the *phoneme sequence* needed to pronounce that word correctly.

Even that isn't quite enough. Sometimes a word's pronunciation depends upon how it is being used. In that case, you also must have some way to figure out what part of speech it is from the structure of the sentence containing it and then apply the correct pronunciation for that context. Or, the context might be determined by the subject matter. In either case, a more global analysis of the sentences is needed to decide which pronunciation to use.

Gender, Inflection, and Emotion Are Other Issues

With a combination of all these strategies, it is possible for a computer to analyze a text string and then produce a phoneme string representing that text string. If those phonemes are pronounced correctly, a spoken sentence will be generated.

Correct pronunciation opens a whole new can of worms. Who is speaking? What gender is the speaker? What age? With what accent does that speaker say things in this language? And what is the emotional content of the sentence? Some of these issues are relatively easy to deal with. Others have only been approximated, so far.

The first step is to decide how the phonemes will be generated. There are basically two choices: one is to synthesize them, and the other is to play back a prerecorded sample of a person saying that phoneme.

If you use a synthesis technique, many parameters can be applied to influence how the phoneme will sound. These parameters enable you to simulate either gender and to adjust for apparent age of the speaker. They also will allow some rough simulation of dialect.

The approach that will yield the best-sounding speech is simply to record actual human beings (of a range of ages and other characteristics) speaking. Then break down those recordings into their phonemes. If you do this and store them in a cataloged fashion, it is possible (although hardly easy) for the computer to stitch the sampled pieces together to pronounce the sentences.

All this tends to produce fairly flat, emotionless speech. So far, computers are not very good at generating the correct emotional flavor for a speech. Still, this is good enough for many purposes. The raw information in a sentence is usually discernible by human beings, if only they can hear each word. The emotional embellishments add a lot to human conversation, but mostly they are used to convey an emotional subtext and we aren't yet in a position to ask our computers to do this for us.

PCs, or even mainframe computers, aren't yet up to analyzing a textual passage and then giving an emotionally compelling rendition of that passage. But then, many people aren't able to do this either. That is one reason why we pay actors to do this for us. So, asking computers to do the job of translating text into speech better than most ordinary people can do that job is probably asking too much. At least for now.

What Is the Current State of This Art?

The many steps I have just described sound rather complicated. They are, but not unmanageably so. People who care have figured out how to do this job fairly well.

Not everyone needs or wants a talking PC. However, if you are blind (or even nearly blind), it can be crucial. For this reason, most of the text-to-speech tools were initially developed for the sight-impaired.

In other contexts, having a PC that talks—especially if it also can listen and understand human speech—can be more than just convenient. That combination, what I call a conversational PC, can be used to support people who are doing a task that requires the use of their hands and eyes.

One example of this is an aircraft mechanic doing a routine maintenance inspection of an airplane. Having a computer that can record messages about what the mechanic is finding and also prompt the mechanic for what parts must be replaced can greatly enhance the mechanic's productivity. In fact, some airlines (and also some railroads) have been doing this for the past several decades using minicomputers. Now it is practical to do the same thing using PCs.

As the PC's capability of analyzing speech input increases, and as this gets applied to performing increasingly sophisticated database accesses, having a talking PC as a surgeon's assistant in every hospital might become standard procedure. We aren't there yet, but it is certainly coming—and yes, these things will probably be commonplace "within the next five to ten years."

Teaching PCs to Listen and Understand

This, of course, brings us right back to the other side of the equation: Having PCs that are capable of listening to humans and understanding. This involves two tasks: Hearing the words and sentences, and then figuring out what those sentences mean.

Hearing and Understanding Is Hard Work

You probably haven't given much thought to how you understand what people say to you. If you have, you realize just how complex that operation is.

First, realize that you don't hear words. You don't even hear phonemes. You hear sounds. Sometimes it is hard to distinguish the wail of a cat from some sounds people make. So you really ought to have sympathy for the designers who have endeavored to make PCs understand speech.

There are, it turns out, two very different ways to speak to a computer. One is the natural way people talk. The other is a highly artificial way to talk that is much, much easier for a computer to understand. After I explain this distinction, I will also address briefly the issue of having a computer that understands one particular person versus one that can understand a wide range of people.

Natural Speech Versus Interrupted Speech

If you have tried to learn a foreign language, you have no doubt noticed that one of the very hardest things to learn is to hear what a person speaking that language is saying. That is, what exactly are the words being spoken? Leave aside their meaning for a moment; just try to recognize what words the sounds represent.

The reason this is hard is that usually we speak rapidly. It seems much more rapid if you aren't familiar with the language. We do this because we seek to convey content as quickly as we can. So we speak essentially as rapidly as a trained listener can comprehend our speech. If you aren't yet a well-trained listener in that language, you will have difficulty discerning the words being spoken.

This suggests that the most difficult aspect of understanding is just this task of deciphering the words from the stream of sounds. This is precisely what the research into making a PC that hears has also told us.

Breaking It Up Makes Hearing It So Much Simpler

Think about what foreigners do when they want to be understood. No, I don't mean that they shout. They slow down. They speak each word clearly and distinctly. That is essentially what we had to do until very recently to get a computer to understand speech. Separate each word by short bits of silence—in effect, make the speaker pronounce each interword space.

This is called *interrupted speech*. With this strategy, the computer's task is made much simpler. Each burst of speech can be counted on to represent one word. So, the computer can compare that burst of sound with a stored sample of all the words it understands and pick the one that matches most closely.

Flowing Speech Is So Much More Natural

Speaking for an extended period in an interrupted fashion is rather tiring, however, and most unnatural. Clearly, the goal must be to have PCs that can listen to a human speaking as humans normally do, and still be able to pick out the words and the meaning. For many years this was like a Holy Grail—out there somewhere to be yearned for and sought but never found.

Now, finally, we have arrived. Sort of. In some fairly limited situations, it is now possible to use natural, connected speech in speaking to a PC and have the PC able to discern what words are being spoken. This only works (so far) for single-speaker recognition, although the best of today's speech recognition programs are capable of storing speech and expressive-style profiles for many different individuals. Each user of the program has his or her own profile, which the program uses to aid in the interpretation of that user's words. Group conversational recognition remains elusive, but individual recognition can approach 97%. That is already quite an achievement.

Phonemes and Context Are Key

Whether you are attempting to make a PC program to recognize interrupted or connected speech, the first step is to attempt to identify the phonemes from the sounds the PC receives. Interrupted speech helps, mainly because the program knows where at least some of the phonemes start (right after each pause). With continuous speech, just the problem of deciding when a new phoneme begins is a fairly tough one.

All natural human languages are redundant. We say quite a few more words than we need to say, just to minimally represent our thoughts. One reason we do this is to give some contextual clues to our listeners to help them identify the words we are speaking from the sounds they are hearing. Naturally, this suggests that a PC program for hearing should also be looking for these same contextual clues. Fortunately, all the good ones do.

In fact, they take this notion somewhat farther—and often a bit more rigidly—than we do. The PC program will have a dictionary of all the words you might say (with their pronunciations), but it doesn't assume that every word is equally likely. Instead, it takes careful note of what you have just said to make predictions about what you will likely say next.

This means that a speech recognition program has at every moment a fairly fixed notion of what you are about to say, based on what it has already recognized. If you suddenly change topics, you can expect that the recognition accuracy will fall until the PC figures out once more what the relevant context is.

If you think about it, this is not very different from what happens to people. If you suddenly jump to a wholly new topic, you can expect your listeners to ask you to repeat yourself. People have the same problems as PC speech recognition programs—although mostly we are much better than those programs at hearing an unexpected word correctly the first time. Still, we are likely to be unsure, and to ask for clarification.

Most speech recognition programs aren't that conversational yet. They simply make their best stab at recognizing whatever you say and let any mistakes simply enter their generated text. You must go back later and clean up those messes manually. (Some of these programs will flag the words it is pretty sure it didn't get right—perhaps by displaying them in a different color—to help you find them when you are in the correction phase.)

Trained Recognition Versus Universal Recognition

People and PC programs can recognize a word only by what it sounds like, and it certainly helps both people and PCs if the same word always sounds the same. This is much more likely to happen if the words are spoken by the same person all the time.

Thus, one way to make a PC speech recognition program work much more accurately is simply to limit it to recognizing a particular person's speech. This strategy has been used for a long time, and whenever it can be applied, it certainly makes the PC program's job much easier.

Single-Speaker Recognition Is Relatively Easy and Reliable

With the single-speaker approach, you first "train" the recognition program by reading some sentences that the program displays. This enables the program to analyze how you say each of those words. Later on, it can apply that knowledge to figure out what words you are most likely saying as you dictate.

You can let other people train the program also, but you must first tell the program each time you change to a new speaker, and let it store each person's pronunciations in a separate profile. When you begin dictating, you first identify yourself to the PC so it will recognize your speech accurately.

Using this single-speaker, trained-recognition strategy—and assuming you are using a very proficient context analyzer—it is possible to get over 90 percent accuracy in recognizing the words spoken, even when the total vocabulary of possible words is many tens of thousands.

Nobody's Perfect

Whether your recognition program has been trained or not, you must realize that mistakes will be made. So, some means of correcting errors is important. If you are using the speech recognition program to enter a block of text, you might choose to enter it all without regard to errors. Later, you can find and correct all the errors. That interrupts the dictation process minimally. But if you are using the speech recognition program to control a process by voice commands, you must catch and correct each error as it occurs. The best way to do this is to have the PC tell you what it thinks you said and have you confirm that before it takes any significant action based on what it heard. If it got the command wrong, you can simply tell it to ignore that command, and then try again to get it to recognize what you want it to do.

Understanding What You Have Heard

So, it now is possible for a PC to recognize what a person says to it. What's the next task? Understanding what those spoken words, phrases, or sentences are telling the PC to do (and then doing it).

The level of difficulty this job has will depend on the context in which you are doing it. If you plan to let your PC listen and then take actions based on what you said to it, you might be able to limit the possible actions enough that it can recognize each command with a very high probability.

But what if you want to have the PC able to engage in a normal, flowing human conversation—with all the interrupted sentence fragments, sudden changes of subject, "ums" and "ahs," and other extraneous noises that this implies? You'll have to accept a lot less reliability in the recognition you'll get, and you will probably have to build in a lot of confirmation loops to check on how accurately the speaker has been heard. Even worse, your PC won't have many clues to let it know whether the speaker's utterances are commands or simply data to be stored.

Indeed, this latter task—making a computer that can participate in a normal conversation so that a human being cannot distinguish the computer from another human—is the benchmark of a true artificial intelligence; so far, it is out there somewhere, but certainly not within our immediate reach.

Generating Useful and Relevant Responses

The last task in making a conversational PC is enabling it to generate meaningful verbal responses. If your PC program has understood the oral input, it probably can generate relevant output. This task seems likely to be the least difficult of our four.

In fact, for some limited contexts, this task is being done right now and very well. Seeing-impaired folks can get their PCs to talk to them, giving them prompts as to what they are to do next, speaking all the error messages, and so on. This works just fine. The talking PC has been invaluable to people with other types of physical disabilities as well. Stephen Hawking, the brilliant quantum physicist, has been able to give lectures and express ideas that have redefined our very understanding of the universe around us through the use of a talking PC that is built into his wheelchair.

However, if you want really general conversations from your PC, you will find that doing this well is harder than anything we are able to do with our PCs today.

How Far Along Are We Now?

What is the current state of the art in this whole area of creating a conversational PC? The answer you will get to this question will depend a good deal on the person you ask and the assumptions that person makes about what you are seeking.

Converting Text to Speech

Many companies now have made products that are pretty good at converting text to speech—provided you don't mind that the speech has little or no emotional embellishment. Some companies let the user add special emotion tags in the text and then their products can do a fair job of adding appropriate inflections to their output—although nothing you would mistake for a real human being. Most of the time, text-to-speech programs are used to read prepared text files or simple canned messages—rather than to speak some complex response the PC generated in reaction to an event input. Dragon System's NaturallySpeaking and IBM's ViaVoice are two of the best PC voice-recognition programs, and each can speak any text you give it. You even can tweak these programs to let your PC sound more or less like a man, woman, or child, and to speak your text with at least some emotional embellishments.

Speech Recognition

The progress in speech recognition in the past few years has been quite dramatic. We have had some fairly good single-speaker (trained) recognition programs for interrupted speech for several years. There are also some very successful applications in which untrained recognition of (some very limited) oral input has been possible.

For the more general problem, it is only in the past couple of years that I could say that it is possible to buy a reasonably good continuous-speech recognition program. Those programs work best when trained properly by the speaker and when the program has had a chance to "read" a lot of text either spoken or written by that speaker to learn that speaker's habits in terms of how he or she puts words together.

IBM's ViaVoice program is one very good example of a product that can do this job acceptably. It requires a pretty hefty assemblage of PC hardware. Don't even try using it on anything less than a 200MHz Pentium with MMX, and you'll do best if you give it lots of RAM to work with (at least 32MB for Windows 95 or 48MB for Windows NT), as well as sufficient disk space to hold all your utterances and the text into which they get translated.

With these restrictions, it is possible for ViaVoice to do a decent job as a dictation assistant with an internal vocabulary of up to 64,000 words or phrases. (A single phrase that is always spoken as a single burst of sound is, so far as any speech recognition program is concerned, a single word.) Words that are not part of ViaVoice's default vocabulary can be added by each user on an as-you-use-them basis.

Dragon Systems has a similar product called NaturallySpeaking. Its hardware requirements and performance are comparable to those of ViaVoice, but to get the very best recognition, you need even more RAM. If you don't have enough, NaturallySpeaking will simply not load its most sophisticated BestMatch recognition algorithms.

Lernout & Hauspie has a product called Voice Xpress, and Philips has one called Free Speech 98. Both are reasonably capable continuous voice-recognition programs, but neither has attracted as many or as favorable reviews as the two market-segment leaders, ViaVoice and NaturallySpeaking.

I also should point out that all these vendors have multiple products in the general area of voice recognition—some tuned more for control of applications and some more for dictation. Before choosing one, you need to review their current offerings. Still, the general concepts I have explained in this chapter should help you make sense of whatever you find has come to market by the time you go looking.

It Takes a Lot of PC to Get the Job Done

I have stressed many times that speech recognition is not an easy task. Indeed, it takes a whole lot of work by your PC. To make this possible in real time, you need a fairly speedy PC. Furthermore, you need one with lots of memory (RAM) and with an adequate sound system.

There are two reasons why you need so much RAM. One is, as I indicated previously, to let the full voice-recognition program load. The other is to have enough RAM to run your application program (for example, a word processor) for which you wish to use voice input and the voice-recognition program and have both of them stay fully in RAM all the time. Windows will swap programs to disk if it runs short on RAM, but that always takes a whole lot more time than just accessing more RAM locations; any time performance is an issue, you want to add plenty of RAM.

Of course, a faster processor will let the voice-recognition program work more quickly—perhaps not better, but definitely quicker. And if your sound card is one that connects to the PCI bus, rather than to the ISA bus, that will very likely help speed the overall process.

In fact, if you have only the minimum recommended system speed and amount of RAM, you'll find that the recognition proceeds by fits and starts. (You'll be well advised not to watch the process on screen while you are dictating. That can slow things down terribly and confuse you as well. Just dictate at length, then check on the results.)

Next, the sound system must be adequate. What does this mean, really? The vendors of the voice-recognition programs all have Internet Web sites, and they post there some information on "approved" computers and sound subsystems. In general, most desktop machines can be made to work, though perhaps not with the sound cards that normally are shipped with them. Many laptop machines are just too electrically "noisy" inside to make adequate audio possible. Before you buy a laptop machine for the purpose of doing voice recognition, be sure that brand and model are on the voice-recognition program vendor's "approved" list.

Finally, we come to the issue of the microphone. This is, it turns out, the most difficult single hardware issue for most voice-recognition users to get right. The issue is twofold: Getting a microphone with enough sensitivity and fidelity (and one able to reject ambient sounds well enough) and keeping it positioned consistently near, but not too near to, your mouth. (Having a quiet room also helps, but that isn't an available option for some users.)

On the left side of Figure 19.1, you see the headset-mounted microphone that ships with Dragon's NaturallySpeaking Preferred product. This is very similar to what is supplied with ViaVoice or any of the other good voice-recognition programs today. And for many users, it turns out to be nearly an optimal solution. (There are better microphones available, for more money, but having them mounted on headsets is what many users seem to prefer.)

On the right in that same figure is the Philips SpeechMike. This is somewhat similar in form and feel to a standard dictating machine's microphone—plus it has a trackball and speaker built in. You can hold this mike near your face and dictate, and at the same time and with the same hand move the mouse and click on things, plus hear the output from your PC's sound system if you like. If you can hold the Philips microphone consistently, it turns out to be one of the best on the market—good enough that you may want to use it even if you simply ignore its trackball and speaker entirely.

FIGURE 19.1
Microphones and their consistent placement are crucial for good speech recognition. On the left is the headset-mounted microphone supplied by Dragon Systems with its Naturally-Speaking Preferred product. On the right is the Philips SpeechMike.

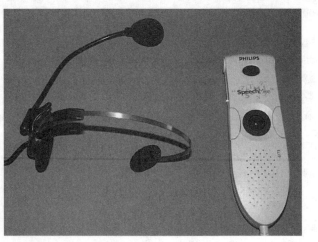

New Skills Are Also Required

Just having the right hardware and software is not enough. You also have to learn how to use it effectively. This implies both that you need to train yourself to do dictation in a consistent manner—and one that won't hurt your voice—and that you need to know when and how to correct the inevitable errors that will pop up even in the very best systems.

All the products take you through a training process. That is important. Also important is "feeding" the voice recognizer a lot of text that you have written or dictated in the past. But there is much more you can learn that will be of great help. Here are a few Web sites I recommend to help you get started:

http://voicerecognition.com/voice-users/

http://www.out-loud.com/

http://www.synapseadaptive.com/joel/default.htm

After perusing the material on these sites, you should have a much better idea of what voice recognition can accomplish today, and of whether you are willing to put up with the demands it places on you and your PC in order to get those benefits.

"Understanding" Oral Input

Both ViaVoice and NaturallySpeaking are intended primarily as tools to enable you to enter text without typing. They aren't really set up to accept lots of commands and have your PC act on them.

Microsoft's product, Voice Pilot, enables you to command your PC orally. It isn't intended for extended textual input. To make the program work satisfactorily, the user must create a structured file of acceptable responses at each stage of operation of the PC. Because of design limitations in that program, this file structure cannot be very complex. Still, it will work, and if you are unable to operate either the keyboard or mouse, being able to run your PC orally can be a godsend.

Generating Relevant Oral Output

As I mentioned earlier, the task of generating relevant outputs to be spoken by a text-to-speech program to create a conversational PC is either pretty simple (if you don't want many alternative spoken utterances) or far too complex for the state of the art (if you want a fully natural conversational capability). So there is no generally applicable answer to where we are in accomplishing this task, other than to say that substantially more work is needed.

What's Next?

Will your PC ever be capable of holding a conversation with you that is as smooth and natural sounding as the ones with the android "Data" on the TV show *Star Trek, The Next Generation*? Ever is a long time. That show is set in the twenty-fourth century, and by then, we might have that kind of capability. But for now, it doesn't look like it's going to be anytime soon.

It is already relatively easy to make PCs speak error messages, instead of beeping at you and putting a dialog box on the screen. It's easy, but do you want your PC to nag you? I predict that having a PC that can nag you will not be very popular. Of course, seeing-impaired people will find the spoken error messages a great advantage.

You should now have a good sense of what the problems are with oral PC input and output and know roughly where we are in solving those problems. Next, I explain other ways that sound and video are being used to enrich the computing experience and to integrate the personal computer with the rest of a person's consumer electronic devices.

PART V

Splendiferous Multimedia PCs

How to "Wow" a Human

Initially, the "killer application" for PCs was Lotus 1-2-3. After we had that program, its popularity made it quite obvious that PCs were here to stay. This one program made a PC so useful to so many people in business that nothing more was needed to ensure the success of PCs in a business setting.

For most of the next five years, almost all PC users used their PCs exclusively to manipulate numbers and words. This meant that displays that could do more than show numbers and words as simple, monospaced text were in effect excessive. Likewise, the capability of making sounds other than a beep was just not a priority for most PC users.

Now, however, PCs with extensive multimedia support are the norm. Competition in these markets is fierce, with top-of-the-line products losing their standing to new products in mere months. Prepackaged PCs today are such that you may actually pay *more* if you try to get *less* in the way of multimedia capabilities. The manufacturers of PCs are thereby suggesting that the "killer" reasons for buying PCs are a growing desire to use the Internet and also to take advantage of the coming convergence between computers and more traditional media, such as television. In fact, new technologies such as Voice Over Internet Protocol (VOIP), will create supersets of existing technologies by enabling you to combine video, audio, and computers into the new age of teleconferencing. Sometime in the future, you'll use a PC, or a computer-like device, to place telephone calls over the Internet.

What Was a Multimedia PC?

In general, PCs handle information. We put information in and get that information out. PCs are therefore acting also as communication devices—they convey information. That's what the first PCs did, and that's what they do today. But in the years since the late 1970s, we've added so many different means by which PCs can convey that information, if it wasn't for the ugly pewter cases, today's PCs would hardly resemble their ancestors. Words and numbers just don't cut it anymore.

Today, we demand that our PCs enable us to work with still images from digital cameras and scanners, full-motion MPEG, DVD, MOV, AVI digital and analog video, and CD-quality digital sound and music. In addition, the sources of this multimedia data are no longer confined to the local hard drive or local area network (LAN). Streaming multi-media technologies such as those provided by RealAudio RM, RAM, and RA files enable users to download multimedia as part of Web sites on the Internet. In other words, you can't do much with a computer today without running into some type of multimedia.

These different *methods* of communication also can be viewed as different *mediums* of communication. What was called a multimedia PC was simply one that could use more than one of these media. Because nearly every PC built today—even a little $500 budget box— has this capability, the term *multimedia PC* has largely become meaningless. Actually, it's been meaningless for quite a while. Some would argue it always was.

The term *multimedia PC* was coined in 1990 by a consortium of product manufacturers called the Multimedia PC Marketing Council—the name was changed to the Multimedia PC Working Group (MPCWG) when they were later absorbed by the Software Publishers Association. Gone are the days when a 386-based PC was a pretty hot machine and CD-ROM drives were just beginning to show up in computer stores. Then, it was already beginning to be obvious that quite a few people were going to be doing some pretty fancy stuff with multimedia in the near future. The MPC Marketing Council felt that this media-rich future would never arrive if no one created a standard against which a PC's multimedia capabilities and performance could be judged. They set out to do just that.

The MPC Council wanted manufacturers to agree to build machines to this new standard, and wanted multimedia program authors to tailor their programs to use *just* those guaranteed features. In order for this to happen, the designers of the new standard had to make it something that could be built and sold at not too high a cost. That meant that they couldn't specify a dream machine; they could only specify a pretty good PC config-uration that could be built affordably using available parts and that would be at least minimally capable of presenting multimedia materials.

MPC1 Through MPC3

Unfortunately, *council* is often just another word for *committee*. By the time the first multimedia PC standard came into existence, it was all but antiquated. Called MPC1, the standard required that a PC must have, at a minimum, a small variety of characteristics—386SX processor or better, 2MB of RAM, VGA display, 30MB hard drive, and so on. It's hard to believe now that this was the state of multimedia PCs only nine years ago!

In May 1993, trying to catch up with technology that had already left them behind, the Multimedia PC Marketing Council came out with a new version of the MPC definition. This one—known as MPC2—had an updated set of specifications. MPC2 also required that not only did a multimedia PC have to have the mandated hardware installed, but that hardware had to meet certain minimum performance standards. These new MPC2 machines required at least a 25MHz or faster, 486SX or better CPU, 4MB of RAM (8MB was recommended), a 160MB hard drive, double-speed CD-ROM, and so on.

In 1995, MPC3 was announced. The technology was moving so fast that parts of this standard were considered to be outdated less than one year later. MPC3 differed from the previous two standards in that it was called a "minimum system functionality, but not a recommendation for any particular system configuration." Moreover, the MPCWG explicitly said that MPC3 did not replace either MPC1 or MPC2. It merely updated and supplemented the list of desirable components for a multimedia PC.

Among many other changes, MPC3—definitely the most long-winded of the three standards—specified at least a 75MHz Pentium class processor with hardware-assisted MPEG1 capability. It increased the minimum acceptable RAM to 8MB and the available hard disk space to 500MB. The MPC3 standard went into great detail to specify how fast the hard disk must be and how little of the CPU's time must be needed to transfer data to and from the hard disk. Likewise, it detailed an upgraded CD-ROM drive, minimum caching for CD-ROM data, and video and audio subsystem specifications.

Certain of MPC3's requirements are so stringent that more than half of the multimedia PC manufacturers have simply ignored them; others were antiquated before the ink was dry. The mandatory system specs of nearly all cutting-edge games have left key aspects of MPC3 in the dust. Most multimedia PC games today have requirements that far exceed what the MPC3 standard defines. Even some business software requires performance and features above and beyond MPC3. Unsurprisingly, shortly after MPC3 was defined, the SPA announced that it was getting out of the multimedia PC specification business. Some of the specs are too weak for most software, and others are so difficult to attain that it's unlikely that any software will actually use all of the capabilities the hardware provides.

Multimedia Today and Tomorrow

Even though the formal specification of what constitutes a multimedia PC is no longer relevant, the technologies that go into supporting multimedia functionality on your computer certainly are. These are the technologies that we rely on increasingly. The capability to actually embed and display pictures into a word processor, ushered in by the Macintosh in 1984, was revolutionary at its time, and that revolution started an evolution that will never end. So, understanding multimedia technologies is no longer appropriate just for cutting-edge, high-end users—nearly everyone will use this technology soon. If you really want to understand your PC, you need to understand how it produces and manages the visual and auditory elements that define our PC experiences.

Screen Output Versus Printer Output

An important point to remember is that most applications featuring multimedia elements (or for which those elements are the whole point) are concerned with presenting information on the PC's video screen (or on some attached video display device, such as a large-screen projection TV). You'll appreciate this fact more if you reflect on what is special about the screen output as opposed to, for example, output to a printer.

> **Note:** Not all video output devices are created equal, so it's important to choose the kind of monitor that best suits your needs. Most desktop computers still use the cathode ray tube (CRT) form of monitor, but some now use the same flat screen liquid crystal display (LCD) technology used by laptop machines. The desktop form of the LCD is bigger because vendors don't have to worry about the size constraints of a laptop form factor. However, the desktop LCD has the same advantages and disadvantages that its laptop counterpart does. Some users think the advantages of LCD displays outweigh the disadvantages. For one thing, you don't have to worry about very low frequency (VLF) and extremely low frequency (ELF) emissions from an LCD, and you'll find that they're less heavy. LCDs also produce a minimum of heat, which is a real advantage in small offices. However, many users find that LCDs also suffer from a relatively poor viewing angle and that the colors aren't nearly as bright. The biggest limiting factor for LCDs right now may be their high price. Expect to pay nearly twice as much for an LCD disply with the same capabilities as a CRT-based monitor.

Images on paper and those onscreen differ in many ways. Originally, of course, printed output was limited to black and white text. For several years, however, full-color, graphics-capable inkjet printers have dominated the printer markets both for business and home users. (There is a plethora of other printers that use technologies such as wax transfer, but these are mainly at the high end of the market.) What you see on paper can now closely resemble what you see onscreen.

Images on the printed page are nevertheless different from onscreen images in a number of ways. By nature, they are static, whereas the screen images can be animated or can even be full-motion video. Additionally, all PC printers can create far more detailed images than any PC video display.

The best video displays offer no more than about 100 pixels per inch. More commonly, a PC's screen display is 72 pixels per inch. Monitor sizes are often larger than the pages that PC printers can accommodate.

Printer resolutions range from a low of 200 dots per inch (dpi) to 4800 dpi. (Most laser printers now offer 600 dpi or 1200 dpi resolution; inkjet printers provide 720 dpi or 1440 dpi resolution.) In contrast, most video displays can show many more individual colors simultaneously than even the best color printers can. However, a printer's much higher dot resolution—despite its generally smaller page size—which means that you can still have much more detail on printed images than you have onscreen. For a brief summary of these ideas, examine the following table.

Paper (Printers)	Video (Monitors)
Dots Per Inch, Commonly	200–4800 dots per inch; 1200 is common 40–100 dots per inch; 72 is common.
Physical Dimensions	8 1/2-by-11-inch (about 13 3/4-inch diagonally) is most common. 6-inch diagonal (the usable area of most 17-inch monitors) is most common.
Dots Per Page or Screen	At 1200dpi, with full bleed (edge to edge printing): 134,640,000. At fixed 800×600 pixel resolution: 480,000.
Simultaneous Colors	Over 64,000, commonly. Over four thousand-million (4,000,000,000).

This difference means that applications that send their output to printers are likely to emphasize the creation of detailed static images (which may or may not be in color). On the other hand, applications that are mainly intended for use onscreen (as is the case for most multimedia applications) are likely to be fine-tuned for the display of animated or video images. These images contain modest resolution, almost certainly using color to carry an important part of their message. Moreover, these video images change rapidly, moving as fast as 15 to 30 frames per second.

Vector Versus Bitmapped Images—Rasterizing and Rendering

Images can be generated and stored inside a PC in two radically different ways: One is called vector art—lines, circles, and curves—and the other is referred to as bitmapped or raster images—pixel images. A piece of *vector art* is a file that contains mathematical descriptions (often called a *display list*) specifying how to generate the image but not the actual image itself. These descriptions break an image down into its component lines, rectangles, and curves.

A vector graphics file must be rasterized (reconstructed out of those components) before it can be presented as an actual image, either onscreen or on paper. Vector images are created with mathematical formulas. For example, to represent a circle, a vector image file would include the circle's center point within the graphic and its radius. Your computer would use these two inputs to draw a raster version of the circle on the display adapter's screen.

One of the biggest advantages of vector graphics is that they can be enlarged or reduced without any loss of quality or definition, so they're resolution-independent. Because the graphic image is defined as a mathematical formula, all the computer needs to do is modify the input parameters as needed to create the appropriate size change when the image is rendered. Vector image files are also normally smaller than raster files in size. This is because only the data that's needed to reproduce the image is stored, not the image itself.

A *bitmapped* image, in contrast, contains the actual pixel image data. Each dot on your display is represented by a specific amount of data in the file. The actual amount of space that each pixel requires depends on the number of colors per pixel used in the image. For example, a 256-color image requires 8 bits per pixel (2^8 color combinations). Your PC's video display adapter simply pumps those pixels to the screen display or printer to have them show up as a visible image.

Some bitmapped images are stored in a compressed form, which means that much or all of the redundancy in that image has been removed by any of several means. For example, the TIF file format enables you to compress the image using one of several compression methodologies. The compression method you choose is important because some methods provide superior results—they produce a very small file that is easily transferred over the Internet.

Unfortunately, some of the most aggressive compression methods also lose a small amount of the graphics data. These are known as *lossy compression methods,* and you should use them only where space is the prime consideration and some loss of detail is acceptable. (We'll talk more about data compression later in the chapter.) Naturally, your PC must reverse any compression process to recover the original pixel data before the image can be presented on the screen.

A bitmapped or raster file contains individual pixels, similar to a real photo. It can be generated by an artist using a paint program or scanned in from a printed original. Raster bitmapped art is resolution-dependent. The resolution of the art determines the size of the file and the sharpness of the reproduction. This type of digital art cannot be enlarged or reduced at will without some deterioration of its quality. (Diagonal lines become jagged if you enlarge the image and detail is lost if you reduce its size.)

Technical Note: A *raster* is a name given to the way in which PCs (and television sets) create images. The display device sweeps across each line of the image, working its way down the screen from line to line. Eventually, all the picture elements (pixels) on each line are drawn, which completes the raster. (The word *raster* comes from the Latin word for *fork*. Think of a fork being dragged from side to side in a region of dirt. It will leave lines in the ground similar to the raster image lines on a video display.) The *rasterizing engine* is a software program or a piece of hardware that takes in the vector art descriptions and produces all the pixels needed to paint the raster.

There is one other major consideration when you're choosing between vector and bitmapped graphics: display speed. The rasterization process for vector art requires relatively more computer power. A graphics coprocessor or an accelerated video card can do much of the work, but some of it must be done by the PC's CPU. This means there are fewer CPU cycles available for other tasks, which may slow some applications, such as an animated presentation, to a crawl and ruin the effect that you're trying to create.

Bitmapped files have an advantage because they're ready to show. All the computer needs to do is send the pixel data to the video screen, and the image quickly appears. As a result, bitmapped images are often faster to display as animated sequences.

It would be easy to choose between bitmapped and vector graphics at this point if it weren't for another problem. Generally, bitmapped images provide a good appearance only at the resolution at which they were prepared. This means that your 800×600 pixel animation may lose some crispness and detail when displayed at 640×480 pixels and look stretched at 1024×768 pixels. (Some image display programs can scale these images, but unless they are specifically directed to do so, bitmapped images will be displayed as received—pixel-for-pixel.)

3D Vector Images

Another kind of vector image is one that specifies objects in full three-dimensional (3D) form. For example, if the drawing you created consisted of a sphere, the vector image file would describe the sphere using a center point and a radius, just as you would with the circle. In this case, however, you'd need to specify an X, Y, and Z axis location for a center point. In addition, you would need three radius measurements for height, width, and depth. (Theoretically, you could get by with a single radius measurement for a sphere, but supplying all three radius measurements enables you to create elliptical shapes as well.)

3D vector images are representational art, just like any other image that we've discussed. The image file contains a 3D description of how to draw an object, but not the object itself. However, 3D image files often go beyond the descriptions found in 2D files to create realistic-looking objects onscreen.

Drawing a 3D image requires a substantially more complex process called *3D rendering*. Besides size and positional information, a 3D image file often includes information about object surface textures, the positions of all of the light sources in the scene, and the point of view from which it is being viewed. The 3D scene-rendering engine then uses all those facts about the objects to construct an image that corresponds to what you would see if you were looking from the specified point of view at the prescribed objects.

There are other considerations with 3D images as well. For one thing, even though an object is fully rendered, the viewer may not be able to see it in its entirety. The object may be partially obscured by other objects in the scene. With both rasterizing and rendering, the work proceeds from the background toward the viewer. This enables the drawing program to create a realistic image that takes the viewer's perspective into account.

In rasterizing, perspective is handled by drawing objects in place and then allowing "nearer" objects to replace those pixels with their own, thus overwriting the hidden portions of farther-away objects. Rasterizing has the advantage of allowing a programmer to create a 3D effect with relatively simple programming methods. The main problem with rasterizing is that the program will waste time drawing pixels that it doesn't need.

In 3D rendering, an attempt is made to decide before actually rendering an object whether it will be obscured or outside the field of view. It is worth spending only the effort of rendering objects that are at least partially visible. The advantages and disadvantages of this method are the direct opposite of rasterizing—3D rendering is harder for the programmer to create, but more efficient in operation.

How PCs Create Compelling Visual Images

To understand the technical tricks used to make the most compelling PC images in some detail, you must know how PCs present images on their screens, and you must understand some things about how people see. I discussed a few of those issues at length in Chapter 13, "Seeing the Results: PC Displays." Here, I am going to discuss other issues of how people see images—issues that are so fundamental that most people have never even thought about them.

You probably think that when you look at something you see it, but you don't. *No one ever sees any objects.* We see, at the literal level (by which I mean our retinas receive), a constantly changing pattern of colored light. Hidden in this pattern are clues from which we can learn about the world "out there." Those clues are almost always ambiguous. We cannot infer with certainty what is really out there just from those clues, but we can and do make reasonable guesses. Indeed, we *must* do that, for without a clear notion of what probably is out there, we wouldn't be able to function.

So if a PC's video display shows us a pattern of colored light that resembles some arrangement of objects, we are likely to interpret that scene as if it actually contained those objects. The more accurately the PC display simulates natural light patterns, the more realistic we say it is: the more we believe what we see. In terms of multimedia, this mostly means that we need enough total pixels, enough possible colors per pixel, and the capability of changing those pixel colors quickly enough for moving images.

If you see something and soon thereafter see a modified version of that same thing, you are likely to interpret what you have seen as movement or change in a single object. You needn't see every stage of the movement or change—just seeing several successive stages in the process is sufficient. This fact, known as the *persistence of vision*, is what makes it possible for motion pictures to work.

Decades before the invention of the first motion picture film, inventors of devices such as the Phenakistiscope and Zoetrope discovered that still images, displayed under the right conditions in rapid succession, could produce the illusion of motion in the viewer's mind. (Most of us have seen these, and similar, early devices in children's museums. Phenakistiscopes, for example, are those slotted disks that spin in front of a mirror. You look through the slots to see apparent movement created from still drawings on the backside of the disk.)

Early developers of movies experimented with display rates until they found a minimum number of images per second that would enable most people to see a continuous motion instead of a succession of snapshots. For the first few decades of motion picture history, moviemakers displayed images at approximately 16 frames per second (fps). Standard film in modern movies runs at 24 fps. In the United States, analog television runs video image sequences at 30 fps (most of the rest of the world uses 25 fps). The 30 fps number for video and the 24 fps number for film are a little deceptive. The reason is that film and video, due to the way they capture images, introduce natural motion blurring into each frame. The motion blur, as it progresses from frame to frame, adds something to the viewers' illusion of motion.

All of these schemes work for the viewer and seem natural, but higher frame rates produce smoother illusions of motion and less flicker—thus, brighter, more convincing images.

Why is all this important? Because it suggests how to fool the brain into thinking it is seeing things that aren't actually there. An early digital artist, John Whitney, once said, "He who controls the pixels controls the image." He simply meant that if you could digitally compute and control each pixel in every frame of a moving picture, you could control the viewers' illusions about what they were seeing. At the time he said this, back in the early 1980s, computers weren't powerful enough to do that for more than very rudimentary types of images. Now they are powerful enough, and we see evidence daily of just how much image manipulation is thereby made possible. (It used to be said, "Seeing is believing." That is simply no longer true—or at least you are well advised not to take that point of view uncritically—as you are probably well aware.)

The patterns of light that fall on each of your retinas are 2D patterns, but the world we invent in our minds to explain those stimuli is in 3D, just as is the physical world by which those patterns were generated. How do we get the extra dimensionality? We can do this in many ways. The most obvious one is by using our two eyes. The patterns that fall on our two retinas differ slightly in ways that hint at the 3D quality of the world at which we are looking. But we don't really need those clues to see the world in 3D. Just cover one eye and look around. Do you have any trouble picking out which objects are nearer and which are farther away? Probably not.

We infer depth from a single eye's view by using what are called *monocular depth cues*. These cues include such things as which objects block the view of portions of other objects. The blocking objects are clearly in front of those they block from our view. Another clue is the relative size of objects. The farther away an object is, the smaller it will appear to be.

You might wonder why this matters. After all, you don't normally cover one eye when you look at your PC. Ah, but both your eyes see the same image on the surface of the PC's video display. Yet, with appropriate use of monocular depth cues in that image, you can become convinced that you are looking through the screen at some 3D scene.

It turns out that these monocular depth cues are more important than the stereoscopic (two-eye) ones. This is why a flat photograph of a scene can still give the illusion that you are looking at a 3D scene. Of course, adding stereoscopic information helps add to the sense of reality. That is why almost all virtual reality systems include a means of creating two independent images and sending each to just one of the viewer's eyes, as I will explain in more detail in Chapter 21, "Immersive PC Experiences." Still, we can create some pretty compelling visual experiences—which is what we're often seeking to do—using only a single video display monitor that's presenting the same image to both eyes.

Making Images with Visual Pizzazz

The simplest images are static ones, and if those images are sufficiently bold and detailed, they can be quite compelling. Adding even a small amount of apparent movement to an image, however, can add a great deal of excitement. For this reason, animation has become commonplace, especially in multimedia applications.

An image on a PC's display screen can involve a lot of information. At a minimum, it will have the standard VGA resolution image (640 pixels per line and 480 lines per image), with each pixel having 1 of 16 possible colors. Such an image has 307,200 pixels, and for each one, half a byte of information is needed to specify its color. This means that if you want to replace one image with another, you must move over 150,000 bytes of information into the video frame buffer.

Many modern PCs have SVGA displays with higher resolutions and higher color depth. To specify this type of image, you must have 3 bytes, or 24 bits, of color information for each of 786,432 pixels (assuming TrueColor images that have sets of 1024×768-resolution pixels that are made up of red, green, and blue triplets). That is 2 1/4MB of data just to specify one static image.

Images with this many simultaneous colors are called *photorealistic,* because they can reproduce almost anything that you can capture on a photograph. Resolution is not nearly as important to the illusion of photorealism as is the number of different colors. Notice that the resolution of normal TV images is relatively modest. At best, a TV can display about 550 pixels per line, and most TV sets don't really resolve more than about 300 to 400 lines in each image. If you want to animate a scene with images this complex—and in particular, if you try doing it by creating a new image for each sixtieth of a second— the video subsystem of your PC has a tough job cut out for it. Also, the CPU and main bus may be taxed to the extreme, shoveling new data to the video display system quickly enough to update the image so often.

There are several ways to cut this task down to size. One way is to use less-detailed images (ones with either fewer pixels or fewer colors per pixel). That works, but it often means settling for a less-compelling visual experience. Another way is to change the image less often or to change only part of the image at a time. One trick, called *palette animation,* sometimes can be used to cut the work down to less than 2/1000 of the original amount. Next, I'll describe next some of these ways that animated or video images can be generated more economically.

For the price of a bit more RAM in the video image frame buffer and a little bit of added switching hardware, you can make the creation of animated imagery a lot simpler. To prevent flicker, the video card normally redraws the entire screen image at least 60 times per second. You must change that image only about 10 times per second to simulate convincing, if jerky, motion. At 30 image changes per second, the effect is as smooth as normal television.

Suppose you have enough frame buffer RAM to hold two complete images. First, draw a complete screen image in one region, and then, while the video output circuitry is scanning through that region 60 times each second to display that image on the screen, the CPU can be using the other region of the frame buffer RAM to create the next image. When that next image is ready, the CPU directs the video output circuitry to switch its focus to that new region, and the new image will appear onscreen within 1/60 of a second. Meanwhile, the CPU can go back to work in the original region of the frame buffer to generate the next image.

If the images are so complex that the CPU must spend a second or more on each one, you will get the effect of a slide show. If it can create wholly new images in less than about 1/15 of a second, the result appears to be a movie. Giving the CPU a whole fifteenth of a second to create an image, however, means cutting the required rate of data pumping from the CPU to the video frame buffer by four over that which would be required to keep up with the full 60-frame-per-second rate used by the video output circuits. Thus, a mere 34MB per second will suffice, even for a 1024×768 photorealistic (24-bit per pixel) movie.

Using a Palette Can Greatly Reduce the Image Data You Need

For many purposes, you don't need photorealistic images. That is, you often can get away with far fewer colors. This certainly is true for graphs and other business graphics, where 16 well-chosen colors can be plenty. Even photographs can look quite good with as few as 256 colors—if they are the right 256 colors for that particular photograph. The most important trick to making really good images with not many colors is to choose the best few colors to use.

The original VGA standard for video cards displayed images of up to 640×480 pixels, with up to 16 different colors simultaneously onscreen. It further specified a color palette that could be any of 16 you wanted, chosen from a much larger set of possible colors. That set of all possible colors for any VGA image includes 262,144 possibilities—more than enough for most normal uses, although it's not quite good enough for full photorealism. (I describe this palette mechanism in detail in Chapter 13.)

VGA displays had only this resolution and color depth for a simple reason. Making a video display with more resolution or more color depth requires more video RAM than could be included in an affordable display at the time that VGA (video graphics array) was first introduced.

The next step was video displays (of VGA-or-higher resolution) that could display 256 simultaneous colors out of some larger palette of possible colors. These displays were amenable to all the same palette animation tricks as the original VGA displays.

Now, with 256 simultaneous colors, it has become quite practical to create dynamic images with very little data having to be transferred from the CPU to the video card as these images cycle through a small number of different forms. First, you must design the image in all its various forms. Figure out a way to color those forms so that each one uses a unique group of colors from the allowable set of simultaneous colors, plus a background color. Then load the palette with a set of numbers that make all but one image appear in only the background color. Thereafter, you need only switch the palette table information to hide the present image and reveal another one, and this process can continue as you cycle through all the images hidden in the original image. This practice is why some programs insist on running in a 256-color video mode, and just won't run at all at any higher or lower color depth.

Of course, RAM prices soon fell. SVGA video display systems became common. We can now create and display much more complex images. Doing so, however, means that we also must manipulate, store, and move much more information for each image.

When Images Must Change More Rapidly Than Your PC Can Draw Them

The output from some multimedia programs includes actual video. That is, these programs attempt to show portions of what amounts to a television program. This potentially involves a huge amount of data being pumped into the video card. When this job is fully and properly done, we call it *full-screen, full-motion video*. That is the goal for much of our multimedia. Until recently, it was often *just* a goal, but nothing stays the same for long.

There are at least three ways in which you can deal with the problem of having massive amounts of data—sometimes, too much data—to display on your PC in a timely manner. First, you can choose to display the video image in a window that is smaller than the entire screen. Originally, a window that was 160×120 pixels was used. A window of 320×240 pixels was also common. The former has only 1/16 as many pixels as a standard VGA screen. The latter has 1/4 as many pixels as a full VGA screen. Naturally, this means you can get away with pumping in 1/16 or 1/4 as many bytes of video information as you would have needed if you were trying to create full-screen, full-motion video.

The second commonly used way to deal with a too-large inflow of video data is simply to drop out some of the frames. If you use only every other frame, you cut in half the number of bytes you must transmit to the video card. (Remember, the video output circuitry is copying the full contents of the frame buffer to the screen 60 or more times each second. That keeps on happening no matter what, so you don't get flickering images if you drop frames. You just get a more choppy or jerky-looking video.)

The third way to deal with this problem is to compress the data. If you "squeeze" out some of the redundancy in the image data, you might be able to reduce the required flow of (compressed) data down in size to something your PC can handle. Of course, before the images can appear onscreen, they must be decompressed. That can be done in software or in specialized hardware that can be added to the video card's circuitry.

Static images are often compressed to reduce their file sizes. Compression saves some disk space and shortens the time it takes to transfer those files over a communications link. The most common ways to compress static image files are by using the GIF, PCX, or JPEG algorithms. GIF stands for Graphics Image Format. JPEG stands for the Joint Photographic Experts Group, which is the standards body that controls this standard.

GIFs and PCX files have been compressed in a *lossless* fashion, meaning that only truly redundant bits are squeezed out, and they all can be returned exactly as they were when the file is decompressed. None of the original image's data is deleted in the compression process.

JPEG, on the other hand, is a way to compress a file that is inherently *lossy*—some data from the original image that is deemed to be redundant is thrown away in the compression process. (As you would expect, lossy compression usually yields smaller compressed files than does lossless compression.) This means that the image resulting from the decompressed file will differ from the original to some degree. The tricky part of these algorithms is in discarding only "unimportant" features of the images. That is, they are designed to make the kinds of "mistakes" when reconstructing images that people are least likely to notice, and they do a pretty good job of that.

All lossy compression techniques have an adjustable setting that controls how much compression they will perform, which implies how much original information is lost. You can set this parameter to a value that makes the damage to your images minimal, or you might need to set it higher to achieve adequate reduction in file size and to achieve your required data flow rates.

If you want to compress a movie (consisting of a succession of digital still images), you can simply apply JPEG compression to a frame and then compress the differences between each frame in turn. This process is sometimes called *motion-JPEG* compression. However, this type of compression is often not sufficient to achieve full-screen, full-motion video. Fortunately, a generally acceptable alternative was found several years ago. A standard describing it was published by the Motion Picture Experts Group (MPEG), who lent the method its name.

The secret to this solution lies in a key fact about video. Most of the time, each video frame is very much like the frame that preceded it. So, if you can somehow record only the changes from one frame to the next, you can lower the required data rate significantly. This process, which is what MPEG compression does, is commonly referred to as *interframe compression.*

There are several MPEG standards: MPEG1, MPEG2, and most recently, MPEG4. (MPEG3 was largely abandoned shortly after work on it began because MPEG2 was found to be sufficient for the HDTV standards that MPEG3 was being developed to support. Nevertheless, the MPEG3 technology is in use.) Each higher-numbered standard is more aggressive and more capable of yielding higher-quality images and accompanying audio with a smaller data flow, and also requires more computing power to do the compression and decompression. (Incidentally, there are other methods by which video images are compressed: Two common ones are Intel's Indeo process and CTi's Cinepak process. Support for the decompression of these two is native to Windows 98, although acceptable results still rely on sufficient processor power.)

MPEG1, which was the first widely supported standard in PC software, starts by degrading the original video image to something equivalent to a 352×288 pixel frame. The audio signal is retained at its original, CD-quality level. The next step in MPEG1 encoding is to convert the video signal from the original RGB (red-green-blue) signals captured by the camera into a color space called YUV.

The MPEG1 standard drops about half of the color information's resolution, which is okay because our eyes are quite tolerant in this regard. It then compresses the signals in a complex manner.

MPEG1 encoding splits up the frames into two or three categories. Some frames, called I frames, are simply sent as-is (or with a compression that is comparable to JPEG for static images). Other frames, called P frames, are sent as the difference between a frame and from the frame just before it. When the third type, called B frames, is used, it becomes the bulk of the frames. These B frames are sent as a difference signal, relating them to both the frame before and the frame after. To reconstruct the original video, it was necessary to place all the frames following the last I frame in memory. For B frames, you must also have the next frame. (This is true whether that next frame is a B, a P, or an I frame.)

By sending I frames every so often, you are protected against losing track of the whole picture. Even if you lose some intermediate frames, when another I frame comes along, you can get back on track. Any loss between I frames, however, will probably mess up the picture until the next I frame was received. Because I frames come more often than one per second, and because most of the time no frames are lost, this degradation is usually quite acceptable. The B frames in particular (and also the P frames to a lesser extent) are greatly compressed compared to the I frames, so the overall effect is a reduction of the digital data rate to an acceptable value.

The MPEG algorithms are very unbalanced and asymmetrical. Doing the compression takes a lot more computing than doing the decompression. By design, this was built in at the outset to make it as easy as possible to build affordable hardware or software MPEG decompressing engines—even at the cost of making the compression job hugely more difficult and expensive. A movie must be compressed only once, but it will end up being decompressed by each viewer's PC (or digital television) every time it is shown. Clearly, it makes sense to unbalance the workload in the way the MPEG designers have chosen.

Most of the latest video cards and some add-on boards for use with DVD drives can perform MPEG2 decompression in hardware. Or, if you have a sufficiently fast Pentium computer, you can get a software MPEG2 decompression program. As hardware speeds and capabilities continue to rise, there's no doubt that in a few years we will have affordable hardware MPEG compression engines available for desktop PCs that can work in real-time. But for now, the compression job is done offline on larger, more powerful computers. Nevertheless, compressing a movie takes far longer than the time the movie will run when it is displayed, in part because to get acceptable results, considerable human intervention and tweaking of the process is necessary.

Animation for Everyone

There are a lot of ways to create animated sequences, but most of them are out of reach of the average user. The equipment required to create them is normally so expensive that the average user can't afford it. Even if you could afford the required equipment, many of these techniques are complicated to implement and require a full-time artist's services.

When the Internet first became the place to go, people wanted to dress up their drab, text-only Web pages with something a little more exciting. Using static graphics allowed them a certain amount of flexibility, but as time passed, static graphics no longer provided the pizzazz that major Web sites required. Webmasters had to come up with some way of creating animated graphics that were not only nice to look at, but easy to download as well.

A favorite way of adding animation to Web sites used by Webmasters the world over is animated GIFs. All that an animated GIF does is pack several pictures into one file. The browser plays these pictures back one at a time, creating the illusion of continuous animation. You can also use special effects to create a slide show using a GIF. The only problem with this approach is the download time—a slide show tends to put quite a strain on the user's download capability.

> **Tip:** One of the least expensive ways to try out animation on your own is to get one of the shareware animated GIF creation utilities that's available on the Internet. One of the better shareware offerings is the GIF Construction Set from Alchemy Mind Works. You can download it from several places. The best place is straight from the vendor at
> `http://www.mindworkshop.com/alchemy/gifcon.html`.

Animated GIF files are easy to understand because they consist of elements that everyone can relate to. The following list describes the common elements that you'll work with.

- Graphics Files—Used to create the animation. An animator would refer to these individual graphics as animation cels.

- Header—Tells the browser what kind of animated GIF is being presented so that the browser can determine whether it can display the animated GIF at all. The header also contains the size of each cel in the animation and the number of colors used for each cel. It also contains a palette of colors that the browser can load to display the cels accurately.

- Control Entries—Determines how much of a delay to place between one cel and the next. One of the nice features about animated GIFs is that you can create special effects by controlling the delay between each cel. The control element also enables you to determine the starting point for the next graphic. This means that you can change just a small part of the display, if needed, to reduce the overall file size. Finally, the control element enables you to specify how to clear the display (if you want it cleared at all) and what special effects to add.

- Plain Text—Allows the animator to add text to slide show–type animated GIF files. This element isn't used when you want to create an animation.

- Comments—Provides information about the animated GIF and the way it's constructed. The browser doesn't use comments in any way; they're only there for the animator's use.

One of the more interesting special effects that you can add to the GIF file as a whole is interlaced display. Interlaced images are displayed one line at a time. It's the effect you see on most Web sites when you're downloading large graphics. Using an interlaced graphic gives users some visual feedback during the download process—it lets them know that the machine hasn't frozen. In most cases, however, you won't want to use this option for animated GIFs, because it takes more time to display an interlaced image. In other words, your animation could end up looking jerky.

As you can see, animated GIFs are a powerful tool that everyone can use. Even though only Webbrowsers were originally designed to display animated GIFs, you'll find them in a lot of places today. In most cases, they're used for small, simple animations that add a bit of sparkle to the display without detracting from it.

Making Socko PC Sounds

In the beginning, the PC could make only beeping sounds. Now it can sing, shout, growl, and play symphonies. Almost any sound you can imagine can be produced on a modern PC, in stere, or even in surround sound. This development is a lot more significant than many people realize. A common view is that images are much more important than sounds, but in certain ways this is very wrong. Sounds convey emotions far more powerfully. You can thrill or horrify someone with an image, but you'll induce deeper feelings of pleasure or send chills up the spine even more easily with the appropriate sounds. Moviemakers know this very well, which is why so much money has been spent on developing and installing the very latest in audio technology at movie theaters. (Watch *Star Wars* with the sound turned off; you'll see what I mean in about five seconds.) Now, PCs are catching up.

The sounds from early sound cards were a lot more interesting than the beeps and clicks that were characteristic of the earliest PCs, but even the low-end cards of the most recent generation are more impressive still. High-end cards, with their five-channel surround sound and powerful subwoofers, can make watching a movie on your PC actually seem acceptable (if not precisely desirable). Break out the popcorn and enjoy!

Before you stop reading and reach for the popcorn, I have a little bit more to explain. To appreciate fully the technological evolution of our modern (multimedia) PC, you must look at how sounds are reproduced and how people hear.

How People Hear

Sounds are variations in air pressure. We hear them mostly with our ears, but also to a degree with our whole bodies. Although we can sense only light with our eyes, we can sense air pressure variations (sounds) with our ears and also our skin—which is especially true for loud, low frequency sounds. Extremely low-frequency sounds can be felt even deeper, causing resonance in our highly porous bones.

Perhaps the most important difference between visual and audible information has to do with the dimensionality of the experience. We receive visual information on the retina of our eyes in an inherently 2D form, and from that our brains construct a perception of the 3D world around us. Auditory information, however, is inherently one-dimensional. The air pressure in the auditory canal inside each of your ears has only one value at any given instant.

By using both your ears and sometimes also the perceptions of sound waves hitting your body, you can tell whether a sound is coming from the left or the right. You even can tell, usually, if it comes from in front of you or behind you. However, you are much less capable of telling whether a sound comes from a source that is on your level, above you, or below you. In a sense, we use our two ears to expand the one-dimensional sounds we hear into a mostly 2D soundscape around us.

It's pretty easy to understand how some parts of our hearing work because of the work done in sonar and other sound-related technologies. For example, direction is usually derived from two primary sources of information in the brain: timing and loudness. The brain compares the time between when the sound arrives in one ear versus the other ear and derives a placement for that sound. It takes a split second longer for the left ear to receive a sound that originates to your right. Because the sound arrives in the right ear first, the brain knows that the sound originates on the right side. The time differential tells the brain just how far to the right the sound originated. In addition, the sound level in the right ear will be slightly higher than the left ear because the sound has to travel farther to reach the left ear. Again, it's not a significant difference, but it is enough to give the brain a cue as to the sound's direction.

The designers of sound reproduction systems have used this kind of knowledge of these and other more arcane facts about human hearing to create a wide range of specialized audio systems. The earliest PCs used some of the most primitive sound placement technologies, such as modifying the sound level in one speaker to reflect the differential between the left and right ears. Modern PCs use some of the most sophisticated sound placement technologies invented, including both sound timing (adding a time delay to either the right or left speaker) and tactile sensation using a subwoofer.

3D audio (such as DirectSound3D, Aureal A3D, and Creative Lab's EAX) is simply a way to assign 3D coordinates to a particular sound. In a perfect world, everyone would have six speakers connected to a Dolby/AC-3 compatible system, allowing true three-dimensional placement of any sound. (Of course, this assumes that someone could actually hear the difference between the five speakers used for Dolby Pro Logic and the six used for Dolby/AC-3.) However, because most people have only two speakers or headphones, 3D technologies today try to simulate these multiple speaker setups. Not surprisingly, there are many ways to perform this simulation. Also not surprisingly, not every technique works for every game or other type of application, or for every hardware configuration. (We'll talk about specific 3D sound technologies and how they work in the 3D Sound section of Chapter 21.)

Because 3D audio is synthesized in most cases, it's not hard to figure out that the environment used to play the sound makes a difference in the level of the 3D audio effect. In many cases, the sound card and application software will use different processes and output methods depending on what the listener's playback configuration is. For example, a sound card may use one algorithm for headphone playback and a very different algorithm for speaker playback.

The difference between headphone and speaker output isn't just the quality of the speakers (although that is a factor); it's the closeness of the speaker to the listener's ears that affects the 3D sound output most. A sound card has to take the sound source's location into account as part of its 3D sound calculations. For example, if you are wearing headphones but the sound card is set for speaker playback, you'll hear few or no 3D audio effects. Because of the differences in sound source location and quality, it becomes very important for games to support and query the user for their listening configuration. This option is usually set on a configuration screen. For example, DirectSound provides a method for telling the sound card which output device the player is using.

Evolving Speaker Technologies

Every loudspeaker works by moving air. It pushes on air to squeeze it (*compression*) and then pulls back to create a region of lowered pressure (*rarefaction*). These low- and high-pressure regions travel away from the loudspeaker at about 1,000 feet a second, in the form of a compressional wave in the air.

The first PCs used a cheap speaker, but that isn't really what made their sound capabilities so limited. The circuitry that drove this speaker could only produce a tone with a fairly harsh timbre and fixed volume. This quality of tone was sufficient to alert the user to an error condition, but was good for little else.

A small speaker can produce only significantly loud sounds in the upper portion of the audible range—that is, high-pitched sounds but not low ones. To make a low-pitched sound, you need a big speaker capable of moving a lot of air. That is why the best sound systems have a relatively big, heavy woofer or subwoofer. (Even the newest flat-panel speaker systems come with a traditional large subwoofer.) Because the lowest-frequency sounds can easily travel through solid objects and aren't very directional, one such speaker is enough. All the directional information in the sounds can come from two or more much smaller speakers. Starting with the MPC2 specification, PCs have had sound systems with stereo speakers for the higher tones, and if they include a subwoofer at all, they would have only one. The audio electronics in these PCs appropriately mix the low end of the audio spectrum from the left and right channels and send that mixed signal to their subwoofer.

Most surround sound systems today include five speakers for the upper-frequency ranges (one of which is usually placed directly in front of you and is dedicated to midrange frequencies, where most human speech occurs) and one subwoofer. The five speakers bring you sounds from the center (but probably above or below your line of sight), from the left and right in front of you, and from the left and right behind you. All of these channels route their lowest-frequency sounds to the one subwoofer, whose position you usually cannot discern just by listening to the sounds it creates.

Creating Beautiful Sounds

Almost any way you make the audio signals that are sent to the speakers will be better than the techniques the earliest PCs used. (Most factory whistles sound better than the earliest PCs.) A pure tone must have a smooth waveform, much like a gentle ripple on a pond. The height of the ripples determines the volume. The time between crests determines the pitch. Absolutely any sound can be made from an appropriate mixture of pure tones. So, if you make a sound system that is capable of reproducing all frequencies of pure tones—each one at any arbitrary loudness, and all of them at once, with no interaction between those tones—you have made a system that can reproduce any sounds you want.

After you have created (or bought) such a sound reproduction system, you need a way to drive it with digital signals. In a PC, this has most often been done with numbers stored in what are called wave files, which most often are given the file extension .WAV. These numbers simply represent instantaneous samples of the sound pressure at one or two microphones. (One microphone is used for monaural sounds and two for stereo—or, with suitable encoding, more than two microphones can be used with the signals being mixed down to two channels for storage and transmission.) These audio samples are taken at equal time intervals, and the exact interval used is set by the quality of the sound you want to record and play back. Also, these sounds can be sampled—digitized—with any of several different degrees of accuracy. This accuracy is typically specified in terms of the number of bits used. (There are several other popular audio formats today, the best-publicized of which is the MP3 format, but the principle of converting digital data back into analog sound is the same. MP3 has become a phenomenon in the online world, after being adopted as the format of choice for college students exchanging near-CD-quality music on the Internet. Several companies have offered hardware to make MP3 portable, and the music industry is even looking into supporting the format.)

If you sample at 22,000 times per second and use 16-bit numbers, you'll get a pretty decent representation of the original sounds. If you double that sampling rate and also use two microphones, you'll get a high-fidelity sound recording—CD quality, in fact— but at the cost of four times as many bytes of data storage. The fidelity increases because your digital sampling rate directly determines the maximum frequency that can be reliably reproduced.

In almost any sound, there are frequency *harmonics* (the mathematics of which is beyond our scope here) that contribute significantly to the *timbre* (a synthesizer term meaning a sound, or a musical term meaning the "color" of a tone) of the total sound. A lower sampling rate cuts out the high frequencies in which these harmonics occur. The result can be a very mechanical, thin, or tinny sound. Research shows that to reproduce a given frequency with an acceptable level of reliability, you must use a digital sampling rate that is no less than twice that frequency. Because the human ear can detect frequencies upward of 22KHz, the 44.1KHz sampling frequency of audio CDs just about covers our entire range of audible sound. (I say "just about" because digital sampling of analog sound is far more complicated than you really need to understand, and there are reasons why a sample rate of even 44.1KHz isn't always adequate.)

Sampling at 44,000 times per second and using 16-bit numbers is a fine way to capture sounds and play them back. In fact, it is probably the most commonly used method—it is how every audio CD is made—but it has drawbacks. One is that these WAV files can become quite large if you record a long audio segment.

One solution to this problem is to build in the capability of synthesizing music. This is usually done by analyzing which sounds each of a large number of instruments makes for each note that it can play. Then, using several pure-tone generators (called *oscillators*) in a specialized FM-synthesis microprocessor chip, it is possible to produce any musical note you can imagine. This is nearly the way it would sound if it had been played on those instruments. At least, that is the idea.

Using this strategy, all you need to store in a file for music to be generated is the list of instruments that will be playing the sounds and then the notes each one plays, indicating for each one how loud it is, what pitch, and how long it will last. That is most of what is stored in a standard Musical Instrument Device Interface (MIDI) file.

A close analog exists between this synthetic music approach and the vector art approach to storing an image. In both cases, the directions for creating the music or image are what gets stored, rather than the actual details of the sound or image. A MIDI sound file is to a WAV file as a vector art file is to a bit-mapped file.

Standards: The MIDI standard was first developed to help professional musicians create quality music using electronic instruments. It is a standard for conveying control messages between different electronic musical instruments. In a professional setup, a keyboard or MIDI guitar will generate MIDI signals that then are sent to a synthesizer where the actual sounds are created. (This is just one example of how such a system might function.)

The MIDI standard allows for several kinds of signals that a typical PC audio system cannot recognize or use. By taking advantage of a preexisting standard, however, every PC can perform as a (somewhat limited) MIDI musical device. You can use a PC to capture MIDI signals from a MIDI keyboard or to send MIDI signals out to a more capable MIDI synthesizer. Today, the best PC sound cards contain synthesizers on a par with better professional ones.

In order to further standardize the PC MIDI experience (and, to a lesser extent, the experience of owning a low-end professional synthesizer), an international consortium of MIDI instrument manufacturers established the General MIDI Standard in 1991. Among other things, this standard describes a fixed set of 128 instruments, a minimum number of simultaneous voices (24, including 8 dedicated to percussive instrumentation), and a minimum number of channels (16, with channel #10 dedicated to percussive instrumentation) over which different MIDI data can be simultaneously sent. Any piece of music that is composed on a General MIDI (GM) instrument can be played back on any other GM instrument and it will sound, for the most part, exactly the same. (The standard does not, to the frustration of many musicians, specify how each instrument sound is to be produced. So each manufacturer's instruments sound somewhat different.) When the GM standard was announced, Roland, Inc. immediately came out with its Sound Canvas device: a rack-mountable keyboardless synthesizer that met the GM specs and was marketed to the PC-using musician.

Shortly thereafter, the shortcomings of the GM standard emerged. Roland extended the capabilities of several of its GM instruments and created its own GS (General Superset) standard. GS instruments adhere perfectly to the GM standard, but music written specifically for a GS synthesizer can take advantage of the GS's additional capabilities. Yamaha has also created a proprietary extension of GM called XG.

In the case of all these standards—indeed, in any case of using a PC to drive thousands of dollars of external MIDI instruments—the PC is functioning as a *sequencer*. That is, it functions as a device that keeps track of the tempo of the music. The PC also ensures that the descriptive MIDI data is sent out to (or is recorded from) all of the requisite instruments in the proper order, at the proper rate.

Unfortunately, the quality of music produced by most sound card–embedded MIDI synths has been disappointing until recently. Mainly, the results disappoint listeners because the analysis of instruments used in creating these synthesizers has been inadequate. No instrument creates every note in the exact same way. The analysis used for early synthesis also ignored the very subtle ways in which the tones fade to silence differently, or in which the resonances of the instruments impact the tones they produce. The result was that early PC MIDI synthesis still produced a comparatively harsh, if tolerable, *representation* of the sounds of traditional instruments. However, no one would confuse it with the real thing.

Tables of Waves Are Even Better

The next step in the evolution of PC music-generating technology was referred to as *wave sound*. This means capturing a sample of an actual musical instrument playing a given note, and then saving all those samples for all the instruments you are interested in (and perhaps for many, if not all, of the notes each one can play). The notes are not broken down into individual pure tones, but instead are simply stored digitally in their messy entirety.

When presented with a MIDI file, a wave sound synthesizer will select appropriate combinations of these prerecorded instrumental sounds and play them back together to generate the desired music. The result can be substantially better than even the best of the earlier synthesizers.

And You Can Do Even Better Still

It's common now to have even better musical synthesizers in midrange PCs. The brand of synthesizer that has set most of the standards in this area is produced by Creative Labs, although there are many other significant players, such as Turtle Beach Systems, Roland, e-Mu, and Kurzweil. Because the Creative Labs SoundBlaster card was the first commercially successful PC sound card, it is the default sound system for many PC programs, particularly games. (Until recently, Creative Labs' products were not taken seriously for professional music purposes, but that is changing.)

New Windows 9x gaming and productivity applications are driving hardware requirements beyond the capabilities of Sound Blaster audio. As OEMs redesign their products to meet the new demands, the Sound Blaster standard is being gradually displaced or enhanced by more flexible programming interfaces with greater capabilities. However, even my Diamond Monster Sound II 300 MX soundboard still includes a Sound Blaster Pro Emulation drive for games and productivity applications that require it. The point is that while we're moving away from the old sound standards, vendors will still have to support them for the foreseeable future.

Creative Labs enhanced its Sound Blaster technology in several ways to incorporate the flexibility and capability requirements of newer applications. The first enhancement was its introduction of what it called its Advanced WaveEffect (AWE) Sound Blaster. This adds a wave sound synthesizer—another microprocessor, separate from the FM synthesizer. The AWE add-on carries the sound samples for all the known instruments in a ROM chip and then plays back mixtures of them as indicated by a MIDI file's contents. These AWE cards also have RAM into which a user can download additional wave samples in groups Creative Labs calls Sound Fonts.

> **Tip:** It may not be apparent at first how to use the Sound Font technology provided by the newer Creative cards. Fortunately, Creative also provides you with Sound Fonts that you can download and work with on your machine. These Sound Fonts add new listening capabilities that you might not have otherwise. You can find out more about the downloadable Sound Fonts at `http://www.sblive.com/liveware/goodies/soundfonts/emu/`. Some of the more interesting offerings at the time of this writing were a set of bells based on those found in Asia, engine startup effects, and even a plunger. Most of the more mundane Sound Font offerings add new instrument capabilities to your sound card.

Having the capability of storing and using user-defined samples enables you to make a MIDI machine that can play more different kinds of instruments. In fact, you can use many sounds—a person speaking or singing, a whole chorus singing, banging on a pipe, an explosion, a car crash, and so on—in place of an ordinary musical instrument.

The most recent Creative innovation is Environmental Audio eXtensions (EAX). This is Creative's vision of 3D sound, and it's based on Microsoft DirectSound3D API. Interestingly enough, this is one of the few cards on the market right now that can provide hardware acceleration for DirectSound3D, which makes games and multimedia applications run much faster. I discuss EAX and the other vendor 3D sound offerings from a user's perspective in the 3D Sound section of Chapter 21.

3D Sound Technology

As I said in the previous section, Creative Labs is far from being the only company working on advanced PC sound synthesis and sound reproduction technologies. A lot of other vendors are working on adding new 3D sound offerings (sometimes referred to as expanded stereo or surround sound) to an otherwise simple stereophonic sound system. In fact, 3D-enabled audio products are available from over 20 sound card and PC makers, including Dell, NEC, Diamond Multimedia, and Turtle Beach. Dolby is one of the leading names in this field, and its Dolby Digital surround sound–encoding strategy is now the industry standard (although it does require five speakers, not just three).

The whole purpose of these new 3D sound technologies is to give you a sound experience that more closely matches what you'll get in the real world. Of course, to really duplicate real-world sounds, you'd have to have the actual objects in the same positions and making the same sounds they would normally make. I doubt even then that you would get a real-world listening experience, because the acoustics in your office are unlikely to match the real world environment that your computer is modeling. As a result, the soundboard has to *model* the 3D sound and present it in such a way that it sounds like the real-world equivalent. A3D and DirectSound3D use head related transfer function (HRTF) algorithms to fool your ear into hearing positional audio from two speakers. These algorithms accept X, Y, and Z access data as input, and then position the object so the user hears it from the correct location.

Placing an object into the right hearing context is fine, but there are some technical limitations that have prevented PC systems from producing the very best sound until now. The first problem is getting good sound quality from less-than-perfect equipment. When you go to a movie theatre (or, if you're lucky enough to have a home theatre) some of the effects of poor acoustics, imperfect recording media, and substandard equipment are mitigated by using one of several sound enhancement technologies, such as Dolby Prologic, which was introduced in 1987. Dolby Prologic normally relies on five speakers: right, left, center, and two surrounds. It is one step up from the surround sound systems originally introduced in 1982. The center speaker helps create more intense 3D effects that can give the listener a better aural understanding of the sound environment. Unfortunately, few PC users have five speakers attached to their systems; it's more likely that they'll have two or, in some cases, four. Fortunately, Aureal also ships a chip that creates a virtual Dolby Prologic sound field from two speakers.

Note: Just to put things into perspective, the most current Dolby specific technology available for PCs is Dolby/AC-3. This system normally requires six speakers: left, right, center, two surrounds, and a subwoofer for low-frequency sounds. You actually get from a PC either two or four speakers' worth of Dolby Prologic (the center speaker is normally missing) and the subwoofer. The most current theatre technology is THX, which was created by George Lucas. THX is more of a certification process than an actual technology. The purpose of THX is to ensure that the equipment in a theatre is the highest quality and that the speakers are placed for optimal sound dissipation.

A3D 2.0 is a new offering from Aureal that branches out from the success of the first version but maintains backward-compatibility with all titles using A3D 1.0. A3D 2.0 includes Aureal Wavetracing, which allows for real-time acoustic reflections, reverb, and occlusion rendering. In layman's terms, this makes sounds behave more like real-life sounds by enabling them to reflect off walls, leak through doors, become blocked by corners, or change as you enter from an outside area into an indoor area. Aureal says that it can also render materials such as stucco, carpets, and deep caverns!

Turtle Beach offers a next-generation Montego A3DXstream PCI-based sound card. One of the best new features to come to the Turtle Beach line is Aureal Semiconductor's A3D Interactive technology for 3D sound positioning with only two speakers or a set of headphones. It will be the first card to use Aureal's new VortexAU8820 digital audio processor chip. The A3D technology is supported in many games from some of the big names in gaming, including LucasArts, Interplay, GT Interactive, Broderbund, Electronic Arts, Sierra On-Line, Ubi Soft, and Activision.

The Montego A3DXstream, with its exceptional 64-voice sound palette, A3D positional audio, and blazingly fast PCI-bus structure, enables you to experience the latest in multimedia audio technology. Dell offers an OEM version on its Dell Dimension XPS D300MHz and D333MHz systems.

One advantage that the Montego has over its competition is that it also supports legacy DOS games. Many of the new PCI cards will run Windows-only games, and a passthrough connection to an ISA card is needed to provide sound for games that aren't compatible with the newer Microsoft sound APIs.

A2D gives those without an A3D-specific processor a CPU emulation mode so they can still get many of the benefits of the technology. A3D API gives developers an interface that supports A2D, A3D, and A3D 2.0. Advanced resource management will be available on current A3D cards and newer Vortex 2 cards.

A3D Authentication Protection will make sure that users will get high-quality playback. A3D 2.0 applications will run with all the hardware features only if the user has an Aureal-certified system.

Microsoft's first speaker-system product, the Digital Sound System 80, includes some innovative features. The system operates in both digital and analog modes. For true digital audio, the system connects to your PC via a USB port, which carries the audio control signals as well as the audio signal.

Windows 98 supports digital audio at the operating-system level. In analog mode, the speakers hook up to your PC through a conventional sound card. The speakers are compatible with older Windows 3.x systems, as well as with Windows 95, 98 and NT. But if you connect them through a sound card rather than through a USB port, you'll lose some of the fancier digital sound features, including higher bandwidth and reduced signal processing, that produce crisper, cleaner audio.

SRS Labs is another leader in this area. Intel has proposed a version of this idea that it refers to as its Realistic Sound Experience (RSX). Microsoft is pushing new sound protocols that go by the names DirectSound and DirectSound3D. All of these companies claim to understand how sounds we hear are modified by the way those sound waves interact with our head and ears. They have applied that knowledge in unique ways to improve the listening experience, both for stereo sound (two speakers) and surround sound (with five or six speakers).

This discussion of MIDI sound generation on a PC is necessarily brief. There are many additional subtle effects that you can use, and these are documented in the literature that comes with the sound cards or your PC. You can get entire books devoted simply to making and capturing music with your PC. One such book is *The MIDI Manual, 2nd Edition*, by David Miles Huber (Butterworth-Heinemann Press; ISBN 0-240-80330-2). Another brilliant resource for computer music—and a dandy doorstop—is Curtis Roads' *The Computer Music Tutorial* (MIT Press, 1996; ISBN 0-262-68082-3). It discusses just about every aspect of computer-based sound, including MIDI and digital audio.

Sound File Formats

I have already told you a little bit about the two most popular sound file formats: WAV and stereo. WAV files store samples of the actual sound pressure, sampled at some fixed rate (commonly 22KHz or 44KHz), with each sample being converted to a 16-bit binary number. Stereo wave files store two sound pressure numbers for each sample time. These two sound pressure numbers correspond to the sound pressures at the two microphones (or to a left and right input signal, if you are creating a WAV file from some other stereo sound source).

MIDI files (the extension is most commonly shortened to MID) store descriptions that a MIDI synthesizer can use to generate sounds. These descriptions must conform to the official standard for MIDI messages. As such, they can be played on or generated by any MIDI musical instrument, from keyboards to synthesizers to PCs.

Audio files on the Internet are sometimes in the AU format. This is like a WAV file, but it is very different internally.

Real Networks has also created a standard for streaming audio files. These RM, RAM, or RA files can be played back as they are being received by Real Player programs. Otherwise, they are like WAV files (with sometimes video information as well as audio).

Finally, I must mention the sound file format that is taking the Web and the world by storm: MP3. This file format enables CD-quality audio to be stored in a relatively compact form. (Typically, an MP3 file will be around 1/10 the size of the equivalent WAV file.) Until very recently, much of the recording industry has mightily resisted the proliferation of MP3 files on the Web because it has the potential to displace sales of CDs or audio tapes. On the other hand, this format has empowered many underrepresented artists to self-publish their work on the Web and make it available to their fans at a very high quality without excessive download times.

Direct Hardware Access

In the days of DOS, direct hardware access was the only way you could create any form of multimedia application because DOS didn't provide any support for these machine capabilities. Windows, on the other hand, provides an almost overwhelming array of functions designed to make life easier for the programmer. In fact, these functions hide the hardware in such a way that a programmer really doesn't need to know much about the specific capabilities of a particular piece of hardware. All that the programmer needs to create is a generic program that will work with the Windows Application Interface (API), and the API takes care of the rest.

Unfortunately, getting all of this free service from the operating system comes with a price. Anyone who has tried creating any type of multimedia presentation using the API knows that while it's not impossible, the resulting application is going to run slowly. This is especially true of the graphics functions provided by the graphics device interface (GDI) subsystem. (Microsoft went so far as to rewrite some sections of the GDI in assembly code to make it faster, but it's still not fast enough for some purposes.) The biggest problem with the various Windows APIs is that Windows needs to control every operation, and it provides several layers of interfaces to do so. An errant application can cause the system to crash; using layers enables Windows to monitor things more closely (although these layers don't always provide the level of protection advertised).

Game developers write applications for one of the most demanding groups in the world. When it comes to speed, gamers often show off their "rigs" like drag racers. Let's face it, DOOM isn't nearly as much fun to play if you can get a cup of coffee and drink it down between kills. Gamers want the action fast, which means game companies have to write code that is optimized for their particular needs.

As a result of Windows emergence as the operating system to use for most business needs, Microsoft's reluctance to update DOS, and the gamer's need for speed, several specialty APIs have appeared on the market that enable the game developer to bypass the Windows API and work directly with the hardware. These APIs are provided with a few caveats that few game developers fail to abide by. For one thing, the API allows a game developer to work with the hardware directly, but only after it notifies Windows that it plans to do so. Another caveat is that the developer has to write with multiprocessing in mind. A gamer will often run a background task while running a game, so the game can't do things to the hardware that will prevent other applications from using it correctly.

The following sections look at the three most popular direct hardware access technologies available to programmers today: OpenGL, Glide, and DirectX. Of the three, DirectX is the most comprehensive because it goes farther than just providing optimized graphics access for the developer.

DirectX

Microsoft's DirectX is designed to make Windows-based computers an ideal platform for running and displaying applications rich in multimedia elements, such as full-color graphics, video, 3D animation, and surround sound. You'll find that this technology is installed as part of the Windows family of operating systems, including both Windows 98 and Windows 2000. Just to make sure you have the latest version (which is 6.1 as of this writing), Microsoft also ships DirectX with many of its products, such as Internet Explorer. Many games and multimedia-oriented applications will also automatically install DirectX components on your system. DirectX is a large set of technologies that include DirectDraw, Direct3D, DirectSound, DirectInput, DirectPlay, and the new DirectMusic.

As with most Microsoft technologies, DirectX has a modular design to make it easy to replace specific components and to decrease the amount of code that needs to be loaded into memory. DirectX is actually composed of several software layers. Each layer performs a specific purpose. The following list describes each layer and what purpose it serves:

- Components—DirectX components represent the top layer of the DirectX hierarchy; most people would have simply called them applications. Obviously, any game or multimedia application that uses DirectX resides at this level. You'll also find that Windows 98 comes with four DirectX components: ActiveMovie, VRML 2.0, NetShow, and NetMeeting.

- DirectX Media—This is the layer that manages all your resources, such as video memory and access to the soundboard. It's the application service level. You'll find several pieces of DirectX here, including DirectShow, DirectModel, DirectPlay, DirectAnimation, Direct3DretainedMode, and VRML.

- DirectX Foundation—All of the system level services appear at this level. When the operating system needs to know what's going on, it will talk to one of the pieces at this level. You'll find DirectDraw, DirectInput, DirectSound, DirectSound3D, and Direct3DImmediateMode at this level.

- Hardware and Network—None of this technology matters if you can't make your PC display believable 3D graphics. It used to be that you could get by with adequate or even cheap speakers when playing a game. That's no longer true. If you want the very best output from your application, you need the hardware to do it. DirectX is more than just some software that helps you get the most from your games and multimedia applications. It also means getting hardware that you would normally expect to find with your favorite stereo. The hardware that I'm seeing today in gaming magazines only serves to remind me that PCs are no longer just machines for work—they're machines for play too.

The programmer-oriented part of DirectX is in the Microsoft Game Software Development Kit (SDK). It is a set of APIs and programming tools that make it possible for programmers to add direct hardware access to their programs without needing to know the specific hardware configuration of each individual computer. For video, this means the programmer can take advantage of the advanced features of a video card, such as 3D, without having to account for the individual features provided by video card vendors such as ATI, Diamond, Matrox, Number 9. It also means that just because your game runs on Windows, it doesn't necessarily have to use DirectX to get good performance. The choice of direct hardware access technology begins as a programmer issue—it becomes a user issue when that program appears in shrink-wrap on a store's shelf.

Now that you have a better idea of what DirectX is, let's look at the individual technologies. The following sections will help you understand how DirectX technologies can help you create a faster multimedia environment—not just for games, but for other kinds of multimedia applications as well.

> **Note:** DirectX was primarily developed for Windows 95. When Microsoft saw how successful DirectX had become and started using the technology for applications, there was a need to add at least some DirectX support to Windows NT as well. Windows NT 4.0 currently supports a subset of DirectX if you install Service Pack 3 or above. Unfortunately, Windows NT 4 adds software-only support for all DirectX components, which means that any hardware acceleration your display adapter provides is lost. Both Windows 98 and Windows 2000 will provide full support for DirectX.

DirectDraw

Moving the data that you need to display from the main system memory to the video adapter can be a time-consuming process, especially when you consider how much memory just one screen of information can consume. Of course, anything the programmer can do to speed up the memory transfer process will greatly enhance application speed and provide the user with smoother animations. One of the ways to do this is to transfer graphics data using a Block Image Transfer (BLIT). DirectDraw's most important capability enables programmers to store and manipulate bitmaps directly in video memory. It enables developers to take advantage of the video hardware's blitter to BLIT these bitmaps from main memory to video memory.

Using a BLIT enhances performance in two ways. First, it's more efficient to transfer data in large chunks than it is to transfer it one bit at a time. In addition, the hardware BLIT operates independently of the CPU and therefore frees up the CPU to continue working on other application needs.

DirectDraw also supports other video card hardware acceleration features, such as hardware support for sprites and z-buffering. *Sprites* enable the application developer to encapsulate individual objects onscreen and move them as single elements. *Z-buffering* helps the video hardware draw distant objects first and close objects last.

Microsoft DirectDraw enables developers to accelerate 2D graphics by providing direct manipulation of video display memory, hardware blitters, hardware overlays, and animation page flipping. It provides this functionality while maintaining compatibility with existing Windows 95-based programs and device drivers.

Essentially, DirectDraw is a memory manager for video memory. Using DirectDraw, a program can manipulate video memory with ease, taking full advantage of the blitting and color decompression capabilities of different types of video hardware without becoming dependent on a particular piece of hardware.

Direct3D

Direct3D is a complete set of real-time 3D graphics services that delivers fast, software-based rendering of the full 3D rendering pipeline (such as transformations, lighting, and rasterization) and transparent access to hardware acceleration. Direct3D is fully scalable, enabling all or part of the 3D rendering pipeline to be accelerated by hardware. Direct3D exposes advanced graphics capabilities of 3D hardware accelerators, including z-buffering, anti-aliasing, alpha blending, bit mapping, atmospheric effects, and perspective-correct texture mapping. Integration with other DirectX technologies enables Direct3D to deliver such features as video mapping, hardware 3D rendering in 2D overlay planes, and even sprites, providing the use of 2D and 3D graphics in interactive media titles.

In the Immediate Mode, Direct3D enables developers to port games and other high-performance multimedia applications onto Windows. Its features include switchable z-buffering, hardware independence, and support for the Intel MMX architecture. Direct3D Immediate mode also supports drawing primitives without the use of execute buffers.

In the Retained Mode, Direct3D simplifies the building and animation of 3D worlds with two new features: animation interpolators enabling the blending of colors, smooth movement of objects, and many other transformations; and progressive meshes that enable the increasing refinement of a coarse mesh over time, helping with progressive downloads from remote locations. Direct3D Retained Mode's features let developers create high-quality 3D applications without wading through low-level object structures.

DirectInput

Microsoft DirectInput provides low-latency support for analog and digital joysticks, with support for alternate user-interaction input devices such as data gloves. Extended capabilities provide support for the special calibration needs of rudder pedals, flight yokes, steering devices, virtual-reality headgear, and other devices. Even though these devices plug into the same game port and are recognized in the same way as joysticks, including them in an application often requires special programming. DirectInput reduces the amount of work that the programmer must do to include an alternative input device, such as a rudder pedal.

From a programmer's perspective, DirectInput has two key benefits over the current standard API functions: support for more types of devices, and faster response times. By working directly with device drivers, DirectInput bypasses the Microsoft Windows message system. Obviously, the impact of DirectInput is less than other technologies such as DirectDraw, but game programmers typically need every bit of time they can get to make the games they're creating fast enough to please even the most serious gamer's tastes.

DirectSound

DirectSound is the audio component of the Microsoft Windows 95 Game SDK. It provides low-latency (that is, quick-response) mixing, hardware acceleration, and direct access to the sound device. DirectSound provides this functionality while maintaining compatibility with existing Windows 95-based programs and device drivers.

DirectSound is a 32-bit audio API for Windows 95 and Windows NT that replaces the 16-bit wave API introduced in Windows 3.1. It provides device-independent access to audio accelerator hardware, giving you access to features such as real-time mixing of audio streams and control over volume, panning (left/right balance control), and frequency shifting during playback. DirectSound also provides low-latency playback (on the order of 20 milliseconds) so that you can better synchronize sounds with other events. DirectSound is available in the DirectX 2 SDK.

DirectSound plays only pulse code modulation (PCM) data formats. Compressed wave formats are not supported. To play compressed wave data, you must first expand the data into PCM format before writing the data to a DirectSound sound buffer. DirectSound supports low-latency sound mixing, 3D spatialization, wave table music synthesis, and direct access to sound devices. As with the other DirectX Foundation APIs, all functions can be fully hardware-accelerated.

DirectSound3D

DirectSound3D is a superset of DirectSound. It enables you to transcend the limits of ordinary left/right balancing by making it possible to position sounds anywhere in three-dimensional space. So, although DirectSound enables you to play normal sounds very quickly, DirectSound3D enables you to tell the user where that sound is located as well.

DirectPlay

DirectPlay is a software interface that simplifies game access to communication services. It provides a way for games to communicate with each other that is independent of the underlying transport, protocol, or online service. DirectPlay contains a set of tools that provide well-defined, yet generalized communications capabilities, enabling players to find game sessions and sites to manage the flow of information between hosts and players.

DirectPlay has three main attributes: a transport-independent way of sending and receiving messages, a service-independent way of creating and communicating with game sessions, and a user interface-independent way of structuring and accessing networked resources such as players. Moreover, because DirectPlay delivers these features via COM interfaces, it is independent of any one language or development environment.

DirectMusic

DirectMusic is an interactive environment for Web site developers and music composers that provides MIDI playback and recording support, DownLoadable Sounds (DLS) support, a software synthesizer, and DLS hardware acceleration. DirectMusic also provides consistent playback, DLS hardware acceleration, and MIDI 1.0 input and output support.

DirectMusic will work in Windows 95 and Windows NT 4.0, but to fully take advantage of all DirectMusic has to offer, you'll need Windows 98 or Windows 2000. That's because DirectMusic needs the new Windows Driver Model (WDM) for hardware acceleration of DLS. In addition, sequencing in Windows 95 and NT 4 will be done in User mode, and DLS will be supported only for the software synthesizer.

The software synthesizer uses the Sound Canvas sound set with GS extensions, a superset of General MIDI (GM), so GM sequences will play correctly. The software synthesizer also gives composers a wider variety of instruments, drum sets, and special effects such as reverb and chorus, along with greater creative control over the way sounds are played. Now, composers can write music specifically for the Sound Canvas instrument set and know that it will sound the same on any Windows system with the software synthesizer.

You'll need a sound card that is DirectMusic-compatible if you want to use your card's synthesizer for DLS instead of the software synthesizer. You may be able to use your existing card—if the vendor provides new drivers.

DirectMusic sequences can be programmed to react to a mouse click or other events by changing the tempo, mood, or other musical aspects, and the Performance Layer can even generate musical transitions when you move from page to page. The result is dynamic, unique music that interactively responds to user inputs. DirectMusic's synthetic sound is certainly no match for the music a good composer can create. However, you may be surprised by its exceptional quality and how the compact format enables the music to travel quickly to your browser and change quickly in response to your actions.

DirectMusic also gives composers access to an almost limitless selection of downloadable sound patches based on DLS. DLS stores instrument sounds in files that can be downloaded to a synthesizer as needed. A single instrument can have up to 12 regions that correspond to different note and volume (MIDI velocity) ranges. Each region can have its own articulation information, such as envelopes to vary pitch and velocity over time, loop points, and MIDI controller inputs.

The concept of downloading new instrument samples to a sound card's RAM is not new. Creative originated this idea when it developed its Sound Font technology. But accessing downloadable samples that can be played on a variety of synthesizers is indeed new. In the past, sound cards from different companies stored their downloaded sounds differently, which meant users couldn't share them and developers found it difficult to create sample sets that everyone could use. The MIDI Manufacturers Association created DLS to solve this compatibility problem. With DLS incorporated into Windows, composers can create any instrument, sample, or sound effect they want and know that it will sound right on any sound card equipped with a DirectMusic-compliant driver.

Even if you don't have a sound card that can use of DLS directly, you are not left out. Microsoft's software synthesizer supports DLS and will work even with non-wave table sound cards.

DirectAnimation

DirectAnimation provides extensive support for such diverse media types as 2D vector graphics, 3D graphics, sprites, audio, and video, and a uniform time and event model. HTML authors can integrate animation using DirectAnimation controls. Authors using

Visual Basic Scripting Edition (VBScript) or JScript and Java applet writers can program Web page animation with Dynamic HTML. Programmers using Java, Visual Basic, and Visual C++ can develop ActiveX controls or full applications that require multimedia support and interactivity.

The DirectAnimation API provides a high-level, easy-to-use API for hosting DirectX Transform in both Web content and applications, and provides a connectivity model for transforms, making it possible to cascade several of them. DirectAnimation also makes it possible to easily use transforms in the context of animation. For example, you can use a video clip or 3D animation as an input to a transform. DirectX Transform technology is also flexible enough to be used alone as a plug-in architecture for any media application.

DirectX Transform

DirectX Transform handles video special effects, such as wipes, ripples, and HeightField transformations, among many other special effects. Wipes are an image transition that takes two input images and produces a combination of the two. Ripples gradually blend and texture one or two input image inputs onto a generated rippling wave geometry. A HeightField transformation that takes an image as input and generates a height field mesh where color intensities are mapped to height values.

Independent content providers can use DirectX Transform to add richness to their Web sites without increasing user download time very much. DirectX Transform implements media components using standard COM objects. It utilizes the richness of COM technology, including packaging, installation, discovery, creation, scriptability, and Web download, as well as COM conventions and implementation methodologies that are well understood by the developer community. The main goals of the architecture include simplicity in implementing transforms, integration with DirectX, and support for transforms that operate on multiple media types.

OpenGL

OpenGL is Silicon Graphics' longstanding and very stable industry-standard API, which was introduced in 1992. This is a vendor-neutral API, which means that it's more open than the other two APIs in this chapter. In fact, more than one vendor sits on the review board that makes changes to the OpenGL specification, including giants such as IBM and Microsoft.

Microsoft originally added OpenGL to Windows as a way to speed up CAD programming. In addition, OpenGL was used for the fancy 3D screen savers that originally appeared in Windows NT. In fact, these screen savers are still the fastest way to see OpenGL in action.

The gaming community started using OpenGL for Windows games over Microsoft's objections. At the time, Microsoft had already introduced DirectX and wanted game developers to use that API instead of OpenGL. Quake was the first game with a large installed base to use OpenGL, but a lot of other games have followed in its tracks. (The fact that there are a lot of games on the market that are based on the Quake engine accounts for at least some of OpenGL's popularity.)

OpenGL is used for some 2D, but mostly for 3D graphics handling. Images are drawn in three dimensions and there's support for shading, texture mapping, anti-aliasing, lighting, and animation. It provides 2D and 3D graphics functions that support modeling, transformations, color, NURBS (non-uniform rational B-splines), fogging (a method of depth cueing that uses a fading effect to blur faraway objects), alpha blending (a graduated shading that uses varying levels of opacity for visual elements), and motion blur. In fact, OpenGL includes approximately 120 commands for drawing graphics such as points, lines, and polygons. OpenGL works in both immediate and retained (display list) graphics modes.

One of the reasons that OpenGL is popular is that it's very portable. You'll find OpenGL supported on a wide variety of platforms, including Macintosh OS, OS/2, UNIX, OPENStep, Python, Windows, and BeOS. Linux and some other operating systems use MesaGL, which is very similar to OpenGL.

In addition to providing enormous flexibility and functionality, OpenGL applications enjoy the broadest platform accessibility in the industry. Applications in the areas of CAD, content creation, energy, entertainment, game development, manufacturing, medical, VRML, and more have benefited from OpenGL's breadth of platform accessibility and depth of functionality.

Although the OpenGL specification defines a particular graphics processing pipeline, platform vendors have the freedom to tailor a particular OpenGL implementation to meet theirunique system cost and performance objectives. Individual calls can be executed on dedicated hardware, run as software routines on the standard system CPU, or implemented as a combination of both dedicated hardware and software routines.

This implementation flexibility means that OpenGL hardware acceleration can range from simple rendering to full geometry, and is widely available on everything from low-cost PCs to high-end workstations and supercomputers. Application developers are assured consistent display results regardless of the platform implementation of the OpenGL environment. Using the OpenGL extension mechanism, hardware developers can differentiate their products by developing extensions that allow software developers to access additional performance and technological innovations.

OpenGL is well-structured with an intuitive design and logical commands. Efficient OpenGL routines typically result in applications with fewer lines of code than programs generated using other graphics libraries or packages. In addition, OpenGL drivers encapsulate information about the underlying hardware, freeing the application developer from having to design for specific hardware features.

Glide

Glide is a graphics-specific API that enables programmers to directly access the hardware. One of the things that makes 3Dfx's Glide API different from the other two APIs that we've discussed so far is that it relies on hardware acceleration. Lots of game programmers love the speed enhancements that Glide provides and develop their games for that API alone. Of course, this means that you have to have the right hardware on your system, along with the correct drivers, to actually play the game in question. Fortunately, at least some of these games are now being written to take advantage of DirectX, because Microsoft has improved the flexibility and speed of this technology so much.

3Dfx introduced Glide along with its Voodoo chipset. This was the first chipset with high-end 3D graphics processing capabilities that were normally found only on expensive workstations such as Sun and SGI at the time. (Vendors such as Matrox and Number 9 did have 3D graphics adapters at the time, but they provided only limited 3D processing capabilities.) The Glide API and the Voodoo chipset were designed to work together to provide maximum performance at a minimal price—3Dfx achieved both goals.

Unlike the other APIs in this section, Glide is also a low-level API that's designed to hide details such as registers, but not designed to provide high-end functions such as display lists or transforms. In fact, there are drivers that enable OpenGL and Direct3D developers to access Glide functionality using the higher-level functions provided in these APIs. Glide is designed to give the developer maximum access to the Voodoo chipset functions, and it doesn't do much work internally. So from a programmer's perspective, Glide is a much harder API to use for writing games, but the extra speed of the resulting application is well worth the effort.

Interestingly enough, Glide has better cross-platform support than the other two APIs. There is a version of Glide that works great on Windows NT 4 (it doesn't matter which service pack you have installed), and another that works on Linux. Glide is also the only one of the APIs discussed in this chapter that will work with DOS. Game programmers who wanted to support DOS had only one choice when it came to 3D programming—Glide. This is another reason that some developers, such as the ones who created Epic MegaGame's Unreal, initially developed for Glide alone.

Will Your PCs Run Your Radio, Wash Your Clothes, and Program Your VCR?

Will your PC soon be controlling your radio, washing machine, and VCR? Sure—or at least it will be *able* to do those things soon. Within the next year or two, don't be too surprised if you see USB-enabled appliances. (Recall that USB, Universal Serial Bus, is a plug-and-play interface that enables up to 127 peripherals to plug sequentially into a single external port, using just a single interrupt and port address.) When USB-controlled appliances become available, if you simply cable one (or many) of them up to your PC (and load suitable software), your PC can converse with that other device—perhaps both interrogating it and commanding it. For a radio, that means finding out whether it is available (plugged in and whatever else it needs), then commanding it to set itself to the station and the volume that you want.

Such innovations could be the tip of the iceberg. We are on the edge of a major shift in how PCs are built and operated. The USB bus (and also the 1394 Firewire bus) is just one part of the story. (See Chapters 16, "Faster Ways to Get Information into and out of Your PC," and 22, "Why Mobile PCs Must Be Different" for more on this subject.)

The Convergence of PCs, Telephones, and Television Is Here—At Last!

For years, we have been reading that PCs, telephones, and television were going to converge. But up to now, actual examples of these phenomena have been few and far apart.

Linking Your PC to Your Phone

PC-telephone convergence has gotten further than PC-television convergence. Many people now routinely look up people or companies in a PC database and then dial the phone with just a click of their mouse. Some companies have equipped their technical support and sales departments with linked PCs and telephones so that when a customer calls, the caller is recognized by caller ID signals from the telephone company. Then the linked PC pops up the customer's previous sales and service call records from the company's master database. There are other examples of PC-telephone convergence, but these are quite typical.

Watching TV on Your PC Now Makes Some Sense

At last, there is some real progress to report on the PC-television convergence front. Digital television is here. And as it turns out, the most practical way to watch it is on your PC.

For several years, it's been possible to get a special video card that has a television tuner. Plug one into your PC and hook it up to a TV antenna or cable, and you can watch TV shows in a window on your PC. You can—but few of us ever really want to do that. The image and sound quality is at best equal to what you could see on a much cheaper stand-alone TV, and often much worse. So why bother?

Now, however, the broadcasting of high-definition television signals with fully digital, CD-quality sound has begun. So far, only a few stations in a few cities are sending out these signals—and then only some of the time. But in the next several years, if the U.S. Federal Communications Commission (FCC) and its peers in other countries have their way, all over-the-air television signals will be broadcast only in digital form.

There are many advantages to this, and—for now—a number of drawbacks as well. Some of the advantages are the potential for much higher resolution images, freedom from "snow," "ghosts," and static, and multiple subchannels within each broadcaster's assigned digital TV channel (which may be used for supplemental information and per- haps two-way interactivity).

For now, with very little programming available, it is hard to justify the high price of a new digital television set. True, you can buy a much less expensive digital-to-analog television signal converter and then play digital TV signals on your normal TV set, but you'll lose all the high-definition quality digital TV is capable of delivering—not to mention the potential two-way interactivity and access to supplemental information.

If you want to see what digital TV has to offer, the best way to do it is to outfit your PC so it can receive and display high-definition, digital television signals. Most modern, fairly high-end multimedia PCs have monitors that can display more resolution than any normal television set, which is more than enough to show off digital television to full advantage. The only restriction is that you must sit closer to your PC's screen than most people do with an ordinary television set. Thus, watching high-definition digital televi- sion will be less of a group experience than ordinary TV watching is.

The cost of enabling a good PC to receive and display digital television shows will be only a small fraction (perhaps less than a tenth) of the cost of a new, large-screen digital television set. The needed decoders are not yet readily available, but you can be sure they will be as soon as the signals they work with are available most of the time and in most television markets. Hauppauge, Panasonic, and Philips have all announced products they promise to bring to market sometime in 1999. Hitachi, Intel, and ATI are among the other vendors contributing to these developments. Surely, very soon there will be more.

For today's PC to work well with the multimedia technology we require of it, it must also have some very special internal parts. In the next chapter, I tell you about some of these special hardware concerns and how they are being addressed.

Immersive PC Experiences

This chapter completes my discussion of PC technologies for standalone desktop and workstation units. It also covers some applications for those PCs when they are connected to other, similar machines. To end this part of the book with a bang, so to speak, I have saved for this chapter the very latest and greatest innovations in what are now sometimes collectively referred to as *immersive PC experiences*.

Just looking at the words in this phrase, you can see that this could refer to any experience using a PC in which you could become fully absorbed. Therefore, even a simple word processor could qualify, if you were able to "get into" using it triumphantly. But as the term is more typically used, immersive PC experiences refers to the types of PC systems and applications that are more likely to engage any user fully—especially ones that address most of our senses.

Software is the starting point for any immersive PC experience. One general software category that fits this description is PC game programs. Most PC games provide intense visual and audio input. A few games can also provide a limited amount of tactile input, provided you have the right hardware. Another type of software that provides an immersive experience is 3D display systems, such as those used for simulators. For example, pilots learn to fly using mockups of the aircraft they'll eventually fly in real life. There is actually one monitor for each window that the pilot would normally have on the plane. In addition, the cockpit controls are fully duplicated so that the 3D display feels completely real. You can get a similar experience at home given the right add-ons to your system (up to and including multiple monitor display with some software and Windows 95/98). 3D display systems are used for more than simulators; many CAD programs also use 3D so that the architect or other engineer can model a real-world device on the computer. In addition, anything that deserves the name *virtual reality*—if there is any such software—might qualify. As you will soon see, there are at least a few other software categories besides these.

A key to any immersive PC experience is that the PC should be providing most of the important sensory input stimuli to the user. I say the important ones because humans have a notable characteristic: We tend to ignore any unchanging sensations. This means that the PC can dominate our sensory experience just by dominating the sensations that change. The fact that you are sitting in a chair or that there might be a pervasive odor in the room might not distract you from the intense interaction you are having with your PC.

This subject is a large and complex one. So, first I'll describe some of the technologies that are being used in these immersive PC experiences, and then discuss the principal applications that have been found for those technologies.

Immersive Technologies

By their nature, most immersive PC experiences tend to be heavily multimedia in character. As such, most of these multimedia experiences use more than a single technology. To understand these technologies, it's best to look at them one at a time.

You have already read about most of the technologies that are used in these experiences. This chapter, therefore, will explore the few, fairly far-out ones that remain. For example, a superior sound system can be assumed to be part of any immersive system. Video, on the other hand, is one area in which a PC might need to be enhanced for some of the experiences that follow. In particular, the PC might need to be able to create 3D scenes.

Simulated 3D

As you read in Chapter 13, "Seeing the Results: PC Displays," any PC that can present photorealistic images can give a strong illusion of three-dimensionality to the scenes it displays. This is because the monocular depth cues in those scenes are normally more important than their lack of binocular depth cues. This is fine for a great many purposes. Lately, though, people have come up with some very interesting applications that require an even more realistic 3D view of something.

There are two levels at which this can be done. The first level is to create a scene with strong depth illusions—so strong, in fact, that you could easily use this scene to discern the true, 3D locations of all the objects in it. This can be done quite effectively using stereoscopic or binocular images.

At the other level, a scene doesn't just appear to be 3D; it really is. You can move your head and look around some of the front objects, bringing objects into view that were formerly hidden. Now that's really 3D!

Fortunately, we don't always need scenes to be *that* three-dimensional. Often it is sufficient to be able to rotate the scene in front of your view. Think of this in another way: If the view on your PC's screen is a 2D image of what is seen by a camera, it might be enough to move the camera around the scene, looking from whatever perspective you want. You also might want to fly the camera *into* the scene, and once there, turn around and look at the back of some objects the camera has passed.

I don't want to suggest that having this type of 2D flying-camera view of a 3D scene is an easy thing to accomplish—far from it—but at least it can be done with some powerful software and a sufficiently high-performance PC. The video display itself doesn't need to be anything particularly special.

3D Modeling Programs and More

The first programs that could create true 3D models of objects were computer-aided design (CAD) programs. They were used by designers and architects to help them visualize their more difficult constructions. (Most simple architecture and design is still done with 2D drawings of various views of the *imagined*, but never actually *imaged*, 3D reality.)

The hardest part of using one of these CAD programs is constructing all the parts and pieces that go into making up the whole object or scene. This is much harder than the traditional 2D drafting techniques—or at least it is a lot more tedious. (Which is, of course, why this technique is not used unless it is really needed.) If, for example, you are drawing an idealized brick (to name something that is very geometrically simple) in a 2D program, you just draw some rectangles and parallelograms by pointing out where each corner of each visible surface goes.

However, in a 3D program, you must not only define each corner's location (and do so for every surface—not just the ones that are visible from a certain point of view), you also must define those corners in the right order.

This matters because the program determines which side of each rectangle is "inside" of the object by the order in which you describe its corners and sides. (Many 3D modeling apps are triangle-based, however.) To be consistent, of course, you want to be able to ascertain the fixed locations and dimensions of the brick's surfaces. You must clarify what is "inside" and what is "outside" of that brick—for each of its six surfaces. Fortunately, these programs now come with libraries of prebuilt parts and objects. For many purposes, you can simply assemble a lot of these building block pieces, perhaps modify some of them, and create your scene or your complex object in far less time than was previously possible.

After you have specified the basic geometry, you also must deal with how each surface is going to look. That is, you must specify a texture and reflectivity for each one. And, if you are going to see anything in the scene, you must specify the type and location of all the light sources.

When you are finished, you can view your creation from any desired place and look at it in any desired direction and with any desired degree of zoom. Furthermore, you can alter the lighting and the camera view dynamically to create a "fly-by" view of the scene. If you really want to get fancy, you might have some of the objects in the scene change their shape, color, or texture as the fly-by takes place.

> **Tip:** As you might imagine, true 3D processing takes a lot of computing power. A powerful graphics processor can take care of that need. However, there's more to it than that. All of this graphics processing also requires moving large quantities of data on the PC bus, which means that the PCI bus might be overwhelmed. Enter AGP. The latest version of this standard is AGP 2.*x*. We talked about this technology in Chapter 13. However, there is one thing you need to know about the display adapters that plug into the AGP slot on your machine. Some of them don't fully adhere to the AGP standard: They really are glorified PCI adapters. For example, display adapters based on the Voodoo 2 and V2100/V2200 chipsets provide only AGP 1.*x* compatibility, which means you won't get everything the AGP bus has to offer. For one thing, these cards transfer data at only 256MBps, not the full 528MBps provided by the AGP 2.*x* specification. Things get a little better with the RIVA 128 and Permedia 2 chipsets because they at least offer off-card texture storage (which enables the graphics adapter to store textures in main memory). If you want to get full AGP 2.*x* capabilities, make sure you get a display adapter based on the Intel 740 or the ATI Rage Pro chipset. You can find out more about Intel's AGP strategy at `http://support.intel.com/support/technologies/graphics/agp/index.htm` and ATI at `http://www.atitech.com/`.

Those of you who are science fiction fans might be able to relate to this technology a little better by looking at shows such as *Babylon 5*. In many cases, the interior scenes were created using a combination of props and specialized CAD programming. However, the most impressive computer-generated scenes from the show were those that took place outside of the ship. Not one of those scenes was created using models, as was done with movies like *Star Wars*. In the case of *Babylon 5*, all of the outside scenes were created within a computer and didn't exist at all in the real world. This use of CAD is called computer-generated imagery (CGI). The number of television shows and movies that rely on CGI today is increasing. You can find out more about this really interesting use of 3D modeling by looking at

`http://www.desktopimages.com/`.

You're likely already thinking that these programs are complex and need all the computing power you can give them. Often, computing the full appearance of each view of the final 3D scene (a process known as *rendering the scene*)—especially a fly-through view of a scene—takes many times as long as the fly-through itself will last. Sometimes graphics design firms use rooms full of very powerful PCs 24 hours a day for many days just to render a short, animated 3D scene.

If you want to get some hands-on experience with this type of program, one relatively powerful, yet modestly priced one is trueSpace from Caligari Corporation, based in Mountain View, California (`www.caligari.com`). There any many others, but this one is a good compromise between power and ease-of-use, and is relatively affordable.

In another use of the same technology, this type of program can be used to create the actual, physical objects that you have designed. In order to do this, the PC on which the design is created is linked to one or more fabrication tools. Then, under the direction of the PC, these tools will either carve up a block of metal or plastic or perhaps build a solid object from a liquid material. This approach is called computer-aided manufacturing (CAM). It is often used to create the prototype of something, which later can be mass-produced by other means. For some items that aren't needed in large numbers, however, this can even be the best way to make all of them.

A related development is the creation of devices that can take an existing 3D object, scan it, and generate the computer model for it automatically. There are several ways to do this, the most complex of which use cameras and are fully automated; others use a 3D pointing device to do this task in a much less automated way.

Virtual Reality Modeling Language (VRML)

The Internet has brought us a new variation on 3D modeling. Most of the time, when people on the Internet are using a browser to view World Wide Web pages, those pages are actually documents created in a language called Hypertext Markup Language (HTML). In Chapter 26, "You Can Touch the World, and It May Touch You, Too!" I tell you more about HTML and its many relatives. Here, I want to focus on just one of those related languages. It is called Virtual Reality Modeling Language (VRML).

Web sites that use VRML can be viewed with any browser that has a loaded and active VRML plug-in. This enables the browser to automatically perform a rendering task— although one almost infinitely less detailed and less complex when compared to that done by one of the 3D design programs like trueSpace. The design itself is contained in the VRML code of the Web page.

This means that you can download the VRML code that describes this scene into your PC. You can then view the scene from any defined vantage point. The characteristics of the objects in the scene and their lighting are fixed by the scene designer. But you, the user, choose the places from which you want to see it and the directions in which you will look at it.

This allows the presentation of information in wholly new ways. If the scene you are viewing is an accurate copy of some real-world place, you can have something of a tourist experience without ever leaving your desk. If the scene is an imaginary one, you can go there when there really isn't any real, physical "there" to go to. There is a new twist on this notion. PC users can insert an avatar into the scene and interact with the avatars of other users also currently viewing the scene. (An *avatar* is a modeled representation of a person, animal, or other entity, possibly with an actual face superimposed on it.)

"Real" 3D Graphics

Good as it is, sometimes a simulated 3D view is not enough. This is especially true if you want several different people to view something from their own vantage points. This is now possible for computer-generated scenes. However, the PC's video system must first be altered in some fairly dramatic ways.

Almost all approaches to creating "real 3D" share one thing: They manage somehow to present a different image of the scene to each of the viewer's eyes. The differences between these left and right views are computed to be just what the viewer would see if he were actually looking at the reality that the computer-generated scene is emulating. (Near the end of this section, I'll mention two true 3D scene generators that don't use stereoscopic images.)

One fairly obvious approach is to create two small monitors and mount them, one in front of each eye. You must add some optics to this to make the monitors appear to be large and located at infinity, so that the viewer's eyes will blend the two 2D views into a single 3D one. The only real problem with this approach is getting sufficiently high-resolution display panels small enough to mount in a pair of comfortable glasses. So far, this technology is able to support only VGA resolution in monochrome or a reduced resolution in color, and it has not yet become commercially successful.

A variation on this has recently been announced by a new company in Seattle, Microvision (www.mvis.com). It has a technology it calls Virtual Retinal Display (VRD). Essentially, Microvision proposes to mount two miniature projectors in a hand-held or head-mounted device that projects images through the pupils of your eyes and directly onto the retinas. You wouldn't be looking at any object outside your eye—the apparatus would simply create the illusion that you were. Microvision doesn't yet sell an end-user product, but its VRD technology might become the basis of a whole family of quite exciting ones someday soon. Keep your eyes peeled for this one.

More common than any two-display approach is a method of producing stereoscopic images using only a single monitor. This is accomplished by running the video display at double the normal frame rate and arranging to show only every other frame to each eye. This enables each eye to see a normal frame rate video image, and the two images will differ in just the right way to cause a stereo image to be seen.

The standard version of this approach in the workstation market is the CrystalEyes product from StereoGraphics Corporation (www.stereographics.com). They also have a lower-priced version for PCs called SimulEyes. Another vendor with a very similar product, called Knowledgevision, is Neotek Automation (www.neotek.com). Its Web site has a well-written discussion of the science behind 3D Vision; if that interests you, go to www.neotek.com/3dtheory.htm.

The systems from both of these companies include special glasses you must wear to see the stereoscopic images their systems create. These glasses have electrically driven shutters that alternately open and close to let first one eye and then the other see the screen. The glasses connect to the PC by a wire, or they can be wireless and receive a synchronizing pulse of light or radio energy from a transmitter on top of the PC monitor. If you've ever seen one of the large-screen format IMAX 3D movies, you've already worn the IMAX PSE glasses, an advanced implementation of this technology.

Still other companies—3DTV, for one—offer projection systems that enable you to put both the left and right eye images on a screen, with each one reaching only the proper eye. This is accomplished by linearly polarizing the light for each eye at a right angle to that for the other eye, and then having the viewers all wear special polarizing eye glasses to enable each eye to see only the image meant for it. This also requires a special type of screen, so the polarization of the light in each image will not be appreciably diminished as it is reflected from the screen. This technology, originally developed jointly by The Walt Disney Company and Kodak in 1981, can be experienced on a theatrical scale at several Disney theme parks and at IMAX-3D theatres.

These are by no means the only technologies that have been devised to give a viewer the perception of a true 3D scene. However, these technologies are currently the most commonly used. Still in development are several very different approaches, one of which is already a product.

This new method uses a spherical mirror whose focal length can be rapidly altered to image the surface of a monitor at a variety of positions throughout a 3D region. At each position at which the monitor is imaged, this approach presents just that portion of the final image that belongs in that plane. Because of persistence of vision, you see the full 3D object apparently just hanging there in space in front of the vibrating mirror.

3D Sound

Just as you can create the appearance of 3D graphics using today's high-end graphics processors, you can also create 3D sound. In fact, there are three popular APIs in place for creating 3D sound today: Microsoft's DirectSound3D, Aureal's A3D, and Creative's Environmental Audio eXtensions (EAX). These three APIs enable programmers to create what appears to be 3D sound, which makes multimedia presentations more immersive because you can actually hear where the sound is coming from.

All three of these technologies work in about the same way. The sound from one speaker is delayed slightly. In addition, sound effects are added and the sound from one speaker might be slightly lower in sound level than the other. This gives your ears the impression that the sound happened first at one speaker, then the other. The amount of time differential and the types of special effects determine just where you place the sound. When working with 3D sound, each object is rendered individually. In other words, the characteristics for each sound coming out of each speaker are different so that you can place different sound sources at different positions in the room. This would enable you to place the sounds that a friend makes at your right side, while those of a monster come at you from the front.

Obviously, the number of speakers you use to create the 3D effect determines just how believable the effect is—how totally you'll be immersed in the experience. Two high-quality speakers with the proper placement are enough to give you sound effects for about 210 degrees (105 degrees on each side of your head). In other words, you'll be able to tell whether someone is to the left or right of you, but not to the back. You'll also get a certain amount of sound representation above and below your head, but again, only toward the front of you and not toward the back. The biggest drawback to using two speakers is that you can't move your head or the effect is ruined. If you hear a sound coming from your right side, moving your head to the right should make the sound louder. However, if the sound card is using two speakers and sound effects to trick your brain into thinking that the sound is coming from the right, the sound won't get louder.

To get a full 360 degrees of 3D sound you'll need a sound card that supports four speakers and one of the surround sound technologies. Using four speakers enables a sound that is supposed to come from behind you to really do so. Unfortunately, most users will find it difficult, if not impossible, to set up a four-speaker system. The reason is fairly easy to understand—no one wants to be tripping on wires as they move around the room.

There are differences between the three programming APIs used to create 3D sound. The easiest to understand is Creative's EAX. All that this API does is add some special effects such as reverb to DirectSound3D. In other words, all you're getting is Microsoft's version of 3D sound with a few additional special effects. Of course, these effects can make the difference between really believing that someone is screaming and knowing that they don't even exist.

DirectSound3D is Microsoft's solution to creating a 3D sound environment. In most cases, DirectSound3D runs as a software-only solution to creating a 3D environment. This means that all of those processor-intensive calculations are taking place on the machine's main processor, rather than on a dedicated soundboard processor. The bottom line is that DirectSound3D gobbles up a lot of processing cycles that developers may want to use for other purposes, such as displaying graphics. Does this make DirectSound3D a poorly designed technology? No, if it's the only technology that you have at your disposal. However, it's important to realize that the speed penalties will affect the quality of presentation that you get.

Fortunately, there are some companies that are planning on support DirectSound3D in hardware. Using hardware acceleration will make it possible to create 3D effects without losing much in other areas of the presentation. If you decide to get software that relies on DirectSound3D and you need the maximum speed from the application, make sure you also install a soundboard that supports DirectSound3D in hardware.

Aureal's A3D API is found on most Diamond Monster sound card products. You can also find it on soundboards that use their special Vortex 1 chip. The API provides only a "wrapper" for the functionality that Aureal provides in hardware. The advantage to this approach is speed. A hardware-rendered sound effect can be rendered faster, which means that the application programmer has more processing cycles to include other sound effects or sound objects. Because of the higher processing speed that it provides, you'll find A3D support in fast-paced games such as Heretic II, SiN, and Half-Life. Obviously, it works just as well for other kinds of multimedia presentations.

> **Note:** Aureal already has plans for making its hardware-based 3D sound even better. The Vortex 2 chip, which may be released by the time you read this, will incorporate Aureal Wavetracing. This is the same physics-based technology used for ray tracing in some 3D graphics boards right now. This kind of mathematical analysis should add just the right amount of shadow and light to the sound to make any aural experience truly convincing.

Of course, the hardware-oriented nature of A3D raises an important question. What happens if the program you're running needs A3D and there isn't an A3D-equipped soundboard in the machine? Aureal will still process the information, but it'll pass the data along to DirectSound3D. In other words, you'll still get 3D sound, but using software instead of hardware.

Computers That Fight Back

An innovative video display and superb audio are enough to create some very powerful immersive PC experiences. If you add to this a way to stimulate the user's sense of touch and the kinematic sense, however, the experiences can be made even more powerful. Most ordinary joysticks accept your movements and translate them into PC inputs, but they don't give feedback other than a spring return to the neutral position. The input devices I am about to mention go well beyond that.

This is the land of the Nintendo Rumble Pak, reactive joysticks such as Microsoft's SideWinder Force Feedback Pro, and similar technologies. The newest entrant to this field, and in some ways the most interesting, is the FEELit mouse from Immersion Corporation.

Some of these devices enable you to point in three dimensions. Others let you push, pull, or squeeze objects, and in the process feel them resist your force. Still others are more like Sensurround sound in movie theatres in the 1970s. The first kind of mechanism is simply a special-purpose input device. The second group is more complex, serving as both an input and output device.

The FEELit mouse proposes to let you feel the edges of objects on your Windows screen, feel yourself dragging icons, and so on. This is an attempt to add a somewhat arbitrary tactile aspect to an artificial experience, rather than (as the others do) simply enabling the user to feel the tactile portion of a simulated, but otherwise perfectly normal, experience.

The actual variety of these input devices and the technologies behind them is tremendous. You can use anything from a simple, inexpensive glove that enables you to control a program by waving your hand, up to a full body suit that will sense every motion of any part of your body—and also will push back on the appropriate parts to simulate what you would experience if you actually moved around in an object-filled scene that, in fact, exists only inside the computer's memory. Combine this last one with a helmet that enables you to see that scene (and perhaps your own body in that scene), and you have the makings of a really convincing virtual reality experience.

Tactile feedback doesn't just include the joystick and mouse. A lot of game players now use surround sound to enhance their gaming experience. The surround sound setup includes four speakers (two front and two back) plus a subwoofer. The subwoofer is the interesting part of the experience. It's not really there to produce a lot of sound that you can hear; the subwoofer produces sounds along the lines of what you can feel.

Imagine for a moment that you're in a jet fighter. Yes, you'd hear a lot of high-pitched noises, and there would be a certain amount of sound from the radio. If the plane was in some type of trouble, you'd hear warning noises. The experience wouldn't end there, of course. There would also be a near constant rumble from the engines. It would be a sound so low that you would feel it more than hear it. That's the kind of sound that a subwoofer is designed to produce. Mix a surround sound system (where you can hear the actual direction a sound is coming from), a subwoofer so that you can feel the rumble, and a force feedback joystick, and you have something that comes close to the real-world experience of flying.

> **Tip:** Some soundboards are better than others at producing surround sound effects. In fact, some boards specialize in it. These boards include software that enables you to tune your listening experience to match the acoustics in your room. They also include multiple input channels so that you can grab sound input from more than one device at a time. If you plan to get the best real-world experience available, make sure you get a soundboard that's up to the task, along with speakers that can handle the sound level.

The tactile experience can go even further. The Intensor by BSG is a standard office chair that includes five built-in speakers—the standard complement for a surround sound system. The speakers are placed in such a way that you'll get the maximum experience from any game you're playing. The subwoofer is actually located in a compartment under the seat, which ensures you'll get the maximum rumble from that jet fighter. However, like a lot of the gimmicks that PC users have been exposed to in the past, this one does have a few potential problem areas. The seat is roomy, but the padding isn't very thick, making long-term sitting a pain. In addition, the controls are right between your legs, which means you probably wouldn't want to use this chair unless you were playing a game. In short, the Intensor provides one way to ensure you're totally immersed in your game or other multimedia experience, but you'll want to have another chair to use for surfing the Internet and other activities. You can find out more about Intensor at

```
http://www.intensor.com/
```

High Data-Rate Communications

One common characteristic of all these immersive experiences is that they involve huge amounts of information. The input and display devices must move those huge amounts of information into and out of the PC at a very high rate if the user is to have a smooth and compelling experience. This is not very hard to do if all the hardware is in one place. But sometimes, the application involves people interacting in two or more locations. Then the demands on the data communications channels can become truly frightening.

No special technologies are used for these high data-rate communications. Just some good old standards such as T1 (1.544Mbps) and T3 (44.736Mbps) telephone lines or fiber optic lines (100Mbps minimum), and so on. Or, in the least demanding cases, perhaps "mere" xDSL or a cable modem will do.

In other words, you need something in the 1Mbps range at a minimum—a 56Kbps modem connection just won't work for some types of immersive technologies, especially those with heavy graphics requirements. (A 56Kbps modem connection will work for steaming video and audio connections, but even so, it's still pretty marginal depending on line quality.) Always remember that a higher-speed connection is better when you're dealing with the technologies we've discussed in this chapter. In fact, graphics are one of the reasons that some companies have moved from 10Mbps Ethernet networks to 100Mbps setups.

There is one caveat: Even though you could get enough bandwidth from a satellite communications link, you probably don't want to use this sort of link if it uses geosyn-chronous satellites. Those satellites are so far out in space, the round-trip travel time of the signals, even at the speed of light, is long enough to introduce noticeable and possi-bly very annoying delays in the interactions between the several participants in your virtual world. On the other hand, a link via some low earth orbiting (LEO) satellites might serve you very well, indeed.

Immersive Applications

What are the uses to which people are putting all of these technologies? You'll not be surprised, I suspect, to learn that games were some of the first ways, and continue to be some of the most popular ways these technologies get used. We are, however, also beginning to find some other valuable ways they can be applied.

Games

Single-user and multiuser games have been popular applications for computers from nearly the very beginning. Even before it was feasible to generate complex graphics, we had Adventure and Star Trek. These early games used only keyboard input and simple character output, so they could be played even on computer terminals that could only display text.

As soon as more visually compelling experiences became possible, computer game designers eagerly exploited these new capabilities. Their customers reacted to these new developments with great enthusiasm, and they pressed the developers of hardware and software for ever more reality and even greater speed in those games. Doom and Myst are two of the most popular examples of how far we have come from the old days of Adventure on a "glass teletype."

Letting a user play against the computer presents one set of challenges for the game designer. Supporting multiple players from different locations who vie against one another in the same game presents a set of challenges that includes all those for the single-user games and a great deal more. For example, here is one place where the issue of high-bandwidth data communication comes into play.

Gamers push the technology, and their enthusiasm has paid for a lot of the new developments. Military gamers also have paid for a big share of them and continue to do so. Computer weapons-training systems are now turning out to be good models for advanced game systems—so as the Cold War winds down, many of the former military hardware and software companies are turning to the game market for replacement income. When these new technologies exist, and especially when they begin to be modestly priced mass-market items, many folks beyond the gaming community will find valuable uses for them as well.

Collaborations

Remember the multiplayer games? We also are seeing that model extended into business applications. Once again, we are using many of the same technologies that gamers have used, but for completely serious business purposes.

Video Conferencing

A major expense for any large corporation is travel. Usually, the reason for having employees travel is so they can attend some meeting. However, with virtual reality technologies, we can make that meeting happen without any two of the participants ever being in the same city. If the meeting is just a chance to talk to one another and to see and hear presentations, it can be accomplished in this remote fashion by using a form of video conferencing.

Virtual Whiteboards

Going one step further, you can now buy *electronic whiteboards*. These are devices that look much like normal blackboards (or whiteboards) on which you draw or write things with markers. When you do so, however, these same drawings can appear simultaneously on a PC monitor in the same room or in a room halfway around the world.

Moving on to the next step, you could dispense with the whiteboard itself and just use a portion of your PC's screen as a shared whiteboard. Then everyone who saw this board on his or her PC screen could also draw on it things that would be seen by all the others, or erase something that someone else had drawn.

This enables the type of meeting in which the participants brainstorm together and take collective notes on the board—again without the participants having to be in the same room, or even on the same continent. At the end, each participant would have a permanent copy of the final result and, if they wanted, a record of all the steps that the group took to get to that result. Microsoft NetMeeting is a strong first try of this type of software.

Virtual Worlds

A good example of this process can be found in the area of virtual worlds. At first, the capability of having a computer generate a purely illusory virtual world in which you could move around, and perhaps even affect the actions going on in that world, was used almost entirely for games.

Architectural Applications

Architects soon realized that they could use this approach to build a building in a virtual world long before it could be built in the real world. Then they could take their clients for a walk through the project. If either the architect or the client decided that a window was in the wrong place or a wall should be a different color, those things could be changed quickly and at very little cost. Thus, architects became some of the primary users of virtual reality as a means of testing their ideas and getting them approved by clients before any final construction plans were ever drawn up.

Educational Applications

The capability of building a virtual building doesn't just apply to ones that have been designed but not yet built. It can also be applied to buildings that have already been constructed—including ones that were built long ago and have long since fallen down or been demolished. Some educators are now in the process of constructing a virtual Rome and a virtual Athens. Several other places are being created as well. This company doing this is CyberSites, Inc. (www.ancientsites.com/as/).

Data Mining

All the applications I have spoken of so far are fairly straightforward uses of the notion that you can build virtual worlds that mimic our own. However, some of the most interesting applications of this technology are used for building virtual worlds that are totally different from our own.

Imagine, if you will, a world in which abstract databases become buildings. Records within those databases become rooms. Then imagine that you can walk or fly through these structures, looking for something you want. Something like this was on Michael Crichton's mind when he wrote his 1994 novel, *Disclosure*. (This was made into a movie later that same year, starring Michael Douglas and Demi Moore. In the movie you can see one visual representation of what this idea might look like.)

Still, I think the most significant virtual worlds will be ones that don't use an architectural model at all. They will, instead, be structured in some fashion that directly reflects the relationships inherent in the data. This will be significant because human beings have an innate ability to perceive patterns. We are, in fact, much better at this task than any computer yet built.

So, if you could make a virtual world out of a large mass of data, with patterns in that world that were meaningful in terms of some real relationships within that data—even though the computer that built that world would not know or understand what those patterns were—putting a human observer into that world might be the most efficient way to discover those patterns.

In a real sense, this could be called data mining. Current efforts go by that name, but are in fact not much more than standard computer-assisted methods of searching through large databases.

No Longer Just for Gamers

I hope you have discovered in this chapter why I think it is very likely that we will be using more and more of these multimedia-enhanced, virtual-world types of immersive PC experiences not only in our leisure time, but also on the job. What was once dismissed as merely for gamers is now becoming vital for business.

This means that the types of PCs we will be buying for all purposes are in many ways going to become more and more alike. Certainly at the very high end this will be true. I think that at the low end there will still be a place for simple, character-only terminals and PCs in many organizations for quite some time to come. But even there, eventually I think we will see voice-responsive speech-enabled, highly graphic PCs replace those character terminals—and when that happens, we'll have some much more people-friendly ways to use computers to do even the most mundane of data access tasks.

In the remaining three parts of this book, I address the special requirements for mobile PCs and talk about how PCs get connected to one another and to the outside world. Chapter 25 discusses PCs that behave as if they were mainframe computers. The final part briefly explores some of the technological underpinnings of the Internet and wraps things up.

PART VI

PCs Are Frequent Flyers, Too

Why Mobile PCs Must Be Different

People who work in more than one location or who must work on the go need something special if they are going to use PCs conveniently and effectively in their jobs. Taking a PC from one location to another has always been possible—after all, the pieces that make up a PC aren't all *that* large or heavy—but it certainly isn't a convenient thing to do. You can use an ordinary desktop PC only when it is set up somewhere, with all the pieces attached and with its power cord plugged into a live wall socket supplying power at an appropriate AC voltage and frequency.

As a result, there is a need for a special kind of PC—one that can be moved from one place to another conveniently. And for some uses, it must also be able to operate wherever it is located, without needing any outside source of power. We call these *mobile PCs*.

From Luggables to Laptops and Beyond

The first PCs were exclusively desktop machines. They had at least three parts: a system unit, a keyboard, and a monitor. Early PC users who absolutely had to have the use of a PC in more than one location either got more than one machine (and carried their data back and forth on floppy disks) or went through the inconvenience of taking their PC with them from location to location, which involved the effort of setting up the PC in each new place.

Luggables

Some manufacturers, including IBM, soon realized that there was a niche market they could serve by providing a portable PC. The first so-called portables were single-box units that included the keyboard, the display, and all the system unit pieces in one handle-equipped case. They were about the size and weight of a sewing machine, and they could be lifted by a single (strong) person. After you set it on a desk, all you had to do to get it working was open the lid, which often contained the keyboard, and plug in the power.

Those early manufacturers called these machines *portable*, but we now refer to them as *luggable* to emphasize their lack of battery power and the fact that you certainly wouldn't choose to carry this type of load around if there was any easier way to get the job done.

True Portables

The reason we had only desktop PCs and luggables for many years was simply that the state of the art of manufacturing electronic circuitry was insufficiently developed. When people knew how to make really compact circuitry that contained all the necessary functionality for a PC, making a truly portable PC became possible.

The early portables were rather heavy and bulky by today's standards. Carrying them all day was no fun. But many people, myself included, did just that because it was the best available way to get PC computing capability on the go.

These portable machines had one important thing that the luggable PCs never had: a rechargeable battery. This meant that not only could you take your PC to your destination, plug it in, and use it there, you could even use it en route—for a short time, at least.

Early battery-powered PCs were able to operate for only a short time before their batteries needed recharging. Later models got better and better, but even today, the issue of battery life between charges is often a troublesome one.

Laptop PCs

The progress of miniaturization did not stop; indeed, it has not stopped, and it shows no signs of letting up any time soon. The second generation of portable computers were small enough to operate on your lap. So, of course, they were given the new designation, *laptop* PC.

Today, this is the most common type of mobile PC. These machines are small enough and light enough (about three pounds) to carry around quite easily, yet they can be as powerful as a good desktop PC. (They aren't so small or light that you can just stuff them into a purse or pocket, but they will fit inside a briefcase or attaché case, or a similar-sized computer case.)

These machines are typically about the size of a piece of letterhead (8.5-by-11 inches), and perhaps one to two inches thick. There are several reasons why this size has evolved as the more-or-less standard size for a laptop PC.

Probably the original reason for designing a mobile PC at this size was so you could put it into a standard attaché case. The designers believed that people would want to carry around their laptop PCs along with their office reports and other similar-sized objects. In fact, this is often done. Because laptop PCs are rather fragile, however, the laptop and those other papers are more often shoved into a specially built, padded, and shock-resistant computer carrying case.

There are two other good reasons for not making the machine any smaller than this size. One is to ensure that the keyboard is large enough to type on comfortably. The other is so the screen is nearly the same size as a desktop monitor.

One interesting exception to the obvious fact that a laptop's keyboard can't be any bigger than its case was a novel portable PC design introduced a few years ago by IBM and referred to as the "butterfly laptop." The keyboard of this machine is split into two parts. It folds in a clever manner when you close the case to make it narrower, and it opens to its full width when you open the case almost like a flower unfolding its petals. All the other laptop PCs have simply had their keyboards fit within the boundaries of their cases.

Thus, we have the size that has worked out to be the best compromise between an adequate-size keyboard and as large a screen as possible, while still fitting into a case that is small enough to carry easily. Still, there are some smaller PCs being made. I'll describe them in a moment.

Figure 22.1 shows a Dell Inspiron 7000 portable computer. This is close to the state of the art in portable computers in 1999. It has a 300MHz Pentium II with MMX as its processor, a 14-inch (diagonal measurement), 1024×768 pixel active matrix screen (with 2X AGP video adapter and drivers to support up to 24-bit-per-pixel color depth), 64MB of RAM, an 8GB UltraDMA/33 hard disk, a floppy disk drive, and a DVD drive (which can play DVD movies, read DVD-ROM discs, and also read CD-ROMs and audio CDs). All that and battery power, too! It has built-in serial, parallel, and IrDA ports, plus two PC Card slots (both of which support the CardBus standard and one of which also offers Zoomed Video support), a USB connector, and an internal 56Kbps modem. You can connect an external keyboard or screen, or output S-video to a VCR or television set. It contains stereo speakers and a microphone, plus it has a proprietary connector for attaching this machine to a docking station to access even more peripheral devices than would fit in this modest-sized case. (If any of these terms are confusing to you, you'll find them defined very briefly in the glossary at the end of this book, and you'll also find detailed discussions of the technologies they represent elsewhere in this book. Either the glossary entries or the index will help you find the appropriate locations of those more extended discussions.)

The first panel in Figure 22.1 shows what the laptop looks like when its top is open. The first callout here points to the included pointing device (a touchpad) with two large buttons below it. Some laptops use other pointing devices (most notably a tiny trackball or a pointing stick), but a touchpad like this one is probably the most common pointing device for this class of machine. The other callouts indicate that the DVD-ROM and floppy disk drives are stacked above one another at the left of the machine.

The second panel shows a close-up view of the left side. Here you can see the covers for the two PC Card slots above the audio input and output connectors and volume control. Also shown is the connector where the external power supply plugs in. This power supply can be used to power the computer to charge the internal lithium ion battery, or it can do both at once.

Figure 22.1
*This Dell Inspiron
7000 portable
computer is typi-
cal of the best of
today's portable
computers.*

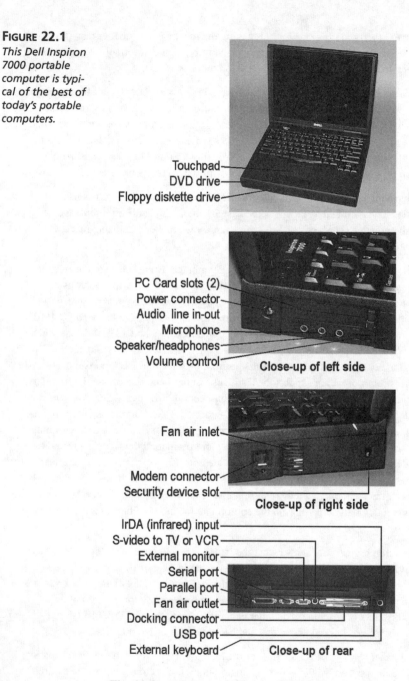

Touchpad
DVD drive
Floppy diskette drive

PC Card slots (2)
Power connector
Audio line in-out
Microphone
Speaker/headphones
Volume control
Close-up of left side

Fan air inlet

Modem connector
Security device slot
Close-up of right side

IrDA (infrared) input
S-video to TV or VCR
External monitor
Serial port
Parallel port
Fan air outlet
Docking connector
USB port
External keyboard
Close-up of rear

The third panel shows a close-up view of the right side. Here you can see the telephone line connector for the modem, the air inlet for the temperature-controlled fan (which runs only when its cooling effect is needed), and a slot for attaching a security cable (to keep the laptop from adding "walking away" to its repertoire of tricks).

The bottom panel of Figure 22.1 shows this mobile PC from the rear. You see here all the connectors it sports to attach to various peripheral devices, plus a connector that enables plugging the laptop into a docking station. Why, you might wonder, have a docking station with all the items that are already included inside the laptop? Some users will want to connect to their office network, hook up an external monitor and pointing device, and perhaps connect a printer and some other local peripherals. The docking station offers a way to do all these things in one easy step.

Fitting everything into this case was something of a tour de force for the engineers. The only way it could be done was by using both the very smallest standard parts and, in many instances, custom-designed parts. Also, these designs leave out some things that are standard on desktop PCs. For example, there are no slots into which you can plug either a standard ISA or PCI option card.

After they've put all the pieces in place, the manufacturers do not encourage end users to open up the case. This is very much unlike the situation for desktop PCs. This makes sense because the parts in a portable are often not only smaller, but also more fragile than those used in desktop units. The makers of these machines often do allow for some limited amount of upgradability. For example, in this portable you can add more memory if you like (up to a total of 384MB). And they have allowed for one option card (which in this machine is the video card, for which there are only two options—4MB or 8MB of video RAM). When this machine came from the factory, the memory sockets were empty. Figure 22.2 shows the two doors on the bottom that you remove to access the add-on memory sockets and the option bay. Also shown is the bay into which the hard drive fits. The connector for the hard drive is at the top of this figure. Adding memory and upgrading the size of the hard drive are the only ways to upgrade this machine from its original factory configuration.

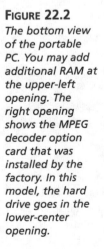

FIGURE 22.2
The bottom view of the portable PC. You may add additional RAM at the upper-left opening. The right opening shows the MPEG decoder option card that was installed by the factory. In this model, the hard drive goes in the lower-center opening.

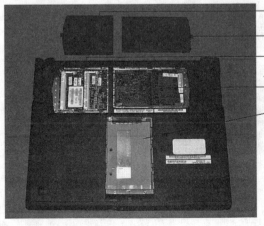

— Cover for memory sockets
— Cover for option card bay
— Sockets for SRAM DIMMs

— video card
— Hard drive bay

Many of the parts in this computer were modified in order to save weight or space. For example, in Figure 22.3, the DVD drive drawer is shown open. You'll notice that almost one-third of the drawer has been cut away. The missing part of the drawer is not important, either for supporting the DVD or CD or for giving the drawer sufficient strength, so it can be omitted safely. The small amount of mass it represents is shaved off the weight of the machine. Such amounts of weight might not seem important, but if you trim away a little bit here and there, the overall weight savings can be quite significant.

FIGURE 22.3

The DVD drive drawer comes out from the front of this portable PC. Notice how the base has been cut away to save weight.

The hard disk drive in this PC is an industry-standard model, but it is mounted in a custom holder that slips into the case and locks in place. In Figure 22.4, you see the drive, flipped upside down and backward and sitting on top of the upside-down laptop. This lets you see the connector on the hard drive and the connector in the open bay into which it normally is fitted.

FIGURE 22.4

The hard disk for this portable PC, removed from its normal place in the lower center of the case.

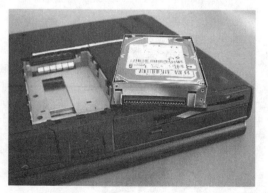

The battery in this laptop is a *smart battery*. This means that it actually contains a small microcontroller and some associated circuitry inside the battery case. That combination enables the PC to learn all about the battery's requirements for charging, as well as its present state of charge. Then it can do an optimum job of keeping the battery charged, without overcharging it, and it can keep the user informed very accurately about how much longer the battery can keep the laptop running. I'll tell you more about smart batteries later in this chapter.

Figure 22.5 shows this battery. Notice the five battery symbols on the left side of the front. Just below each one is an LED, and to the right of all of them is a button. Press this button and the appropriate number of LEDs light up, depending on the amount of charge in the battery (from 20 percent up to 100 percent, in 20 percent increments). At the lower right, you see the connector by which the battery links itself to the PC. It has more than two terminals because the battery must not only supply power, but also must communicate with the PC over what is termed the System Management bus.

FIGURE 22.5
The special "smart battery" used in this laptop.

Just as desktop PCs are gaining in power and dropping in price every year, so are laptop PCs. These trends show no signs of abating anytime soon.

In the past, it was common for laptop PCs to receive upgrades (to a new generation of CPU chip, for example) months to years after the corresponding upgrades were introduced for desktop machines. Now, however, the manufacturers are starting to introduce some new upgrades in mobile PCs first.

The one feature that laptop PCs have had for years and that is still rare on desktop machines is the PC Card slots (most of which now are the improved version referred to as CardBus slots, perhaps with Zoomed Video support as well). Of course, the major reason why these slots are not so common in desktop machines is because those machines have internal I/O bus slots (mostly PCI) instead. At one time, it seemed likely that desktop PCs would soon come with PC Card slots to permit easy exchange of information with digital cameras and other peripherals that use a PC Card slot for their interface. Now, however, it seems more likely that those peripherals will be using USB if they are going to link directly to a PC. Alternatively, they may use CompactFlash or SmartMedia memory cards. In that case, you will use a suitable adapter that will accept those memory cards and will in turn connect to one of the standard ports on a desktop PC.

New, Thinner Laptops

In the past year, we have seen a new development in laptop computers. While the standard size and shape of laptops got more powerful and packed with ever more features—in the process becoming more and more capable of replacing desktop PCs—"road warriors" who needed only very good PCs for doing a limited number of tasks have convinced manufacturers to offer an entirely new category of laptop computer.

These are the ultra-thin laptops. Sony pioneered this trend with its Vaio model, but now all the major laptop makers are jumping on the bandwagon. The Dell equivalent is the new Latitude LT. These machines have very good keyboards and screens that are nearly as large and nice as the high-end "regular" laptops. The overall size of these new machines is about the same as a normal laptop in all but their thickness; they are approximately half as thick as a regular laptop, and they are much lighter. To achieve these benefits, they have been designed without built-in DVD (or even CD-ROM) drives or floppy disk drives, and they also lack many of the other features common to today's high-end laptops, such as our example, Dell Inspiron.

Sub-Laptop PCs

One recent addition to the lineup of portable computers is the family of very small portables, which are still too large for most pockets (although some of them will fit in a jacket's outer pocket), but which can easily fit into a purse or zippered notebook. These computers, which include the Toshiba Libretto, usually come with about an eight-inch (diagonal) screen, Windows 98, a built-in modem, and support for one PC Card (usually Type I or Type II). These devices have been selling phenomenally well in what might have seemed a tiny market just a few months ago: people who want what is fundamentally a full-featured notebook that is shrunk by about 30 percent.

One step down from these "miniature notebooks" are the handheld PC (HPC) or *PC Companion* models, as they are increasingly called. These devices, including Vadem's Clio and the HP Jornada 820, are approximately the same size as the Toshiba Libretto, but run only Windows CE Pro, not full-on Windows. Other than the price difference—HPCs are currently selling for about $500.00 less than the Toshiba Libretto and its kin—it's rather hard to fathom the appeal of these devices. On the other hand, the bottom dollar is often, the bottom dollar. Whether this class of sub-laptop will do well or will flounder will be determined exclusively at the cash register.

Miniaturization did not stop at the HPC or PC Companion phase. There are some good reasons to be very glad that it did not. After all, we now have cellular phones that fit in a shirt pocket. Why not full-fledged PCs that do so as well? Microsoft is pushing this idea with its Windows CE operating system. With the introduction of version 3.0, Windows CE started to look pretty good; but of course, it still has its limitations, and it certainly has some fierce competition.

The main competition for Windows CE-based products are devices referred to as *personal digital assistants* (PDAs). The most popular of these is the Palm Pilot from 3Com Corporation. These devices, in general, are capable of storing a database of contact information, an appointment calendar, and often a collection of memos or a to-do list. Some also include game programs. Some PDAs enable you to enter data as handwriting. Others use tiny keyboards. Many of them also have some means to be connected to a PC and to synchronize their data with similar data files on the PC. This enables entry of masses of data into the PC followed by a simple download to put that data into the PDA. In other cases, the link is accomplished by an infrared beam to an IrDA port on your PC.

The next generation of Palm Pilot (the Palm Pilot VII) will include wireless connectivity by radio to a proprietary network, to be called Palm.Net. This will extend the uses of the Palm Pilot to include a form of Internet access. Suitably modified Web pages will be able to serve up data and accept requests from these new Palm Pilots over this wireless network. Just how useful this will be—and more important, how much market acceptance it will get—cannot be assessed yet.

PDAs are limited (at least today) in what they can do. On the other hand, some hand-held PCs (HPCs) can do significantly more than a simple PDA. For example, they can run spreadsheet programs, word processors, database programs, and communications programs. With a version of a cellular phone linkup, these machines can even be used to surf the Internet quite effectively.

One of the great beauties of PDAs is that they are optimized for just the few tasks they are supposed to perform. They don't attempt to be full PCs with all the generality that implies. This means they are often cheaper than the present generation of Windows CE hand-held PCs.

Of course, as Microsoft improves Windows CE and as the hardware makers learn how to stuff ever more goodies into those little packages, we will no doubt have some pretty amazing hand-held PCs. But because they'll be too small to have a "real" keyboard (by which I mean one that is large enough for touch typing), they might not become a mainstream item until they have the power to understand speech. That will come, I have no doubt. However, because it takes at least the power of a 200MHz Pentium with MMX and 48MB of memory to do good voice recognition now, and because a hand-held PC with that combination of resources is yet to be seen, I suspect it will be some time before we have hand-held PCs that are up to the task of good voice recognition.

Until we get to that stage, PDAs that clearly are not PCs will have a secure niche in many of our pockets and purses. After all, they do whatever limited jobs they are designed to do quite well. Those jobs have turned out to be the things people value even when these devices cannot also be used for power word processing, demanding graphical design work, and so on.

Lessons to Be Learned from Portable PCs

That was a fairly fast overview of the progress to date in mobile computing. There are, I think, some very important lessons we can learn from looking more carefully at that history.

Space Constraints Lead to Proprietary Parts

As I previously said, cramming all the power of a desktop PC into a package as small as a laptop is no easy feat. Just look at your desktop PC for a moment. Think about all the space it takes up. Notice, if you will, the mass of cables and connectors it contains. Now consider what you would have to do to put all those pieces into such a tiny box.

The only way to do this (so far) is to use at least some proprietary parts and some industry-standard parts designed especially for mobile PCs. This means that it isn't possible to build your own laptop as easily as building your own desktop PC. You can't just go to the nearest computer superstore and buy a case, plus a bunch of parts to go in it, and end up with a laptop PC.

The biggest implication of this is that the number of each different kind of part that gets built is much smaller for those parts that are used only in a particular model of laptop or other mobile PC. This means that the cost of those items for mobile PCs is likely to be significantly higher than the equivalent items for desktop PCs.

As just one example, memory modules (SIMMs and DIMMs) for desktop PCs are a commodity item; they are made by many different companies, and for the most part are interchangeable. There is only one size for a DIMM or for a SIMM. However, memory modules for laptop computers come in many different shapes and sizes, and they often cost several times as much per megabyte as the standard memory modules used in desktop PCs. (Recently, the higher-end laptops have begun to use standard memory modules, a trend we can only be grateful has begun to take off.)

This is only one example of the main reason why laptop computers cost more (for a given level of performance) than their desktop brethren. It is the direct result of their having to use proprietary designs in order to put all the pieces a particular manufacturer wants to include into such a cramped space.

Space Constraints Limit Upgrade Possibilities

There is another lesson we can learn from the history of mobile PCs. When you build a desktop PC, you put its "guts" into a system unit case. Normally, that case is noticeably larger than it absolutely must be. This is done so it can have unused slots and bays for optional cards and drives, making upgrading that desktop PC pretty easy.

The only upgrades that are possible for a typical mobile computer are those that were contemplated by the manufacturer and allowed for in that particular model's design. Other than functionality that can be added via PC Cards, there are no option slots for additional technologies. No spare drive bays, either. You may be able to swap the floppy disk drive for another hard drive, a CD-ROM drive, or another battery if the manufacturer of your laptop PC chose to give you those options. Some do, but many don't.

The main way mobile PC makers have addressed this limitation is by offering *docking stations*. These are boxes into which you can plug your entire mobile PC. They have some I/O slots and drive bays, plus some additional connector spaces on the rear panel for additional I/O connectors.

There is one big drawback to using a docking station. It takes up enough room and is sufficiently nonportable that you likely will use one only at a desktop location. So really, the docking station is a way to convert your mobile PC into a deskbound PC temporarily.

Docking stations are a little like the expansion chassis that were offered for desktop PCs 15 years ago. Back then, PCs were cramped inside, and you couldn't add much in the way of upgrades without running out of slots or bays. So, if you wanted, you could buy a second system unit without a CPU and hook it to the main system unit. Then you could put any additional plug-in option cards or drives into that expansion chassis.

This strategy soon disappeared from the desktop marketplace for the simple reason that it was expensive and cumbersome. And with the improvements in electronic miniaturization, it became possible to put almost anything one might want within a normal-sized system unit. Something similar might very well happen in the mobile computing field. Only this time, in addition to the seemingly inexorable (and even accelerating) trend of ever-smaller and more capable electronic devices, the driving force will be the rise in popularity of the Universal Serial Bus and the IEEE 1394 bus. When those bus designs are sufficiently well established, I expect to see laptop PCs that have only those types of connectors (plus perhaps PC Card slots) for attaching peripherals, upgrading system memory, and so on. If this comes to pass (as the proponents of those two standards are passionately sure will happen), we might come to a point where upgrading a mobile PC is as easy and inexpensive as upgrading a desktop machine. (Also, by the time that this happens, so much more functionality may come "standard" inside the full-featured laptops that their owners will find little reason to want to upgrade them.)

Space Constraints Mean Greater Control

The flip side to all these limitations in the design of mobile PCs is that the manufacturer has much more control over what they contain and how they work, because they are mostly fixed in their features and use proprietary parts.

Therefore, mobile PCs aren't subject to nearly as many weird problems as desktop PCs. They just don't have the chaotic mix of parts from different manufacturers tucked inside, so the makers can feasibly test almost all the possible variations of each of their models before shipping them to customers. This is simply impossible for a general-purpose desktop PC, which can have any of several thousand different add-on pieces put in it by the customer after it is shipped from the factory.

For this reason, mobile PC makers have been much more successful in getting their products to work well with energy-saving features than the desktop PC makers have. Of course, the fact that battery power is such a precious resource has also impelled the mobile PC makers to work harder toward this goal.

When Enough People Want Something...

As electronic devices continue to shrink, it becomes more feasible for a laptop manufacturer to include more and fancier devices inside their machines. And as the market for these machines expands, the number of folks demanding certain features increases. The inevitable result of this is that "full-featured" laptops are getting more like desktop PCs all the time. One way this happens is simply by including more of the desktop PC items (which now are small enough to fit). Another way is that manufacturers now have enough of a market to justify creating custom parts that implement popular functions that were formerly unavailable in such small form factors or with such low power consumption.

Indeed, soon the price, performance, and functionality distinctions between a "pretty good" laptop and a "pretty good" desktop PC may nearly vanish. We're seeing one example of this trend in the rapidly falling prices and improving size and performance of high-resolution, active-matrix LCD screens. This has led to laptops with screens as good as desktop PCs, and to flat-screen LCD panels for desktops becoming nearly as popular in some quarters as conventional CRT (cathode ray tube) screens.

Power Is Precious on the Road

Speaking of power and how precious it can be leads me right into my next topic: Battery power for PCs on the road. The main reason you have a battery in a mobile PC is so you can compute when you aren't near a wall outlet. Other advantages include being untethered so you can use your PC as you wander around the office, even though you might be close to power outlets. You can also keep your PC going during a brief power outage when it is running on AC power. That last advantage points out something that many people might not realize: Virtually every mobile PC has a built-in uninterruptible power supply or UPS.

That's why batteries are important. It is important to understand how they work and how to help them do their job well so they don't let you down at some inopportune time.

Smart Batteries

Anytime you use battery power for a computer, you must face a serious problem: How do you know when it is time to recharge or replace the battery? When must you stop and save your work, or risk losing it when the battery voltage falls too low to keep the computer running normally?

Laptop computers have long come with a battery gauge applet. The original versions of these programs claimed to report how much battery life remained at all times. How can they do that? And can they really do it accurately?

Typically, these programs depend on a manufacturer's experience with certain batteries of a given type. They also make assumptions about the probable power load that the computer represents, based on which parts of it are powered up. Each second, one of these programs decides what fraction of the total battery life must have been used and reduces its report of remaining battery life accordingly.

This procedure doesn't actually monitor the battery itself, so it is quite possible (especially for an older battery that is nearly worn out) for the battery to run out of juice before the battery gauge thinks it will. Conversely, you might be prompted to shut down your PC unnecessarily because the battery gauge applet thinks your battery is nearly exhausted, when in fact it still has plenty of power to continue for quite a while longer.

Clearly, the right way to go about all this is to put more "smarts" into the battery—build into it some monitoring circuitry that can watch the actual condition of each cell in the battery independently, and then have it report to the computer how it is doing. A side benefit is that such a smart battery not only tells the computer that it needs to be recharged, it also can specify what recharging current should be used and when to stop that recharging. Making batteries and computers that work together in this fashion is precisely what the manufacturers of batteries and laptops have been doing.

(Less worked on so far is a corresponding sort of power-smarts that could also be added to the PC to enable it to reduce power to various parts of the PC, not only when they are not being used, but sometimes when they are, in order to stretch battery life to some user-designated value. For example, if you are doing something that is not "compute-bound"—that is, the time taken to do things doesn't critically depend upon the speed of the CPU, perhaps because mostly you are waiting for data to come off a DVD or CD—the system might save power by reducing the CPU clock frequency.)

Two standards have evolved regarding smart batteries: one called, as you might expect, Smart Battery System, and one called (less obviously) the System Management Bus (SMB). These two have been put together by a consortium of battery manufacturers, Intel, and other interested companies.

The Smart Battery System (SBS) specification is built upon the capabilities of the System Management Bus. That standard, in turn, is built on another standard promulgated by Philips Semiconductors called the I^2C (Inter Integrated Circuit) bus. (Other examples of this bus show up elsewhere in PCs. In Chapter 13, "Seeing the Results: PC Displays," I describe one of those other uses, namely the VESA ACCESS.bus, also known as the Data Display Communcations (DDC) standard.)

You can learn more about these three related standards and their specifications at these Web sites:

```
http://www.SBS-Forum.org/
```

```
http://www.powersmart.com/
```

```
http://www-us.semiconductors.philips.com/  {search on I2C, then look in other
documents}
```

The SMB is simply a specialized application of the I^2C bus. This bus requires two wires (plus ground) and optionally supports two more. It communicates control information at a relatively slow rate (under 1MHz) between different parts of a system. The SMB standard allows multiple "master" devices.

When systems are built according to the SBS specification, they permit the use of multiple types of batteries, including "dumb" batteries and smart batteries with various "chemistries" (for example, NiCad, NiMH, lithium-ion, or the newest lithium-polymer batteries). In all cases, the system is able to interrogate the battery and, if it discovers that the battery is smart, learn many things about it. First, it can learn what type of battery it is. Next, it can learn what charging current is appropriate for it, and what the fully charged voltage will be. And it can find out how long this battery will last under various rates of discharge. Finally, it can also interrogate the charger available for that battery and, depending on which of three defined levels of smarts that charger has, direct it to do the appropriate things to keep the battery charged and the host system informed about the battery's state of charge to a very high degree of accuracy (approaching 1 percent in many circumstances).

With such a smart battery, and with a PC that knows enough to use that battery's smarts, you could interchange different types of batteries freely. Pop in an alkaline-air smart battery today and run your PC until that battery is dead. Put in a lithium-ion smart rechargeable tomorrow and recharge it as necessary.

If you have a PC that has the hardware and software support (system management bus and appropriate additions to the system BIOS), by all means you should use smart batteries. Then you can really believe what that PC's battery gauge tells you.

Extending Your PC's Battery Life

Whatever type of battery your portable PC uses, and no matter how long it lets your computing sessions last between recharges or battery replacements, you probably wouldn't mind if it lasted a little while longer. At the very least, you could save some hassles and money. So, you must learn some steps you can take to extend your battery's life, and also learn when not to take those steps that might compromise your efficiency. Not every power-saving idea that you find touted in some computer magazine makes good sense for the way you use your computer.

Use AC Power Whenever Possible

Use AC power whenever you can. Shouldn't that be obvious? No, it really isn't. Here is a caution I must give you about doing this: Almost every PC that can run on rechargeable battery power includes a battery charger. This is true even when you might think it isn't. If your PC has a battery eliminator or any other way to power it from the AC line instead of from its internal battery, most likely the power supply inside it (or in the box in the middle of the cord or in a cube at the end of the power cord that goes into the wall) is really a battery charger.

Does this make a difference? Yes. First, this means that while you are running on AC power, you are at least trickle-charging your PC's internal battery. Most of these power supply designs will charge a depleted rechargeable battery and then, when your PC is full of charge, they will not shut themselves off completely. They will cut back to supplying a slight trickle of current to keep the battery topped off. This is done because rechargeable batteries lose some of their charge over time just by sitting there. You may think of it as if there were a small load on the battery inside its case. Even if you don't pull any current out of its external terminals, the battery will slowly die on its own.

Most of these power supplies assume that your PC has its battery in place (and that the battery isn't *really* dead—by which I mean that the battery can still accept a charge even if it doesn't currently have much of one in it).

Normal power supplies for PCs convert AC power from the wall into DC power. This involves taking the alternating current (AC), which is simply alternating positive and negative waves of electric power, and turning them into a steady supply of direct current (DC). To do this, however, they must store some electrical energy internally to bridge the times when the wall socket isn't supplying any voltage or current. Those are the times between the waves of positive and negative voltage. Normal power supplies store this energy in capacitors. Because these capacitors enable those supplies to filter out the pulses inherent in AC power and thus provide a steady DC output, they are called *filter capacitors*.

Power supplies for PCs with internal batteries can enable the internal battery to do most of this energy storage task. In effect, they enable the battery to run the PC for short periods of time, 120 times each second. After each one of these intervals, the power supply replaces the charge that was withdrawn from the battery.

> **Warning:** You must have your PC's battery in place (and it must not be dead) if you are going to run your portable PC on AC line power. That is true for almost every PC with a rechargeable battery. It is not true for a mobile PC that doesn't have a charger type of power supply—its AC power supply won't be depending on the battery to help it do its job.

One big benefit you get from the strategy I have just described (and that is used in almost all rechargeable battery–powered PCs) is that when you run this type of PC from the AC power line, you are in effect running it on a UPS. Thus, you are automatically protected against brownouts, surges, spikes, and power failures.

Don't Recharge Inappropriately

Clearly, if you run your PC on battery power for very long, you will have to recharge that battery at some point. Most manufacturers recommend that you discharge the battery all the way and then recharge it fully. They don't approve of partial discharge and recharge cycles.

This is most important if you have a Nicad battery in your PC, because partial discharge and recharge cycles cause the battery to lose capacity through the "memory" effect. It also is a good idea to use a full discharge and recharge cycle even for batteries that are built using one of the other popular chemistries.

Having a spare (and fully charged) battery with you is a good idea if you are using your PC away from AC power. That way, when the first battery is depleted, you can swap batteries and keep on computing. Then, at the next convenient time, you can recharge the depleted battery, making it ready for use when the swapped battery becomes depleted.

I must make another point about appropriate and inappropriate recharging. Every battery chemistry implies a different terminal voltage and a different optimum charging scheme (in terms of how much current to use and how to taper it down to the trickle-charge value as the battery approaches full charge). Because this is so, the designers of PCs that use rechargeable batteries design their power supplies with a knowledge of which kind of rechargeable battery their PC is going to use. The exceptions to this are the newest PCs that are designed to use smart batteries. These PCs often include chargers capable of charging nearly any kind of rechargeable battery, and they listen to the battery first to find out what kind it is and how they can charge it optimally.

Naturally, for this latter approach to work, any battery you use in such a PC must itself be a smart battery. An ordinary battery without those smarts can't tell the PC what kind it is or what its needs are. (And so the charger must fall back to a worst-case assumption and handle that battery in a very conservative and probably nonoptimal manner.)

> **Caution:** If your mobile PC doesn't support smart batteries, don't ever replace its battery with one that uses a different chemistry scheme. Doing that could damage the new battery, the PC's power supply, or both.

Use Power-Saving Settings

The battery in your mobile PC supplies power so your PC can do its job. If your PC can be configured to require less power, the battery will be capable of supplying it with adequate power for a longer time. This fairly obvious insight is behind various strategies that have been implemented in most mobile PCs; you can make the PC use less power whenever you don't really need it to be using the maximum.

In practice, this means that if you aren't currently accessing your PC's hard disk, there is no reason for it to be spinning; this is also true for your CD-ROM drive. Also, if you aren't doing anything with your PC, the display can be turned off. Perhaps the most exotic approach is that you can slow down the CPU clock speed anytime it is waiting for you to press a key or move your mouse. Each of these strategies will reduce the total power consumption of the PC.

However, these savings don't come without some associated costs. For example, it takes a few seconds to get a turned-off hard disk back up to speed. So if it has been shut down to save power, you will have to wait those few seconds before you can access it again.

This whole issue of power saving has much broader implications than just extending the life of a mobile PC's battery, so I will continue this discussion in the next section on the ecologically sensitive PC, which is in this chapter because the mobile PC makers have been leading the rest of the industry in this regard (for good and obvious reasons).

The Ecologically Sensitive PC

From almost the beginning, people realized that doing everything they could to reduce a PC's power consumption was important for portable, battery-powered PCs. It is now becoming clear that the same issue can be important for desktop units as well.

Is This Really Necessary?

When PCs were young and there weren't many of them, the total power consumption of all the PCs in the world was insignificant in the big picture. Now that there are hundreds of millions of PCs worldwide and many of those PCs are being left on all the time—sometimes for some very good reasons, such as being able to respond to incoming messages—the issue of how much power they consume is becoming a rather important one.

Overall, electrical power is one of the major ways in which modern societies use energy. Its usage contributes significantly to pollution problems. So for both economic and environmental reasons, it would be nice if we could drastically curtail the use of electrical power by our PCs.

Still, you have a PC because it enables you to accomplish some things you couldn't do without it. Therefore, you are likely to use only those energy-saving strategies that don't get in your way. When saving energy and doing useful things conflict, you have to compromise based on your personal evaluation of the trade-offs.

PC Power Management Overview

You can save power consumption by your PC in two ways: Limit when you have it turned on, and cut down on the power it uses while it is turned on.

The Ultimate Power-Saving Method

The ultimate way to save on the energy used by your PC is to turn it off. That, of course, defeats the purpose for which you got your PC. But you don't need to keep it on when you aren't using it.

There has been a debate in this industry for a long time on just this point. Some folks have pointed out that hard disks are stressed most when they are started. Likewise, most of the electronics in a PC are stressed more by changing temperatures than by a constant temperature. So perhaps you are shortening the overall life of your PC by turning it off when you aren't using it. On the other hand, your PC clearly will last longer if it is almost always shut off, and it almost certainly will use less total energy as well.

Peter's Principle: When to Turn Off Your PC

The real question is not "Should you turn off your PC when you aren't using it?" but "For how long do you have to anticipate that you won't be using your PC before it is clearly better to turn it off rather than leave it on for your next use?"

My personal take on the matter is that anytime you anticipate using your PC again within less than about eight hours, it probably makes more sense to leave it on. If you are going to go away from it for longer than that, it's probably a good idea to turn it off.

You should ask yourself another question before deciding: What hardware and tools are running on your PC that might help minimize its power consumption? For example, the monitor frequently uses more energy than all the other parts of the PC put together (other than a laser printer). So, if you have arranged to have the monitor shut itself off or turn itself down to some very low level of energy usage whenever you aren't actively using the PC, you can justify leaving the system turned on more of the time. The Microsoft- and Intel-sponsored OnNow Initiative and the so-called "Instantly Available" PCs it proposes to create will merely be the endpoint of this process—and those PCs you truly will never need to turn off (except if and when you or someone else is going to open them up and work on them).

Another issue to consider is whether your PC is running on a UPS. If it isn't, spikes and surges on the power line can damage it more easily (although you should have a good surge protector in place, in any event). Brownouts or power failures of even a short duration can disrupt your PC more than a shutting down and restarting. If I were not using a UPS or at least a good surge protector, I'd turn off my PC rather more often.

Saving Power While Your PC Is On

I just mentioned one way you can save power without turning off your PC totally: Shut off the monitor when it isn't being used. You can do this manually, but it is even more effective if you arrange to have your PC do it automatically. You can have it do several other things automatically to save power, as well.

What the Hardware Must Do

To power down different parts of your PC selectively and under software control, the parts in question must be able to interact appropriately with that controlling software. Naturally, you can never completely turn off power to a gadget that must be able to respond to a software signal asking it to turn on, but you can let it power down everything but the tiny part that listens for that wakeup signal.

A common example in most homes is a television set that can be turned on using a remote control. Some part of the TV set must be listening for the infrared signals from the remote control in order to respond to them.

Modern Energy Star monitors can be commanded to go into any of several states of reduced power, from nearly all the way off (except for that tiny monitoring part) up to almost completely on but with the screen image blanked. The reason for having several power levels to which the monitor may be powered down is that it takes different amounts of time to recover from each. The lower the power, the longer it will take to get back into full operation.

The hard disk can be turned off when it isn't needed, and modems can be powered down (with just enough circuitry left powered that they can come back to full operation when they detect an incoming call). Almost all printers now have power-saving modes that drop their consumption to nearly nothing until you issue a print command. Certainly, if you printer doesn't support power-saving, it should be turned off when it's not needed.

Perhaps the most interesting of the various power-saving features is that the clock speed of the CPU may be reduced. All modern PC processor chips (and many of the other chips used in a PC) are made using the complementary metal-oxide semiconductor (CMOS). One important fact about a CMOS circuit is that it uses almost no power to sit in one state. Every time you change the state of a portion of the circuitry, however, some small chunk of electric charge will make its way through the circuit from the power lead to the ground lead. The size of the chunks of charge that fall through each time are fixed. So the average rate at which charge flows, which is to say the average current through these devices, is directly proportional to the number of state changes that are taking place within them during each second.

The power dissipated as heat in the chip is simply the average current through it multiplied by the voltage on the power lead attached to the chip. Therefore, power is also directly proportional to the number of state changes per second.

One thing CPU manufacturers have done and continue to do is work to lower the voltage needed to power their chips. Originally, all chips used 5 volts (except for a few that used 12 volts). Now, most of the key circuits are designed to work at 3.3 volts, or 2 volts, or in some cases as little as 1.8 volts. We very likely will see that number fall yet further as the manufacturers learn even better ways to make their products work with minuscule power.

The lower the voltage applied to the chip, all other things being equal, the lower its power dissipation. But a given chip must have some minimum voltage in order to operate. There may or may not be a minimum frequency at which it must be "clocked" in order to work correctly.

Some CPU chips can have their clocks slowed down arbitrarily. They can't go any faster than the rated maximum speed without risking miscomputing, but they can going as slowly as you like without any bad consequences. As you reduce the clock frequency, you also reduce the power the CPU chips draw from the battery or other power source.

Other CPU chips have some minimum speed they must go. They are like a man riding a bicycle. Depending on the man's skill, it is possible to ride quite slowly, but he probably can't actually stop the forward motion of the bicycle completely without having it fall over (assuming he doesn't put his foot on the ground). The reasons are different, but many CPU chips cannot run at less than some minimum speed without forgetting what they are doing.

Furthermore, the memory in our PCs is mostly DRAM, which, I remind you, stands for dynamic random access memory. They must be refreshed at least a few thousand times per second in order not to forget the information they are holding.

However, it is often possible to reduce the clock speed of the CPU from several hundred million cycles per second to perhaps one million. Doing so will reduce the power requirements of the CPU chip, the memory chips, and all the other CMOS chips that are running at the same frequency by the ratio of the normal operating clock speed to the slowed-down clock speed.

Reducing the clock speed of the CPU can save you up to 99 percent of the energy drain on those chips when you aren't actually using them. Really sophisticated energy-saving circuits can apply this strategy not only when you walk away from your PC, but anytime that it is waiting for you to do something.

So, if you are doing some word processing, each time you type a key, the PC must do something with that. If it finishes its work before you press the next key, it can slow down its clock until you press the next key. In effect, you make the PC run just fast enough that it is always working, but never faster than necessary. This clever trick works with virtually no downside to it. The reason is that you can slow down or speed up the clock any amount you like in almost no time, and the circuitry needed to do this is minimal.

On the other hand, powering down the monitor or stopping the hard drive from spinning means that when you are ready to use them once more, you have to wait up to several seconds for them to recover from their rest and get back up to speed. So, you really don't want to do that every time you aren't using them for just a few seconds or a few minutes. Only when you really pause in your use of the PC for many minutes are you likely to have the screen image disappear. The hard disk may stop turning if you don't access any files on it for many minutes. If it does, you may experience an annoying delay when you next want to save a file, load a new program, and so on.

These are some of the possible ways the hardware can reduce the average power it consumes while still enabling you to compute at more-or-less full speed whenever you want. If your PC can take advantage of all these features, you might be able to leave it on almost all the time with very little energy wasted. However, the hardware cannot do all of this by itself.

What Software Must Do

To make the hardware pieces turn off or on, slow down, or whatever else at just the right times, some program must tell them what to do and when. The programs that do this in a modern PC are a part of the motherboard BIOS that is dedicated to this purpose. These programs can only activate or deactivate the hardware; they don't know when you want those strategies to be applied, so you need some way to tell these programs what you want.

You can do this in two ways. One is through some entries in the motherboard BIOS setup program. (Normally, you access this program with some special keystroke at a prescribed point in the bootup process.) Here, for example, you might be able to specify whether you want the hard disk to stop spinning when it hasn't been accessed for the length of time you specify. (Usually, you won't be able to enter just any time you like, but rather you must pick from among several fixed options.)

Another level at which your PC may be programmed, or configured, for more-or-less power savings is through an operating system applet. Thus, the operating system might monitor the programs you are running and decide, which of the energy-saving options it should invoke. Again, you can tell it (by making some choices in a setup dialog box) how you want it to do that job.

APM, ACPI, and OnNow

Microsoft and Intel are pushing very hard to get PC makers to standardize their methods for power management. The first big push was called APM, which stands for Advanced Power Management.

APM defines four power management states for any controlled device (PC or otherwise): Ready, Stand-by, Suspended, and Off. Each of these represents an increasingly lower state of power consumption, and probably an increasingly longer time to return to the Ready state.

Most PCs today support APM, as do most monitors and many other devices. The APM approach, however, has not proven to be sufficiently flexible or powerful to meet the full need. Mainly, this is because APM focuses on control of the system board functions and a fairly crude level of control of peripheral devices. More fine-grained control, and control that permits intelligence from the motherboard to take action independent of the CPU, are two desirable additions that APM simply cannot support.

With the introduction of Windows 98, Microsoft (and Intel) have shifted the focus to a newer, better standard called Advanced Configuration and Power Interface (ACPI). This new standard will require smarter BIOS programs as well as ACPI-enabled peripherals. It takes time to create these things and then for them to spread throughout the installed base of computers. So, despite the very considerable promise of ACPI, at this time it is a technology to watch, and not yet one you will want to insist on using.

When the OnNow and Instantly Available PC initiatives have run their course, we can look forward to having PCs that all support ACPI fully. Thus, they'll be able to save the maximum amount of energy and yet be ever ready to spring into action to do our bidding, and to do so with almost no perceptible delay. You can learn more about ACPI, OnNow, and the Instantly Available PC at these Web sites:

http://www.teleport.com/~acpi/

http://www.microsoft.com/hwdev/onnow.htm

http://www.microsoft.com/hwdev/pc99.htm

A Recommendation Regarding "Green PCs" at This Time

I have mentioned several times that there can be a cost to you when you use energy-saving strategies. I mentioned a few of these costs, such as the delay you will experience each time you access some file on the hard disk after a long period of not using the disk, if you have programmed your PC to turn off the disk drive when it isn't being used.

One of the more serious problems may happen if you have your PC turned on and connected to a phone line or network. You may be running some program that monitors the phone line or the network for incoming messages. You expect that whenever a message arrives, the PC will snatch it and do something with it. If your PC has powered itself down too far, however, it might not be able to come back to full operation in time to catch the beginning of the message. If so, the cost of your power-saving strategy defeats the purpose of leaving your PC on in the first place. You might as well have saved even more energy by simply turning your PC off.

To be sure you won't get stung by a scenario such as this, you might have to run some tests. Configure your machine for power savings, and then check to be sure it can respond in time to all the important stimuli you expect it to receive. If it works flawlessly, congratulations are in order; you configured it appropriately. (You might be able to save even more power by using some more aggressive settings in the power savings setup. If you try reconfiguring, repeat all your tests to be sure.)

Most of what I have said to this point is "a counsel of perfection." That is, it really only applies if everything works exactly as it is supposed to work. Unfortunately, not all PCs work perfectly all the time.

So if yours is a desktop PC, you may find that you must forego many of the potential power savings just because if you don't, your PC will crash even more often than it normally does. The crashes to be concerned about are those that happen just as the PC is attempting to recover from some power-reduced state. If it locks up then, try turning off one or more of the energy-saving strategies and see whether that keeps it from crashing.

Laptops are likely to be better at using power-saving strategies without causing problems—mainly because their makers have a lot more control over the total hardware and software configuration. You simply cannot customize them nearly as freely as you can a desktop unit.

So for now, I suggest that you experiment with energy-saving strategies, but only if you are willing to test each one to see whether it works without any undue problems on your PC with your added hardware and software. Don't be surprised if you find you can't use all the energy-saving features you might like to use.

Eventually, the industry will get this all figured out and we will be able to use all those features freely. Energy-saving strategies will be a good thing for us as PC users, as citizens in a society that is increasingly burdened by pollution, and, of course, as payers of the electric bill.

Mobile PCs at Home and in the Office

Finally, before leaving the topic of mobile PCs, I must mention a new trend: buying a laptop PC that is so powerful that you end up using it on your desktop. It becomes your only PC, but because it is a portable battery-powered one, you can use it anywhere.

What to Look for in a Multipurpose PC

The most important thing is to be sure the portable you get is powerful enough to do the computing you want to do at your desk. For a long time, that would have meant buying an outlandishly expensive portable. But nowadays you can get virtually the same power in your portable as you can in a similarly priced desktop unit. You will have to pay a premium for the portability, but not very much. The main thing you will lose is the flexibility that goes with an easily reconfigured desktop unit.

The next most important thing to do, in my opinion, is to get a good keyboard for use on your desktop. You should also get a good mouse, a graphics tablet, or a larger trackball. You can get more than one of each if you want to use your PC on several desktops, or get ones that you are willing to pack up and carry with you when you travel. Whenever you are in any location for more than a brief time, take the time to attach the external keyboard and mouse or whatever. Laptop PCs keyboards are sometimes okay, but I find a full-size, ergonomic keyboard far preferable for any extended use. (I have yet to find a laptop whose built-in pointing device satisfied me. So far, I think of them as necessary evils to use when you can't attach a mouse or the like.)

I find that USB connectivity is wonderful for this purpose. In Figure 22.6, you see the example laptop connected to a Microsoft USB-enabled keyboard, a Microsoft USB-enabled mouse, and a Microsoft Sound System—all via an inexpensive four-port USB hub. Only one cable attaches to the laptop to support all this functionality. (The sound system does require a separate power connection to an AC line; all the rest can work off the power available across the USB bus. Of course, if you plan to work for a long time, plugging in the laptop power supply would also be a very good idea.)

Microsoft Digital   Dell Inspiron 7000   Micro-Connectors
Sound System 80   UH-144 USB hub

FIGURE 22.6

With USB accessories, connecting an external keyboard, a mouse, and even a high-quality sound system to a laptop computer can be delightfully easy.

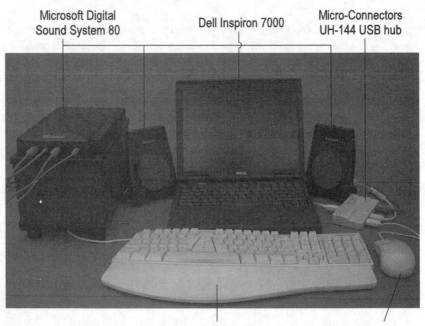

Microsoft Natural Keyboard   Microsoft USB
with USB adapter   Intellimouse

I used to have to say also that you should have a separate, high-quality monitor for each desktop on which you use your laptop. But now that high-resolution active-matrix LCD screens have become commonplace and affordable, they are included in most of the better laptops. Therefore, I can now drop that recommendation, but only for folks who have one of the newer laptops with such a "desktop-quality" screen. If yours doesn't have one, you may also wish to add a quality monitor to your list of desired accessories at each location where you plan to spend much time computing.

Docking Stations Add Back Lost Flexibility

A docking station allows you to attach your external monitor and keyboard to it permanently. You can also attach your office network cable, a phone line, a printer, and whatever other peripheral gadgets you might want to use when your PC is docked.

You still have a portable PC. Just slide it out of the dock whenever you want to use it on the go. When you slide it back in, once more you have a fully supported desktop PC system with all the right peripheral devices. For this strategy to work well, the PC must know whether it is docked, and in each case it must do the right thing. In particular, it must load the correct device drivers to support the peripherals that are attached to it and not act as if they are still attached later when you undock your PC.

PC operating systems are not yet fully up to this task, but they are getting there. Each new generation is a little better at the job. Still, for now, you will likely want to power down your PC each time you are ready to dock it or undock it—no matter what your PC's user manual might say about its capability to safely dock with the power on.

What I have just described is how a docking station can add convenience to a portable PC at an office or home desk. What it also can do is give you back the flexibility you lost when you opted for a portable instead of a desktop unit. This is because a good docking station will typically have some I/O slots (at least ISA, and maybe PCI as well) and some drive bays, plus a power supply, an array of port connectors, and so on. This means that when your portable is docked, it can have more things added to its basic hardware configuration than are permissible in its ready-to-travel state. Of course, if you use this flexibility, you are on your own. In the process, be sure you don't make your nicely stable laptop into one of the all-too-typical, fragile desktop units that will crash if you look at it cross-eyed. One way to deal with this problem is to configure your PC so it doesn't use nearly as many of the energy-saving strategies if it is running on line power as it does when it is running solely on battery power.

Summary

Mobile PCs are different from other PCs intended for desktop or file server use. Mainly, the mobile PCs have been carefully designed to be the absolute minimum size and weight possible for their feature set. This means they generally are less flexible about accepting upgrades than other PCs and often are more stable in their operation as a result.

Mobile PCs use batteries. Battery technology is complex and constantly improving. If you can get a PC that accepts standard size batteries or, even better, smart batteries (and your PC knows how to use those smarts), you will be much happier with them than with a normal, old-fashioned battery.

Whatever battery strategy you use, reducing your PC's power needs helps extend that battery's life. Modern mobile PCs are pretty good at doing this in several ways. Many of those same strategies can be applied to desktop PCs, but for now you might want to pass on most of them because they also often bring along some additional instability.

Mobile PCs are so good now that, with a docking station and an external keyboard, mouse, and monitor, they can serve very well as a desktop PC replacement. No longer is a mobile PC useful only when you are on the road.

Even smaller PCs and PDAs have their place in our computing world. As the technology improves, they may come to assume ever larger roles in our lives. But for now, nothing smaller than a laptop is likely to serve all the uses we have for our PCs.

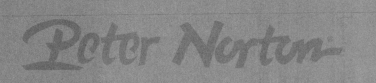
Peter Norton

PART VII

The Connected PC

The PC Reaches Out, Part One: Modems and More

The previous chapters talked about an isolated PC. Some of the PCs I have discussed are loaded with features, and they might even have some of the necessary hardware to become connected with other computers, but the PC didn't have to be connected to anything outside itself. This part of the book (Chapters 23, 24, and 25) is all about how a connected PC differs from an isolated one.

In this chapter, we will look at connecting PCs to other computers with simple direct connections, as terminals to large computer systems, with standard telephone modems, and across high-speed communications systems.

Reaching Out, and *Really* Reaching Out

Some PCs are connected only slightly. Others reach out a little bit, and still others reach way out—perhaps all the way across the globe—and connect to many other computers. To make this clear, we can organize them into four realms of connectedness. But before I talk about those four realms, I want to describe the smallest ways in which a PC can reach out.

A Really Short Stretch

The shortest links from a PC are those it has to its own peripherals. But in one view, all the attached peripheral devices are really just parts of the PC itself. With modern PCs, the keyboard and screen are clearly essential parts of the PC, yet they are in separate housings and are connected to the system unit in much the same manner as many of the other peripheral devices, such as a printer, an external disk drive, a scanner, or an external modem.

So, the shortest linkages considered in this chapter are the ones that take a PC from an essentially isolated state into an interconnected state (connected to at least one other general-purpose computer). The minimal form of such a connection is two PCs directly linked to one another (and to no other computers) by a cable or infrared light beam. This is probably done most often when a laptop computer is linked to a desktop computer. This is frequently done to enable easy transfers of files from one machine to the other, or to enable the laptop computer to print a document on a printer attached to the desktop machine.

The most common method used for this type of link is a cable that connects a serial or parallel port on one of the computers to a similar port on the other computer. A relatively new method involves connecting two PCs via their USB ports. You can use several different software programs with this simple type of hardware connection. Data transfer rates vary across connection types and software programs from a general maximum of 115 kilobits per second (Kbps) for a serial connection to as much as 12 million bits per second (Mbps) for a USB connection.

Starting with version 5.02, DOS has included two programs designed for use in exactly this situation. Running INTERSRV.EXE turns one of the two computers into a file and printer server. Running INTERLNK.EXE on the other computer enables it to access those services across the link between the two. Windows 95 and Windows 98 have a Direct Cable Connection facility that does much the same thing.

Before either of those programs was developed, several commercial programs that linked PCs for file transfers and printer sharing were available. These programs have been continuously improved and are still popular. Laplink is probably the most popular. (These third-party programs have been enhanced and are now capable of general remote control operation of a PC. I will tell you more about such usage for them under "Remote Control of a PC" in Chapter 24, "The PC Reaches Out, Part Two: Through the NIC Node.")

The Windows Direct Cable Connection facility and the original versions of Laplink and its competitors use a cable connected between a serial port on one PC and a serial port on the other PC, or linking parallel ports on each machine. These connection methods allow data transfers at rates up to a few hundred Kbps for a standard port and up to 1,000Kbps for the new Enhanced Capability Port (ECP) used on most newer PCs.

But now you have a new and better way to interconnect two PCs. The latest version of Laplink, as well as products from Belkin and other vendors, enable you to link PCs over a Universal Serial Bus (USB) cable. This works only if you are running Windows 95B (which is also sometimes called Windows 95, OSR2) or Windows 98, because they are the only versions of Windows that support USB connectivity. Windows 95, OSR2 required that you download and install a service pack to add the necessary drivers to support USB. The advantage to using USB for the inter-PC connection is that it can carry data at least 10 times faster than is possible with even the fastest type of PC parallel port, which is, in turn, considerably faster than the fastest of the standard PC serial ports. It is possible to connect PCs in a way that allows even faster data transfer, but that requires specialized networking hardware. I'll discuss such *local area networks* (LANs) later in this chapter, and in more detail in the next chapter.

Four Realms of PC Connectivity

The first realm of connectivity covers those PCs that are each wired directly to a single central computer, which might be a mainframe or a minicomputer. When they are communicating with that central computer, these PCs are acting essentially like old-fashioned "dumb" terminals (by which I mean just a screen, keyboard, and perhaps a pointing device such as a mouse—no CPU and no local data storage capability). Later in this chapter, in the section "Direct Wire Connections," I'll explain why it often makes more sense to use a PC for this task than to use the dumb terminal that once was so common.

The second realm of connectivity occurs when several autonomous PCs in the same general area are connected to one another (and perhaps also to one or more central computers). This is a LAN and is the most common way that PCs are connected in businesses (and some homes) today.

The third realm is when several LANs are linked together into a *wide area network* (WAN). This enables all the computers in each LAN to communicate over an inter-LAN link to any of the other computers in any of the other connected LANs. This scheme gets around the fact that LAN interconnection technologies are limited in the distances that they can cover between computers. Many large corporations have set up WANs to connect their far-flung offices.

Finally, we have the realm that includes PCs that are capable of establishing connections with huge numbers of remote computers of all types and sizes. As more and more PCs are becoming connected to the Internet, this is fast becoming the most common category of connected PC.

Permanent and Transient Connections

Some PCs are permanently connected to one or more other computers. But many PCs connect to those other computers only when they need to.

Direct Wire Connections

PCs that are permanently connected to one central host computer often use a simple direct cable from the PC's serial port to a terminal server on the central computer. This is the same type of connection used by dumb terminals. Because the PC is much more than just a keyboard and screen (plus perhaps a pointing device), it can do more than just act as a terminal, however. When it is acting as a terminal, we say that it is in a *host session*. The rest of the time it acts just as if it were an isolated PC. (Some IBM minicomputers and mainframes use the TwinAx or 5250-style connection system, and others use the 3270-style Coax system. Using a PC as a terminal on either requires installation of a specialized adapter card.)

While it is in a host session, such a PC can log the session to its local hard disk. This can serve as an audit trail, or it could be reviewed at a time the host computer was unavailable in order to analyze aspects of a previous session. Furthermore, this ability can be particularly useful in debugging problems on the host or connection system. When it's not in a host session, the PC can do anything any other standalone PC can do. Therefore, if a host connection is needed for only a portion of the day, the rest of the time the PC can be used to do useful work without having to rely on the host.

PCs that are connected to several other autonomous computers via a local area network can use any of several different kinds of permanent connection methods. Some names you might have heard of for this type of connection include Ethernet, Token Ring, and Arcnet. These same connections can be used to access distant LANs across a WAN, if the LAN to which this PC is connected has a WAN connectivity as well. I will describe all this technology in Chapter 25.

Transient Wired Links

Although having your PC permanently connected to other computers can be very convenient, sometimes it just doesn't make sense. Portable computers are an obvious example. If you are traveling, your portable computer doesn't need to be constantly linked to the office LAN or to the Internet. The freedom that comes with unhooking the wire can be a very valuable one. It's possible now to keep connected without using a wire link, but that isn't yet very common for portable PC users. Even those who have these links don't use them all the time, for reasons of cost if nothing else. Recent innovations in wireless networking, especially for the small office/home office (SOHO) environment, may cause this situation to change in the near future. But until the competing standards groups settle their differences, not much commercial activity is likely to occur.

Permanent interconnection is also not the best approach when computers in a home or office are remote from the computers to which they only sometimes must connect. You can save a lot of money by having that computer connected only when the link is being used.

Even if your PC is permanently connected to some other computers, there might be some types of distant connection that you occasionally want, but that needn't be available to you except when you need them. A transient link often makes sense in this situation, mainly to save money and facilitate sharing expensive resources.

The most common method of transient connection is to use a modem and a dial-up telephone line. Your PC causes the modem to dial a distant computer, and when the connection is established, you can exchange information with that distant computer just as if your PC were wired directly to it. In addition to using a traditional modem, there are digital options. ISDN is one such option, which is completely digital and allows higher connection speeds. ISDN is like regular modem calls over standard telephone lines in almost every other regard.

Wireless Links

You don't need to have a cable to link PCs to other computers. The two most common technologies for this purpose are radio links and optical links. The *radio links* are mostly used for transient connections with distant computers. These links use a modem plus a radio transceiver (possibly a cellular telephone) just as some other PCs use a modem and a normal, wire-based telephone connection. In most respects, these links function just the same as a modem-to-phone-line link.

Until very recently, most wireless connectivity solutions were targeted at corporate users. That meant that they were focused on the highest possible speed for data transfer. In fact, they were often able to transfer data as fast as over a wired link (usually around 10Mbps). Now, however, the focus for most wireless connectivity solution providers has shifted to the consumer and the creation of home LANs. These new wireless links operate typically at about 1Mbps. This is only about one-tenth of the speed of a slow office network (and one one-hundredth the speed of many, faster office networks), but it is comparable to the speed of a USB link, and the industry believes that it will suffice for most home and consumer uses. (One of the more inventive methods of creating a home network uses the house electrical wiring for its data connection.)

Optical links are most often achieved using infrared light. Some LANs use this medium of data transmission, and the Infra-red Data Association (IrDA) standard includes a high-speed protocol for just this use. A more common example is to link a portable computer to a desktop machine via their IrDA ports. This can be done either to transfer some files or to let the portable computer use a printer that is attached to the desktop machine. Some printers have their own IrDA ports built in. They can be used by a portable PC directly, without needing any help from a desktop PC. The printer simply becomes one of the portable computer's peripheral devices, albeit one that is only sometimes connected to it.

Modems and More

I've just told you that modems are commonly used to make transient connections between PCs and other computers. You probably already knew that. Now let's look into exactly what modems are and how they work.

Reaching Out and "Byte-ing" Someone

Motorola used the phrase "Reach out and byte someone" in its advertisements for modems. I've always rather enjoyed this clever play on the slogan used by the telephone company to promote voice calls: "Reach out and touch someone," because modems are how we send bytes of digital data over a normal voice-grade telephone line.

A modem is an interface device. It connects on one side to your PC and on the other side to a telephone line (or in some cases, to any one of a number of other types of connection systems).

The name modem stands for MOdulator/DEModulator (once capitalized in the acronym MODEM but now more commonly written simply as modem) because a modem has both a modulator and a demodulator built into it. What, you ask, are they? A good question. And why are they needed? That's another good question.

"Yodeling" PCs

Most PCs sold today include a modem, either built-in or attached to it. When you use the modem to connect your PC over the phone line to a distant computer, you are likely to hear many strange sounds coming from the modem's speaker. You might have wondered what they are and why you need them.

Built-in modems most often are built on cards that plug into the now-antiquated ISA bus, and external modems used to be made to connect to a PC's serial port. For a brief period, some external modems were introduced that could connect to a PC's parallel port as a means of achieving higher speed.

Laptop owners have had the option of using a PC card (formerly called PCMCIA card) modem. Each of these options was the best choice for some users, but now we have an even better one—and it is one that will work well for almost every PC user.

I am speaking of the new USB modems. These are external modems that plug into a Universal Serial Bus port. You have to have a fairly modern PC to have this feature, and you must be running an operating system that supports it (which at this point means Windows 95 OSR2 with the appropriate service pack or Windows 98), but if you meet those requirements, this is the clearly best option when selecting a new modem.

One way a USB modem excels is that the USB port is able to support data transfers at speeds far greater than anything a serial port can manage. (This doesn't speed the modem's connection to the outside world; it just ensures that there isn't a bottleneck between the modem and the PC.) Another advantage is that you can freely plug or unplug any USB device at almost any time without upsetting the PC at all. And you don't have to worry about IRQ or I/O port address conflicts. The plug-and-play operating system takes care of all that for you. Last, but not least, a USB modem frees a slot in your PC—and enables you to use a PC without any ISA slots, which is certainly where PC manufacturers are heading. (See Chapter 16, "Faster Ways to Get Information into and out of Your PC," for more on the USB bus.)

The sound you hear when your modem begins a remote connection session is essentially your modem "talking" to another modem at the other end of the phone line. The different strange tones normally go on for several seconds, and then the modem shuts up. Actually, the modems continue making their strange sounds. You just don't hear them because normally the communication software application that operates the modem tells it to turn on its loudspeaker until the two modems have successfully "negotiated" a connection, and then to shut off its speaker for the duration of the call.

This enables you to hear your modem trying to connect—and if you understand what you are hearing you can tell how well it is doing. If you hear a person talking at the other end, you know to disconnect your PC because you haven't reached a modem. After the connection is established properly, by shutting off its speaker, the modem saves you from having to listen to all that screeching the rest of the time your PC is connected.

Why Modems Are Needed

The standard telephone network was designed for one purpose (carrying human voices in conversation) and is now being used by many of us for a totally different purpose (carrying lots of digital data back and forth). The characteristics of the two types of signals are very different. The telephone network functions acceptably for human voices; it simply cannot carry digital data as such.

> **Note:** There are some exceptions to that last statement. I'll cover them in the "Keeping It Purely Digital" section later in this chapter. For now, let's focus on the normal kind of telephone line—called a Plain Old Telephone Service (POTS) line, for which this statement is true.

Why can't ordinary phone lines carry digital data directly? Human voices are sounds that cover a range of frequencies from roughly 30Hz up to about 10KHz. That is, we make vibrations in the air that fluctuate no more than 10,000 times per second and no less than around 30 times per second. Any sounds outside that range are inaudible to most of us. We don't even need to hear all those frequencies in order to understand what someone else is saying.

Therefore, to save money and for other technical reasons, the phone companies have limited the bandwidth of their normal voice-grade lines to a maximum of about 3KHz and a minimum of around 100Hz. This lets enough of the sounds we make get through for most normal conversational purposes.

You may be wondering if the fact that a human voice produces an analog (that is, a continuously variable) pressure wave as opposed to a digital signal is somehow important here. It is not. The whole issue, from the point of view of signaling theory, is how rapidly the signal on the channel may be varied. That depends on the bandwidth. As I will explain in a moment, modems create tones (including sometimes very nonmelodious tones) to represent the digital bits you actually want to transmit.

Digital data is sent over a phone line in a serial manner. That is, the data is sent one bit at a time. You can have either synchronous or asynchronous connections. A synchronous connection just pumps out the bits of each byte one after another, all in synch with some clock. An asynchronous connection sends out all the bits for 1 byte, plus some start and stop bits to tell the receiving computer where the data begins and ends (and perhaps a parity bit to verify its accuracy), and then waits a little while before sending out the next byte. There is no necessary connection between the clocks at the two ends of the link.

Technical Note: Normally, in PC applications, modems operate asynchronously. The main exception to that is if you are running an error-correcting protocol such as V.42; then the modems will switch to a synchronous data transfer mode. This change is invisible to the user, but it results in some improvement in data throughput (as well as a lot more assurance, thanks to the error-correcting aspects of the protocol, that your data got across the link okay).

The use of error correction requires that the modems on both ends of a connection support the same protocol (V.42). This compatibility is becoming more common as computer users and connection services upgrade to newer modems.

The limit on the frequencies at the low end is no problem for people talking, but it is as much of a problem as the limit on the high end for the transmission of digital data. To see this, consider a digital message that consists of 1 million 0 bits followed by a 1 bit, then another million 0 bits, then a million 1 bits. If this message were converted into voltages in the synchronous serial manner, it would be a constant voltage almost all the time. This long time between voltage alternations constitutes a very low frequency signal and is equivalent to silence. Nothing would be happening on the link, and the receiving end wouldn't know whether it was still connected or not.

One solution to this problem is simple enough: Use the data values to modulate a tone signal. The tone for a 0 bit is different from the tone for a 1 bit, but at all times there is some tone being sounded. That way, the signal is always there for the receiver to hear.

This is how early modems worked. But this strategy doesn't allow pushing the maximum number of bits over the phone line in each second. Essentially, it uses only a few of the many frequencies the phone line is capable of carrying. By using more of those frequencies simultaneously, we can send many more bits each second—just as modern, high-speed modems do today.

In order to understand just how a modern modem does this trick, it's necessary to distinguish between two terms that are commonly confused: *bits-per-second* (bps) and *baud*.

What's a Baud?

In honor of Emile Baudot, a nineteenth-century French telegrapher who invented an early transmission code, we use the term *baud* as the unit of speed in data communications—or misuse it, as is more often the case, in writings and conversation about PC communications.

Technically, 1 baud means 1 symbol per second. (Think of one change in the state of the transmission medium per second.) A symbol can represent any number of bits—the maximum number for a particular connection is set by the characteristics of the transmission medium and of the transmitting and receiving devices. At very low data rates, each symbol is normally used to represent a single bit.

In a slow modem (carrying data at 300bps or less), each bit is represented by two tones, one for a 0 and the other for a 1. At higher data rates, more tones are used. If you used 512 tones, you could encode 9 bits simultaneously. (In fact, instead of using 512 discrete frequencies, modern modems use a combination of fewer individual frequencies but delay some of those signals by a variable fraction of a cycle (phase modulates them) to convey more information.

If you are unclear about why 512 tones imply that you can carry 9 bits by a single one of those tones (2 to the 9th power is 512), I invite you to go back to Chapter 3, 'Understanding Bits, Nybbles, and Bytes." There you will find the relationship spelled out in great detail.

A 300-baud modem uses 1 symbol per bit, so the baud rate and the bits per second are both 300. At higher data rates, the common practice is to send signals that stand for one of a larger set of possibilities. That means that each symbol carries several bits of information. If there are 512 possible symbols (signal states), then each one carries 9 bits of information. This is what is done in a V.34 (28.8Kbps maximum data rate) modem when it is operating at its maximum data rate. In this case, the actual baud number is only one-ninth of the number of bits per second. Thus, a 28.8Kbps modem is actually just a 3.2 kilobaud modem. But you'll never see that latter value in an advertisement for these products—it just doesn't sound impressive enough!

When Modems Talk to Each Other and to Their PCs at Different Rates

Until very recently, all PC modems used a serial port. (The few parallel port modems are the only exception. Even the USB modems, which don't plug into a serial port, are using a version of serial data transmission—as the full name for USB, Universal Serial Bus, suggests.)

The serial port hardware does two necessary things. First, it converts the data from parallel bytes into a stream of single bits. It also adds some very necessary start, stop, and parity bits. The modem converts these bits into tones (called "modulating the carrier with data") and sends them over the phone line.

At the other end there must be a similar modem that will convert the tones back into digital bit levels (called "demodulating the data"), and the serial port will convert those bit streams back into parallel bytes. (Refer to Chapter 15, "Understanding Standard PC Input and Output," for a detailed discussion of how serial ports work. Refer to Chapter 16 for the details on USB.)

Note: Internal modems are built on plug-in cards you put into a slot inside your PC's system unit, usually on the ISA bus. They include all the hardware for a serial port on the plug-in card. External modems attach to a serial port either on your PC's motherboard or on some other plug-in card. Internal modems draw their operating power from the PC's power supply. External modems use a separate power supply.

There are some important implications in these differences. If you put an internal modem into a PC, you must be sure that its serial port doesn't conflict with one that is already in the machine. Conversely, if you want to use an external modem, you must be sure your PC has a serial port available for it, and it must be one that will work fast enough to support the modem. A serial port that supports data rates of 57.6Kbps or greater is preferred for 28.8Kbps modems, and a minimum of 115Kbps is required for 56Kbps modems.

Why must the serial port be able to work more than twice as fast as the modem? There are several reasons. First and often, the controlling fact is that data compression is often used in modem protocols. That means that more bytes of data are sent to the modem than it sends out to the receiving modem at the other end; and when receiving data, the decompression the modem means it must be able to send more bytes to the PC than came across the telephone line. Second, there is some operational overhead because the PC must sometimes send commands to the modem. These are additional bytes that must flow over the PC-to-modem link that don't also have to travel over the telephone line.

The most important point in all this is that the modem-to-PC link must not be the bottleneck. If ever the modem is frustrated in sending its data to the PC, some of the incoming data will be lost. This is not acceptable, so we routinely set the serial port speed to at least twice the modem's maximum data rate over the telephone line—and even then sometimes that turns out to be not quite good enough.

External modems have a feature that has endeared them to computer support people. They have line and process status lights on their front panels (at least most of them do). These are wonderfully informative about the modem's activity and state, and provide extremely useful troubleshooting information.

Finally, having a separate power supply means that you can turn off an external modem without turning off your PC. This is sometimes useful to reset a modem that gets "hung." It also can be a security precaution, because if the modem is turned off there is no way anyone can "reach into your PC" via the phone line.

Of course, if you use a USB modem you get even greater freedom and ease-of-use; because it is a fully Plug-and-Play–compatible device, the operating system takes care of preventing resource conflicts, and you need only have the modem plugged in when you wish to use it.

The data serializing and the bit-stream modulation (and the inverses of those actions) are two distinct processes. The first process (serializing the outbound data) occurs in the serial port, as does the deserializing of the inbound data. The second process (modulating the outbound bit stream onto the carrier and demodulating the inbound tones into an inbound bit stream) occurs in the modem.

There are jargon names for each of these processes. If you read about the *DTE rate*, it is a reference to the rate at which the PC's serial port (or USB port) is sending and receiving bits of data. If you read about the *DCE rate*, that is the speed at which bits of data are flowing over the telephone line. (These terms, *DTE* and *DCE,* were first used to stand for the devices. DTE is data terminal equipment, and DCE is data communications equipment. Now they also are used for the gender of the serial port on each, and as a reference to the processes on either side of the modem.)

These two processes can run at the same rate. Often, we run the connection from our PCs to our modems at one rate, and run the modems at a different rate. For this to work, the modem and the serial port must be able to buffer some of the information, and also to tell one another when they are ready to send or receive additional data. All modern modems and PC serial and USB ports have those features.

Sometimes modems "compress" the data they send over the phone line. That is, they look at a stream of bits and figure out a way to encode that information more compactly (getting rid of redundancy) by using a standard method. The receiving modem uses the inverse of that method to reconstruct the original bit stream. This lets the modem send more data across the link (more bits per second) than the physical baud rate that it is using would seem to allow. But it can do this only if the data it is receiving has redundancy in it. (I described this general concept in Chapter 3. Please refer to that chapter if you are having trouble understanding this discussion.)

To keep a modem that is doing data compression busy—that is, to keep it sending "compressed" information across the link at the maximum speed of which it is capable—you must send the data to it from the PC somewhat faster than it will be going across the modem-to-modem link. You also must take the received data away from the modem just as fast. This is why we commonly set our serial port data rate anywhere from two to four times faster than the nominal maximum bits-per-second data rate the modem can support over the telephone line.

The optimum rate multiplier to use depends on how much redundancy there is in the data you are transferring. Text typically compresses to one fourth of its original size. ZIP and GIF files don't compress at all. Some graphics, spreadsheet, and database files can compress to as little as a tenth of their original size.

You also should be aware that often when you see a message about how fast you are "connected," the speed refers to the number of bits per second (even if it is called the "baud") at which data is flowing between your PC and your modem—it doesn't mean the speed at which the modem is sending and receiving bits on the phone line. Therefore, if the connect speed you see reported seems to be faster than you thought your modem could go, that's the reason. Nothing to worry about, but just be aware of which speed you are discussing.

A factor that bears on this is the wide use of the V.34 modulation, which negotiates the actual data transmission rate independent of PC interaction and does so continuously during transmission. Although this is an excellent line noise compensation feature, it leaves the computer able to report only the data rate at which it communicates with the modem.

Standards—The More the Merrier!

In order for a modem link to work, the modems at both ends of the link must be compatible. That is, they must use the same methods for modulating and demodulating the carrier signal, compressing the data, and so on.

Over time, modems have changed a lot. Even simple, inexpensive modems today are vastly more capable than the best (and most expensive) ones were just a few years ago. This means that we have many standards for modems.

Initially in the United States, the Bell Telephone Laboratories defined all the standards used for modems. Now, however, the usual standards are set by an international standards organization. For many years, the relevant organization was the CCITT,(International Telegraph and Telephone Consultative Committee). That role has now been taken over by the International Telecommunications Union (ITU), which is an organization that serves in an advisory capacity to the United Nations. Thus, the new designations for modem standards carry the prefix ITU-T (instead of CCITT). The CCITT was internationally staffed and headquartered in France. Its successor organization, the ITU, is headquartered in Geneva, Switzerland. As a consequence of this heritage, virtually all ITU documents have been written originally in French and later translated into English with the occasional interesting results.

The ITU-T standards didn't just spring up out of nothing. Usually, some company comes up with what it regards as a "breakthrough" that lets it make a modem that performs in some way very much better than any previous ones. That company will, of course, market the heck out of the idea and try to get everyone to buy its modems. But this wonderful new feature will work only when one of these special modems is talking to another of the same kind of modem. Eventually, the manufacturer decides that it is in its interest to get a formal international standard to cover this new feature. Then (if it *is* a commercially successful feature) every modem maker will put it into its products, and at that point all of those modems, no matter what brand, will be able to use that new feature when talking to any of the other modems that include support for it. That is when an international standard develops.

Some of the commonly used data communication standards for modems include: V.32 for 9600bps; V.32bis for 14.4Kbps; V.34 for 28.8Kbps; V.42 for error control; V.42bis for data compression; V.FC, a proprietary version of 28.8Kbps (now superseded by V.34);

MNP2-4 (various error control protocols developed by Microcom and given to the industry); MNP5 (data compression; less efficient than an alternative standard called LAPM, but both are used by V.42bis); and MNP10 (data compression optimized for cellular telephony). The newest of the ITU-T standards is V.90, which are used in what are called "56Kbps" modems. (See the section later in this chapter on "Modem Speed" for a full discussion of just what these strange beasts can do.)

Modems can also be used to send and receive faxes. When they send and receive faxes, they conform to a different set of CCITT (now ITU) standards, bearing such monikers as V.17 for 14.4Kbps faxing and T.30, the fax protocol itself.

A quality, modern modem will support all of the standards I have just listed (and probably several more). You can set your communications software to send a message to the modem when you begin a communications session configuring the modem. This sets values in a series of registers, and those values tell the modem which of those standards it is to support during the present call.

Even if you ask it to work at its maximum possible speed, the modem might discover that the modem at the far end isn't capable of working that fast, or that the line between them is too noisy or distorts the signals too much.

In that case, the two modems negotiate some slower speed at which they will carry on the conversation. They will, that is, unless you (or the person at the far end) have instructed your modem (again through commanded register settings) to accept no less than some high standard. In that case, the modems will just hang up the phone whenever they run into a problem.

Similar configuration issues apply to error correction and data compression protocols. You must tell your modem to use them, and the other modem must agree to do so.

Must you configure your modem? Probably not. Many people use communication software provided by their modem manufacturer, by an online service (such as America Online) or by an Internet service provider, or software that is built into their PC's operating system. In any of these cases, that software is probably preconfigured to command your modem correctly for that use. Note, however, that these preconfigured settings are more likely to be biased toward trouble-free modem installation than to optimal performance.

The only time most users must ever worry about their modem configurations is if they are setting up communications programs that will use their modems for calls to local bulletin board systems or some other destinations for which no "standard" software is provided. In that case, you must look at the documentation that came with the modem, check with the manufacturer, or check with a Usenet newsgroup. Here are a couple of URLs where you can start:

```
http://users.aimnet.com/~jnavas/modem/faq.html
http://www.rosenet.net/~costmo/
```

Varieties of Fancy Modems

When you go shopping for a modem, you are likely to feel overwhelmed by all the different jargon terms and different features claimed for various models. Because this is such a rapidly changing field, it's impossible to tell you about every one of the terms you may encounter. But I can tell you about some of the more popular and important ones.

Data, Fax, or Voice?

First, you must realize that modems are frequently used for at least two and sometimes three different jobs in PCs. One is data communication. This is what you use when you surf the Internet. It also is what you need to send and receive email or to transfer files. The second main use is for sending and receiving faxes. A third use is for handling voice phone calls (with the help of an additional telephone handset or other equivalent hardware). A voice-capable modem can be used for simultaneous voice and data communications on a single phone line if the other modem supports this mode of operation.

A modern variation on this idea is called Voice over IP (VoIP) and refers to routing voice phone calls placed on ordinary (analog) telephones—with their signals converted into digital data—over the Internet to an appropriate receiving box that can convert that digital data back into analog form and deliver it to another person's normal telephone that is connected to that receiving box. This has been a niche application so far (mainly used in large corporations), but it appears that within a very few years almost all voice calls will be handled in this fashion instead of going over the traditional public switched telephone network (PSTN).

Knowing this, you must decide which of these tasks you want your modem to do. You don't have to buy a modem that does all three unless that is what you want. On the other hand, if all those capabilities come at an acceptable price, there's no drawback to your modem's being able to do something you don't need or want it to do. And, someday you might change your mind.

Most modems advertise in big type their maximum speed when used for data communication. The present standards for fax transmission don't permit sending that sort of information quite as fast as the newest and fastest data modems, so the lower fax speed usually is not mentioned on the box. Be assured that if you buy a "data and fax" modem, it will support the relevant standards and will send and receive faxes at the proper speed.

One kind of data, fax, and voice modem just routes different calls to the appropriate software or hardware. That is, if this type of modem is in your PC, and if you are running the appropriate program to monitor the modem, then when a fax call comes in, your fax software will be launched and the fax will be received. If a data call comes in, some data communications program will be launched. For voice calls, your PC may start ringing.

Another, newer type of combination modem goes by either the acronym ASVD (Analog Simultaneous Voice and Data) or DSVD (Digital Simultaneous Voice and Data). These modems can carry data and voice information over the same line at the same time. Don't buy an ASVD modem unless it supports the V.34Q ITU-T standard for this. These modems can transfer voice or even music at the same time a data file transfer is going on.

With suitable sound hardware (microphone, speakers, and sound card, or telephone handset or headset) attached to your PC you'll be able to hold a conversation with a person at the other end of the link even as you are sending or receiving data. You'll very likely be able to hold *full duplex* conversations (with both people speaking at once), which is better than the usual speakerphone-type limitation of *half duplex* conversations (in which one person speaking cuts off the other one). Full duplex conversations require a sound card that supports this feature and using a headset with a boom microphone adds a great deal of convenience.

This technology can be used to collaborate between two workers who are sharing their thoughts as they work on a common document. Another use is in gaming when two players can "taunt" one another as they play. One projected use—and it might prove to be one of the most valuable—is for technical support.

With a voice/data modem on your PC as well as on a technical support person's PC, and if you are each running suitable remote control software, the technician might be able to ask you about your problems, then actually take control of your PC to fix them for you.

DSVD modems conform to a different ITU-T standard (V.70). These modems digitize the voice signals and simply insert that digital data into packets that are sent along with the file transfer or other digital data being communicated across the link. These modems are a little more expensive, and they aren't up to handling music, but they may support a higher speed of overall data transfer.

As with all other modem technologies, both ASVD and DSVD require that both modems have the feature for it to be used.

Modem Speed

Analog modem speeds have pretty much peaked. The present standard best speed is either 33.6Kbps or 56Kbps. The 33.6Kbps modems do what you would expect from their name; the 56Kbps modems, on the other hand, are probably not quite what you think they are.

The 33.6Kpbs models can transfer data simultaneously in both directions at up to 33.6Kbps. This takes all the bandwidth that is commonly available on a standard (POTS) voice-grade telephone line. In fact, it requires a very good connection to get this full speed. Many times, using these modems doesn't result in any faster file transfers than if you use a 28.8Kbps modem, and possibly hardly any faster than a 14.4Kbps mode.

Still, you want a V.34-compliant modem because this standard is the most "intelligent" one. These modems are better able to adapt to changing line conditions than earlier protocols allowed. And, they can be upgraded in various ways more easily.

We are in a transition phase for what are called "56Kbps modems." Up to late 1997, there were two competing (and *not* interoperable) methods manufacturers used to make these work. U.S. Robotics (now a part of the 3Com Corporation) made modems it called x2 modems (because they promise twice the speed of an older-style V.34, 28.8Kbps modem). Rockwell and its partners in this venture, Lucent Technologies and Motorola, called their version K56Flex.

Fortunately, the ITU has now adopted the V.90 standard that encompasses both of these approaches. A typical modem you buy today will support one of these two older approaches—and it will work with V.90-compliant modems as well. This backward compatibility is important, for a new standard of communication is useful only when the modems at both ends of every link you try to establish understand the same standards. If you have a slightly older modem, you may be happy to hear that it is probably upgradable to full V.90 compatibility—often by merely downloading a file and "flashing" the non-volatile RAM in the modem with this new programming.

There is one thing that all these different kinds of "56Kbps" modems have in common: They achieve their faster speed for downloading (data inbound to your PC) by sending data in that direction faster than in the outbound direction. This uses more of the available voice line bandwidth for the high-speed direction, at some limitation to the speed in the reverse direction. Also, even at their very best, they cannot pump data across the line at the full, theoretical maximum of 56Kbps. The telephone regulatory agencies won't allow that. Thus, the actual download speed is limited to, at the very best, around 53Kbps (with line noise often limiting it to a good deal less than this), and the upload speed is never faster than 33.6Kbps.

The most common application of this lopsided data rate arrangement is for connection to the Internet. In this instance, you will usually send short strings of commands and receive large image-laden responses. Be aware that your Internet service provider (ISP) must use digital phone lines for 56K service; in practice, this means ISDN.

So, only if you are using these beasts with an optimum quality telephone line will you get anything more than 33.6Kbps throughput, and then only in one direction at a time. Furthermore, unless you are using a USB modem, you must be sure that you have a serial port that can accept the data at the appropriate rate. If data compression is being used, it's possible that the highest-standard PC serial ports (running at 115Kbps) will not suffice.

There is one more way to speed up your modem communications. If you have two voice-grade POTS telephone lines, you may be able to effectively double your connect speed by using two analog modems connected to the two telephone lines simultaneously. Windows 98 and Windows 95 OSR2 include Multilink-PPP support, which is what you'll need to make the two modems share the load gracefully. Or, you can get third-party software to do this (and Diamond Multimedia's Shotgun product claims to add the capability of releasing one of the two lines for an incoming voice call without losing the data connection). This is new technology, so remember that "your mileage may vary" and it might not work with your ISP.

Cable Modems and Satellite Modems

Many of the community access television (CATV) cable companies are now getting into the Internet service provider (ISP) business. They usually offer a small box that splits your TV cable in two. One branch goes to your normal television cable box for tuning channels and displaying them on your television set. The other branch will likely go to either an internal ISA or PCI card or it might be possible to get a box that will connect to a USB port.

These boxes are not really "modems" because they use purely digital signals on both the link from them to your PC and to the cable company's "head end."

The only analog links are from the cable modem to the television set and to your telephone, if the cable operator also offers voice telephone service (as some are now starting to do). In a way, they are closer relatives to the xDSL services that the local telephone companies are beginning to deploy (and which I discuss in some detail later in this chapter).

Nonetheless, these new boxes are called *cable modems* (which is no different from the way the terminology gets misused when one speaks of an "ISDN modem"). Some cable operators offer a combined box with both the cable modem function and the normal cable tuning function rolled into one unit. These devices will let you download information at a very high rate (from 1–10Mbps). They might also let you upload information at a comparable rate.

The basic problem with cable modems is that cable operators must redo all the amplifiers in the system to enable two-way communication, and then they also must do something to ensure that the bandwidth of their cable doesn't get overloaded. As long as only a few customers are using cable modems, they will work wonderfully well. But if they are extremely fast (and they should be *at least* five to ten times faster than any analog modem) and also don't cost too much, then lots of people will buy or lease them, and soon you might find that the cable is choked with data and the cable modem is no longer capable of running as fast as it is supposed to run. Only time will tell whether this solution will be viable and in any way better than the phone-line connected options.

Another variation on this theme is coming from some of the providers of direct broadcast satellite television. These companies offer small dishes you can buy or lease that will enable you to receive hundreds of television channels. Some of them are now also offering the option of Internet access. (DirecPC is one trade name for this Internet access service from Hughes Network Systems, the same company that offers satellite TV service under the trade name DirecTV. Hughes also offers a combination of the two called DirecDuo. This particular Internet access service offers up to 400Kbps downloads, but all uploads are limited by your normal modem-to-ISP link.) DirecPC has offered the same ways for connecting to your PC as were mentioned above for cable modems, an ISA or PCI card and, most recently, a USB connection.

Although satellite systems have excellent bandwidth, they do suffer from a noticeable lag time between inputs and responses. This will impact such applications as online games and Internet fax transmissions. The facsimile protocol definition, T.30, places strict time-out and signal time separation requirements on all fax transmissions. These time dependencies are critical and cannot be easily stretched, which could lead to an apparently insurmountable problem of using a transmission medium that introduces long delays. Hughes Network Systems has at least partially solved this by having a computer at its ground station acknowledge receipt of each packet before those packets are uplinked to the satellite, rather than depending upon the ultimate recipient PC to return the acknowledgment packet. Then, when that ultimate receiving PC does return its acknowledgment, the HNS computer absorbs it. A DirecDuo antenna is shown in Figure 23.1.

FIGURE 23.1

A DirecDuo antenna provides both Internet downloads and digital broadcast television signals from a pair of nearby satellites in geosynchronous orbit.

This mostly means that some subset of the potential channels is being reserved for Internet downloads. Uploads will happen over your normal phone line. Your receiver will decode the channel it has been assigned and it will broadcast (just to you!) whatever Web page you have indicated you want by the information you uploaded over the phone line.

Again, this seems like an option that will be very nice for the early adopters—until the word gets out and too many people want to use it. Then it might well fall flat on its face for want of sufficient channels to serve all the subscribers. Of course, if the provider can keep adding satellites and channels as fast as it adds subscribers, the scheme will work out just fine.

Much the same problem is faced by all Internet service providers, for they must add new dial-up lines and modems as they add subscribers in order not to give busy signals to too many callers, and they must also add more bandwidth on the other side to the Internet, not to bog down everyone. However, putting up another satellite to get more channels is a much more expensive proposition than buying a bunch of modems or even hooking up another T1 line.

Hughes Network Systems says that it has ample capacity for the near future on a dedicated satellite (its DirecTV service uses three other satellites), and that it has international agreements in place to let it place many more satellites in geosynchronous earth orbit, plus many more in low earth orbit when it needs additional capacity.

Hughes Network Systems also notes in its user agreement that you are not guaranteed 400Kbps download speeds. If lines get too congested, they will simply throttle down all users in order to ensure fairness of access.

Is It Real, or Is It Simulated?

Most modems are complete products with all the necessary hardware in the box (or on the board). External modems are just like internal ones, except that they have a power supply that internal modems don't require. (External modems also offer some nifty LED lights. These aren't vital, however, and you can get a program to simulate most of them in a corner of your PC's display screen if you really want "lights" for your internal modem.)

But some modems are very different from all the rest. These special modems have only hardware enough to do a portion of the job of a modem. The rest of the job is done by your PC's CPU by running some special software. Other, nonstandard modems are different in yet another way. These "modems" use general-purpose digital signal processors (DSPs) with a program running in them to simulate a modem. IBM's M-Wave modems are built this way.

The modems that use your PC's CPU obviously cost the manufacturers less to build, so they should cost you less money to buy. If your PC is relatively new and fast, the modem probably will work just fine. Also, upgrading them is particularly easy, because that most likely just means loading a new program onto your hard disk.

If you want to do any data communication when your PC is running in real mode (using DOS as the operating system), there is one subset of this genre to watch out for: the so-called "Windows Modem." Because it uses a Windows program to "finish" the work of making these modems function, they will be useless unless Windows is running.

The idea behind the DSP-based modems (for example, IBM's M-Wave) is that the same hardware can also be programmed to do other things. Thus, one plug-in card could, in principle, serve as a modem, a sound card, a scanner interface, and more. In practice, these combinations have not proven very popular.

Do I Need a New Modem?

If all you have is an older modem, is buying a newer one necessarily a good idea? That depends on what you do with your PC and just how old your modem is. If you have a

14.4Kbps modem, you will see about a tripling of speed by getting a new modem. That might be worth the cost to you if you do a lot of Web surfing on the Internet, or it might be worth very little if all you do is send or receive occasional email.

If your present modem is a 28.8Kbps modem, the first thing to do is check with the manufacturer. Many of them can be upgraded by "flashing" a new program into their onboard ROM. If this is possible, it certainly will be the way to go, even if there is a modest cost for the upgrade. If your modem needs a new "data pump" chip, sending it in for an upgrade still might be worthwhile.

Otherwise, this is a good time to buy a new modem. They now go about as fast as they are likely to go. Of course, I suggest that if your PC is able to use it, you'll be better off buying a USB modem than an older-style serial (or internal) modem.

Even faster access to the Internet or other online information services will be provided by a cable or satellite modem. Not everyone lives where he or she can get cable modem service. Internet access via a satellite downlink is available over much of the planet (but it is usable only where there is also a landline telephone link to an ISP). With the coming deployment of low-earth orbit satellites (for example, the Iridium system), we may soon have two-way satellite Internet services available even in the remotest areas.

There are only a couple of exceptions to this advice. If your telephone company offers, or soon will be offering, some version of xDSL, you may wish to wait for that. The second exception pertains if you think ISDN is for you. (You'll learn more about both possibilities in the next section.)

Keeping It Purely Digital

The POTS voice-grade telephone lines that you probably use in your home, and may be using in your office as well, are analog communication channels. A *wire pair*—two copper wires, separately insulated and normally twisted together in a loose helix—carries electrical signals that are an analog of the sound pressure that represents the speech signal being transmitted. When you use these lines for data transmission, you first must convert that digital data into the electrical versions of some special sounds; then, at the other end, you convert them back into digital form.

There are several ways to avoid that double conversion and get faster, more reliable data communication. They all cost more than a POTS line—in some cases, a lot more.

The phone companies are all converting their central offices and long-distance lines from analog to digital. When you use a POTS line for digital communication, the signals will almost certainly get converted back and forth between analog and digital forms more than twice. This only strengthens the case for using a purely digital approach.

Integrated Services Digital Network (ISDN)

The simplest step up from analog to digital is to use an ISDN (Integrated Services Digital Network) line. There are several flavors of ISDN. First is the so-called Basic Rate

Interface (BRI). This offers you two data channels at 64Kbps (B-channels) and one control channel (D-channel) at 16Kbps. The combined data rate on both B-channels is 128Kbps. The D channel normally cannot be used for data connectivity; it is used to provide information and call management. With this service, you will usually get two phone numbers. You can receive a call on either number, and even receive two simultaneous phone calls, using both channels at the same time.

If you do this, each call will get one of the B-channels, and data can flow across this channel at 64Kbps if the data channel is not in use, or at up to 56Kbps if it is. If you place only one call from your computer, and if your computer software and ISDN "modem" support channel-bonding (and if the modem at the other end of the connection does also), you can get a single channel of 112Kbps or 128Kbps, depending on the state of the D-channel.

The interface box you must use to connect your PC to an ISDN line is called an ISDN modem. This is a bit of a misnomer, because no modulation or demodulation of the digital data is involved. The only time a modem-like function happens in these boxes is when you use the extra POTS line jack they typically offer. Some offer one and some offer two POTS jacks. You can hook a normal analog phone or fax machine to such a jack and use it as if it were connected to a normal POTS line. You can even use this jack for one B-channel while using the other B-channel for a digital call placed by your PC.

A more expensive version of ISDN is the Primary Rate Interface (PRI). This offers 23 B-channels and a 64Kbps D-channel, with a total data transfer rate of about 1.5Mbps when all channels are used at once.

This sounds pretty good. And it can be, or not. There are some real advantages to an ISDN connection. First, the line is purely digital. That means it either doesn't work at all—which is relatively rare—or works at its full speed. There are no issues of negotiation to determine an acceptable speed for the present line conditions. That means you can initiate an ISDN connection in a fraction of a second rather than in the up to 30 seconds it can take an analog modem pair to settle on how fast they are going to talk to one another. If you can get channel-bonding to work, your data rates will be at least twice as great as the best analog modems can provide.

There are also some severe drawbacks to using ISDN. One is cost. In most places, it costs anywhere from a little bit to a lot more than a POTS line to get an ISDN line. A normal analog telephone service line usually costs $20 to $30 per month. An ISDN line typically costs two to three times as much. The first-time setup charge for an ISDN line can run anywhere from free (if you get a special offer) to $500 for a remote location. However, because ISDN has two "lines" bundled together, it might be a good option for those who would buy a separate modem line anyway.

Calls that are "free" local calls on your POTS line can be toll calls on an ISDN line. There are some areas of the country where ISDN lines are what is called "metered service." This means you even pay to connect to local numbers. However, most metered service has been removed or made optional. For you to take full advantage of an ISDN line, the other end must be digital as well; however, you can use your ISDN line to serve the host end of a V.90 56K modem connection. This cannot be done with an analog line.

Channel bonding doesn't always work. Some ISPs won't guarantee that it will work for every call, though often it does. Many ISPs charge you double for calls when channel bonding happens, but only the normal rate if it fails. This variability means you can't count on getting the full 128Kbps data rate just because you want it.

T1, Fractional T1, and Other Very High-Speed Connections

Before ISDN was available, the phone companies routinely leased special high-bandwidth, non–dial-up lines to companies that needed that service. These lines, which are still available, come in several denominations. One of the most popular is called a T1 line. This line can handle 1.544 million bps, the same as a PRI ISDN line. Some companies have leased T1 lines from the phone company and then turned around and leased a fraction (some number of the 24 multiplexed "fractions" of the T1 line) of their bandwidth to other companies. That allowed companies with a smaller appetite for bandwidth to get it at a lower cost than a full T1 line.

The main difference between these options and ISDN is that whereas ISDN is a dial-up network connection (so you place calls to wherever and whenever you want), a T1 or fractional T1 line is a leased line. You are always connected to the phone company (and always paying it for the service, whether you are using it or not). As a result, these connections generally cost more than ISDN.

Before there was ISDN, telephone companies sought to solve this need in a different way. They offered a dial-up service called *Switched 56*. This is a dial-up connection to the Public Switched Telephone Network (PSTN) that can carry 56Kbps of data.

There are other phone company offerings, such as Frame Relay and ATM (Asynchronous Transfer Mode). These are both full-time connections like T1 but, whereas T1 is a widely used means of carrying both data and voice communications, Frame Relay and ATM tend to be used exclusively for high-speed data and are much less common. Both Frame Relay and ATM are packet strategies for shipping lots of data quickly across a network that may be shared by many users.

Very large companies sometimes need even faster data rates. The phone companies offer something called T3 service (45Mbps capacity), and for the super-hungry, OC12 through OC48 (2.4Gbps) services (an optical-fiber service standard). If you really think you need one of these levels of data capacity, you will need very specialized assistance. You must talk to the phone company, and you probably also want to hire a consultant to help you define your needs and the best solutions to them.

Optical-Fiber Communication Channels

Some cable TV operators are using fiber links from their "head end" equipment (where they receive the downlinked signals from the satellites and convert them into the various channels of TV signal you get on the cable to your home) to distribution points in each neighborhood. Eventually, they may even put in optical-fiber links to each individual home.

If your company (or home) has optical-fiber cable coming to it, you can attach to that for the ultimate in high-bandwidth communication—provided that someone on the other end is prepared to accept your flood of bits and send them to the right ultimate destinations, and to send back to you a similar flood of data bits from wherever you request. For now, though, this is not a commonly available option. Still, it is something to be watching for. When it comes, it will be more bandwidth than we know how to use (so far). Of course, by then, we probably will want even more! (See Chapter 25 for more on optical-fiber data communications channels.)

xDSL

A new wave of technologies is coming from your local phone company. They carry names such as ASDL, HSDL, and xDSL. A new variation on this theme, recently adopted as a standard by the ITU, is called G.Lite.

All these technologies use the traditional copper wire pair that makes up a POTS analog phone line to carry data at much higher rates. This is accomplished by changing the connection switch to a digital switch at the point where your copper wire lines reach the telephone company's central office. Some of the proposed switch types will support voice calls in a manner similar to ISDN.

The ASDL (Asymmetrical Subscriber Digital Link) variation of this idea uses the POTS line pair as a purely digital link, and it shoves much more data across the link in one direction than in the other. Unlike on the 56Kbps modems, however, on an ASDL line the high-speed direction can be reversed whenever you want. (However, because some overhead is involved in the switch, you can't do it very often without cutting down on the overall data throughput.)

HSDL (High Speed Digital Link) is an improved version of ASDL. xSDL covers both of these and some more variations as well. G.Lite is a consumer-oriented version that will offer up to 1.5Mbps in the inbound direction (for downloads) and 512Kbps for outbound (upload) data. This version is supposed to be deployed by the various local telephone companies throughout the U.S. in early 1999, but many observers think that timetable is impossibly optimistic.

These are technologies in the laboratories and are being tested in the field in a few places. Unless you happen to live or work in one of those test areas, they are not yet options you can select. But they will be soon—or so the phone companies keep telling us.

Which Way Should You Go?

Analog or digital? Which way should you go? Maybe you can have it both ways. Some Internet service providers offer both ISDN and analog modem dial-in ports.

In order to take advantage of this option, you must have both an analog modem and an ISDN modem (or a device that is a combination of both). If you only occasionally need really fast Internet access—but when you want it, you really want it—this combination approach may make sense to you. Just check out what the minimum costs are and see if they are acceptable.

A different choice is whether to use one of the always-connected options (cable modem, T1 line, and the like) or a dial-up connection. You get a lot of advantages from a constant connection—and one very big disadvantage. One of the advantages is that you don't have to make a conscious choice to connect to the Internet—it's just there, all the time.

The disadvantage is simply the flip side of that coin. Your system is wide open to outside intruders all the time, and some program on your PC might decide to reach out to the Internet to get something and bring it in. You won't necessarily be aware of what these outside programs are doing to your PC until it is too late to stop them. So, if you do opt for a constant connection, you'll likely need also to invest in a firewall or other security measure to control what comes into your PC when you aren't looking.

Summary

Connected PCs offer some capabilities that standalone PCs simply cannot match. In this chapter, I described the most common ways that PCs get connected to other computers through a modem link and briefly described some of the things they can do when they are connected in that way.

In the next chapter, I continue this discussion about connected PCs, but focus on connections to or through a network using a network interface card (NIC).

The PC Reaches Out, Part Two: Through the NIC Node

In Chapter 23, "The PC Reaches Out, Part One: Modems and More," you learned about PCs that are connected to a single other PC by a direct wire (between their serial, parallel, or USB ports) or by an optical means You also learned about various ways PCs can be connected to other computers by using a modem of one kind or another.

I mentioned that the most common way PCs are interconnected in offices and some homes is by a local area network (LAN). This chapter focuses on LANs and the things to which they are connected, and on some of the software you need or might want to take advantage of your PC's connections to other computers.

Because the technologies are so similar, I will sometimes make reference to "networks" that connect multiple peripheral devices to a central computer, or to more than one computer. A growing trend is for standalone devices—for example, a hard drive or a printer—to be connected directly to a local area network rather than to a single computer.

The NIC Node

The network interface card (NIC) is one of the most potent devices for expanding the capabilities of your computer. It joins your computer to a connected collection of others in such a way that all can share hard disk storage space, data files, peripherals (such as printers and modems) and messaging facilities.

A Number of Network Designs

The idea sounds simple enough. A local area network is a way to hook together many PCs so they can exchange information. But the actual practice can become pretty complicated. There are many ways to go about achieving this connectivity. Because the subject of networks is so large, I will focus on some of the enabling technologies, and those only in their more popular implementations.

This section first discusses the wiring schemes that are most commonly used. Then you learn about some popular ways to organize the exchange of information over those wires.

Many Topologies

Topology is the branch of mathematics that studies the ways things are connected to one another. It ignores the sizes and shapes of those things, and looks only at their connectivity. In reference to LANs, the term topology refers to how each PC is connected to all the others in a logical sense, without regard to the physical arrangement that accomplishes this connectivity.

Figure 24.1 shows several common LAN topologies. In each case, I have also indicated one or more of the common network cabling schemes that use that topology. The USB LAN is in fact designed for connecting peripheral devices to a host computer rather than for connecting computers to one another.

FIGURE 24.1
Some common LAN topologies.

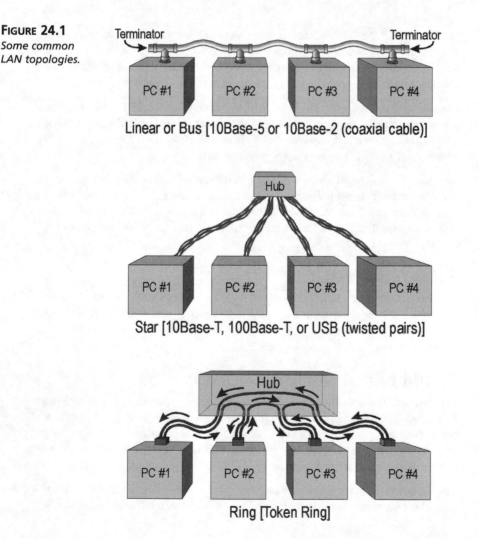

Linear or Bus [10Base-5 or 10Base-2 (coaxial cable)]

Star [10Base-T, 100Base-T, or USB (twisted pairs)]

Ring [Token Ring]

Bus or Linear Networks

The top portion of Figure 24.1 shows what is sometimes referred to as a *bus topology*. The most common examples of this scheme are the 10Base-2 and 10Base-5 wiring schemes used in many Ethernet LAN installations. (Ethernet itself is a prescribed way of using the cable, as I will explain later, and it doesn't require any particular form for that cable.) 10Base-2 uses a thin, flexible coaxial cable. The nickname for this wiring scheme is *thinnet*.

The 10Base-5 wiring scheme also uses coaxial cable, but it is a thicker, more rigid cable. This makes setting up such a network harder, but the larger cable can carry the network signals much farther than the thinnet cable without unacceptable attenuation. The 10Base part of the designation refers to the maximum data rate of the network (10Mbps). It also indicates that this rate includes transmission of the overhead information necessary to demarcate and address the data. The numbers 2 and 5 are numeric designations that identify the length and type of wire used for the connections. 10Base-2, for instance, is good for approximately 200 meters on coaxial cabling. Likewise, 10Base-5 is good for approximately 500 meters on thick cabling.

The figure shows the taps for each PC as BNC T-connectors attached to the PCs (or actually to the network interface adapters installed in those PCs), with the cable made up of short pieces going from PC to PC. At each end of the bus, the open side of the T-connector is capped with a *terminator*. This is a device that connects an appropriate resistor between the center conductor and the shield of the coaxial cable. The result is that any electric signals arriving at the terminator are fully absorbed; none of those signals gets reflected back along the bus. These reflected signals are sometimes confused with genuine data, which is why terminators are required.

This is the common way to set up thinnet. In contrast, 10Base-5 commonly uses penetrating taps clamped onto a single, continuous backbone cable with terminators installed at the ends of the cable. Although 10Base-2 is easier to pull and connect, 10Base-5 is more durable and enables longer cable runs and greater immunity from stray electrical noise.

Star Networks

The middle portion of Figure 24.1 shows a *star network*. This is a very common way to connect multiple devices to a central one. Here, you see a hub connected to each PC by a set of twisted-pair cables. These wires (essentially high-grade telephone lines) are inexpensive to manufacture and very easy to install.

It's important to realize that although the hub is shown as if it were at the center of the network, in a star wiring scheme all the signals that arrive at the hub on any cable are immediately sent back out on all the other cables. This means that the hub is a data interchange point. In effect, all the cables are simply wired in parallel, and thus any signal put onto one shows up on all. That makes this logically very much like the bus topology shown at the top of this figure. (This logical similarity is why this kind of wiring scheme can be used interchangeably with the bus topology for Ethernet LANs.)

Star topologies are used for many different kinds of networks (meaning different cable designs as well as different methods for using those cables). Though preceded by ArcNet, the most common use of star topologies for PC LANs is for Ethernet. This variety of Ethernet is usually called 10Base-T, and each cable (referred to as Category 3 or better cable) has four unshielded twisted pairs (UTP) of copper wires. (The same signal carried over an optical fiber is called 10Base-F.) As with 10Base-2 and 10Base-5, the name 10Base-T implies a maximum Ethernet data rate of 10Mbps. The same wiring scheme, if it is of a high-enough quality (termed Category 5 in the industry) can also be used to carry 100Mbps or 1000Mbps (1Gbps). 3Com is currently marketing a fiber version of 1Gbps Ethernet. If the network is used in this way, it is called 100Base-T.

Another star topology "network" is the *Universal Serial Bus* (USB). This is not a network in quite the same sense as Ethernet. USB is a network for transmission of data from peripheral devices to a PC host computer, rather than a means of connecting multiple PCs to one another; still, the connectivity topology for USB is identical to that for 10Base-T.

Modified Star Networks

A simple star network has every node connected directly to the hub. But in many cases it is more practical to have a multilayer, modified star network. In this form of networking (which is used for Ethernet and USB networks), each device that is connected to the hub can be a controlled device, another hub, or a combination of the two. The wiring in these networks can, thus, be a multiple branched tree rather than a pure star network in which every device connects back to the root hub. (You'll find more information on USB in Chapter 15, "Understanding Standard PC Input and Output.")

Ring Networks

The bottom portion of Figure 24.1 shows a *ring network*. The most common example of this is a token-ring network. Here, you see a MAU (Multistation Access Unit) and a cable from it to each of the PCs. MAUs are analogous to hubs in an Ethernet environment. In a token-ring network, data must go into each PC and back out again, through the MAU and on to the next PC, until the data has made a complete circuit around the ring.

The MAU just connects the outbound data path from each PC to the inbound path to the next PC; it does nothing to the data as it goes by. In fact, you could build a ring network without a MAU just by connecting each PC to both its neighbors. The reasons to use a hub (besides the fact that the token-ring specification calls for one) are that it makes setting up the network easier and the network itself more robust. MAUs automatically disconnect PCs that are powered off, and in certain types of network card failures.

The token-ring specification is also frequently referred to by its name of the defining standard organization's name, IEEE 802.5. (IEEE is the acronym for Institute of Electrical and Electronic Engineers.) Token ring specifies both the physical cables and connectors and also the method in which they are used. I discuss the token-ring method for handling data in the section "Token Ring," later in this chapter.

Fibre Channel

Optical fibers can be used to carry digital data in the form of light pulses. These fibers can carry much higher data rates than any kind of metal wire, because light waves have a much higher frequency than electrical signals carried over wires. The telephone companies are now using this on their "backbone" connections. Many large companies also use optical fiber links for very high data rate communication within their facilities (in their LANs).

Most electric power transmission companies string optical-fiber cables alongside their metal power-carrying wires. (In this last case, the reason is not so much the high data rate the optical cables support as it is the complete immunity to electrical noise enjoyed by any purely optical channel.)

The standard protocols for using optical cables are Fiber Distributed-Data Interface (FDDI), High Performance Parallel Interface (HIPPI), and Fibre Channel (FC). These protocols were developed especially for use on optical connections, but they can be and are often used on copper wire links as well. This is particularly true in what are termed storage area networks." (I'll explain just what this sort of beast is in Chapter 25, "PCs That Think They Are Mainframes: Multiprocessor PCs and Other Servers.")

Optical-fiber links can take either one of two physical forms. In one, the laser whose output is modulated to carry the data is operated in a single mode. That means there is only one frequency and phase to all the light it emits. A different way to use the laser is in a multimode fashion, in which many similar yet slightly different light waves are emitted together. Lasers that operate in single mode are more expensive to make, but the signals they generate can be sent reliably over much longer optical fibers, which can justify their higher cost in certain applications.

The principal advantages of optical LANs are high speed (starting at 100Mbps, to well over 1Gbps with Fibre Channel), total immunity to electromagnetic interference (including different ground potentials at each end), and the capability of spanning much longer distances than is feasible with copper LANs (in fact, up to 10 kilometers between devices with the Fibre Channel protocol). It is also very difficult to intercept data flowing over an optical connection because the connection itself must be interrupted to install a tap. On the down side, optical fibers are vastly more expensive than copper wire and much more difficult and expensive to install and maintain.

The greater distance capability comes in two parts. First, optical networks regenerate the signals at each node. (This is shown in Figure 24.2 by having the cables enter each box on one side and exit from the other.) Thus, their length limitations apply only to the internode distances.

The principal disadvantages to a purely optical network are the higher cost of the hardware, vastly higher installation costs, and the greater fragility of the connections. These factors have made many companies more interested in overhauling their copper wire networks (known quantities) than jumping head first into optical network upgrades at this time. (Indeed, the Fibre Channel protocol itself has proved so valuable that it is now found ever-increasingly on copper-wire systems.)

A particularly valuable variation on simple Fibre Channel that is highly favored for use in storage area networks is what is termed *Fibre Channel with a Dual Arbitrated Loop*. This configuration is shown in Figure 24.2. Here, there are two ports on each of the hard drives, and twin optical cables link from the PC's network interface card to all of them. If any link fails, the other side of the pair of links can take over the data load seamlessly.

In this discussion, I have only scratched the surface of this important standard and its related developments. You can learn much more about Fibre Channel and HIPPI at the following URLs.

For FC:

`http://www.fibrechannel.com/technology/tech_frame.htm`

`http://www.t11.org/`

For FDDI:

`http://www.cisco.com/univercd/cc/td/doc/cisintwk/ito_doc/55773.htm`

For HIPPI:

`http://www.hnf.org/tech.htm`

FIGURE 24.2
Fibre Channel net-works can use either single or dual sets of opti-cal links (or cop-per wires, for shorter distances). The dual arrange-ment offers both higher speed and the added safety of redundancy.

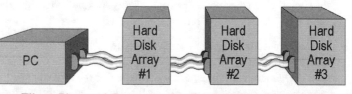

Fibre Channel System with Dual Arbitrated Loop

Linking Two LANs

Often, people want to link several LANs together to let any computer on any of the linked LANs exchange data with any other computer on those linked LANs. If you have two or more bus LANs, you could simply hook them together end-to-end. (Remove the terminators from the ends you want to connect and substitute a cable from one to the other.) Then you'd have simply one larger bus LAN.

Similarly, if you have two or more star LANs, you can hook them together by linking their hubs. (Most star LAN hubs come with a special expansion port for just this purpose.) Two ring LANs could be combined into one larger ring. Just break each ring in one place and hook them together to form a single, larger ring.

All those ways of combining two smaller LANs into one larger LAN will work (assuming that they are close enough physically for the physical topology to support the link), but it often is not a good idea. It's better to link the two LANs by an interLAN connection box (called a *router* or *bridge*) of some sort.

This is particularly vital if you want to link a bus LAN to a ring or star LAN. When linking dissimilar topologies, you absolutely must have some type of router to pass signals from one LAN to the other.

A router is, in fact, a computer running a suitable program to examine each arriving data packet's *envelope* (the portion of the packet that specifies who sent it and where it is supposed to go) and then send it on its way to the correct attached LAN. This routing function effectively isolates a connected network from packet traffic that is not addressed to it, providing a considerable efficiency savings. A router may also translate the physical protocol (the method of handling data packets). A bridge is used to connect two networks with the same topologies.

One reason for using a router between two LANs rather than directly connecting them is that the router can isolate data traffic on one LAN from that on the other. That is, any data packets that originate on one LAN and are addressed to another computer on the same LAN have no reason to leave that LAN.

If you can keep all the "local" packets within each LAN and only exchange the "long-distance" packets, you will keep the data traffic congestion on each LAN to the minimum possible value. For this reason, one of the most common prescriptions for speeding up a sluggish LAN is to break it into segments and connect them to one another with routers.

To factor into this equation, however, you need to pick a "routable" protocol to run on your network. The simplest networking protocol of all—NetBEUI—has the smallest overhead due to a number of reasons, key of which is its inability to be routed. The following list shows common protocols in alphabetic order and their ability to be routed:

Protocol	Routable
CLNP	Yes
DECnet	Yes
DLC	No
IPX/SPX	Yes
LAT	No
NetBEUI	No
PPP	Yes
PPTP	Yes
SLIP	Yes
SNA	Yes
SNAP	Yes
TCP/IP	Yes
X.25	Yes
XNS protocols	Yes

The inability to be routed substantially restricts the size of a network you can grow to by preventing the protocol from being transmitted across a router. Nonroutable protocols can be used only on a LAN or across a bridge or brouter. Bridges, routers, and brouters are discussed in more detail later in this chapter.

A variation on this idea is shown in Chapter 25 in the section "Interconnecting Multiple Central Computers."

Note: A *broadcast storm* is a sudden flood of messages that clogs your transmission medium, reaching or nearing 100 percent of your bandwidth. A broadcast storm slows down the network and can even prevent clients from using the network. The most common cause of a storm is a malfunctioning NIC, but it can also be caused by high levels of traffic.

If your network ever suffers a broadcast storm, the best tool for troubleshooting is a *protocol analyzer* that can identify the source of the storm. If it turns out to be a faulty NIC, you must immediately remove that machine from the network until the card is changed. However, if you determine that the problem is due to high utilization, you need to use switches, bridges, or routers to segment your network.

Many Hardware Protocols

The wiring plan alone doesn't fully define a network. The next level of definition specifies how those wires will be used. In particular, it specifies the signals the wires will carry and how they are to be interpreted.

All networks organize data into packets. The purpose of this packaging is to enclose each message in an envelope that describes (at a minimum) who is sending it and who is supposed to be receiving it.

Ethernet

Ethernet is a strategy for exchanging data between linked computers. Every computer has an address. In some networks, each computer is assigned an address by some central arbiter or based on which segment of the network it is hooked to. Ethernet is different in this regard. Every Ethernet NIC (network interface card) ever made has its own, unique serial number. That is the address that Ethernet uses to route each packet of information that is sent to that device.

The most clever concept in the Ethernet protocol is its means of resolving an inevitable conflict that will arise whenever you have multiple "speakers" that can each start speaking at any time. On a network, this means that their signals will be mixed together, and the result is a muddled mess that none of the "listeners" can understand.

Carrier Sense, Multiple Access with Collision Detection (CSMA/CD) takes care of this problem. First, any Ethernet device will listen to the signals on the bus to be sure no one else is talking. Then, if it wants to speak, the device will start doing so.

First, each device waits for some random amount of time (all the while listening to see whether any other device starts speaking in the meantime). If some other device starts speaking while the first device is waiting, the first device won't begin speaking until the bus is quiet once more. If, by chance, two devices start at virtually the same instant, both will soon realize it and they'll each stop and wait a random (and therefore probably different) amount of time before they attempt to speak once more.

You'll often hear people refer to any link using the CSMA/CD strategy as "Ethernet." This is common, but technically it is incorrect. The inventor of Ethernet, and the IEEE standard defining it, both say only the original 10Mbps version is "true" Ethernet. The IEEE has published a standard it calls IEEE 802.3 to fully define this particular 10Mbps networking standard.

Any alternative scheme that uses CSMA/CD is perhaps best referred to as a networking scheme that uses the Ethernet protocol. (A version called Fast Ethernet transfers data at 100Mbps, exactly 10 times as fast as the original Ethernet with the same protocol. Versions that run at 1000Mbps are referred to as *Gigabit Ethernet*.)

The CSMA/CD strategy works a lot like the way people talk in a polite conversation. And it works just fine—as long as there aren't too many folks trying to express themselves.

Similarly, on an Ethernet, if there isn't too much data "traffic," it all works splendidly. But if the bus is almost always busy, some devices may find it hard to "get a word in edgewise." Because the Ethernet NIC sends out data only when it has some message to convey, the size limit for an Ethernet network is set by how much total conversational content the entire collection of connected computers wants to exchange, rather than the number of connected PCs.

Ethernet has become very popular. In part, this is because it can use almost any wiring scheme that can support an adequately high rate of serial bit transmission. Also, in its 10Base-T (or 100Base-T or 1000Base-T) star configurations, the fact that the failure of any one of the connected computers or of any one segment of cable will not cause the network as a whole to fail is a great advantage. Only the one computer that failed (or whose cable to the hub failed) will drop off the network. Of course, a hub failure would bring down the entire network, but because the hub is so simple, that is a much less likely event.

Some other aspects of Ethernet's popularity have to do with the fact that its competition had some drawbacks. ArcNet preceded Ethernet into general usage but was much slower, though it tended to be more reliable than early Ethernet implementations. IBM's token ring was just that—IBM's. Their proprietary attitude did much to discourage its adoption. What probably pushed Ethernet over the top of the acceptance curve was its general adoption by operators of minicomputer systems running under the UNIX operating system.

The main drawback to Ethernet is that there is no guarantee that every PC will "get its turn to talk" as soon as it needs to. Thus, a super-congested Ethernet can simply fail to convey some of the messages it is supposed to convey in time to satisfy the timeout requirements of the software attempting to use it. This prompts more attempts to send the data that ultimately result in a broadcast storm. This makes it essential that the next higher level of organization of the communication over the network uses some form of error detection and correction. (That job is done by any modern network operating system that supports Ethernet.)

Token Ring

Token ring is a very different way to handle the same problems. IBM devised token ring to require a ring or star-ring topology network. Each device sends messages out by one port and receives messages on a different port. All the devices are hooked together by a link to a neighbor on each side, with the ends being looped back (see the bottom portion of Figure 24.1).

Only one block of information is circulating on the ring at all times. Sometimes that block is a minimal packet called the *token*. At other times, one or more messages is attached to it. Each device on the ring has an address. Every message starts with a header saying who is sending it and to whom it is addressed.

Whenever a PC receives a block of information, it scans the block looking for messages addressed to it. If there are any, it will remove their content but leave their headers (addressing information). These headers are now marked to say that the messages for which they were the envelopes have been received. If this PC has any messages to send, it will append them to the end of the information block as it sends the whole thing on to the next PC in the ring. Finally, if there are any headers in the block that were put there by this PC and marked that their data was properly received, it removes them.

This strategy is in some ways more complex than CSMA/CD, but in other ways it is simpler. Most important, it certainly guarantees that each and every message is received by its intended recipient, and that every PC gets a chance to send a message every time the token passes by it.

However, this approach requires that every PC on the ring see and handle every message that is going to any PC on that ring. It also absolutely requires a ring topology. Any break in the ring, or the failure of any one of the connected computers, will cause the MAU to bypass that system in order to preserve network integrity.

Other Layers in the Network Strategy

The overall strategy for a network must include more than simply specifying the wiring scheme and data packet handling protocol. It also must tell about how programs within each connected computer are to communicate over that network. The OSI model is a well-defined, seven-layer model for networking.

This model divides networking tasks into seven fundamentally different layers to make it easier for the industry to explain the different operations that take place in successful networking. The seven layers are shown in Figure 24.3 and are most easily remembered with the mnemonic *All People Seem To Need Data Processing*.

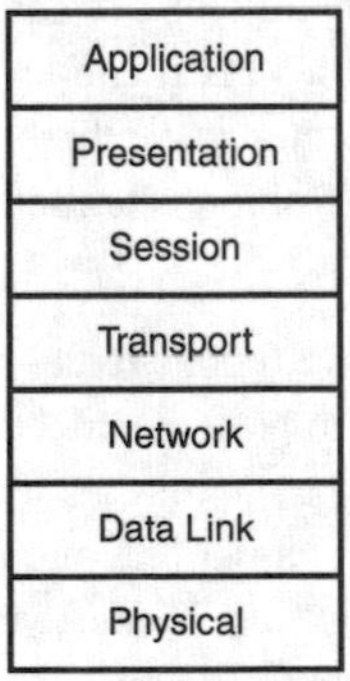

FIGURE 24.3
The seven layers of the OSI model from top to bottom.

| Application |
| Presentation |
| Session |
| Transport |
| Network |
| Data Link |
| Physical |

The Application layer is the interface to network services—it interacts with the user. The Presentation layer translates between the Application layer and all others. It also provides redirection, encryption, and compression. The Session layer establishes the rules that will be used for communication between two machines, and the Transport layer—as the name implies—handles network transmissions. The Network layer is where addressing and switching take place, and the Data Link layer handles error checking and other elements related to link control. The Physical layer interfaces with what you can actually see and touch: the NIC, cable, and so forth.

So far, I've explained the two lowest-level layers in the OSI model. The other layers are all components of the network operating system (NOS) software that runs on top of this enabling hardware connection. I'll tell you a little bit about them in the "Some Common NOSes" section later in this chapter.

LANs, WANs, and Virtual Private Networks

LANs can be connected to one another by the use of a router or a bridge. If the connected LANs are local to each other, the result is simply a larger LAN (but one that will operate more efficiently than if the segments were connected directly, without use of routers or bridges). If you connect several LANs that are physically spread out over a wide area, the result is called a *wide area network* (WAN).

Many large companies have leased high-speed phone lines to connect the LANs in each of their offices in different cities around the world into one large WAN. The benefits of doing this are very similar to those you find in linking multiple LAN segments with routers or bridges. You can get from any computer in the entire system to any other, and yet purely local data traffic is kept from clogging up the larger-scale connections.

Of course, leasing these permanent, high-speed telephone links that might span continents and even oceans can be expensive. Altenatives include a *virtual private network* (VPN), and Frame Relay.

The idea behind a VPN is simply this: If you can protect your data packets from snooping eyes well enough (with encryption, for example), you can ship them back and forth over the public Internet without fear. Essentially, a VPN is simply a set of software pieces that you can use at each LAN location to send and receive these encrypted data packets over the Internet. Connecting two sites in this fashion is termed *tunneling* via the Internet.

Because local Internet connections are quite inexpensive (compared to dedicated transcontinental telephone lines), this will enable you to have the effect of a WAN without its usual cost. Of course, you must make some compromises. Perhaps the most important one is that you will have to put up with the fact that Internet connections do not, so far, have a guaranteed latency or throughput capacity. That is, you never know just how long it will take to get some data from one site to another. However, you can minimize this by sticking to a single ISP for all the locations you are trying to connect. This ensures that all your traffic stays on the ISP's network and is more directly under its control.

Some Internet service providers (ISPs) are working together to devise a higher class of service they can offer their customers, in which one can be assured of a fixed, low latency (time to get the first byte of a message to its destination) and minimum guaranteed throughput (guaranteed amount of data you can send per second). If these plans work out, you will at least be able to balance the cost savings of giving up a dedicated WAN link against the speed loss you will experience by using Internet tunneling. Until that time, however, VPNs are a chancy proposition. They are okay for some purposes and totally unacceptable for other, more critical ones.

> **Note:** Although they are less expensive than WANs, VPNs have two important drawbacks. First, VPN packets travel the less-than-private servers of the Internet. No matter how well encrypted, these packets can be readily intercepted and therefore possibly decrypted by any unscrupulous cyber-thieves. Second, because the Internet is loosely managed, there is no guarantee that your packets will arrive on time, or for that matter, at all.
>
> If you're not sending time-critical or highly sensitive data, VPNs do serve as an inexpensive replacement for a true WAN. (See the discussion of Quality of Service (QoS) in Chapter 26, "You Can Touch the World and It May Touch You, Too!")

Frame Relay is a digital technology that uses variable length frames and assumes error checking is done by other devices, and you have a high-quality network transmission capability. By making those assumptions, it is able to not perform some of the operations that are normally performed and thus increase network speed and performance. Error checking, you will recall from earlier in this chapter, is a function of the Data Link layer, and thus Frame Relay works at the second layer of the OSI model. Frame Relay typically runs at speeds up to 1.544Mbps.

Host Connectivity

You might get the idea from what I've said about networks to this point that they are just a means for connecting PCs. Of course, that isn't true. Networks are used to connect all kinds and sizes of computers to one another.

One use for networks is to replace the direct wiring of terminals to mainframe computers. I mentioned near the beginning of Chapter 23 that often today companies are replacing their old, "dumb" mainframe (or minicomputer) terminals with PCs. They can still use a serial cable to connect these PCs to the central host computer. Then running host connectivity software on the PC will make it act as if it were a dumb terminal.

Replacing an inexpensive dumb terminal with a more costly PC can make sense because the PC can do so much more. Not only can you use the PC to send keystrokes to a host computer and receive screens of information back, you also can save that information to local storage. When you exit from the host session, you can use the PC to do other tasks (including local processing of the information you just retrieved from the central computer). With the newer PCs and their operating systems, it is even possible to concurrently access a host and perform other tasks as well.

If you use a LAN as the link from a PC to a host computer, even more possibilities are available to you. Now, in addition to starting a host session, you can communicate from your PC to any other computer on the LAN, and you can do local processing, too. Connecting PCs in this way provides the ultimate in flexibility.

The NIC Node Needs a NOS

Whenever you add new hardware to a PC, you must also add some software to enable the PC to use that hardware. Network software is no exception. Having a BIOS ROM on a network interface card is common. That ROM contains some basic device driver programs to activate the hardware on the card. However, the job that a network does is so much larger, and so much farther abstracted from the role of mere hardware, that a simple device driver is not enough.

What Is a NOS and Why Do I Need One?

A network brings into a PC a whole new realm of resources and possibilities. To manage this new realm one needs a new operating system called a *network operating system* (NOS).

Please don't be confused by this. On the server, the NOS will be the only operating system running, but the NOS doesn't in any sense replace the PC's main operating system. Instead, on the PC it augments the existing OS, adding new capabilities to manage the new possibilities inherent in the network setup. What might confuse you about this is that some modern PC operating systems, such as Windows for Workgroups (version 3.1x), Windows 9x, and NT, bundle a NOS with the main OS. UNIX is an older operating system that also does this. In contrast, Novell NetWare, for example, adds network interface driver software to the PC's existing operating system to facilitate network operations, and includes a NOS only for the server.

The main purpose of a network operating system at the client level is to allow the user of one computer to see some of the resources on some distant computers as if they were resources on the local computer. Think of your computer as the "local" machine and all the other computers as the "remote," or "foreign" ones.

Using a suitable NOS and network connection you might be able to "map" root or some subdirectory of a remote computer as if it were the root directory of a local drive (this will give it a local drive letter). As an alternative, you might simply be able to browse that remote drive using the Windows 9x Explorer program. Either way, you can load programs from that drive or, if you have permission to do this, save files there. Some other kinds of resources that can be shared across a network include printers, scanners, and modems.

Big problems face the designers of network operating systems. First, they must be able to keep track of all the connected resources. Second, they must be able to deal with many different kinds of connected computers and to make sense of the file systems on each one, translating filenames and path locations as necessary to make the distant computer's files look as if they are just like the local ones. Then, when a file is transferred, there might be an additional translation task to make the foreign file show up in the format and in compliance with the naming convention expected for that type of file on the local machine.

The first of these is the directory and name problem. For small LANs it isn't too bad, but for a very large WAN it can be tough. The Internet is so large and so dynamic (and without any central control) that the directory job has in some ways proven to be beyond our present ability to solve it fully.

> **Technical Note:** The step of translating file formats isn't always done. However, it is an important one if you want to give the local computer user the illusion that those foreign files are just like the ones stored on the local machine. One example is that on a UNIX computer, text files normally have only a line-feed character at the end of each line, whereas on a DOS or Windows machine, text files always end each line with a two-character combination (carriage return plus line-feed). This seemingly trivial difference has a big impact on the way the data in the file is displayed.

Some Common NOSes

Many different network operating systems are in use today, but only a few of them have a significant market share. The first to be developed for DOS-based PCs were add-ons to the PC's operating system, whether that was DOS or DOS plus Windows. Later generations of PC operating systems have included some or all of the functionality of a NOS within the basic PC OS.

Most networks can be classified into one of two categories. The first are those that use a File Server and Workstation model (also called Client/Server, but a more correct use of this term is discussed in the section "Client/Server Computing," later in this chapter). The second are Peer-to-Peer networks. Some NOSes support just the first of these models. Some have been designed primarily to support the Peer-to-Peer model, but in fact those NOSes can support both Peer-to-Peer and Client/Server.

File Server and Workstation Networks

The notion of a File Server and Workstation model of networking is this: All the important files reside on one or more central computers (called file servers). Each person uses a workstation, which is a computer connected to the file server by the network.

When you do some work on your workstation, you get the needed data files, and perhaps some of the applications as well, from the file server. You load them into your PC and do your work with them by running application programs in your machine. When you finish, you save your data files back onto the file server. Often these networks also have central printers, and any user wishing to print a document will direct it across the network to the printer.

Novell's NetWare is the most popular network software used in the PC world. Windows NT Server is rapidly gaining marketshare and may soon exceed NetWare in the amount of servers deployed. UNIX, with its decades-long history of supporting many different kinds of computers and its robust built-in support for networking, is the most popular network operating system for networked computers other than PCs. Both of these NOSes are primarily intended for use on a File Server and Workstation model of network.

Historical Aside

Many "flavors" of UNIX exist. Originally developed at AT&T's Bell Laboratories, UNIX was initially given away to universities. AT&T did not offer support; it just gave them the program source code. The universities had to provide their own support.

In the process, they often modified UNIX to meet their own special needs. In particular, the University of California in Berkeley created a flavor now known as Berkeley Software Development (BSD) UNIX.

A commercial company, Santa Cruz Operation (SCO), markets another very popular variation. And fast becoming the favorite for UNIX users in the PC world is Linux. Linux is particularly enticing because it is available free, complete with source code. You can buy a copy (and get some technical support from your vendor), or you can download a copy or get one from a friend freely and then have at it, making any changes you want, all without any copyright violation.

There are several advantages to file server–based networking. One is that all the critical files live on just a few, central machines. Professionals can oversee these machines, keeping them running smoothly, and those professionals can be counted on to do all the prudent file management tasks, including backups. The users of the workstations needn't concern themselves with those pesky details that can be so crucial—and whose omission can be so tragic when a PC's hard disk crashes.

This arrangement also neatly separates the work of serving as librarian to many (the job of the file server) from that of working with the individual files' contents (the job of each workstation). This helps balance the workloads of the different computers in the network.

The file server might have very little work to do for any one user—just retrieving a few files—but it must do that same job for many, many other users at the same time.

Another advantage is that a user can "log in" to the network from any workstation and do the same things pretty much anywhere. Because the files all live in the central repository, they can be accessed from any connected workstation just as well as from another.

Of course, this is not a perfectly true statement. Some workstations might have more RAM than others. That can matter if the task you want to do requires a huge amount for manipulating large graphic files, for example. Also, to save time and network traffic, the network administrator might have installed many of the more popular applications on local hard disks in the workstations. But if the one you need hasn't been installed on all the workstations, that can limit your freedom to log in from anywhere and still do the same kinds of work. One solution to that is to have a central copy of every application that can be used if there doesn't happen to be a local copy on a particular workstation.

Another problem with the connect-anywhere paradigm is access management. Windows NT, in particular, is designed around the workgroup organizational principle and organizes workstations and servers into workgroups and domains. If a user does not have access to a given domain, he or she will not be able to log into a server in that domain.

Peer-to-Peer Networks

The other general kind of network uses a peer-to-peer model. This means that, in principle, all the computers that are hooked together are equal. In particular, any computer on the network can be configured to share some or all of its local resources with the users of the other computers on the network. That means each computer can become a file server (or a printer, scanner, or modem server). But at the same time, those computers are also workstations.

You don't have to share any resources you don't want to share in this type of network. That is, each workstation can be configured to have none, some, or all of its resources shareable. When you do share a resource, you can attach a password to it, and only those other users who know the password for that particular resource will be able to access it. Some Peer-to-Peer networking systems do allow passwords to be assigned to the user, not to the resource, but they are rare.

Windows 9x has a further refinement of having two kinds of access control: user-level, in which passwords are specified for specific users and groups, and share-level, in which a password is assigned to each resource. User-level access control in Windows 9x is available, however, only if you have either a Novell or Windows NT server that can authenticate passwords. This is something that a traditional Peer-to-Peer network wouldn't have. Peer networking support for PCs is now included, at no additional cost, in Windows for Workgroups, Windows 9x, Windows NT, Windows 2000, and OS/2 Warp.

One advantage to peer-to-peer networking is that users can exchange files among themselves directly. With the file server model, file sharing between workstations can happen only in a two-step fashion: First, one user uploads the file to the server. Then the second user downloads it from the server. By using passwords that are shared selectively, one can share files with only some of the other workstations. (This can also be accomplished on a file server, but it requires that the administrator of the file server set up differing access rights for different directories, and that the users be grouped according to which access rights they are to be given. This discourages an ad hoc decision by one user to share files with another user, yet keep them private from all the rest.)

Another important advantage to peer networking, from the user's standpoint, is that it is closer to what the PC revolution has been all about: getting away from central control of the computing resource. There is another side to this, of course. The people in a company who are responsible for all the computing hardware and services have a much harder time keeping track of who is doing what on a peer network. Often, the central system administrators choose not to back up files stored on individual workstations, in which case users must assume that responsibility for themselves.

Some Networks Blur This Boundary

Windows NT and OS/2 both are marketed in two versions: one intended for file servers and one for workstations. The intention is to support the file server plus workstation type of networking and also enable you to set up peer networking if you want.

Windows NT Server not only supports workstations running Windows NT Workstation, but also workstations that are running Windows 9x or DOS plus Windows for Workgroups, version 3.x. OS/2 Warp supports all those types of workstations plus workstations that are running OS/2 Warp.

In a mixed network, some machines might be designated as file servers. They can be repositories for most of the shared files, and perhaps also for many shared applications. But the individual workstations can also be configured to share some of the files, printers, and modems that they have locally with any other workstation user. So, with the built-in NOS functionality of these operating systems, you can have the best of both worlds. (Or, from the point of view of a curmudgeonly computing services manager, the worst of both worlds!)

Protocol Differences Between Networks

Networks exchange packets of information, but they don't all format those packets in the same ways. I mentioned previously that there is a formal, seven-layer OSI model for networks. The details I told you previously dealt only with the bottom two layers. The NOS products I have mentioned all do the work of the other five layers, but sometimes in different ways.

Popular Packet Protocols

Novell NetWare uses a packet protocol named IPX; UNIX uses TCP/IP; and Windows for Workgroups, Windows 9x, and Windows NT can use NetBEUI, although they prefer

TCP/IP for moderate-to-large networks. You can have packets of more than one kind circulating on a network, but the only computers that will see each kind of packet are those that are running a NOS that understands that format of packet.

It's also possible to add support to a NOS for packets of one or more styles other than their native kind. Thus, you can add a TCP/IP protocol stack to Netware or Windows for Workgroups. Windows 9x, NT, Windows 2000, and OS/2 include optional components for just this purpose.

> **Note:** If you intend to access the Internet, you have to have a TCP/IP protocol stack on your PC. Or, you must access the Internet via a gateway, proxy server, or firewall computer that will translate all the packets you send or receive across the Internet from IPX (if you are on a Netware network) to TCP/IP as they leave, and back again for the packets that come in.
>
> A gateway will just convert packet protocols. A proxy server will also translate network addresses for all the internal computers to a single address that is visible on the external network. A firewall does both these things and one more: It filters out any "bad" packets going either in or out, basing its decisions on rules that can be set by the network administrator.

There is, in principle, no problem with having any number of protocol stacks on your PC. The practical situation is often different from the ideal, however.

If you are running real-mode network drivers, they will take up some significant portion (several hundred kilobytes, typically) of your PC's precious first megabyte of main memory. If you run too many of them, they will use up too much of that space. Your PC will be connected to all manner of different network clients, but it won't be capable of doing anything useful after it connects to them.

Protected-mode operating systems, such asWindows NT, Windows 2000, OS/2, UNIX, and to an extent, Windows 9x can put their network support modules into extended memory. That helps a lot. But you still are using up memory for this purpose, so you must be sure not to scrimp on memory in your PC if you are planning to load multiple protocol networking support.

Another key reason for reducing protocol stacks is reducing bandwidth usage. Many OSs announce their presence periodically on every protocol they have loaded. In addition, they may have to try several protocols before finding one to communicate with a specific target machine. All of this adds considerably to the packet traffic on a network and propels administrators to reduce the protocols that they use.

How Do You Choose Your NOS?

If you are using a PC that is running DOS plus Windows for Workgroups, Windows 9x, Windows NT, Windows 2000, or OS/2 Warp, you already have a NOS built into your

PC's OS. However, that doesn't mean you must use that NOS. You may decide to add support for another NOS (most commonly for NetWare). Mainly, you will do this if you are going to connect your PC to an already existing NetWare network. Some of these OSes have NetWare client support built in; others require the addition of a device driver for that purpose.

Normally, you choose your NOS based on what you want to do with it. Or, you make your choice based on what NOS is already in use by the computers to which you want to connect.

Most file server and workstation computer networks are set up by a company's central Information Technology (IT) department. They will choose the NOS and you must simply go along. (On the other hand, they'll do most or all of the hard work of getting your workstation up and running. You only have to learn how to use it.)

If you are setting up a small network, you probably will choose one of the peer networks. Setting them up is much easier than setting up UNIX, Netware, a Windows NT Server, or a Windows 2000 Server.

Other Software for the Connected PC

In this chapter and the previous one, I've told you about network software and about communications software for accessing other computers via a modem or other, similar link. What about other software that is useful only for connected PCs?

I'll just describe briefly some broad categories of this type of software, so you will be aware of their existence. If you must get one of these programs, you'll have to assess your needs carefully and then compare the various options you have to see which one will best meet your needs.

Client-Server Computing

File server and workstation networking is often confused with another term: client/server computing. But, in fact, they are quite different concepts.

Simple file server and workstation computing usually has all the applications running on the workstations. The file server just "serves up" the files on request. Real client/server computing splits the computing work between the workstation (client machine) and the central server. A prototypical example might be an online transaction processing application (OLTP) for airline or theater ticket reservations. The central computer maintains a database (for example, of airline seats that are available on all the flights of a particular airline or of theater tickets available for certain shows).

The workstation accesses this database by sending queries and commands to the central computer. The actual accesses to the database, either for reading a record or for updating it, are done by the server. But the client computer can also do some significant computing work. In particular, it will be responsible for drawing all the (perhaps graphically complex) screens that present the database information to the user in a pleasant manner. The client workstation might also do some cost comparisons and route optimization calculations locally. Finally, it might be accessing more than one central computer if the travel arrangements involve comparing the available seats on many different airlines.

Another example is found in the X-Windows protocol. Originally developed for UNIX machines, there are now some X-Windows applications for PCs as well. In this case, the jargon gets turned around somewhat.

An X-Windows server is a program that runs on a workstation. It receives commands from a program running on a distant machine, and in response it "serves up" the requested images on the workstation screen. The program that is deciding what to have displayed is running on the distant machine and is called the X-Windows client program. One X-Windows server can serve many X-Windows clients, showing the images commanded by each one in a separate window on the workstation's display screen.

Finally, an Internet browser such as Internet Explorer or Netscape Navigator uses a type of client/server operation. The browser is a program that runs in your PC, and its main job is to present the data it receives from the distant computer. Using that browser, you can run programs in those distant computers or you can download programs from them that then run in your computer as temporary or permanent additions to your browser.

> **Note:** A modern innovation in client/server computing is to break down this type of work into three layers. The *front end* is the program that runs in the workstation. The *back end* program is, for example, a big mainframe database that keeps track of lots of transactions. Between these two is a layer of *middleware* that coordinates the requests for access to perhaps several different databases (each on its own back-end computer) from the many different workstation client front-end computers. Most companies implement the rules by which they are run, called *business rules,* in middleware.

Fat Versus Thin

You might also have heard about *fat clients* and *thin clients.* Essentially, this distinction refers to what capabilities the workstation hardware has. If it has its own hard disk, stores most applications locally, and just requests data files from the server (and returns them when it is finished updating them), it is a fat client workstation. (Another name for this kind of beast is simply a PC.)

If, on the other hand, it has more nearly the hardware limitations typical of an older, dumb terminal (just a screen, keyboard, and perhaps a mouse or other pointing device), it is a very thin client (sometimes called a network computer or NC). All it can do is ship commands off to the central computer to be applied there by an application running on that central computer and then display whatever that central computer sends back.

An almost-as-thin client might have a substantial amount of computing power, and maybe a lot of RAM, but no hard disk. It must load every program, as well as all its data files, from the central computer. But it still can do the computing work with those files locally. (Any temporary files it creates will have to be created on the central machine, of course.)

What are the advantages of fat versus thin clients? Well, generally, the fat client minimizes network traffic. Only data files travel to the server, and those only after they have been fully massaged at the workstations. But, if it is possible for the user to save data on the local hard disk, it is also possible for any data so saved not to be backed up with the central machine backups. If that is done, and if the local PC hard disk dies, that data will be lost.

Also, if an upgrade to an application is installed on the central machine, any thin clients get the benefit right away. Fat clients must be individually upgraded before they are able to receive those benefits. (Of course, it might be possible to do those upgrades more-or-less automatically, in which case this advantage becomes minimal.)

If the network fails, a thin client is useless. A fat client is a full PC and can do anything a not-connected PC can do whenever the network is down. Although networks are fairly stable, they do crash from time to time, and this can be a significant advantage for the fat clients.

Finally, fat clients put more control and power in the hands of the individual user. This, politically, is the right thing to do. At least for well-trained users it is.

Thin clients are fine for a temporary employee or one who is relatively unskilled at using a PC. Fat clients are preferable in the eyes of most power users. I'll return to this issue at the end of Chapter 26.

> **Note:** *Fat* and *thin* do not always have to refer to computers, but can also be used to reference client programs. The same principles apply, but instead of focusing on the physical machine, the focus shifts to the software application.

Remote Control of a PC

Remote access to a PC, once gained, can provide you with two distinct possibilities for operation: acting as a remote node, and remote control. In the former, you establish a connection and then work from the remote site as if you were just another workstation (node) on the network. The best example of this is Dial-Up Networking.

Remote control programs, on the other hand, are another category of software that has been especially designed for use on connected PCs. These programs enable one person, sitting at a PC, to see the screen output from, and supply keystrokes to, a program that is running on a distant PC. Usually, the program on the distant PC also puts its output on that PC's screen, and it also listens to that PC's local keyboard. The remote "controller" is simply able to see and activate that program remotely at the same time the local user is doing so.

From the very beginning, DOS has provided something like this in its CTTY command. That redirects the *console* (by which DOS means the keyboard and screen) from the physical keyboard and screen to a serial port. Then, if you have a dumb terminal attached to that port, you can use the computing power of the PC on the remote screen and keyboard of the terminal.

But when you do this, you cannot also see the screen displays on the PC's own screen, nor will any keystrokes you enter on the PC's keyboard reach the running program. True remote control programs go well beyond what the CTTY command offers.

Why would you want such a program? One good reason is for training. Others are for software maintenance and telecommuting (working on the office workstation/LAN from home via dial-up access).

If you are responsible for supporting several PC users, and if you cannot easily go to the desk of each one whenever a problem arises, being able to see the screen displays and actually type commands into that PC from a remote location can be very helpful. The alternative is to ask the user at the PC to read to you what the screen display says, and then try to talk the user through the correct keystroke sequences to do whatever tests you may decide to try.

Anyone who has had to do this knows that this process is at best arduous, and at worst disastrous. Many times the PC's user doesn't understand enough to know what to notice on the screen, or cannot seem to understand well enough just what to type (or not to type) in response to verbal requests over a phone line.

One potentially serious limitation to remote control software is that of the screen resolution it supports. If the local and remote PCs have screens with very different resolutions, it often is necessary to compromise on some resolution both PCs can support before the remote control software will work. Recent versions of these products (such as Norton's pcANYWHERE) are capable of adjusting to discrepancies in resolution and other screen properties relatively gracefully.

What can be worse is that these programs tend to be quite slow. If you are linking to the remote PC over a phone line, you will find that this type of link simply is not fast enough to support the full speed with which a modern PC can redraw the screen. One way some of them try to compensate is to use data compression. Another way is to send only the high-level Windows API calls instead of the actual screen information. Both help, but neither approach solves all the problems.

However, most remote control programs now come in network versions (which may run on TCP/IP, IPX, or NetBEUI protocols between the PCs), and most of these networks are fast enough to draw the screen images at least reasonably fast. Therefore, I recommend that if you have a choice, you connect remote control programs to the target PCs by a network connection whenever possible.

Workgroup Computing

Finally, I must at least mention one of the hot jargon terms of the day: *workgroup computing*. This is supposed to mean some type of program or programs, commonly called GroupWare, that enable people in different locations, each equipped with a PC, to work together in some meaningful way. Lotus Notes, the most popular GroupWare, enables a group of users to set up chat databases to discuss or share work files, as well as coordinate workflow and track a document or other object as it moves throughout the group (routing). Notes works equally well when executing on a local LAN, a group of LANs, or on a WAN. Microsoft Exchange Server is the main competitor to Lotus Notes in the scheduling and data sharing functions, but it does not support file share coordination.

Video Conferencing

One application that has been much touted is *video conferencing,* in which a video camera and microphone are in place at each location. Each person sees on his or her PC's screen images of several or all of the other participants, and hears all of them. The notion is that this will replace travel in some situations where workers must have a meeting but aren't already in the same general locale. The software necessary to implement video conferencing is included in Microsoft NetMeeting, or can be purchased separately from a number of vendors.

Shared Whiteboards

You can add to this a *shared whiteboard* experience. This is done by running a program on each of the connected PCs that sets aside a portion of each PC screen for a scratchpad and then enables users at any of the connected PCs to write on this scratchpad with their pointing device. (You can distinguish the marks made by different users by using a different color for each user, or you could use color for another meaning—the choice is up to the group.)

Group Calendaring and Scheduling

Another groupware application is *shared calendaring*. This means having a calendar program for each person on which he or she can note appointment and meeting schedules. But then it is also possible, if these PCs are connected, for an authorized person at any one of them to search all (or a selected subset) of the calendars for a suitable time to hold a meeting, and then to enter that meeting on all those (selected) calendars remotely. This can shortcut a lot of telephone tag and greatly facilitate getting together groups of very busy people.

Shared Word Processing

Some word processors are also group-enabled. The idea here is to enable a dispersed group of people to work on a document together. Everyone sees the current document on their screens. If they are enabled to make changes, any of them can move the cursor, type characters, cut and paste, or otherwise edit the document. This can be combined with an oral conversation if the PC-to-PC links include a voice capability (as would be the case if, for example, they are linked with simultaneous voice and data modems, described in Chapter 23, or if they are networked together and at the same time a suitable networked-telephone program is available to all the users).

Summary

Connected PCs offer some capabilities that standalone PCs simply cannot match. In this chapter, I described the most common ways that PCs are connected to other computers and briefly described some of the things they can do when they are so connected.

In the next chapter, I tell you how PCs also are moving into the realm formerly occupied only by mainframes or minicomputers. Most of these PCs are used as file servers and thus are connected to many other PCs. But in some cases, the specialness of the PCs I will be describing comes from having more than one CPU inside their chassis, rather than from the linking of it to other PCs, each with its own CPU.

PCs That Think They're Mainframes: Multiprocessor PCs and Other Servers

Interactive computing began with massive mainframe computers connected to huge numbers of terminals. The terminals were simply keyboards and screens, with no local computing power. This development began about 40 years ago.

The next stage of interactive computing saw the emergence of standalone PCs (less than 20 years ago). Then, those PCs became networked (mostly in the past decade). This introduced two new variations on the original mainframe-plus-terminals model: the file server-plus-workstation networking model and the client-server model of distributed computing.

After this, elementary PCs became attached to mainframes in lieu of dumb terminals. Finally, today, we are seeing many of the central computers in those distributed computing environments being replaced by "super PCs." In this chapter I'll describe some of those super PCs and explain what distinguishes them from ordinary desktop PCs.

Analyzing the Need

Most desktop PCs today have far more raw computing power than even the largest of the mainframe computers built 40 years ago. Because those mainframes were able to handle dozens, or in some cases even hundreds of terminals, it seems reasonable to suppose that today that job could be done by a simple PC.

However, our expectations for any such central computer on a large network have grown over the years right along with the power of computers. For example, consider that 40 years ago all terminals were capable of displaying only characters. Now we expect many of our workstations to show us a richly graphical screen image. The central computer is often responsible for managing much of what we see on those screens and doing so for anywhere from dozens to hundreds of them. Thus, it would be a mistake to simply grab any old PC and put it in service as if it were a modern mainframe computer. The scales of processing power have advanced for the entire processor span, from microcomputers to mainframes.

Context Matters: Two Prototypical Uses for a Central Computer

To successfully replace a mainframe (or a minicomputer) with a PC, the first step is to carefully analyze what the mainframe computer does and then make sure the PC is capable of doing those same things. To accomplish this, we must distinguish between two prototypical applications for which those central computers are used.

File Servers to Workstations

The least demanding use of a central computer is as a simple file server. In this scenario, the central computer is connected to a network of workstations, and it serves up files to those workstations upon request.

In this case, the central computer must have a lot of input/output (I/O) capability. The actual computational task it must accomplish is quite limited, but to keep track of all the open files, and to cache the most recently accessed ones for every user, the central PC must have a lot of RAM (and, of course, a lot of disk space).

To do this job well, you may need only a moderately powerful CPU, but it might need to be supplemented with additional microprocessors that are customized for and dedicated to just the work of handling all that I/O. The so-called "I2O" (Intelligent Input-Output) industry initiative describes just such an approach. Intel's i960 family of CPUs is an example of this kind of microprocessor. (See Chapter 15, "Understanding Standard PC Input and Output," for more on this topic.)

Back-End Processor for OLTP System

A much more demanding application, and one more typical of how networks of computers are used these days, is as the back-end processor for an online transaction processing (OLTP) system, often called a database server. Here, the central computer must perform essentially two kinds of tasks. One is the simple serving up of files (or, more commonly, of records from within large database files). The other task it must do involves searching those database files for appropriate sets of records. This involves all the same requirements as the file server and workstation scenario plus a substantial amount of actual computing work. So, this is a file server and workstation system plus. Other network configurations might require different, but similar, tasks from their central computers. Client/server systems, for example, have the central computer serving up information and also running various server-end application programs. Again, this type of system looks a lot like the simple file server-plus-workstation model, but it goes well beyond that in terms of what the central computer will be expected to do.

These sorts of mainframe-replacement PCs demand something quite different from what is appropriate for a pure file server. Depending on the size of the system you are trying to build, it may be necessary to have multiple PCs connected in a "cluster," or you may need multiple CPUs within a single PC. And you may need to add several I2O subsystems as well. I'll expand on both these approaches later in this chapter.

Reliability Is Key

In all these cases, one of the most essential requirements for the central computer is reliability. After all, if a workstation computer fails, only one person is put out of business until it is fixed. But if the central computer fails (in these centralized networks), the entire network of workstations becomes nearly useless until the central computer is repaired.

Some centralized networks use multiple central computers. Failure of a single central computer might or might not take down the entire network. Or, it might knock out a segment of the network. True peer-to-peer networks, on the other hand, usually continue to run quite nicely if one or more of the workstations fail.

Of course, if you are using a workstation that is accessing files at another workstation and that remote workstation fails, you can't continue that task. You still have the rest of the networked resources at your disposal to do other tasks, however.

Steady Electrical Power Prevents Many Problems

To ensure the reliability of your central computer, power it from an uninterruptible power supply (UPS). This is essentially a box with two power supplies and a set of batteries. One power supply converts incoming electrical power from the AC line to DC power at the voltage of the battery. This electrical energy is used both to recharge the batteries and to power the secondary power supply.

The secondary power supply can work in one of two ways, depending on whether it is an external or an internal UPS. An external UPS will have a secondary power supply that converts the battery voltage back into AC voltage at the same voltage and frequency as the incoming electrical power. Essentially, this box sits between your computer and the wall socket, and it makes its output look just like the wall socket's output, but without the noise spikes, brownouts, and interruptions that are typical of the power you will get from any normal electrical outlet.

Warning: Some UPS secondary power supplies create outputs that really aren't kind to PCs. These boxes are intended to make AC electrical power—of the sort that a heater or motor might need—but they aren't complex enough to provide a true simulation of the sinusoidal waveform your PC expects. If the UPS you are considering produces a square-wave output, don't get it. The best way to get the right system is to verify that its output is listed as a sine wave in the unit's specifications.

Other unsuitable UPSs are able to switch over to battery power only after a delay period that may be short for people, but which is agonizingly long for a PC. Unless your PC's power supply is oversized, it will likely need to be supplied with input power pretty much nonstop. The UPSs I am referring to here may go by the name *standby* (as opposed to something suggesting that their output circuitry is always on). Not all standby UPSs are unsuitable—but many are, so check carefully the specifications, especially the specification for the switch-over time. Anything over about twenty milliseconds is likely to be too long.

Internal UPSs, on the other hand, are replacements for the power supply that lives inside your PC's system unit. In these units, the secondary power supply directly converts the battery voltage into several different, closely regulated DC voltages that the PC uses internally.

For a file server, you will usually use an external UPS. Only a good-sized external UPS will be able to store enough electrical energy to keep your file server humming during a typical power outage. Good UPSs also have an output port that sends signals to the PC it is powering to alert it to power failure.

A monitoring program can keep track of when and for how long the UPS has been providing power. As the UPS's batteries begin to fail, the monitoring program can send messages to alert the users of the attached workstations that the network will be shutting down shortly. Then, the monitoring program can automatically do an orderly shutdown process for the server before the UPS is finally unable to continue supplying power. It should be noted that the average UPS has the capability of keeping its associated PC powered up for several minutes. This time is generally provided for an orderly shutdown, not for continued work.

Peter's Principle: Save Your Data from Destruction and Save Yourself from Major Frustration: Use a UPS

I recommend an internal or external UPS for all the workstations on any network (or, in fact, for most standalone PCs). You can get small capacity units fairly cheaply. Replacements for the internal power supply can cost little more than the supplies they replace.

Not only will these units enable the user to continue working at a workstation in the event of a brief power outage, they also will do a better job of filtering out noise spikes and other power-line anomalies that, if passed through, might cause computer errors.

Block Lightning and Static Electric Shocks

Protecting computers from lightning and surges can become a complex topic, with all the different methods of diverting these electrical energies from reaching the delicate circuitry of your PC.

The first protection that must be considered is providing an adequate ground. That third prong that people still break off from time to time to make the plug fit in an older two-prong outlet is a safety device that helps to protect your computer—and to protect you.

A ground line gives electrical energy a place to go if the normal path is interrupted. This prevents, or discourages, the energy from trying to find a path through you or your PC's components.

Surge suppressors, which prevent harmful levels of electricity from reaching your computer, use the ground line to divert that energy away from your PC.

You can get surge protectors for the network cables also. I recommend using surge protectors in addition to a UPS backup system. You also must surge-protect any modem phone lines or other paths by which a lightning surge might enter your network.

It is generally a good precaution to surge-protect each system piece's power connection and any signal connection to another system. Don't forget "hidden" parts, such as network hubs, routers, and the like. If they use line voltage, they need protection.

Plugging your UPS into a surge suppressor might seem a trifle redundant, but it is good insurance. Two specifications to look for when selecting a suppressor are power-dissipation capability and circuit protection. Power dissipation is the measure of the suppressor's capability of withstanding use, as measured in joules; a larger number is better. Circuit protection refers to the fact that a PC is (or should be) connected to an electrical outlet by three wires. Power spikes can occur across any or all pairs of these wires, and a good suppressor should have "three-way protection" to deal with this.

As a last comment on surge suppression, I'll point out that it is possible to get a whole-building surge suppressor. That is a very good idea, especially in areas with lots of lightning storms. These devices must be installed by a licensed electrician. And remember, even if you protect the building, it may help to also protect the individual devices—and most especially remember that you must be concerned about spikes that may come into the building over network cables or phone lines as well as over the main electrical power feed. If your work environment has a low humidity—even just at certain times of the year—you might need to drain off static electric charges from the users before they touch the workstation keyboards or disk drives. If you don't, users might get charged up enough by simply walking to their desks to deliver potent zaps able to kill a workstation or, in the worst case, an entire network. Many companies sell simple grounding pads— often in the form of a mousepad—which you can touch before touching your PC. These pads are designed to slowly (over a second or two) drain the static electricity off your skin, so you won't feel the kind of nasty shock you experience when you instantly drain off static by, for example, touching a metal doorknob after walking across a carpet. These pads connect to your home or office's electrical ground or to the metal case of your PC—which is connected to your office's ground through its power cord.

Backing Up Data Is Even More Crucial on a Network File Server

By now, most PC users know that file backups are important. And many of them perform backups regularly. If you are in charge of a file-server-based network, this task becomes even more vital because many users' files are at risk. If you don't do backups and verify them regularly you are running a very real risk of having a whole flock of people justifiably mad at you. Chapter 6, "Enhancing Your Understanding By Exploring and Tinkering," addresses backup strategies.

Error Correction Codes to the Rescue

Modern PCs are inherently quite reliable machines. Still, they do have the occasional hiccup. We routinely depend upon the Error Correction Codes (ECCs) that are stored along with our data on every PC hard disk to save us from data loss when those devices fail to work perfectly. Almost always, that approach succeeds. (You just don't know how very often this happens. Possibly as frequently as several times per day, a typical PC hard disk will fail to read from the disk surface some data it has been asked for. But in virtually every instance, it is able to supply the requested data flawlessly—by reconstructing what the data must have been from the data it could read plus the ECC information.)

It is perfectly possible to extend this approach to ensuring reliable operation in spite of actual, although brief, hardware failures by adding ECC to the data stored. More and more, precisely these steps are being taken in the large PC-based systems I talk about in this chapter.

RAID Makes Sense for Servers, for Sure

In Chapter 9, "You Can Never Have Too Much Closet (or Data Storage) Space," I told you a little bit about RAID mass storage systems. These redundant arrays of independent disks are arrangements of multiple hard disk drives with a special controller. Eight levels of RAID have been formally defined. Each provides some level of protection above and beyond that which you will get from the disk drives themselves. For ultimate performance and reliability enhancement, you can combine two or more of the RAID levels in one storage system.

RAID Level 1 uses simple *disk mirroring*. That is, each disk has a twin that holds exactly the same information. Every time you write anything to disk drive A, it goes to both drives A and B. If one of the two drives fails, the controller will stop using it (but continue to use the other drive as if nothing happened), and it will notify the system administrator that this disk must be replaced. After replacement, the contents of the remaining disk drive are simply copied to the new drive. This approach works okay, but it requires buying twice as much total disk capacity as you would need if you stored only a single copy of all your data.

A variant of disk mirroring is called *disk duplexing*. Disk duplexing is identical to disk mirroring except that disk duplexing requires that each of the two disks be on a separate controller. There's a slight performance improvement when using disk duplexing over disk mirroring, because commands can be transmitted to the drives on a separate bus.

The most popular version, RAID Level 5, can be made to store the data, plus a parity bit for every byte, on multiple disk drives (as few as three, or as many as you want). Because all the data and the associated parity information from each file are spread across all these disks, you can expect to recover all of it flawlessly, even if one of the disks in the array dies totally.

The best RAID implementations often enable you to *hot swap* a failed disk drive. Hot swapping means you can take out the dead drive and replace it with a good one without having to shut down the system.

After you have replaced a dead drive, you must load it with an image of the data that used to be on its predecessor. Depending on the RAID software you have implemented, this might happen automatically, or you might have to go through some steps manually.

Another benefit to some of the RAID implementations is that they may enable you to access the information stored in the disk array more rapidly than if the disk drives were simply connected as individual drives to the PC. Also, by using an array controller, you can attach more total capacity and still give the illusion that it is a single volume. This may be a substantial benefit, provided your operating system is able to handle such a large disk volume efficiently.

I won't go into all the other details of the different RAID levels. If you want more technical information, you should absolutely check out Distributed Processing Technologies' Web site at

```
http://www.dpt.com/library.htm
```

You will find additional—though less useful—"official" discussions at the RAID Advisory Board site at

```
http://www.raid-advisory.com
```

and more information including some pictures that may help you understand this topic at

```
http://www.hp.com/storage/array/trraid.html
```

Storage Area Networks

A new development in reliable and high-performance data storage for PCs is what is termed a Storage Area Network (SAN). This is a collection of hard disk arrays, probably organized as several RAID subsystems, connected together by a high-speed network (often Fibre Channel) and connected to *more than one PC*. The unique quality of the SAN approach is that it allows many PCs to access each hard disk simultaneously. This adds reliability. (If one PC fails, it is no more catastrophic than if one hard disk dies.) It also adds to the overall system performance. You may wish to reference the "Ring Networks" section in Chapter 24, "The PC Reaches Out, Part Two: Through the NIC Node," for a closer look at this connection scheme.

To learn more about SAN, go to one of these URLs (for the Fibre Channel Loop organization or the Storage Networking Industry Association, respectively):

```
http://www.fcloop.org/SAN/FAQs/default.htm
```

```
http://www.snia.org/
```

Note: Storage Area Networks are commonly used in *clustered* environments, in which more than one machine behaves as if it were a single machine. This increases reliability.

Blowing by the Bottlenecks and Piloting Past the Pitfalls

The details of how to build and optimally configure the central computers for a network vary depending on what that network is to do, and also on which network operating system you will be using. However, many of the issues are common to every type of network and all network operating systems (NOS). When you understand these issues, you can see pretty easily how to apply that knowledge to your own situation.

The Workstation-to-Central-Computer Connection

The first issue to be dealt with in any network is providing adequate connectivity from the workstations to the central computers. I include the possibility of multiple central computers here for several reasons.

You might want to have multiple file servers simply to have enough file storage capacity as well as the ability to access all that storage quickly. Also, using multiple file servers is an effective means of breaking down the network connecting them to the workstations into several independent segments. You can also provide some redundancy, so the network can keep going even if one of the central computers should fail.

Direct Serial Connections to Each Workstation

If you are setting up an OLTP application, you might connect each workstation to the central computer by its own private serial cable. Certainly, this was the original way this type of network was built. But this approach can be problematic if you want to use a PC for the central computer, especially if you have a lot of workstations to support. Fortunately, better approaches are now commonly available.

Normally, a PC can have at most four serial ports. You can get plug-in port expander cards that will increase that number to a few dozen. Beyond that, you must use a separate communications processor, either in its own box linked to the file server over some high-speed data path such as a SCSI bus or a plug-in I/O subsystem such as the I2O cards mentioned earlier in this chapter.

Typical Network Connections

The more common way to set up OLTP systems and almost any other type of file server-based system of workstations, is by connecting all the computers, both workstations and file servers, via a network. As I told you in Chapter 15, many alternative networks are available: The most popular are Ethernet and Token Ring. Large Ethernet networks are often implemented using a mixture of 10BaseT, 10Base-2 and 10Base-5 cables (running

at 10Mbps) plus some similar cables on which the signals are running at 100Mbps or
even 1Gbps. Some of these cables will be optical-fiber cables instead of copper. Smaller
Ethernet networks installations use unshielded twisted-pair wiring—called 10Base-T (or
100Base-T) for Ethernet.

The simplest way to achieve the needed connectivity is simply to put a suitable network
interface card (NIC) into each workstation and each file server. Then, connect all of them
using a single network cable (or, if you are using a star topology, a single hub). This
works, but if the network is going to carry a lot of traffic, or if many workstations are to
be connected, you can do better by using a slightly more complex scheme.

You can gain a lot of throughput simply by segmenting the network. The simplest way to
do this in a system that has only one file server is to put multiple NICs into that server
and connect a different network cable to each. This totally separates all the data traffic
that goes between the file server and the workstations on one segment from all the traffic
on all the other segments. However, each NIC will use up an IRQ, an expansion bus slot,
and some port addresses, which means you cannot have many of them in a single PC.

Some NICs have a ROM that must reside at some specific memory address. Using even
two of these in one PC would cause a conflict. So, if you wish to use the strategy I am
discussing here, no more than one of the NICs you use may have such a ROM. (Future
versions of the PCI bus standard may permit resolving this sort of memory address conflict; negotiations on this point are still in process in the relevant standards committee.)

Another way to segment your network is to use a high-speed backbone, perhaps using
100Base-T or Gigabit Ethernet. At intervals on that backbone cable, attach a router/hub
that connects a separate 10Base-T or 100Base-T network to your individual workstations.
This is a common approach, but there are many others. Whatever works well is fine.

Interconnecting Multiple Central Computers

Arguably, a better way to segment your network is to use multiple file servers and let
each one serve also as a router. To implement this approach, put two NICs into each file
server. Connect groups of workstations to one of the NICs on each file server, and interconnect all the file servers via another network cable attached to their second NIC. (You
can combine this approach with the previous one by having each file server connect to a
separate high-speed cable with each one supporting multiple segments of lower-speed
network cable to groups of workstations. Then, the real "backbone" cable becomes the
one interconnecting the file servers.)

Figure 25.1 shows one example of this arrangement schematically: three file servers
connected by a backbone network. The backbone is shown as running at either 100Mbps
(for a small system) or at 1Gbps (for a larger system). There are fifteen workstations
(numbered PC #1 through PC #15) in this network, arranged into three segments of five
workstations each. These segments are shown as running at one-tenth the speed of the

backbone network cable. This is just about the relationship you want. In this example, it seems likely that the data traffic on any one of the segments would reach saturation of that segment's capacity before the backbone reached saturation. This is true even though file requests may have to be routed over the backbone to a more remote file server.

FIGURE 25.1
One good way to arrange multiple file servers so that they segment the network that serves the workstations.

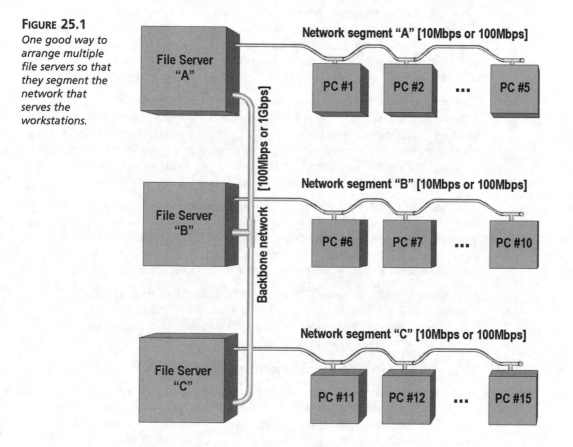

This approach also enables you to divide the workload among the several file servers. Assuming the demands for data coming from the workstations is fairly evenly divided among those workstations, and if each segment has an equal number of workstations, this should balance the load across all the servers. If you know that some workstations are much more demanding than others, just put fewer of them on each segment or file server to give them the level of service they require.

Input-Output Bandwidth Issues

Connectivity is one thing. Achieving acceptable throughput is another. The NICs in your file servers, in particular, will be called upon to deliver lots of bits of data as rapidly as possible. Each file server must talk to many workstations (and also to the other file servers), whereas each workstation talks only to the file server to which it is connected.

Be sure to use a good, fast NIC and place it on a fast bus. In today's PCs, this means using an SCSI-3 fast and Fast Ethernet PCI NIC, or a Fibre Channel PCI NIC. Also, use multiple NICs and multiple file servers as necessary to divide the workload until no one file server and no one NIC within a file server is overloaded.

For a simple file server, this is the main issue. The actual CPU type and speed are much less important, although you don't want to build a network of any size these days around a file server that uses a 486 or earlier CPU.

If your file server is also running server-based applications or doing major work as an OLTP back-end processor, the CPU speed may indeed be an issue. I'll talk a little more about that point in just a moment.

Don't Put Too Many Workstations on a Single Server

If you use the file server loop, with each file server supporting a number of workstations as your networking model (as I just suggested is often the best approach), then you must be careful not to overload any of the file servers. Remember, they now are serving as routers to all the other file servers, in addition to their jobs as file servers and perhaps server-based application execution engines. Alternatively, you can connect the servers through separate routers.

Workstations, Logins, and Processes: Which Number Matters Most?

All this talk of too many workstations brings up another issue: What is the relevant number to look at? The easiest to count is the number of workstations on a given segment of your network. But that might not be an extremely important number.

Much more important is the number of users who are logged in to your network from workstations on that segment. And beyond that, the number of sessions each one might have going at once is important. Finally, each session may have multiple processes or threads that are active, and each one of these adds to the overall load as well.

In the end, the numbers you care about most are the megabytes of data traffic on the network cable and the number of independent processes each file server is expected to support. Unfortunately, those are also the hardest numbers to estimate in advance. Wise network administrators get and use good monitoring programs to give them a constantly updated picture of the load on their network segments and also on their servers. That way, a valid judgment can be made about the correct numbers of workstations to hook up to each server.

Server RAM and Disk Space

Network operating systems have to do many of the same jobs as the operating system of a standalone PC or workstation, but the jobs they perform are sometimes much more demanding. To do their jobs properly, they must be given plenty of RAM and plenty of disk space. How much do you need, and why is it a more serious issue for a file server or back-end OLTP processor than for a workstation or desktop PC?

The hardest challenge faced by most file servers is simply handling the input-output demand. They must be able to access a huge number of different files simultaneously.

Think about what goes on in a typical desktop PC. By design, it is a single-user computer and probably is running at most a few processes at once. Each of those processes opens a few files and reads or writes information in those files. That operating system must maintain pointers to those files, and for optimum efficiency, it must cache the most recently read or written sectors for each one in its disk cache.

Now look at the file server's perspective. It must maintain all those pointers for each user's processes, and it must cache the most recently read or written sectors in each of the files accessed by each of those processes.

A modest-size disk cache that would be more than sufficient for a single-user PC will quickly be overwhelmed by the data flowing to and from the hard disk or hard disk array on a file server. That would render the disk caching virtually worthless.

Network operating system documentation may tell you about the amount of RAM you need per user. Unfortunately, the number you are most likely to find quoted tells you only about the absolute minimum amount of RAM needed to keep track of the files that each user has open, rather than the optimum amount you want to supply in your servers to let them create sufficiently large disk caches for each process. NetWare, for example, recommends (demands) about 16–32KB of RAM per user that is logged in (the actual amount varies by the version of NetWare).

A more realistic value for the optimal amount of RAM per user is at least 1MB. (The corresponding numbers for other NOSs are likely to be similar, as they all face common issues.) Those numbers should be applied per process, if some of your users are running multiple processes at once. For a network with a few tens of users, this recommendation is not too hard to meet. You can put several hundred MB or even a few GB of RAM in the typical PC that is intended for use as a network file server. And you certainly should.

If your network's central computers are also expected to run server-based applications or do OLTP back-end processing, you need even more RAM to hold those applications in addition to all the file pointers and cached data that the simple file server holds.

This recommendation becomes a problem when you have a large network (or one with lots of processes). When the number of processes passes a few hundred, it's impossible to get a PC that can hold enough RAM to do what you want it to do. The NOS might be able to address as much as several GB of physical RAM, but the motherboard memory sockets usually just cannot hold that much. (There are now a few exceptions to that statement. Some memory manufacturers, Siemens Semiconductors for one, have recently introduced DIMMs that each hold 1GB, and you can expect the PC makers to introduce server models that can use these DIMMs to support up to 32GB of RAM per PC. Still, no matter how large this limit grows, it is still a limit, and often that is the most important fact to know.)

If your network must support too many users and thus requires too much RAM for any one PC, you have another compelling reason to go to a network configuration that has multiple interconnected file servers. Load up each one with its maximum possible RAM until you have enough in the total of all the file servers to support all your users' processes properly.

Sometimes More MIPS Are Needed

I made the general point earlier that simple file servers are most burdened by the amount of input and output they must do. Back-end OLTP processors and file servers that are used to run significant numbers of server-based applications, on the other hand, may actually become *compute-bound*. That is, they may be limited in what they can do not by the speed of their network attachment or their disk arrays, but rather by the speed of their CPUs.

There are only two possible solutions. You can either add file servers or beef up the processing speed of each file server. If you choose to speed up each server, you must choose to buy the fastest CPU available or use multiple CPUs within each file server. (Of course, to get the very fastest performance you can, do both.)

The fastest CPUs for Windows NT file servers are the Alpha processors from Digital Equipment Corporation (DEC), a longtime minicomputer manufacturer recently purchased by Compaq. However, these machines are not really PCs. For UNIX file servers, you might want to use a Sun, IBM, or HP workstation—again, not a PC. If you want to use a super PC as the central computer, then for any of the popular NOSs you should use a Pentium II with the fastest available clock speed. In some situations, you can even increase that speed if you get a PC that contains multiple CPUs. (See Chapter 7, "Understanding PC Processors," for information on the upcoming processors from Intel and its competitors. As I write this, a Pentium II is the best you can do from Intel, but by the time you read this, there well may be a better choice on the market.)

Can Multiple Processors Help?

Mentioning multiple CPUs within a single PC brings up a whole new topic, and one that is just beginning to get the attention it deserves. This is the field of multiprocessor PCs.

Multiprocessing Is Different from Multitasking

Multiprocessing is very different from multitasking. *Multiprocessing* refers to using more than one CPU in a single computer. *Multitasking* refers to using one CPU for more than one computing task at a time.

You most likely multitask all the time on just about any PC. If you run Windows (including Windows 3.*x*, Windows 9*x*, or Windows NT), many things will be going on in the background that you are unaware of. And, you can intentionally start up several different programs and let them run at the same time. The same is true if you are running OS/2 or UNIX (including Linux) as your PC's operating system. Even a pure DOS machine can be doing some multitasking—for example, if you are doing background printing using the DOS PRINT command.

What appears as PC multitasking is actually an illusion. It is accomplished at a hardware and operating system level through *task swapping* among all the different tasks that are to be done "simultaneously." This means that the operating system directs the CPU at intervals to save all the "context" of what it is doing, and then to turn its attention to the next task.

One task after another gets a little bit of the CPU's attention. Eventually, all of them have been served and the CPU is directed to resume the first one. This swapping from one to another to the next and finally back to the first task keeps going constantly. Windows 3.*x* relies on cooperative multitasking, which means that it doesn't move on to a new task until the running task tells it that it may. This can lead to very choppy multitasking or even a total failure of multitasking. For this reason, all the other popular PC operating systems use preemptive multitasking. In that approach, the CPU is interrupted at fixed-time intervals so it will be sure to give some of its attention to each of the current tasks during every second of its operation.

If these *time slice* intervals are short, the user won't notice them and instead will see the PC apparently doing all those tasks at once. That is ordinary, everyday multitasking.

Multiprocessing is a whole different animal. This means having more than one CPU in a computer and somehow dividing up the work among all the CPUs. Many different schemes have been used to accomplish this, but in order for any of these schemes to work, the operating system must be able to divide the total workload into many separate tasks. Obviously, this can be done if each one is a separate program that has been launched by a separate user. But it can also be done within a single program in which different functions are routed to different processors.

When Multiprocessing Doesn't Help

Multiple processors don't always help. If you have a program that does one thing after another, a step at a time, and each step depends on the ones that have gone before, there is no way that using more than one processor will help speed the work of that program.

At the opposite extreme, suppose you have a program that does the same information-processing task over and over, each time applying it to a different set of data. The data to be used for all these different times of repeating the common task is all available at the beginning. You could speed up the program enormously if only you had as many processors as you had sets of data to process. Then each one could be working on its own set of data at the same time as all the others.

Of these two examples, the first is a highly linear program, but the second one could be rewritten for massively parallel processing, with great benefit. Most things we do with our PCs fall somewhere in the middle, and the majority lean toward the linear processes. A file server is one of the least necessarily linear problems, because we could, in principle, be serving each workstation's requests in parallel with all the rest. So for a file server, more than almost any other PC usage, using multiple processors can help.

But it will help only if two conditions are met: The hardware must be able to perform the multiple calculations in parallel without getting confused, and the software must know how to spread the work over all the processors.

Both these conditions can be met in a properly designed file server PC. But creating those PCs has turned out to be anything but easy. Still, the potential benefits are great, and many folks have given it a try—some have succeeded quite nicely.

What's Hard About Multiprocessor PCs?

Managing multiple processors is not a trivial business. The operating system must be much more sophisticated than is required for properly managing the traditional, one-processor PC. The hardware, furthermore, needs to be specifically tailored to take advantage of the additional processor' presence. As the complexity of both our needs and the tools we use to address those needs increases, multiprocessing will become more common. Hardware and software manufacturers are already preparing for this evolution, doing the research required to solve the unique problems such a system presents.

Hardware Issues

There are several hardware difficulties in building a multiprocessing PC, and there are a number of different ways of dealing with them.

The first issue any multiprocessor system must deal with is how to keep the processors from conflicting with one another as they access memory, caches, hard disks, and other resources in the computer. You can give each CPU its own bank of main memory. If you have a program that consists of many parts that can be run in parallel, you can simply load one part into the memory of each CPU and let each do the job with which it is presented.

The opposite extreme is to use only one pool of main memory, but add in some special hardware features (sometimes called gates, flags, or semaphores). These are mechanisms that can be used to tell a particular processor to wait a moment while another processor is doing whatever it must with the contents of main memory, then letting the first processor do what it wants in the same area. (If the two processors are trying to access very different addresses in main memory, there may be no conflict in letting them both do their access at the same time, but only if each has its own independent bus connecting it to the main memory.)

Sometimes there will be only one pool of main memory, but there will be a separate Level 2 cache for each CPU. (This assumes each CPU has its own Level 1 cache on board its chip.)

Another issue that must be dealt with when a PC contains multiple CPUs is how to coordinate the activity between them. There are two basic approaches to this:

- Asymmetric Multiprocessing—A single CPU is the master arbitrator for all functions in the PC. The operating system typically runs on this CPU, and all applications run on the other CPUs.
- Symmetric Multiprocessing—There is no single master arbitrator. The operating system utilizes a series of low-level data structures to control which task each processor is assigned.

Most PC operating systems are symmetric multiprocessing–based. They don't assign a single processor to arbitrate. Instead, they utilize some memory to control which processor is doing what.

In some large multiprocessor computers, the asymmetric multiprocessing approach is used. A Master CPU is given just this one job of supervising all the others. In those computers, typically, there are many other CPUs (a dozen or perhaps a few hundred) that all perform as peers, under the direction of the Master CPU.

In PCs, though, it's more common to have only a few CPUs. In fact, the most common configuration today uses only two CPUs; four CPUs are the next most common. In these cases, it would be a waste to let one CPU do nothing but manage the others. So, these systems all use some form of symmetric multiprocessing.

Software Issues

As you might imagine, the software to run multiprocessor computers is as diverse as the hardware configurations used in those computers. Indeed, the software must be designed with a knowledge of exactly how the hardware pieces can all work together, which means that any substantial change to the hardware configuration requires a totally new approach to the operating system's design.

The most important thing a multiprocessor OS must do is allocate the CPU resources among the processes (also called *threads*) it runs. That is, each program must have been broken down into independent threads, or chains of steps, to be taken. For each thread, there must be a set of data on which it will operate. Then the OS can send each thread with its data to a particular CPU for execution.

If the program must at some point combine the results from all the different threads, the OS will have to choose just one CPU to do the work of combining them. At that time, it can assign the other CPU or CPUs to any other thread tasks that may be pending, perhaps for some totally different application program.

How can the OS know whether each thread is independent of all the others? This question is important, because if any two or more of the threads act on the same data, they might have to run sequentially. When these threads belong to totally separate programs, the OS knows it is safe to allocate different threads to different CPUs.

More commonly though, the different threads are parts of the same overall process. Certainly, this is true of the file accesses being performed by a file server. In these situations, the only way to take advantage of multiple CPUs is for the author of the application program that is running to explicitly designate which threads can be run in parallel and which cannot. (For a file server, the relevant application is the one doing file-access management on behalf of all the network users. This is actually a portion of the network operating system running on top of the basic OS for the computer.)

At this stage of development, not a lot of PC application programs have been optimized for multiple CPU PCs, but among those that have are some of the most widely used products available. Adobe Systems, for example, has implemented multiprocessor support in its 32-bit flagship products—including FrameMaker, Illustrator, Photoshop, and Premiere—under Windows NT, Macintosh, and Sun SparcStation operating environments. You'll notice correctly that these tools are all graphics- and calculation-intensive, and Adobe began its multiprocessor support work over three years ago because the tasks this type of program performs are so suited to parallel processing.

Both DOS, with or without Windows 3.x, and Windows 9x have no notion of what to do with anything more than a single CPU. So putting in a second CPU and running the PC on any of these OSs is just a way to waste money and electricity.

Windows NT and OS/2, on the other hand, know how to use two or four CPUs simultaneously. Some flavors of UNIX know how to use even more CPUs. In any of these cases, there remains the question of whether the applications running on top of the basic OS kernel have been written to take advantage of multiple processors whenever they are available.

Summary

PCs are now so powerful that it can be very practical to use them as if they were mainframe computers or super-powerful graphics workstations. Both of those kinds of computers used to be far beyond anything a PC could do, but that no longer is the case.

(There are more powerful mainframes than any PC and more powerful workstations, but for many applications that used to require a mainframe, mini, or dedicated graphics workstation, a high-end PC is now more than adequate.)

Configuring a network and a PC to serve as its central computer requires looking at a lot of different issues that are of particular importance. The most important issues are input/output speed, providing enough central PCs to support the total load, and balancing the workload among all the central computers.

Multiprocessing PCs (those with more than one CPU) can be most helpful for graphics and digital video workstations, file servers, and other central computers in a network. The PC industry as a whole is just beginning to develop and standardize the possibilities of using multiple processors to speed up PCs. As we try to get more computing out of these boxes, though, this territory may become invaluable. There is only so much speed we can gain from wider buses and faster clock rates. At some point—barring an unforeseeable breakthrough—we also will need to use multiple CPUs working in parallel. For the majority of tasks we perform on our PCs, however, widespread utilization of multiple processors remains where it has been for the past two years—on the horizon.

PART VIII

PCs, the Internet, the Future, and You

You Can Touch the World, and It May Touch You, Too!

The Internet: Certainly, you've heard of it. Perhaps you use it daily in your work or for recreation. But do you understand what it is and how it works? The Internet is growing at a truly amazing rate. Very few things, if anything, have grown so rapidly and continued to do so for so long. Today it has changed virtually everything about the world of PCs. Tomorrow it might change virtually all aspects of our lives.

In this chapter I want to cover briefly some of the technology that is behind the Internet and its amazing growth and impact. This won't make using the Internet any harder or easier, or more or less useful, but it might scratch an intellectual itch or two.

What Is the Internet, and How Does It Work?

The Internet is a network, in many ways just like an office network. It connects many different computers together for the purpose of exchanging data. What's so different about the Internet is its scope. It is an interconnection of many smaller networks. Its scope is global. The number of connected computers is almost unimaginable, and its penetration into the ways we use our PCs to work and play is getting deeper by the day.

Also, the Internet—unlike every network of which it is composed,—is not something that is under anyone's control. No single person or organization is responsible for the Internet. Aspects of it have been entrusted to this group or that, but overall it is one of the most amazing demonstrations of a functional anarchy—quite possibly one of the few in all of human history.

The Internet Both Is and Is Not Like Any Other Network

At the technical level, the Internet (sometimes called simply "the Net") is very much like any other network. It consists of computers that are connected together and that exchange packets, which carry information. Some of these computer-to-computer links are permanent ones; others are made temporarily to facilitate a particular data exchange and then broken once more.

One way in which the Internet is unlike many networks is its degree of massively redundant interconnectedness. For any given two locations in most networks, there are at most a few paths to get from here to there. On the Internet, however, there are usually a huge number of alternative paths. (Still, in some key places, a substantial portion of the Internet can be temporarily severed from all the rest by just one mistake on the part of a backhoe operator.)

Another difference is the wide variation in the value of the data stored in the many connected computers and available to all who seek to access it. Most other networks connect computers belonging to a single company or organization, and those computers mainly store similar kinds of data with similar value to the people who make up those organizations. The Internet is, to put it bluntly, a mess in this regard.

Although you can't trust everything you find on the Internet, it is one of the most universally accessible, if not the richest, lode of information on the planet. After you learn to navigate around "the Net" and validate what you find there with a combination of careful consideration of the apparent source of the information and cross-checking with other sources, you may find that you turn to the Net more often than to almost any other information resource (I know I do)—simply because it will have proven to be the fastest way to answer most of your questions.

Furthermore, many people are now finding their natural communities of like-minded people via the Internet, without regard to their actual, physical locations. People who share interests on such divergent topics as flower arranging and terrorism have setup discussion and information sharing forums on the Net that span the planet. Whether this is a wonderful or a regrettable development for our society is something I will leave to sociologists to debate.

Internet Protocols

Although the Internet is, in general terms, like any other network, it also has some things about it that are special. For example, the Internet was built around a data transmission protocol that was designed just for it. Furthermore, most of the higher-level protocols used to control various kinds of network-mediated transactions were first developed for use across the Internet or its predecessors.

Of course, like almost any great success in any field, these have now been adopted for use in a wide assortment of networks, including some that aren't connected to the Internet at all. One of the hottest areas of development in many businesses now is what are termed *intranets*, which is simply copies of the Internet model on a smaller scale for use within a single organization.

Transmission Protocols, Gateways, and Firewalls

Just about any network carries data from place to place in packages called *packets*. You can think of them as being in many ways like letters inside envelopes. The letter is the data load being carried. The envelope provides information on the source and destination of the packet. One way in which network data packets differ from most letters carried in envelopes is that the packets are too small to hold an entire message. So, almost all files that are transferred over networks—and a file is what corresponds to a letter in our analogy—must be broken down into many small pieces. As Figure 26.1 shows, each one is enclosed in its own "envelope" (packet), and includes as header information the addresses of source and destination, as well as the sequence number of this particular piece of the "message" (file).

FIGURE 26.1
The envelope analogy as it relates to data.

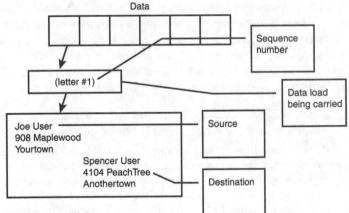

Note: Another analogy to help you understand what is going on is to think of shipping boxes instead of envelopes. If you order a large number of items from your favorite online shopping site, your order comes in a number of different boxes. Each box contains a portion of your order, and has the destination and sender address on it. Additionally, there is a sequence number on the box ("3 of 7") to easily let you see if all of the order came or not.

There are many alternative ways for a packet to find its way from the source to the destination. Because any one of those routes can be more or less congested at any given instant, it is quite possible for the packets that make up a single message to travel from the source to the destination via many different routes.

The implication is that the packets might arrive out of order. This is where the sequence number comes into play. The receiving software examines the envelopes and sorts them into the right order. It also acknowledges receipt of each one. If the sending software doesn't get an acknowledgement within a reasonably short time, it will assume the packet got lost and resend it.

One way this strategy can fail is if the link between sending and receiving programs has a high *latency*. This means simply that packets take an unusually long time to get from one point to another. That can happen even though the rate of data flow is very high, just because the overall distance to be traveled is very long. This is one of the salient characteristics of any link that must bounce off a satellite, for example. In this case the sending program may get tired of waiting and resend and resend packets *ad nauseam*. This, of course, doesn't really help things. Instead, it just clogs up the channel.

One way around this difficulty is a strategy called *TCP Spoofing*. Here, an intermediary is set up to receive and acknowledge packets midway, or just before the high latency portion of the link. The intermediary then forwards the packets over that high latency link and waits more tolerantly for the ultimate receiver to acknowledge their receipt. The satellite ground station responds to the sender in a timely manner and then, in what amounts to a separate conversation, sends the packets to the ultimate recipient and listens for acknowledgements with due allowance for latency.

Peter's Principle: When It Really Must Get There

If you, or any application programs you are running, want to be sure that each message sent out is received, ask the receiving person or programs for acknowledgments. Some programs do this automatically; many do not. In particular, email across the Internet can be an iffy proposition. So, for any important messages, I always include in the message a request to the recipient to reply immediately just so I will know that he or she has received my message.

The main protocol, itself actually a set of related protocols, that describes how the Internet shall carry packets of information is called *Transmission Control Protocol/Internet Protocol (TCP/IP)*. Like most of the other standards that describe how aspects of the Internet work, TCP/IP was developed by and then published (on the Internet, of course) for comment before it finally is adopted as a standard. The survival of the Internet as an operating medium of communication has depended upon the voluntary compliance with those standards by all the organizations, companies, and individuals whose computers make up the Internet.

Local area networks of PCs and larger computers have been built using many different wiring strategies and network operating systems (NOSs). I described several of these in Chapter 24, "The PC Reaches Out, Part Two: Through the NIC Node." Each NOS has its own preferred protocol for handling packets, although some are capable of supporting some other protocols as well.

Historical Aside

The reason behind this proliferation of protocols is twofold. First, companies make serious financial investments to support the development of their products. In order to protect those investments under patent law, companies devise unique, proprietary methods of doing whatever it is that their product is supposed to do. Government agencies award patents to unique processes (or devices) to enable the patent owners to better defend themselves against theft of their work.

Of more direct benefit to us as individual users, however, is the reality that technology evolves. As it does so, better ways of doing things—better protocols—are conceived that could not have been conceived in the past. Implementing these better (more efficient, more economical, safer, or whatever) protocols often means abandoning the past. People will, of course, choose to implement these new protocols on their own time frames, so it takes a very long time, often, for old protocols to die, leaving us with a wide array of options. Of course, to maximize the appeal of a new protocol, it must emulate old protocols, if necessary, thereby maintaining backward compatibility.

The most common NOS for PC LANs is Novell's NetWare. Traditionally, NetWare has used the proprietary protocol suite IPX/SPX. SPX (Sequenced Packet Exchange) is built on IPX (Internetwork Packet Exchange), and is a connection-oriented packet structure. All NCP (NetWare Core Protocols) were built on SPX (contrast this to Windows NT, which is built on SMB _ Server Message Blocks).

Recent versions of NetWare also support TCP/IP, but you must be careful. Until NetWare 5, there was support, but not fully integrated support in the Novell line and thus not all functions could be performed over TCP/IP. More and more network administrators are supporting and migrating to TCP/IP on their organizations' internal networks, as well as on links to the outside world. Which protocol an administrator decides on can make considerable difference when interacting with addressing schemes and routers. If the network must maintain TCP/IP anyway, such as for internet access, it doesn't make sense to burden routers with routing a additional packet type: IPX/SPX. Likewise, it does not make sense to manage another set of routing tables (one for TCP/IP and one for IPX/SPX).

Routers connect different network segments. When the packets traveling on the different segments use different transmission protocols, the router is responsible for translating between them. In effect, the router hardware opens the "envelope" of each packet, extracts the contents, and then places them in a new envelope that is properly addressed for travel on the next network segment.

Some routers are more than just packet shufflers; they also serve a security function. (Think of them as combination postal worker and security guard.) Some of these routers are called *firewalls*. They examine each packet they receive and test it against various rules. If it passes, they send the packet on to its destination.

Some of these rules might involve not passing packets coming from certain, untrusted source locations. Other rules might actually look inside the envelope and decide which packets to pass based on the data they contain. The person who configures the firewall has the responsibility to set up the correct set of rules to give the owner of that firewall the level of security that it was bought to provide.

A side effect of a firewall might be to disguise the true source of packets when it forwards them. This can be both helpful and a great inconvenience. Here is one common example: A company can give the appearance to the outside of having only a few Internet addresses, but in fact have on the inside a great many more. This allows the company to better control the flow of information in and out of its networked systems. Its marketing Web site can remain easily available to the general public while its confidential financial information remains accessible to a trusted few, but safe from the prying eyes of the rest of us. This sort of firewall router is often termed a firewall with *proxy server* functionality. The essential difference between it and a simpler firewall router is that the proxy server version will also set up a correspondence between the internal and external addresses for each conversation it permits to pass through its wall of safety. This correspondence will last only as long as that conversation does. Therefore, the external addresses can be reused as much as necessary while the "true" internal addresses of the users remain fixed.

This can be inconvenient when you want to carry on a conversation over the Internet with a computer that insists on knowing who you are. The firewall simply might not allow that type of conversation. The conversation you wanted to have might prove to be impossible to hold, unless you have a way of working around this roadblock. (Often, such workarounds are available; you just have to ask your network administrator in order to learn about them.)

One way that this hiding of internal IP addresses can be extremely helpful is in dealing with the limited supply of Internet addresses. At the hardware level, each computer on any TCP/IP network, from a small office LAN to the entire Internet, must have one or more IP addresses, or 32-bit numbers. Naturally, with only 32 bits in those addresses, there can be no more than approximately four thousand million of them. (See Chapter 3, "Understanding Bits, Nybbles, and Bytes," if you aren't clear as to why this is so.) Each computer's IP address must be unique in that computer's world—which is to say among all the computers that it can see directly via the TCP/IP protocol.

Technical Note: IP addresses are commonly expressed as four numbers separated by decimal points, sometimes called dotted-decimal notation. Each of the four numbers is a decimal expression of the value of one of the four bytes that make up the total 32-bit IP address. So, for example, the IP address of 206.85.92.79 is equivalent to the 32-bit number 11001110 01010101 01011100 01001111. (This IP address happens to be the one assigned to the primary domain name server, or DNS, at Earthlink, my Internet service provider.)

Overlaid on—and completely independent from—the IP address scheme is a more human-friendly naming scheme for computers and their users. Rather than referring to a computer as 11001110 01010101 01011100 01001111, or even as 206.85.92.79, it is easier to remember it by a name such as SALES, GOOFY, or any other you want to assign it. This text value is known as a *host* name, and can be used when referring to the computer in such things as email. Thus, John's e-mail address is john@agoodman.com. This says that his username is john, and his mail account is accessible at the computer host named agoodman in the top-level domain com.

There are a limited number of top-level domain names, and mostly they indicate either the type of computers in that domain or the country where the computer is located. The most common top-level domain name is com, which stands for some type of commercial entity. The net top-level domain refers to computers belonging to companies that provide Internet services. The gov top-level domain name includes most U.S. government entities. The edu top-level domain includes most colleges and universities.

Any time you specify a computer's domain name, as in Symantec.com, that name must be translated into the computer's IP address. This is done by sending a message to some Domain Name Server (DNS), which will either know the translation or know which computer to ask.

Eventually, this process brings back to the requestor an IP address that it should use in place of the host and domain name. Then, when messages for a user at a certain computer arrive there, that computer looks in its table of usernames to determine in which actual mailbox it is to put that message.

When the IP address scheme was first proposed, it seemed like four billion addresses were surely going to suffice for a long time. But with the incredible growth of the Internet, it is now proving to be a too-limited supply. The way in which those addresses were originally parceled out to organizations further limited the number that any one group could use. Hiding large numbers of internal addresses behind a proxy server type of firewall is one way some companies are getting around this shortage. A name that you may encounter for this process is *Network Address Translation (NAT)*.

A pure *proxy server* router is an alternative to a firewall in this context. It is a computer that does the address hiding and protocol conversions, but doesn't do the rule-based packet filtering that is the essence of a firewall computer.

This is a problem now, but in the next few years we can expect a new generation of IP addresses (referred to as IPv6) to arrive with double the number of bits. Ipv6 addresses are 16 bytes long, written as eight hex numbers separated by colons (each hex number standing for 16 bits). Surely, *that* number of address possibilities will suffice for a long time—even if the Internet continues its exponential growth for many more decades.

Assuring Quality of Service

The new Internet that is being developed today, based on IPv6 addressing, also will have a number of other important new features. One of the most eagerly awaited is support for *Quality of Service (QoS)*. This is a new protocol that lets one tag packets by the importance of their getting where they are going in a timely manner.

There are many reasons why one might want to use this feature. One is if you are sending a "streaming" multimedia file. This could be a movie or TV show, or a song, and so forth. Whatever it is, the intention is that the recipient will play it immediately, as it is coming over the Internet. (Another example would be a telephone conversation that was routed over the Internet. This very "hot" new topic is often referred to as "voice over IP" or VoIP.)

If you are going to enjoy playing such a streaming multimedia file, it had better keep coming all the time until it is through. Likewise, to enjoy talking to someone in a telephone conversation you want not to have any long delays in the transmission of your speech or that of the other party.

The other reason for wanting quick and consistent packet delivery might simply be that you value your message very highly, and in particular its timely delivery. Think, for example, of an order to one's stock broker to buy or sell a security that is rapidly changing its price. Any inadvertent delay might cost you a great deal of money.

Of course, everyone would *like* to have his or her messages go over the Internet at the fastest possible speed. But are you willing to pay extra to get that service? Some people will be willing, at least some of the time. This is why it is important to have a way to differentiate those packets whose quickest possible delivery is most important. Then users and ISPs can negotiate what level of service they'll get, and what they will have to pay for that service.

Other Common Internet Protocols

The TCP/IP set of protocols handles the problems of routing packets from place to place and reassembling messages in an adequate manner. (There is still the nagging problem of ensuring that UDP messages actually do get where they are going, but that can be handled at a higher level with an additional acknowledgment protocol of some kind.)

Other Internet protocols deal with higher-level transactions. For example, the File Transfer Protocol (FTP) specifies how one computer can ask another computer to send it a copy of one or more files. Various mail protocols deal with how to handle email.

(These include protocols for addressing messages and maintaining virtual mailboxes.) The Gopher protocol lets you access information on a remote computer arranged into a hierarchical menu. The rlogin and Telnet protocols are for remote logins; they specify a way in which you can convert your computer into a terminal to some remote computer (provided you have an account on that remote computer). *rlogin* stands for "remote login" and is used from one server to another on the same network, while telnet stands for "terminal network" and is used from one server to another wheyther or not they're on the same network or not.

Some of the more recent additions to the family of Internet protocols are ones used in connection with the World Wide Web. Even more protocols are being proposed all the time, and no doubt some of them will be adopted as official Internet protocols at some future time.

One standard whose popularity is growing is "multicasting." This means that when you send a digital video to multiple recipients, instead of sending actual copies of each data packet to each recipient, the data packets can carry multiple addresses and be sent to all those places in the most efficient manner possible. (That is to say, a packet might travel over most of the distance from you to your recipients before being copied into the video player program at each recipient's location. Thus, on almost all the links, only one copy of each packet would have to be transmitted.)

As TV and radio broadcasting over the Internet continues to grow in popularity, the importance of multicasting will continue to grow along with it. Right now, there are many Web sites that offer something very much like a radio or TV broadcast. But the way they work today requires that a separate copy of every data packet be sent from that site to each of the (most likely a huge number of) receiving computers. The consequent growth in the Internet's total traffic could be sharply limited if almost all of those duplicate packets could be avoided—which is precisely what multicasting promises to do.

Please keep in mind that all these protocols are voluntary standards. Someone proposes one, a committee of volunteers discusses and publishes it for additional commentary, and then it gets adopted and published as an official Internet standard. However, that doesn't ensure that anyone will actually use it. Still, this process has proven to work remarkably well. The truly useful protocols do get widely supported by hardware and software vendors soon after (or in some cases well before) their official adoption.

A Lot More Than Just Data Is Out There

The beginnings of the Internet can be found in establishment of the ARPAnet by the U.S. Defense Department's Advanced Research Projects Agency in the late 1960s. The agency had only a few, limited goals in mind when it set up this novel experiment.

The Early Internet Had Limited Uses

One thing the original designers of the ARPAnet hoped to accomplish was to provide a means of sharing some otherwise wasted computing resources in widely separated places. Thus, for example, if a researcher at the University of California in Los Angeles wanted to do something but his local computers were all busy, he might send his job over the ARPAnet to a computer in Upsala, Sweden. If it was the middle of the day in Los Angeles, it would be late in Upsala, and possibly their computer would be idle. If it was, his job could be sent there from Los Angeles, run there, and the results could be returned to Los Angeles sooner than the job could be run in Los Angeles (where it would have to wait for a computer to become available). To promote this goal, the ARPAnet had to support remote logins, file transfers, and a few other simple functions.

The other principal use envisioned for the ARPAnet was as a testing ground for this and other ideas about networking. Experiences with these two uses of the ARPAnet led the DOD to expand it to what eventually became the Internet.

Almost as an afterthought, the designers decided it would be handy to provide a mechanism that would allow a user at one computer to send messages to people who were near one of the other computers connected to the ARPAnet. This would allow the network researchers to talk among themselves as they did their experiments on the network. While they were at it, they made the mechanism available to anyone who wanted to use it—provided that each person had an account on some computer connected to the ARPAnet.

To everyone's surprise, email soon turned out to be the most highly valued aspect of the ARPAnet and, later, of the Internet into which that network grew. Even today, email is one of the main reasons why people start using the Internet.

Decades passed with little change in the kinds of things people did on the Internet. Email ruled. Throughout the 1970s, file transfers became the next most important use, and remote logins were the third. Perhaps the most appreciated of the new uses for the network were real-time chat facilities and multiperson games, the use of which exploded in the early 1980s.

The World Wide Web Brought the Internet to the Masses, and Vice Versa

Starting in 1993, the World Wide Web (also called "the Web") came into being. Internet usage exploded, and it continues to explode even more daily. Some people confuse the Internet and the World Wide Web. They are definitely *not* the same thing. The World Wide Web (WWW) is simply one of many uses of the Internet.

If you liken the Internet to a system of highways, the WWW is somewhat like the practice of commuting to work. It is something that happens on the Internet. This definition tells you that it is something that lives or happens on the infrastructure that is the Internet, but it doesn't tell you much about just what the pieces are that make up the Web or how they are accessed.

What Exactly Is the World Wide Web?

The World Wide Web is the entire collection of resources that you can access, from anywhere in the world, over the Internet by use of a Uniform Resource Locator (URL, also called a Universal Resource Locator). These resources take many forms, including textual documents, static graphic images, video clips, and programs.

The notion of a URL is a very flexible, powerful, and important one. Any complete URL has at least three parts. The first part of any full URL is a keyword that tells what protocol must be used to access this resource. If the URL starts out `http:`, it points to a resource that will be accessed by using the Hypertext Transfer Protocol (HTTP). This is the means used to request *Web pages*, which are files that have been formatted in accordance with the Hypertext Markup Language (HTML) specification.

If a URL starts out `ftp:`, it specifies a resource to be accessed by use of the FTP protocol. Another common keyword is `mailto:`, which specifies that this URL tells you where to send an email message. Finally, the keyword `file:` specifies a resource file located on your local computer.

The second and third parts of a full URL locate the resource in question. The second part is the name of the computer where this resource can be found (in the case of a file) or that contains the intended destination (in the case of a `mailto:` URL). The third part is the name of the resource (or destination) on that computer.

Here is an example of a full URL:

```
http://www.w3.org/TR/REC-html40/
```

The first part of this URL is `http:`, so you should know that it is pointing to a resource that is to be accessed using the HTTP protocol. The second part of this URL is `//www.w3.org/`, which specifies the computer we are referencing. In this case, it is the computer that holds all the activities of the principle WWW standards group. The third part, `TR/REC-html40/`, specifies the particular resource on this computer, which in this case is the current specification for the HTML language.

Warning: One point that must be stressed for PC users is that at least the third part of any URL is case sensitive, which means capital letters and lowercase letters are treated differently. So, in this example, if that last part were typed as `TR/WD-HTML40/` or as `tr/wd-html40/` (or any capitalization other than what I've shown in the preceding full URL), the resulting URL wouldn't necessarily point to the HTML specification document. Most likely, it wouldn't point to any resource at all. The second part of any URL (the machine name) is the only part that is guaranteed to be not case sensitive. The best plan is for you always to scrupulously follow the case you see when copying a URL. Doing so will save you from many failures to link to a resource.

continues

> That part of the URL must be stressed for PC users, in particular, because most file accesses on a PC aren't case sensitive. You can pretty much ignore capitalization of all filenames (and sometimes you'll see Windows 9x, in particular, change the capitalization for you spontaneously). That is totally different from how most other computers in the world treat filenames. This means that PC users might have picked up a bad habit of ignoring case in filenames, which will not serve them well when accessing resources on the WWW.

The HTML standard also defines the notion of a *relative* URL and a *fragment* URL. The relative URL simply is all or a portion of the third part of a URL. The first two parts are defined implicitly by context. Thus, if an HTML document includes a reference to `./images/BigBlueCar.gif`, this is a pointer to a particular Graphical Interchange Format (GIF) image file located in the `images` directory (a subdirectory of the current directory—as indicated by the "."). If you were moving back from the current directory, ".." would signify one directory back, whereas "/" as the first character would signify the root directory.

> **Warning:** Notice that the directory separator symbol is the forward slash character ,not the backward slash normally used on PCs. This is due to the Internet having been traditionally the domain of UNIX servers. The UNIX operating system uses the forward slash for this purpose, and all Web servers adhere to this for compatibility reasons.

A *fragment* URL is a normal URL (full or relative) that has a # character (sometimes called a hash mark, or a pound sign) at the end, followed by a name. This name refers to a region within the resource pointed to by the URL. This form is commonly used to position your view of that resource so you can immediately start reading at the named location. Here is a sample of a fragment URL:

```
http://www.w3.org/TR/REC-html40/intro/intro.html#h-2.1.1
```

This points to section 2.1.1 of the specified document. The section name evidently is `h-2.1.1`, and the document name is `intro.html`. That document describes the World Wide Web, and this section describes URIs (Uniform Resource Identifiers) and URLs.

Another variation on a URL that you may have encountered, and wondered about, is one that includes a tilde in the third section. For example:

```
http://www.earthlink.net/~joeblow/images/neatpix.jpg
```

In this URL, the tilde means that one or more subdirectory layers have been omitted. The tilde and the characters that follow it, up to the next forward slash character, point to that subdirectory below the host's root whose name is given by the characters following the tilde character. (This can work reliably only if that name appears only once in the directory tree being searched. Because normally that name is the login name of a user of that computer, this uniqueness is pretty well guaranteed.) This usage seems quite common among ISPs and Web page hosts, but it is not specified in the URI or URL definitions,.

Technical Note: If you really want to know the full, gory details of all the different ways a URI can be described, you may wish to look at the official W3 Consortium "Request for Comment" document (RFC 2396) that describes them. Here is that URL. But be forewarned. This is a *very* geeky document. In it you will also find links to other, related documents.

```
ref HYPERLINK http://www.ics.uci.edu/pub/ietf/uri/rfc2396.txt
http://www.ics.uci.edu/pub/ietf/uri/rfc2396.txt
```

What Is HTML?

Web pages are essentially small files of HTML-encoded text. This is a relatively simple example of a more general class of formatted files described by an international standard that was devised many years ago, called the *Standard Generalized Markup Language (SGML)* specification.

You can access an HTML document by using what is called a *user agent*. This most commonly is a Web browser, such as Internet Explorer or Netscape Navigator, but it can be a text-only browser, such as Lynx, or a program that reads an HTML file and then pronounces it out loud for a blind user.

Basically, HTML files are just text files, but they contain some special blocks that indicate various things other than normal textual content. What I have referred to as the special HTML words or blocks are formally referred to as HTML *elements*. The beginning of an element of HTML is often indicated by a start tag. For example, <HEAD> would mark the start of the header region. The end of that element is indicated by an end tag which is identical to the start tag except for the insertion of a forward slash right after the opening angle-bracket symbol. For our sample case, it would be </HEAD>.

Not all elements must begin or end with a tag. Sometimes, these locations are implied and don't need to be explicitly specified, although most of the time the start tag (at least) is needed.

HTML elements serve one of three general kinds of function. Some, such as HEAD, TITLE, and BODY, specify general areas within an HTML document. (The HEAD area holds general information about the document—information that your user agent, which normally is your browser program, will use but will not display. The TITLE area, which fits inside the HEAD area, contains the title that will show up in your browser's title bar. The BODY area contains the essential content of the page.)

The second kind of element specifies a format for some portion of the content. This could include the font, color, or location of some text, or the size of a frame to hold an image, and so on. In the latest version of the HTML specification, however, this kind of HTML element is discouraged.

Instead, authors of Web pages are encouraged to use style sheets to define the appearance of various items. If that is done, this second kind of element becomes not the description of a style, but merely a pointer to a named style. Using style sheets in this way enables you to separate the content from its appearance. This lets you make many pages that resemble one another by preparing just one style sheet and referring to it in all those Web pages.

The third kind of element specifies some external resource. This might be an element that causes that resource to be included in the current page. The most common example of this are the elements that cause images (commonly in GIF or JPEG files) to show up on a Web page, or it might be an element that links to another resource. This is best exemplified by a hyperlink, which loads a new Web page when you double-click on it.

Other uses for this third category of HTML element include loading a music file and launching a program to play it, or loading and running a Java applet, and so on. (I'll explain what a Java applet is later in this chapter.)

Here is a small sample of HTML code. This extract from the copyrighted source code was taken from an actual Web page (for the Exploratorium hands-on science museum in San Francisco—one of my favorite museums), with its permission. I have omitted most of the lines of code in this Web page, because they didn't show any new principles beyond those shown in the lines you see here. If you want to see all the lines of code (and also see what they look like with all the images loaded, and so on.) then point your browser to this URL:

```
http://www.exploratorium.edu/
```

When you have connected to the site, you can use the source-code viewing option of your Web browser program to see the HTML coding of the page. (Any Web site owner may, of course, change the content of that Web site at any time. What you find there may differ from what I am showing you here, but the principles used will be the same.)

Now for the HTML code sample. The ➡ character at the beginning of some of the lines indicates that those lines are really continuations of the line just above them. So imagine that the page is wide enough, and that you stack every such line at the end of the line just before it.

```
<HTML>
<HEAD>

  <META NAME="Description" CONTENT="Exploratorium ExploraNet- the online home
➡ of the Exploratorium, a hands-on museum of science, art, and human
➡ perception in San Francisco. ExploraNet provides interactive online
➡ exhibits and exhibitions, activities, science news, and publications,
➡ as well as general information about the museum. Online since 1993.">
  <TITLE>Exploratorium: ExploraNet</TITLE>
</HEAD>
<BODY BGCOLOR="#ffffff" BACKGROUND="images/back.gif" LINK="#bcac58"
VLINK="#b7acb7">

<TABLE WIDTH="517" BORDER="0" CELLSPACING="0" CELLPADDING="0" HEIGHT="585">
<TR>
<TD WIDTH="122" VALIGN="TOP" HEIGHT="584" ALIGN="CENTER">
➡ <P><IMG SRC="images/palace_anim3.gif" WIDTH="102" HEIGHT="120"
➡ ALT="The Palace of Fine Arts"
ALIGN="BOTTOM" NATURALSIZEFLAG="0"></P>

…

<TABLE WIDTH="90%" BORDER="0" CELLSPACING="2" CELLPADDING="0">
<TR>
<TD WIDTH="8%"></TD>
<TD WIDTH="92%">The Exploratorium is a museum of science, art, and human
➡ perception with over 500 interactive &quot;hands on&quot; exhibits.
➡ Each year more than 600,000 visitors come to the Exploratorium, over
➡ 90,000 students and teachers come on field trips, and more than 2000
➡ teachers attend professional development programs which focus on
➡ inquiry-based teaching and learning in the K-12 classroom. </TD>
➡ </TR>
</TABLE>
</P>

<P><CENTER><FONT SIZE=-1>&copy; The Exploratorium 3601 Lyon Street San
➡ Francisco, CA 94123 Tel: 415-563-7337</FONT></CENTER></TD></TR>
</TABLE>
</BODY>
</HTML>a
```

Extending the HTML Standard

I said that HTML is a subset of SGML. Successive versions of HTML have incorporated more and more of the features of SGML. But SGML was developed to describe documents intended solely for printing on paper. Now, with the full capabilities of computers and the vast variety of the World Wide Web, that isn't nearly a broad enough vision.

Many different groups have worked at extending the notion of what all might be included in the hypertext language of the Web. Like all Internet standards, these ideas are first developed by individuals or companies, then proposed and debated on the Internet, and finally adopted by a standards group, most often the World Wide Web Consortium (W3C).

One group has proposed adding what it calls Cascading Style Sheets (CSS). This is a means of specifying the appearance (formatting) of Web pages both as they will appear on screen and when they are printed to paper—and doing so independently from the specification of the content of those pages.

A very different approach to extending HTML has been the creation of what is now called the Extensible Markup Language (XML). This is not merely a set of new terms for the markup language; it is instead a set of meta-markup language terms. That is, it defines how the markup language may be dynamically extended. The developers' intention is to make it possible for anyone to create his or her own private extension to HTML in a way that everyone else can understand.

One example of this is the new Adobe-developed, and proposed, W3C standard called the Precision Graphics Markup Language (PGML). This is essentially a blend of Adobe's PostScript and Portable Document Format (PDF) standards, and it is explicitly an example of the sort of extension XML contemplates.

A related development aims to define something called XSL, which you may have guessed stands for Extensible Style Sheets. This would permit extending the CSS standard in much the same manner as XML does for HTML.

To learn more about these topics, you may wish to check out these URLs:

```
http://www.w3.org/TR/REC-html40/     (for the HTML, version 4.0 specification)

http://www.w3.org/TR/WD-css2         (for the CSS, version 2 specification)

http://www.w3.org/TR/WD-xml          (for the XML specification)

http://www.w3.org/TR/NOTE-XSL-970910 (for the XSL proposal)

http://www.w3.org/TR/1998/NOTE-PGML  (for PGML proposal)
```

Sometimes a Browser Isn't Enough

The two main HTML user agent (browser) programs used on PCs today are Microsoft's Internet Explorer and Netscape's Navigator. Dozens of alternative browsers are available, however, plus add-on modules for many word processors to let them edit and save HTML files. All these browsers can read and display an HTML file. They mostly can also display some of the embedded graphic images. In particular, most HTML browsers understand GIF and JPG (JPEG-compressed) files. So, if an HTML element in a page specifies that a GIF or JPG file should be loaded and displayed, the browser will do just that.

However, none of the browsers understands every graphics file format in common use. For example, I don't know of even one that will display EPS (PostScript graphics) files.

So, while you can put in an HTML element that specifies that a certain EPS file should be loaded, when the browser reads that tag it will not be capable of fully complying with the instructions. Instead, the browser will pop up a dialog box that points out that it is being asked to load a file of a type it doesn't know about, and it will offer to go to a page of plug-ins to see if there is one there that would be helpful. If you have an OLE 2–capable application for viewing those files, Internet Explorer will allow you to see them.

What's a Plug-In?

What are plug-ins, and how do they work? Essentially, they are small helper programs that add to the functionality of your Netscape browser. The same function exists in browsers other than Netscape's but there they are called add-ins, ActiveX controls, and Plug-ins. These will be discussed separately later, but for now consider the concepts behind all of them.

When a modern Web browser loads, in addition to loading its own program code into memory, it also loads any plug-ins that you have previously installed. Then, when it is scanning Web pages, if the browser encounters an element that specifies acting on a resource of a type it doesn't understand, it will check to see whether any of its loaded plug-in programs understands this type of resource. If such a plug-in exists, the browser will hand over control to it, pointing it to the resource in question as it does so. After the plug-in has finished processing that resource in whatever way it has been programmed to handle it, the plug-in will pass control back to the Web browser.

Whenever any modern Web browser encounters an element that asks it to do something it cannot do natively and that none of its loaded plug-ins can handle, the browser is built to prompt the user and then, if the user wishes, to look for a suitable helper (plug-in) program that will be capable of handling that type of request. If a suitable plug-in can be found, you can download and install it into your Web browser for use during your next session using that browser program. (At present, you may need to close the browser before you can install a new plug-in because, until very recently, browsers load plug-ins only when they themselves load.)

Dozens of different plug-ins are now available for both Internet Explorer and Navigator. (Because the two browsers integrate with plug-ins in subtly different ways, each plug-in must be written to work with a specific browser.)

I have been using Netscape Navigator, version 4.5 for a fairly short time. Already, I find that I have 12 plug-ins installed for it. Here is my present list, as it is presented to me by Navigator (for illustration purposes only):

- Windows Media Player Plug-in Dynamic Link Library
- ZipSurfer
- Netscape vCalendar Plug-in v.4.0
- Shockwave Flash 3.0 r8

- RealPlayer(tm) LiveConnect-Enabled Plug-In
- QuickTime Plug-In for Win32
- Netscape Default Plug-in
- Netscape Media Player, Audio Streaming Plugin, v.1.1.1516
- Cosmo Software browser plugin for viewing interactive 3D content on the Web using Netscape 3.x/4.x on Win95/NT
- Headspace Player Stub for Netscape Communicator
- NPAVI32, avi plugin DLL
- Sound Player for Netscape Navigator, v.1.1.1515

Plug-ins are programs, and as such they may be written using any of the many PC programming languages. These days, they most often will be written using C, C++, or Java.

> **Warning:** This approach in creating helper programs is very general. It enables the programmer of the plug-in to make his or her program do just about anything that any other PC program could do. This means that you'll probably want to download and use only plug-ins that you get from a trusted source. Otherwise, you could be making a home for a "Trojan Horse" program that will do who-knows-what damage to your data at some inopportune moment.

Making Web Pages Responsive: CGI Scripts

By the very nature of the concept, HTML is mostly about displaying pages of information. Then, whenever you click on some hyperlink, your browser will summon a new HTML page to display. These pages can include not only the text that is in the file pointed to by the URL used to load the page, but can also include graphics images, video clips, or other (HTML) text pages inside a frame.

That sounds fairly staid, but Web pages today are often dynamic and highly interactive creations. You might find that displayed pieces change when you move your mouse pointer over them. When you enter information into a form, that form could add boxes, change colors, or otherwise indicate that it had received and was acting upon your input.

How is this done? Having the HTML code on the Web page you are viewing causes some program to load and run as well. That program can be either one that runs on the Web server, or one that runs in your PC.

For most of the time that the World Wide Web has existed, the dominant way of doing this job has been to use CGI scripts. In fact, a recent survey of the WWW suggests that about two thirds of the pages are just static HTML, and almost all the rest are made more active by the use of CGI scripts. Very few use any of the highly talked about new methods such as ISAPI, Netscape's server API, and Active Server Pages (ASPs)—server-side alternatives to CGI. Complementing the server side are VBScript, and JavaScript (both being client side-technologies). Still, with all the push those new technologies are getting, we can expect them to become much more prevalent in the next couple of years.

Common Gateway Interface (CGI) is a standard type of program which communicates with the Web server to produce custom Web pages. It is similar to a DOS batch file, but with considerably more power. A CGI script can be launched by an element on any Web page you may be viewing. These CGI scripts are mostly written in a language called Perl. This is an interpreted language (like BASIC), although now there are also compilers for Perl (just as there are for BASIC).

Any CGI script can be interpreted on-the-fly from its source file form (much like a DOS batch file is), or it can be compiled into a binary program. Either way, it will do the same thing. The advantages to the compiled version include both that it can run faster and that it will be less vulnerable to a hacker attack. The disadvantage is that the author must go through an extra compilation step after completing and debugging the interpreted version of the script.

A general property of all CGI scripts is that they are server-side scripts, which means they are programs that execute on the Web server. You access the server with your browser by pointing to some HTML page. That page is downloaded to your PC, and its contents are displayed on your PC's screen. However, any reference it contains to a CGI script will be sent back to the Web server and will cause the script to be executed there. The results of this execution are returned to the browser.

The good aspect to this, from the Web server administrator's viewpoint, is that only CGI scripts that are properly installed on her machine can be run in this fashion. That gives the administrator a chance to check all the CGI scripts that the users of this machine might want to load before they are made active.

The good thing, from your point of view, is that whatever those CGI scripts do, they do it on the distant machine. Only some response HTML-tagged text can make its way from that script into your PC.

The bad thing about this strategy, is that it has the potential to be quite slow—especially if your connection to the Internet is clogged. You may do something at your end that triggers a CGI script at the remote end of a long and sometimes congested link. It can be many seconds or even minutes before the intended action is taken at the remote computer and evidence of it arrives back at your PC. This is okay for some purposes for which CGI scripts are used, but it isn't really suitable for the type of quick-response interactivity that is becoming more and more popular today.

So, how can one get really snappy, exciting animation and interactivity out of a Web page? Move the programs that make all that excitement happen over from the Web server to the PC (or other computer) that is viewing the Web page.

What's All This Jive About Java? And What's an ActiveX Component?

This is where ActiveX, VBScript, Java, JavaScript, and Java Beans come into the picture. The first two I just named are from Microsoft; Java and its siblings are from Sun Microsystems.

So the first question is, "What's Java?" Your second question should be, "Why should I care?" To some people, Java is just a new programming language. To others, it is nearly a religion.

Actually, everyone agrees that Java is a new programming language. It is heavily object-oriented. It was devised partly by simplifying C++ and partly by looking carefully at what programmers really need in today's world of distributed, multiplatform computing.

Java has some special qualities. These qualities have moved it up from merely another computer programming language to its present exalted status as the most-probable long-term Microsoft killer and the carrier of the torch for cross-platform interoperability.

Sun's phrase for all this is "Write Once, Run Everywhere." The essential idea is that it, or someone, will create a Java Virtual Machine (JVM) for each computer platform (computer hardware plus operating system). Then, anyone can write a Java program and it will run unchanged on every platform that has a JVM. This is not the first time someone has proposed something like this, but the need for cross-platform support has never before been greater, and now might be the first time that the idea has a fighting chance to succeed.

One reason for this optimism about Java is that Sun is giving it away, and many people who are nervous about Microsoft's dominance are supporting it. The pressure has, in fact, become so intense, that even Microsoft is supporting it—although Sun claims that Microsoft is doing so in a way that both violates the latter's license agreement with Sun and jeopardizes the platform-independent nature of Java.

Java Basics

This sounds fine, but a bit abstract. Okay, let me give you a few more details and see if that will help flesh out the picture for you. Java, in its original form, is an interpreted language. The interpreter is a part of the JVM.

Microsoft wrote a JVM that became a part of its Internet Explorer (IE). Microsoft repeated this for each platform version of IE that it has released. (This means a separate JVM for the Windows 3.x and Windows 95 environments on a Wintel PC, as well as one for the Macintosh.) Netscape wrote another one for each version of Navigator or

Communicator. This means all the difficult hardware and operating system–dependent details have been handled by them. Now you or anyone else can write a Java application, and so long as all the JVMs out there can interpret everything that is legal in a Java program, your program will run on all the platforms with JVMs.

This is not new. Essentially, the notion of a JVM is similar to a software simulator that runs on one platform and in the process makes it look like another platform. Thus, we have SoftPC, a program with versions for the Macintosh and NeXT computers that emulate the PC well enough that you can run almost any PC program on those "foreign" computers quite nicely. There is a problem with SoftPC and all the other emulators that use this idea, however. They are slow. Very slow.

Critics of Java said right away that it would fail simply because any Java program was bound to be ever so much slower than a well-optimized program to do the same task that had been written in a language especially devised for the platform on which the program was to run. Java proponents answer that this might be true, although they hope to narrow the performance gap soon, but the savings in programmers' time in not having to prepare a version of every program for every platform is so great that it will outweigh any performance problems. Besides which, the huge and rapid improvements in processor power are making even the most inefficient software run at acceptable speeds.

So far, that seems to be pretty much true—within some limits. There are two main uses for Java at this time. One is to create Java applets. These are little programs that run in conjunction with a Web browser, usually. The other use is to create full-scale, standalone applications.

Although Java applets are not all that abundant in numbers so far, they have been quite well accepted in the Internet world. Java stand-alone applications have not. The main reason is that what Java applets are doing, so far, is so simple that even with a 10-fold degradation in performance (over the comparable C program), they run fast enough. The limiting factor in most Internet-related applications is the speed with which Web pages and other resources can be downloaded—not the speed with which the applets that can be included in those downloads run when they are on your PC. When it comes to stand-alone software applications, however, such as an office suite, performance is nearly everything. Corel tried to write a Java version of its WordPerfect office suite, but it just didn't take off in the marketplace.

One way in which Java applet performance can be improved is by adding to the JVM a Just-In-Time (JIT) Java compiler. This is a program that receives the Java source code and spits out native binary code for the platform on which it is running. This binary code can be reused whenever the Java source code recycles through a given portion of its source code. With this and other careful tweaks, Java is now showing some fairly respectable performance numbers—not yet catching up to C or C++, but getting quite close.

Security Issues and Java

Java's natural home is the Internet, where programs written in Java can be downloaded over the Net into different computers. This diversity of computers goes far beyond the matter of their hardware and operating systems. They are also owned by a huge diversity of people and organizations. This raises some serious security concerns. When you are Web surfing, you are reaching out and touching many different computers all over the world. Some belong to companies you have heard of; others belong to companies or individuals who are total strangers to you.

If you load a Web page that causes some CGI script to execute on the remote computer, that is surely okay—at least as far as you are concerned. No matter what the CGI script does, it isn't going to be capable of hurting the files in your computer because a CGI script is what we term *server-side* scripting.

Now consider how things change if you download a program (Java applet or whatever) into your PC and run it there. It could possibly do some severe damage to your data. You don't really want to download it unless you can trust the people who wrote it not to have a hidden agenda with a malicious twist or unless you can assure yourself that you have protected your PC against any and all rogue programs.

Generally, we don't know enough about who is behind many of the Web pages we access to confidently extend much trust. Many people worry about giving their credit card numbers to a merchant over the Internet. Actually, this is no worse, in general, than handing your card to a waiter at a restaurant. The waiter could copy down your credit card number just as easily as a snoop could take it off the Internet on its way from you to the merchant. Furthermore, with the consumer protection laws that are in place in the United States, at least, your liability is fairly limited no matter what the waiter or Internet snoops might try to do. On the other hand, a rogue program in your PC...why, it could be worse than anything I want to contemplate!

The designers of Java were well aware of these concerns. Therefore, they made sure that their JVM design would build in as many safeguards as possible. First, any Java source code that arrives at the JVM is examined to be sure that it is valid Java source code, and that it doesn't attempt to do anything that might compromise the security of the user's PC or its data. In most Java implementations, this means it cannot do any file accesses on your disk drives, and it can communicate with only the remote computer from which it came.

Second, the JVM looks at any precompiled Java byte-codes and does similar checks on them. The name given to all of this process is "keeping the program in the sandbox." That is, confine the program to doing only innocuous things and you will keep your data safe.

This sounds like a wonderful approach, and it is pretty good, but there are two nagging problems. One is that sometimes the restrictions (such as no file access on the local disk drives) may be too severe. They just won't let you do some interesting and important things you might want to do. Second, the programmers who wrote the various JVMs are human. They make mistakes. Some of those mistakes might compromise system security.

Indeed, several security holes have been found (and patched) in the Java sandbox, and more are probably lurking out there, just waiting to be found. You can only hope that the "good guys" find these holes before the "bad guys" do. In the meantime, each user has some control over what degree of exposure she wants her PC to have; options settings in each browser allow her to restrict a variety of Java-related actions.

Microsoft's Answer to Java: ActiveX Components

Microsoft responded to Java's rapid rise to prominence with an initiative of its own. It announced and has been actively pushing the notion of *downloadable active components*. These are mini-programs that you can download to do specified tasks. In a way, they act much like Java applets or Web browser plug-ins—except that they load off the Internet and run in your PC all at once, rather than having to be "installed" and your browser restarted before they work.

One big difference from Java applets is that ActiveX components can do anything any other program on your PC can do. No sandbox concept is connected to them. Microsoft instead says the right way to assure yourself that your data is safe is to download and run only ActiveX components that come from trusted sources. They have included a mechanism for putting in unchangeable digital certificates inside each ActiveX program. If you set your browser's security level sufficiently high, only those ActiveX modules that come from organizations with their own trusted certificates will be allowed to run.

In a way, Microsoft has simply proposed expanding the sandbox from a subset of the possible actions inside your PC to encompass all the programmers at all the trusted companies in your universe. Once again, this sounds pretty good. But how will it turn out in practice? I think it is still too early to say for sure.

The Java Beans Answer to the ActiveX Challenge

"Ah," say the Java devotees. "we can do just as well in a similar, yet different way." They propose writing small program pieces they call Java Beans. These are similar in their limited functionality to ActiveX components. Like ActiveX objects, Java Beans can communicate with one another, so you might have a Java Bean that presents a button for the user to press. When that happens, this Java Bean will pass a message to another Bean. That Bean may then print something. The Beans for buttons and printing are very different, and each is capable of doing only a single thing. However, by communicating and cooperating, they can add up to a whole program.

Like ActiveX components, Java Beans can live in your PC for a long time. In contrast, full Java programs (applets) are usually downloaded each time you access a Web page that offers them, and they are run in your PC until you leave that page, after which they are discarded.

JavaScript Is a Whole Different Animal

JavaScript is something else again. The JavaScript language is simply a syntax for putting some active programming statements in a Java-like form inside an HTML Web page. When your browser reads this Web page, it will see and execute the JavaScript lines. This will make it do what amounts to running a program on your PC, but that program needn't be downloaded separately from the Web page of HTML code. (You can store JavaScript in a file with extension .js either on the Web server or on the local PC, and then load it by a reference in a Web page. That, however, defeats much of the specialness of JavaScript.)

The nearest Microsoft relative to JavaScript is VBScript, which is mainly a language for controlling Microsoft applications and operating system activities. Just as Microsoft has "improved" Java to make it run more efficiently on a Windows machine (and in the process "breaking" the platform independence that was always one of Java's greatest selling points), VBScript will work only in a Microsoft world.

How will all this play out? You'll just have to stay tuned to see. In addition to the normal competitive pressures that govern what (if anything) people will do with products from different manufacturers, this contest is complicated by a legal battle between Sun and Microsoft over whether or not Microsoft may elaborate (and thus alter) Java in ways that make it better for Windows users and programmers, but which in the process essentially block Sun's vision of "Write Once, Run Everywhere." Like most legal battles, this one could take many years to play out fully.

Jini Is Java's Newest Kin

You may have heard a new name recently, and noticed that it was somehow connected to Java. That name is Jini. In fact, this is a specification Sun Microsystems is also promoting, in this case to let Java programmers write code to work with almost any gadget that might be connected to a network. So far this is only a proposal, but it could turn out the be the way that Java gets extended down into the littlest smart objects in our daily lives, from refrigerators to alarm clocks. Stay tuned…this could be something significant—or a total bust. It's too early to tell, just yet. And if you want to keep current on this topic, one URL you can watch is this one:

```
http://java.sun.com/products/jini/
```

Be Careful: It Can Be a Dangerous World Out There

I cannot leave this whole area of discussion of Internet-related dangers without mentioning computer viruses. They exist, and they *can* hurt you—or more precisely, your data. A virus cannot do any damage until it gets control of your PC. Just arriving there isn't enough.

If you should be so unlucky as to download and run a program that has been infected, you possibly will infect many other programs on your PC. Some day when one of them runs, you might discover that this particular virus has the nasty habit of wiping out some of your files, locking up your machine, or—worst of all—reformatting your hard disk.

Even worse, you can get a computer virus and infect files on your machine by downloading and then just *examining* certain types of data files. Many spreadsheet programs have an autorecalculate function. If the virus infects the program which that function actually is, then when the spreadsheet autorecalculates, it could be infecting other files at the same time.

Similarly, if you load a Microsoft Word document (or a document created for almost any other mainstream, high-end word processor), it could have some Word (or equivalent) macro viruses in it. If one of them is attached to the Autoexecute macro, simply loading that file into Word to look at its contents could suffice to activate the virus. At that point, the virus can infect other files on your disk drives or even across your local area network.

The computer virus threat has been around for quite a long time. That goes both for viruses that infect program files (including the boot sector of your disk drives) and for those that infect spreadsheets, word processing documents, or other data files. The good news is that if you take some sensible precautions, you can avoid having any serious data loss when a virus strikes your PC.

The most important of these steps is to frequently complete incremental backups of all your critical data files. Another step is to use a good virus-scanning program (with an updated set of virus signatures) to check out each new program or major application data file you receive before you run that program or load that data file.

The bad news is that it is much harder to remember to do this—and in some cases may be impossible to do—if you receive these files across the Internet. This will only become worse if Microsoft gets its way and we blur the line between the desktop and the Internet even more than it is today.

Already, if I happen to click on a URL in a word processing program, I might find that my dial-up networking program has run, I am connected to the Internet, and my Web browser has been launched and is loading up the resource indicated by the URL on which I clicked. I have done this by accident more than once. It can be unnerving to know that you might have just invoked an untested and untrusted program. (You may have installed an antivirus program—or a utility program that includes this special sort of antivirus program as a component—in which case that program will very likely scan all incoming documents and attempt to block any that are infected with a computer virus program. That *might* work—but only if the scanning program is frequently updated to know about all the latest viruses that are out there, and even then it also might sometimes fail to work anyway. The "antivirus technology" people use is pretty good, but it still is not perfect.)

Summary

The Internet has a lot to offer. Most of it is wonderful; some of it is terrifying. If you educate yourself about the dangers as well as the opportunities, however, and if you practice some simple safe computing habits, you can make sure that the balance of your Internet experiences is a good one. I hope that the information I have presented here helps you to see more clearly just how that may be done.

Looking Back and Looking Ahead

You've made it. We are at the end of our tour inside your PC. I expect that now you know a lot more about the technologies that can be found there. You probably also know about a lot of technologies that aren't in your PC yet, but which you will have an opportunity to add in the near future.

Furthermore, you now can see the shape of that great tsunami that is about to inundate all of us: the Internet. Its leading edge is already here, and we are all feeling its effects. When it *really* hits us in earnest, the effects will be greater still. However, because you had the good sense to read this book, you will be among the lucky ones. You will be equipped with the knowledge you need to be able to surf that tsunami successfully.

Learning from the Past and Predicting the Future

We all hope to learn from our past experiences. If we are very good at it, we might even be able to discern, however dimly, what the future will hold in store. In this section, I'm going to offer just a few observations I've made about our recent past and some speculations about what might be our common future—all in the context of what PCs are, have been, and seem likely to become.

The Big Story of the Recent Past: The Internet

I think few would argue with the observation that the most important development relating to PCs in the past couple of years has been the explosive growth of the Internet and its consequent insinuation into virtually every corner of computing on the planet. There have been a lot of other developments in the PC world, including the emergence of new generations of CPUs, new operating systems, and so forth. But driving many—or perhaps even most—of those changes has been the need to adapt to the influence of the Internet.

What's the Next Big Story?

Here I'm going to go out on a limb. Not very far, but a little way. If the big news of the past two years has been how the Internet has affected all of PC development, I think the next two or three years will see a similarly large impact from the coming "convergence" of PCs with telecommunications of all kinds, and with the world of entertainment. Another equally significant trend is that PCs are now capable of very good voice recognition. This means that soon everything from handheld devices to entire homes and offices will be capable of being controlled by vocal utterances, instead of the often-awkward pressing of tiny keys or tapping of a stylus on a too-small screen.

Right now in my office, I have a telephone that includes an answering machine and some networked PCs with various attached peripherals, including a couple of printers, one of which is an All-in-One machine (meaning it includes fax and scanning capabilities). Will my telephone always be separate from my PC? Maybe not. Has changing from a stand-alone fax machine to an All-in-One altered the way I work? At least a little bit. Faxing has become a more computer-integrated process, so I have a log of everything I send or receive.

Combining the power of a PC with the functionality of a telephone and a fax machine permits some very interesting new possibilities. For example, if my telephone and my PC become one, every call I make can be automatically logged, and for every incoming call I can see instantly the data I recorded the last time that person called me. I can also find someone in my PC database and then place a call to that person with just a mouse-click. I can also use my computer to screen calls using caller ID. These are merely a few minor ways in which PCs and telephones can be made to work together usefully.

Still, just because combinations of these functions are being made into devices now, there is no certainty that every office will take advantage of these new possibilities any-time soon. In fact, I think that the working acceptance of this sort of integration of telecommunications with PCs will proceed at a fairly modest pace. But it will continue; of that I am quite sure.

Games have always been one of the first ways that new PC hardware gets pushed to its limits. Gamers and game programmers can never have too much speed, or sound that is too good, or nearly enough of anything else to sate their desires. So I expect gamers to push the envelope, and for that to continue to help drive developments in our industry. However, games are hardly the only way people entertain themselves. Indeed, for many people, the thought of playing a computer game is abhorrent, or merely distastefully irrelevant to their lives. For them, entertainment is more likely to mean going to the ball game, theater, or opera—or just quietly reading a good book. Will PCs evolve in ways that change those experiences? I hope so. And I believe so.

Already, PC hardware is evolving in ways that enable you to take an electronic copy of a book on a hike, to the beach, or perhaps just into the bathtub or bed. These *e-books* make it possible to acquire and read books in whole new ways.

The different models now reaching the marketplace differ in their details, but all permit you to download many books into one small and very portable object, and then read whichever ones you want, make annotations, and search for particular words or phrases. Thus, when you happen to wonder when a particular character last appeared in the story, you can pause in your reading, instantly scroll back to wherever that might have been (the PC having found that place for you), jump back once more to where you interrupted your reading, and continue the story.

I know I have often wished for such a capability when I was reading a paperback novel, and really felt I needed it when studying a textbook. This sort of nonlinear reading will seem more and more natural as we spend more time on the hyperlinked World Wide Web.

Theaters may soon come equipped with instant translation tools to help attendees hear the dialogue in their native language. Or, during the intermission you might want to look up all the other plays some performer has been in and see if you can better understand the interpretation he or she is giving in tonight's show.

Television channel-surfing is one activity that is being affected, and very powerfully. When you get 500 channels of cable or satellite TV, finding out what you want to watch among that flood of offerings can become an overwhelming task. Digital cable connections are available that will alert the user when certain programs come on, control access to various channels, program pay-per-view movies, and even assist with programming your VCR.

What about the "smart clothes" I mentioned in Chapter 1, "The View from Afar?" What about houses that respond to voice commands. ("Jeeves, bring me my coffee, please," or "Jeeves, turn down the heat, and open the kitchen window, please.") Those things may come into common use, but I certainly don't expect to see them in very many households in the next several years. More immediately, we can expect to see the microprocessors in our VCRs, microwave ovens, and the like become more capable and helpful in the use of those appliances.

A long time ago, an astute observer pointed out to me that when new inventions come along, the time it takes for society to "digest" them, which is to say to make them integral parts of our lives, seems to depend much less upon what those inventions are or the technologies behind them, and much more on various economic realities, plus some psychosocial realities about how very hard many people find accepting any significant kind of change in their lives. These considerations usually mean that the integration of a profound new technology takes several decades.

However, I have to admit that PCs have been a somewhat special case. After all, the whole notion of an IBM PC is less than twenty years old. Look how far it has come so far. Perhaps these PC-related societal changes will also proceed at an unprecedented pace.

I'll end this section with one safe prediction: The future of PCs and their growing impact on our lives will be anything but dull. Ours is an interesting time in which to live. Having said that, I must also point out that the Chinese sometimes curse a person by saying, "May you live in interesting times." I can only hope that you and I will find the interest brought to our lives by PCs in the future to be an overall benign or even beneficial one.

Our Tour Is Over But the Journey Is Not

I must warn you. Our tour is over, but your journey most definitely is not. PC technology is expanding and advancing constantly. Keeping current is a tough job, even for those of us who work at it full time. So don't relax totally; keep your eyes and ears open. Armed with the fundamental understandings you have developed here, you should be able to make more sense than most average observers of each new trend or new, fancy product.

How the Story Comes Out Depends, in Part, on You

I've told you a complex story about what our PCs are and how they got that way. It's a story that will continue, and the really good news is that how it comes out depends at least in part on you. That's right. You can influence your own (and others') future. You and millions of people like you shape the future daily as you make your buying choices and as you make your views known in other ways.

To cite just one example, a few years back a major company in the industry proposed to publish on the Internet a database of all the companies and individuals in the United States. Many people were horrified. They feared that their privacy would be intruded upon intolerably, and so they spoke up. The company in question was deluged with email, conventional letters, and phone calls. The overwhelming majority of them were critical of the plan. The company backed down.

Even while explaining at great length how their plans weren't really a threat to anyone's privacy, they reversed their course completely. They still published information about companies, but all the data they had on individuals was not placed on the Internet.

That's just one example of how you, acting in concert with others, can definitely affect the industry. Beyond this group power, you also must remember your personal power over your personal PC, which leads me directly to my next topic.

Remember, It's *Your* Personal Computer; *You* Are in Charge

That's right: It is *your* personal computer, which means *you* are in charge of it. Perhaps someone else paid for it. Maybe that person or organization even maintains it for you. But you have it because you are entitled to a personal computer. You have the right (and the responsibility) to decide when and how your PC is used. Don't abdicate this responsibility to anyone else. Keep yourself informed about the possibilities. Then be vocal with your opinions.

Make, and then implement, your choices in whatever ways you can and need to make your PC work for you in just the way you want it to. Resist the efforts of central administrators to take away this power.

The rise of PCs has meant a great leveling of many corporate power structures. It also helped end the Cold War and has contributed mightily to the massive political changes we are seeing in our world. It has brought "power to the people," many of whom were formerly quite powerless—or thought they were. It would be a shame if we let this power slip through our fingers.

Please keep on learning about PCs and everything else that interests you. This is the best way to keep yourself mentally alive and interesting both to yourself and to others. If you come across something really interesting—perhaps something you think would help others learn more about their PCs, or simply something about PCs that fascinates you—I welcome hearing about it. You can send me email at

`john@agoodman.com`.

I'm pleased you have chosen to spend this time with me, and I hope to see you on our mutual journey sometime in the future.

Glossary

Here is where to come when you see a word or phrase that you don't recognize. Many times the brief definition you will find here will satisfy your curiosity (or remind you of a more extended discussion you have read previously). In other cases you may wish to follow the italicized pointer at the end of the definition to the chapter or chapters in which I discuss that concept at greater length, or you can look in the index for additional pointers. The bold-faced words or phrases in the definitions indicate items defined elsewhere in this glossary.

Numbers and Symbols

1284 (aka IEEE 1284)   IEEE (Institute for Electrical and Electronic Engineering) standard number 1284 is the formal description for the various forms a PC **parallel** port may take. This includes the original PC parallel port, the bidirectional parallel port, the EPP (Enhanced Parallel Port), and ECP (Extended Capability Port). *(Chapter 15)*

1394 (aka IEEE 1394)   IEEE (Institute for Electrical and Electronic Engineering) standard number 1394 is the formal description for what began as Apple Computer's **FireWire** very high-speed **serial bus**. *(Chapter 16)*

3DNow!   An addition to the normal set of instructions for **x86** processors introduced by AMD and now supported by several **CPU** manufacturers, these are mainly intended to accelerate processing of 3D intensive game programs. The 3DNow! instructions are similar in concept to the **MMX** instructions, but they support both **integer** and **floating-point** instructions and data. They followed Intel's introduction of MMX and preceded its introduction of the **KNI** instruction group that does a very similar set of things. This standard is also supported by the Microsoft **DirectX** multimedia driver in its version 6.0 and beyond. *See also* **MMX, KNI,** and **SIMD**. *(Chapter 7)*

A

access time   *See* **latency**.

ACPI (Advanced Configuration and Power Interface)   The modern way for the **operating system** to control the power consumption of system components. Intended to replace **APM** when it was introduced with Windows 98. However, not all systems and peripheral parts are yet ready to support ACPI. *See also* **ASL**. *(Chapter 23)*

Active Directory   Microsoft's proprietary means for providing and accessing directory information over a network. Contrast with **LDAP** and **NDS**.

ADSL (asymmetric digital subscriber line)   An **asymmetric** form of purely digital data delivery over conventional telephone lines. *See also* **G.Lite** and **xDSL**.

AGP (Advanced Graphics Port)   A **bus** that connects the video processor to a portion of **main memory** through the **Northbridge** chip. This bus operates at full system bus speed, and an AGP video card is, therefore, much faster than a **PCI** video card. *(Chapter 16)*

ALU (Arithmetic Logic Unit)   The component of a **CPU** that is responsible for performing integer math functions as well as making logical comparisons.

AML (ACPI Machine Language)   The compiled form of **ASL**. *See also* **ACPI**. *(Chapters 18 and 23)*

AMR (Audio-Modem Riser)   An Intel term describing a plug-in card carrying **analog** circuitry (for both audio input and output and for connection to a **POTS** line) that fits into a special socket on a motherboard. This is a part of Intel's newest initiative to standardize motherboards for PCs.

analog   A signal, as with audible sound, that possesses continuous variances, as opposed to discrete variances. Contrast with **digital**.

APM (Advanced Power Management)   The first standard means of specifying system-level control of power consumption by various parts of a PC. This standard was introduced by Microsoft and Intel in 1995 with Windows 95. It is now being supplanted by **ACPI**. *(Chapter 23)*

ASL (ACPI Source Language)   A **p-code** language used to express control concepts for a **BIOS** that is **ACPI**-compliant. *(Chapters 18 and 23)*

asymmetric   In the context of data transmission, a scheme in which data can be received and sent simultaneously by dividing the total available **bandwidth** into two **channels**, each of which has a different **throughput**.

asynchronous   Two or more events that are not synchronized in time. In the context of data transmission, a process by which data is sent or received at a variable rate. Contrast with **synchronous**.

ATA (AT Attachment)   A standard that defines how hard disks and similar devices may be attached to a PC (based on the **ISA** interface). This is the formal name for what is more commonly known as **IDE**. *See also* **ATAPI**, **EIDE**, **IDE**, and **ISA**. *(Chapter 16)*

ATAPI (ATA Packet Interface) An extension to the **ATA** standard allowing support of devices other than hard disks (for example, CD-ROM drives) over the ATA interface. *See also* **EIDE**, **IDE**, and **ISA**. *(Chapter 16)*

ATM In the context of computers, **Asynchronous** Transfer Mode, which is a communications **protocol** for **packet-switched** data communication that uses very small (53-byte) **packets**; often used for very high-speed networks. *(Chapter 24)*

ATSC (Advanced Television Standards Committee) The standard for all-**digital** transmission of television signals, now beginning to be implemented. *See also* **DTV**, **interlaced scan**, **progressive scan**, **NTSC**, and **PAL**. *(Chapter 13)*

ATX A standard design for PC motherboards, based on the IBM PC/AT motherboard's design. ATX features a rotated design that promotes better airflow, attached **parallel** and **serial** connections, and other improved features. *See also* **NLX** and **WTX**.

availability A term that refers to the fraction of the time that a computer system is available for useful work. A "high availability" system is a very reliable one. (This concept has been an important one for large computer systems for years; it only recently has become an issue for PCs, because they have moved up in capability and are now doing some of the jobs formerly reserved for mini- and mainframe computers.)

B

b versus B In this and many other books and technical magazines, *b* stands for a bit and *B* stands for a byte (8 bits). *(Chapter 3)***back-side bus** Modern **CPUs** for PCs have two data buses communicating with **memory** at different speeds and for different purposes. One, termed the **front-side bus** or **system bus**) goes to the **Northbridge** chip and then on to **main memory**, **AGP** video, and the **PCI** bus. The second (back-side) bus goes only one place, to the Level 2 **cache** memory. This bus operates at the full speed of the CPU core or at half that speed; the front-side bus operates typically at a small fraction of the core speed. *See also* **DIB**. *(Chapter 7)*

bandwidth The capacity of any data path, whether **digital** or **analog**, to transmit data. With specific regard to PCs, bandwidth is commonly expressed in terms of bits or bytes per second.

biometrics The study of means for measuring unique properties of individuals, and the devices that do this job. Examples include retinal scanners, fingerprint scanners, iris scanners, face recognition systems, and voice recognition systems. These devices are now becoming common as authentication means to permit users access to a network or other restricted resource, alternative to passwords, keys, smart cards, or the like.

bps Bits per second, also written *b/s*. (Contrast with *Bps,* meaning bytes per second). Similarly, Kbps and Mbps refer to thousands and millions of bits per second, respectively, and KBps and MBps refer to thousands and millions of bytes per second, respectively. *(Chapter 3)*

BRI (Basic Rate Interface) One of two ways you can get **ISDN** pure-**digital** telephone service. In this **protocol**, two **channels** for data transmission are defined, each of which operates at 64Kbps, in addition to a third channel that is used for control purposes, which operates at 16Kbps. *See also* **ISDN**.

bridge A means of connecting two or more **LAN**s. Bridges may convert between different data transmission **protocols** and may filter which of the data packets received from any one connected LAN gets passed on to each of the others. Contrast with **router**. A device that couples different buses inside a single PC or links two PCs or other, similar devices. A **PCI**-to-PCI bus is one example of this. Additional examples: The **Northbridge** chip serves as a bridge between a PC's front-side bus, the AGP bus, and the PCI bus. *(Chapters 16 and 25)*

bus A formal specification of an interconnection between two parts of a PC. A full bus specification must include the logical, physical, electrical, and timing aspects of the interface. *See also* **point-to-point**. *(Chapter 4)*

bus clock The small fraction of a PC's total **system clock**, which regulates the steps on the *PCI* and *ISA* buses and elsewhere within the PC. *(Chapters 7 and 16)*

bus contention A situation in which two or more devices connected to a **bus** seek to use that bus at the same time. *See also* **deadlock**, **CSMA/CD**, and **semaphore**.

C

C-RIMM (Continuity RIMM) An empty RIMM module that does not provide any additional **memory** to the system in which it is installed, but which is needed to fill any empty RIMM sockets on the system's motherboard. (Direct **Rambus** memory subsystems require that all available memory sockets are filled at all times). *See also* **RIMM** and **S-RIMM**. *(Chapter 11)*

cable modem A device that allows two-way data transmission over a **CATV** cable, typically for access to the **Internet**. Contrast with **ISP** and **direct broadcast television**. *(Chapter 24)*

cache A temporary holding place. Cache **memory** is the term used to describe a very fast yet small amount of **RAM** that is used to hold data on its way into or out of the **CPU**. A disk cache refers to some RAM that is used to hold data on its way to or from a disk drive.

Cascading Style Sheets (CSS) A standard for attaching style information to **HTML** documents. This allows precise control over the formatting of those documents (whether they appear on a screen or are printed on paper), independently from the specification of the document content. *See also* **XML**. *(Chapter 27)*

CATV (Community Antenna Television) The formal name for what most people call simply cable television. *(Chapter 24)*

CD   Pressed optical discs for storing digital audio data. *(Chapter 9)*

CD-R   Recordable optical discs that can be written to by means of a laser, but only once for any place on the disc. *(Chapter 9)*

CD-ROM   Pressed optical discs used to store digital data for specifically computer-related purposes, including programs and any kind of data file. *(Chapter 9)*

CD-RW   Recordable optical discs that can be written and rewritten to by means of a laser. With suitable software, these may function like very high-capacity floppy diskettes. *(Chapter 9)*

CDDI (Copper Distributed-Data Interface)   A **protocol** for high-speed data transmission over copper-wire links, derived from **FDDI**. *See also* **HIPPI** and **Fibre Channel**. *(Chapter 25)*

CDPD (Cellular Digital Packet Data)   An industry standard for transmission of **digital** data (currently at 19.2Kbps) over a cellular phone network.

CDSA (Common Data Security Architecture)   An industry initiative to define hardware-based security measures for PCs, **DVD** players, and other consumer electronic devices that may be used to access copyrighted data.

channel   Any pathway over which data may be moved.

channel bonding   A term that describes using the two or more data channels of an ISDN connection simultaneously to increase the data transfer rate. *See also* **Multilink-PPP**. Contrast with **modem-bonding**. *(Chapter 24)*

chipset   The electronic logic chips that are needed to connect and control all the different parts of a PC motherboard. In most modern PCs, this is almost entirely contained in two **VLSI** chips called the **Northbridge** and **Southbridge** chips. *(Chapter 16)*

client/server   Refers to a way of partitioning the workload for a given application between a central machine (the **server**) and many attached **workstations** (the clients). *(Chapter 25)*

clock   Used as a noun, a timing mechanism, used to keep multiple parts of a PC in sync with one another. Used as a verb, the process by which two or more processes within a PC are synchronized to occur at the same time. *See also* **system clock** and **bus clock**.

clock jitter   *See* **jitter**.

clock skew   *See* **skew**.

Codec (compressor/decompressor)   A program or **device driver** that is capable of extracting viewable video and analog audio from a compressed, combined **digital** data stream.

collision   Two devices attempting to use the same resource simultaneously.

CompactFlash Card   A standard **bus** and module design initially intended for add-on **memory** for hand-held PCs, **digital** cameras, and other similar devices. This standard is now being extended (in its second generation form, referred to as **CompactFlash Card II**, or **CFII**) to include devices such as miniature hard drives, and for use in larger systems, such as very thin laptop computers. Contrast with **SmartMedia**, which does not include the flash memory controller circuitry in the removable module. *See also* **Solid State Floppy Disk**. *(Chapters 10, 11, and 12)*

compile   With respect to computer program code, the process of turning a high-level computer language's instructions into machine code and storing that code in a file that the computer can later execute. Syntactic programming errors can be caught in this process without the program actually being executed. Contrast with **interpret**.

compression   Reducing the size of a data file either by removing redundancy (lossless compression) or by removing both redundancy and some inessential information (lossy compression). *(Chapter 13)*

CPU (Central Processing Unit)   The device within a PC that does the bulk of the information processing. *See also* **ALU**, **FPU**, and **microprocessor**. *(Chapter 7)*

CSMA/CD (Carrier Sense Multiple Access with Collision Detection)   The **protocol** that defines **Ethernet**. A method of utilizing a **bus** topology where all devices have free access to the media (multiple access). Devices first listen to make sure the line is available (carrier sense), and then attempt to transmit. In the case of two devices transmitting at precisely, or nearly, the same moment, the error is detected (collision detection), and each device waits a pseudo-random amount of time before attempting to retransmit. *(Chapter 25)*

D

deadlock   A condition in which two processes are each stalled, waiting for the other to complete. *See also* **bus contention** and **semaphore**.

device driver   A program that enables a piece of software or the **operating system** itself to activate and use a hardware device. A program that enables a piece of hardware to be treated as if it were something different. *See also* **DLL** and **VxD**.

DHTML (Dynamic HTML)   An enhancement to **HTML** that permits defining pages whose content will change after they have been downloaded to the client machine. Specifically, it extends the ability of **scripts** to change the HTML page on which the scripts are hosted. The browser can read the DHTML code and display its content differently as the user takes certain actions. *See also* **HTTP**, **CSS**, and **XML**. *(Chapter 27)*

DIB (dual independent bus)   Intel's name for the two buses going from the CPU to other parts of a PC. *See also* **front-side bus** and **back-side bus**. *(Chapter 7)*

DIMM (Dual Inline Memory Module)   A small printed circuit board (**PCB**) carrying multiple **memory** chips mounted on both sides of the board and with independent electrical contacts on the two sides of the PCB. Contrast with **SIMM**. *(Chapter 11)*

DirectX   A collection of **operating system**–level tools that provide for greater ease in the programming and utilization of multimedia content in a Windows environment.

disc   Within this text and throughout most of the industry, this spelling refers specifically to optical storage media.

disk   Used generically to refer to any data storage device using magnetic or optical techniques.

diskette   A magnetic-based floppy 3.5-inch or 5.25-inch data storage device.

dithering   A means of approximating a value that is not representable directly by interpolating between two sources whose values average to the desired value.

DLL (dynamic link library)   A file that contains one or more programs that may be referenced by some other program. A DLL can be loaded by the **operating system** only when needed, or it may reside in **main memory** indefinitely. *See also* **VxD**.

DMA (Direct Memory Access) controller   A controller that can be programmed by the **CPU** and then left to move a block of data from one region of **main memory** to another, or to or from an **I/O port** without further CPU attention. *See also* **Ultra-DMA**.

DNS (Domain Name System)   A system that supplies actual numeric **IP address**es that correspond to a named resource on the Internet or any other network using **TCP/IP** as its data transmission **protocol**. Sometimes used to refer to a specific computer that performs this task, as Directory Name Server. *See also* **URL**. *(Chapter 27)*

DOCSIS (Data Over Cable Service Interface Specification)   A developing standard for adding two-way data communication to a conventional Community Antenna Television (**CATV**) system. When it is complete, this will define the means by which cable **modem**s will interface with the remainder of a CATV system.

DOS (disk operating system)   Originally named to contrast with the **operating systems** that preceded it, this term simply indicates a computer's OS, which is loaded from disk-based storage when the computer is powered up. (Older computers had their operating systems loaded from tape or stored permanently in circuitry.) *(Chapter 17)*

double buffering   A strategy in which two temporary storage areas are used to hold data moving either to or from some device. Commonly used in 3D graphics acceleration schemes, which benefit dramatically from one video buffer being able to be filled while a second one is being emptied.

DRAM (Dynamic Random Access Memory)   **RAM** modules (or chips) that can retain information only if they are refreshed at frequent intervals. Contrast with **SRAM**, **Flash Memory**, and **ROM**. *(Chapter 11)*

DSP (Digital Signal Processor)   A special-purpose **CPU** that is designed specifically to support calculations appropriate to signal processing. Often used in **modems** and other devices within or attached to a PC, as well as in specialized instruments.

DTCP (Digital Transmission Content Protection)   An international standard (for both the PC and entertainment industries) specifying how **digital** content is encrypted to permit only authorized uses (for example, play but don't copy) from devices such as **DVD** drives.

DTV (Digital Television)   A group of standards for purely **digital** television image transmission, including various resolutions for the images. *See also* **interlaced scan**, **progressive scan**, **NTSC**, and **PAL**. *(Chapter 13)*

duplex communications   Refers to data flowing in both directions through a **channel**. Thus, full-duplex means data flows both ways simultaneously, and half-duplex means the data flow alternates between one direction and its opposite.

duplex printing   Printing on both sides of a page.

DVD   Originally standing for **Digital** Video Disc, and then for Digital Versatile Disc, this term now is just DVD. An optical disc of the same size as a **CD** but capable of holding far more data. Like CDs, DVDs come in several kinds. DVD-ROM is analogous to **CD-ROM**. *(Chapter 10)*

E

ECC (Error Control and Checking)   A methodology by which errors at the bit or multiple-bit level in RAM may be intercepted and corrected as that data is being sent to the CPU. Contrast with **parity**. *(Chapter 11)*

EDO RAM (Extended Data Out RAM)   This variation of **DRAM** technology enables the **CPU** to address one location while still reading data from a previous one, thus increasing the speed with which data may be read from **memory**. This has been the workhorse form of DRAM in high-end PCs for the past several years, but it has been replaced in desktops and low-end servers by **SDRAM**. *(Chapter 11)*

EEPROM (Electrical Erasable Programmable Read Only Memory)   An integrated circuit design for the creation of **NVRAM** modules. Functions as **ROM** (read-only) at all times, except under specific conditions in which new content can be downloaded electronically.

EIDE (Enhanced Integrated Device Electronics)   An improved version of the **IDE channel** definition, permitting use of **LBA** (Logical Block Addressing) for very large hard disks, booting from CD-ROMs and similar devices, and so forth. *See also* **ATA**, **ATAPI**, **IDE**, and **ISA**.

encryption   A method by which data is rendered secure and unreadable to anyone who does not possess a proper password or decryption key.

EPROM (Erasable Programmable Read Only Memory)   An integrated circuit design for the creation of **NVRAM** modules that require exposure to ultraviolet light to erase their contents.

Ethernet   The common name for **CSMA/CD**. True Ethernet operates at 10Mbps data transmission speed. Ethernet-like standards have been developed that operate ten and one hundred times that speed, referred to often as **Fast Ethernet** and **Gigabit Ethernet**, respectively. *(Chapter 25)*

Eurocard   A class of circuit boards that use pins (96, in the current European-defined standard) rather than an edge connector. These boards form the core of the CompactPCI initiative, which is concerned with producing PC-compatible hardware designed for ruggedness and durability.

extranet   An **Internet**-like network, but one that links a company with its suppliers and/or customers and is not generally accessible to persons outside those groups. *See also* **intranet**.

F

Fast Ethernet   An **Ethernet**-like networking standard that operates at 100Mbps.

FC-AL (Fibre Channel Arbitrated Loop)   A redundant cable design for a Fibre Channel link to provide security against cable failure.

FDDI (Fiber Distributed-Data Interface)   A **protocol** for high-speed data transmission over optical fiber links. *See also* **CDDI**, **HIPPI**, and **Fibre Channel**. *(Chapter 25)*

Fibre Channel (FC)   A standard for networking and high-speed data access, using optical fiber and/or copper wires as the physical medium. The Fibre Channel **protocol** currently supports 1Gbps (gigabits per second) and 2Gbps data transfer speeds, with a 4Gbps version forthcoming. *(Chapter 24)*

firewall   A router that selectively filters packets from the "outside" to prevent unauthorized access to internal systems. *(Chapter 25)*

FireWire   *See* **1394.fixed point**   A way of storing and manipulating numbers that can be expressed within a predetermined number of bits, and with an implied decimal point location within that number. This method gives all numbers the same absolute precision (minimum difference between distinguishable numbers) and also implies a maximum size to those numbers. Contrast with **floating point**. *(Chapter 3)*

Flash Memory   A type of nonvolatile, electronic, random-access **memory**. These modules hold data indefinitely even without power being applied to them continuously (though power is required to read those data). Using a special process, the data held in a

Flash Memory module may be changed. This latter process is termed *flashing the memory*. Contrast with **DRAM**, **NVRAM**, **SRAM**, and **ROM**. *See also* **CompactFlash**, **SmartMedia**, and **Solid State Floppy Disk**. *(Chapters 10, 11, and 12)*

flicker   A very annoying property of images on a display device (for example, a video monitor) that aren't refreshed frequently enough to fool the eye into thinking they are static (or continuously displayed moving) images. Too much flicker will cause severe eyestrain and headaches. *See also* **refresh rate**. *(Chapter 13)*

floating point   A way of storing and manipulating nonintegral numbers of almost any size. *(Chapter 3)*

form factor   A jargon term referring to the physical size and shape of an object.

FPU (Floating Point Unit)   The subcomponent of a **CPU** that is dedicated to the processing of floating-point (non**integer**) math. Contrast with **ALU**.

frame rate   A measure of how quickly (expressed in frames per second) video or animation can be presented on a display device. *(Chapter 13)*

FSB (front-side bus)   Another name for the system **bus** that connects the **CPU** to the **Northbridge** chip in a modern PC. *See also* **back-side bus** and **DIB**. *(Chapter 16)*

G

gamut   The range of possibilities. Mostly encountered in PCs in connection with discussions of color, where the gamut for a given technology refers to the extent of its capability of showing a wide range of colors. *(Chapters 13 and 14)*

GART (Graphics Address Remapping Table)   A mechanism used by all **AGP** cards to permit them to find the data they use from main memory, even as the **linear address**es of that data may be shifted around by the CPU's **page table** mechanism. *(Chapter 16)*

GIF(Graphical Interchange Format)   One of the two most common graphic file formats in use on the Internet. *See also* **JPEG**. *(Chapter 20)*

Gigabit Ethernet   An **Ethernet**-like network type that operates at 1000Mbps (1Gbps).

G.Lite   A new standard being adopted by the **ITU** (International Telecommunication Union) as its standard G.992.2. This standard describes a variant form of **asymmetric digital** subscriber line (**ADSL**) that includes 1.5Mbps download speeds and 384Kbps upload speeds. Probable adoption is slated for mid-1999, with products arriving in stores around the same time. *See also* **ADSL** and **xDSL**. *(Chapter 24)*

Global Descriptor Table (GDT)   A table that is built in **memory** before any x86 processor can go into **protected mode**. The contents of this table specify the regions of memory that every task may access. *See also* **Local Descriptor Table (LDT)** and **Translation Lookaside Buffer (TLB)**. *(Chapters 8 and 11)*

H

HDSL (High-speed Digital Subscriber Line) *See* **xDSL**.

HID (Human Interface Device) A term referring to any object by means of which a human might interact with a computer (examples: keyboard, mouse, telephone, and fax machine). This term also refers to a standard that classifies such devices, to assist in supporting them in software.

HIPPI (High Performance Parallel Interface) A **protocol** for high-speed data transmission, which uses a multiwire link. Used almost exclusively as a point-to-point supercomputer channel. *See also* **CDDI**, **FDDI**, and **Fibre Channel**. *(Chapter 25)*

HomePNA (Home Phoneline Networking Alliance) A consortium and the standard it has developed to allow **Ethernet**-style networking of PCs in homes and small offices using the existing telephone wiring, rather than dedicated network wiring. This approach permits continued use of those same phone lines for normal voice calls, and it is compatible with the *splitter-less Universal ASDL* standard.

hot-swap The capability of removing and replacing components of a computer (for example, a hard disk drive) without having to shut down the PC. This capability is inherent in any devices attached via either a **USB** or an **IEEE 1394** connection, and it may be provided for other devices by a special hardware interface.

HPC (Handheld PC) A computer that is a PC (able to run a version of **Windows**, most commonly **Windows CE**) and yet is very small and highly portable. Contrast with **PDA**.

HSM (Hierarchical Storage Management) A general term for a strategy that moves less often used data files off the hard disk onto some less rapidly accessible storage medium, such as an optical disc in a jukebox, and then when the data are even less often used, offline to an external archive.

HTML (Hypertext Markup Language) A subset of the Standard Generalized Markup Language (**SGML**) used in **Internet**- and **intranet**-based Web objects, this standard has gone through several generations, each one taking more features from SGML and enabling more elaborate and precise Web page definition. *See also* **HTTP**, **CSS**, **DTML**, and **XML**. *(Chapter 27)*

HTTP (Hypertext Transfer Protocol) The standard way that Web browsers request pages of HTML code from a Web server. This **protocol** defines, among other things, the **URL** (uniform resource locator) methodology used to communicate client-side requests to a **DNS**. *(Chapter 27)*

I

I²C (Inter Integrated Circuit) bus   A **bus** standard promulgated by Philips for communication at relatively low speeds over a very simple two-wire (plus ground) link between parts of a system. This multiple-master bus strategy is used in the **System Management Bus (SMB)** for communication with **smart batteries**, smart chargers, and their hosts (mostly laptop computers and cellular phones, so far). *(Chapter 23)*

I2O or I₂O (Intelligent Input-Output)   An Intel-sponsored standard for computer subsystems designed to handle several hundred simultaneous I/O transfers, under control of a subsidiary processor, thus relieving the main CPU of that burden. The standard calls for a cross-platform architecture that is specific to neither a particular device nor operating system. *(Chapter 15)*

I/O port   A hardware interface between the **CPU** and some external device. Each I/O port has a **port address** or a range of adjacent addresses (of which the lowest one is called the base address). These addresses form a separate address space from that of **main memory**. The devices attached to I/O ports may be inside the PC or outside of it.

ICC (International Color Consortium)   A standards organization and the standard it has promulgated for color matching across multiple input and output devices. *(Chapters 13 and 14)*

IDE (Integrated Device Electronics)   The common name for the **ATA** standard. Originally a description of peripheral devices (such as a hard disk drive) that contained all the control and interface electronics necessary to connect them to a PC, this now (especially in its **EIDE** form) refers to a standard way of connecting any of a large variety of peripheral devices to a PC. *See also* **ISA** and **EIDE**.

integer   A whole number (positive, negative, or zero) that has no fractional part. Integer arithmetic is a means for doing mathematical calculations in which all the numbers are assumed to be integers. Contrast with **real number**. *(Chapter 3)*

interlaced scan   Forming a **raster-scan image** by drawing every other line on the screen in turn (typically from top to bottom), and then going back and filling in the missing lines. This is the method prescribed in the **NTSC** standard for television images, which is the television standard in the USA. Contrast with **progressive scan**. *(Chapter 13)*

Internet   The collective name for all the networks worldwide that are connected to one another and that use the **TCP/IP protocol** suite.

Interpret   The process of translating a high-level language statement into machine code form, and then immediately executing the result. Contrast with **compile**.

intranet   An **Internet**-like network or series of servers based on the same **TCP/IP** suite of **protocols**, but one whose scope is limited logically and perhaps also physically so that it can be accessed only by users within one corporation or other entity *See also* **extranet**.

IP (Internet Protocol)   The standard method for communicating over the physical links that make up the **Internet**, this is in fact a collection of standards, each tuned to the needs of a particular transport medium.

IP address   A number (currently 32 bits long, but in **IPv6** slated to be extended to 128 bits in length) that specifies a unique device in a **TCP/IP**-based network. Conventionally, this number is written as four decimal numbers (each in the range 0 to 255) separated by periods (for example, 125.14.95.5). A **DNS** is used to "resolve" names of resources to their equivalent IP address. A reverse-DNS search refers to looking up the name of the resource by reference to its IP address. *See also* **URL**. *(Chapter 27)*

IPv6   A standard proposed for the next generation **Internet Protocol**. Its primary purpose is to dramatically increase the number of servers and resources that can be made simultaneously available over the **Internet** and provide significant enhancements to Internet-related security technology.

ISA (Industry Standard Architecture)   The design of the bus slots used by IBM for option cards in the original PC and PC-AT models, later adopted by all clone PC manufacturers as the standard way to attach peripheral devices to a PC. This also was the source for the design of the **IDE** and **EIDE** channels. The ISA bus doesn't support many features now considered essential (or at least highly desirable) for peripheral connectivity and so is being phased out of new PCs.

ISDN (Integrated Services Digital Network)   A dial-up, but purely digital alternative to conventional, dial-up, analog **POTS** telephone service. It comes in two flavors, with **BRI (Basic Rate Interface)** service having two 64Kbps signal channels and **PRI (Primary Rate Interface)** service offering 23 64Kbps signal **channels**. *(Chapter 24)*

ISP (Internet service provider)   A vendor that offer a variety of ways to connect to the **Internet**. Usually, these means it includes a link that takes place over a leased or dial-up telephone line. Contrast with **CATV**, **cable modem**, and **direct broadcast satellite**. *(Chapter 24)*

ITU (International Telecommunications Union)   A body of governments that makes recommendations and defines standards with regard to **digital** telephony.

J

jitter   Refers to the degree of inconsistency of the spacing of the "ticks" of a **clock** signal. *See also* **skew**.

JPEG (Joint Photographic Experts Group)   Refers to a standards body, and to a **digital** still-image compression standard they have promulgated. *See also* **GIF, Motion-JPEG**, and **MPEG**. *(Chapter 20)*

K

KNI (Katmai New Instructions)   A further elaboration of the **x86** instruction set, this uses streaming SIMD instructions that speed other kinds of operations, including **floating-point** processing, not originally included in the **MMX** group of new instructions. Katmai was the internal name for Intel's Pentium III, prior to its market introduction in early 1999. *See also* **3DNow!**, **MMX**, and **SIMD**. *(Chapter 7)*

L

LAN (local area network)   A connection between multiple PCs created in order to facilitate the sharing of application programs, data files, and resources (such as printer or modems) within a restricted geographical region, such as within a single building. Compare with **WAN** and **VPN**.

LAPM (Link Access Procedures for Modems)   Now the primary **protocol** for **asynchronous**-to-**synchronous** conversion, flow control, and error detection and correction in V.42 **modems**. These modems also support the **Microcom Networking Protocols (MNP)** Classes 1–4 as an alternative way of accomplishing these same things. *(Chapter 24)*

latency   The delay after issuing a command before it begins to take effect.

LBA (Logical Block Addressing)   A scheme devised to enable PCs to support IDE hard drives of greater than 500MB capacity.

LDAP (Lightweight Directory Access Protocol)   A standard method for working with TCP/IP-based servers, accessing hierarchical directory information and extracting specific data from those systems. This standard is a proposed basis for the creation of a universal Internet-based telephone directory. Contrast with **NDS** and **Active Directory**.

Linux   A very popular "open source" **operating system** for PCs created by Linus Torvalds and based upon UNIX. The proper pronunciation is said to be "Lih-nucks." *(Chapter 17)*

Local Descriptor Table (LDT)   A table that is built in **memory** for each task running on an x86 processor before it can go into **protected mode**. The contents of this table specify the regions of memory that task may access. *See also* **Global Descriptor Table (GDT)** and **Translation Lookaside Buffer (TLB)**. *(Chapters 8 and 11)*

logic gate   A transistor or collection of transistors that are used within a **CPU** or other circuit to perform logic-related analyses such as AND, OR, NAND, and NOR.

LVDS (Low Voltage Differential Signaling)   A common means of sending signals across some of the more advanced, high-speed **bus**es inside a PC. This uses a pair of wires with signals that move in opposite directions to represent each data transition. The receivers for this system look only at the difference in voltage on each such pair of wires to sense the arrival of each data transition, thus helping them ignore any superimposed noise signals (which commonly are going to be similar in size and sign on both wires).

LS-120   Also called a *Super-Floppy diskette,* this is a diskette (and corresponding drive) that can use either traditional magnetic means for recording data in exactly the same format as on a standard floppy diskette, or with enhanced positioning assistance from an optical head following prerecorded optical tracks on special floppy disks, it can record approximately 100 times as much data.

M

main memory   The pool of **RAM** and **ROM** that the **CPU** can address directly. Some of this is on the motherboard; portions may reside on a video card or some other option card (Various devices in a PC may also have some RAM or ROM, but if it isn't addressable by the CPU, it isn't a part of main memory.) *(Chapter 2)*

memory   The space, comprised of a variety of types of RAM chips, in which a computer performs its work.

memory address   Every location in **main memory** where data may be held has an address. This binary number is used by the **CPU**, the **DMA controller**, the **cache** memory controller, and any other hardware that must read or write that data from or to that location. The collection of all the memory addresses the CPU can address is called its *memory address space.*

Microcom Networking Protocols (MNP)   Originally a proprietary set of **protocols** used only in Microcom modems, many of them are now available to all and they have been adopted widely. Classes 1–4 are an alternative to **LAPM** within the V.42 modem standard. Class 5 provides a standard for data compression during transmission. MNP 10 is a special version that supports cellular phone connections, which often suffer from brief interruptions that otherwise would cause the modems to lose their connection. *(Chapter 24)*

MIDI (musical instrument device interface)   A standard way of connecting music generation, recording, and playback devices such as synthesizers with each other, with keyboards and other input devices, and with PCs over a low-speed **serial bus**. This also refers to a way of encoding music and other audio program material so that it can be sent over a MIDI bus and played back by a synthesizer.

MIME (Multimedia Internet Mail Extensions or Multipurpose Internet Mail Extentions)   A broad and extensive standard for attaching data objects of any kind to an **Internet** mail message (or a message traveling over any network using the Internet **protocols**). This includes compressed files, audio files, video files, and more—and the standard includes a means for defining new types of attachments as desired.

MIP-mapping (Multum In Parvo)   A technique used to smooth the appearance of textures that have been mapped onto 3D images.

MMX (Multimedia Extensions)   Intel's extension to the x86 instruction set (57 new instructions) using the **SIMD** technique to speed multimedia-related calculations. This standard has been adopted by the industry, and these new instructions are now available on all of the newest clone **CPUs** as well as on Intel's CPUs. *See also* **3DNow!**, **KNI**, and **SIMD**. *(Chapter 7)*

modem (modulator and demodulator)   Technically, this name refers to a device that converts digital data into analog tones and back again. It now has been extended, however, to include some purely digital devices, such as **cable modems** and **ISDN** modems. *(Chapter 24)*

modem-bonding   Refers to using simultaneously two **analog** modems connected to two separate voice-grade POTS telephone lines in order to double the achievable data transfer rate. *See also* **Multilink-PPP**. Contrast with **channel-bonding**. *(Chapter 24)*

motion-JPEG   A way of compressing multiple frames of picture information, such as in a movie, which utilizes JPEG **intraframe** compression, and various other **interframe** compressions. Variants are often found on **Codecs** on video capture cards. *See also* **MPEG**. *(Chapter 20)*

MP3 (Motion Picture Experts Group, audio layer 3)   A subset of MPEG1, this standard defines a way to compress audio files very effectively without losing much of the quality. It is fast becoming the standard way to sell audio over the **Internet**. *See also* **MPEG**. *(Chapter 20)*

MPEG (Motion Picture Experts Group)   A standard body of engineers and others in the movie and television industries, and to several compression standards it has promulgated for **digital** motion picture data compression. MPEG2 is now the standard for digital television and **DVD**-based motion images. MPEG4 is the latest standard, based largely on Apple Computer's proprietary **QuickTime**. *See also* **JPEG** and **motion-JPEG**. *(Chapter 20)*

Multilink-PPP   The dial-up **protocol** most commonly used to "bond" two **ISDN** digital **channels** or two analog modem channels to achieve double-rate data transfers. This capability is included in Windows 95 OSR2 and Windows 98. *See also* **channel-bonding** and **modem-bonding**. *(Chapter 24)*

multiprocessing   Using multiple CPUs to perform one or more **processes** simultaneously. Contrast with **multitasking**. *(Chapter 26)*

multitasking   A single CPU working on more than one task at a time. The central processor (**CPU**) is switched between the different tasks so frequently that it gives the illusion that all are being attended to all the time, even though in fact, only one is being worked on at any given instant. Contrast this with **multiprocessing**. *(Chapter 26)*

N

NAS (Network Attached Storage)   Storage devices that can be attached directly to a network and then accessed by all the other devices (for example, PCs) on that network. Contrast with **SAN**. *(Chapter 26)*

NAT (Network Address Translation)   A process by which private IP addresses, used within a closed network such as an **intranet,** are converted into public Internet-compatible IP addresses. After the implementation of IPv6, such stopgap measures will likely be unnecessary.

NDS (Novell Directory Services)   Novell's proprietary means for providing and accessing directory information over a network. Contrast with **LDAP** and **Active Directory**.

NetBEUI (Network BIOS Extended User Interface)   Unroutable protocol designed with simplicity and speed in mind. For use with the NetBIOS networking structure.

NLX   A standardized low-profile design for PCs. This design features a motherboard with a riser card, with all option cards plugged into the riser card. *See also* **ATX** and **WTX**.

Northbridge chip   A **VLSI** chip (part of the motherboard **chipset**) that connects the system bus (from the **CPU**) to the **AGP** port, **main memory**, the **PCI** bus, and the **Zoomed Video** bus. *(Chapter 16)*

NTSC (National Television Standards Committee)   The standard video signal format used in the United States. It specifies interlaced scan, 30-frame (technically, 60 fields, each of which is half of an interlaced frame) per second images. *See also* **interlaced scan**, **progressive scan**, **DTV**, and **PAL**. *(Chapter 13)*

NVRAM (non-volatile RAM)   A general term referring to any of a wide variety of technologies that support electronic data retention even when external power is removed, yet permit that data to be changed when desired. Some of the technologies this encompasses include **EPROM**s, **EEPROM**s, **Flash Memory**, and battery–backed-up **RAM**.

O

OBE (Out of Box Experience)   Refers to how easy or hard a customer finds it to set up a new computer.

OLTP (On-Line Transaction Processing)   Large database applications, such as airline or theater ticket reservations systems, that are simultaneously accessible from many terminals or connected PCs. *(Chapter 25)*

OOP (object-oriented programming)   A style of programming that bundles data and procedures (called *methods*) into black boxes" with defined interfaces but hidden interiors. These program boxes are arranged in a hierarchy via the concept of *classes* and *inheritance*. *(Chapter 18)*

operating system   The software that manages and schedules resources within a computer; the underlying programs that enable application programs to operate the hardware. **DOS**, **Windows**, **OS/2**, and **Linux** are some of the currently popular operating systems for PCs. *(Chapter 17)*

OS/2   Joint Microsoft-IBM–developed **operating system** that Microsoft no longer supports or develops. IBM continues to sell OS/2, but in numbers small enough to allow OS/2 to be considered a niche product. *(Chapter 17)*

P

p-code (pseudo code)   A way of reexpressing a computer program in an alternate form that is closer to, but not the same as, machine code. A p-code interpreter can then very quickly interpret and execute the p-code. This approach enables editable programs that still perform almost as well as compiled programs. *(Chapter 18)*

packet   Specified arrangement of data and address information. A packet is the basic building block of a protocol. Many different formats of packets have been defined for various packet-delivery data communication protocols. *(Chapter 24)*

packet-switched data services   A means of carrying many different messages on the same circuits by breaking each one into many small **packets**. All the packets are sent, serially, across the circuit, one after another, and each is routed correctly to its own destination based on address information carried within the packet. Contrast with **PSTN**. *(Chapter 24)*

PAL (Phase Alternation Line)   A television signal format used in video equipment in some parts of Europe and Asia. With 25 frames per second, it is incompatible with NTSC (30 frames per second) signals used in North America. *See also* **interlaced scan**, **progressive scan**, **DTV**, and **NTSC**. *(Chapter 13)*

parallel   Sending data more than one bit at a time by the use of separate wires for each of those bits. Contrast with **serial**.

parity   A methodology through which errors at the single-bit level in RAM may be intercepted before that errant data is sent to the CPU. Contrast with **ECC**. *(Chapter 11)*

PCB (Printed Circuit Board)   A card made of an insulating material coated with metal that is then etched to form a circuit, or several such cards laminated together to make a multilayer PCB. This technology is used to create motherboards, plug-in option cards, and memory modules.

PCI (Peripheral Component Interconnect)   An Intel-sponsored standard, now very widely deployed, for connecting peripheral components to computers. This bus design is essentially replacing the ISA bus in PCs, and it also is used in many industrial computers with a totally non-PC design. Originally only a 32-bit bus operating at speeds up to 32MHz, it now supports both a wide (64-bit) and fast (66MHz) version as well. *See also* **PCIx**.

PCL (printer control language)   Hewlett-Packard's page description language. Originally designed as a limited program for its first laser printers, it has now, by its present version 6, become a very competitive alternative to Adobe's **PostScript**. Printers with support for PCL built in can be sent a much more compact description of a page to be printed than is possible for a "dumb" printer that can only put pels on a page. *See also* **pel**, **pixel**, and **PostScript**. *(Chapter 14)*

PDA (Personal Digital Assistant)   A common term for small, extremely portable digital devices that do not provide the full functionality of a PC. One of the most popular examples of this class of device is the Palm Pilot. Contrast with **HPC**.

pel   The smallest physical unit of an image that a given device (display or printer) can produce. Contrast this with **pixel,** which is the smallest unit of image information in a file or that is delivered to that output device. *(Chapters 13 and 14)*

PGP (Pretty Good Privacy)   One of two proposed ways to enhance the security of Internet mail, both by encrypting the content and by insuring authenticity of the claimed sender. PGP uses a public key scheme in which data is encrypted by the use of a key (password, if you will) that is available publicly. This data can be decrypted only through the use of a privately held key which is mathematically related to the public key. In this way, anyone who knows your public key can send you content that only you can later read. *(Chapter 27)*

pipelined   A term describing any process in which several steps may be started before the first one is finished. A way of speeding up calculations by beginning later steps while earlier steps are still being worked on. This is applicable to many component parts used in a PC.

pixel   The smallest logical unit of a raster image. This is an "atom" of the image and can be specified in terms of its color according to any of several color models. Contrast with **pel**. *(Chapters 13 and 14)*

point-to-point   A term used to describe a data path that joins a source with a single destination. Contrast with a **bus connection,** in which the source may broadcast a message to several destinations simultaneously.

port address   The location in memory that the **CPU** uses to manipulate data through a physical **I/O port**.

PostScript   This page description language by Adobe was introduced with the first Apple LaserWriter. This is a full computer operating system (complete with file system and I/O control, and so forth), but it is one designed specifically to address the needs of a printer, video terminal, or other two-dimensional imaging device. *See also* **Cascading Style Sheets**, **PCL**, **PGML**, and **XML**. *(Chapter 14)*

POTS (Plain Old Telephone Service) Analog   Telephone service (voice grade line) using a separate single pair for the connection to each telephone. The normal sort of telephone service used in homes and offices in the twentieth century. *See also* **PSTN** entry. Contrast with **xDSL** and **VOIP**. *(Chapter 24)*

PPGA (Plastic Pin Grid Array)   A standard packaging methodology for integrated circuits in which the contacts are formed as a rectangular array of pins on the bottom of the package. These packages can then be installed in a socket, in particular of the **ZIF** design.

PPTP (Point-to-Point Tunneling Protocol)   A protocol used to create a Virtual Private Network (**VPN**) over a public **packet**-switched network (such as the Internet). *(Chapter 25)*

Precision Graphics Markup Language (PGML)   An application of XML to support a more graphically precise specification of the appearance of Web pages and documents destined for a printer than is possible within normal **HTML**. Providing an alternative way of specifying formats to that included in the CSS standard, PGML was developed by Adobe, and is based on its **PDF** (Portable Document Format) and **PostScript** page description languages, but extends them in several ways that are important for Web pages such as **progressive rendering** and transparency.

PRI (Primary Rate Interface)   One of two forms of ISDN. Provides 23 64Kbps data channels and 1 64Kbps signaling channel. *See also* **ISDN**.

process   A computer program or a part thereof consisting of a set of defined steps that are to be performed to achieve a specific goal.

progressive rendering   Drawing an image first in low resolution, then refining it one or more times at successively higher resolutions. This strategy is often implemented in **GIF** and **JPEG** files used on the Web to enable viewers to see the basic image quickly and then, only if they decide it is worth waiting for the rest of the image details to be downloaded, see it in its full resolution. *See also* **PGML** and **resolution**.

progressive scan   Forming a **raster-scan image** by drawing each line on the screen in turn (typically from top to bottom). Essentially all PC video displays use progressive scanning to form their images. Contrast with **interlaced scan**. *(Chapter 13)*

protected mode   In 386-and-later processors, a mode of operation that enables the **CPU** to perform 32-bit wide operations and use a flat **memory** model. Contrast with **real mode**.

protocol   Most simply, a defined, standard methodology for achieving some goal.

proxy server   A computer that links a **LAN** with an external network (such as the

Internet) and hides the network addresses of internal machines from the view of anyone connected to the external network. Contrast with **firewall**. *(Chapter 13)*

PSTN (Public Switched Telephone Network)   The normal telephone network used for dial-up calls. One circuit connection is established for each call and maintained for the call's duration. The PSTN also is often referred to in data communications circles as POTS service. *See also* **POTS**. Contrast with **Packet-switched data services** and **xDSL**. *(Chapter 24)*

Q

QoS or **QOS (Quality of Service)**   A somewhat nebulous term, covering various means of guaranteeing that a data link will manage to provide a given application that uses it with at least some specified minimum level of **throughput** and some maximum **latency**. The **USB** and **FireWire** standards include QOS provisions for some devices while allowing others to send data on an as-bandwidth-is-available basis. Some **Internet ISP**s are starting to offer special, higher-cost services with some QOS guarantees, and the next generation of the Internet will include QOS support in its design. *(Chapters 16 and 27)*

QuickTime   An Apple-developed compact file format for encoding video and audio program material. Now the basis for the **MPEG4** standard.

R

RAID (Redundant Array of Inexpensive Drives)   A collection of hard disks attached to a special controller that distributes the stored data across those disks in a way that maximizes speed of access to the data and/or minimizes the risk to those data when one of the disks fails. There are many different arrangements in common use, **RAID 0** (sharing data nonredundantly across multiple disks to improve performance, but not reliability), **RAID 1** (also known as disk-mirroring, which improves reliability, but not performance) and **RAID 5** (which provides an economical balance of redundancy with capacity, and works well in disk arrays with any number of disks from two up) are the most popular. *(Chapters 9 and 26)*

RAM (random access memory)   The volatile, electronic, read/write, random-access memory that is used mainly to hold programs and data while they are being used in your PC (as opposed to disk storage where those files reside when they are not in use). *See also* **DRAM, EDO RAM, SDRAM, SRAM**, and **RDRAM**. Contrast with **ROM** and **Flash memory**. *(Chapter 11)*

rambus   *See* **RDRAM**.

raster-scan image   Any image that is formed by drawing lines of dots. This term is generally applied to a video display device, but it could also be used to describe the output from most printers. *See also* **interlaced scan** and **progressive scan**. *(Chapter 13)*

RDF (Resource Definition Framework)   A **W3C** standard designed to help control the uses of information transferred across networks, including the Internet. *See also* **P3P**.

RDRAM (Direct Rambus DRAM)   A type of random access **memory** module and a memory architecture using these modules. Its primary distinguishing feature is that data and **clock** signals flow through the group of modules on **parallel** paths with matched time delays, thus allowing much faster clocking than is feasible with conventional memory architectures. *See also* **DRAM**, **EDO-RAM**, and **SDRAM**. *(Chapter 11)*

real mode   A mode of operation in which later Intel-compatible processors behave like the original 8088 processor, capable of addressing only 1MB of RAM and using a memory paging model. Contrast with **protected mode**.

real number   Any number (positive, negative, or zero) including both whole numbers (**integer**s) and ones with a fractional part (examples: 4.17, -0,0025). *(Chapter 3)*

refresh rate   How frequently the image on a display device is redrawn. *See also* **flicker** and **frame rate**. *(Chapter 13)*

resolution   How finely an image is defined, spatially. This can be separately defined for the image and for the image display (or printing) devices. *See also* **pel** and **pixel**. *(Chapters 13 and 14)*

RIMM (Rambus Dual Inline Memory Module)   A DIMM that carries DRAM modules for use in a Direct **rambus memory** subsystem. These devices are designed to let data and **clock** signals flow through them in **parallel** paths with carefully matched lengths and propagation delays. *See also* **C-RIMM** and **S-RIMM**. *(Chapter 11)*

Ring 0   The lowest level (most privileged) at which programs can operate on an Intel **x86** processor. This is where the **kernel** of an **operating system** must run, and in Windows it also is the locus of a number of additional operating system components. Compare with **Ring 3**. *(Chapter 11)*

Ring 3   The highest level (least privileged) at which programs can operate on an Intel **x86** processor. This is where user programs run (including all Windows application programs.) Compare with **Ring 0**. *(Chapter 11)*

ROM (read-only memory)   This term is applied to several, very different things. When it is applied to electronic **memory**, it refers to the memory chips that hold programs and data that do not change and must always be accessible to the processor in a PC, or to the memory chips that hold programs and data in, for example, a modem. Applied to a **CD** or **DVD**, this refers to a version of those digital storage media that can have data manufactured into them only at the factory (as opposed to –R, -RW, or -RAM variations whose data can be written by the end user). *(Chapters 10 and 11)*

router A means of connecting two or more **LAN**s that use the same protocol together, filtering which of the data packets received from any one connected LAN gets passed on to each of the others. Contrast with **bridge**. *(Chapter 25)*

S

S-RIMM (SDRAM replacement for a RIMM) A way of packaging SDRAM chips on what appears to be a RIMM module but is actually a more conventional SDRAM **memory** system building block. These devices will be used to fill RIMM sockets in Direct **Rambus** memory subsystems if RIMMs are not yet available in sufficient supply. *See also* **RIMM** and **C-RIMM**. *(Chapter 11)*

SAN (Storage Area Network) A standard, based on **Fibre Channel**, for connecting multiple data storage devices (typically large hard drives) to multiple hosts. This arrangement is commonly used in a very large server or server farms," because it permits very high-speed data transfers and redundant access, thus ensuring both high **performance** and high **availability** for the storage system. Contrast with **NAS**. *(Chapter 26)*

SCSI (Small Computer System Interface) This standard for connecting peripheral devices (commonly hard disks) to a computer has gone through many generations of improvement. **SCSI1, SCSI2** (including its **Ultra-** and **Wide-** variants), and **SCSI3** devices are all in common use today. Further, this standard formed the basis for other, more advanced interconnection standards, such as **USB** and **FireWire**. *(Chapter 16)*

SDRAM (Synchronous DRAM) The latest generation of DRAM memory modules, supplanting **EDO-RAM**, first in workstation and other desktop PCs and later in servers. SDRAM chips are able to transfer data in a single clock cycle because their operations are synchronized with the system clock. *See also* **RAM, DRAM, RDRAM**, and **SDRAM**. Contrast with **SRAM, Flash Memory**, and **ROM**. *(Chapter 11)*

SECC (Single Edge Contact Cartridge, also referred to as an SEC Cartridge) Intel's method of packaging its **CPU**s in modules that contain the CPU and Level 2 **cache** memory. *(Chapter 7)*

semaphore A flag value that is stored in some location that is accessible to multiple devices that are contending for control of a bus or other resource. When the semaphore value is set, it indicates that the resource is in use. When it is reset, the resource is available for use. *See also* **bus contention** and **deadlock**.

SEPP (Single Edge Processor Package) Intel's name for a board-level packaging that fits into a **Slot 1** or **Slot 2** CPU module socket. Used as an alternative to its **Socket 370**–compatible designs for certain Celeron processors. There are also third-party adapters that use this form factor to support CPUs that plug into a Socket 5, Socket 7, or Super7 socket on motherboards with a Slot 1 socket. *(Chapter 7)*

serial Sending data one bit at a time. Contrast with **parallel**.

Serial Presence Detect   An industry standard way of permitting the motherboard system logic (the **chipset**) to access an **EEPROM** that is included on some memory modules (**DIMMs**, **RIMMs**, and so forth) via the I^{2}C bus to learn what the capabilities and operational requirements are for that module. *(Chapter 11)*

server   A term commonly used to denote a computer (that might be a PC, a mini-, or a mainframe) whose main use is to store and "serve up" information for use on attached **workstations**. In **client-server** applications, this central machine may also be used to do some significant portion of the data processing workload. *(Chapter 25)*

SGML (Standard Generalized Markup Language)   Subject of a formal, international standard, this is an elaborate scheme for "marking up" a document to indicate the nature of various elements in a textual document, including how they shall be displayed on a printed page or display screen. The World Wide Web on the Internet was initially designed to use pages that were defined using a small subset of the SGML markup codes, called **HTML**. *(Chapter 27)*

SIMD (single instruction, multiple data)   The technique used in both **MMX** and Katmai New Instructions (**KNI**), both of which are additions to the normal **x86** instruction set. This technique places multiple data items into a register, then performs a common operation on all of them simultaneously. *See also* **3DNow1**, **MMX**, and **KNI**.

SIMM (Single Inline Memory Module)   A small printed circuit board carrying multiple **memory** chips. Although there are usually electrical contacts all along one edge on both sides of the PCB, the contacts that are directly opposite one another are electrically connected and do not function independently. Contrast with **DIMM** and **RIMM**. *(Chapter 11)*

skew   The amount by which a data signal may get out of step with its associated **clock** signal. *See also* **jitter**.

Slot 1   The Intel standard for SECC **CPU** modules first used in the Pentium II. This is a 242-pin socket and all the CPU modules that fit into it run their L2 cache memory at half the processor core frequency. *See also* **Super-7 socket**. *(Chapter 7)*

Slot 2   Intel's newest standard for SECC **CPU** modules. This is a 330-pin socket and all the CPU modules that fit into it run their L2 cache at the full speed of the processor core. *(Chapter 7)*

Slot A   AMD's answer to Intel's **Slot 1**, the Slot A uses DEC (Compaq) Alpha bus protocols. It is the socket for which AMD has designed its new K7 **CPU** module, and it may also be used for future CPU modules, both from AMD and other x86 clone CPU makers. *(Chapter 7)*

SMART (Self-Management and Reporting Technology)   Newer hard disks are able to inform the **operating system** when errors occur in a way that suggests the drive may soon fail altogether. When this is supported by a utility program (or by the OS), drive failures can be anticipated and data saved from loss.

Smart Battery System (SBS)   A standard for batteries with embedded intelligence, allowing communication between smart batteries, smart battery chargers, and host systems (mostly laptop PCs and cellular phones, so far). *See also* **System Management Bus (SMB)** and **I2C**. *(Chapter 23)*

SmartMedia cards   In contrast with **CompactFlash**, a SmartMedia card contains only flash **memory** chips and not the controlling electronics required to access those chips. *See also* **Solid State Floppy Disk**. *(Chapters 10, 11, and 12)*

SMIL (Synchronized Multimedia Integration Language)   An extension to HTML to support multimedia documents in which synchronizing the sounds with the video portion is critical.

SMTP (Simple Mail Transfer Protocol)   A widely used protocol for exchanging messages, not restricted to mail or used only on the Internet.

SNTP (Simple Network Time Protocol)   A simple **protocol** for synchronizing **clocks** (including PC clocks) across a network, or worldwide.

Socket 370   Intel's name for its next-generation, 370 pin socket. This **ZIF** socket physically resembles the Socket 7, but has many more pins. Intel introduced it with its newest Celeron **CPU** models in early 1999. Compare with **Socket 7, Socket 8, Slot 1,** and **Slot 2**. *(Chapter 7)*

Socket 7   The standard socket used by Intel Pentium processors and by their clones from AMD, Cyrix, and IDT-Centaur. This was the last of the Intel-specified **CPU** socket designs that it licensed to its competitors *(Chapter 7)*

Socket 8   The Intel design for a **CPU** socket used for the Pentium Pro. *(Chapter 7)*

SODIMM (Small Outline Dual Inline Memory Module)   An industry-standard miniaturized version of the DIMM commonly used in mobile PCs.

Solid State Floppy Disk Card (SSFDC)   A very small form factor **memory** card design (trade-name **SmartMedia**) mainly used in certain digital cameras. Contrast with **CompactFlash** cards. *(Chapters 10 and 12)*

Southbridge chip   A **VLSI** chip (part of the motherboard **chipset**) that connects the PCI bus to the **ISA** bus, mouse port, keyboard port, **USB** and IEEE **1394** (**FireWire**) ports, **IDE** (or, usually, **EIDE**) channels (to hard disks, **CD-ROM** drives, **DVD** drives, and so forth), and any floppy diskette drives in the PC. Contrast with **Northbridge** chip. *(Chapter 16)*

SRAM (Static RAM)   **Memory** chips or modules in which data can be held indefinitely without **clock**ing (but only so long as power is applied to the chips). Because this is a relatively expensive kind of memory to make and it can be made to operate very rapidly, it is most often used in PCs in relatively small quantities in the system's cache memory. Contrast with **DRAM, Flash Memory,** and **ROM**. *(Chapter 11)*

Super-Floppy   *See* **LS-120**.

super-scalar   The capability of a **CPU** of performing multiple instructions within each **clock** cycle.

Super7   A trademarked term used by AMD and the other "clone x86 **CPU**" makers, and by motherboard manufacturers supporting those chips, for an enhanced version of Intel's **Socket 7** *(Chapter 7)*

symmetric   In the context of data transmission, a method of enabling data to be sent and received simultaneously by dividing the total available **bandwidth** into two **channels**, each of which has the same **throughput**.

synchronous   Two or more events that occur at the same time. In the context of data transmission, a process whereby data is transmitted or received at a fixed rate. Contrast with **asynchronous**.

system bus   *See* **front-side bus**.

system clock   The circuit that synchronizes all actions of all of its principal parts. Normally, this runs at the same speed as the CPU (or perhaps half or twice the CPU speed). *See also* **clock** and **bus clock**.

System Management Bus (SMB)   An application of the Philips **I$_2$C bus** now used in PCs to interrogate memory modules, and in **smart batteries** and the systems that use them (such as laptop computers and cellular phones) to control power consumption and learn how to recharge those batteries safely. *See also* **Serial Presence Detect** and **Smart Battery System (SBS)**. *(Chapter 23)*

T

TCP/IP (Transmission Control Protocol/Internet Protocol)   The basic **protocol** used for data transmission on the **Internet**, and now on many **intranets** and other **LAN**s. This is a reference to both a physical layer control and the next higher-level control of the process of communication over a data link. It still refers to a fairly low level of control of the communication, and is normally "supervised" by higher-level protocols such as **SMTP**.

texture mapping   The process through which 3D objects are given the illusion of possessing physical surfaces.

throughput   Generally, the speed at which a computer processes data. A means by which the rate at which data is moved across any suitable path or channel is measured. Commonly expressed in terms of bits per second. **Translation Lookaside Buffer (TLB)** A special hidden register inside the Intel **x86** CPUs that holds values read from the Local or Global Descriptor Tables (**LDT** or **GDT**) in memory and that are used to calculate addresses for future accesses to memory. *(Chapter 11)*

U

UNC (Universal Naming Convention, also known as Uniform Naming Convention)
A standard way of specifying a resource (typically a file or peripheral such as a printer) on a network, it consists of two parts. The first identifies the host computer's name; the second identifies the shared resource's share name. Example: \\computer\resource *(Chapter 27)*

Universal Plug-and-Play (UPnP) A new Microsoft-proposed standard to extend plug-and-play behavior from PCs to a host of diverse devices, including traditional consumer electronics (TVs, VCRs, and so forth) and new, data-enabled appliances.

UPS (uninterruptible power supply) A battery–backed-up power supply that can continue to provide good quality electrical power (for awhile) even when the input source fails. *(Chapters 4 and 26)*

URI (uniform resource identifier) A standardized way of representing resources, especially on the Internet. There are two broad classes of URI, and some resources may fall into both categories. The first and most well-known is the **URL (Uniform Resource Locator)**. This specifies a resource by how you get to it. The other broad category is the URN (Universal Resource Name). This names a resource which must continue to have a globally unique and persistent name even when the resource ceases to exist, becomes unavailable, or is physically moved. *See also* **URL**. *(Chapter 27)*

URL (uniform resource locator) A special case of **URI (uniform resource identifier)**. A URL specifies an accessible object on the Internet, primarily by describing how to access it. A URL consists of three parts. The first names a protocol for accessing that object. The second is the name of a host. The last part names (specifies as a path) which object on that host is being addressed. *(Chapter 27)*

USB (Universal Serial Bus) A medium or low-speed **serial bus** using a transmission derived from the **SCSI** bus **protocol**, but permitting "hot plugging" of devices. This is fast becoming the preferred way to connect peripheral devices to a PC, except for those few that require super-high–speed connections. (Those peripherals at present are usually connected via a **SCSI** bus, or are plugged directly into the **PCI** bus, but soon most of them will migrate to the new IEEE **1394** bus. The USB bus also will take over the special-purpose ports on a PC, for mouse and keyboard. *(Chapter 16)*

V

VBA (Visual Basic for Applications) A Microsoft programming language based on Visual Basic that it now includes in all its office application programs. This facility enables any user of these programs to automate their operation and, in some ways, to modify their functionality. *(Chapter 18)*

VLSI (Very Large Scale Integration)   A manufacturing technique that allows making very complex integrated circuits. Commonly used for **CPU**s, PC **chipset**s, **DSP**s, and certain other very complex logic circuits. Complexity in these circuits is measured in numbers of logic gates they include. SSI (Small Scale Integration) circuits contain only a few dozen gates at most. MSI (Medium Scale Integration) circuits may contain a few hundred or thousands. LSI (Large Scale Integration) circuits contain tens of thousands of gates, and VLSI circuits now routinely include several million gates.

VoIP or VOIP (Voice Over IP)   An umbrella name for an assortment of hardware and software products aimed at moving most or all voice telephone calls off of the **analog** public switched telephone network (**PSTN**) and onto **digital** networks using **Internet** Protocol (**IP**).

VPN (Virtual Private Network)   A strategy for using the **Internet** to connect two or more **LAN**s in physically distinct locations over an encrypted channel. *See also* **PPTP**. Contrast with **WAN**. *(Chapter 25)*

vSynch   A synonym for vertical bandwidth, expressing the frequency with which a display can be completely refreshed.

VxD (Virtual Device Driver)   The x in this name stands for "anything." (Thus a VKD could be a virtual keyboard driver, or a VDD a virtual display driver.) These are small programs that augment the operating system at its lowest level (**Ring 0**) and thus can be made to do anything and to directly access any portion of the hardware.

W

W3C   *See* **World Wide Web Consortium**.

Wake On LAN   A strategy for making it possible for a PC that is in a powered-down state to be returned to full power-on status when it receives a signal across a **LAN**. This is useful for managing many PCs from a central location.

WAN (wide area network)   A very large area network arrangement similar in function to a **LAN**, but typically extended over a much broader geographic region. A **WAN** will typically use dedicated wire or microwave links to connect the constituent LANs, as opposed to the connection of LANs over a shared medium that is characteristic of a VPN.

WDM (Windows Driver Model)   Microsoft's latest specification for the creation of **device drivers**. Device drivers written in compliance with this standard will work both in Windows 98 and in Windows 2000.

Windows   Microsoft's overall name for its most popular family of PC **operating systems**. This family includes the original Windows 1.0–3.11 programs, which were simply graphical user interfaces (**GUI**s) loaded on top of **DOS**; Windows 95 and 98, which were more complete integrations of DOS with the GUI; Windows NT, which is a fully rewritten 32-bit operating system based on the Windows model for user and program interactions; and Windows CE, which is the reduced version of Windows for use on handheld PCs (**HPC**s). *(Chapter 17)*

Windows CE   The version of Microsoft Windows that is intended for use on handheld PCs and for embedding in settop boxes and other "information appliances."

WINS (Windows Internet Name Service)   A means for letting Windows machines using **NetBIOS** networking protocol find and access resources with **IP addresses**.

Wintel   A nickname for any computer based on the Intel **x86 CPU** architecture and running some version of Microsoft **Windows**.

workstation   A term commonly used to denote a computer attached to a central **server**. This often implies a computer with more power (speed; amount of RAM; size, number, and/or resolution of the attached video display or displays; or other significant attributes) than the usual desktop PC. *(Chapter 25)*

World Wide Web Consortium (W3C)   A membership organization, jointly hosted by MIT in the USA and CERN in Europe, which adopts and publishes standards for the World Wide Web (and, by extension, for any **LAN**, **intranet**, or **extranet** using **Internet** and **WWW** protocols). *(Chapter 27)*

WTX   A new standard design for PC **workstations**. This design stresses accessibility and modularity and is intended for very high-powered PCs. *See also* **ATX** and **NLX**.

WWW (World Wide Web)   This term refers to the collection of machines connected via the Internet that serve and use information in accordance to **HTML** and related protocols. This is essentially an application using the **Internet** as infrastructure, and it has become one of the most commonly used of those applications (along with email and file transfers).

X

x86   The family name for the Intel **CPU**s used in various generations of PCs (starting with the 8088 and continuing through the 80286, 386, 486, and Pentium processors.) This name also includes all the compatible CPUs made by AMD, Cyrix, and others. *(Chapter 7)*

xDSL   Any one of several standards for digital communication over normal copper twisted-pair telephone wires from a home or office to some convenient (for the telephone company) point where analog POTS signals can be separated from the all-digital xDSL ones.. *See also* **ADSL**, **HDSL**, and **G.Lite**. *(Chapter 24)*

XML (Extensible Markup Language)   A standard way to describing database objects for display within a Web page. This standard augments HTML (with or without CSS, PGML, and so forth) to make Web pages that can be automatically updated with data extracted from a database in any of several standard database formats. *See also* **CSS, DHTML, HTTP, HTML,** and **PGML.** *(Chapter 27)*

XSL (extensible style language)   An extension to XML to enable, among other things, search engines to access and index text contained within a Web page graphic. *See also* **CSS, DHTML, HTTP, HTML, PGML,** and **XML.** *(Chapter 27)*

Z

ZIF (Zero Insertion Force)   A socket design in which there is a lever that removes all pressure on the pins while the device is inserted or removed, and then applies pressure to them all concurrently to provide reliable connections.

zoomed video   A high-speed data channel from a PC Card bay directly to the graphics accelerator in the video display subsystem. *(Chapter 16)*

Index

E

P

Q

S

Y-Z